On The Road To FREEDOM

Footprints On Indian History **1937 -1947**

Part II

Sudip Kar Purkayastha

Vitasta

Let Knowledge Spread

Published by
Renu Kaul Verma
Vitasta Publishing Pvt Ltd
2/15 Ansari Road, Daryaganj
New Delhi - 110 002
info@vitastapublishing.com

Set ISBN 978-93-82711-82-7
ISBN 978-93-82711-43-8

Reprint 2018

The views and opinions expressed in this book are the author's own. He is solely responsible for the facts and authenticity of the quotes and sources used for this work. The publisher is in no way liable for the same.

Cover and Layout Design by Vitasta Publishing Pvt Ltd
Printed by Vikas Computer and Printers, New Delhi

To

Young Indians in whose
hands lie the Destiny of India

CONTENTS

ACKNOWLEDGEMENTS

Foremost, my sincere thanks to Prof Manjula Bose, who first inspired me to write books.

Many thanks to the staff and officials of the National Library, Kolkata and its 'old newspaper' section; National Archive of India, New Delhi; State Central Libraries at Kankurganchi, Kolkata & Cubbon Park, Bangalore; and Raja Rammohun Roy Library Foundation (RRRLF), Kolkata. In particular I thank Samir K Banik, my friend and former official of the National Library, Kolkata and Shri Mrityunjoy Ghosh, AL&IO of RRRLF for his their help and cooperation.

I am grateful to Vitasta and my publisher Renu Kaul Verma for taking up the manuscript and Papri Sri Raman, my editor, in particular.

I have sincere appreciation for my nephews Indraneil and Tonmoy for their useful feedback on the manuscript.

I have been the beneficiary of an intellectually stimulating and emotionally supportive familyambience. Thanks to my brothers and sisters for their encouragement and valuable feedback. I can never thank my wife Jaya and sons Rituraj and Siddhartha enough for their silent, self-effacing support and also their never-ebbing encouragement throughout thislong journey that has lasted six years. I must make a special mentionof Siddhartha, who has been an inseparable part of this project in everypossible manner—arranging numerous books from India and abroad,going through manuscripts and offering valuable suggestions, besideshandling the entire computer operations. This book embodies his contribution all through

Prologue

The story of India's struggle for independence from the powerful British Raj is a fascinating one. After the East India Company set up their hegemony across the subcontinent, the Indians waged their first major battle in 1857, in a bid to throw off the company's chains. It was carried out by large number of disaffected Indian sepoys of the Company, led by several valiant commanders and a number of native rulers distinguished for their valour, strong antipathy for the British and love for the motherland. The vehemence of that struggle, the gallantry and the spirit that were on display, supreme sacrifices offered by numerous named and unnamed heroes and the interminable nature of the armed challenges that kept cropping up over and again across the vast swath of the subcontinent, especially in its central and northern parts, kept the British rulers in a state of panic and dread.

That the British could come back from the precipice of certain disaster and re-establish their grip over the vast territories they had lost to the 'rebels' in a matter of months, owed primarily to the help they received from the Maharaja of Nepal (a Hindu kingdom in the Himalayas), and various native princes ruling states including inter alia Patiala, Nabha, Kashmir, Indore, Gwalior, and Hyderabad. They also got their lifeline from Indian sepoys who continued to be loyal to the Raj, in particular those belonging to the Madras regiment as well as the Sikh soldiers. Before 1859 came to an end, the Company, albeit with considerable difficulties, managed to crush the armed uprising completely. Significantly, however, they paid a heavy price for their misgovernance. They lost their possession of the colony of India to the British empire. Her Majesty's Government assumed the governance and Queen Victoria held out to Indians assurances of justice and fair play.

The Indian armed challenge against the colonial rulers had, thus, burst forth intensely in a small window of time and thereafter fizzled out rather quickly. The assurances and the promises that were held out by Her Majesty's Government had a pacifying effect and Indians, generally, looked forward with some measure of optimism to the future. Interestingly, the next round of Indian challenge against the British Raj sprouted forth rather soon. But unlike 1857, the standard bearers of the new challenge were the educated middle class intelligentsia who propagated the mantra of *swaraj* across the country and the masses. Carried by the agency of these new-look soldiers, the yearning for freedom gradually got etched on to the consciousness of the vast masses, and the series of movements eventually consumed the British Raj in 1947.

The early symptoms of the disenchantment of Indians with HMG began to manifest as early as in the 1870s, due to the condemnable attitude and actions of the government in handling the ruinous bouts of famines and famine victims. That a psyche of disdainful racial discrimination alone could be the engine of such apathy and indifference was confirmed by more racially-biased legislations that followed in close succession. In hindsight, the mega celebration of the coronation of Queen Victoria in India in the year 1877 could be seen as a politically significant event. It was apparently benign but, in fact, began to trouble, vaguely or otherwise, thinking Indians. Unseemly in the context of the widespread epidemic and extreme human miseries, this event went on with great fanfare for days while the poor famine victims were dying in hundreds and thousands. The heartless festivity stood in stark contrast to the British claim that HMG was the most civilised of all governments in the contemporary world.

This book begins its story from that signal event and meanders its way through the corridors of seventy long years to end in 1947.

The intervening period of seven decades witnessed various strands of struggles by the Indians against the Raj in quest of *swaraj*. The impatient revolutionaries wanted to expel the colonial rulers 'then and there' and resorted to violent means. The constitutionalists explored the parliamentary route to secure the right of self-government from the Raj consensually. Then there were two huge non-violent mass movements led by Gandhi, the like of which the world had never experienced, before or after. But the British Raj frustrated every such challenge, sometimes with an iron hand, some other times with feigned magnanimity and diplomatic finesse but above all by driving deep wedges amongst their Indian adversaries on the basis of religion and castes. They cultivated the Muslim fears about losing their due share of political rights to Hindus in a democratic polity with commendable success. Thus, barring very few occasions, the struggle of the mainstream Indians, led by the Congress Party, failed to enlist the support of the majority of the Muslim community. On several important junctures the Raj was able to fight some of its toughest political battles in India by gathering strength from the Muslim League. The two, in fact, shared a cosy relationship based on a 'quid pro quo', with the common objective of stalling the mainstream challengers' aspiration for *swaraj* and a united independent democratic India.

In 1941, Churchill, the new British prime minister, had made it crystal clear that the British government had no intention to abandon HMG's vast Indian empire. Till mid 1940s, the Raj showed no desire to cast away the brightest jewel from the British crown. But the ordeal undergone in course of the Great War during 1939-45 compelled them to rethink after the war was conclusively over, and the Raj had chance to reflect. Though the Allies eventually managed to win the war, Britain suffered heavy losses of human lives and it was nearly devastated in terms of physical assets and financially ruined. With regard to their Indian empire, they were subjected to another torment. The impact of the Indian National Army on the armed forces, their mainstay in the colony, had shaken their confidence badly. By 1946, for the first time, the Raj seemed to be in a mood to abandon its Indian empire, albeit reluctantly. This presented the Indians with an unprecedented opportunity to enter the post-war world as a united independent country.

Unfortunately that did not happen. The gulf between the Congress, representatives of the mainstream Indians and the Muslim League, the chief spokesperson of Muslims in the country proved to be unbridgeable. Significantly, the distrust that Jinnah harboured about Gandhi in 1947 seemed to be far greater than what Sir Syed Ahmed had displayed towards the Congress in 1885. The failure of two premier political bodies to come together, even after the lapse of a period as long as sixty-two years or more, constituted a telling commentary on the success of British diplomacy and the mindset of Indian politicians. Before they left, the Raj took their last revenge on their disloyal Indian challengers by granting them dominion status on the condition that they agreed to divide the country. The two parts of India walked into freedom amidst rivers of blood.

The above narrative is only the broad contour of the story of India's freedom struggle. The readers may find the details, spread out over eleven chapters in two parts, engrossing. The saga of the Indian struggle is a wide-spectrum account of human instincts, emotions and actions. It embodies stories of many opposites on the part of political actors—raw courage and cowardice, temperance and greed, supreme sacrifice and abject selfishness, straight-forward dealings and chicanery, clear-headed and muddled thinking. It recounts the momentous 'movements', the likes of which the world has never seen and the abrupt manner in which they were withdrawn. It describes the clashes of great ideas and also of the titans. It tells the stories of blind faith of the followers in their leaders as well as endemic mistrust between great leaders themselves. It is glorified by the spirit of peace and nonviolence and yet it has been stained by the blood of fratricide. It chronicles the subtle political art of 'divide and rule' practised by successive Viceroys and the British government in London to perpetuate the British rule in India. On the whole, the wide spectrum of Indian challenges to the British, apart from having been a freedom movement for four hundred million people, it also constitutes a captivating political story that has universal educative value. Most certainly, it has many lessons for the people of independent India and they can ignore it only to their great disadvantage.

The book has shortlisted the milestone events during the period 1877 to 1947, presented them to the reader in the newspapers style of those times, together with insightful analysis. The 'political analysts' and 'political observers' referred to in the book represent the author's analysis and interpretations based on his extensive study of history. The items presented in the style of 'editorials' are to be taken as the author's view.

The book has two part. The first part, divided into four chapters, tracks the events that occurred till the end of 1936, together with their analysis. The second part spreads into seven chapters, deals with rest of the period till 15 August 1947.

The author has done extensive research of available materials in multiple domains including inter alia documents, books, newspapers, magazines, websites and attempted to piece them together in a time sequence by furnishing the relevant dates, wherever available. At the same time, the readers are cordially welcome to suggest improvements in any form for incorporation in future editions.

The author may be reached at sudipkarp@hotmail.com

ONE

UNEASY TRANSITION

1937 - 1939

UNEASY TRANSITION

CONGRESS,BRITISH TWO FORCES IN INDIA: JAWAHARLAL
There Is A Third Force, It Is Muslim India: Jinnah

January 3, 1937, Calcutta: Electoral campaigns by political parties are in full swing. Congress is clearly ahead of the rest. It has a smooth-oiled election machine, with Vallabhbhai Patel as the main organiser and Jawaharlal, the chief campaigner. He is on a whirlwind tour of the provinces and is receiving an overwhelming response everywhere.

Interestingly, although the Congress, by deciding to contest the election, conceded defeat on its longstanding tussle with the government on the issue of the new constitution, Jawaharlal, undaunted, is trying to use the election to the advantage of his party. He is attempting to convert the election into a kind of referendum, asking people to choose between the Congress and the British government. He is suggesting that these two are the principal adversaries and all other parties have to choose a side; to vote against the Congress would be to vote for continuation of the British domination.

The text, tone and tenor of Jawaharlal's election speeches cause great irritation to Jinnah. He finds the 'two adversaries only' theory abhorrent. It challenges not only the political weight of the Muslim League but his own personal worth as a leader. Breathing fire and brimstone, an irate Jinnah has thundered, 'I refuse to line up with the Congress. I refuse to accept the proposition. There is a third party in this country and that is Muslim India... we are not going to be camp followers of any party'. Jinnah was addressing a rally[1] at the Muhammad Ali Park here. Political analysts are observing some distinct changes of late in Jinnah's stance. The election manifesto of the League carried many demands, secular and economic in character. But in the present utterance, Jinnah is not calling the Muslim League as the 'third party' but the 'Muslims' as that 'third party', vesting the religious grouping with a communal overtone.

Communists Make Foray Into CSP National Executive

January 1937, Faizpur: In recent times, the Communists in the country are, in accordance with the directives of the Comintern, trying to come closer to the Congress. The Comintern's changed policy favours forging popular front against the imperialist regime. In India, the Congress has been playing a stellar role in mobilising wide range of forces for the national struggle and happens to be the principal mass organisation fighting for national liberation. However, the Communists feel the Congress has not been able to sufficiently energise and activate the movement at the level of the proletariats as there has been a disconnect between its bourgeois leaders and the poor masses for long years. This issue was addressed to an extent in 1934 when the left-leaning Socialists in the Congress came together and formed the Congress Socialist Party, providing scope to the Communists to work using a Congress platform. Now, in the third annual session of the CSP, the Communists have, as a part of their new strategy, been able to achieve a deep penetration into its leadership too. Several Communist leaders have been included in the CSP national executive. The Communists want to develop and broaden the Congress so as to transform it into a powerful anti-imperialist front.

Provincial Elections Come To An End

February 1937: Elections to eleven British Indian provinces which began last month, have now concluded. This was the first election held under the Government of India Act 1935. The two main political parties contesting the election are the Indian National Congress and the All-India Muslim League. However, in provinces like Punjab, Bengal, Sind and the NWFP, the regional parties also seemed to have emerged as strong political forces. All eyes are now set upon the results.

Electoral Verdicts: Congress Top Gainer, Secures Absolute Majority In Five Provinces

February 1937: The election results of eleven provinces are out. Amongst the political parties, the Congress has emerged as most successful. It contested in 1,161 general seats and won more than 700 of them. It also contested 58 seats reserved for the Muslims and won 26, most of these in the NWFP. The party has achieved clear majority in five provinces, viz. Bihar, Central Provinces, Madras, Orissa and United Provinces. It fell marginally short of the half-way mark in Bombay. In all these six provinces, it can form ministry provided it takes a political decision to do so. It has emerged as the largest single party in Bengal and Assam, and achieved majority in the NWFP together with the Khudai Khidmatgar of Khan Abdul Ghaffar Khan. However, its performance has been miserable in Punjab and Sind. The Muslim League's overall performance has been very poor in comparison. Out of 491 Muslim seats, it has won only 106. Its best performance has been in Bengal where it secured 38 out of a total 117 Muslim seats, finishing second after the Congress in terms of total tally. It fetched some seats in Hindu majority provinces, especially UP. In the Muslim majority province of Punjab, albeit marginally, the party failed miserably, securing only a single seat out of a total of 84. In the clear Muslim majority province of Sind, it failed to open account. In the most heavily Muslim-dominated province of the NWFP, the League drew a blank. The bottomline is, it would not be in a position to form government in any province on its own strength. Out of the main regional parties, the Unionist Party emerged with a majority in Punjab. In Bengal, the Krishak Praja Party, though considered as the third largest party after the Congress and the League, has acquired huge political importance, as the Congress and the League do not see eye-to-eye in the province.

Congress Euphoric But Needs To Introspect Jinnah Upset And Needs To Introspect Too

February 1937: Though the Congress has achieved much greater success than the rest, the election result has also shown many chinks in its armour. Despite being the oldest and the most organised political party, it could secure clear majority only in five out of eleven provinces. Its results were very poor in Punjab and Sind. In Assam it was expected to secure majority of its own but fell far short of the half way mark. Most importantly, in the reserved constituencies it won only 26 out of 491 Muslim seats. On the whole, despite being ahead of all others, the party's claim of being the real representative of all Indians cutting across religion has been busted. This truth hitherto concealed and now exposed could, henceforth, be used by both the government and also its native political adversaries. Critics say, this could be seen as a serious political loss to the party.

The Muslim League has become even more upset. The League, led by Jinnah, failed to consolidate Muslim votes in the election. Rather the Muslims across the country and especially in provinces where they are in majority displayed their distinct preferences for regional parties over the League. This has come as a major blow to the League's vision of organising the Muslims in the country under one banner as a separate nation. With no prospect of laying hands on office unless joining a coalition, the League is realising its path ahead has grown complex and thorny.

Jinnah has become aware that to steer the League to its destination would call for consummate diplomatic skill. He is a much-mellowed and worried person now.

Unionist Party Keeps Up Its Victory Run In Punjab

February 1937, Lahore: In keeping with its traditional hold over Punjab, the Unionist Party, led by Sikandar Hayat Khan, has secured single party majority in the recently held provincial election. It has won as many as 95 seats out of a total 175, whereas the Indian National Congress has managed to win only 18 seats. This is a stunningly weak performance by the premier national party. It has, at best, managed a tenuous hold over the province, its influence confined only to limited sections of Hindu voters in urban areas. The plight of the Muslim League is more miserable.

The Unionist Party was formed in 1922 with secular economic agenda. It positioned itself as the protector of the interests of the rural population, cutting across religion. Its secular agenda and commitment to rural causes helped it win previous elections in 1923, 1926, and 1934. Last year, Sikandar Hayat Khan took over the reins of the party, following the death of its popular leader, Fazli Hussain. This year it witnessed a pleasant repetition of past performances.

Muslim League Bites Dust, Fakhr-e-Afghan Stands Tall

February 1937, Peshawar: Electors of the NWFP have rewarded the tireless efforts put in by Khan Abdul Ghaffar Khan and his elder brother Khan Abdul Jabbar Khan, popularly called Dr Khan Sahib, amongst Pasthun peasantries in the NWFP. Ghaffar's struggle against the colonial rulers and their cohorts, viz. the big Khans in the province, appealed to the freedom-loving people and this has reflected in the election result.

Despite patronage and covert support by the governor and the bureaucracy, the Muslim League has failed to establish its presence in the province's legislature. The Congress, in coalition with the Khudai Khidmatgar, is set to govern the strategically-located border province with an overwhelming Muslim population. The election result has, to an extent, salvaged the dent the Congress suffered elsewhere in India about its claim that it represented Indians of all religions, especially the Muslims.

Bengal Electors Deliver A Polarised Verdict

February 1937, Calcutta: In the provincial election, Congress has emerged as the single largest party in Bengal, winning 52 seats followed by the Muslim League, with 39 seats and the Krishak Praja Party bagging 36 seats. The legislature has a total of 250 seats. Out of these three parties, the achievement of the Krishak Praja Party has been most spectacular. Having been founded only last year, the party, with a secular agenda, has been able to attract widespread support, especially of the poor peasantry cutting across 'religion'. Its leader, the maverick Fazlul Huq, had raised the election slogan of 'Daal Bhat' meaning 'rice and pulses' for all. And it has worked wonders.

Neither the Congress nor the Muslim League has got absolute majority and being antagonistic to each other, the two parties forming a coalition ministry is out of question. With these two parties being principal contenders cum adversaries, the Krishak Praja Party holds the key to the coalition government.

Congress Is Reticent About Ministry Formation

February 1937: The Congress is a divided house on the question of acceptance of office. Prior to the election, it was a hypothetical issue. Now it must make up its mind. The party has been against many provisions of the new constitution, more particularly those relating to the federal legislature and government. Yet, it has ended up lending some measure of legitimacy to the constitution by taking part in the election. Now, forming the ministries may be interpreted by the people as the party's final approval to the GOI Act 1935. In particular, the Congress Socialist Party leaders within the Congress have been vehemently opposing 'acceptance of office'.

Besides inner dissensions, the party runs another grave risk—not having access to adequate power and financial resources to carry out its own policies and programmes. Although provincial autonomy is being touted by the British Raj as a gift of the new constitution to Indians, the fact is, the scope and powers of the provincial governments are not absolute. The Governor General will continue to wield such extensive power that the provincial autonomy, for practical purposes, runs the risk of being compromised. The net result will be the incongruence between heightened public aspirations and the party's restricted capacity to deliver. The mismatch could generate and escalate public grievance against the party and damage its image.

On top of everything else, the constitution gives an overriding power to the governor of every province to suspend the constitution and assume all the powers of the government. Section 93 gives the Governor power even to dismiss the provincial government. The hanging of a sword over the head constantly makes the position of such a government most precarious.

In view of all these factors, a number of leaders are not in favour of forming government in the provinces. They feel forming government under these disagreeable conditions can not only create frustration in the leaders and ordinary Congressmen but, and more dangerously, tempt them into corrupt practices.

What Holds Back Congress From Office Acceptance?

Way back in 1934, Rajendra Prasad, as Congress president, had observed that nearly 80% of the central revenues were being spent by the government on army and other fixed charges like pays, allowances, pension etc, thus leaving a meagre 20% subject to vote. Now that the prospect of government formation is facing the party, the uselessness of 'office acceptance' is being felt all the more. It would be simply impossible to implement Congress' policies and programmes for reconstruction of the nation with a paltry and inelastic purse.

Moreover, the real powers shall effectively rest in the hands of the Governor General. In the provinces, the governors shall have far-reaching powers including even dismissal of the elected government. Jawaharlal feels Congress can lose much and gain little from these exercises. By accepting the office after having rejected the constitution, the Congress shall stand self-condemned. Congress leaders would lose themselves on compromises and communal tangles. With responsibility far outstripping authority, Congress will not be able to do much and soon dissatisfaction shall spread all over the country. Besides Jawaharlal, Subhas is also against taking up governance with limited power and sees a distinct possibility of Congress ministries getting mired in corruption. On the whole, Congress is diffident on this issue.

Critics say that the British regime is aware of the multifarious problems the Congress ministries would face and the certitude of the pitfalls that would lie ahead of them. The regime, they say, wants the Congress to be exposed as incompetent to govern and also prone to corruption.

AICC GIVES CLEARANCE FOR MINISTRY FORMATION

March 16-17, 1937, Delhi: The AICC has passed a resolution permitting the 'acceptance of office' in provinces where the Congress commands majority in the legislature.

Before putting the resolution to vote, there was animated debate. The opposition to the resolution came from right, left and centre. If veteran leader like Malaviya criticised the move, so did Jawaharlal and also Socialist leaders like Jayprakash Narayan and Masani. It was a core question of 'credibility' as some of the antagonists argued—the party had fought the election on the very plank of its opposition to the new constitution and its pledge that it would try to end this constitution on being elected. The protagonists, on their part, made a distinction between the federal part and provincial part of the constitution. They contended the party's major opposition has been in regard to the 'former'.

That part of the constitution itself was nowhere in the realm of implementation as both the Muslim League and the princes of the native states were opposed to it. The League feared the federal election will lead to Congress hegemony in the central legislature, whereas the princes apprehended they would lose a good measure of their autonomy in a federal structure. On the provincial issue, the protagonists contended that the recent Government of India Act abolished diarchy in the provincial government and granted them full autonomy. The only issue was that, although all departments were transferred to the charge of elected ministers, those were subject to very substantial discretionary powers, safeguards and reservations retained by the governors.

Congress leaders had opened dialogues with the Viceroy to secure a written assurance from the British that the governors in provinces would not exercise such powers but the government has been refusing to oblige.

In the AICC, Gandhi has resolved this problem by adding a clause to the draft resolution that says that the Congress can accept office, subject to the condition that the leader of the Congress Party in the provincial legislature 'is satisfied and able to state publicly that the as long as he and his cabinet act within the constitution, the governor will not use the special power of interference or set aside the advice of ministers.'[2] With its incorporation, the resolution was passed with 135 votes in favour and 78 votes against.

Critics, however, feel that the manner in which the Congress has been successively diluting its hard, puritan stance on the issue of the new 'constitution' does not bode well for the party. They point out that the attraction of powers and perks has set in motion a dangerous dynamics and that the party has begun an inexorable journey to a dead end and obvious infamy, which none would probably be able to prevent, including Gandhi.

Subhas Released Suddenly

March 17, 1937, Calcutta: Soon after landing in Bombay in April last year, Subhas was arrested and confined to his brother's house at Kurseong, a hill station in north Bengal, far away from politics—provincial or national. By the end of last year, his health again began to deteriorate and in December he was brought to Calcutta for treatment. But he continued to be under arrest. At long last, tonight he was suddenly released from the Medical College Hospital in the city.[3]

Political analysts opine that the British government did not want Subhas to be free before the provincial elections were complete. They have been aware of his charisma and mass appeal and apprehended that his participation in election propaganda could sway the voters of all communities in favour of the Congress across the country, more so in Bengal.

Proclaim Political Objectives Of Indian Muslims: Iqbal

March 20, 1937: Iqbal has been disturbed by Jawaharlal's speech delivered yesterday at All-India Convention of Congress Legislators and also by the recent Congress activities, especially aimed at winning over Muslims. Today he has written to Jinnah, stressing the need to counter such attempts. He has suggested the need to hold an the All-India Muslim League Convention in Delhi and invite all the elected members of the provincial assembly and the AIML leaders. Iqbal stressed upon the need to proclaim the political objective of the Indian Muslims as a distinct political entity.

He also wanted it to be emphasised that Muslim cultural problems were no less important than their economic difficulties. In an obvious hint to Jawaharlal and the Congress, Iqbal suggested that clear enunciation of the political objectives of the Indian Muslims would ensure that they would not lose sight of their cultural entity in the face of political device or intrigue by their adversaries. Interestingly, Iqbal has pointed out the possibility of using the new constitution to the advantage of the Muslims. He has written that it provides opportunity to reorganise Indian Muslims. Jinnah himself has been thinking on such lines. On 9th of this month he had indicated the preparedness of both the League and the Muslims to make best use of the constitution for whatever it was worth. Iqbal's communication has come as a reinforcer.

Muslims Must Live Or Die As A United Nation: Jinnah

March 21, 1937, Delhi: Jinnah is presiding over the council of All-India Muslim League. The League is still nursing its electoral bruises. Jinnah is finding it difficult to reconcile with the outcome. It was expected that Jinnah would be self-critical but his utterances in the council have surprised and shocked all nationalist Indians. In his speech, Jinnah stressed that the differences between Hindus and Muslims were not due to lack of nationalism among the Muslims, but because of differences between the cultures of the two.

Then he exploded a bombshell, saying, 'Muslims must unite as a nation and then live or die as a united nation'.[4] As late as in the poll campaign, he used to refer to the Muslims as a 'community'. Post-poll, in a significant shift, he has begun to address the Muslims as a 'nation'. Thus, he is insinuating that the nationalism of Muslims would be different from the nationalism of the Hindus, or the rest of Indians. It seems Jinnah is now bringing Iqbal to real politik. The council has adopted a resolution urging the need to take immediate steps for setting up branches of the AIML at the provincial and district levels across the country.

According to political observers, intense political reactions on the part of Iqbal, Jinnah and the AIML coming in quick succession have been caused, in no less measure, by the Jawaharlal-initiated programme of mass contacts by the Congress with the Muslims which seeks to address the problems faced by Indian Muslims, essentially through economic terms.

Jawaharlal Initiates Muslim Mass Contact Programme

March 31, 1937: Communal politics and communal leaders have been competing with the Congress for long. Though the Congress has left the Muslim League way behind in the provincial elections, Jawaharlal, the Congress president realises that the League may be down but certainly not out and can hit back in several ways. Ominously, amongst some of the regional parties, which achieved some measure of success in recent elections, it is possible to notice clear communal orientations.

Jawaharlal, however, has acquired a new confidence to tackle these communal leaders. It stems, in part, from his grounding in socialism and the remarkable electoral success of the Congress. Buoyed, he has concluded that the communal problem in the country is not so insurmountable—it is a political creation and not a religious one and that its roots lie at economic depravity of the poor Muslim masses. The communal riots or disturbances are instigated by landlords and other vested interests to preserve and serve their own narrow class interests. Jawaharlal reckons that the need for independence and its interlinkage with problems such as the removal of poverty and unemployment are the same for the Muslim masses as they are for their Hindus, Sikhs or Christian counterparts.

He feels the vexed communal problem can be redressed by a set of policy actions by the government. He has also diagnosed that the Congress failures in the past to handle the communal issue, as in the case of the Lucknow pact or the Khilafat movement, arose because it relied upon a few communal leaders and came to an understanding with them, instead of addressing the needs of the community at large. He does not want to repeat the mistake. He feels the Muslim League represents a group of Muslim leaders, however estimable they may be, from the economically affluent sections whose class interests are distinct from those of the poor Muslim masses. He wants the provincial Congress committees to establish direct contact with the masses and take up their causes. Jawaharlal feels, once their economic grievances are removed by appropriate government policies, the communal leaders will become defunct.

Today, he has issued a circular[5] from the AICC office laying down a broad framework of this initiative. He has instructed each provincial Congress to appoint a special committee to undertake the task of increasing Congress contacts with the Muslim masses, both rural and urban. He has also assured them support from the AICC and announced his plan of setting up a separate department to help in this task with advice, leaflets, pamphlets etc.

Gandhi, who has taken note of Jawaharlal's recent initiatives, wants to wait and watch. Political analysts, however, say that Jawaharlal is possibly trying to oversimplify a complex issue by interpreting it in purely economic terms. This is in sharp contrast to Iqbal's interpretation of communal relations and his description of Muslims as a separate nation. Significantly, in its recent council meeting, the Muslim League leadership has already decided to confront the fledgling Congress initiatives head on.

Unionist Party Forms Government In Punjab

March 1937, Lahore: Sikandar has formed a coalition government in which his Unionist Party is joined by legislators of Khalsa National Party and Hindu Election Board, representing the non-Congress Hindu leaders. It may be recalled that the Unionist Party secured single party majority in the election but has chosen to form a coalition ministry that makes the ministry representative of all three major religious groups. The Indian National Congress with 18 legislators and the Shiromani Akali Dal with 10 legislators, together with a few others from smaller parties are sitting in the opposition bench.

Congress Pushes Krishak Praja Party To League's Lap

April 1, 1937, Calcutta: The election result in Bengal had created tension and uncertainty, as neither the Congress nor the Muslim League could achieve majority and the Krishak Praja Party, led by Fazlul Huq, emerged as the third largest party. Congress, being the single largest party, could have staked its claim to form a coalition ministry with like-minded parties. But, it has been taking a long time to decide as a matter of principle whether or not to accept office. In the meantime, the Krishak Praja Party had approached it for a coalition, but the provincial Congress could not give its nod.

The scope for coalition also existed between the Krishak Praja Party and the Muslim League. But, there was, for some time, a diplomatic tussle as to who would take the initiative. Eventually, the League blinked first and proposed to the Krishak Praja Party to form a government together. The coalition has now materialised. Fazlul Huq took oath as the premier. His cabinet has six Muslim and five Hindu ministers. Of the former, only two belong to his Krishak Praja Party and four are from the League, reflecting the numerical strength of the two parties in the legislature. The League has driven a hard bargain by capitalising on its numerical superiority and the helplessness of the provincial Congress.

Political analysts say, the Congress has lost an important opportunity to fight against communal politics across the country by forfeiting the chance to form the government in Bengal, the province that has the largest Muslim population. And, ironically, the party was eminently qualified to govern, being the single largest party in alliance with the Krishak Praja Party, a Muslim-dominated secular and energetic political formation.

I Add My Voice To Nation's Welcome to Subhas: Tagore

April 6, 1937, Calcutta: At the end of long periods of prison, exile and internment, Subhas, the charismatic young national leader, was released by the government on 17th of the last month. He was in a hospital in the city at that time, undergoing treatment and recuperating slowly. He is due to return to the centre-stage of the Indian struggle for independence and this has become a cause for countrywide jubilation.

In Calcutta, the capital of his home province, the people are so excited that they are celebrating today as 'All Bengal Subhas Day' to felicitate him. A mammoth meeting was held in Shraddhanand Park in north Calcutta where some six organisations of various hues garlanded him as a mark of honour and respect. Tagore, the revered poet and Noble laurate, has joined, saying: 'I add my voice to the nation's welcome to Subhas'.[6]

Jawaharlal Prime Mover Of Muslim Mass Contact

April 1937: Jawaharlal, the Congress president, has been taking some concrete steps to increase contacts with the Muslim masses. On the last day of the previous month, he had issued a circular to all the provincial Congress committees drawing their attention to this issue. He has started a dedicated cell in the AICC to monitor and control the required activities and put young Kunwar Mohammad Ashraf, one of his trusted persons, in its charge. Ashraf shares Jawaharlal's Socialistic perceptions about the need to redress economic woes of the Muslims. He has begun his work in earnest.

Jawaharlal realises the importance of effective communication to build up rapport with the Muslim masses. He has ordered that the Congress pamphlets and notices be bilingual—in both Devnagari and Urdu scripts. Jawaharlal's personal conviction and enthusiasm have been exerting influence over the provincial Congress committees so much that the programme for mass contact with the Muslims has begun even in distant Madras though, according to reports, little, if any, attempt was made to secure the views, or personal commitment of C Rajagopalachari, the premier of the province. On the whole, the reports show that the programme has been able to generate good measure of response from the Muslims. Particularly poorer sections of the community seems to be slowly warming up to the Congress. Enrolments are rising.

Panicked League Searches For Organisational Response

April 1937: The responses to the Congress' Muslim mass contact programme have, so far, been encouraging. This is causing concern in the League leaders. Not only did they fare poorly in the recent elections, now this Congress method of trying to build direct bridge with the Muslims has forced them to view the new rival initiative with much anxiety. Jinnah and Iqbal have been bitter about Jawaharlal's programme. Maulana Shaukat Ali has warned that the effects of such a programme would lead to a 'fearful catastrophe'.[7] Simultaneous with issuance of threats and warnings to the Congress, the League is realising the need to build a strong organisational framework like that of the Congress, to be able to widen its influence and mobilise the country's Muslims under its banner.

HITLER PROPS UP FASCIST FORCES IN SPAIN

April 27, 1937, Madrid: Indian politicians, who have been anticipating 'break out' of war between European nations and a consequent realignment of powerful nations in the continent, sighted the early signs when Adolf Hitler's Germany interfered in the internal politics of Spain. That country has been undergoing civil war for past some time, with the left wing Republicans and the nationalist rebels fighting each other bitterly.

The armed forces of the country, led by General Franco, have been against the programmes and policies of the incumbent Republican government. Within the Republicans again, a section is committed to defend the constitution whereas another section looks at the ongoing internal strife as a pad for launching Social revolution. General Franco finds this completely unacceptable.

Hitler, noted for his anti-Communist bias, has, in a blatant move, sent German bombers to help General Franco's forces against the Republicans. In an unprecedented and horrific military action, the German fighter planes pounded the Basque town of Guernica yesterday. This is being seen as an ominous signal in the continent. Britain is upset at Hitler's growing political aspiration and muscle flexing. It is keeping a close watch.

Give Fitting Reply To Nehru's Atheistic Socialism: Iqbal

May 28, 1937, Lahore: Iqbal is worried about the turn of events since the results of the provincial elections were out. The reverses suffered by the League and the successes of the Congress have dented his dream of uniting the Muslims as a separate nation and advancing the goal of securing a separate state for them. The Muslims of the country have distributed their preferences across a spectrum of parties. The Muslim League, supposed to be the architect of the 'separate nation', has received a very low level of endorsement than what Iqbal, Jinnah or other top leaders had expected. Still worse, Iqbal has also been peeved at the manner in which Jawaharlal has been addressing the communal question—the latter's overt neglect of the religious content and analysing it in terms of economics and class interests. Iqbal finds such argument as virtually amounting to denying the political existence of Muslims. He has been greatly irritated by the Muslim Mass Contact Programme of the Congress, although he seems to have taken cognisance of the importance of meeting the economic demands of poor Muslims.

In the backdrop of these unsavoury developments, Iqbal has urged Jinnah to respond to the emerging challenges with urgency. He has written to Jinnah, requesting him to address the issues relating to the economic problems of the Muslim masses failing which, he expressed his fear that, they would have no interest in the League. Iqbal believes most of the problems the Muslims face in the country would get resolved if the Shariat was properly followed—this would ensure the right of subsistence to every one. Since the enforcement and development of the Shariat was impossible in this country without a free Muslim state or states, Iqbal has again urged Jinnah to raise the demand for a separate land for the Muslims. He reckons this would be the best reply Jinnah could give to Nehru's atheistic socialism.

GOVERNMENT FORMATION IN PROVINCES

Viceroy Urges Congress To Take A Practical View

June 22, 1937, Delhi: Nearly three months ago, the AICC had accorded conditional approval to the party to form ministries in provinces. However, the leaders of the provincial Congress failed to extract a commitment from the governors on the issue of exercising 'special powers'.

The governors refused to assure them, arguing that any guarantee or assurance undertaking not to exercise a constitutional power would be improper and against the constitution. Some sections in the government buttressed this contention, saying that such assurances would prevent the governors from discharging their constitutional obligations to the minorities and other vulnerable sections in cases of emergencies. The government's stand thus froze the Congress initiatives.

To resolve the impasse, Lord Linlithgow, the Viceroy, has now taken a subtle initiative. Without giving any formal assurance or guarantee, he has furnished elaborate reasoning to establish that the Congress was being unduly apprehensive of the 'provisions' in the 1935 Act, which had nothing to do with day-to-day governance, and constituted the special responsibilities of the governors that were restricted in scope to narrowest limits.

In those rare occasions, the minister or ministers, who disagreed with the governor's actions taken under special power, could always publicly disassociate themselves. On the whole, the Viceroy, sought to convey that the government could not really commit any unconstitutional act by giving a formal guarantee, as the Congress was seeking and that the Congress ought to exercise practical wisdom and ought not to either dither or hype up the issue.It appears that the government would not like to commit itself any more. It is now for the Congress to take a call.

Viceroy's Exposition Of Constitutional Provisions

The Viceroy, anxious that the British Raj's new constitutional reforms in India do not seem suspect in the eyes of the world, intervened to break the stalemate between the Congress and the provincial governors. Today he has issued a highly diplomatic statement.

Without formally guaranteeing that the governors would not exercise their special powers, the Viceroy said that the Congress' apprehension of the governors exercising special powers to impede or challenge ministers in day-to-day administrative matters was not justified. He clarified that the governors' special responsibilities were restricted in scope to narrowest limits.

In ministerial field there could be no interference, save in respect of matters with regard to which a governor is empowered to exercise his individual judgement. If differences arise in such matters the ministers could publicly disassociate themselves from such decisions of the governor. The question of severing partnership between the Governor and his ministers will arise where the ministers feel their credit and position were hopelessly undermined by a particular action by the governor in exercise of his responsibilities under the Act. But such circumstances are most unlikely to arise in ordinary circumstances.

The Viceroy added that the design of parliament was to avoid any such clash of opinion as would be calculated unnecessarily to break down the machineries of the government, or to result in the severance of that fruitful relationship between the governor and his ministers, which is the basis of the Act. What the Viceroy has done is a careful, lucid exposition of the positions of the governors and ministers. He did not give any assurance that the Congress has been seeking. At the same time, he gave a message that the British government was anxious to keep the special power of the governor in reserve so long as an obvious emergency did not make the 'use' of such power indispensable.

CONGRESS TO FORM GOVERNMENT IN PROVINCES

July 7, 1937, Wardha: On 22nd June, the Viceroy had stated that the essence of provincial autonomy was the cooperation between the governor and his ministers. Following this, the governors stated that their intention was not to provoke conflict with the ministers but to resolve them. Congress has interpreted that because of circumstances and events that have since occurred, it will not be easy for governors to use their special powers. Based on such general statements and interpretation of political situations, the Congress has now decided to take the plunge to accept office. The working committee has passed a resolution[8] today, permitting Congressmen to 'accept office where they may be invited thereto….' But the resolution makes it clear, the office is to be accepted and used to work in accordance with the lines laid down in the Congress manifesto and further, to implement the Congress policy of combating the new constitution on the one hand, and carry forward the constructive programme on the other. Gandhi has drafted the resolution.

Gandhi Returns To Active Politics, Congress Gears Up For Battles Ahead

July 17, 1937, Wardha: In the middle of 1934, Gandhi had announced his retirement from the Congress. Since then, he has been keeping away from the hustle and bustle of politics and Congress activities. During this period, he has been in the thick of constructive activities including development of villages, prohibition, communal harmony, and especially removal of untouchability. Notwithstanding his reluctance, the Congress repeatedly got in touch with him, whenever in need for guidance.

Post elections this year, it has become very difficult for him not to get involved in Congress affairs at least at the policy level. On 26th February, following the election results, Jawaharlal and other top Congress leaders came down to Segaon for his guidance and the working committee also held its meet there, on the following two days. Again, it was under his guidance that the AICC held a meeting on 16 March in Delhi and passed an important resolution demanding assurance from the governors about 'non-interference' as a condition to accept office in the provinces.

When this resolution generated a bitter political dispute with the Raj, the Congress again went to him for guidance. Eventually, he played a key role in guiding the working committee in passing the resolution in favour of accepting the office, together with a set of safeguards. It is true that he has ceased to be a member of the Congress and has not revoked his 'retirement decision' formally. However, facts suggest that he is again emerging as the party's nucleus and its key decision-maker. Today, he has written an article in *Harijan* laying down a set of guidelines for the Congress ministries and conduct and behaviour expected of the ministers. It looks almost certain that he will be at the centre stage of the Congress before long.

Shape Your Lifestyle To Match Semi-starved Masses

July 17, 1937, Wardha: Though Gandhi has not yet fully returned to Congress activities, there are indications that he is in the process of doing so. Today he has issued a set of guidelines[9] in *Harijan* meant for the Congress ministries in the provinces. There are two parts: general and specific. He has described the GOI Act 1935 as a feeble attempt by the British to replace the rule of the sword by rule of majority, with the hope that in course of working under the new constitution, Indians will come to regard their exploitation as a blessing in the end. Gandhi asked Congress legislators to thwart the intention of the framer of this new constitution by implementing the Act in a way not intended by the Raj, and refraining from using it in the way intended by the latter.

Having said this, Gandhi laid down a number of specific actions for the Congress ministries like: a. immediate implementation of 'prohibition', making 'education' self-supporting and stop financing of education from 'liquor' revenue; b. transforming jails into reformatories and converting them into workshops; c. making 'salt' free for the benefit of the poor; d. ensuring that all purchase of cloth are of khadi; e. focussing more on villages than the cities.

He laid strong emphasis on lifestyles and conduct of the Congress legislators. He warned them: 'We are the poorest nation on earth, many millions living in semi-starvation. Its representatives dare not live in a style and manner out of all correspondence with their electors...'Finally he said, if at the end of their endeavours, if the Englishmen or Anglicised Indians can be made to see the 'Indian' which is the Congress view point, 'the battle is won by the Congress and complete independence will come to us without shedding a drop of blood'.

'Busybody President' Of The Congress

July 26, 1937: Jinnah is yet to fully recover from the shock of the electoral reverses. To add insult to injury, Jawaharlal's unique analysis of the communal problem, prescription for its remedy and plans to establish direct contacts with the Muslim masses over the heads of League leaders have been irking him a great deal. In particular, he is not able to withstand Jawaharlal's 'Muslim Mass Contact programme'. Jinnah has been disparagingly referring to Jawaharlal as 'the busybody president of the Congress' who seems to be 'carrying the responsibility of the whole world on his shoulders and must poke his nose into everything except minding his own business'.[10] Jawaharlal's approach and his Muslim mass contact programme seem to be creating a steely resolve in Jinnah to prove that it is indeed the Muslim League that can bind the Muslim masses together and is their true representative.

Congress-League Feud Over Ministry Formation In UP

July 1937, Lucknow: Post election, the relationship between the Congress and the Muslim League has been progressively worsening. Another serious misunderstanding has arisen in the United Provinces on the issue of forming a coalition government. The two parties had developed serious differences on the number of cabinet berths and pre-conditions. They sparred and parted company.

Each has its own story. The Congress denies having had a pre-poll understanding with the League to form a coalition ministry. It achieved a single-party majority in the province and could form ministry of its own, but it still invited the League legislators as a measure of goodwill and for the sake of communal harmony. However, the League sources claim that the two parties indeed had an electoral understanding and the Congress even supported some of its candidates against the candidates of the Agriculturist Party. The Congress clarified that, the Agriculturist Party (AP), a party of the landlords, was its prime rival in UP, and its support for the Muslim League candidates against the AP candidates was, therefore, only strategic.

Whether or not there was a pre-poll understanding, both the parties, through a series of talks and negotiations, had, for past some time, been sending clear signals that they were working towards a coalition ministry. Local League leaders, Chaudhury Khaliquzzaman and Nawab Ismail Khan, were reportedly in talks with Congress leaders, including Jawaharlal, MAK Azad, GB Pant, JB Kripalani and Narendra Dev for securing two cabinet berths out of a total of six. If that was to be acceded to, the Congress, already under compulsion to give a berth to its Muslim member Rafi Ahmed Kidwai, faced the prospect of having three Muslim ministers, ie. half of the cabinet. That looked disproportionately large in a substantially Hindu majority province.

There were claims for additional berths from its own Muslim members too. Following a long-winding, tortuous and complex scheme of negotiations which included Jinnah's intervention and warning to the UP Muslim League body against an understanding with Congress at the provincial level, the initial negotiation and agreement of the above two local League leaders with the Congress came under stress. On its part, the Congress also came under great internal pressure against conceding two cabinet berths to the League. Finally, the party imposed a set of stringent conditions on the local League leaders, if they hoped to be inducted in the cabinet. According to reports, these conditions are indeed tough and signify the near dissolution of the legislative body of the League in the United Provinces. The League leaders have rejected the Congress conditions and thereby the prospect of the Congress-League coalition government has practically ended.

Anticipating the failure, the League has begun intense propaganda across the country by projecting itself as a victim. It is trying to tell the Muslims across the country that the Congress is loathe to sharing power with the Muslims.

'Conditions' The Congress Wants League To Accept

July 1937, Lucknow: The local Muslim League leaders say the negotiation broke down as Congress went back on its assurance that two of the League leaders would be made ministers and later changed it to only one. According to the Congress, it was prepared for 'two' ministers, but the League leaders were not prepared to accept the attendant conditions. It is difficult to find out the truth. However, here is a list giving the gist of the conditions[11] that the Congress wanted the League members to accept:

a. The League members would fight the new constitution, which was an election plank of the Congress;
b. The League members would resist the introduction and implementation of the 'federal' part of the constitution;
c. The League members would lay stress on the demand for setting up a Constituent Assembly;
d. The League members would wind up the League group in UP legislature, including the UP parliamentary board;
e. All the league members would become full members of the Congress without necessarily severing connection with the League and also without being required to specifically take the Congress pledge;
f. No Muslim League candidate would be put up in future elections in the province;
g. The League would commit to resign from ministries and legislatures in case of resignations by Congress members.

MUSLIM LEAGUE'S BYELECTION STRATEGY
Blunt Exploitation Of Religious Fundamentalism

July 1937, Bundelkhand: The rivalry between the Congress and the Muslim League has escalated to a new high over a byelection in the United Provinces. In Bundelkhand, a reserved constituency, a byelection has been announced upon the death of the Muslim League legislator. The Congress, now bolder and more confident of its reach and appeal to the Muslims, courtesy the hard work being done by the Muslim mass contact committee, has decided to field Nisar Ahmad Shervani, a well-known person as its candidate against the League nominee, Rafiuddin Ahmed. With this move, all hell has broken loose. For the first time perhaps, the Muslim League leaders have begun to bluntly appeal to the religious sentiment of the voters.

In a statement, the League has asked Muslims to come together as they had been 'ordered by God and His Prophet to support the Muslim League candidate in Bundelkhand to give a crushing reply to the non-Muslim organisation so that in future, it would not dare to interfere in the affairs of Muslims.'[12] Its cadres are fanning across villages shouting anti-Congress and anti-Hindu slogans. In a cleverly contrived election campaign, the League has been trying to make the Congress and the Hindus look synonymous and mobilise Muslim voters on religious lines. Congress leaders are greatly upset at this blatant communal politics.

Muslim League Raises Bogey Of 'Islam In Danger'

July 1937: Muslim League has been skilfully using the coalition ministry fiasco in UP to justify the need for a separate Muslim state. It is urging the Muslims to look at the UP incident as a model of things likely to be seen in the future, once a government is set up on the centre under the new constitution. It is contending that only those Muslims who are prepared to join the Congress would have a share in the government to the exclusion of the larger Muslim community. It has also begun raising the bogey of 'Islam in danger', to play on the fears of the Muslims in the country. It seems, the League is getting some measure of success through these crude, fundamentalist strategies to influence the Muslim minds.

Result Is Out – Bad Blood Spills Over

July 1937, Bundelkhand: Though the Muslim League candidate has won the Bundelkhand byelection, the contest was close and he managed to win by a margin of 727 votes while the electorate numbered around 7,500[13]. The defeat was moderated by the fact that the Congress led two out of three constituency segments and evoked good measure of support in the rural pockets. The result has further embittered the relationship between the two parties. The League is feeling the heat of the Congress programme of Muslim mass contact. It is also upset at the growing confidence of the rival Congress in fighting a reserved seat in this fashion.

My People Are The People Of India: Jawaharlal

July 1937: The Muslim Mass Contact (MMC) programme of the Congress has been arousing heat and controversies in the country. The communal leaders are growing angrier by the day. On April 21 this year, Maulana Shaukat Ali had, in a press statement, issued a veiled threat that the Congress programme of MMC could lead to fearful catastrophe. To that, Jawaharlal, possibly in a tacit reference to the failed Khilafat movement, which the Maulana steered as one of the key leaders, responded that it was futile to seek understanding with communal leaders and groups. Jinnah, enraged at Jawaharlal's utterances, commented that the latter was speaking in a manner as if he were a sovereign authority. Jawaharlal, however, expressed resentment at what he described as the League's obstructionist strategies to what were Congress' ordinary political work amongst the Muslims. But Jinnah finds the Congress programmes and activities as abominable, unauthorised, and 'uncalled for', trespassing into the legitimate and exclusive political territories of the League. Now he has warned that the Congress' MMC is fraught with serious consequences. Earlier this month, Jinnah warned Jawaharlal to stay off the Muslims and advised him: 'There is plenty of scope for… Mr Nehru to improve his own people, the Hindus…'. just as the League should try to improve the Muslims. This attracted a sharp rebuff from Jawaharlal who replied that, 'Not being religiously or communally inclined', he ventures to think of 'my people' 'as the Indian people as a whole.[14]

Congress Forms Government In Provinces

July 1937: In provincial elections, the Congress got clear majority in Madras, United Provinces, Central Provinces, Bihar and Orissa. Rajagopalachari formed the government in Madras on 15th of this month. Before the end of the month, Congress has formed ministries in other five provinces, viz. United Provinces, Central Provinces, Bihar, Orissa and Bombay. In Bombay, the party has gone for a coalition government as it did not have simple majority.

Madani Advocates Composite Nationalism, Writes To Iqbal

August 1937, Deoband: The Congress started its Muslim Mass Contact programme on economic presumptions—highlighting the need to remove poverty and backwardness of the vast poor Muslim masses and pulling them closer to the party in the course of carrying out relevant programmes. It has now received a boost with a section of the Islamic clergy supporting the campaign. Included in the above have been leading Ulemas of Deobond and of Jamiyat al-Ulema. Husain Ahmad Madani, a co-founder and president of Jamiyat al-Ulema, has appealed to people of his community to join the Congress to accelerate the freedom struggle. He is in favour of developing a composite nationalism in the country. However, conscious of the fact that Muhammad Iqbal, another highly influential Muslim leader, has been propagating a contrasting ideology by calling Muslims a separate nation and urging them to unite, Madani has written to him to bring in clarity at the ideological level in the country, especially for the Muslims. Madani has argued that the word 'qaum' could be applied to any collective group and its basis could be any of religion, common habitat, race, colour or craft.

He also expressed the opinion that present-day nations are made by homelands. Citing England, he has pointed out how members of different faiths living in that land constitute one nation. Madani has expressed the need to get rid of British rule so that the Muslims are able to practise their faith freely. Since they were not strong enough to win their freedom all by themselves, they needed help from the non-Muslim communities. He is thus viewing the support to the Congress in the overall context and urging Muslims to join the party and strengthen the movement for freedom.

Ambedkar Introduces Bill To Abolish Khoti

September 17, 1937, Bombay: Bhimrao Ambedkar has ensured that a good number of legislators from the depressed classes were elected into the provincial legislature. As many as 14 members of the Indian Labour Party have been elected to the Bombay provincial legislature in February this year. This is about 90% of the seats reserved for the depressed classes. He is also setting examples before them as to how to keep alert eyes on and empathise with the problems of the depressed classes and bring in legislations to redress these. Today he has introduced a bill in the Bombay legislature that seeks to abolish the 'Khoti' system of land tenure in the Konkan region. The objective is to end the tyranny of the 'Khots', who happen to be an intermediary, authorised by the government to collect land tax and ill treat the hapless villagers, besides keeping a portion of the revenue collected with them. Congress, the dominant coalition partner ruling Bombay, has not been in favour of the abolition of the system but only intends to reform it. Ambedkar is undeterred and prepared to go the long haul. He has introduced another bill to release the Mahar untouchables from a system of forced slavery, ie. to work for the government as slaves. He is putting his background as a lawyer to good use in carrying out a strong legislative campaign to improve the lot of the weaker sections.

Prisoners of Cellular Jail End Prolonged Hunger Strike

September 24, 1937, Port Blair: Now that Indian political parties have formed governments in the British Indian provinces, political prisoners are growing hopeful of better treatment including release. Severely oppressed by jail authorities and living under harsh conditions in the infamous cellular jail here, about two hundred prisoners, mostly freedom fighters from Bengal, went on a hunger strike on 24th July this year demanding repatriation to mainland India and also release from the prison.

The sufferings in the prison here have become almost proverbial. Their hunger strike found an immediate resonance in the country. In mainland India, many political prisoners began hunger strike as a sympathetic gesture. Telegrams were sent by Gandhi, Subhas, Tagore, Jawaharlal and Fazlul Huq, the prime minister of Bengal, to the prisoners assuring them of support while urging them to end their strike. On 29th last month, all but seven prisoners ended their hunger strike and had wired to Gandhi expressing gratitude to him and the nation that their cases were being pursued with the government. The seven prisoners had, however, been continuing with their hunger strike despite intermittent requests by Gandhi to end the same. Eventually, today they have suspended their strike. The government has been initiating steps to repatriate the island prisoners to the mainland.

Sikandar Hayat Makes Peace With Jinnah

October 14, 1937, Lucknow: Punjab forms an important component in Jinnah's stratagem to form a separate state for Muslims. However, the performance of the Muslim League in the province in the recent election has been pathetic. Though Punjab happens to be a Muslim majority province, the voters here have simply looked the other way and supported the Unionist Party led by Sikandar Hayat. Casting away his disappointment, Jinnah has made a strategic move to overcome the roadblock to his scheme by inviting Sikandar to join the Muslim League with all the Muslim legislators of his party.

Both Jinnah and Sikandar are in Lucknow in connection with a session of the Muslim League. Following their talks here, the two leaders have arrived at an understanding which is set to determine the future relations between the two parties. According to League sources, it has been decided that both the parties will continue to function in cooperation.

All Muslim members of the Unionist Party will sign the creed of the AIML and join it while continuing their membership with their existing party simultaneously. In future elections to legislatures, the coalition will support candidates put up by either. Muslim legislators, who are elected on or who accept the League ticket, will constitute the Muslim League Party in the legislature. While the existing coalition will continue, it will be open for the League to forge coalition with any party which pursues fundamental principles, policy and programme consistent with that of the League.

According to sources close to the Unionist Party, this is a simple arrangement whereby the Muslim members of their party would continue to be Unionist in Punjab and Leaguers outside the province.

It appears, the two sides somewhat differ about the exact features of the pact. However, to both the leaders, the pact at present looks politically expedient. Sikandar, being confident of his own popularity and mass appeal, is not unduly worried about its fallout in Punjab. To him, he can manage its outcome in local politics whereas the support of the central leadership of the League would be useful at the all-India level for more than one reason. As for Jinnah, he has been able to bring an important Muslim majority province under his sphere of influence, even if nominally, for the time being. What the AIML had failed to accomplish through a hard-fought election, Jinnah has begun to achieve it by means of deft political negotiations.

Enlist In Thousands With Muslim League: Jinnah

October 15-18, 1937, Lucknow: Jinnah is growing increasingly hostile to the Congress and making every effort to polarise Muslims in favour of the League. While delivering the presidential speech[15] at the Muslim League session here, he has criticised the present leadership of the Congress for alienating the Muslims and pursuing a policy, which he said, is exclusively Hindu centred. He has charged that the Congress governments in six provinces, by their words, deeds and programmes have shown it over and again that the Mussalmans cannot expect any justice or fairplay at their hands.

He has criticised the Congress highcommand for speaking in different voices without any genuine concern for the Mussalmans. He contended that: 'One opinion is that there is no such thing as Hindu-Muslim question and there is no such thing as minorities' question in the country. The other high opinion is that if a few crumbs are thrown to the Mussalmans in their present disorganised and helpless state, they can be managed.' But Jinnah warned the Congress that these leaders are sadly mistaken and that 'the All-India Muslim League, has now come to live and play its just part in the world of Indian politics…'

He has implored people to rally round the Muslim League flag saying, 'Enlist yourselves by hundreds and thousands, as quickly as you can, as members of the All-India Muslim League, provincial Leagues, district Leagues, organise yourselves, establish your solidarity and complete unity.' He has then sought to encourage their insularity from the mainstream, saying: 'Eighty million of Mussalmans in India have nothing to fear. They have their destiny in their hands, and as a well-knit, solid, organised united force can face any demands and withstand any opposition to its united front…'

Political Realignments Begin In Punjab

October 1937: The Sikandar-Jinnah pact has surcharged the political atmosphere in the province. In the opposition bench, the Akali Dal has begun coming closer to the Congress. Amongst the supporting parties in the treasury bench, viz. the Khalsa National Party and the Hindu Election Board, there are visible disappointments. But these are of little significance, as the Unionist Party has a single party majority in the assembly. Any intra-party squabbles alone may be of consequence, if at all. There are no such signs and Sikandar is in complete control of his party men.

I Signed My Death Warrant, Laments Nariman
Nariman Utterly Unreliable, Says Gandhi

October 29, 1937, Bombay: While forming the government in Bombay, there was factional divide in the Congress and a contest as to who should lead the government. At the end, Vallabhbhai Patel settled the row. BG Kher was chosen to head the government over Khursheed Nariman, another charismatic, dynamic and competent party leader. On this issue, a deep discontent emerged and continued to simmer within the party. Complaints were made to Gandhi that Vallabhbhai decided the issue on communal consideration, choosing Kher, a Hindu over Nariman, who happened to be a Parsee. Even Abul Kalam Azad, a senior Congress leader, held the same opinion. Offended at the allegation, Vallabhbhai agreed for an independent enquiry. The enquiry gave him a clean chit and its findings were accepted by Nariman.

However, Nariman retracted later. In a statement issued from Mysore, he said he had earlier accepted the report under duress — as he was told Gandhi's health would be affected otherwise, implying if he continued to pursue his allegation and aggravate the issue. In hindsight, he said, he realised he had committed a grave blunder and in fact signed his own political death warrant by accepting the enquiry report. The working committee is not amused and is contemplating action against Nariman. Gandhi has been upset too by Nariman's statement and has found it extraordinary. Today he has written[16] about Nariman's conduct, expressing a great degree of pain that the latter's statement has caused him. Gandhi wrote, Nariman's statement was a distortion of facts and surely his health had nothing to do with Nariman's 'confession'. He has written that by his 'Mysore recantation'; Nariman has proved himself 'utterly unreliable'. Gandhi said he has placed relevant papers with the working committee. It is likely that the latter may impose a harsh punishment upon Nariman.

Kisan Sabhas Clash With Congress Governments

October 1937: Right since the formation of the All-India Kisan Sabha (AIKS) in April last year, the oppressed peasantry in the country has been acquiring confidence to stand up to the atrocities and injustices of the British. Swinging into action, this new body, in a matter of four months, formulated a 'Kisan manifesto', putting forth a slew of radical demands including abolition of zamindari, cancellation of rural debt, and also substituting the system of land revenue with a graded structure of agricultural income tax. After the Congress governments took over reins in several provinces, the farmers were enthused and the Kisan Sabhas were hoping to initiate several reforms with help from the government. But their last three months of experience have been rather disappointing.

Things are particularly bad in Bihar where the Kisan Sabhas allege that the Congress government has been acting under the influence of the zamindars. They are bitter that in several instances of confrontations between the farmers and the landlords, the latter have been leveraging the state power and ensuring use of police and military. Farmers are being intimidated by false cases and arrests. The zamindars are also reportedly strengthening their private armies. Undaunted, the farmers who have organised themselves under the AIKS and local Kisan Sabhas have been preparing for a long fight to secure their rights.

Under such circumstances, the AIKS has started to move away from the Congress. It appears that the apex body has begun to gradually come under rising Socialist and Communist influences. Significantly, AIKS has adopted the red flag as its banner.

Support For Mysore People's Struggle AICC Resolution A Paradigm Shift In Congress Policy?

October 31, 1937, Calcutta: The ongoing people's movement in Mysore and the Congress involvement therein has been causing tension amongst Congress leaders. In a meeting held here today, the AICC has passed a resolution protesting against the repressive policies of the Mysore government, and its suppression of civil liberties of people including the right of speech, assemblage and association. The resolution, after wishing the people of the state success in their legitimate, non-violent struggle, went far beyond and appealed to people of both the Indian states and British Indian provinces 'to give all support and encouragement to the people of Mysore in their struggle against the state for rights of self-determination'.[17] Such open support to the people's movement of states was simply unthinkable in the past. Many Congressmen feel that Jawaharlal's involvement has been instrumental in securing the AICC's full support.

Gandhi Proposes Subhas As Next Congress President

November 1, 1937, Calcutta: Gandhi, on an important political visit to the city to ensure repatriation and release of Andaman prisoners, has been staying at the house of Sarat Bose, Subhas's elder brother. Today he has written a note to Vallabhbhai, expressing his displeasure over the manner in which the issue of prospective punishment to Nariman was dealt with, by the working committee. Gandhi has also been unhappy about the AICC resolution suggesting an interventionist policy in favour of the people's movement in Mysore state. Jawaharlal, the Congress president, played a key role in that initiative. In his note, Gandhi has made no effort to disguise his displeasure on this issue and wanted all members of the working committee loyal to him, to resign in protest. He has advised Vallabhbhai accordingly.

In the same note, he has also revealed his mind about the next Congress president. Significantly, he has not mentioned about another term for Jawaharlal. Instead, he has expressed his choice for Subhas, though not without reservation: 'I have observed that Subhas is not at all dependable. However, there is nobody but he who can be the president'.[18]

Why Gandhi Wants Subhas As The Next President?

In recent years, there has been emergence in the Congress of a strong block comprising the left nationalists as well as the Communists. Although it is not a cohesive and disciplined group, its members are trying in their own way to influence the macro policies of the party, which are at variance with that of Gandhi in many respects. This has been leading to occasional frictions, as happened over the last two years.

The orthodox Congress, led by leaders like Vallabhbhai, and swearing loyalty to Gandhi, are controlling the composition of the cabinets in various provinces, thus wielding the lever of power, where the left block has little say.

With the two blocks thus positioned, Gandhi has reportedly indicated his choice of Subhas as the next president. Political analysts say he must have made several discreet calculations in arriving at his choice. First, Subhas being a favourite of the left block, the selection recognises their importance. Second, the administrative power through provincial governments being controlled by the orthodox faction, the presidency to the other faction would act as a balancing factor. Third, the orthodox faction, slowly getting accustomed to the role of governance, seems to be losing the will and spirit to wage struggles or conduct movements. The left blocks, comparatively distant from the perks and privileges, still retain the urge and stamina for struggle. A president from their block can keep the spirit high.

Gandhi probably knows that having left out Jawaharlal, he has no other choice than Subhas to represent the left block.

This Resolution Is Ultra Vires: Gandhi
When I Don't Understand, I Can't Act Otherwise: Jawaharlal

November 13, 1937, Wardha: Gandhi had expressed his reservations about the AICC resolution on Mysore in an article in the *Harijan*. He made it clear that he did not hold any brief for Mysore and he would, in fact, like the Maharaja to reform many things. He was, at the same time, emphatic that it was Congress policy 'to give an opponent his due'. More importantly, he pronounced his verdict on the very validity of the resolution. Referring to an earlier AICC resolution passed in April 1936, in Lucknow on a relevant issue, Gandhi wrote, 'In my opinion, the Mysore resolution was ultra vires of the resolution of non-interference'. This hit Jawaharlal hard as he had played a key role in regard to the adoption of the resolution. Though upset, Jawaharlal refused to give in to Gandhi's sweeping comment. With regard to the 'ultra vires' observation, he has written to Gandhi today, saying he cannot conjure with any such provision. He continued: 'You have censured the AICC and me for the course we pursued. I have not yet understood how and where I was wrong and so long as I do not understand it, I can hardly act otherwise.'[19] The tone and tenor of Jawaharlal's letter betrays a new trend of thinking in matters relating to States' People's Movement.

Unrest Engulfs Indian Labour Under Congress Rule

November, 1937: The Congress Socialist Party has been disillusioned by the high-handed manner of the provincial Congress governments in dealing with political dissent. It has taken exception to the prosecution of six of its members in Ahmedabad for the simple reason that they had helped distribute pamphlets of the banned Communist Party of India in a public meeting that was to be addressed by the Congress president. This incident was criticised in *The Congress Socialist*. It was noted that these regimes did not even consider Gandhi's advice—that the government ought to consult the provincial Congress committee before taking any action against a Congress worker. The party has also held that the reasons for unrest and discontent in workers are legitimate while noting that, 'There is a wave of intense unrest among Indian labour. Strikes have become the order of the day all over the country.'[20]

Clearly the Congress governments in provinces have a long way to go to secure the confidence of the workers and also the Socialist members of their own party.

SAVARKAR ESPOUSES CAUSE OF HINDU NATION
Reminds Hindus Of Their Glorious Past

December 10, 1937, Ahmedabad: His impeccable track record as a fierce Hindu Nationalist has made VD Savarkar a natural choice for the post of president of All India Hindu Mahasabha. Here Savarkar is presiding over the nineteenth session of the Mahasabha. His presidential speech is being considered by political observers and analysts as controversial as well as politically significant, especially coming at a time when Jinnah and Muslim League have been raising demands of a separate land for Muslims.

Savarkar, in his speech, has defined terms like Hindu and Hindutva and made a strong case for a resurgent assertive Hindu nation. He has made out a strong case for encouraging and promoting Hindu nationalism. Hindus, he has contended, by being the vast majority of India's population, constitute the bed rock of the country. There is nothing objectionable about Hindu nationalism as it never sought to infringe on an equal just right and liberties of any other population group of India. On the contrary, he claimed, Hindus have suffered maximum struggle and undergone enormous sacrifice for liberating India from the British rule.

Savarkar has expressed the resolve of Hindus to create an independent united Indian state, where all population groups will live with equal rights, signified by the formula of 'one man one vote'. The language in the country should be the one spoken by the majority of its people. The script also should be adopted based on the same consideration.

Savarkar has observed that amongst all non-Hindu population groups, the Mohammedans have, in particular, not agreed to such conditions of equality. Referring to the history of antagonism spanning over past several centuries between Hindus and Muslims, he has identified the latter as a separate nation, whose love for India as their motherland has been but a handmaid to their love for their Holy land, meaning the land where the religion they profess originated, which was outside of India. They have customarily withheld their support to the freedom struggle unless they were given some special rights and privileges like separate electorates, adoption of Urdu as national tongue (even though it is spoken by only a couple of crore of people) and so on.

Savarkar has been more critical of those 'unity hankers' amongst the Hindus who hastened to truncate the 'Vande Matarm' song because Muslims won't tolerate it. The communal question was a real one that could not be suppressed by merely refusing to recognize it. Like a deep-seated disease it warranted diagnosis and treatment.

Savarkar wanted Hindus to continue with their struggle for liberation whether or not the Mohammedans of India join in. In the event the latter have a design to set up Mohammedan rule in India, the Hindus, Savarkar warned, must stand up on their own feet, fight and liberate themselves from any non-Hindu yoke, whether British or Muslim or any other. In the latter part of his speech, Savarkar condemned the apologetic attitude in some Hindus to proclaim themselves as Hindus. Reminding the Hindus that they were born of the lines of Shri Ram, Shri Krishna, Shivaji, Rana Pratap and Govind Singh he exhorted them to be proud of their great heroic past and rise up to the challenges that lay before them.

TRANSFORMATION OF VD SAVARKAR

Over decades, Savarkar, an ardent advocate of Hindu cultural and political nationalism, has undergone a radical transformation in his philosophy and political thinking. He was an atheist and had begun his political life as a political extremist committed to drive the British away from India by force. He wrote a book titled, The Indian War of Independence, based on the Sepoy Mutiny of 1857, which got him instant recognition amongst patriotic Indians.

The British government banned the book, apprehending it would encourage sedition in India. But, it was published in Netherlands,

France and Germany, and smuggled into India. This book was widely circulated and it kept inspiring growing tribes of freedom fighters. Savarkar had made an abortive attempt to stage a revolution against the colonial government.

In that connection, he was arrested and deported to the infamous Cellular prison in the distant Andaman, where he faced severe persecution. In the solitary confinement, Savarkar had time to introspect and analyse and he began to develop a political philosophy about Hindu cultural and political nationalism.

AMBEDKAR OBJECTS TO THE WORD 'HARIJAN'

January 22, 1938, Bombay: Gandhi has been using the term 'Harijan' to refer to the people belonging to the depressed classes and Congressmen are following this usage. However, not everyone agrees with the aptness of the term. Some say it betrays a condescending attitude on the part of the Caste-Hindus, and that instead of breaking the caste barrier in the Hindu community, it compartmentalises the depressed classes for eternity by sticking a label to them as a collective body. What is truly needed to bring this vulnerable population at par with the rest is not such 'gimmicks' but extending them the full range of civil rights.

A serious dispute broke out in the Bombay legislature, when the Congress sought to introduce a bill where the term 'Harijan' was used to refer to the depressed classes. Bhimrao Ambedkar objected to the usage of this term. He argued, if untouchables were 'people of god' as the movers of the bill in the Congress claimed, then others would be 'people of monsters'. However, the Congress did not agree to make any changes in the term introduced by Gandhi. Ambedkar felt bitter, walked out of the House with other legislators of the Independent Labour Party, as a mark of protest against the government for 'using its majority in a tyrannical manner'.[21]

Whether or not the word is dropped from the bill, Ambedkar's walkout has attracted the attention of the nation to this issue. It is likely to be debated more and more in every section of society.

Subhas In London

January 1938, London: Subhas is presently in England. This is his first visit here since 1921, when he had returned to India after resigning form the Indian Civil Services. Though he was in Europe during 1932 to 1935, the British government gave him an impression that his entry into England was banned and thus managed to block him from visiting that country, despite his keenness. However, the present occasion is completely different. The government has imposed no ban, placed no bar. There is an air of expectation and rumours of his taking up the mantle of the Indian National Congress. At Victoria Station, large number of associations and organisations of Indians like Friends of India, the Swaraj League, the Congress League, the Indian Political Group, the Oxford, Cambridge and London Majlis and several others have congregated to extend him a warm reception.

President-elect Subhas Meets European Leaders

January 1938, London: Subhas has received the news that he has been elected as the next Congress president. In England, important British leaders including Clement Attlee, Ernest Bevin and Stafford Cripps have received him warmly. This trip is qualitatively different from his earlier forced exile of two years in Europe, when he was constantly chased by secret agents and dissuaded from entering England. Now he is being seen as the premier of the most important political party of India, with the people and the media of this country keen to know his views on various issues including Indian political aspiration, Indo- British relation, and international relations.

Everywhere, while delivering speeches, Subhas is making it very clear that India led by the Congress wants to frame her own constitution. In the meanwhile, he is also warning that under no circumstances should the British go ahead with the implementation of the federal part of the constitution as envisaged under the 1935 Act, which would be a blunder.

Subhas spent about three years in Europe, during 1932-35 when he had travelled extensively across the continent, interacted with political leaders, and developed his own political insight into the emerging political situations. In the process, he detected quite a few dormant volcanoes waiting to explode. And in such eventualities, he also identified the opportunities that would open up before India to unshackle herself from the British chain.

Now that it has been confirmed that he has been elected as the Congress president, he is looking at the news as more than a formal compliment—with a sense of great responsibility. He feels an opportunity has arisen before him to factor in his understanding of the international situation into his role as the president of the Congress, to shape the policies of that great organisation and prepare Indian people to strike the British government hard at the appropriate time. He is sure that India must not miss the coming opportunity yet again—her children must not commit the same blunder that they did during the First World War.

God Give You Strength To Bear Jawaharlal's Mantle – Gandhi Wires Subhas

January 23, 1938 Calcutta: Subhas has returned from Europe. Today is his birthday. Upon arrival, he has received a welcome message from Gandhi reading: *Welcome home. God give you strength to bear the weight of Jawaharlal's mantle. Love. Bapu.*[22] However, considering Subhas's past track records as a fiercely uncompromising leader with independent, uncluttered thinking and opinion on national and international issues, political observers are not sure if he, as the new president elect, would view his responsibility in the manner Gandhi would like him to do.

Trouble Brews In The Central Provinces

February 15, 1938, Nagpur: Even as the Congress is poised to hold its fifty first annual session in Haripura enthusiastically, serious infighting has gripped the Congress government in the Central Provinces. That province has both Marathi speaking and Hindi speaking regions. The cabinet, led by Marathi speaking prime minister Dr NB Khare, has ministers from both the linguistic groups.

A political storm has been blowing in the province for past some time over a protracted confrontation between Khare and his three cabinet colleagues. RS Shukla, DP Misra and DK Mehta, belonging to Mahakoshal, a Hindi speaking area of the province. Khare suspected they were plotting against him and has accused them of bribery and nepotism.

DP Misra and his two colleagues, in turn, alleged that Khare was in league with the British governor and planning to remove them. This controversy has been taking a toll of the public image of the Congress Party. In this ongoing tussle, top leaders like Vallabhbhai Patel, Rajendra Prasad and Maulana Azad are irritated with Khare and they have also been sharing their perspective with Gandhi.

A Village Transformed Into A Town

February 1938, Haripura: This is the first major Congress session to be held after the Congress formed government in various provinces. The venue itself has been so organised as if to celebrate that transformation. A small city, Vithal Nagar, named after the departed veteran Congress leader Vithalbhai Patel has been constructed in the Haripura village. Built under the caring guidance of Vallabhbhai and the reception committee members, this small temporary city is spread over two miles and three-fourth of a mile wide and has been provided with modern facilities like waterworks, electricity, post & telegraphs, telephone line and roads. Adorned with fifty-one gates to commemorate the fifty first session of the Congress, the city is also well illuminated. There is great enthusiasm amongst both local people and Congress workers, who are looking ahead to the commencement of the proceedings.

Subhas Gets Rousing Reception

February, 1938, Haripura: Haripura marks the fifty-first session of the Indian National Congress. Subhas's presidential car was driven by fifty-one bullocks and it went through fifty-one gates of honour. On the way to the venue, he acknowledged the cheers of a highly enthusiastic crowd. One of the distinguished patriots and crusaders for

India's freedom, he has been marked for his youth, enthusiasm, and compassion for his countrymen. Generally perceived to be belonging to the anti-Gandhi camp, the fact that he was elected as Congress president suggests that a kind of understanding between him and Gandhi has been reached. Much of the exuberance and enthusiasm seem to be in recognition of this fact.

Young, Charismatic Subhas Presides Over Haripura Session

February 19, 1938, Haripura: Subhas is 41, a young president and a charismatic leader. His political career since 1921 has been exceptionally eventful—a saga of repeated confrontations with the government, numerous arrests, exiles and internments. The Congress was deprived of his service during last year's election campaign as he was interned for almost a year then. There had been speculations as to what would have been the impact on the electoral outcome, if he were allowed to campaign for the Congress.

Subhas has been known to be a man, who would follow his own convictions and never compromise with principles. In the late 20s and early 30s, when the Congress had inner debate on the 'dominion status' issue, he was steadfast about 'complete independence' instead of 'dominion status'. On that issue, he had even crossed sword with Gandhi. Long period of suffering in prison could not wane his spirit a wee bit to fight relentlessly for the freedom of India. His forced exile in Europe in recent years and his interactions with the eminent leaders in that continent have given him an unique understanding of international politics and situations. To vast number of party workers and delegates, his spirit, maturity and vision is precious.

Subhas Makes It Clear He Will Be His Own Master

In his presidential speech, Subhas has made several important points, which are distinct departures from the past. He wants the Congressmen and Indians to be ready to take advantage of the impending war in Europe. He foresees that it will be a great continental war, which will create enormous pressure on the British to defend itself against strong adversaries. Subhas reckons that this will present India with the right opportunities to extract her freedom. At the same time, he has also made it clear that he does not have any feeling of animosity towards Britain. He has said, 'Once we have real self-determination, there is no reason why we should not enter into the most cordial relations with the British people.'

On the Government of India Act 1935, Subhas has condemned the statute as the 'pittance of self government' while continuing to retain control in the British hand. He said that this made the constitutional reforms a mockery. He felt this new constitution imposed on unwilling Indians must be fought at various levels. He has laid emphasis on a strong central government, which while unifying the country, should also be able to put all the minority communities and provinces at ease by allowing them large measures of autonomy in cultural and governmental matters. To the delight of the Socialist delegates, he advocated the relevance of socialism, though not communism, as a system that could cater to the needs of the Indians. Significantly, more than half of his speech was on national reconstruction and the problems India was likely to face after the British left the country.

He has expressed a sense of urgency for the Congress to draw up a master programme of national reconstruction. His exposure to the economic planning model of various European countries and especially, the success of the Socialistic model of planning in the USSR in improving the economic condition of her people in a short time frame, have convinced him of the need of putting in place a mechanism that can hasten the pace and scope of industrial and economic development of the country. He has announced a 'national planning committee' and urged Jawaharlal to take charge of it.

On the whole, he has given enough hints that while he realised the necessity for Congress unity, he would also not hesitate to mould its policies if he could, to reach the goal of freedom.

New President Focuses On National Reconstruction

February 1938, Haripura: Subhas has listed poverty, illiteracy and diseases as the major problems afflicting India. To solve these, he has stressed upon the need for scientific production and distribution, which can be effectively carried out only along Socialistic lines. Subhas said that the first thing India's national government would have to do is to adopt a planned approach. This would require setting up a commission that would, in turn, draw up a comprehensive plan for reconstruction. He has given a road map:

Measures to tackle increase in population;

Radical reform in land system, abolition of landlordism;

A comprehensive scheme of industrial development under state ownership and control, as mere agricultural development will not be able to solve the economic problems of the country;

Planning Commission to decide which of the home industries could be revived.

CONGRESS' INTERNATIONAL POLICY

Subhas And Jawaharlal Have Radical Differences

February 22, 1938, Haripura: Although both Subhas and Jawaharlal have had sufficiently long exposure to Europe and European politics in recent years, they differ radically as to the manner in which India should handle the evolving political situation in that continent. Whereas Jawaharlal is adherent to a strong idealistic approach of an international hue, Subhas is a pragmatic nationalist who feels that every country should determine her foreign policy in narrow national interest. Thus, Jawaharlal is keen that the Congress denounces Japanese occupation of China and also the fascist aggression in Europe. He is keen about the internal political system of the countries concerned. But Subhas has made it clear in his presidential speech that India should not be influenced by the internal policies of any country or the form of its state. He has quoted the example of Soviet Russia, a Communist country which has not hesitated to form alliances with non-Socialist states if that suited her own interest. He said that India should look at her own interest and not mind using help from Britain's enemies, if these helped advance the cause of Indian nationalism, whether these came from Germany, Italy or Japan. Such significant differences of opinion amongst two top leaders portend to difficulties in the formulation of 'war time' policies by the Congress.

New President's Agenda Displeases Gandhi

February 1938: It is true that Subhas's appointment as the president of the Congress was unanimous and obviously carried Gandhi's endorsement. However, since his taking over, Subhas has been chalking out priorities for the organisation which are not liked by Gandhi or his loyalists. For example, Subhas as the new president, envisioning an impending European war, has been trying to harden Congress' attitude against the British with a view to wresting freedom for the country. According to the Gandhian camp, these are wrong priorities and needless at this time. Then, Subhas has launched a National Planning Committee for drawing up a comprehensive plan of industrialisation for national development. Gandhi, personally, has been against industrialisation and therefore finds this unwarranted. Subhas, however, is undaunted—he is determined to pursue his own line.

States' People's Movement: Congressmen Can Participate

February 1938, Haripura: The gradual evolution of a pro-active Congress policy-regime in favour of the States' People's Movement, which reached a new height due to Jawaharlal's involvement in Mysore, has generated intense debate in the Congress. A powerful group, mostly pure Gandhians, are opposing the recent trend—Gandhi himself had reservations on the Congress role in the southern episode. He and former president Jawaharlal had clashed on the issue last year.

At Haripura, the working committee at first took up a resolution that called for disbanding of Congress committees in the princely states and declared that no Congress work should be carried out in the states without its consent. However, the left wing of the Congress put up fierce resistance to any such move.

A compromise was reached under which the existing Congress

committees would be allowed to continue under the direction of the Congress working committee, but they are not to engage in parliamentary activities or to launch direct action campaigns under the Congress banner. This means that the Congress as an organisation, would not participate in the internal popular agitation in the states. But a new route has now been declared open—individual Congressmen would be allowed to render further assistance to States' People's Movements in their personal capacities. Few leaders, especially Gandhi, Jawaharlal, and Patel have their own spheres of influence amongst princely states and they will be in a position to make use of the new policy.

Controversy Over Release Of Political Prisoners Two Premiers Resign, Then Withdraw

February 1938, Lucknow and Patna: Congress, in its election manifesto, had promised that upon forming the provincial governments it would release all political prisoners. However, it has not been easy for the party to implement this agenda to people's expectation, as the governors in the provinces, especially so in the United Provinces and Bihar, refused to accept the Congress ministry's recommendation on the release of these prisoners in large numbers. In both UP and Bihar, many political prisoners have been languishing in jail for long. Besides, since the second half of last year when political prisoners from Andaman began to be repatriated to India, their number in these two provinces have shot up further. On the issue of their release, the Congress entered into confrontation with the Governor General. The issue grew so complex that GB Pant, the premier of UP and Srikrishna Sinha, the premier of Bihar, tendered their resignation on the15th of this month as a mark of protest.

With both sides hardening their stance, Gandhi had to intervene. In a press statement issued a couple of days ago, he argued that the decision to release political prisoners was a matter of both right and responsibility of the provincial ministry, as the provinces have been bestowed complete autonomy. It was, of course, for the provincial ministries to take a call on the merit of such decisions including the need to be assured of the future behaviour of the released prisoners and the governors ought to rely on his ministers' judgement rather than try to fetter their functioning. Gandhi, as a solution, suggested that the governors may be left free to declare that they did not want to usurp the power of the provincial ministries and that they relied on the latters' decision, who incidentally had complete responsibility in the matter. On the other hand, it was for the provincial ministries to ensure the merits of the assurances they received from the political prisoners they were set to release. The confrontation between the two sides seemed to be coming close to a solution. The prime ministers of both UP and Bihar have now withdrawn their resignation.

Communal Relations Deteriorate
Gandhi And Jinnah Unable To Sort Out Differences

February 24, 1938: Since the last election, the communal divide has been on the rise due to the ceaseless propaganda by the Muslim League. Jinnah has been feeling that Jawaharlal and Congress leaders close to him are aggravating the issue by their unhelpful approaches. So he has written to Gandhi to intervene. On 24th of last month, Gandhi while ruling out his personal involvement in any talks but accepting the proposal suggested[23] that Jinnah first begin discussion on the issue with Maulana Abul Kalam Azad, on whom he depended for decisions on communal issues and problems. However, this has incensed Jinnah who is feeling slighted by Gandhi's suggestion. In a point blank attack, he has written to Gandhi that there should be no doubt left about the Muslim League being the one authoritative and representative organisation of Muslims of India. In the same breath, he has also tried to corner Gandhi by describing him and the Congress as representing the Hindus of the country.

Jinnah says, further progress in talks would be possible only on the above basis. Gandhi is obviously disturbed by Jinnah's accusation. What is causing more disquiet all around is that the League has been able to attract more and more Muslims to its communal stance in recent months.

League's Discontent Against Congress Governments

March 1938: Discredited with the election results and with no role in governance in any province except Bengal, the League is adopting a new strategy with an eye to 'vote bank' politics. It has set up a mechanism to collect the details of alleged discrimination and ill-treatment meted out to the Muslims by the Congress governments. It is a fact that the Congress governments in various provinces have been struggling with several issues of governance due to inexperience.

In the process, after the initial honeymoon period, public discontents has begun to surface in towns and villages. However, observers say that these governments, notwithstanding their other shortcomings, cannot be blamed for communal bias. But the League is keen to project them as anti-Muslim. It is ready to go any length and adopt any means to achieve its political purpose. Such has been its enthusiasm that people are encouraged to report not only actual but also exaggerated accounts of difficulties or problems faced. Some times, stories are also being planted at the League offices. Stories, actual and imaginary, have begun doing the rounds across the community and it is raising the communal temperature.

Raja Of Pirpur To Probe Congress Atrocities

March 20, 1938: The council of the Muslim League has aggravated the communal disharmony in the country by a seemingly political move. In its council meeting held here, presided over by Jinnah, it has appointed an eight member committee under the presidentship of Raja Syed Muhammad Mehdi of Pirpur—to investigate into the hardship, maltreatment and injustices imposed on the Muslims by the provincial Congress governments and submit a report to the League.

In another resolution, it resolved to re-designate the volunteer corps of the League as 'The Muslim National Guards of India'.[24] Political analysts say that there is little substance in the allegations of atrocities and the League, out of power in most provinces, has resorted to this step to hype a non-issue to polarise Muslims of the country.

Muslim League's Rising Ambitions

April 17-18, 1938, Calcutta: AIML held its special session here, and Jinnah presided. AK Fazlul Huq, the premier of Bengal was the chairman of the reception committee. One of the resolutions adopted in the session praised the efforts by the Fazlul Huq ministry in Bengal and Saadullah ministry in Assam in resisting Congress machinations to break the fronts and exhorted Muslims to extend wholehearted support to the ministries in these two provinces.

Building of coalition with the regional Muslim power groups seems to be a part of Jinnah's strategy to establish the hegemony of the Muslim League over the entire Muslim community in India. Though the League does not independently run government even in a single province, Jinnah is trying to bring the Muslim-dominated regional parties running provincial governments under the overall control of the League. Last year, he had worked out an arrangement with Sikandar Hayat Khan, the Punjab premier and the leader of the ruling Unionist Party in Punjab. He has also been able to convince Fazlul Huq to become a member of the League. To this list, he added Muhammad Saadullah, who has been running a minority government in Assam with the blessings of the provincial British governor. Ministries in two other Muslim majority provinces, viz. Sind and NWFP, still have no allegiance to him or the League. Jinnah is planning to bring them under the influence, if not control, of the League. A steely resolve is working in him—to make the League the sole representative of Muslims in India.

Comrade Lenin Wasn't Born In This Country: Vallabhbhai

April 1938, Saran: Notwithstanding a Congress government being in charge in Bihar, farmers' unrests are spreading far and wide and Kisan Sabhas are leading the poor peasants' movements against their oppressors. Some of the Kisan Sabha leaders are deeply influenced by socialism and Marxist philosophies. Within the Congress, the Congress Socialist Party (CSP) leaders, unlike their orthodox counterparts, are lending active support to the Kisan movement. There are many in the CSP who believe in socialism and also class struggles. Advocacy for socialism, marxism and class struggles by the left-wingers has been the cause of a cold war between

Gandhian leaders and the Congress Socialist Party over past couple of years. Vallabhbhai is strongly against the Marxist philosophy and he has been vexed by the ongoing conflicts on the issue in Congress. Now, on a tour of Saran district in Bihar, he has given vent to his dissatisfaction. The district has been in the eye of a storm—facing repeated bouts of peasants' protests. Expressing his resentment against the Marxist leaders, he said: 'Comrade Lenin was not born in this country and we do not want a Lenin here. We want Gandhi and Ramchandra. Those who preach class hatred are enemies of the country.'[25]

The impatience implied in the statement has surprised many, especially those knowing Patel as the leader who had taken up cudgels on behalf of the oppressed farmers and led the famous and successful Satyagraha a decade ago in Bardoli.

League Sole Representative Of The Muslims: Jinnah

June 6, 1938: Shedding aside the ignominy of the poor electoral performance. Jinnah is consistent in his attempts to position the Muslim League as the sole representative of Indian Muslims. He is using a fork strategy. First, he is claiming that the League is the sole representative of the Muslims. Second, he wants to rob the Congress of its right to represent the Muslims. As such, he has caused the Muslim League to pass three resolutions, which seek to edify these claims. One of the resolutions even goes to stake the League's claim to represent other minorities as well.

In tł e aftermath of the election, Jinnah had a torrid relationship with Jawaharlal, the previous Congress president. Now, with Subhas taking over the mantle, he has made a strategic move to obtain the Congress' endorsement to the League's stand on the basis of these three resolutions. Subhas has, on his part, pointed out to Jinnah, the absurdity of the League's claims, citing facts like the presence of many eminent Muslim leaders in the Congress, the Congress' running a popular government in NWFP, a province with overwhelming Muslim majority, and other compelling reasons. On the insistence by the League that the Congrees cannot nominate Muslims as members of negotiating committees, Subhas summarily rejected the demand. He, however, urged Jinnah to join hands with the Congress to realise the common destiny.

Jinnah has sensed his move would not cut ice with the new Congress president. As such, in a clever diplomatic shift, he shot back a reply that the League needed no endorsement from the Congress on its claim of being the sole representative of the Muslims. Jinnah said it has been a settled fact right since 1915 when the Lucknow pact was signed between the League and the Congress. No one questioned this fact, Jinnah argued in his reply, till the Jinnah-Rajendra Prasad dialogue in 1935. Jinnah argued that the matter was referred to the new president, primarily to clear the doubts that arose in the context of Jawaharlal's claim that there were only two parties in the country— the Congress and the British government. In any case, Jinnah made it clear, the League will remain steadfast on its resolutions.Subhas is clearly upset at such intransigent, unamenable and unreasonable attitude of the League leader. He may put up the matter to the working committee for further deliberation.

In Europe For A Break, Jawaharlal Finds No Peace

June 1938: Jawaharlal was in the thick of domestic politics for two years when he steered the Congress as its president in 1936 and 1937. Significantly, right since July last year, the Congress has also been running governments in several provinces and that put additional pressures on its top leadership, including him, to resolve multiple problems within the limitation of the new constitution.

Besides, during the last few months, he had developed differences of opinion with Gandhi on some issues like the AICC resolution on supporting people's movement in the Mysore state, disciplinary proceedings against Nariman and generally a lenient approach towards the left-wing in the party. By November last year, it was clear that Gandhi was considering a new president for the Congress. Combination of circumstances encouraged Jawaharlal to undertake a visit to Europe. This getaway, he surmised, would be a welcome break and re-energise him. Known for his anti-Nazi stand, he avoided an invitation by Germany and instead arrived at Barcelona in the middle of this month. However, instead of acting as energiser, this visit is generating new kind of anxieties in him. Spain has been bleeding due to a civil war. Its Republican government has been exposed to the risk of being overthrown by the country's military chief, General Franco with the assistance of Hitler.

Austria has already been annexed by Germany and Czechoslovakia is almost cowering at the prospect of an impending German invasion, as both Britain and France have shown little courage to face the German dictator. Upset at these developments, Jawaharlal has thereafter travelled to Paris and London, where he canvassed in favour of democratic forces. This month, during his visit to London, he discussed the case of Indian independence with the labour leaders of Great Britain.

Jawaharlal's Solidarity With Spanish Republicans

June 1938, Barcelona: Spain is undergoing a bloody civil war. Its Republican government is under siege by General Franco — the right wing army general. Hitler's Germany and Mussolini's Italy are abetting Franco to bring down the Republican government. German bombers are raiding Spain's territories. Jawaharlal is presently in Barcelona and he is a sad witness of the incessant bombing on this beautiful city. To him, this is not only a confrontation between the Republicans and Franco, but part of a larger battle between the progressive and reactionary forces across the world. He has expressed his solidarity with the Spanish people.

Political Crisis Engulfs Central Provinces

June 1938, Nagpur: On the running dispute between Khare and his cabinet colleagues, Gandhi, seemingly convinced of Khare's indiscretion, wrote in *Harijan* on 4th June that Khare made the charges against his colleagues recklessly and spitefully. Khare visited Gandhi to present his side of the case but he was not encouraged. Upon return to his province, Khare asked the three ministers, viz. Shukla, Misra and Mehta to tender their resignation. But all the three, under advice from Rajendra Prasad, have dug in their heels and refused to oblige. This has raised the political temperature in the capital.

Jawaharlal Criticises Fascism And Imperialism

July 17, 1938, London: Jawaharlal is in Europe. He has reached England from Spain. Today he has addressed a gathering of about 5,000 in the Trafalgar Square on the second anniversary of the outbreak of civil war in Spain. In his speech, he has dwelt on the similarities between fascism and imperialism and criticised Britain's foreign policy.

Wardha Scheme Creates Schism Between Communities

July 1938: Gandhi, as the supreme ideologue of the Congress Party, has been laying down the principles and priorities for the Congress governments in the provinces. However, his followers have been finding it difficult to make the transition from agitation to good governance, a skill for which they were not trained. What is more, they are quickly getting addicted to the loaves and fishes of 'office'. Almost a year has passed since the party assumed offices in various provinces, but not much has been achieved in terms of good governance. The die-hard supporters, of course, are highlighting the Congress governments' achievement in regard to releasing political prisoners, abolition of zamindari, writing off agricultural indebtedness of poor farmers and so on. But, Kisan Sabhas and the Socialist faction within the party are questioning the veracity of these claims.

Of several good cannons of governance propounded by Gandhi, one that has been taken rather seriously by the Congress governments has been the Wardha scheme of education, a brainchild of Gandhi. Based to a large extent, on the principle of 'activity learning', the scheme aims at holistic development of students while ensuring that their education becomes self-financing. But even in regard to this, the provinces are more going by the letters of the scheme than appreciating its spirit and underlying philosophy. Gandhi took keen interest and lent guidance in shaping the Wardha scheme, as he wanted it to be a vehicle for nation-building and to groom future citizens of India right from the school level.

The scheme was inaugurated in February this year. Sections of Muslims have been uncomfortable with some of its features like singing of 'Vande Mataram' and use of the Hindi language. In the process, they have been ignoring the core features of the scheme that train the students for vocations, instil in them self-confidence, build their character and help them grow as worthy citizens.

To make matters worse, the communal elements and especially the Muslim League workers have been out to convince the Muslims in general that the 'scheme' itself is against Islam. Their main criticisms are that the scheme (a) promotes the idea of a single nation; (b) imposes Hindi as the medium of instructions by undermining the Urdu language; (c) imposes Hindu culture over Muslim students; (d) makes it mandatory for all students to sing Vande Mataram; (e) requires Muslim children to bow before Gandhi's photograph. The whole scheme is becoming a victim of malicious propaganda.

Khare Outwits His Opponents

July 1938, Nagpur: Khare, unable to get resignation of his three cabinet colleagues, has in a clever move tendered the resignation of his government, which has led to the dissolution of the whole cabinet. When the governor asked him to form a fresh government, he constituted a new cabinet with alacrity, completing the task within 24 hours, leaving out the dissident three former ministers. In another deft political move, he inducted a Harijan member in his new cabinet.

The Congress Parliamentary Board took serious view of Khare's action and also suspected the role of the British governor behind these unfolding events. It has summoned Khare to Segaon.

Khare Should Lose His Head: Gandhi

August 8, 1938, Segaon: As the intra-party conflict snowballed into a major crisis, Khare visited Segaon and in Gandhi's presence, he was reprimanded. He confessed to having committed an error of judgement and gave it in writing. But when Gandhi added further admission to the script in his handwriting, Khare refused to sign the revised draft. Sensing that the point of 'no return' was reached, Khare defied the authority of the Congress Parliamentary Board (CPB) and also threatened that he would contest for the leadership of the legislature party.

In view of these unsavoury developments, the CPB resolved that Khare was guilty of indiscipline and unworthy of holding high office. Following this condemnation, Khare resigned as prime minister. He is now accusing the top leadership of fascism and attacking both Vallabhbhai and Gandhi for throwing him out of the Congress. He is also alleging that Gandhi objected to his action of including a Harijan minister because this would raise 'impossible ambitions amongst Harijans'.[26] In response to Khare's fresh allegations, Gandhi sought to chastise him suitably. Today he wrote[27] in the *Harijan* reminding the critics: 'They say this is fascism, pure and simple. But they forget that fascism is the naked "sword". Under it Dr Khare should lose his head.' At the same time, he reminded them that the Congress was the very 'antithesis of fascism' and that it can boast of having the willing and hearty obedience of its followers, including Dr Khare 'so long as they chose to belong to it.'

BENGAL BECOMES COMMUNALLY SURCHARGED

August 1938, Calcutta: The Muslim League-dominated coalition ministry, led by Fazlul Huq, has been through various means and measures, promoting communal tension and disharmony rather than addressing the genuine problems of the people of the province. It may be recalled that as Fazlul capitulated to the Muslim League and turned to be the League's spokesperson, more than twenty legislators of the Krishak Praja Party (KPP) grew disenchanted with him and they have been sitting in the opposition. Now the opposition, led by Sarat Bose, has brought a set of no confidence motions against individual ministers. According to KPP legislator Tazimuddin Khan who spoke in support of the 'no confidence', the coalition ministry has been instrumental in spreading a false and insidious cry of 'Islam in danger', thus vitiating the air of the province. The communal venom and the government role in regard to promoting this has been threatening the freedom of opinion and speech and also the civil liberties of the people. Intimidation and assault are replacing reasons and arguments, he contended. Shyamaprasad Mukherjee, the Hindu Mahasabha leader, condemned the repression unleashed on the rights and liberties of one particular community. He also castigated the government tendency to resort to the bogey of 'Islam in Danger' every time its unworthy policies and actions were exposed.

There has been much firework in the legislature debates from which one thing is evident—that Bengal is in the throes of a grave communal crisis, unless remedial measures are taken in time.

Although the Treasury bench was very uncomfortable in facing the charges, the coalition government somehow averted the crisis by sheer numbers. The 'no confidence' was defeated by 130-111 votes. The Congress leadership is realising the folly in abdicating its role in the ministry formation last year, even though it had emerged as the single largest party in the poll.

Trouble Brewing In Rajkot

August 1938, Rajkot: A dark cloud has been gathering over Rajkot, a native state in the western part of the country for some time. The trouble began after the death of its popular and sagacious ruler, Thaokre Saheb Lakhajiraj. His son Dharmendra Sinhji, a weakling, under the influence of his diwan Durbar Virawala initiated a set of unpopular policies that sought to curb the legitimate political aspirations of the states' subjects.

Gradually, the new ruling regime imposed severe restrictions on political activities by the states' peoples, which compelled the latter to begin a movement to protect their rights. The popular discontent became so widespread that the movement soon engulfed the state. The workers of a cotton mill went on strike, demanding better working conditions. Eventually, the people raised the demand for the revival of the Kathiawar Rajkiya Parishad so as to be able to effectively put forth their views and demands. The ruling regime, upset and angry at the spiralling protests, sought to suppress the movement using harsh measures.

In recent years, the Congress has been adopting pro-active policies in regard to States' People's political activities. In the Haripura Congress, although an organisational intervention was ruled out, clearance was given to Congress leaders to participate in such movements in their individual capacity. Vallabhbhai Patel, undisputedly the strongest Congress leader in this part of the country, has intervened. It is expected that this will lift the peoples' movement to a new level.

Subhas Helps Congress Form Ministry In Assam

September 20, 1938, Shillong: A political emergency arose in the eastern most province of British India when the minority government led by Saadullah faced with a 'no confidence' motion, tendered his ministry's resignation. The provincial Congress Party has been of the opinion that Saadullah government's wrong policies, especially one in favour of illegal immigration, have caused Assam significant harm and 'policy correctives' must be applied forthwith. However, the provincial Congress, led by Gopinath Bordoloi, was not able to muster adequate number of legislators to form a coalition government. As such, Bordoloi had sent an SOS to the Congress president to help the provincial party out.

Assam, with its small population spread over vast lush green landscape in the hills and the plains and in particular, in the verdant Brahmaputra valley, has been a standing invitation for illegal immigrants from neighbouring Bengal, especially the Muslims. The immigration has actually been an ongoing process but gathered momentum under the Saadullah ministry. Unless checked immediately by appropriate government policies, this could assume a huge dimension and pose threat to the demographic profile of the province.

In the provincial election, the Congress emerged as the single largest party in an assembly of 106 members. However, as it fell short of the half-way mark and also failed to take due initiative for a coalition, the British governor, Robert Reid, applying his discretion, allowed a minority government led by Saadullah to take over the reins. Saadullah cobbled up nine members to constitute a provincial Muslim League and governed with 'near total' reliance upon the British bureaucracy in the province. Due to its unpopular policies, the minority government was recently confronted with a 'no confidence' in the legislature, when Saadullah tendered his resignation.

Upon this, the Congress got a chance and it opened up negotiation with the Tribal Party and others for a coalition but it fell short of two members. Desperate that the party must take over the governance to protect the province's interest, Bordoloi had urged the highcommand to help. Upon this, Maulana Abul Kalam Azad landed here, studied the situation and opined against the Congress forming government, as it did not have the majority. But his ruling did not assuage the feeling of insecurity of the local Congress. Bordoloi sent an SOS to the Congress president, urging help.

Subhas, the Congress president, quickly grasped the urgency and intricacies of the situation and landed in Shillong himself by setting other appointments and engagements aside. Through his charismatic personality, power of reasoning and persuasion, he solved the problem of the 'two' seats. Subhas paved the way for the formation of a Congress-led stable 'coalition ministry' in Assam before he returned from Shillong. Today, Gopinath Bordoloi has taken oath as the head of the provincial government.[28]

Poor Performance Of Congress Ministries Leaves Gandhi Disillusioned

September 24, 1938: Past apprehensions about the pitfalls that lay ahead of the party in the event it decided to accept office, are coming true. Indians had very high expectations from the Congress governments as distinguished from the colonial British regime which had been traditionally seen as oppressive and exploitative. Unfortunately, these provincial governments have delivered little and exhibited large degrees of ineptitude. In several respects, they have given poorer accounts of themselves than their colonial counterparts. Their task has been rendered difficult due to their lack of experience in governance, increasing friction with the bureaucracy and constant political opposition by the Muslim League. But their worst enemy has been their own proneness to corruption.

There are allegations of corrupt practices against Congress ministers and leaders. In less than nine months' time since formation of the ministries in provinces, Jawaharlal grew restive about the falling standards of their functioning. In April this year, he wrote to Gandhi lamenting that the Congress is losing the high position it built with so much labour. He added that the Congress ministers have sunk to the level of ordinary politicians, devoid of principles and their work was governed by day-to-day opportunism.[29] Another top leader, Rajendra Prasad has also been bitter. He has observed ruefully that every legislator wants to be a minister.

But the most disillusioned man is perhaps Gandhi himself. Writing in *Harijan,* he has expressed his anxiety[30]: 'It is difficult to cope with correspondence that I am having from several places about violence, untruth and corruption in the Congress.' Even though he was against arriving at any hasty deduction about the Congress politicians, he still felt that violence, untruth and corruption have made inroads enough to warrant drastic measures in order to prevent decay overtaking the great organisation. Gandhi is pained a good deal to see that the Congress ministers have been losing the spirit of dedicated public service and turning to be power addict. He has always believed in the 'bottom up' approach and felt that the Congressmen could begin the national reconstruction work even without possession of the formal power of governance.

The true power could be generated by mutual cooperation and service at the local level. As such, Congressmen could have used their government in the provinces to give strong pushes to the programme of national reconstruction. He wanted Congressmen to use the legislature for public service. He had also issued moral and ethical guidelines for the Congress ministers. Unfortunately his initiatives are proving barren and those who are at the helms of the governments are paying him only lip service.

BRITAIN, FRANCE ACQUIESCE TO GERMAN EXCESSES

September 30, 1938, Munich: Hitler has kept European countries in tenterhooks with his territorial ambition in general and intention of immediate annexation of Sudetenland of Czechoslovakia, in particular. His rationale behind the latter is the demographic profile of that area—majority of the people being German speaking. A four nation conference began here yesterday with Britain, France and Italy participating in addition to Germany. Though her fate was being decided, Czechoslovakia was not allowed in the deliberation—a delegation from her land was kept waiting outside. Based on an Italian proposal introduced by Mussolini, an agreement has been reached ceding Sudetenland to Germany on the condition that the latter would guarantee safety of rest of Czechoslovakia. Neville Chamberlain, prime minister of Britain and his French counterpart Edouard Daladier, have flown back after signing the pact.

According to political analysts, the message of the conference has been that Neville Chamberlain and Daladier have meekly submitted to the aggressive German dictator, dashing hopes of all democracy lovers across the world. This pact has exposed the soft underbelly of the mythical British power. Back in India, Subhas is more convinced that the time is ripe for serving a timed ultimatum to the British to quit India.

Jawaharlal's Obsession With International Politics

Dark clouds of war are billowing over Europe. The democratic nations, many of them wounded and bruised, are trying to come together to defend themselves against Nazi Germany and Fascist Italy. Jawaharlal, a worried person, is in England to profess the Indian National Congress' support to the democratic camp led by Britain. In an interview to the Manchester Guardian, he said, 'Indian opinion is entirely anti-fascist and that a free India would unhesitatingly throw itself behind democracies in a war with fascism.' His statements carry weight as a heavyweight Indian leader, even if he no longer continues to be the president of the Congress party.

Britain's politicians, possessed of the gravity of the forthcoming war and keenly appreciative of the value of India's willing cooperation to Britain's war efforts, wanted Jawaharlal to commit more, particularly in the matter of 'collective security' and 'peace front'. Driven by his spontaneous sympathy for the democratic camp, Jawaharlal has declared his support for these measures too. But some of his British leftist friends felt that he is committing on behalf of the Congress more than what is warranted.

They pointed out that by declaring support for the 'peace front', he is ignoring the interests of the colonised and the working classes, as that meant pledging support for a war that was aimed to benefit the capitalist and the imperialist forces.

To the Communist Party of Great Britain (CPGB), Jawaharlal presented the resolution that was drafted by him and passed in the Haripura Congress.

That resolution referred to 'collective security' but made India's participation contingent on being a free nation. Jawaharlal presented the resolution as an endorsement of the 'collective security' pledge by the Indian National Congress. Seemingly influenced by his assertion, CPGB in its own resolution welcomed the Indian Congress' position in favour of collective security. When some of the Independent Labour Party delegates protested that the resolution gave a wrong impression that Indians were prepared to fight for collective security, Jawaharlal accepted that the resolution did not contain all that was agreed upon in Haripura, but insisted that it was compatible with the Haripura resolution.

Critics say that in his over enthusiasm to profess Congress support for the democratic camp, Jawaharlal stretched the Haripura resolution to an unacceptable extent. At the outset, that resolution was a conditional one and the support was offered only on the condition that India was granted independence. As such, it was ethically incorrect to use it in the CPGB resolution.

CIVIL LIBERTY DOES NOT INCLUDE VIOLENCE: GANDHI

Oct 5, 1938, Wardha: The AICC session held in Delhi on 26th of last month witnessed an unseemly confrontation between the orthodox leaders and the leftist groups. Besides corruption, the Congress has also been afflicted by a simmering tension between these two groups on ideological issues. The latter has not only been talking Marxist jargons like 'class struggle', some of them have been resorting to 'violent actions' in provinces and publishing their ideas for wider audiences. The Gandhian faction brought a 'civil liberties' resolution to put a brake on such trend.

It said that some Congressmen are advocating class war, including murder, arson and looting in the name of civil liberty and warned the public that 'civil liberty does not cover acts of or incitement to violence or promulgation of palpable falsehood'.[31] Condemning these trends and tendencies, the resolution reinforced the Congress tradition to support measures defending life and property of the people and urged the provincial governments to introduce these in the respective provinces. Many radicals opposed the resolution and proposed amendments. When these were rejected, they walked out.

Gandhi has commented[32] on the incident in an article in the *Harijan* today. He has taken strong exception to such undemocratic tendencies on the part of some members, who by their actions have been weakening the Congress while it is engaged in a life and death battle against the most experienced and organised empire in the world. He has gone to the extent in observing that those who are against the fundamental policies of the Congress should decide whether they would serve the Congress and the country better by remaining outside rather than being inside and resorting to obstructionist policies.

Arrests Of Political Prisoners, Schism In Congress

October 1938: Political arrests and treatment of political prisoners have been sensitive issues in India. In its election manifesto, the Congress had promised release of political prisoners and this has now become a matter of raging controversy. On the issue of fresh political arrests, differences are emerging within the top echelon of the party. At the core are the left wing and Communist political workers. Gandhi is against a blanket approach irrespective of the type of offence committed by a political worker. In *Harijan* he has written that in the seven Congress ruled provinces, some persons are seemingly under the impression that they can say or do what they like. He reminded them that civil liberty is not criminal liberty. He also wrote that there are vast possibilities for application of non-violence in various fields, including politics and Congress ministers having faith in non-violence will explore these, but 'whilst they are doing this, or whether they do so or not, there is no doubt that they cannot ignore incitement to violence and manifestly violent speech even though they may themselves run the risk of being styled violent.'[33]

Jawaharlal, known for his sympathy with the left and Socialist political workers, is apprehensive of the provincial Congress governments taking tough line against them. He has been upset by the aggressive approach of Rajagopalachari government in Madras and KM Munshi, the home minister in Bombay. To apply a check on indiscriminate arrests of these workers, Jawaharlal attempted to cause CWC to pass a resolution that Congress ministries would not embark on arrests and prosecution of Socialists or leftists without the working committee's prior approval. However, orthodox leaders like Rajagopalachari, Patel and others have foiled his attempt.

Azad Threatens To Resign, Vallabhbhai Backs Subhas

October 1938: The Congress party had formed a coalition government in Assam last month after Subhas, the Congress president, visited Shillong and helped remove the obstacles. But it seems that the impasse is not yet over. In the central office, senior leader Maulana Azad was not happy at the turn of events—that a Congress ministry was finally set up in that border province against his recommendation. Since then, he has been making his unhappiness known to the top leadership. Not only does he find this ministry formation against the principle of the Congress, which provided the 'majority' in the legislature as a pre-condition for acceptance of office, but he has also been accusing Bordoloi of resorting to corrupt practices to secure the support of the additional two legislators.

In the resultant moments of crisis for Gopinath, Subhas, the president of the party, vouchsafed for his integrity. Unconvinced, Azad thereafter threatened to resign from the Congress Parliamentary Committee as a mark of protest and apparently to mount pressure upon the party. However, Vallabhbhai, the chairman of the committee refused to budge and stood by Subhas's decision.[34] Knowing the authority and clout of Vallabhbhai Patel in the party organisation and on matters involving the provincial governments, Azad may not push the matter further. Gopinath can breathe easy.

WAR CLOUD DARKENS OVER EUROPE

German Forces Arrive In Czechoslovakia

October 1, 1938, Prague: In March this year, Hitler had just shoved 'unification' scheme down the throat of Austria, leveraging the presence of the Nazi elements in Austria. The nationalist Austrian Chancellor, Schuschnigg, who had refused to merge with Germany was somehow got rid of. The new Austrian Nazi Chancellor, Arthur Seyss-Inquart, planted by Hitler had then invited German troops to Austria to prevent disorder. The grip over Austria only whetted Hitler's hunger for more territories. Thereafter he claimed authority over Sudetenland, a Czech border area. That move had clearly unnerved both Britain and France and leaders of the two countries flew to Munich. But at the end they meekly acquiesced to Hitler's fancy reasoning. The Czechs had a treaty with the French but the latter left them in the lurch, unwilling to confront Hitler. The Czechs themselves were prepared to fight, but they got no moral support from the bigger powers and had to reconcile with their fate. Today, Hitler's army has crossed the Czech border to take control of Sudetenland. Germany's aggression and Britain's timid attempts at reconciliation are being watched worldwide, including by the Congress in India. Jawaharlal has been horrified by this development and he has, in fact, given up hopes for Britain.

Subhas, the Congress president, had anticipated this development. Right since his taking over as the president, he has been warning about the impending war in Europe and asking for preparedness on the part of Indians to seize the opportunity that would arise in consequence of the war. He is sure if the lever is pressed at the right time, the British will have to leave India and that the right time has almost arrived. However, the Gandhian faction is against any such move. To them, priority is the running of ministries in various provinces and continuing with the parliamentary proceedings.

An Overtly Muslim Majority Province With A Feeble Muslim League Is Anachronistic: Jinnah

October 1938, Karachi: One of the major demands of the Muslim League since the 1920s was for a separate province of Sind to be carved out of Bombay, a decidedly Hindu majority province. This demand was accommodated in the Government of India Act 1935 despite Congress reservations on more than one ground. The new province with a distinct majority of Muslim population, added to the number of existing Muslim majority provinces of NWFP, Bengal and Punjab. It was also to strengthen the hands of the League in its political negotiations with the government and the Congress.

But the provincial election results administered a shock to the League where it could bag a meagre three seats out of a total strength of thirty-three in the legislature. The electorate betrayed their lack of confidence in the abilities and goals of the League and gave fractured verdicts in favour of several regional parties and independent candidates. Currently Allah Bux, a prominent leader of the Sindh Ittehad Party— a regional party, is running a coalition government with the support of Congress and independent Hindu legislators. The current state of affairs in Sind is hurting the League like a thorn in its throat.

Jinnah does not want to lose time to gain Sind for the League. He wants the people of Sind to feel that it is simply anachronistic for such an overtly Muslim majority province to have a feeble Muslim League in the overall political structure. As such, he wants the full weight of the All-India Muslim League to be felt by the people of Sind. To impress them of the growing strength and clout of the League, he wants to showcase here the prime ministers of Bengal and Punjab who have already become members of the League. And leveraging upon its all-India strength, Jinnah wants to give a clarion call to the Muslim leaders of various regional parties in the province to gather under the banner of the League and carry out its cherished goal of creating a separate state for the Muslims. Clearly, the process is utterly communal and would push the people of the province from their long-held secular political outlook. But Jinnah seems determined to go ahead with his plan.

To achieve these strategic objectives, the Muslim League has given a call for a mega conference to be held in this port city, which would be attended by top league leaders from across the country.

Muslim League Makes Political Statement In Sind

October 12, 1938, Karachi: The gala conference of the Sind Provincial Muslim League is about to conclude here. It opened on 8th of this month at Napier Road here. For five days, it has been drawing large crowd. Top leaders of the All-India Muslim League from all over the country have converged here. The star attractions include Sikandar Hayat Khan, the prime minister of Punjab and Fazlul Huq, the prime minister of Bengal, both of whom have become members of the League though they are still heading their own regional parties in the respective provinces.

The League had done commendable groundwork before the conference was formally inaugurated. It convinced important local leaders like GH Hidayatullah, GM Syed, Abdullah Haroon and Abdul Majeed Sindhi to join the League. These new enrolments have given a huge boost to the League's image in the province. Of them, Abdullah Haroon has been the chairman of the reception committee. In his welcome speech, Haroon had focussed on the key theme, ie. the need of an independent federation for Muslims of India

After the deliberations, Jinnah set about the challenging task of building a credible structure for the Muslim League in the province. He has held meetings with the members of the legislative assembly and formed the Muslim League Assembly Party, to be led by Sir GH Hidayatullah. It is being heard that even Allah Bux himself was prepared to be a part of the exercise on the condition that the League would support him as the premier of the province. But this was not done and Jinnah is happy, for whatever has been achieved towards the image makeover of the League in this strategically important province. Political analysts say the conference has attained much of the political objectives of the League not only in Sind but also nationally. Jinnah has been successfully pursuing his strategy of plucking the ripe fruits in provinces for the League, to make good the electoral failures.

Subhas Chairs First Meeting Of Industries Ministers

October 1938: Subhas, as the Congress president, has been keen about a planning committee that would initiate an exercise aimed at planned development of India. He introduced the idea in the Haripura Congress, and has been trying to explore ways and means to take it forward. He has been keen that Jawaharlal takes up this challenging task that has profound implications on India's future. Jawaharlal not only has a Socialist outlook and international exposure, but also wide acceptability amongst the left as well as the right, which would help in putting the committee on a firm foundation. Subhas has been trying to persuade Jawaharlal to accept this onerous responsibility. In the meanwhile, he has chaired the first meeting of the industries ministers of Congress ruled provinces. This is likely to help the planning committee to take off.

Jawaharlal Upset At Criticism Of His International Policy

November 1938: Since his return from Europe to India, Jawaharlal has been upset that only few Congress leaders share his eagerness on the issue of committing India to Britain's war efforts with or without condition. The Congress Socialist Party members strongly felt that such enthusiasm on the part of Jawaharlal was unwarranted as the imperialists to whom India's support was committed by him were poised to fight the impending big war to protect their own interests, which was of little concern to India and therefore 'collective security' was a non-issue. Still worse, Jawaharlal was upset to see that sympathy with fascism has been somewhat growing in the country among communal parties. There was little support for Spanish Republicans and great deal of passive resistance against taking in Jewish refugees into India, issues that Jawaharlal held close to his heart.

Jawaharlal Is The New President Of AISPC

November 1938: The States' People's Movement has got a boost with Congress veteran Jawaharlal taking over as the president of the All-India States' People's Conference. The political aspirations of the subjects of the native states have been growing steadily. They tend to look at the political rights of the people in British India as benchmark to set their own expectations. The dissatisfaction with their curbed entitlements in the semi-feudal setups has been causing them deep unrest.

The rulers of most of these states, instead of improving upon quality of governance, have been indulging in repressing popular movements with British help. Such tendencies have been creating a spiral of protest and repression. Against this backdrop, Jawaharlal's taking over as a key leader of their movement has begun to generate new hopes and optimism. Jawaharlal, on his part, seems to realise the need to organise the states' people's Movements with a sense of urgency. He is sprucing up the organisation in a bid to infuse a new life into and bring the states' people's Movement to some kind of alignment with the mainstream national struggle.

Raja Of Pirpur's Report On Alleged Congress Atrocities

November 15, 1938: The Syed Muhammad committee has submitted its reports today to the League, listing out alleged atrocities committed by provincial Congress governments in seven provinces. It has identified three principal areas, viz. singing of 'Vande Mataram', Tricolour and Cow protection. It has also listed the atrocities on individual Muslims and discriminatory government policies against the League. The report has been signed by the Raja of Pirpur and five others.

Congress Squanders Chance To Form Ministry In Bengal Yet Again As Gandhi Does A U-turn

December 15, 1938, Wardha: Since the formation of the Krishak Praja Party (KPK)-Muslim League coalition ministry in Bengal last year, the League, by virtue of its numerical strength, has been the dominant partner and it has been doggedly pursuing its communal politics. As a result, the government has been derailed from the KPK's secular agenda and communal tension has begun to pervade the entire province. Subhas and his brother Sarat, both of them popular across both the communities, wanted to put an end to the current regime by decoupling Huq and his KPK from the League. An understanding was reached to replace the present coalition by a partnership among the KPK, the scheduled caste legislators and the Congress, which Huq was to take over as the head of the new coalition government. NR Sarkar, the finance minister in the current government, was to play the key role in this make over. He was to resign on the eve of the budget, forcing the government to collapse whereupon the new coalition would take over.

Though apparently not an ethical political operation, Subhas and Sarat chose the strategy in greater public interest, more importantly to cleanse the government of the ghost of communalism. Having decided upon the arrangement at the provincial level, Subhas had paid a visit to Wardha to discuss the matter with Gandhi and obtained his nod. But for reasons best known to him, NR Sarkar had a rethinking on the issue and decided to backtrack. Without consulting Subhas, he went to Wardha and met Gandhi in the company of two eminent persons from Bengal—one of them MAK Azad a senior Congress leader and the other, GD Birla one of the top-ranked Indian industrialists. Azad expressed his opposition to topple the Muslim League ministry in a Muslim majority province like Bengal. Birla too opposed the idea, reportedly because he felt the change of government with the Congress substituting the League on the coalition would harm his business interests. With each of the trio expressing opposition, Gandhi reportedly changed his mind on the issue and sent a letter to Subhas through Sarkar asking him to abandon the scheme. Gandhi has referred to the exhaustive discussion he had with the three over the Bengal ministry. Today he wrote: 'I feel... that the best way of securing comparative purity of administration and a continuity of a settled programme and policy would be to aim at having all the reforms that we desire, carried out by the present ministry.'[35]

No Meeting Ground Between League And Congress

December 16, 1938, Wardha: Subhas, the Congress president, has presented Jinnah's letters, together with the three resolutions of the Muslim League to the working committee. In his letter, Jinnah had specifically mentioned the bases on which the Congress-League negotiations could proceed henceforth. The working committee found it impossible to agree with these demands. Today, Subhas has written to Jinnah saying that the Congress cannot start negotiation w ith the League on the basis of the conditions put forth by the latter. With this expression of disagreement, the communal issue is likely to come back as a burning question in the country.

Three Gentlemen More Important Than Congress President: Subhas

December 18, 1938, Bombay: Subhas has been deeply upset by Gandhi's sudden change of position on such a serious matter that impinged on political future of a large and politically-sensitive province like Bengal, and that without taking into confidence the apex provincial Congress leadership and the Congress president. Subhas has replied to Gandhi's letter angrily. He has said, 'The position, therefore, is that you attach more value and importance to the views of these three gentlemen than to the views of those who are responsible for running the Congress organisation in Bengal.'[36] His reply expresses shock, surprise, pain and a criticism of the wisdom of Gandhi's new decision. His great dismay over the manner in which Gandhi decided on such a critical issue is reflected in these words: 'It has astonished me that you did not feel it necessary to even consult me before you arrived at a decision on such a serious matter...'

But it seems, once Gandhi has decided, Subhas's outbursts may not change the Congress stand. Critics say that the Congress has committed yet another blunder by dithering on the plan, giving scope to the Muslim League to cement its position and communalise the political atmosphere in a province that has the largest Muslim population in the country.

Political Rationale Of Congress Ministries

As Congress president, Subhas, has been contemplating ways and means to increase Congress' bargaining power in negotiations with the British regime. For this, he wants the Congress to be a part of the government in all the eleven provinces. Presently it is running its own government or participating in coalition governments in eight of the eleven provinces. Subhas wants Congress to participate in the governance of the remaining three provinces of Bengal, Punjab and Sind. This would, Subhas feels, enable Congress to talk to the British government on behalf of all the eleven provincial governments. The implication is that even without reaching that elusive Hindu-Muslim settlement, which the British have been using as a stick to beat the nationalists with, Congress will be able to officially represent the people of British India and its negotiation with the government will not be seriously handicapped, even if there is no settlement with the Muslim League. Second, he wants to raise the acceptability of the Congress to Indians across communities. Having taken note of the vicious and motivated ongoing campaign by the Muslim League against Congress ministries, Subhas has also written to Gandhi that the party should itself hold enquiry on the grievances of Muslim population against its ministries. This would assure the minorities that the Congress is anxious to understand their problem and remedy them as humanly as possible. Subhas suggests that if the above two sub-goals are achieved, the Congress can forcefully place its demand for complete independence with the British government, by the time the Congress holds its next annual session. Further, against the backdrop of a tense international scenario, the British would not be able to easily reject the Congress demand. In the event they do so, Congress should begin satyagraha after giving due notice to the regime.

Now Gandhi's action in the Bengal matter has thrown the entire plan into jeopardy. Out of the three non-Congress Muslim majority provinces, Bengal was the best bet for introducing Congress-coalition government as it is the single largest party here and, therefore, commands considerable political clout. Bengal also happens to be the province with the largest number of Muslims. As such, Congress in governance here could have salutary effect upon communal harmony in the country. This golden opportunity has been wasted!

Bihar Congress Ministry Curbs Peasant Movement

1938, Patna: The provincial Congress government in Bihar is adopting a high-handed approach in dealing with the peasant movements. The core driving force behind the movement is the conflict between the interests of ordinary peasants and the landlord community. The installation of Congress government had created high hopes in the peasant class that now their grievances would be looked into and interests shall be protected.

On the ground, quite the contrary is happening—the government is siding with the zamindars. Unfortunately, even the provincial Congress committee is betraying impatience in dealing with the peasant movement and its leaders. Twenty years ago, in 1917, the British government had banned the entry of Gandhi to Champaran. Now the Saran District Congress Committee has asked a leader of Swami Sahajananda Saraswati's stature not to tour the district as this might create unrest among kisans and tenants. Everyone knows the Swami's exceptional contribution in energising the Bihar peasantry. People find the approach of the Congress leaders nothing but ironical and sad.

Kisan Sabhas Tussles With Congress Governments

1938: The relationship between the Congress and the Kisan Sabhas has grown more complex after formation of Congress ministries at various provinces. These Sabhas have been functioning in various places like Awadh, Gorakhpur, Darbhanga, Medinipur, Kheda, Guntur etc, spread across provinces. In several places, the Sabhas and the local Congress units have been competing for the support of the peasantry and as such their roles have become adversarial than complementary. Barring some Sabhas like those led by Vallabhbhai Patel, which were welcomed in the Congress camp, most others have been facing a tough time. Some of them are being handed down raw deals by Congress ministries, sometimes worse than the British dispensation.

In the initial days following the formation of the Congress ministries, there was great enthusiasm in the peasantry. The peasants and workers, assured of a fair hearing of their longstanding demands by indigenous governments, accelerated their agitation against the vested interests. The Congress governments, however, have been against such over enthusiasm. As a result, these segments were unable to realise the true implications of civil liberty. What is worse, instead of guiding, the Congress governments are coming down heavily on many of them. The peasantry and the Kisan Sabhas are dismayed to see the indigenous governments using strong-arms tactics and often siding with the big landlords.

In Bihar, after the Congress took over reins, the enthusiastic kisans had attempted to regain the control of 'bakasht' land through Satyagraha. They have been anguished to find the Congress government coming to the aid of the zamindars and using police repression to silence them. Not stopping at that, the latter are also carrying out vilification campaign to malign Kisan Sabhas and their leaders.

Bakasht Land – A Key Conflict Area

The demand to end ill treatment of the vast multitude of farmers tilling 'bakasht land' has remained one of the key focuses of the All-India Kisan Sabha. In 'bakasht land', the zamindars give the farmers only the right to till and extract rent in return. The latter retain the right to bring in new tillers who agree to pay higher rent and other tributes and evict the current farmers. This inherently inequitable arrangement puts the vulnerable tillers eternally at the mercy of the zamindars and enables the latter to perpetrate oppression on them in several forms.

The system had a free run with the silent approval of the British regime. In the provincial elections, the All-India Kisan Sabha enthusiastically campaigned in favour of the Congress amongst the peasantry in the hope that the Congress government would redress the longstanding grievances of their members, including the sufferings of the 'bakasht' tillers. The formation of the Congress government was celebrated with wild cheers in the countryside. But unfortunately, the Kisan Sabhas are growing disappointed as the Congress government seems to be siding more with the zamindars.

Bihar Government Suppresses Kisan Movement

1938: Rahul Sankrityayan is in Saran district to lead a protest movement of peasants and workers. He went on a prolonged fast to protest against atrocities and injustice inflicted on these poor people by the landed gentries with tacit support of the local bureaucracy. He was arrested with his co-workers by the Bihar police. In prison, they were denied the status of political prisoners. In justification, the government has alleged that Rahul is not engaged in the Kisan movement here for political reasons but promoting his self-interest. Rahul a famed litterateur, is also a venerable leader, well known for his commitment to the public causes. The people at large, here, are not lending any credence to the government statement. In fact, the Congress government is bringing itself into disrepute by resorting to such vindictive course of actions.

Muslim League Whips Up Communal Passion

December 1938: Since July last year, the Congress has been running government in several large provinces where Muslims are minorities. The League appointed an eight-member Committee led by Raja Syed Mohammad Mehdi to tour these Congress ruled provinces to collect data and details about government injustices to the Muslims. As the committee members are surveying the Muslim masses and recording complaints—spontaneous or induced, facts or exaggerations, real or imaginary—Jinnah is hyping the issue to the great irritation of the Congress Party and its provincial governments. He even attempted to persuade the Viceroy, albeit without success, to get a royal commission appointed to enquire into these alleged atrocities.

Neither the British governors of these provinces nor the Viceroy himself, are taking Jinnah or the League on these matters at face value. During a meeting with Jinnah, Viceroy Linlithgow has made it plain that his government has found no specific instances of atrocities by provincial Congress ministries.

However, Jinnah is undaunted. He is busy in building political capital for the League by escalating communal hatred.

Out on an extensive tour of the provinces, Jinnah is lecturing to whip up communal feelings—he is equating Congress with Hindu.

Gandhi Under Attack From Communal Muslim Leaders

Gandhi is realising that the heydays of his popularity with the Muslim people are over—gone are the Khilafat days! The events since the second round table conference have been adding to the gulf between him and the emerging Muslim leadership. The current stock of Muslim leaders is growing increasingly assertive and dismissive of the Congress. Gandhi's problem has been compounded because of poor quality of governance by the Congress ministries in various provinces, which gave the Muslim League a chance to launch a campaign against the Congress. Gandhi obviously could not escape criticism, being seen as the last point of responsibility. His Wardha scheme of education has come under particularly severe attack from the League.

It appears that as Jinnah has been emerging as a leader of growing stature and strength among the Indian Muslims, Gandhi is getting increasingly alienated from the latter. Since last year, Jinnah, a wily politician, has begun attempts to completely polarise politics. He has been claiming that the Muslim League alone represents India's Muslims and that the Congress can speak only for the country's Hindus. Unfortunately, Gandhi, these days, does not have many influential Muslim leaders around him like he had in the 1920s to establish his credential as much as the leader of the Muslims as of the Hindus. Though Maulana Abul Kalam Azad holds senior position in the party, he does not have significant mass base. Gandhi can, of course, try to reduce the gap by directly talking to Jinnah. However, Jawaharlal and Azad are against giving importance to communal leaders. In May this year, Gandhi, exasperated, had publicly said that the work of Hindu-Muslim unity now belongs to the younger generation. Jawaharlal, on his part, considers communal leaders like Jinnah as political reactionaries and feels Congress ought to reach the Muslims directly. Accordingly, he made Congress launch a countrywide Muslim Mass Contact programme. This scared the Muslim League and prompted it to raise its anti Congress pitch and feed the Muslims with various stories—many of these, fabricated and distorted. Things are not becoming better and Gandhi's stock as a leader of the Muslims is on a downtrend.

Kisan Sabhas Mull Satyagraha In Bihar

December 1938, Patna: The farmers' unrest is spreading across Bihar. While ruling the province for past about one-and-a-half year, the Congress government has taken little initiative to address the grievances of the poor peasantry. In districts like Darbhanga, Saran, Champaran, Arrah, Patna, Gaya, Monghyr and Bhagalpur, 'bakasht land' snatched by the zamindars from the tenant farmers on diverse pretexts has been a prominent issue.

Congress ministers are reportedly siding with the zamindars, leaving the farmers in the lurch.On the 3rd and 4th of this month, the Bihar Provincial Kisan Sabha resolved to use Satyagraha as its weapon of struggle to defend and protect peasants' interests. Rahul Sankrityayan, a prominent scholar and peasant leader, has advocated use of Satyagraha in every district. In accordance therewith, the Kisan movement in Bihar is taking the shape of direct action. The Congress ministry in Bihar is much displeased and preparing to suppress the challenge with state power.

Release Of Political Prisoners
Sharp Differences Emerge Within Congress

1938: The issue of the release of the political prisoners has been causing internal dissensions in the Congress. It is becoming clear that the prime ministers of several Congress-run provinces do not hold identical views.

No doubt, it was one of the electoral promises made by the

Congress and the stand taken by the prime ministers of Bihar and the UP corresponded to that pledge. But, the premiers of Madras and Bombay are making it clear that they do have serious reservations on this matter. Rajagopalachari, the Madras premier, has not been keen to release political prisoners. His reservations about Communists are well known. In October last year, he caused Baltiwala, a Communist leader, to be arrested and that too under a repressive criminal law, which the Congress always condemned.

In Bombay BG Kher, prime minister, has also not been enthusiastic in adopting a soft line towards political prisoners. There, KM Munshi, the Home Minister, is even more aggressive. Instead of releasing the political prisoners, he wrote to the Viceroy to put the CID in Bengal in touch with the Bombay CID so that the unwanted leftists and Communists could be traced.

Such hostile attitude towards the left wing and Communist leaders, charging the political detenus under repressive laws and putting them under surveillance by the indigenous governments have been causing much hurt and ill feeling across the country. Some critics say that such approaches on the part of the Congress governments make them no different from the British regime.

Subhas Determined To Contest For Presidency

December 1938: The Gandhi loyalists, who overwhelmingly dominate the working committee, have conveyed to Subhas, their suggestion that Subhas should not try for re-election.

He is clearly perturbed. In hindsight, Subhas is possibly realising the mistake of not having included at least a few members from the left camp in the working committee. Now most of the working committee members, including Rajendra Prasad, JB Kripalani, Bhulabhai Desai, Jamnalal Bajaj, Shankarrao Deo, Jairamdas Daulatram led by Vallabhbhai are opposing his re-election, in unison. Even Jawaharlal is not in his favour. However, Subhas is determined to contest. He insists that he must do so to ensure that the policies initiated during his presidentship continue in the critical period that lie ahead. He says he can, of course, move aside if any other from the left camp is nominated for the post. Otherwise, he has made it clear that he would certainly contest.

Ban Removed On Bose's *The Indian Struggle*

1938: *The Indian Struggle,* written by Subhas, has earned wide acclaim in the Western press. However, it was banned by the British Indian government. Now the ban has been lifted. In the book, Subhas has criticised both Gandhi and Gandhi loyalists. He criticised the latter for having 'mortgaged their intellect' to their master.

He has more unkind words for them. The release of the book in India has earned him some instant and powerful enemies within the Congress. Subhas, as Congress president, through a set of programmes and policies has already upset the British regime. The timing of lifting of the ban this year seems to be intriguing.

If Azad, Jawahar Don't Want, Pattabhi Only Choice: Gandhi

December 21, 1938, Segaon: Gandhi has not been happy, not even comfortable with the prospect of Subhas being re-elected. Subhas's strong views on the imperative of using the international war situation for India's independence are not acceptable to him.

These directly challenge his doctrine of 'non-violence', as both creed and strategy. He is also witnessing increasing trends of violence all around — in the international arena, within the country and even within the Congress organisation. The leftists are growing increasingly assertive and many of them are talking of class struggle. The peasants are also resorting to violent demonstration for their rights under the banner of the Kisan Sabhas. Under such circumstances, he is sure, Subhas, the most popular leader from the Socialist group, must not be put in the saddle once again. Prior to Subhas, Jawaharlal, who was identified with the leftist wing too, served as president for two consecutive terms. Now Gandhi wants one of his loyal followers to take over.

He had spoken to Maulana Abul Kalam Azad but the latter refused, saying in the present circumstances, the post would be a crown of thorns. Knowing his mind, Gandhi offered it again to Jawaharlal, who even though a left candidate, would be much more pliant than Subhas. Gandhi has sent Jawaharlal a wire saying: 'If you want to try again, please do. If you won't or he won't listen, Pattabhi seems to be the only choice'.[37]

TWO

From Governance Back To Agitation?

1939

From Governance Back To Agitation?

SUBHAS STANDS FIRM, TO CONTEST AGAINST GANDHI'S WISHES

January 1939: Subhas has served a term of one year as Congress president and he would like to be at the steering wheel for another term to galvanise the party into action and wrest freedom, taking advantage of the war in Europe. Subhas is convinced that a highly vulnerable British Imperialism at this juncture presents an unprecedented opportunity to India to snatch her freedom. At the same time, he has understood that Gandhi is not prepared to make use of the war. He is therefore bent upon seizing the moment, seeking re-election as Congress president. He wants to force the issue with the British at once.

Subhas is keen that the Congress serve an ultimatum upon the British government, demanding independence within six months and also simultaneously begin preparation for a national struggle. But Gandhi has ruled out the question of a national struggle now or even in the near future. In fact, right since September 1938, Gandhi has been consistently arguing that a national struggle is out of question in the near future, whereas Subhas has been convinced that India was internally more ripe for a revolution than ever before and the impending international crisis would give Indians an opportunity for achieving their emancipation. Owing to sharp differences of opinion on a number of issues including that of launching a serious struggle at this juncture, the Gandhian camp is not prepared to offer him a second term. But his own conviction about the correctness of his strategy is inspiring Subhas to contest the election. The left and the socialists, large in numbers, are backing him.

A Confrontation Seems Unavoidable

January 1939: Subhas is more convinced than ever about his prognosis of the looming war. He wants Congress policy initiated under his presidency to continue to take advantage of the war to secure India's independence. He wants the Congress to launch a national struggle to evict the British regime if they do not leave on their own.

Gandhi is cautious. He was the leader of two important national struggles and knows the pulse of people. His reckons that the party is not left with sufficient energy to launch another national struggle at this juncture. During 1932 to 1935, the government had repressed Indian people and political workers, ruthlessly. Yet another handicap is plaguing the Congress—the two years in the 'office' has made the party workers and the leaders accustomed to a comfortable life style and emaciated them of spirit and resilience. He has another reservation and that a serious one—Gandhi feels that it would be ethically incorrect to hit the British when they are in distress. Therefore, at this critical juncture, he does not want the party to get swayed by Subhas's highly activist policies. He has been thinking of a new president who would listen to and address these concerns.

Subhas, on his part, is thinking the issue as non-negotiable. The chance to secure freedom is real and ought not to be missed. He has communicated to Gandhi that he was personally not keen for a second term and would be agreeable to any other candidate from the leftist camp to lead the party so that the national struggle is led to its logical conclusion.

A couple of factors have made differences between Subhas and the Gandhian camps irreconcilable. First, Subhas has been keen about a candidate acceptable to the Leftists to ensure the continuation of policies that he has begun. The Gandhian camp, however, is arguing that the Congress policies are determined by the AICC and working committee rather than the president and as such the argument does not hold good. Second, Subhas has criticised most of the working committee members, who happen to be orthodox Gandhians, of coming to a understanding with the British government on the 'federal' part of the GOI Act 1935.

The latter has taken this as baseless accusation and one that casts aspersion on their integrity. Emotions are running high as the president has been accusing his own cabinet members. Gandhi himself has taken exception.As a result of the combination of such circumstances, a contest has become inevitable and it is likely to be keen.

Subhas enjoys high popularity amongst the Left camp which happens to be numerically stronger than the orthodox camp loyal to Gandhi. The Left camp is rallying behind him. Subhas has also been trying to convince Jawaharlal to support his cause. But Jawaharlal is not responding in any decisive manner. He seems keen to be seen being above factions. Under these circumstances, the two sides, viz. Gandhi loyalists and the Leftists are preparing for the impending battle.

Spain's Republican Regime On Verge Of Collapse

January 26, 1939, Madrid: The political situation in Europe is deteriorating further. In the civil war raging in Spain, the Republican government is on the brink of defeat. General Franco, supported by Hitler and Mussolini, has won a series of victories against it. He seems determined to uproot the Republican regime from Spain. More than three hundred thousand Spaniards are reported to have been killed in the hostilities. Today Franco's troops have entered Barcelona and the vanquished Republican army members are crossing into neighbouring France. The fall of Madrid is imminent. The European continent is gradually turning into a big theatre of war.

In India, Subhas is finding his prognosis coming true, one after another. He is seized of thoughts as to what ought to be the Congress policies to take advantage of the unfolding events.

Congress Presidential Election – Rivals Gather Strength

January 28, 1939: A tough presidential contest is on hand. As Gandhian leaders under Vallabhbhai are marshalling resources, a consolidation in the Left camp is also evident. Subhas's consistent and bold commitment to stand for Socialist causes, even in the face of opposition by the High Command, are reasons for his high popularity amongst the socialists and Communists. On the eve of the election, the CPI organ *National Front* made a direct appeal to the electorate in his favour—it has carried the banner headline 'Vote for Subhas'. Earlier, in an editorial, PC Joshi had proposed that Subhas must be re-elected to lead the nation in the critical times that lie ahead. Radical Congressmen are combining with socialists, Communists, and followers of MN Roy to defeat the Gandhi-nominated candidate.

SUBHAS RE-ELECTED PRESIDENT
Gandhian Leaders Are Surprised, Shocked

January 29, 1939: The result of the Congress election on which a million eyes were riveted, is out. In a stirring contest Subhas has defeated Pattabhi Sitaramayya, Gandhi's nominee, by 1580 to 1375 votes. The result has come as a shocking surprise to Gandhi and his loyalists. It has also demonstrated an unprecedented unity in the Left camp.

The Congress socialists, Communists, Royists and the Kisan Sabha members all closed their ranks behind Subhas, pulling off this victory, which was considered nearly impossible, given Gandhi's undisputed sway over the Congress organisation for over the past two decades and the unity and discipline of the Gandhian Congressmen under the stewardship of Vallabhbhai. The Left ambition to ascend to the driver's seat of the Congress—the premier political organisation of the country, which appeared in the realm of attainment under the charismatic leadership of Subhas, galvanised all of the Left camp's constituents in this battle. Their grit and determination got even stronger, driven by a rumour going around that some orthodox Gandhian Congress leaders have entered into an opaque understanding with the British government to accept even the 'federal part of the constitution'. To the Left, that would be nothing less than backstabbing. Subhas himself has been much exercised over the issue and and has brought it before the electorate.Given the hold of the Gandhian leaders not only over the organisation but also the various provincial governments, this victory acquires special significance.

The result has created a commotion because it signified, for the first time, an open and successful defiance of Gandhi's authority in the party. Political analysts have sat down to analyse the reasons behind it and its future implications.

Pattabhi Sitaramayya's Defeat Is My Defeat: Gandhi

January 31, 1939, Bardoli: Gandhi has issued a statement[38] on the result of the presidential election, which is being viewed by political observer and analysts as highly significant. The statement is forthright, it lays bare his mind and gives a signal of the hurdles that lie ahead of the re-elected president.

Gandhi, while admitting the fait accompli '...Shri Subhas Bose has achieved a decisive victory', made his own opposition to Subhas abundantly clear, '…from the very beginning I was decidedly against his re-election' and proceeded to give reasons thereof. He elaborated: 'I do not subscribe to his facts or the arguments in his manifestos. I think that his references to his colleagues were unjustified and unworthy.' He then made the burden of 'defeat' weigh light on Sitaramayya by taking over the cross upon himself with a prophetic statement, 'Since I was instrumental in inducing Dr Pattabhi not to withdraw… the defeat is more mine than his.'

Thereafter, he addressed the electorates and the victor in sharp words. His self-deprecation, 'It is plain to me that the delegates do not approve of the principles and policy for which I stand', disguised his assessment of the low maturity level of the electorates and unworthiness of the re-elected president, which became evident, when he pronounced, 'After all, Subhas Babu is not an enemy of his country. He has suffered for it...' Then came his barbed ridicule, ' ...In his opinion, his is the most forward and boldest policy and programme...' At the end, Gandhi issued a veiled warning. Calling his orthodox followers as the 'minority', Gandhi said, 'The minority may not obstruct on any count. They must abstain when they cannot cooperate'. Gandhi's statement has sent a clear message that Subhas, though, has won the electoral contest, has a gruelling battle ahead.

Native States Are Suckled By Imperialism: Jawaharlal

February 1939, Ludhiana: Jawaharlal took over as the president of the AISPC last November. Since then, he has recruited new members to its steering committee, converted the monthly journal *The States' People* into a weekly one, launched a fund-raising campaign, established a research office and dispatched mobile observers across states to report on ground situation.

His global exposure made him see that the semi-feudal states have been collapsing like a pack of cards all over the world. He surmises that these 550 plus princely states in India would be no exception to that worldwide trend, once the British withdrew from the country. In the session of the AISPC, he observed:

'Offspring of the British power in India, suckled by imperialism for its own purposes, it (princely order) has survived till today, though mighty revolutions have shaken the world and changed it, empires have collapsed and crowds of princes and petty rulers have faded away. That system has no inherent importance or strength; it is the strength of British imperialism that counts. For us in India, that system has in reality been one of the faces of imperialism. Therefore, when conflict comes, we must recognise who our opponent is.'[39]

It is clear he is realising the need for the Congress and its leaders to intervene more decisively with a sense of urgency so that the states' people's struggles are synchronised to the extent possible with the national movement in the British India.

In the Tripuri session of the Congress, a decision is likely to be taken to connect the activities of the two organisations, viz. Congress and the AISPC. Meanwhile, here the AISPC has sought to engender the next level of momentum. It provided for a mechanism of joint meeting of the AICC with its own standing committee. With Jawaharlal being both its president and also a top-ranked leader of the Congress, the future programmes and policies of the AISPC are likely to show increasing influence of the Congress and also consolidation of peoples' movement in British India and Indian states.

Jawaharlal has expressed the need to keep the movements in native states non-violent. This, some crticis say, is probably to ensure that Gandhi does not disapprove of gradually increasing involvement of Congress leaders like him in the states' people's causes.

EXODUS FROM CONGRESS WORKING COMMITTEE

February 22, 1939, Wardha: In his first reaction to the news of the presidential election result last month, Gandhi had given an indication of the shape of things to come in the way of Subhas. Referring to his orthodox followers as the 'minority', he had said, 'They must abstain when they cannot cooperate.' Subhas did realise the import of the utterances and he has been attempting all these days to secure Gandhi's approbation to his re-election. Ignoring Gandhi's harsh criticism, he professed that it would be his aim and object to try and gain Gandhi's confidence. But all his efforts have so far gone unheeded.

The working committee has been scheduled to meet here on the eve of the Congress session in the Tripuri. However, Subhas, being seriously ill, had sent a request to the members through Vallabhbhai to postpone the meeting till the Tripuri session to be held next month. The Gandhian members of the working committee, who have been fuming right since the presidential election, have become more antagonised at this development.

They are finding in this request for deferment, the Congress president's lack of confidence in them in taking important decisions in his absence. Today, twelve of them, in a seemingly concerted action, have tendered their resignations to the president. The remaining three are Subhas and his brother Sarat besides Jawaharlal. It is being heard that Jawaharlal, though did not formally tender his resignation, has issued a statement, which is making most people think that he too has done so. In the letters of all the twelve members, the reasons stated in support of the resignation are identical: 'We feel that the time has come when the country should have a clear-cut policy, not based on compromise between different incompatible groups of the Congress. It is but right therefore, that you should select a homogenous cabinet representing the view of the majority.'[40] According to some political observers, the unified action, common draft and the tenor of the letters suggest that Gandhi himself has a hand in the matter.

Congress Session Begins, Political Intrigues Loom Large

March 10, 1939, Tripuri: The Congress session has begun here. In stark contrast to the previous session at Haripura where the ambience was one of hope and enthusiasm, Tripuri seems to be enveloped by gloom, despair and political intrigues. Subhas, the re-elected president, has been seriously ill and has started from Calcutta for Tripuri with 104° F temperature.

The delegates here seem to be affected by all-round uncertainties, not only because of the intra-party differences but also the evolving international situation. The German juggernaut has been rolling on the continent. Closer home, Japan has embarked on a conquest of China. Significantly, the top leadership of the party is divided over the question of the 'use of the international situation'.

The party is required to take some crucial decisions here, like what role does it envisage for itself and India in relation to the war that has already begun raging in Europe and is likely to engulf Britain sooner than later. Ironically, two top leaders holding opposite views on the matter would not be participating for practical purposes. Gandhi, on his part, has made it known that he would not be able to attend Tripuri, as he was too occupied with the affairs of Rajkot. Subhas could not attend the working committee meeting at Wardha earlier owing to illness. Though he is present here, his poor health would deter his effective participation in deliberations.

The Gandhian working committee members are present with their supporters in full strength. They have come here with a definite plan. As regards the Left bloc, its main constituent, viz. the Congress Socialist Party led by Jayaprakash Narayan, has arrived with the largest contingent.

States' People's Political Struggle Subhas Wants Congress Support To Be Comprehensive

March 10-12, 1939, Tripuri: The Congress session is in progress here but Subhas, the re-elected president, is ill and therefore his presidential speech was read out in the session by his brother Sarat Chandra Bose. Subhas has expressed concern at the British regime being in league with the rulers of the Indian native states in most places. Gandhi's bitter experience at Rajkot recently has been a clinching evidence of such a nexus. In present circumstances, the Congress, he felt, should draw closer to the people of the states.

Earlier, the Congress had put a ban on certain form of political activities being conducted in the name of the Congress in the native states. He has said now the ban is being lifted. He also said, the work of guiding the popular movement in the states for civil liberty and responsible government should be conducted by the working committee, on a comprehensive and systematic basis.

Subhas Wants Ultimatum To British Government

March 10-12, 1939, Tripuri: In the presidential speech that was read out, Subhas said the time has come to raise the issue of 'swaraj' and submit India's national demand to the British government in the form of an ultimatum, and give them a certain time limit. If no reply is received or reply is unsatisfactory, Congress should resort to mass civil disobedience. Although the Left, radicals and many of the common congressmen are enthusiastic, Gandhi himself is against any such action at this juncture. Most of the former members of the working committee, being staunch Gandhians, are predictably not in favour of this approach.

In accordance with the presidential speech, a bold resolution demanding self-determination 'within six months' under threat of 'civil disobedience' was introduced but it was defeated for want of support. Instead, a resolution has been passed that places a demand for 'swaraj' but does not mention a time frame.

Leftists Want Subhas To Seize Initiative

March 10-12, 1939, Tripuri: The constituents of the Left camp want Subhas to make use of the opportunity provided by a favourable verdict in the presidential election. They want him to form a Left-dominated working committee, and carry forward the national struggle, free from the fetters of Gandhian ideology. MN Roy wrote to Subhas that Gandhi himself had admitted defeat, and now the Congress must be given a new leadership, entirely free from the principles and pre-occupations of Gandhism. In regard to the constitution of the working committee, the Communists want the presence of a Leftist group in the executive, whereas the Congress Socialists insist on a majority. It is clear that the Left camp wants the re-elected president to seize this unique opportunity. However, Subhas seems to be thinking otherwise. He apparently wants all groups of the Congress to be with him. This seems to be impossible, though.

Assault On 'Rebel' President Imminent Right-wing Leaders Sharpen Their Knives

March 10-12, 1939, Tripuri: The right wing of the Congress, led by Vallabhbhai, has dealt a fatal blow to the re-elected president. GB Pant, a member of the working committee and prime minister of UP has introduced a resolution in the subjects committee which proposes to take away the independence and autonomy of the Congress president to choose his colleagues in the working committee, by subjecting the exercise of cabinet formation to Gandhi's approval.
Resolution[41] reads:

'In view of various misunderstandings that have arisen in the Congress and the country on account of controversies in connection with presidential election and after, it is desirable that the Congress should clarify the position and declare the general policy.

a. This Congress declares that adherence to the fundamental policies which have governed its programme in the past years under the guidance of Mahatma Gandhi and is definitely of opinion that there should be no break in these policies and they should continue to govern the Congress programme in future. This Congress expresses its confidence in the work of the Working Committee which functioned during the last year and regrets that any aspersion should have been cast against any of its members;
b. In view of the critical situation that may develop during the coming year and in view of the fact that Mahatma Gandhi alone can lead the Congress and the country to victory during such crisis, the Congress regards it as imperative that the Congress executive should command his implicit confidence and requests the president to nominate the Working Committee in accordance with the wishes of Gandhiji.'

Pant Resolution – Deadly Blow To Elected President

March 12, 1939: The resolution introduced by GB Pant, apparently an emotional one aimed at re-establishing the exalted position of Gandhi in the organisation, practically rendered it impossible for the president to pursue his policies and programmes forming part of his election manifesto. The Congress constitution gives an unfettered right to the president to choose his colleagues in the working committee. As such, the resolution seemed to be ultra vires the constitution. However, Subhas did not disallow it, possibly not to hurt the already-ruffled feelings of Gandhi himself and the Gandhians.

Soon after introduction of the resolution, its ramifications were beginning to be felt. It forced the delegates to choose between the leadership of either Gandhi or Subhas. The matter became more complicated due to introduction of another resolution that proposed putting before the government a 'national demand for independence'. Subhas wanted it in the form of a 'timed ultimatum', backed by a 'threat of nationwide disobedience'. On the issue of a time frame, Gandhi has been very clear—he felt that the nation was not ready to launch another big movement at this juncture. Jayaprakash Narayan, the prominent leader of the Congress Socialists, also held a similar view. Further, he has also been convinced of the indispensability of Gandhi in any nation-wide movement, if and when launched.

On the issue of the 'national demand', therefore, Congress Socialists led by Jayprakash supported a resolution that did not mention any time frame. As regards the Pant resolution, which practically compelled delegates to choose between Gandhi and Subhas, they decided to abstain. This came as a huge blow to Subhas, as the Congress Socialists formed the largest bloc in the Left camp. Their absence allowed the Gandhian bloc to push their way through. Eventually, the Subjects Committee passed the resolution by 218-133 votes.

Congress observers say, the resolution has far-reaching impact and can make it untenable for the president to continue in office. Subhas has a clear and distinct political approach, radically different from Gandhi. As such there is simply no way he can form a working committee satisfying the conditions imposed by the resolution.

Congress Socialists Abstain, Tilt Scale Against Subhas

According to political observers, the adoption of the Pant resolution is likely to create an unprecedented situation in the Congress. Though it is against the tenet of the Congress constitution, the president allowed its introduction, thereby giving scope to his detractors. To their credit, Gandhian leaders made deft political moves creating pressure upon the president to do what they wanted him to.

They made a forceful exposition of their case while introducing the resolution in the open session. Pant said, 'if the delegates wanted Gandhiji back they had to prove it to him'.[42] He tactfully positioned it, trying to make it less controversial by suggesting that his resolution was 'for Gandhi', and 'not against Bose'. There was visible confusion in the Left camp. When the issue was projected to them as a 'mutually exclusive choice' between Gandhi and Subhas, most delegates had to rethink. They felt the indispensability of Gandhi's leadership in any future nation-wide struggle. However, MN Roy and few others opposed the Pant resolution in its present form. But the amendment was defeated. Although Subhas had support from the radicals, Communists and a section of the Congress Socialists, the majority of the Congress Socialists abstained from voting, paving the way for passage of the Pant resolution.

HITLER IS IN THE HRADZIN PALACE

March 15, 1939, Munich: Six months ago, Hitler had annexed Sudetenland—the Czech province with a concentration of German speaking people. In hindsight, that was a mere 'entry move', giving a vague ethical justification for German aggression, which would be followed by gobbling up the whole country. At that time, he had presented Prague with a set of impossible conditions coupled with veiled threats. In the meanwhile, German agents were busy in creating wide-scale disorders in Czechoslovakia, preparing the ground for Hitler's intervention. It was becoming clear that Hitler's demands were nothing but ruses to establish German hegemony over Czechoslovakia. Today, Hitler has ended the suspense by exterminating democracy in that country together with robbing its independence. He reached the Hradzin Castle, the ancient palace of Bohemian kings and lately the residence of the president, and raised the German standard here. This seems to be the final stroke in the annexation of Czechoslovakia.

The whole of Europe has been shaken by this brazen assault. But neither Britain nor France is able to gather sufficient courage to resist the marauding German army. They seem to be under-estimating the imperialistic ambition of Hitler and engaging in self-deception that they, or their colonies, would not attract his growing greed.

Gandhi Writes To Subhas, 'Initiatives Are On You'

March 24, 1939: New Delhi: Subhas continues to be ill. He is convalescing in Jealgora near Dhanbad. Still not able to attend to his duties as the new president, he has been writing to Gandhi to sort out the problems that has arisen in the wake of the Pant resolution.

Deeply hurt by that resolution, which has put him to an impossible situation, Subhas has been corresponding with Gandhi urging his intervention to resolve the problem. On several key issues including inter alia taking advantage of British in the impending war situation, he has serious differences with Gandhi. Unless he has freedom in choosing his working committee members, he cannot afford to carry out his policies. However, the Pant resolution robs him of this freedom. In his missives, Subhas had questioned the propriety of the Pant resolution which takes away the unfettered right given to the Congress president by the Congress constitution to select the members of the working committee. He has desired to have Gandhi's guidance as to how to form the working committee in the prevailing circumstances.

Gandhi is fundamentally opposed to Subhas's policies on taking advantage of the war that includes serving ultimatum on the British, nationwide civil disobedience and such others. He is convinced that the nation is not ready for another big movement now. In such circumstances, he feels the last thing he can do is to be a facilitator of Subhas's programme and policies. In a wire reply,[43] Gandhi has now told Subhas that the resolution seemed quite clear and that the initiative is on Subhas. Gandhi has also mentioned that if Subhas is not able to attend the national work due to health, he should adopt the only constitutional course open to him—an unmistakable hint that Subhas ought to resign. These suggestions, per se, are betraying Gandhi's bitterness and lack of patience at Subhas's re-election and continued absence from office due to illness.

WAR CLOUD OVER EUROPE
Congress' Multiple Strands Of Thinking On India's Role

The war situation in Europe is becoming increasingly grim. It seems likely that before long it will reach the doors of Britain. Against such backdrop, a political discourse has begun within the Congress as to what ought to be the role of India. There are differences in perspectives. In fact, serious differences on this issue between Gandhi and Subhas were partly responsible for a contest for the presidency of the party. Three distinct strands of opinions are doing rounds. Jawaharlal is clearly supporting the democracy camp led by Britain. Last year he had visited that country and issued public statements pledging Indian support to the pro-democracy camp. His over-enthusiasm in this matter and interpretation of the Haripura Congress resolution in a particular way exposed him to criticism back home. However, he is steadfast in his personal opinion and keen to influence the Congress policies in favour of Britain and its allies. Gandhi has a different view. He is a firm believer in the creed of non-violence and as such, does not want India to support either of the warring parties whether Britain or Germany — Allies or the Axis. Subhas is singularly concerned about India's independence. He is looking at the war as an opportunity to wrest India's freedom. If Britain does not concede to India's demands, the colonial regime must be pushed out of India through nationwide Satyagraha. He is also completely open to enlist the support of Britain's enemy nations to secure independence. The choice of the allies, he feels, should be decided along the lines of narrow self-interest of Indian nation adopting an unsentimental approach. In a letter to Jawaharlal, he has written that '... it is no use condemning countries like Germany and Italy on the one hand and on the other, giving a certificate of good conduct to British and French imperialism.'[44] As far as the orthodox leaders, they have no distinct opinion on the issue and they are ready to follow the lines decided by Gandhi.

With such wide differences marking the political thoughts of its major leaders, formulating a 'war-time policy' is posing a tough challenge to the Congress.

Anger Over Presidential Election Explodes Gandhi Hints At Cleaning Up Congress Stable

March 30, 1939, Jealgora: After Tripuri, a seriously ailing Subhas has been recuperating here near Dhanbad. Since his arrival here, he has been in a series of correspondences, especially with Gandhi and Jawaharlal, in a bid to tide over the crisis facing him. Pant's resolution is now hanging around his neck like an albatross. He has not been able to work out the riddle—to form a committee that enjoys Gandhi's confidence, yet with whom he can carry forward his policies and programmes. His ill health is posing additional hurdles restraining him from initiating any vigorous initiative. As a result, the task of forming the working committee is in a limbo. He ought to have finished the exercise by the end of the Tripuri session.

From Gandhi's recent communication, it was apparent to Subhas that the delay in forming the working committee is causing Gandhi disquiet. He had even suggested that Subhas could resign if he was unable to discharge the president's duties because of prolonged illness. Subhas was hurt and felt that Gandhi's suggestion was unfair. In reply, he wrote questioning Gandhi on this point and citing precedents of presidents in the past continuing to hold office while in prison. Subhas also expressed his unhappiness over the roadblocks put up by the rightists, whom he described as 'Gandhites' and urged Gandhi to intervene to restore national unity. He sought a definite guidance on the formation of the working committee and mentioned that he would be compelled to part ways in the event he did not have freedom in selecting members of his cabinet.

Gandhi has now responded, saying that since Subhas considers Pant resolution as ultra vires the Congress constitution, his choice of committee should be unfettered. Gandhi has written,[45] 'Assuming therefore that your policy has the backing of the majority of the AICC, you should have a Working Committee, composed purely of those who believe in your policy'. Gandhi said if Subhas is to function as president, his hands must be unfettered. Then came a threat. Gandhi warned 'So far as the Gandhi-ites (to use that wrong expression) are concerned, they will not obstruct you. They will help you where they can, they will abstain where they cannot. There should be no difficulty whatsoever, if they are in a minority. They may not suppress themselves if they are clearly in a majority.'

Thereafter, his anger burst forth on the presidential election result and his resolve to overhaul the electorates that brought the recent debacle: 'What worries me, however, is the fact that the Congress electorate is bogus and that, therefore, majority and minority lose their full meaning. Nevertheless, till the Congress stable is cleansed, we have to manage with the instrument we have for the time being.' Before concluding Gandhi also mentioned 'terrible distrust amongst ourselves', which has made joint work impossible.

Shareef Report On Muslim Persecution

March 1939: SM Shareef, a Bar-at-Law, was appointed by the Bihar Provincial Muslim League to survey and report on the alleged atrocities by the Congress government of Bihar on the Muslims of the province. Shareef has submitted his report. His report displayed tendency to generalise things based on few cases, and it levied unsubstantiated accusations. His main observations are imposition of cow protection and Hindi on Muslims, as well as interference with their religious practices. Political observers say that the findings are highly exaggerated and driven by political motives.

Subhas Urges Gandhi To Save Congress And The Country From A Calamity

March 31, 1939, Jealgora: Subhas and Gandhi have been engaged in long correspondence though no solution is in sight. Gandhi has delivered Subhas one important message—let him form a homogenous working committee of his choice but he must be able to secure AICC approval for his programmes and policies. The Gandhian camp has been certain that Subhas will not be able to re-enact the presidential election result when large number of Congress Socialist Party delegates had supported him against Sitaramayya. Gandhian leaders are already speaking about an imminent split in the Congress Socialist Party (CSP), with a block going against Subhas.

Subhas has today written[46] to Gandhi, emphasising the need for unity in the Congress and urging him to take immediate initiative and intervene to save Congress and the country from a calamity. He pointed out that the Gandhian faction was bringing pressure on him to resign. His resignation and parting of ways, Subhas warned, would begin a civil war and weaken the Congress. He also made it clear that quite contrary to the belief of Gandhian leaders, barring a small section of official CSP, the bulk of the Congress socialists were with him. In the event of a split, he predicted that the Congress will be deprived of radical youthful progressive elements.

GANDHI LAYS DOWN FINAL ROADMAP
Subhas Has To Take The Call

April 2, 1939, New Delhi: Gandhi seems to have realised Subhas's vulnerability and also sensed the impending victory of the rightist bloc, headed by Vallabhbhai in the coming AICC session in Calcutta. Giving clear indications that he is no longer amenable to entreaties and persuasions nor afraid of threats by Subhas, he sent a long wire which said it all:

> Posted Full Reply Your Letters. My Advice Therein Is Irrespective Of Pandit Pant's Resolution And In View Diammetrically Opposite Views Held By Two Schools Of Thought You Should Forthwith Form Your Own Cabinet Fully Representing Your Policy. You Should Frame And Publish Your Policy And Programme And Submit The Same To A.I.C.C. If You Secure Majority You Should Be Enabled To Carry Out Your Policy Unhampered. If You Do Not Secure Majority You Should Resign And Invite A.I.C.C. To Elect A New President. Given Honesty And Goodwill, I Do Not Fear Civil War. Love, Bapu.[47]

'How Are Our Views Diametrically Opposite?' Subhas

April 6, 1939: Gandhi's wire has compounded Subhas's worries. In continuing with what is increasingly appearing to be an elusive search for a solution, he has sent yet another communication[48] to Gandhi. In it Subhas has sought to establish that their views are not diametrically opposite as Gandhi suggested. In proof, he has quoted the 'National Demand Resolution' which was recently passed in Tripuri with the support of the Gandhi-ites. Subhas has contended that the import of that resolution is not radically different than the ultimatum that Subhas had proposed. He has clarified that as Congress president he has not proposed any violent movement but suggested the launch of a nationwide non-violent civil disobedience movement, which is not contrary to the principle of non-violence.

Subhas is possibly seeing injustice in Gandhi's suggestion that he should secure majority approval in the AICC in respect of his policy and programme, when his stand has already been justified by his election as the president. He has let his feelings be known in this regard and also made it clear that he has no desire to stick to office even for 'one day', unless he can thereby advance the public cause, as he understands it.

Give Us A Chance! We'll Try To Justify Ourselves: Subhas

April 10, 1939, Rajkot: Subhas was upset at Gandhi's refusal to bring about a reconciliation between the two factions in the Congress and Gandhi's insistence that he went ahead to form a cabinet of his own choosing. Gandhi's last cable of 2nd April was simple, straightforward and rigid. Following this, Subhas on 6th instant urged Gandhi, in the event he formed such a working committee, to express his confidence in his cabinet and give them a chance to work for one year to serve the country. He had implored: 'I would earnestly request you to give me your vote of confidence till next Congress. If, in the meantime, we fail to justify ourselves by our service and suffering, we shall stand condemned before the Congress...'[49] In such an eventuality, they would deserve to be kicked out of office, he contended. Subhas also mentioned that Gandhi's vote of confidence would also mean the confidence of the AICC.

But today, Gandhi has rejected even this appeal. He made two critical points. First, he expressed his inability to interpret the controversial 'Pant resolution' and left it to Subhas to do his own interpretation and act accordingly. Second, he informed Subhas: 'I cannot, will not, impose a Cabinet on you… nor can I guarantee approval by the AICC of your Cabinet and policy. It would amount to suppression... If you do not get the vote, lead the opposition till you have converted the majority.'[50] He mentioned that the two of them saw things so differently that there was no common platform between the two on the political or even economic issues. Gandhi, therefore, advised that they had better work along own lines and in their own ways.

ITALY BARES ITS FANGS, ANNEXES ALBANIA

April 12, 1939, Tirana: Italy has annexed Albania today. It may be recalled that Hitler's forces have already annexed Austria and steamrolled Czechoslovakia. It appears Mussolini just does not want to be seen as a meek, second rate power in the Axis camp. Both his ego and dangerous ambition for territories seemingly set him up for the invasion of Albania. It is reported that even the king of Italy, viz. Victor Emmanuel III, thought Mussolini's plan as an unnecessary risk.

Notwithstanding, Mussolini had given an ultimatum to Albania at the end of the last month, following which his forces invaded the latter's territory on the 7th of this month and negotiated the Albanian resistance without much difficulty. Today, the seal of approval for the Italian annexation finally came from the puppet regime that Mussolini has set up in Albania. The Albanian parliament has voted to unite their country with Italy. It is clear, the Axis power is running its juggernaut over the continent. Competitive conquests by the Axis nations are making things worse. The worries of the Allied powers are growing by the day.

My Hope Has Been Cremated In Rajkot: Gandhi

April 24, 1939, Rajkot: The unrest in Rajkot had come to a head in August last year when a general strike was observed in the state against government repression. Vallabhbhai endorsed the popular agitation against the ruler, and demanded new elections to the representative assembly, limits on princely withdrawal from state treasury, reductions in land revenue and cancellation of monopolies granted to few businessmen that worked to the detriment of the common people. Following this, there was a multi-party negotiation involving him, the diwan, the ruler and the British political agent in Rajkot.

This resulted in a settlement. Vallabhbhai called off the satyagraha movement in exchange of the ruler agreeing to a privy purse and the appointment of a committee to recommend reforms. He was to recommend seven out of the ten committee members. However, post negotiation, the ruling regime, reportedly at the instigation of the British governor, again hardened its attitude. After Vallabhbhai submitted his list of nominees who were Brahmins and Banias, the state government cleverly advocated that the committee should be more representative of the state's demographic profile and especially include, Rajputs, Muslims and Depressed classes.

This led to a stalemate. Gandhi himself arrived at Rajkot. He even approached the Viceroy and the latter suggested arbitration by Sir Maurice Gwyer, the British chief justice of India. Maurice endorsed Vallabhbhai's list but, still, the state administration did not budge. Gandhi went on a fast unto death. But the ruler and his diwan did not relent. On the contrary, the Rajputs and Muslims in Rajkot, reportedly at the behest of the ruling regime and as a part of a deeper political intrigue against the Congress, threatened to launch their own Satyagraha. Worse for the Congress, the leaders of Muslims and backward classes in British India joined the issue and began arguing for separate representation of their community in the reform committee. Things got so messy that Gandhi admitted his failure and withdrew from the imbroglio.

It has become clear how fragmented the Indian polity has turned out to be and also the loss of control of a leader of Gandhi's stature on various segments of people. He is clearly a shattered man. Today he has issued a press statement[51] saying that Rajkot seems to have robbed him of his youth and that suddenly he has begun feeling old and being weighed down by the knowledge of decrepitude. He also lamented: 'I never knew what it was to lose hope. But it seems to have been cremated in Rajkot.'

Rajkot Leaves Gandhi Devastated

Rajkot has virtually shattered Gandhi. Given that it is his home turf, his absolute sway over the Congress, his liberal access to the highest echelon of the colonial government in Delhi and his own political experience and acumen, the failure to persuade the ruling establishment of this small native state seems nothing less than a fortuitous stroke of ominous destiny. The obdurate

> state government refused to give him any space and on the contrary handed him a gloomy defeat by chicanery and intrigue. It countered his much-haloed and sacrosanct vow of a 'fast unto death' by engineering an ill-motivated counter Satyagraha. The last straw was the scary prospect that the problems of Rajkot might spill over into the British Indian provinces, inducting the Muslims and the Depressed classes within its fold. At that juncture, Gandhi possibly deemed it appropriate to withdraw, without realising his political goal, a rare occurrence in his long political career.
>
> In Rajkot, Gandhi became involved in an agitation where his local repute, mediatory skill and access to Delhi could do little to alter the attitude of the state government or set up a successful non-violent model for States' People's Movements. Gandhi had staked too much but nothing came at the end. The course of events has even affected his health. It has left him devastated and handed him a sense of defeat.[52]

Gandhi Reluctant To Help Subhas

April 29, 1939, Sodepur: Gandhi has been staying at the outskirts of Calcutta but he may not attend the AICC being held in the city. In his communiqué of 10th April, he had made his mind abundantly clear. In few cables sent thereafter he reiterated the same position. Today he put the last nail on Subhas' hope.

To a desperate request that Gandhi nominate the working committee members himself, he has written[53] to Subhas, 'I feel myself utterly incompetent to do so. Much has happened since Tripuri. Knowing your own views and knowing how you and most of the members differ in fundamentals, it seems to me that if I give you names, it would be an imposition on you.' Once again, for the last time before the fateful AICC meet was to be held, Gandhi reiterated that Subhas was free to choose his cabinet. The only lifeline he suggested was that Subhas could reach an agreement with the ex-members of the working committee on the relevant issue. At the end, he hoped, '...I hope, however, that whatever is done will be done with mutual goodwill.' As regards Subhas, this is his last input for the AICC session as Gandhi would not attend it. He is likely to leave for Brindaban in a couple of days.

Political analysts say that Gandhi knows better than anybody else the impossibility of the ex-members reaching an agreement with Subhas. They feel Subhas is certain to face a hostile opposition in the AICC session and he is left with little option.

Subhas Resigns, Rajendra Prasad Takes Over

April 29-May 1, 1939, Calcutta: The AICC session has concluded here. Gandhi has not attended. Therefore, the chance of any last minute reconciliation between Subhas and the Gandhian camp has fizzled out. In the session, Subhas presented a letter from Gandhi, read out its contents and explained how the Pant resolution and Gandhi's own directives to work out a solution in consultation with the Gandhian leaders have put him in an impossible situation.

He explained that, as the president, he would like the working committee to be a composite one that should be able to command the confidence of the largest number of Congressmen. As it was impossible to reconcile these contradictory conditions, he tendered his resignation to enable the AICC to find a solution to the imbroglio.

Jawaharlal then moved a proposal, asking Subhas to withdraw his resignation and suggested that the members of the previous year's working committee be retained, barring two who are seeking to discontinue for health reasons. These two posts, Jawaharlal said, should be filled by Subhas according to his choice. Subhas, however, felt this did not address his need for a composite Working Committee. Sarojini Naidu, in chair, felt Subhas's statement was vague. Jawaharlal withdrew his proposal. Sarojini then wanted the session to elect a new president. Following these developments, Rajendra Prasad has been elected as the new president. He would finish the presidential term until the next full Congress session.

The new president has formed his working committee. Both Subhas and Jawaharlal excused themselves from the new committee. Two new members have been chosen from Bengal They are

Prafulla Chandra Ghosh and Dr BC Roy, both of whom are known to be Gandhi loyalists. These two selections seem to be serving dual purposes—to assuage the feelings of hurt in Bengal owing to Subhas's ouster and second, tighten the grip of the the Gandhian camp over the provincial Congress.

Subhas Creats 'Forward Bloc', Plans To Galvanise Left

May 3, 1939: Subhas is convinced about the correctness of his policies and wants that the Congress must not lose the golden opportunity that the evolving war situation is presenting to the country. His efforts to influence and guide the Congress as its president at the present critical time have been frustrated due to the machination by the rightist Gandhian camp, but he does not see this as the end of the road. Recognising that the constituents of the Left camp are disorganised and, therefore, deprived of a legitimate and decisive say in the Congress policy, he has proceeded to bring them under one banner. For this purpose, he has announced the formation of a new grouping within the Congress and christened it the 'Forward Bloc'.

The object of the Bloc is to rally all radical and anti-Imperialist progressive elements in the country on the basis of a minimum programme, representing the greatest common measure of agreement among radicals of all shades of opinions. Subhas's objective is clearly to bring all of the Congress Socialists, Communists, Royists and members of the Kisan Sabhas under the banner of the bloc and influence the Congress policies in a significant manner.

Congressmen Take Part In States' People's Movements

May 1939: The decision in the Haripura Congress that Congress leaders could involve themselves in the States' People's Movement in their individual capacity had given a huge fillip to the peoples' democratic aspirations and their movements in the princely states. Tripuri Congress this year gave further momentum to this process by allowing greater cooperation between the Congress and the AISPC. As a result, the peoples' movements in the states are both getting stronger and attracting severe repression by the respective regimes, aided by the British.

Many protesters have been jailed and injured and a few even killed. Notwithstanding the setback Gandhi suffered at Rajkot, several top Congress leaders including Jawaharlal Nehru, Vallabhbhai Patel, Pattabhi Sitaramayya, Jamnalal Bajaj, Harekrishna Mahatab and Nabakrishna Chaudhury are giving the people leadership across several Indian states. Political analysts say at last the Congress seems to have appreciated the need and importance of helping the popular movement in the states and is making conscious attempts to merge the two streams of movements in British India and the Indian India.

I Feel A Cripple Without Jawaharlal, Says Gandhi

May 5, 1939, Brindaban: Gandhi came here from Sodepur. He had left Subhas in Calcutta to face a hostile AICC session. He seems to be a tired person these days. Earlier, he had emerged physically and mentally shattered from Rajkot. Within the Congress, although his followers were able to force Subhas to resign as Congress president, the Left forces have begun to galvanise under the former president and they have started to defy Gandhi's decades-old authority over the organisation. The unfolding events are causing him both distress and anxieties. Communist Party of India members, who refused to support Subhas against him a few months ago in a bid to keep unity in the national struggle, have begun to move away from the mainstream Congress. They are mulling the prospect of joint struggle with the newly-formed Forward Bloc.

According to political observers, Gandhi has come to develop a feeling of loneliness and unease that he does not have the young men's understanding and support. The approaches and strategies of the Muslim League these days have been causing the Congress further disquiet. The League not only remains as irreconcilable as ever but it is also trying to fish in troubled water by offering communally motivated support to the government.

Gandhi is distressed. He feels lonely even within the Congress. There are only a few who genuinely understand his philosophy and method of action. Amongst them, he has come to depend on Jawaharlal the most. Though he admits that there are differences between him and Jawaharlal yet, he does not consider these to be significant. In an interview to the Gandhi Sevak Sangh, he disclosed his dependence on Jawaharlal: 'Without[54] him I feel myself a cripple. He also feels more or less the same way'. Then he added, 'Our hearts are one'. Political observers see in Gandhi's statement a clear sign that he is looking at Jawaharlal as his political successor.

Subhas Initiates The Left Consolidation Committee

June 21, 1939, Bombay: Subhas formed Forward Bloc to bring the Leftist forces under a single banner. But the trend of events of late suggests that Congress Socialists, CPI, Royists and Kisan Sabhas are unwilling to merge their identities in the Forward Block. Thus, in the All India Forward Bloc Conference being held here, Subhas has announced the formation of the 'Left Consolidation Committee'. This committee would have equal representatives from each of its constituents, including the Bloc, and it will try to influence the Congress policy in favour of serving the government with an ultimatum, use the international situation to India's advantage to secure her freedom and also build up a Socialist India, post-independence.

Muslim Mass Contact Programme Is Withering

June 1939: At last there are reasons for the Muslim League leaders to smile and rejoice. As the membership register of the League is bulging, the recent reports from the rival camp indicate that the Congress' Muslim Mass Contact programme has begun a downhill journey. For the lay public, this may sound strange especially after the Congress made steady headway in Muslim enrolment for some time. However, to the insiders in the party, it would not be such a surprise for more than one reason.

First, the Muslim Mass Contact programme has been too much dependent on only one leader, viz. Jawaharlal who had conceived it too. As the Congress president he had pushed it hard, giving it support through competent personnel, budget and other resources. The fact that he is no longer the Congress president is making a difference. Then, most of the orthodox right wing Congress leaders have been at best passive, if not hostile, to the scheme.

With the increasing enrolment of Muslim members and their growing aspirations for higher positions in the organisational hierarchy, including seats in the provincial Congress committees and also as members of the legislatures, these leaders have begun to put up roadblocks to the programme including withdrawal of financial support. There have been conflicts in regard to demands for seats on the provincial Congress committees, election tickets and so on. The combined impact of these unfavourable developments has begun to take its toll. The euphoria is over and disappointment is large.

Fissures Within Left Consolidation Committee

July 1939, Calcutta: Following the formation of the Left Consolidation Committee (LCC) last month, there were some meetings and negotiations in the initial days. However, differences have begun to surface soon thereafter. MN Roy has been critical of the working of the Congress Socialists. It may also be recalled that many Communist Party members have penetrated into the Congress Socialist Party and their differences with the original CSP members over important issues are becoming prominent. In recent days, the two groups have been engaged in confrontations over the control of the branch offices. As such, the LCC has not been able to achieve much of the purpose for which it was constituted at the first place. Its constituents are often not able to take a united stand to be able to influence the Congress policies.

Subhas Defies Highcommand, Holds Demonstration

July 9, 1939, Calcutta: During 24 to 27th last month, the AICC in its session held in Bombay, had passed amongst others two resolutions that generated good measure of dissatisfaction amongst party segments. One of them restricted the scope for staging Satyagraha in provinces. It said, '…no Congressman may offer or organise any form of satyagraha in the Administrative Provinces of India without the previous sanction of the Provincial Congress Committee concerned.'[55] The other one, while stressing upon the need for cooperation amongst the Provincial Congress ministry, the Provincial Congress Committee, and the Congress Party, laid down some ground rules about each one's turf. Thus, it said that the Provincial Congress Committee could not interfere with the discretion of the ministries in administrative matters but may draw the latter's attention privately to any particular abuse or difficulty. In case of difference between the two in matters involving policy, reference should be made to the Parliamentary Subcommittee. The resolutions were drafted by Gandhi himself.

Subhas has been of the opinion that both these resolutions would act counter to the cause of the nation and therefore, ought to be protested forcefully. The first resolution strangulates the scope for building up mass movements across the country while the second one would encourage a drift towards constitutionalism. In other words, this new mechanism would increase the influence, power and authority of the provincial ministries at the cost of the Congress organisations. Subhas thought it fit to stage extensive protest against these dual measures and gave a call to hold countrywide demonstrations against the dictatorial attitude of the central leadership.

Subhas had expected that the Left consolidation committee would play an important role to ensure the success of the protest call. But, the issue, ironically, has wedged deep divisions among the LCC members. After showing early enthusiasm and support to his call, the majority constituents of the committee backtracked. The CPI and the Socialists began to stress on Congress unity, which they felt was put to jeopardy by Subhas's call. MN Roy felt Subhas's call was a blunder. By 6th July, all major constituents of the LCC had withdrawn from the protest programme. The breakdown of the unity at such a critical juncture seems to have sounded a death knell to the consolidation committee. However, Subhas, undeterred, has gone ahead with the protest and held a large demonstration here with the full backing of the Bengal Provincial Congress Committee.

Subhas Removed As BPCC President

August 11, 1939: Since May, when the Forward Bloc was formed, the Gandhian leadership of the Congress has been perturbed by the growing opposition from the Left block led by Subhas. It had been waiting for an opportunity to strike back. The 9th July rally held by Subhas in defiance of both the directives of the working committee and the incumbent Congress president has provided it with the opportunity. The fact that a clear schism had already arisen in the Left camp concerning the 'protest demonstration' has made its action less risky.

The Congress working committee has treated Subhas's action as a grave act of indiscipline and disqualified him as the president of the Bengal Provincial Congress and also to be a member of any elective Congress committee for three years from this month. Subhas's reply to the 'show cause' did not satisfy the party. The resolution drafted by Gandhi and passed by the working committee, stated that it had given 'anxious consideration' to Subhas's action and his reply to the Congress president but thought that the right course for Subhas would have been to appeal to the working committee or the AICC on his areas of concern.

Unconvinced about the notion that every member is free to interpret Congress constitution as he likes, which would be a sure prescription for anarchy, the working committee felt that 'it will fail in its duty if it condones the deliberate and flagrant breach of discipline by Shri Subhas Chandra Bose'. Therefore, for his grave act of indiscipline, the Committee has resolved, 'Shri Subhas Chandra Bose is declared disqualified as President of the Bengal Provincial Congress Committee and to be a member of any elective Congress committee for three years as from August 1939.'[56]

As regards many other responsible Congressmen and party officials who participated in the programme, the Committee refrained from taking action 'as they acted under the inspiration of Shri Subhas Chandra Bose'. However, the committee left the onus of taking corrective action on the provincial Congress organisation for the sake of maintaining discipline, especially if these members did not express regret for their actions.

Purge Of Subhas Sympathisers Continues

August 1939: After the expulsion of Subhas, Gandhi loyalists have been after the members of the Congress Socialist Party, Krishak Praja Party and Swaraj Party inside the Congress, whomever they suspect as Subhas sympathisers or who, they perceive, can question Gandhi's policy and authority. Many members of these organisations, who were working on the Congress platform, have been identified and expelled from Congress. Critics say Gandhi has been insistent on this purge.

HITLER AND STALIN JOIN HANDS – EUROPE SHIVERS

August 23, 1939, Moscow: After Czechoslovakia, is it the turn of Poland to be the victim of Hitler's imperial design? Germany's latest military manoeuvres seem to signal so. After a meek capitulation in Munich and remaining a passive spectator in Hitler's conquest of Czechoslovakia, both Britain and France were preparing to resist any further fascist aggression against democratic countries.

An Anglo-French military mission was scheduled to arrive in Moscow to thwart a possible attempt by Germany to annex Poland in the neighbourhood of Soviet Russia. However, taking the world by surprise, Adolf Hitler and Russian leader Joseph Stalin have, today, signed a mutual non-aggression pact implying that the two nations would not use force against one another or join hostile alliances with other powers. The treaty between fascist Germany and the Socialist Soviet Russia has been spreading confusion, disquiet, and panic across countries, especially in the democratic camp led by Britain. The ramification is far and wide. A feeling has begun to pervade that the countries are turning self-obsessed and throwing ideologies to the wind.

In India, now the impact of the war has begun to be felt. In terms of political reactions, the pro-democracy camp, led by Jawaharlal, is feeling the need to stand by the side of Britain with greater determination. But the Indian Communists have begun to identify virtues in this pact. Some of them say the pact will limit the extent of the war. Describing the current war as an 'imperialist undertaking', some of them are also justifying Germany as the lesser of the two evils. To Subhas, Forward

Bloc and other aggressive nationalists, the treaty has greatly added to the vulnerabilities of Britain and reinforced their conviction that the time is ripe to force the issue of freedom of India upon the British.

Gandhi Against Achieving Freedom By Violence

August 27, 1939: The accelerating 'war situation' in Europe and the aggressive stance towards the British Raj adopted by a section of political India, especially those led by Subhas, have been building up pressure upon Congress top leadership to clarify the party's stand. Gandhi has issued a press statement today in this connection. Referring to two letters he has received from two ladies in London, urging him to give voice to his message and act on the basis of 'non-violence' in war-ridden times, he has, besides stating the relevance of 'non-violence', also ruled out any scope of violence in relation to securing freedom for India. He said:

'I cannot emphasize my belief more forcibly than by saying that I personally would not purchase my country's freedom by violence even if such a thing were a possibility.'[57] Some critics say this signifies Gandhi's desire for an image of a global statesman, at the same time sharply criticising those who have been advocating the launch of movements against the British government to force the issue of India's freedom leveraging the 'war situation'.

GERMAN TANKS ROLL INTO POLAND

September 1, 1939, Warsaw: After inking pact with Stalin, Hitler has wasted little time. Today morning at about 6 am, German tanks have entered Poland. With no opposition coming from neighbouring Russia, German forces are advancing into the country without much difficulty. However, reports from London suggest that Britain is viewing this latest act of German aggression as the last straw on the camel's back. Winston Churchill, who has been opposing the policy of appeasement of Chamberlain all along, was invited today to join the war cabinet as the First Lord of the Admiralty and this is expected to bring in a radical change in Britain's approach to Germany and other fascist countries.

BRITAIN DECLARES WAR ON GERMANY

September 3, 1939, London: Britain has declared war on Germany today. In a matter of hours, France has followed suit. Britain has also appealed to all members of the Commonwealth to join the crusade. In Delhi, the Viceroy declared India as a belligerent party and issued an Ordinance assuming widespread power for suppression of internal disorder. In India, Subhas was addressing a strong gathering of two hundred thousand people in the sea beach of Madras city today when the evening newspaper carrying the news was handed over to him. The news confirmed his prognosis of the European situation.

VICEROY DRAGS INDIA TO THE GREAT WAR
Indian Political Parties Not Consulted

September 3, 1939, New Delhi: While Great Britain has declared war on Germany, here in New Delhi, Linlithgow, the Viceroy, has formally declared India to be a party in the war. His unilateral announcement has taken the whole political establishment of India by shock and surprise. True, Britain in recent times has been under severe pressure by the ongoing victories of Germany, and it needed the wholesome support of India, in the form of both men and material, quite badly.

But the Viceroy did not deem it necessary even for once to consult the native political dispensation—whether the Imperial Legislative Council or the Congress, the most important political party—which has been running government in majority of the provinces. It may be mentioned that last year, when Jawaharlal had visited England, there were several requests made to him to make the Congress commit India's support to the democratic camp. The issue of India's joining initiatives like 'peace front' and ' collective security' were hotly debated, with the underlying objective of securing the willing consent of the Indians, to help Britain and others in the democratic camp in the war efforts against fascist forces. But now, all those initiatives have been disdainfully aba ndoned, her free will was laid to the dust and at one single stroke India was forced to join the 'war'. The Congress is unable to bear this indifference and neglect.

India Baffled, Humiliated

September 4, 1939, New Delhi: The Viceroy's announcement has left India both baffled and humiliated. In a swift follow-up action, the Viceory today called the Chancellor of the Chamber of Princes to canvass war support for Britain. Though a section of people do sympathise with the democratic countries led by Britain in their fight against the fascist forces, many nationalist Indians are feeling insulted at the manner in which such a serious decision has been thrust upon them. A comparison with other Commonwealth countries is adding insult to injuries. Britain had urged those countries to join the war and the decision was to be taken by their respective Dominion Parliaments. India, on the contrary, was being dragged like a captive beast to the sacrificial altar, as if Indians had no mind, no opinion!

My Own Sympathies Are With Britain, France: Gandhi

September 4, 1939, Simla: After the British government dragged India unilaterally to the rapidly-escalating war, the Viceroy has been preparing himself to withstand a series of protests and unrests. True to his apprehension, political India has begun to boil. However, he got an unexpected reprieve from the most important political leader of the country—Gandhi.

Linlithgow had sent a telephonic invitation to the top political leader of the country to the summer capital. Gandhi responded to the call immediately. While entraining in Delhi for Kalka, a big crowd sang slogans in chorus: 'Mahatma Gandhi ki Jai' and 'We do not want any understanding'. At the Viceregal lodge, Gandhi made it clear that he came to the meeting in his personal capacity. However, Linlithgow took heart as Gandhi said his sympathies lay with Britain and France on purely humanitarian ground. As the meeting progressed and the destruction of the House of Parliament and the Westminster Abbey by German bombs seemed probable, Gandhi reportedly broke down and became disconsolate. In a statement[58] to the press about the meeting, Gandhi said he had emerged from it empty handed and without any 'understanding'. If there is to be an 'understanding' it would be between the Congress and the government, he clarified.

According to political analysts, notwithstanding Gandhi's clarification, his words of sympathy in favour of Britain and France have enormous political ramifications and these may be leveraged by the government for its own benefit.

Jinnah For Muslim Cause – Viceroy For Indian Support

September 4, 1939, Simla: As the war in Europe has now engulfed Britain completely, the Viceroy is trying to drum up support from Indian political parties and states. After Gandhi, it was Jinnah, the tallest leader of Muslim League, who was invited to visit the Viceregal lodge and be talked to. Jinnah has reportedly told Linlithgow that Muslim League would support the war effort if, and only if, Muslims' interests are protected to its satisfaction in any future Indian constitution. He wants the government to recognise the Muslim League as the sole spokesman for India's Muslims and has sought a veto over constitutional reforms.

Condemning Congress governments in provinces for attrocities on Muslims, he wanted them to be dismissed. Significantly, he did not ask for any immediate steps towards independence, for which he was ready to wait. Satisfied with his discussion with the Viceroy, Jinnah seemed to be in favour of the Muslims helping the government by extending honourable cooperation at this critical and difficult juncture. The Viceroy is somewhat relieved to get such assurance from a prominent leader, even if communal. He has also the support from the native rulers and also depressed classes leaders.

We Are Not Out To Bargain With The British: Jawaharlal

September 8, 1939: Providing another major relief to the British Raj, in an interview to the *Associated Press*, Jawaharlal has made a significant statement which is perceived by many to reflect his true feelings on the issue of war support to the British, notwithstanding the position the Congress might eventually adopt. While there are growing demands, for using the 'war situation' to wrest India's freedom, he emphasised: 'We have repeatedly stated that we are not out to bargain. We do not approach the problem with a view to taking advantage of Britain's difficulties.'[59] This is in sharp contrast to the stand taken by Subhas and a large section of the Leftists. Jawaharlal seems to be squeezed between his ideological compulsion to support the Allies in their war against the fascists and the imperative for India's independence, which is being steadfastly denied by the British. He has described the ongoing war period as a time of 'inner torment'.

Negotiations For Federal India Suspended During War

September 11, 1939, New Delhi: Viceroy Linlithgow has announced that all negotiations for establishing a federal India will remain suspended till the end of the war.

Declare Your War Aim – Congress Tells The British

September 10 to 15, 1939, Wardha: Notwithstanding his deep emotion in support of Britain and France that came into visible display during his meeting with Viceroy Linlithgow few days ago, Gandhi, through a press statement, had made it clear that the issue of 'war support' was a matter to be discussed and decided by the Congress and the government. The working committee met here and discussed this critical issue for a week. There have been different strands of opinion in the party and those are to be resolved.

Subhas, though suspended from the party, was specially invited. Amongst others special invitees were Jayaprakash Narayan, Narendra Dev and MS Aney. Jinnah was invited too, but he was unable to attend. In the meeting, Subhas opined that the struggle for freedom should begin at once. He also said, if the Congress working committee did not take necessary steps, the Forward Bloc would consider itself free to act as it thought fit in the best interest of the country. There was a realisation that between the imperialist and the totalitarian forces, there was little to choose from, unless the cause of Indian independence was advanced. Since Britain has been claiming that she has been fighting for freedom and democracy, it became incumbent upon her to declare as to how she intended to apply these principles to India. After week-long discussion, the Congress working committee has adopted a lengthy resolution asking the British government to declare its war aims. The issue of war support would hinge on that.

Gandhi differed in regard to the modalities of rendering 'help' for the war-efforts. He wanted whatever support is to be given to the British should be made available unconditionally and on a purely non-violent basis. However, he did not want to force his opinion. Rather he appreciated[60] the 'tremendous responsibility' that the working committee had to discharge and that 'it could not take the purely non-violent attitude'. In the circumstances, Gandhi urged all Congressmen to support the CWC decision and not fritter their energies in petty squabbles and party strife.

Author Of Statement An Artist: Gandhi Praises Jawahar

September 15, 1939, Segaon: The resolution adopted by the working committee was drafted by Jawaharlal. It considered the impact of the war on countries across continents, and examined the pattern of confrontations between the Nazis and the Fascists on one hand, and the imperialist countries masquerading as democratic forces on the other. By pointing out the radical gap between the 'utterances' and the 'real motives' of the imperialist countries like Britain and others, the document questioned why they were not implementing democracy in the countries ruled by them while claiming simultaneously that they were fighting for 'democratic freedom'. If Great Britain is indeed fighting for democracy, then she ought to end imperialism and establish full democracy in India and give Indian people rights of self-determination by allowing them to frame their own constitution through a constituent assembly.

The resolution took a dig at the rulers of the Indian states who are offering their support and resources for the cause of 'democracy' in Europe while they were denying it to their subjects by taking help from the British. Taking a highly principled stand that transcended narrow geography the resolution committed India's support to the British on the condition that the war would be fought for eradication of both fascism and imperialism and not to protect the imperial structure with its extant possessions, rights and privileges. Coming to the 'operating part', the resolution has demanded to know the aim of the war: 'The Working Committee, therefore, invite the British government to declare, in unequivocal terms what their war aims are in regard to democracy and imperialism and the new order that is envisaged, in particular, how these aims are going to apply to India and to be given effect to in the present.'[61] Gandhi has issued a press statement [62] today in praise of Jawaharlal, the author of the statement. Describing him as an 'artist', Gandhi said that the statement was addressed not only to Indians or the British and the British people but also to all the nations of the world including all those who are oppressed. 'He has compelled India, through the Working Committee', Gandhi said, 'to think not merely of her own freedom, but of the freedom of all the exploited nations of the world'.

Political analysts are, however, not so sure of the efficacy of this document on the practical, calculative, diplomatic and war-hardened British regime. They feel the stand of the Congress working committee, as reflected in the statement, appear vague, general and somewhat philosophical. It does not reflect an urgency for India's freedom, but rather mixes up the issue with broader universe of exploited nations and it is mired in complex, confusing ideological nuances.

We Must Drive British Away: Forward Bloc

September 1939: Though Congress has refrained from taking a final stand on extending war support, the party has hinted it could do so provided the British war-objectives are acceptable. Forward Bloc, on the other hand, has made it clear that it does not want the British to win the war because India could hope to be free only after the defeat and break-up of the British empire. Not willing to repeat the mistakes of World War I, when Indian cooperation to Britain was reciprocated by the Rowlatt Act and the Jallianwalabagh massacre, it has been in favour of wresting freedom of India from the British by using the war situation. Right since May this year, Subhas has been touring the country. Over last several months he has conducted hundreds of meetings and spread his message loud and clear.

The Communist Party of India, though it did not support Subhas in his parting battle with Gandhi in the aftermath of the Pant resolution, is now coming closer to the Forward Bloc. Both are working on programmes of general strike and mass upsurge in India. They also aim at transforming these to even armed uprising, should that be necessary, to drive out the British. The politburo of the Communist Party has stressed upon the need for the revolutionary utilisation of the war crisis for the achievement of national freedom.

Realpolitik-al Snub To An Ideology-obsessed Congress?

October 17, 1939, New Delhi: Even as the political parties, the Congress in particular, have been waiting anxiously for His Majesty's government to clarify the war objectives, and the future constitutional arrangement and other related issues, the Viceroy has today issued a lengthy statement[63] for the entire Indian audience.

At the outset, the Viceroy has acknowledged the Indian anxiety on these issues. He mentioned having met and discussed these with not less than fifty-two important people, representing different interest groups since the outbreak of the war. Those interactions, he noted significantly, have convinced him of the existence of many different outlook, demands and solutions.

On the basis of these and the policy of His Majesty's government, the Viceroy clarified that it was not possible to state the aim of the war at this point and that a definition of the objective can come only at a later stage of the campaign. No less importantly, a statement of the 'aims' cannot be that of a single ally. At the same time, he wanted to reassure Indians that it was just and fair, 'We are fighting to resist aggression whether directed against ourselves or others', and also altruistic: 'We are seeking no material advantage for ourselves… We are... looking beyond to lay the foundation of a better international system… We... long for peace; but it must be a real and settled peace, not an uneasy truce interrupted by constant alarms and threats.'

On the future of constitutional arrangement, the Viceroy gave expression to His Majesty's government's desire 'to further the partnership between India and the United Kingdom within the

Empire to the end that India may attain her due place among the great Dominions.' On the new constitution provided by the GOI Act 1935, he expressed satisfaction on the working of the 'provincial' part but indicated that in the light of the changed circumstances, the government intended to modify the 'federal' part when the time comes.

He promised that the government would confer with several communities, parties, interests and the princes on the constitutional scheme at the end of the war. In this connection, he specifically pointed out that His Majesty's Government has noted the strong urging by the minority on 'the necessity of a clear assurance that full weight would be given to their views and to their interests in any modifications that may be contemplated.' He followed this up with an assurance saying that it was unthinkable for the government to attempt to plan afresh or effect any modification without taking counsel from all concerned interest groups. Finally, he expressed great satisfaction for both the 'spiritual' and 'material' support of India and Indians to His Majesty's Government in the war efforts. He suggested that India, having noted the ideals and objects of the government in pursuing the war, is eager to lend her support to a common cause in 'harmony with her past history and her highest traditions'.

He has also suggested setting up a 'consultative group' to channelise Indian desire to associate with the war efforts. This group is to comprise representatives of all major political parties in British India and of the Indian princes and it would be presided over by the Governor General.

Congress Asked For Bread And Got A Stone: Gandhi

October 18, 1939, Wardha: According to political analysts, the Viceroy's statement has come as a strong rebuff to the Congress for more than one reason. First, he makes it clear that there are many different strands of thinking amongst Indians, with their unique outlooks, demands and solutions and the Congress happens to be one of those 'many'. He obviously sees a role for himself as the arbiter.

Second, if the Congress working committee's statement

was a detailed discourse on political ideology dwelling on differential impact of forces like Nazis, Fascists, Imperialists upon several hapless exploited nations of the world, the Viceroy's statement is simple and straight forward. He divided the world in two camps: good and evil, and projected that His Majesty's Government was fighting for the former and hence merited the support of India and Indians. It has been an exposition of 'realpolitik' and it intended to expose the irrelevance of intricate questions of 'political ideology' in the extant circumstances.

Third, the Viceroy has made it clear that India must not expect complete independence—she must rest content with the 'dominion' status. Fourth, he has given an unmistakable hint that at the end of the war, the government would like to change the 'federal' part of the GOI Act 1935, taking into account relevant factors especially the Muslim League's view point. This signalled the British intention of playing the 'divide and rule' game more vigorously. Last but not the least, he has by a single stroke sought to project that Gandhi's sacred principle of 'non violence' has few takers and little relevance because he claimed to have found Indians of various classes eager to associate themselves with the British war efforts.

The Congress has been deeply upset at the statement. Gandhi has issued a statement to the press that vents his frustration with the incorrigible British tendency to play the 'divide and rule' game with the Indians. He has given up the hope to cooperate with the British, saying: 'So far as I can see the Congress will be no party to it, nor can the India of Congress conception be a partner with Britain in her war with Herr Hitler.' Gandhi lamented: 'The Congress asked for bread and it has got a stone.'[64]

Jawaharlal Tries To Build Bridge, Jinnah Indifferent

October 18, 1939, Wardha: Jawaharlal has written to Jinnah intending an early meeting to find a solution to the vexed Hindu-Muslim question. Clearly upset at the response of the Viceroy to the Congress communiqué, Jawaharlal has noted there is no way left but to reject the Viceroy's suggestion. Jawaharlal is hopeful that Jinnah will take a similar stand too. Political analysts, however, feel the two leaders are looking at the issue from very different platforms. For Jawaharlal, it has become indispensable to secure Jinnah's cooperation to be able to create pressure on the British. On his part, Jinnah has been demanding that the Congress recognises the AIML as the sole representative of Indian Muslims. This has been vehemently opposed by the Congress. According to analysts, in these circumstances Jinnah would rather cooperate with the British if they agree to consider the League's demands.

Last month the Viceroy had announced the suspension of the federal part of the GOI Act, and that has heartened the AIML with the hope for greater accommodation in days to come. Today the Viceroy's specific assurance implying that the government would consider the League's views while reviewing the 'federal part' of the 1935 Act has brought the League closer to the British regime.

Muslim League Sees Hope In Viceroy's Declaration

October 22, 1939, New Delhi: The working committee of the AIML has met here and considered the Viceroy's statement on Britain's aim regarding India. The League has taken a diametrically opposite view than that of the Congress. The working committee of the League has praised the statement and seen in it a new charter of hope for the minorities as it promised the Muslims an effective say and control over all future constitutional arrangement. In the circumstances, the Committee authorised Jinnah, should he be satisfied, to assure its cooperation to the British for prosecution of the war.

CWC Wants Congress To Exit From Provincial Ministries

October 22-23, 1939, Wardha: The working committee of the Congress has met amidst deep disquiet over the Viceroy's declaration. It is upset that its request to declare the war aims, which it said was made not only on behalf of Indians but millions across the world, was discarded, with such impunity. In the lines of the Viceroy's lengthy declaration, the Working Committee read the naked desire to perpetuate the old imperialist policy, the abominable attempt to hide the true British intention behind the curtain of the so called 'differences' between Indian political parties, and, blatant use of the 'minority' card.

Having considered all relevant issues, the Committee has resolved that as a first step, the Congress ministries in the provinces would be asked to tender their resignation. To the countrymen has been issued a call to dissolve all differences and unite in the cause of India's freedom. Its message to the Congressmen has been to remain prepared for all circumstances and eventualities, but at the same time show restraint in their actions and deeds. They were expressly warned against resorting to any hasty action including civil disobedience, political strikes etc. According to political observers, the latter part of the instruction are aimed at protecting Congressmen from the influence of Forward Bloc, Communists and others who are aggressively pursuing the cause of freedom.

Congress Ministries Instructed To Resign

October 27, 1939, Madras: The Viceroy's response to the Congress resolution is being seen by the party as a rebuff. It also betrays an imperial disdain towards the substantive part of the party's resolution. The Congress has been infuriated and in its meeting held four days ago, the working committee decided that its ministries in eight provinces ought to lay down the office. Today Rajagopalachari has tendered the resignation of his ministry in accordance with the party policy.

According to many political analysts, the 'resignation' decision has been taken in a hurry and under pressure of competitive politics, lest the Forward Bloc, the Communists and other aggressive nationalists gain substantial mind-share of the country's freedom loving people. They contend this decision may extract a heavy political cost from the Congress in the form of loss of negotiating power vis-à-vis the government and strengthening of the communal parties, especially the Muslim League.

Viceroy To Protect Minorities Interests

November 5, 1939, New Delhi: Viceroy Linlithgow had invited Gandhi, Rajendra Prasad and Jinnah here to explore the possibility of moving beyond the mechanism of the 'consultative group'. He wanted to expand his executive council through an agreement between the two major parties—the Congress and the Muslim League. The exercise began four days ago. Linlithgow wanted the two parties to discuss the provincial positions to be able to suggest agreement proposal in respect of the proposed expansion of the 'executive council' (EC) at the centre. The provincial position included one irritant, ie. the League's oft-repeated but ill-founded complaints against the provincial Congress governments' ill-treating the Muslims.

The Indian leaders discussed the relevant issues over the last few days but failed to sort out their fundamental differences. The Congress, however, asserted that the issue on hand was not communal but a political one. The party also refused to consider the offer to join the EC until the HMG clarified its 'war aims'. Today, the Viceroy issued a statement[65] lamenting the lack of agreement. But he declared his commitment to continued attempts to build a consensus among the major parties. In this regard, he has given unmistakable hints that he would zealously safeguard the interests of the minorities. He observed that 'There are strong and deeply rooted interests which are entitled to the fullest consideration...'. He made it clearer: 'There are minorities which are great in numbers as well as great in historic importance and in culture. Those are all factors to which full weight has to be given.'

Pampered Jinnah Pitches Up Demands

November 5, 1939, New Delhi: The bonhomie between the government and the League has been on the rise. Though it has formally withheld active war support till the British government complied with its communal demands, the League has been extending assistance to the government by way of tacit and silent support. Today, Jinnah tried to leverage the growing closeness by placing a slew of demands to the Viceroy. He wrote asking for the reconsideration of the GOI Act 1935 de novo after the war concludes.

Till this was done, he wanted an assurance that the government would not make any major declaration or enact any constitution without consent of the two major communities. Jinnah additionally wanted to have some say over the deployment of Indian troops, while deployed outside India—that they must not be used to fight a Muslim power or country. Jinnah also supported the pan Islamic solidarity by insisting that the reasonable demands of Arabs in Palestine should also be met.

Congress Quits In NWFP, League Heaves Sigh Of Relief

November 7, 1939, Peshawar: Unlike most other British Indian provinces, the British tried to maintain the NWFP as a virtual feudal pocket. They have been, for long, acting in cohort with the big landlords and tribal chiefs to suppress the masses and also keep them in perpetual poverty.

These landlords and tribal lords have been made the supporters and patrons of the British rule, and as a quid pro quo, they were conferred honorary appointments as magistrates and subordinate judges. In 1937, the Congress ministry led by Dr Khan Sahib, the brother of Khan Abdul Ghaffar Khan, had assumed office amidst huge public enthusiasm. Over the last two years, Khan Sahib initiated a series of the people friendly measures such as land reforms, release of political prisoners and propagation of the Pasthun language. He also put the big khans in place by stripping them of the honorary appointments conferred by the British. This endeared the Congress government to the masses, who are fiercely independent by nature and lovers of freedom.

When the Congress ministry tendered its resignation today, disappointments was writ large across this predominantly Pasthun province. But the British governor is happy. So also are the big khans. The governor had been alarmed at the rising popularity of the Congress Party and the Khan Brothers. He wants to hit at the root of these by promoting a sustainable political counter-weight to the Congress in this province. Reckoning that resignation by the present government will provide him with such an opportunity, governor George Cunningham is reportedly thinking in terms of actively encouraging the Muslim League. For the time being, the province has been put under governor's Rule.

Zetland Rejects Congress Claim On Minority Protection

November 7, 1939, London: The statements by top British officials, whether in India or abroad, betraying their determination to leverage the 'communal' card for imperialist goals, are aggravating Congress' agonies. A couple of days ago, the Viceroy, while projecting the enormity of the disagreement between the Congress and the League on the constitutional question, had hinted at the kind of priority the government intended to attach to the minority issue.

Today, in his address[66] to the House in London, Lord Zetland, Secretary of State, highlighted the difficulties posed to the Muslims in the Congress-ruled provinces and the need for some accommodations on this count. He criticised the Congress for its insistence on a declaration by His Majesty's Government about 'India's independence' and its claim that it would thereafter sort out the communal issue through the mechanism of a 'constituent assembly,' to the satisfaction of the minority communities. He has made it plain that it is impossible for the government to accept these Congress demands.

Gandhi Hopes Dialogue Will Resolve Communal Tangle

November 7, 1939, Sevagram: Though the British government has just brushed aside its resolution and Jinnah too is in no mood for a dialogue unless his 'League as the sole representative' demand is accepted, the Congress is still banking on the hope for reconciliation with the League. Today Gandhi expressed hope that the talks between Jinnah and Jawaharlal will resume and produce a basis for a lasting solution of the communal tangle.

Governor Props Up Minority Government In Assam

November 17, 1939, Shillong: Congress ministries in the country have begun to resign since the last month, with Rajagopalachari putting up papers first in Madras. In Assam, things have been complex considering the bitter experiences of immigration in the past. The resignation by the Congress ministry is likely to have an adverse impact. But the final decision by the provincial Congress has been in alignment with the party policy. Following the decision of the Assam Provincial Congress Committee taken on 7th of this month at Sibsagar, the Bordoloi government has tendered its resignation two days ago.

There was wide disagreement over the resignation decision in the province for understandable reasons. Even the central leaders of the Congress are reported to have harboured divergent views on the propriety of such a decision. Subhas, although, no longer a decision-maker in the Congress, had for past sometime been impressing upon-Gandhi to exempt Congress government in Assam from resigning. He had referred to past experiences of the province under the Saadullah government, and pointed to its unique vulnerabilities that could be used by the British governor or a pliant successor government to promote communal discord.Significantly, as soon as Linlithgow declared India as a party to the war two months ago, Saadullah and his party rose to pledge loyalty to and support for the King Emperor and appealed to Indians to stand by Britain in this difficult and uncertain time.

Now Saadullah has been rewarded and he has been allowed to form his second minority ministry in the province. He is determined to support British war efforts and also advance the goal of Muslim League simultaneously. A prisoner of the central decision, the provincial Congress is watching helplessly.

Congress Committee To Escalate Noncooperation

November 22, 1939, Allahabad: Though more than two months have passed since it first demanded that the British government declares its war aims, the Congress has practically achieved no political goal, but managed to lose its political clout by relinquishing ministries in the provinces. The government, with help from the League, the princes, and other sympathetic parties and groups, have been carrying on the war-related activities without any hindrance. There are reports from several parts of the country about war extortions from Indians, including even those of low economic means. But the government has been keeping its eyes and ears closed. Gandhi himself has written as well as cabled, bringing several such atrocities to the notice of the Viceroy.

Today the working committee has met again to chalk out its road map. It criticised the British government for being selfish, insensitive to Indian demands and for brazenly using the 'minority card' with ulterior motive. At the same time, it laid strong emphasis on demand for India's independence and the right of the Indian people to frame the country's constitution through a constituent assembly. The Committee has flagged these as core conditions to enable the Congress consider cooperation with Britain. The Committee has dwelt on the constituent assembly in detail—that it should be elected on the basis of adult franchise while retaining separate electorates for such minorities who desire them and ensure that the number of these members in the assembly reflect their numerical strength.

The Committee reckoned that the first step of the Congress protest was withdrawal of its ministries in the provinces. It declared that the policy of noncooperation must continue till the British government accepted its demands. In the meantime, though the Congress would continue to strive for a honourable settlement with the British government, it would resist all attempts to coerce Indians to war activities against their willingness, albeit using non-violent means. The Committee exhorted the Congressmen to prepare themselves through constructive activities like spinning, communal harmony and abolition of untouchability.

DOORS OF POWER OPENING FOR MUSLIM LEAGUE

November 27, 1939, Delhi: In compliance with the central directives, the Congress ministries began to resign a month ago. The first to resign was Rajagopalachari's ministry in Madras on 27th October. It was followed by resignations in UP, Bombay, Bihar, Orissa, Central Provinces, NWFP and Assam. Now, the governors are ruling most of these provinces under Section 93, with the help of nominated advisors. As a result of the abdication by the Congress, the Muslim League has come to acquire greater access to power in British Indian provinces. It is dominating the coalition ministry in Bengal. In addition, the prime ministers of Assam and Punjab are nominally members of the League. Saadullah has been recently anointed as the prime minister of Assam by the governor, whereas Sikandar Hyat Khan of the Unionist Party in Punjab happens to be a member of the League under a dual membership pact.

The League is also trying to establish its grip over Sind and NWFP, taking advantage of the Congress decision to quit. Political observers say, it is bizarre to see how the balance of political power in British Indian provinces changed all of a sudden—Congress opting out of power in eight out of eleven provinces and the League starting from almost nothing to now establishing some kind of grip over three provincial governments and eyeing another two provinces.

Observe Friday, 22nd As Day Of Deliverance: Jinnah

December 2, 1939: Jinnah has been greatly relieved at the Congress ministries resigning in several provinces. Today he has issued an appeal to the Muslims to observe Friday, 22nd December, as the 'day of deliverance and thanksgiving', as a mark of relief that the Congress governments have at last ceased to function.

Jinnah Irked By 'Constituent Assembly' Bug

December 8, 1939: In recent days, Jinnah has been upset over repeated demands raised by Gandhi in his press interviews and writings in favour of a 'Constituent Assembly'. According to Gandhi, the idea of 'constituent assembly' was introduced in the Congress by Jawaharlal in the 'war objective' resolution and it has been in use since then. Gandhi felt that this was an advanced 'mechanism of democracy' and though he had scepticism about it initially, he soon became a 'convert' and realised its indispensability in solving the communal question by allowing various communities to be present in the assembly, safeguarding their own interests. Gandhi spoke about its utility to the News Chronicle in October and to The Hindu in November. In an article captioned, 'The Only Way' in the Harijan on 25th last month he made a strong case for Constituent Assembly. Jinnah has been irritated by Gandhi's repeated pleadings in favour of this novelty. To him 'democracy' per se is not fit for Muslims in India as this would mean an inevitable Hindu Raj. Today he has expressed his surprise and irritation over Gandhi's new-found commitment to the 'Constituent Assembly.'[67]

Jinnah Wants Royal Commission To Probe Atrocities

December 13, 1939, Bombay: The League had appointed the Pirpur Committee to investigate into alleged atrocities on Muslims in the Congress ruled provinces. Based on that Committee's report, which is strongly believed by knowledgeable circle to be biased and partisan, Jinnah has issued a statement demanding that the government appoint a Royal Commission under the chairmanship of a Lord of the Privy Council to go into the issues of injustices, allegedly perpetrated on the Muslims by the Congress ministries in the provinces. Political analysts say, this is more of a political strategy on the part of Jinnah to step up pressure upon both the British government and also the Congress, with a view to securing advantages in future negotiations. Given the fact that the Viceroy and the provincial governors have radically different assessments on this issue, they feel Jinnah's demand is unlikely to be considered.

Accept League As Sole Representative Of Indian Muslims

December 13, 1939, Bombay: Jinnah has written to Jawaharlal, laying down the condition for a dialogue on the communal settlement. He wants the Congress to first accept the fact that the

Muslim League is the authoritative and the representative organisation of the Muslims in India. With an unfriendly government acting as the umpire between the two parties, Jinnah's patently communal stand is causing the Congress anxiety.

League Celebrates Congress Exit From Provinces

December 22, 1939, Bombay: Political India has not been unanimous in reacting to the Congress' decision to withdraw its ministries from several provinces. Although the Congress and its sympathisers are claiming it as a major sacrifice to push the agenda of India's independence, some consider it as political brinkmanship and yet some others are rejoicing over the decision.

Jinnah had called upon people to celebrate today as the 'day of deliverance'. For nearly-two and-half-years Jinnah had been upset due to the Congress running governments in majority of the provinces. He is both relieved and delighted that the Congress, on its own, has forfeited that political advantage. His critics say he sensationalised the issue by calling upon the people to celebrate today as a day of deliverance. This may well help him in churning out further political capital.

Ambedkar And Periyar Join 'Day Of Deliverance'

December 22, 1939, Bombay, Madras: Interestingly, Jinnah's call of 'day of deliverance' initially seemed to many as a politically immature and patently communal action. However, the public perception began to change when two other prominent leaders of the depressed classes, viz. Ambedkar and Periyar, also issued similar calls. Of the two, Ambedkar has a strong feeling against the workings of the Congress governments in provinces.

He is reported to have said that the he ought to have taken this initiative himself ahead of Jinnah.[68] In the south of the country, another prominent Dalit leader, Periyar, also called his supporters to celebrate the day for identical reason. Besides, the small group of Anglo-Indians seemed to be happy at the Congress decision. They are making common cause with the anti-Congress camp. Much to the consternation of the Congress, all of them have joined to celebrate the 'Day of Deliverance'. Today the AIML celebrated the day with much fanfare at different places. In Bombay, large number of people gathered at Mahomedali Road where Jinnah and Ambedkar addressed them.

Talks With League No Longer A Proposition: Jawaharlal

December 30, 1939: In the heydays of the Congress following its victory in provincial elections in 1937 and early success of his own Muslim Mass Contact programme, Jawaharlal was dismissive about the communal leaders and loathed to talk to them for settlement of the Hindu-Muslim issue. However, the recent success of the League and Jinnah in communalising the Muslim community and gradually weaning them away from the Congress has compelled him to try for 'one-to-one' dialogue with Jinnah. Gandhi, especially, has been advising this course.

The recent conflict with the Viceroy and the resignation of the Congress ministries has added to the urgency of the conversation. Unfortunately, while he was hoping to be able to build a joint front with Jinnah against the British, Jinnah's call for 'day of deliverance' has shaken his sensibilities to the core. Today, Jawaharlal has issued a statement indicating that the dialogue with Muslim League through Jinnah would no longer be a proposition. He also charged that Jinnah is keen to protect British rule in India.

A Grim Picture Of Muslims In Congress-ruled Provinces

December 1939: Even though the Congress ministries are out of governance, the political propaganda against them by the Muslim League is in full swing. Fazlul Huq has published a pamphlet listing out Muslim sufferings under Congress rule in which he has mentioned ban on Azans, attacks on mosques, noisy Hindu processions near Muslim places of worship, forbidding cow slaughter etc as examples of Congress' atrocities.

So far three reports, including the present one, have been submitted listing out atrocities by Congress governments in provinces on Muslims and their acts of political persecutions against the Muslim League and its supporters. The other two were by the Raja of Pirpur Syed Muhammad and SM Shareef. Political analysts, however, say the accounts furnished by these reports are often exaggerated, hyped up and in several cases outright false. They say the League has been using these as political instruments to accentuate communal divide in the country and wean away Muslims from the Congress.

THREE

Groping In Darkness

1940-1941

Groping In Darkness

We Must Honour Guarantees To Minorities: Viceroy

January 10, 1940, New Delhi: Even as the tremors generated by his October declaration last year continues to shake political India, the Viceroy today spoke to the country again, clarifying the government's position on relevant issues. He made it clear that His Majesty's Government has the Dominion Status of the Westminster variety as its objective for India. But before that is granted following the conclusion of the war, the government would be agreeable to reopen the GOI Act 1935 and use Indian opinion for its modifications. In the meantime, as an immediate earnest on the part of the government, he has agreed to expand his executive council by including small number of India's political leaders into it. On the sensitive issue of minorities, he has reminded everyone about the government's commitments to their claims and especially those to the Muslims and the Scheduled Castes: 'There are the insistent claims of the minorities. I need refer only to two of them - the great Muslim minority and the Scheduled Castes - there are the guarantees that have been given to the minorities in the past; the fact that their position must be safeguarded and that those guarantees must be honoured.'[69]

I 'd Thought I Had Gained Subhas As A Son: Gandhi

January 13, 1940: A number of distinguished Indians have been requesting Gandhi for removal of the ban on Subhas for the sake of a unified national struggle, but Gandhi has remained unfazed. Last month, Noble laureate Rabindranath Tagore had requested him to have the ban on Subhas lifted and his cooperation cordially invited in the paramount interest of national unity. But Gandhi has not been convinced. Today he has written in *Harijan* expressing his opinion in public. He made no secret of the fact that he had played a key role in imposing the ban:

'The love of my conception, if it is as soft as a rose petal, can also be harder than flint. My wife has had to experience the hard variety. My eldest son is experiencing it even now. I had thought I had gained Subhas Babu for all time as a son. I have fallen from grace. I had the pain of wholly associating myself with the ban pronounced on him.'[70]

Subhas Urges National Struggle Against British

January 1940: Subhas has been touring the country, exhorting Indians to join the Forward Bloc against all the reactionary forces—whether of Imperialism or within the so-called nationalist camp. Many are listening and responding. Subhas has been talking of freedom of India with a sense of urgency and he wants the country to take advantage of the war situation. He wants a national struggle to begin 'here and now'. He has also been warning people against the potential tendencies in the Gandhian leaders to compromise with the colonial government.

He has criticised some Leftist and CSP leaders who have been shying away from the struggle and siding with the Gandhian camp. Jawaharlal is clearly upset at such a campaign. He has called Forward Bloc an 'evil'. Gandhi, in a recent letter to Andrews, wrote: 'I feel that Subhas is behaving like a spoilt child of the family...'[71] Senior leader SS Satyamurti feels that the Bloc is not helping the cause of the struggle against the British but helping enemies of the Congress and the country.

He Has Forsaken All For Country – Gandhi On Jayaprakash

March 12, 1940, Sevagram: Congress Socialist Party leader Jayprakash Narayan was arrested last month in Jamshedpur while he was addressing an anti-war gathering in that eastern industrial town. Gandhi has high opinion of Jayprakash and he has found the government action unwarranted. Today he has issued a statement[72] praising the sterling qualities of the passionate, young socialist leader: 'He is an authority on socialism... He has forsaken all for the sake of the deliverance of his country. His industry is tireless. His capacity for suffering is not to be excelled...' Gandhi has lamented that instead of allowing the fight with the Congress to develop along its natural course, the government has chosen to precipitate the matter. At the end of his communiqué, he has urged the government to set this wrongful action right if it was done without due deliberation and unless it was the outcome of a pre-arranged plan.

Anti-compromise Conference Would Disrupt National Solidarity: Jayaprakash Opposes Subhas

March 1940, Ramgarh: Subhas has issued a call for holding a massive 'anti-compromise' conference at Ramgarh. Dismayed at the diffidence and inertia of the Congress in launching a national struggle against the embattled British regime, he has invited the entire Left forces to the conference to prepare for an assault.

However, a large section of the Congress Socialist Party does not concur with his views. Jayaprakash Narayan, the prominent Congress Socialist Party leader has voiced his strong opposition[73] to the proposed Anti-Compromise Conference, scheduled to be held at Ramgarh. Claiming that the Ramgarh session of the 'Congress' would be the biggest anti-compromise conference, he has dismissed the suspicion that the Congress Working Committee is going to enter into an alliance with imperialism and abandon the cause of independence.

At this juncture, he has contended that another conference (by the Bloc) would disrupt the Congress and destroy the national solidarity. Commenting that 'The entire background of the

Conference is disruptive' he has made it clear that he would not associate with the proposed conference.

Communal Fire Rages, Allah Bux Ministry Burns

March 18, 1940, Sukkur: The Muslim League has been making intermittent attempts to establish its grip over the provincial government of Sind. However, Allah Bux, heading a secular government was cruising along putting his skill at managing coalition partners to optimum use. The coalition was enjoying the support of Hindu legislators—both Independents and Congress members, which has been an eye sore for the League. For almost a year, the League has been hatching a plan to communalise the ambience of the province by making use of a simmering tension between Hindus and Muslims over Manzilgah, a prominent building in Sukkur in the shape of a mosque.

Though the Hindus of the province claim ownership of Manzilgah, it has been under the actual control of the government as the Muslims have been building up pressures to get its possession on the ground of religious sentiment. In March this year, the working committee of the Sind Muslim League took up the issue and decided to use it to mobilise the Muslim community against the Allah Bux ministry.

In accordance with a well laid down plan, the local Muslims at first waged an aggressive movement to gain control of the building, which was resisted by the Allah Bux government. However, things went out of control as the Hindus, claiming ownership of the building, supported the government initiative. From October onwards, hundreds of Muslims went to Manzilgah to occupy the building and being stopped, they courted arrests. The stories of government actions against the devout Muslims flared up the majority passion. The League managed to spread the flame across the province and a wildfire of communal hatred began to consume large number of Hindu lives and properties.

As fallout of the riots, the Hindus suspected Allah Bux's competence to give them security and protection. Thereafter, as a number of Hindu legislators withdrew their support, the coalition government collapsed. The Muslim League is looking at the success of its strategy with glee. At long last it has been able to realise one of its strategic goals, to embitter the relationship between the two communities who have been living together peacefully for ages in the province. It seems certain that the wedge that has been driven will not be easy to remove.

The Cast Is Now Moulded, Destiny Has Set Its Seal On It

March 19, 1940, Ramgarh: Maulana Abul Kalam Azad is presiding over the Congress session here. The party is holding important deliberations, as it has to face twin enemies simultaneously—a hostile government and a vicious communal force ie. the League. As Jinnah is stepping up his campaign that Muslims are a separate nation, Azad has thought it fit to offer a serious rebuttal. In his speech, Azad, has countered the 'two-nation' theory of Jinnah and Muslim League, saying:

'It was India's historic destiny that many human races and cultures and religions should flow to her… One of the last of these caravans... was that of the followers of Islam. This came here and settled here for good. This led to a meeting of the culture-currents of two different races... This fusion was a notable event in history. ... Eleven hundred years of common history has enriched India with our common achievement.' Referring to the common achievements in the field of language, poetry, literature, culture, art, dress, manners and customs etc. he said, 'This joint wealth is the heritage of our common nationality and we do not… want to go back to the times when this joint life had not begun… The cast has now been moulded and destiny has set her seal upon it. Whether we like it or not, we have now become an Indian nation, united and indivisible.'[74]

However, critics say despite Azad's impressive oratory, Congress may not be able to convince the Muslims in general, given Jinnah's sustained and planned propaganda aimed at communalising them. The Congress has been following an 'ostrich policy'. What is needed is a vigorously pro-active policy to attract Muslims into the party mainstream.

Congress Rebuffs Viceroy, Mulls Civil Disobedience

March 19, 1940, Ramgarh: In the session under progress here, the Congress has passed a resolution disapproving the Viceroy's unilateral declaration of war on the part of India and using Indian men, material and resources. It also stated that nothing less than complete independence is acceptable to India and Indians.

The resolution says, the British Government's declaration of India as a belligerent party without reference to India's people and exploiting her resources in the war is an affront to them. From the circumstances it is clear that the British government is carrying on the war fundamentally for imperialist ends. Under the circumstances, Congress cannot be directly or indirectly, a party to the war. Congress has declared that nothing short of independence can be accepted by the people of India. People alone can shape their own constitution and determine their relations to other countries through a constituent assembly elected on the basis of adult suffrage.

The resolution emphasised the imperative of the mechanism of the constituent assembly to safeguard the interests of all recognised minorities. It pointed out that the Congress does not admit the right of rulers of Indian States to come in the way of India's freedom. Difficulties raised in relation to states were British creation. The resolution, while stating that the Congress withdrew its ministries in several provinces to dissociate itself from the war, added that such a step must now be followed by the civil disobedience movement to which it would resort to as soon as the Congress organisation is considered fit for the purpose or in case circumstances so shape themselves as to precipitate crisis. Gandhi will take the responsibility to declare civil disobedience when he is satisfied that Congressmen are strictly observing discipline and carrying out constructive programmes presented in the Independence pledge.

You Cannot Make Me Your General On Your Terms

March 18-19, 1940, Ramgarh: The Congress is introspecting and deciding on the future course of action at Ramgarh. Gandhi is attending the meeting. None of the talks of high ideology, internationalism, emancipation of the exploited nations, guaranteeing minority rights through constituent assembly et al. could dilute the steely British resolve to exploit India ruthlessly. Clearly out of depth, the party has brought back the old war veteran Gandhi in the driver's seat. On his part, Gandhi wanted to see, talk and listen to the Congressmen who would be his army in the ensuing battle. Though his soldiers are dying to hear his 'march' order, Gandhi pleaded for restraint and preparation. While speaking[75] to them, at the outset he cautioned them that at the present moment conditions were not propitious for 'immediate launching of campaign'. But when it would be launched, Gandhi wanted his terms and conditions to be followed without a question: 'You cannot make me your General on your terms'. And then he made it clear that there was no question of launching civil disobedience 'until I feel that you are ready'. He also vested them with great responsibilities that 'you have therefore to purify every Congress Committee and make it a satyagrahi unit'.

As Gandhi was busy in outlining his strategy, the party went full steam in political sloganeering. Breathing fire against the British regime for its treacherous way in involving India in the war, and for pouring scorn over all its appeals and overtures up till now, the party adopted a resolution[76] that roared: 'nothing short of complete independence can be accepted by the people of India...'. As regards the much-awaited Satyagraha, the resolution did not indicate any time-frame for the movement and left it to Gandhi, the supreme commander. The resolution asked Congressmen to make themselves worthy as soldiers through discipline and constructive programme and be ready to take a plunge when Gandhi feels satisfied about their fitness and sounds the war bugle.

Ramgarh Pulsates With Political Gatherings Forward Bloc Aggressive – Congress Cautious

March 19, 1940: Ramgarh is engaging national attention these days. As the Indian National Congress is holding its session to decide on the harsh government response to its well-intentioned offer, another conference, jointly convened by the Forward Bloc and the All-India Kisan Sabha is also underway. Swami Sahajanand is presiding. Its tone and tenor are strident, militant and unambiguous. The proceedings of this conference stands in sharp contrast to that of the Congress, which seems to be somewhat confused and now doing a U-turn, after a failed bid at eliciting a favourable response from the government.

The joint conference of the Bloc and the Kisan Sabha is a culmination of a series of meetings held by Subhas across the country against the colonial regime and in favour of freedom. He began the exercise last October by holding an anti-imperialist conference in Nagpur. Criss-crossing the country over these last six months, he has been urging Indians to make a paradigm shift in their thinking on the issue of national struggle and freedom. He has been attacking some of the sacred cows of Gandhian policies, eg. spinning, as having become inadequate and irrelevant for a new age struggle. At Ramgarh, he has given the call for an immediate All-India struggle with 'no rest or break, nor any side-trekking' as happened in 1932. Subhas is emphasising that every blow received by Britain in Europe would make it loosen its grip on India. It was now for the Indian people to make an immediate demand for the transfer of power to them through a provisional national government. Recently, in the weekly magazine *Forward Bloc,* he had appealed to all Left wing workers and leaders not to be hindered by sluggishness of the rightist Congressmen. He said the latter do not understand the aspirations of the Indian masses and have ceased to represent them.

He is repeating his warnings in Ramgarh. It is reported that the Bloc's conference is drawing huge crowd, more than the Congress session. It is causing quite a concern in the Congress camp. After all, the issue involved is highly emotive and people can easily swing in favour of the political formation that is taking a more confident, decisive and courageous step.

Let Conference Sounds Death Knell For Compromise

March 19, 1940, Ramgarh: Subhas has charged the Congress leadership as being listless, indecisive, demoralised, and engaged in only passing 'red-hot' resolutions which unfortunately have been neutralised by 'Mahatma Gandhi' and other right wing leaders so much so that the 'realistic' British government has ceased to take that organisation seriously any more. In an obvious reference to the Congress Socialist Party, Subhas has criticised a section of the Left for being apologists of the Congress right wing leaders and condemning this Anti-Compromise Conference and even attempting to sabotage it.

In these circumstances, Subhas has called upon the entire Left to come together and wage an unflinching national struggle against imperialism. This should be the only focus at this juncture and the battle for 'socialism' could be waged at the next stage he has contended. Subhas wanted the conference to send a clear warning to both the colonial ruler and its Indian allies and sound the death-knell of compromise with imperialism.

National Struggle Is Not Congress Prerogative

March 19, 1940, Ramgarh: Swami Sahajanand, the undisputed leader of the Kisan Sabhas, while addressing the Anti-Compromise Conference, criticised those who insinuated as if it was the monopoly of the national organisation like the Congress alone to announce the beginning of a National Struggle. In an implied reference to the rights of other nationalist forces to begin the crusade, especially when the Congress was acting in fits and starts, he said such a struggle could be a slow process and also partial but, of course, it would develop into a gigantic movement. Voicing his deep concern for the miserable plight of the toiling masses, Sahajanand said the campaign against slavery has already begun and this would be a continuous process. There was no need to announce the struggle for freedom at intervals nor could such struggle be started by announcement by any great organisation or person.

Communists Out To Strike British Raj Hard, CSP Wary

March 1940: As the Congress and the Forward Bloc-Kisan Sabha combine are holding separate sessions in Ramgarh to formulate their respective policies towards the colonial regime, the Communists have put in their chip to raise the political temperature much to the chagrin of the British. They have announced a new line called the 'proletariat path', which advocates that the weakened state of the British Empire during the wartime should be used to hit them hard. Towards this end, the doctrine suggests the party should give a call for general strike, stop payment of taxes and rent and mobilisation for an armed revolution. It is clear that after deserting Subhas during his confrontation with Gandhi, the Communist Party has now moved quite close to his stance in terms of stridency and militancy. The Congress is upset at the development.

The Congress Socialist Party, which in recent years witnessed significant Communist infiltration in its rank and file, is upset with the Communists' latest strategy not only because of its excessive radicalism but also due to the apprehension that they might inundate the party and take over the reins. As such, with active support from the mother party, viz. the Congress, the CSP leadership has embarked on a vigorous purging exercise—to expel Communists from its fold.

LEAGUE DEMANDS HOMELAND FOR INDIA'S MUSLIMS

March 22-24, 1940, Lahore: In a sensitive political environment where the British are fighting Germany with their back to the wall, the League is upset by the Congress demand for 'complete independence' and its discomfort is further aggravated as other aggressive nationalist organisations spearheaded by the Forward Bloc have already been vigorously pursuing programmes to expel the British from India.

For the League, it is more important to secure a separate homeland for Indian Muslims before India gets her independence and the British leaves the subcontinent. The League has held its session here under the presidentship of Jinnah. Moved by Bengal prime minister Fazlul Huq, in its general session, the League adopted a momentous resolution[77] on the following lines:

- It stated the federal part of the Government of India Act 1935 was not acceptable to Muslim India;
- It welcomed the Viceroy's declaration of 18 October in as much

as it provided for a review of the plans and policies underlying the GOI Act 1935 with concerned parties, interests, and communities but it insisted that the entire Act be reconsidered de novo. The resolution demanded that the revised plan must have the approval and consent of the Muslim India;

- It stated that in order to be acceptable to Muslim India, any constitution plan must be premised on following basic principles:
  a. The geographically contiguous areas to be demarcated into regions and these be so constituted 'with such territorial adjustments' as may be necessary that the areas in which the Muslims are numerically in a majority, as in the north-western and eastern zones of India should be grouped to constitute 'independent states' in which the constituent units shall be 'autonomous and sovereign';
  b. The constitution to provide adequate, effective and mandatory safeguards for the protection of religious, cultural, economic, political, administrative and other rights and interests of minorities in these units and regions and similar safeguards to be provided in the constitution in other parts of India where the Muslims are in a minority.

The session authorised the working committee of the League to frame a scheme of constitution in accordance with the basic principles and also providing for 'the assumption finally by the respective regions of all powers such as defence, external affairs, communications, customs and such other matters as may be necessary'. Political observers say, unless neutralised urgently, the resolution may potentially cause a paradigm shift in the nature and course of political struggle for independence and the British response thereto.

This resolution seems to be Jinnah's strategic response to the repeated demands by Jawaharlal and Gandhi for 'independence' and framing of constitution through the 'constituent assembly,' on democratic principles. Jinnah has, through this counter response, sought to segregate Muslim India from the rest and have its own system of compiling the constitution.

THE 'PAKISTAN' RESOLUTION – AN INSIGHT

The Muslim League has been very sensitive about the prospect of a wholesale application of the Western democratic institutions in India. Time and again, the League ideologues have made it clear that such a system may have relevance in the West. However, in India, this issue is determined on the basis of religion and ethnicity. As such, applying Western democracy in India will force the Muslims to the status of permanent minority and put them at the mercy of the majority Hindu community. To safeguard against any such possibility, right from the time the political representative system was introduced under the Minto Morley reforms, Muslims have been obtaining protection under the separate electorate system. Now the League ideologues are going a step further and issuing appeals to the Muslims to rise as a separate nation on the basis of their religion. This would ensure the logical culmination of the long years of political struggles for the Muslims, they contend.

The League ideologues have been using history - factual or fabricated, to prove their theory of the Muslims being a separate nation. They maintain that though the Hindus and the Muslims have been living in the subcontinent for centuries, they remained as two discreet, disparate population groups deeply divided not by mere religions but also almost every form of social order, customs and manners. Notwithstanding the coexistence of nearly a millennium, the two communities do not interdine, intermarry and even prefer to avoid physical proximity. On top of all these, the two communities fought each other bitterly for political supremacy till the time the British conquered the land and created an undivided India, giving birth to the speculation of single nationhood for all of India. The League is against this concept of 'territorial nationalism', which it deems as a byproduct of Western political system.

The resolution has, without expressly mentioning the name of 'Pakistan', defined a separate homeland for the Muslims as the goal of the Muslim League. The resolution calls for creation of independent states in the north-west and the east of India where

Muslims are in majority. It may be significant to note that Jinnah is considering Pakistan not as an end but a means to an end. He wants a separate homeland where the Muslims of the country can live in their individual and collective spheres, in accordance with the teachings and requirements as set out in the Holy Quran and Sunnah. Pakistan, comprising these independent states, is expected to cater to this lofty aim. It appears Jinnah is positioning his idea of Pakistan with dexterity, calculated to appeal to the religious emotion of the Muslims.

According to some political analysts, the Congress does not seem to have realised the full implication of this communal development on their dream of an independent undivided India. They are too busy with their ideological rumblings, much of which are theoretical and sentimental. They also do not appear to be aware of the fact that Muslim support is quickly slipping from beneath their feet.

LEAP OF FAITH OR A POLITICAL STRATEGY?

The Congress forfeited much of its political power by withdrawing from governments in eight provinces. Ironically, however much the party wished this action to be seen as a martyr's sacrifice for the cause of India's freedom, the lack of popularity of its former provincial governments evoked inadequate sympathy for it among the masses. The Muslim League, on the other hand, has been quietly adding to its political clout, both in the provinces as well as in the centre.

Over last one year, much of the energies of the Congress have been dissipated over intricate ideological debates, which have, at the end, left the British regime irked and antagonised. The League, on the other hand, has been busy playing realpolitik. It sprung to forge a framework of cooperation with the government on the condition that the government gave a guarantee to protect the interests of the Muslims in the future constitution and negotiations.

Jinnah has chosen this 'chaotic time' to lead the Muslim League to pass a resolution in its current session in Lahore, asking for a separate homeland for the Muslims of India. With it the League has given a signal that it was no longer interested in the talks about federalism. For past few years, more specifically, since the breakdown of negotiation for a Congress-League coalition government in UP, talks of Muslims as a separate nation and a separate homeland for them were gaining ground. Poet Iqbal had built up its philosophical foundation and Rahmat Ali, the Muslim student in Cambridge, coined a name - PAKISTAN, for that homeland. Now the Muslim League under Jinnah has given it a political expression.

Significantly the resolution does not make a mention of the name 'Pakistan'. However, to everyone, it is clear that it refers only to that separate homeland for Muslims for which Rahmat Ali had coined that name. Many are calling it as the 'Pakistan Resolution'.

All these days, the demands of the communal Muslim parties were confined to separate electorates, provincial autonomy and residuary powers to the provinces within a federal structure. Now the resolution has exploded like a bomb upon India. This is a demand for partitioning the country and could issue forth only out of deep-seated abhorrence and intolerance for other sister communities. Except for communally-surcharged persons, all others even amongst the Muslims are finding it not only shocking but also impracticable. Several Muslim organisations like the Arhars, Jamiat ul-Ulema, Shia Political Conference have expressed their unhappiness and reservations.

According to some political observers, there is lack of genuineness on the part of the League in making this demand because it knows very well that barring predominantly Muslim inhabited provinces of NWFP and Sind, the remaining Muslims are scattered almost all over India. Their migration to the Promised Land is just impractical. They feel, the League may rather use the resolution as a bargaining chip in its future negotiations with the government and the Congress.

A Slave Has No Obligation To Defend His Slavery: JP

March 26, 1940, Jamshedpur: Jayaprakash Narayan was arrested here last month for delivering anti-war speeches. To the magistrate hearing his case, the passionate Socialist and the leader of the Congress Socialist Party has made no attempt to defend himself but owned up his action proudly. Pleading guilty of the charge brought against him, Jayprakash said in a statement[78] that both German Nazism and British imperialism were evils and that the Indians can be no party to such a war which is being fought in the interest of imperialism. He made it clear that it was the patriotic duty of every Indian to stop the British from using India's resources for its imperialist goals. It was for the British people, he contended, to decide whether they wanted a Nazi victory or own victory with democracy at home and in India. He said the government brought charges against him for impeding the production of munitions and other supplies for war purposes. Accepting them, he clarified that he considered such actions as duties even if these constituted infringement of laws of the foreign government established in this land by force. On the charge that he was endangering the defences of the British India, Jayprakash pointed to the hidden incongruity: '...I think the irony of it cannot be lost upon us. A slave has no obligation to defend his slavery. His only obligation is to destroy his bondage.' His spirited statement has begun to make great impact on the people of India.

Jinnah's Stock Is Steadily Rising In Delhi And London

March 1940: There are wide-ranging reactions to the resolution passed by the Muslim League asking for separate homeland for Muslims in India. Jawaharlal has tried to discard it by calling it as Jinnah's fantastic proposal. Gandhi is shocked and regarding it as the demand for vivisection of the country. Rajagopalachari is disgusted and he has described Jinnah's statement—that considered a united India as the cause of most of 'our troubles'—as a manifestation of a diseased mindset.

Lord Linlithgow, the Viceroy, however, seems to be a happy man. The British government has been irritated by the continued opposition of the Congress to its war efforts. Jinnah's resolution has struck at the very root of Congress' assertion that it is the voice of the whole India. Possibly, the Viceroy's desire is to let the Congress and the League fight this new issue out. In the meantime, Britain will have a free run in drafting men and material for its global war efforts.

The British are finding Jinnah an important ally in the present times as the latter has promised the League's support for the war on easier conditions, unlike the Congress which would not settle for anything less than independence. Jinnah's warning that people should not be fooled by Gandhi's Satyagraha campaign, aimed at coercing the British into a tight corner in these difficult times, has reportedly brought him closer to the war-ravaged British regime. Thus, as the government is viewing top Congress leaders with suspicion, Jinnah's stock has been steadily going up in both Delhi and London. Before taking important policy decisions, the government seems to be eliciting his views.

How Can Descendants Of Converts Be A Separate Nation, Wonders Gandhi

April 1, 1940, Sevagram: For past some time, both Iqbal and Jinnah have been insisting that the Muslims are a separate nation but Gandhi and the Congress did not accord due seriousness to their statements, possibly discounting these as a political gimmick. But the Pakistan Resolution has changed all that and Gandhi is no longer able to ignore the issue. Quite upset, he has sought to establish the absurdity of such a claim on the ground that both Hindus and Muslims in India belong to the same racial stock. He has raised this question in *Harijan*:

'The vast majority of Muslims of India are converts to Islam or are descendants of converts. They do not become a separate nation as soon as they became converts… Hindus and Muslims of India are not two nations. Those whom God has made one, man will never be able to divide.'[79] However political observers say, the League leaders are using the 'separate nation' plank for political end. To them, Gandhi's writings are emotional froths and unlikely to make any impact.

Gandhi Feels He's Losing Grip Over Muslim Countrymen

Recent developments, and particularly the Pakistan resolution, have made Gandhi realise that his appeal to Muslims has eroded perceptibly. Even in the 1936-37 winter election period, Congress had much better image amongst Muslims. The new generation of Muslim leaders under a strident Jinnah are growing more disdainful of the Congress. The inadequate performance of the Congress ministries during 1937-39, aggravated the problem, leading to the loss of Gandhi's appeal to Muslims. All the while the Muslim League has been trying to exploit the Muslim grievances and alienation to its advantage. Gandhi seems to have no effective political strategy to tackle this challenge. He is trying to simplify the issue by stating that communal amity between Hindus and Muslims would be impossible as long as the British government remained in India. Gandhi insists that Britain has to leave first and only then Hindus and Muslims will come to their senses, even if that means shedding each other's blood in the process. However, Jinnah is of the firm opinion that the communal problem must be resolved before the British leave India and the key to it lies only in a separate homeland for Muslims. Such radical differences in perceptions and unwillingness of the Congress to take the problem head on and with due urgency are only signalling the difficult days that lie ahead.

The Gulf Between Gandhi And Jinnah Is Widening

To the Congress, the international relations, the ideological imperatives of non-violence and the question of 'war support to Britain' seem to be much more compelling issues than the threat of an explosive communal discord. They are clearly not able to realise the significance of the Pakistan resolution, which can potentially engulf the whole country in communal politics, in years to come. One way of mitigating the problem would have been to initiate a Gandhi-Jinnah interaction years ago. But Jawaharlal came in between by suggesting that the

Congress should ignore leaders like Jinnah and go for direct contact with the Muslim masses. After the Congress began its Muslim Mass Contact programe under Jawaharlal's guidance and following some measure of success, Gandhi felt that the work of Hindu-Muslim unity could be better tackled by the younger generation. But, Jinnah, a shrewd strategist, alarmed by the Congress' Muslim Mass Contact programme, began to insist and repeatedly so, that Muslim League alone represents India's Muslims and that the Congress can speak only for the country's Hindus. He has been repeating this so often and with such vehemence that by now many Muslims have begun to believe in his propaganda. As a result, the two top leaders have drifted gulf apart from each other, especially over the last three years. The Pakistan Resolution of the League has come as a stark reminder of that fact!

Non-League Muslim Parties Oppose Demand For 'Pakistan'

April 27-28, 1940, Delhi, Today a large number of members of non-League Muslim parties assembled here to register their opposition to the Muslim League's demand for Pakistan. Allah Baksh, prominent leader from Sind, presided. Few prominent non-League Muslim organisations, viz. Nationalist Muslim Party, Jamiat-ul-Ulema, All-India Momin Conference and Majlis-i-Ahar have come together to form the Azad Muslim Conference. They have been mobilising various shades of Muslim opinion against the League's call to divide the country.

The conference also issued a call for a constituent assembly to draw up the constitution for India. It wanted the assembly members to be elected on the basis of adult suffrage. At the same time it wanted an overriding provision that the constitution must provide such safeguards for protection of all legitimate Muslim interests as may be recommended by the Muslim members of the constituent assembly. Political analysts feel the conference, by its unique stand, may not satisfy either the League or the Congress fully.

Civil Disobedience Hurts India's Honour: Jawaharlal

May 20, 1940: The issue of war support to the British has become controversial. Subhas has been spearheading the anti-British movement. However, Jawaharlal, known for his obsession for international politics and sympathy for the democracy camp, has issued a statement that should cheer the government up a wee bit. He said that by launching a civil disobedience campaign at a time when Britain is engaged in a life and death struggle would be an act derogatory to India's honour.

I'm Here Not To Preside Over End Of Empire: Churchill

May 1940, London: Since taking over as the prime minister of Great Britain from Neville Chamberlain on 10th of this month, Winston Churchill, a war veteran and seasoned, tough politician, has been generating hope and confidence in his countrymen. They are expecting him to be able to marshal the country and the empire's strengths against the fascist forces. Churchill has been very possessive about the British colonies and India in particular. This may be music to the ears of his countrymen, but appear as anathema to the Indians. Churchill recently laid bare his mind when he said he has not become the prime minister to preside over the liquidation of the British empire. He also said:

'We have no intention of casting away that most truly bright and precious jewel in the crown of the King, which more than all our other dominions and dependencies, constitutes the glory and strength of the British empire.'[80] His utterances are warming the hearts of Britons, but sending an ominous signal to the freedom-loving people of India.

We Don't Seek Freedom From Britain's Ruin: Gandhi

June 1, 1940: Though the government has been acting tough, trampling civil liberties and herding his disciples into prison, Gandhi has not lost hope. Today, writing in *Harijan,* Gandhi referred to an article of Rammanohar Lohia published in it, pleading for immediate civil disobedience to enforce world peace. Differing from Lohia, Gandhi has advised restraint. He has argued that in the present atmosphere, it would be impossible to keep such a movement Non-violent and disciplined. Gandhi apprehends that any false step may seriously undermine the great moral prestige of the Congress. No less importantly, he does not seem to have lost hope on the British sense of justice and fair play. In the article captioned 'Not Yet', he has pleaded with Indians not to embarrass the British at this juncture. He opined that even if the British suo motto do not declare India a free country, Indians should wait till 'the heat of the battle in the heart of the Allied countries subsides' and the future becomes clearer. He sounded his opinion clearly: 'We do not seek our independence out of Britain's ruin. That is not the way of non-violence.'[81]

Allied Retreat Before Scorching German Attack

June 4, 1940, Dunkirk: In his quest for conquest of Europe, Hitler had sent troops to invade the 'low countries' on the night intervening 9 and 10 May. Startled, both Britain and France despatched strong contingents of troops to thwart the German advance. These forces coalesced with Belgian troops to put up a united front, but failed to resist the invading Germans. To their horror, the German army then rushed to the coast along the English channel, in a bid to cut off the Allied forces and exterminate them.

Almost trapped in the northern part of France, the Allied forces planned to slip out through the port of Dunkirk. But sensing the Allied design, German troops rapidly moved towards Dunkirk and launched a pincer attack with assistance from their mighty airforce. While the besieged armies, with assistance of the Royal Air Force, struggled to keep the advancing German troops at bay, the Allied nations organised a desperate 'evacuation operation' to ferry their soldiers out of the entrapment.

In a unique and hurriedly set up operation that began on May 27, the Allies deployed assortment of destroyers, merchant ships and hundreds of little ships including even fishing vessels to evacuate over 330,000 British, French, Belgian, Pole and Czech soldiers and carried them to safety in England. Today the last batch of the entrapped soldiers left Dunkirk even as the German military managed to dismantle the last line of defence and enter the port. About 30,000 Allied soldiers are likely to have been taken as prisoners.

The inability to contain the German aggression and such abominable capitulation have hit Great Britain hard and dented its prestige badly. According to available reports, over 68,000 British soldiers were killed or wounded or captured in course of this operation.

French Government Abandons Paris

June 14, 1940, Paris: Post-victory in the battle of Dunkirk, the German juggernaut continued to roll over the French land. Four days ago, the scared French government abandoned Paris. Today the German army entered the capital city.

Our Help Has A 'Price' – League Reminds HMG

June 15-16, 1940, Bombay: The Muslim League Working Committee met here. Through a resolution adopted here, the League has sought to remind His Majesty's Goverenment that the latter has indeed, been a beneficiary of the League's stand on the issue of 'war support'. Not only that the League never created any difficulties for the government in its prosecution of war, it has left all the League-dominated provinces free to cooperate with the government. At the same time, the committee has made it clear that the League too has a set of expectations and demands before the government. Its resolution states in particular about the League's demand that HMG should make no declaration regarding any future constitutional problems or any vital issues connected thereto.

We Are Unable To Go Full Length With Gandhiji : CWC

June 17-21, 1940, Wardha: The Congress seems to have tired out in its strict adherence to the sublime ideology of 'non-violence' in an imperfect world filled with violence, intrigue and chicanery. Significantly, the ideal-driven resignation by the Congress ministries have made the party lose power of governance in eight provinces but brought it little moral halo, much less the image of a 'martyr'. The bottom line is, it could not reap political dividend from an act of enormous sacrifice. On the contrary, Jinnah leveraged the issue for the League's benefit. Then, while the Congress has been moving away from a working relationship with the British over the last one year fighting over principles, its Ramgarh resolution hinting at a programme of civil disobedience has begun to push it even further from the government. All along this period, causing the Congress irritation and dismay, Jinnah has been coming increasingly closer to both Delhi and London by extending tacit League support for the Allied war efforts.

In the circumstances, some members of the CWC, led by Rajagopalachari have begun to question the steadfast, unexceptional adherence to the principle of 'non-violence' by the party. A question, though academic at present, has begun to be discussed by the members of the committee as to—if India were granted independence by the British—whether helping them in their war efforts as a free country would not be a departure from the principle of 'non violence'? The working committee discussed these issues over five long days and a clear schism has emerged between Gandhi and the majority of the committee members.

At the end of the discussion, the committee has released a statement[82] saying that while it held 'the Congress must continue to adhere strictly to the principle of non-violence in their struggle for independence, the Committee cannot ignore the present imperfections and failings in this respect of the human elements they have to deal with...' Examining the relevant factors and circumstances, the committee has come to the conclusion that 'they are unable to go the full length with Gandhiji...' Consequently, the committee has decided to absolve Gandhi from future programme and policies that the Congress has to pursue as are appropriate in the conditions prevailing in India and the world.

Gandhi And CWC Choose To Walk Different Paths

June 21, 1940, Wardha: Gandhi is not happy with the statement and stand of the working committee on 'war support', albeit conditional. Although he had, at the time Britain joined the war, made an extemporaneous statement that he would want the Congress to give unconditional non-violent support to Britain, later on he possibly realised that, examined against his own exalted moral touch-stone, there cannot be any non-violent support for a violent cause, in whatever form or way it may be. Now he is not in favour of extending support to any party to the war. He even wants India to adhere to non-violence, not only as a means of national struggle for independence, but also as a free country. He has reiterated his firm resolve that he cannot give up or dilute the central philosophy of his life for political expediency. For the working committee, however, Gandhi's position has been too doctrinaire. As such, the CWC has decided to ignore Gandhi's view in formulating its future position. Possibly, for the first time in the history of the party, it seems Gandhi and the Congress Working Committee are poised to walk two different paths.

Hedgewar Breathes His Last, Mantle Of RSS Passes On To Golwalkar

June 21, 1940, Nagpur: Today Dr Hedgewar, the chief of the Rashtriya Swayam Sevak Sangh (RSS) has breathed his last here. Under his energetic stewardship the Sangh has been able to spread its branches and activities in different parts of India. His long trusted follower M S Golwalkar has taken over the reins. Golwalkar has been known for his prodigious intellect, outstanding oratory, spirit of service and sacrifice and above all exceptional organising abillity. Large numbers of swayam sevaks feel confident that the Sangh will continue to march forward under the new chief. One thing is however interesting. Unlike several political parties whose priority has been to drive out British to secure freedom the Sangh values man making and character building and considers these as pre-requisite for setting India free and restore her to past glories.

Hitler Visits France, Two Countries Conclude Armistice

June 23, 1940, Compiegne: Today Hitler has arrived in Paris on his first visit to the French capital. Both Germany and France yesterday concluded an armistice at Compiegne by virtue of which Germany has secured control over France and access to her strategic ports in the Channel. German forces can now leverage these ports and air bases for invasion of Britain. At last Great Britain now lies exposed. On her part Britain has been practically left alone in the continent to carry on the war against Hitler. It is now looking to the US for military supplies. However, its primary dependence is upon Commonwealth countries and especially India, from which it has been liberally drafting men, material and even money in the form of public debt to support its war activities.

Jinnah Assures Cooperation, Hedges 'Two Indias' Claim

June 27, 1940: Simla, The Muslim League has adopted a cold, calculative and strategic approach with regard to extending help to Britain during the war. Earlier, to ensure that the organisation could produce an alert, flexible response to the changing situation, its working committee had, by a resolution, on 15th of this month, authorised Jinnah to conduct negotiations with the Viceroy. Today, in an interview with the Viceroy here, Jinnah tried to advance the League's cause at the expense of the Congress. He reportedly assured the Viceroy that the League is ready to cooperate from inside, by being part of the executive council. Jinnah, however, made it clear that any declaration that the government makes in regard to the consideration of the future constitution of India should not preclude the League's demand for creating two Indias.

Chance To Strike At the British Overdue
Subhas Meets Gandhi, Jinnah And Savarkar

June 1940: Subhas has been keenly watching the course of the war in Europe and reckoning that the hour to strike the British in India has become overdue. While in the Congress, he, as its president, had been trying to impress upon his party colleagues precisely about such an opportunity but the Gandhian camp failed to appreciate his prognosis. Now, he has made another frantic attempt to convince Gandhi. He went to Gandhi with a passionate appeal to launch a countrywide-campaign of passive resistance without further delay. But Gandhi felt Subhas's way was wrong.

He continued to be of the opinion that India was not prepared for a fight and any attempt to precipitate things would do more harm than good to her. Amongst other top Congress leaders, Jawaharlal too held a strong view against unsettling the British.

He had issued a politically important statement on these lines last month. Subhas has realised it would be in vain to expect the Congress to take advantage of the war situation—it would continue to wait indefinitely for the good sense to dawn on the British government. Following his meeting with Gandhi, Subhas met Jinnah. Predictably, Jinnah, busy in building a coalition with the British against the Congress to secure a separate homeland for Indian Muslims, did not evince interest in his proposal.

Subhas also banged the door of Savarkar, the leader of the Hindu Mahasabha but failed to persuade him to take a plunge against the British. At the end of an urgent and hectic mission, Subhas has come back to Calcutta. He has planned a protest movement to shift the 'Holwell monument'—a vestige of British victory of Bengal, from the heart of the city. He expects this will strengthen nationalist feelings amongst both Hindus and Muslims against the British.

War Spreads To Africa, Italy Challenges Britain In Egypt

June 1940: Now Italy has sparked a war in North Africa where its colony in Libya borders Egypt, a British protectorate. According to available reports, the Italian army is expected to challenge British interests in Egypt. This is an additional source of worry for Britain.

Government In Fire-fighting Mood, Subhas Arrested

July 2, 1940, Calcutta: Subhas had given a call to observe 3 July as a protest day demanding removal of the Holwell Monument. The dismantling of the monument could, many surmised, mitigate the two-centuries-old stain of infamy that the British sought to attach to Siraj-ud-Daulah, the last independent ruler of Bengal. In the provincial ministry led by Fazlul Huq, many Muslim legislators, reflecting the mood of their community, have been strongly supporting the cause. However, the government has been wary of Subhas using the occasion to accelerate his anti-British movement. Today, a day ahead of the proposed protest, the police has arrested Subhas under the Defence of India Act.

Lay Down Arms, Invite Herr Hitler: Gandhi
Britons Urged To Fight Nazism With Nonviolence

July 2, 1940, Sevagram: As the flames of war keep engulfing scores of nations, Gandhi perceives his role not only as an Indian leader but also as a world statesman. To him, non-violence is a creed and not strategy and he has already made it known that he will not compromise on the issue even if that resulted in India's continued servitude. He is proud of the fact that India's freedom struggle, led by the Congress has earned attention and admiration across the world because it has been carried along the principle of non-violence. He is convinced that the key to the present global crisis lies on the application of the principle of non-violence, which alone can bring back sanity in the war intoxicated nations.

Gandhi has written an open letter[83] in *Harijan* addressed to the British people. Written in the context of Britain's war with Germany, he has urged:

'I want you to fight Nazism without arms, or, if I am to retain the military terminology, with non-violent arms. I would like you to lay down the arms you have as being useless for saving you or humanity. You will invite Herr Hitler and Signor Mussolini to take what they want...Let them take possession of your beautiful island, with your many beautiful buildings. You will give all these but neither your souls nor your minds. If these gentlemen choose to occupy your homes, you will vacate them. If they do not give you free passage out, you will allow yourselves, man, woman and child, to be slaughtered, but you will refuse to owe allegiance to them….'

However, contrary to his expectations that the British people would take cue from his advice, his letter has reportedly begun to evoke a variety of emotion in the target audience, starting from stunned disbelief to bitter criticism.

Congress Is A Political Organisation, It Works Not For Nonviolence But For Political Ideal: Rajagopalachari

July 3-7, 1940, Delhi: In sync with the deliberations and conclusion reached at the Congress Working Committee meeting in Wardha held last month, some of the working committee members have been actively considering war support to the British, provided this ensures India's freedom. To MAK Azad, the Congress president, 'non-violence' has been a matter of policy, not creed. He also has no qualms about Indians taking up the 'sword' if that ensures the country's freedom. His feelings have been, 'If freedom could be obtained by fighting, we would certainly participate in the war.'[84]

If Azad's strong feelings have been acting as an emotional force influencing the members of the Committee, Rajagopalachari has offered an intellectually compelling justification[85] for departing from 'non violence' to achieve a just political goal. He contends that he 'could not go with Gandhiji, on his conception of the state' because the Congress 'is a political organisation not working for non-violence but for the political ideal'. He also issued a statement mentioning the hard reality which has been that the Congress was 'working in competition with other political parties.'

Rajagopalachari's views have found wide acceptance amongst Committee members. Two stalwarts, viz. Jawaharlal and Vallabhbhai have taken up the case. The dual influence of emotion and reasoning has been clearly in evidence in the meeting of the working committee being held here. The majority of the members seem to be in favour of lending war support to the British regime, albeit with appropriate conditions.

Congress Compromises On Principle, Promises War Support

July 3-7, 1940, Delhi: The Congress had talked tough at Ramgarh and put the government on notice. It gave out the signal that Gandhi, the veteran of many battles, was back on the saddle and the civil disobedience could be launched any time, then onwards. But the wily government, possibly encouraged by a slew of tough pre-conditions that Gandhi imposed on his army of followers before he would launch a movement, chose to ignore the Congress anger and treated the party's threat as harmless occasional outburst.

But things have worsened since then. India has been croaking under pressure of British war efforts. Even the common folk of low means are being squeezed in the name of the war. Against this background, the Congress Working Committee has been meeting here since 3 July to chalk out the next course of action. Its deliberations have been marked by a strategy re-think. The majority veered round the view that the party should not continue to be overburdened with the ideology of non-violence, but adopt a pragmatic approach on the issue of war-support. This new strand of thinking has been showing up in the party for the last one month. It has now found expression in the form of a historical resolution here. The resolution offered active war support from the Congress to the British government on two core conditions: first, His Majesty's Government must make an unequivocal declaration on Indian independence; second, it must agree to the setting up of a provisional national government such as to command the confidence of all elected elements in the central legislature and secure the 'closest cooperation of the responsible governments in the provinces.'[86] In return, the Congress has agreed to 'throw its full weight into the efforts for the effective organisation of the defence of the country.'[87]

This is the first time that the Congress has openly come out of its age-old traditions of 'pure non-violence' and offered to actively associate with the war efforts. It challenged the tenets of Gandhi's policy and that led to intense intra-party debate. Drafted by Rajagopalachari and endorsed by the party strongman Vallabhbhai, the resolution was advocated by its protagonists on the plea that this departure from 'non-violence' was strategic and solely for the sake of country's freedom. Though Gandhi did not consent to this departure, he did not oppose it actively, either. At least five members were against it 'on principle' but they abstained, facilitating its adoption.

THE MYSTERY BEHIND THE DELHI RESOLUTION

The sudden change in strategy assuring active war support to the British in contravention of the age-old principle of non-violence by the Congress has taken millions by surprise. However, political analysts are not astonished though they have divergent views on the political rationale of the party's action.

One section of analysts feel that those Congress leaders, who have been sympathetic to the British and the Allied powers, promoted this resolution to throw a lifeline to the latter as the Allies have been gradually collapsing before the Axis offensive. According to another section, the resolution has been actuated by the pressure of the Pakistan Resolution, passed by the Muslim League recently. They contend that the Congress is hurriedly trying to arrive at some kind of a settlement with the British government, before the Muslim League manages to escalate the Pakistan issue to a point of 'no return'. This section opines that unlike the general impression of a serious internal dissension on the resolution, there has been a intra-party consensus on it. To buttress their finding, they are citing Gandhi's tacit endorsement of the proposal, even though it openly violates his commitment to 'non-violence', both, as a policy and creed.

Gandhi – Lone Traveller In His Doctrine Of Nonviolence

Gandhi has now been left almost alone in the strict adherence to the path of non-violence. One of the major discords that had compelled his parting with Subhas was the latter's readiness to explore every means, non-violent or violent, to secure India's independence. As the Congress president, Subhas wanted India to use the international situation and help from Britain's enemy nations, if necessary, to expel the British regime. On that occasion, the top echelon of Congress leadership stood by Gandhi's side.

But within an year of Britain's joining the war and after its receiving repeated drubbings from Germany, most of the top leaders like Jawaharlal, Maulana Azad, Rajagopalachari and others are finding Gandhi's insistence on using 'nonviolence under all circumstances' impractical. Jawaharlal is eager to provide war support to Britain and her allies. Azad has openly declared that the Indian National Congress is not a pacifist organisation but an instrument for achieving India's freedom.

Azad and several like-minded leaders felt, if freedom could be obtained by fighting, India may participate in the war. To them, between Nazism and democracy, India's place ought to be in the democratic camp. However, India could not take part in the ongoing war till she is given independence—meaning she could participate in war as a free nation fighting for the cause of democracy on her own volition and conviction. To them, non-violence should be a matter of policy and not creed.

Gandhi is indeed hurt that his own long-time followers could discard a powerful ideology in which he has put his heart and soul for mere political expediency!

In the international arena, the rapidly escalating tension and armed conflicts between nations convinced Gandhi that the key to international peace is in the adoption of the principle of non-violence. He not only used available opportunities to air his opinion, but early this month wrote an open letter in 'Harijan' addressed to Britons asking them not to fight Hitler but oppose him by spiritual force. But instead of appreciating his suggestions, there has been widespread criticism.

Gandhi has practically no support, in Indian or international politics, to his doctrine of 'nonviolence under all circumstances' or his insistence on 'nonviolence' as a creed. The current global war and the war-induced situations have put his belief to a rigorous test, indeed.

AICC Endorses Working Committee Resolution

July 27-28, 1940, Poona: The AICC in its session held here, has endorsed the resolution adopted by the working committee in Delhi. Though that resolution was in contravention of Gandhi's creed of non-violence, it was considered as justified for the sacred cause of India's freedom. A question, though academic at present, still remained as to the use of armed forces in India after she secured her freedom. To address this question, another resolution was adopted here. It said that in the present circumstances, the party is unable to declare that the principle of non-violence should be extended to India's national defence.

Pressure Mounts On Congress President, Repentant Congress Leaders Find Middle Path

July 1940: In the Delhi session last month, while passing the resolution offering conditional war support to Britain, the working committee of the Congress had abandoned Gandhi's ideology. In fact, the working committee, while recognising the impracticability of Gandhi's views on the matter, had earlier in Wardha absolved him of responsibilities of the Congress programmes and left him to tread his own path, pursue his convictions. However, since then some of the top leaders who have, for long, been his ardent loyalists began to suffer pangs of conscience. None of them could forget that India's freedom struggle has reached its present height only under Gandhi's leadership and his steadfast adherence to non-violence. Therefore, on such a fundamental issue, they did not want to desert their supreme leader. Post Delhi, Vallabhbhai changed his view and soon some more leaders began to waver.

Thereafter, recently Rajendra Prasad and several other working committee members wrote to Azad, the Congress president, that they firmly believed in Gandhi's views on war and desired that Congress should adhere to them. Since the Congress president held a contrary view, ie. in favour of war support, and which he brought into play in the recent AICC session in Poona, these leaders said they had no option but to offer their resignation. However, not to embarrass Azad, they agreed to continue as long as their differences did not have any immediate practical application. If, however, the British government accepted the terms of Congress resolutions, the participation in the war would become a live issue in which case they would have no option but to resign. Azad has written back accepting their position and urged them to continue as members of the working committee till then. Political observers say, given the indifference of the British government to Congress and its demands for India's freedom, the differences between the two camps in the party are likely to remain a mere academic issue.

The Gandhi loyalists, therefore, can bask in their professed commitment to the principle of non-violence. On the flip side, it looks certain that such a schism may deter Congress as an organisation, to take any effective steps for India's freedom in the times ahead.

Viceroy Ignores Congress Offer Of War Support

August 8, 1940, New Delhi: Even as the Congress was eagerly waiting for a favourable response to its offer of war cooperation, the Viceroy has issued a statement[88] today that has come as a shock to the party. In the statement, he just ignored the Congress offer for cooperation. Adding insult to injury, he has recorded his observation of India's eagerness about making greater contribution to the war efforts and stressed upon the need to promote national unity to achieve that purpose. Completely ignoring the Congress demand for 'complete independence' and almost snubbing the Congress leaders, he reiterated His Majesty's Government's objective to grant 'dominion status' to India after the war.

In the meanwhile, the Viceroy has proposed a mechanism that would serve two purposes: (a) larger participation of Indians in governance at the federal level; (b) chanellising the Indian support for the ongoing war. Accordingly, he has announced the plan to expand the Governor General's executive council to include certain number of representative Indians and setting up of a War Advisory Council to consist of Indian representatives from the states and the national life of India as a whole.

In what would be music to the ears of the League, the Viceroy has made it clear that in any revision in the constitution, full weight would be given to the views of the minorities. He has held out the assurance that at the appropriate time, the government will facilitate framing a new constitution on the basis of Indian conception of social, economic and political structure of Indian life. While he seemed to be reconciled to a mechanism like the constituent assembly to devise the framework of a new constitution at the end of the war, the Viceroy has reiterated his October declaration about HMG's concern 'that full weight should be given to the views of the minorities in any revision brought out.'

Political analysts say the Congress strategy that was formulated to alienate Gandhi, has not paid off. The Viceroy seems to have derived further strength from the League's Lahore resolution and he seems determined to use it to torment and chastise the Congress.

You Have To Be Fully Nationalist Or Frankly Communal Gandhi Rebuffs Master Tara Singh

August 16, 1940, Sevagram: Over the last few months, Sikh leader Tara Singh has been anxious for multiple reasons like the League's demand for Pakistan, its growing proximity with the British regime by virtue of extending war support and the declining ratio of Sikhs in the British Indian army. Recently, he had written to MAK Azad, Congress president, urging Congress not to prevent recruitment to the army and sent a copy of his letter to Gandhi.

Gandhi has been upset at such an attitude on the part of persons taking part in the civil disobedience. Today he has sent a letter, almost reprimanding the Sikh leader, saying that there was nothing in common between Tara Singh and the Congress and that while the former believed in the rule of the sword and always thought about 'my community', the Congress was committed to non-violence and thought about the whole nation. Gandhi charged that Master Tara Singh's civil disobedience was purely a branch of violence and that by being in the Congress, he was weakening both his community as well as the Congress. Gandhi has practically served Tara Singh with an ultimatum to choose between two mutually exclusive options: 'You have to be either fully nationalist or frankly communal and therefore dependent upon the British or other foreign power'.[89]

Congress Urges People To Condemn Government

Aug 18-22, 1940, Wardha: Congress is sad, dismayed and angry at the Viceroy's response to its offer of 'war help' which was made, ironically, by going against the very fibre of the organisation. In a meeting being held here since 18th August, the working committee has adopted a resolution rejecting Viceroy Linlithgow's declaration. It has charged the government with ignoring Indian aspirations and continuing with its autocratic and irresponsible system of governance. The committee has sharply criticised the government for its mischievous use of the 'minority card' when the Congress has been repeatedly assuring that the minority interest would be adequately protected through the mechanism of constituent assembly and this, in agreement with the minority groups.

The committee expressed its astonishment and disappointment at the government's rejection of its proposal for the formation of a 'provisional national government' with the elected representatives of Indian people in the central legislature. It concluded that the government, instead of working with the elected representatives at the legislature is keen to gather together and carry on with such dissentient groups and individuals who oppose the wishes of the majority of people of India. The resolution therefore called upon the people to condemn the attitude of the British government by means of public meetings and also in the legislatures through their elected representatives.

These Hammer Strokes Must Weaken The Chain That Binds India: Gandhi On Lohia's Arrest

August 25, 1940, Sevagram: The government has been pouncing on Congress leaders at the slightest provocation. Rammonahar Lohia, a bright Socialist and one of the co-founders of the Congress Socialist Party, was arrested for his anti-war speech and writings. In the court, this highly educated, enlightened and spirited Socialist leader had referred to his peace plan for the world on the basis of democracy, independence, constituent assembly, freedom of movement and settlement in any part of the world, social equity, total disarmament etc. He declared that he bore no ill will against any people. As regards the British, he said that though the 'British have done evil to us, but I do not want to do evil to them'.[90] The judge was effusive in his praise of the young Socialist and found him 'a highly intellectual and cultured gentleman, a man of high principles and morals whose honesty of purpose nobody can doubt...'[91] At the same time he found it important to keep him in confinement so as to protect the relations between the government and the masses from his influence. He pronounced two years of rigorous imprisonment for the accused.

Today Gandhi has written in *Harijan* about Lohia and the 'sentence' imposed by the court. While lavishing praises on this high-minded and spirited Socialist leader, Gandhi has criticised the nature of punishment pronounced. Disillusioned with the government's way of handling the ongoing peaceful protest movement, he has both lamented and warned: 'Dr Lohia and other Congressmen's imprisonments are so many hammer-strokes that must weaken the chain that binds India. The government is inviting the Congress to start civil disobedience and deliver the last blow... It is a pity.'[92]

Congressmen Rush Back To Gandhi For 'Road Map'

August 29, 1940, Wardha: In the working committee meeting held here a few days ago, the July resolution offering Congress support to the war came under sharp criticism, especially by the members intensely loyal to Gandhi. They insisted that the resolution to be passed here must express repentance for having disobeyed Gandhi and offering war-support against the very fabric of the Congress organisation. The subsequent events had conclusively established, they contended, that the departure from the core Gandhian principle of 'non-violence' was wrong not only ethically but politically as well. Some even went to the extent of discovering virtue in the Viceroy's rejection of Congress offer of 'war cooperation' in as much as it came 'as God-sent escape from a false and untenable position'. The resolution eventually passed did not express these sentiments, deferred them to be defined in future meetings but, the members keenly wanted the party to again go back to Gandhi, most experienced in the art of political negotiation.

Gandhi did not disappoint them. He agreed to step into the driver's seat. The AICC is scheduled to meet next month on 15th in Bombay and it is expected to take some momentous decisions. Today Gandhi has written to Linlithgow[93] seeking an appointment, preferably before the next meeting of the Congress policy-making body. Drafted in his characteristic style of using both persuasion and veiled threat, Gandhi has brought to the notice of the Viceroy growing instances of war exactions and the top officials grabbing inflated salaries on the pretext of the war at the cost of vast poor masses of India. He has also expressed his fear of the government coming down on civil liberties of the Indians. 'If things go on as they are and if the Congress remains supine', Gandhi expressed his fear, 'the Congress will die a slow death'. Then he delivered the threat: 'The profound differences between Congressmen and me are practically bridged.' Having dwelt upon the forces in operation, he tried to keep the door of negotiation ajar by adding 'If I cannot help the British Government, I do not wish to embarrass them'. At the end of the letter, Gandhi has made the object of the appointment clear, which would be to avoid all possibility of an error of judgement and to put before the Viceroy his case 'before taking any irretrievable step'.

FREEDOM STRUGGLE IN INDIA AND CHINA
Gandhi, Mao Zedong Follow Contrasting Strategies

August 1940: Indian nationalists have been sympathising with the vast Chinese population on fighting grim battles against imperialist Japan's brutal aggression over past few years. The Japanese propped up a puppet government in northern China and their writ now run across vast swathes of the Chinese land. Though Chiang Kai-shek and his nationalist army made efforts to expel the Japanese, they could achieve precious little against much superior military might of their enemy. At last the Chinese seems to have found an answer. Communist leader Mao Zedong's Red Army, comprising peasants from the countryside, are accomplishing a formidable task. This peasant army has no aircraft, mechanised transport or adequate artillery. But they have indomitable courage, abundant patriotism and extensive mass support. They have been waging guerrilla war against their formidable foes, using local people as their shield and the local homes and huts as their abode. The Japanese are having a hard time and they are on the retreat at several places.

To several well-informed Indians, the success of common people of China under Mao Zedong is an inspiring story. However, Gandhi, the tallest Indian leader, is steadfast in his commitment to 'non-violence' and he has a different roadmap for getting rid of the British from India. The mode of struggles against imperialism in China and India, indeed, are in sharp contrast with each other!

Muslim League Rejoices Over Viceroy's Announcement

August 31- September 2, 1940, Bombay: A meeting of the working committee of the AIML was held here at Jinnah's residence and the emerging political developments were discussed. If the Viceroy's response last month to the Congress conditional offer of war cooperation came as a blow to that party's leadership, the Muslim League has welcomed the declaration with open arms.

It is particularly delighted about the Viceroy's assurance that the government would not accept any constitutional framework or system of government, which did not contain adequate safeguard for the minorities and protect them from the domination by majority community. The League considered it as the legitimate reward for its tacit support to the British war-efforts.

The Muslim League Working Committee has described the declarations of the Viceroy and the Secretary of State as a considerable progress in recognising their approach, their point of view, and the stand taken by the League on behalf of Muslim India on the issue of the future constitution of India. The working committee, in a reciprocatory gesture, removed the ban on its members accepting membership of the 'war committees'. However, the committee reminded that before it could extend 'full cooperation' there were other demands waiting to be conceded to. The committee made it conditional upon the Viceroy's clearing those points with Jinnah.

GERMAN BOMBERS BEGIN TO POUND LONDON

September 7, 1940: Following the fall of France, Hitler has been planning invasion of Britain to complete the conquest of the continent. According to reports, he has been attempting to secure decisive air superiority before launching a land invasion. German bombers began attacking military targets in Britain early last month. However, some of the bombers managed to drop bombs even on civilians due to inaccuracy, but at times even by design. On 24th last month, German planes had dropped bombs on central London which invited a sharp retaliation by Britain. At prime minister Churchill's instructions 81 RAF bombers raided Berlin and continued bombing the city for three succeeding days. Hitler found such an offence by the underdog, Britain, an act of intolerable audacity. In a public rally held a couple of days ago, Hitler thundered that he would raze London to the ground.

Today the German air force began to carry out this sombre threat, issued by their Fuehrer. An enormous fleet of nearly a thousand aircrafts, comprising both bombers and fighters, and forming a nearly 20-mile wide bloc invaded the London sky and began to pound the city in a 'shock and awe' operation. Londoners have been shaken at the enormity of the invasion and viciousness of the attack. Worse still, reports indicate that Hitler may not stop the bombardment unless Britain is made to sue for peace.

Congress Comes Full Circle, Repents Disobeying Gandhi

September 15-16, 1940, Bombay: The AICC concluded a two-day meeting here. One of the important purposes was to formally repent for the working committee having disobeyed Gandhi and having decided to depart from his principle of 'non-violence' earlier this year. In a resolution,[94] drafted by Gandhi himself and moved by Jawaharlal, the AICC deplored the British government for rejecting the Congress' conditional war support offered vide 7 July resolution, intending to keep India under its subjugation indefinitely and initiating a policy of suppression of public opinion against war and the war efforts.

Noting the grave situation that surrounded the national freedom movement now, the resolution stated that, 'The Congress is pledged under Gandhiji's leadership to non-violence for the vindication of India's freedom'. In such circumstances, the resolution added that the AICC 'therefore, requests him to guide the Congress in the action that should be taken'. It also made clear that the 7 July, Delhi resolution by the working committee and the AICC resolution adopted in Poona endorsing the Delhi resolution no longer applied and they have lapsed. The present resolution has made it clear that the policy of non-violence 'continues,' notwithstanding anything contained in the previous resolutions which may have generated apprehensions in this regard. Not stopping at the past lapses, the AICC went on to make commitment to non-violence in the times ahead. It said that the AICC 'firmly believes in the policy and practice of non-violence not only in the struggle for swaraj but also in so far as this may be possible of application in free India'.

OFFER OF COOPERATION WITHDRAWN
Congress To Fight For Freedom Of Expression

September 15-16, 1940, Bombay: The AICC met here to discuss its next course of action. In its resolution, the committee also made it clear that it cannot submit to the British government's policy that denies India's natural right to freedom and which suppresses the free expression of public opinion. The resolution said, the Congress, driven by spirit of Satyagraha, does not want to do anything that would embarrass the government, but such self-restraint cannot be taken to the extent of self-extinction. The resolution further said the Congress has no desire at present to extend Non-violent resistence, should this become necessary, beyond what is required for the protection of the liberties of the people.

It is being learnt that the Congress is in no mood to compromise on the issue of free expression of public opinion. Towards this aim, launching some form of civil disobedience, as may be decided by Gandhi, was considered.

'Let Our Voices Be Heard' : Gandhi's Moral Appeal

September 15-16, 1940, Bombay: In the AICC session held here Gandhi has spelt out a strategy[95] that would be so calibrated as to not embarrass the British government or to dislocate their war efforts, but at the same time register moral protests by Congressmen against the British dragging India into the war and carrying on with it to protect its own imperialist interests. Gandhi said, though the Congress did not want to embarrass the British government, it could not invite self-extinction as well. The government policies and actions would wipe out the Congress if it was not allowed to freely express the opinions of Indians against the war efforts, he contended. Gandhi has emphasised that the liberty of speech and expression will be the focus of the upcoming movement, and he hoped both the Congress and the government will play fair.

Gandhi has argued that the British government has been claiming to the world that the Indians are lending them war support voluntarily, while the Congress has been insisting that the war has been forced on the Indians. He said the Congress would not grumble if the British government can get people to help them in the war efforts without being subjected to any kinds of pressure other than moral. At the same time, he implored, 'but let our voices also be heard'. He wanted the government to give liberty to the Congress to educate people against the war efforts without resorting to violent means.

Gandhi made it clear that the Congress would not go for any confrontation with the government at this stage. He said he would not want to embarrass the government, nor want to dislocate their war efforts. He has also ruled out mass civil disobedience. He plans nothing more than individual civil disobedience as the tool of protest. But then he does not want the movement to extend beyond what is required for the preservation of the liberties of the people. His aims are captured in his core message: 'We do not wish to embarrass the Government. At the same time we do not wish to carry the policy of non-embarrassment to the point of suicide.' Interestingly, Gandhi has hinted that these cautious, calibrated and measured protests too can be avoided if the government permits him and the Congress freedom of speech against the war efforts. Gandhi said if the Congress can get a declaration from the British government that it can carry on anti-war propaganda and preach non-cooperation with the government in their war efforts, there will be no civil disobedience. However, before launching the movement, he is planning to meet the Viceroy to make the Congress stand clear.

Germany, Italy And Japan Sign Tripartite Pact

September 27, 1940, Berlin: Today Germany, Japan and Italy have signed a tripartite pact here. It provides that these three countries would mutually assist in the event anyone is attacked by another country which is not already involved in the ongoing war in Europe or in China. They have agreed to an arrangement whereby Japan has recognised the leadership of Germany and Italy in establishment of a new order in Europe and these two European nations accepted Japan's leadership in the establishment of a new order in Greater East Asia. In practical terms, it may protect Germany and Italy from direct US intervention in

Europe while these two Axis forces would support Japanese annexation of the colonies of the Western nations in Southeast Asia, which they have forfeited because of their defeat by Germany, or which they might lose in the days to come. The pact comes into effect immediately and would remain in force for ten years at the end of which, the parties may examine the need for its renewal.

IMPLICATIONS OF THE TRIPARTITE PACT

The tripartite agreement just concluded in Berlin has been signalling the prospect of the European war turning global. The three signatory countries have agreed, in collaboration with each other, to overthrow the existing colonial order and establish their own hegemony across the continents. Towards that objective, they have been sensing US as a major hurdle and they have attempted to neutralise her possible intervention in the present and future war through this mechanism.

Though US has not yet entered the war, it has been helping Britain by providing destroyers, bombers and fighter planes through sale as well as 'lend and lease' facilities. This is clearly delaying the German ambition to conquer Britain. But Allies want more. US President Roosevelt is under pressure to enter the war on the side of the Allies. On the other side, Germany wants to pre-empt US intervention in the European war by creating the spectre of a Japanese attack on the US in the Pacific.

Japan has a conflict of interest with the US in China. It runs a puppet government at Manchukuo in north China, and has a 1.5 million strong troop presence across the country. Presently, it has an effective control over the bulk of coastal China. Its ambition of a victory over entire China has been resisted by the nationalist government. Holed up in the western China, the nationalist government has been doggedly fighting Japanese aggression with critical help from the West, particularly the US. Since July this year, President Roosevelt has restricted export of American aviation fuel and scrap metals to Japan to loosen her grip over China. Such a trade ban has been hitting the Japanese war industries badly.

There are more reasons for Japan to act against the US. The defeats of European colonial countries, in particular the Netherlands and France, by Germans months ago have been making them forfeit their colonies in Southeast Asian regions. With Britain tottering against German attack, her colonies in Asia are likely to join that list. Japan finds in the discomfiture of these European countries, an unique opportunity to annex and or befriend their lost colonies. Significantly, Japan announced a Greater East Asia Co-prosperity Sphere in August this year, encompassing Southeast countries like the Philippines, Malaya, Burma, Thailand, French Indo-China, Netherlands East Indies, eastern parts of Siberia, parts of Australia and New Guinea. Japan wants these countries to supply food and raw material for Japanese industries and in return accept Japanese exports. Japan wants to make it mandatory for these named countries to join this 'new order' and proposes to penalise the non-conforming country.

Anticipating Japanese design, the USA, in the spring this year, shifted the main base of its Pacific Fleet from California in the west coast to Pearl Harbour in the Hawaii in the east. From its new base, the fleet would be in a position to monitor and address any possible Japanese aggression in the entire Southeast Asia including the Philippines where the US has stationed a large body of soldiers. In another significant and futuristic step, Roosevelt on 19 July has signed a 'Two-Ocean Navy Act', providing for two fleets for the Atlantic and Pacific and nearly doubling the US naval capability on an urgent footing. In a nutshell, the US is determined to block Japanese design by throwing the dual noose of economic sanction and naval force around Japan's neck. To overcome these irritants and realise her territorial ambitions, Japan considered co-prosperity, a treaty not only useful but essential.

The tripartite pact has been viewed keenly by political observers in India as well. Since the war started in Europe, there are now indications that the war might touch Asia.

India Remains Gagged, Gandhi Fails to Persuade Viceroy

September 30, 1940, Simla: In accordance with the strategy recently decided upon in the AICC meeting concluded in Bombay, Gandhi went to Simla and met Viceroy Linlithgow three days ago in a bid to exclude any communication gap and make the latter see the Congress viewpoint. However, Linlithgow, made it plain that the government would not allow liberty to the Congress to preach against war in public. Today Gandhi has written[96] to Linlithgow, referring to their meeting and recording his laments over the lack of agreement: 'It is unfortunate that we have not been able to arrive at an agreement on the single issue of freedom of speech.' However he refused to give up hope. Continuing, Gandhi wrote: 'But I shall hug the hope that it will be possible for the Government to work out their policy in the spirit of the Congress position...'

But political analysts do not foresee any chance of the Viceroy changing his position, given the 'life and death' struggle Great Britain is engaged in and the likelihood of the dislocation that the Congress preaching would cause to the ongoing war efforts.

Vinoba Bhave Taken Into Custody

October 21,1940, Paunar: Before launching the much-awaited individual civil disobedience, Gandhi exercised due care and held extensive consultations with the working committee. Vinoba Bhave, the first person to offer the Satyagraha, was chosen thoughtfully, taking into account his impressive background and his supposed ability to take up such a highly-sensitive mission. Vinoba was one of the inmates of Gandhi's ashram who joined almost at its inception. Over the years he has emerged as a distinguished educator, social reformer and one dedicated to public cause. He later on set up his own ashram in Paunar village, not far from Wardha and has attracted large followings. Besides these extraordinary accomplishments, Vinoba has been an ardent advocate of Indian independence and also a strong anti-war activist.

Vinoba started his Satyagraha at the Paunar village four days ago. He began with an anti-war speech before a gathering of about three hundred People. This was the first case of Gandhi's much-publicised individual civil disobedience. The government waited and watched for four days, possibly to figure out the potential of the Congress programme. Today it pounced on the Satyagrahi. Vinoba has been taken into custody under the Defence of India Rules.

'I Might Give Away The Only Thing I Have—My Life'

October 30, 1940, Wardha: Even before the newly-launched Congress movement could attract adequate public attention, the government has begun to use strong-arm tactics by threatening the Press against giving coverage of Satyagraha-related news, without previously referring these to the Chief Press Adviser of the government in New Delhi. It issued advisories to the editors, drawing to their notice the penal provisions of the Defence of India Rules, in this regard. Gandhi has been greatly upset after a notice was served on the editor of the *Harijan* on similar lines. The government imposed censorship upon news related to Satyagraha by Vinoba Bhave including his speeches. Gandhi held it to be an affront to civil liberty and wrote to the Viceroy for remedy. On the 24th of this month, the Viceroy sent a reply, that couched in fine legalities, refused to address Gandhi's concerns. On that very day he announced temporary suspension in the publication of *Harijan*, *Harijan Bandhu* and *Harijan Sevak* as a mark of protest against attempts to throttle press freedom.

The reply sent by Linlithgow, whom Gandhi has been deeming as a friend for a long time, has shocked and saddened him. He held a seven-hours long discussion with Jawaharlal today on related issues. In his long reply[97] to the Viceroy's letter, Gandhi interpreted the latter's message: 'Reducing your language to simple terms you tell me that I must be punished if I do not behave myself...' Gandhi pointed out that by his action, the Viceroy has proved to the world that the British government could not conduct the war for India, without stifling India's public opinion. Gandhi has been particularly saddened at the government approach while he, on his part, has shown great sensitivity to the British position in the ongoing war: 'I ask you to believe me...in every single step I have taken, I have thought of you and your people...'

At the same time, possibly realising that no amount of reasoning, persuasion or entreaties would be able to melt the iron heart of the Viceroy, Gandhi attempted to use his ultimate weapon. Squeezed between the government's diktat and his moral duty to not allow non-violent protests perish by default, he added in his missive to Linlithgow: 'I might, therefore, give the only thing I have in me to give - my life. I told you about the possibility of a fast, prolonged or unto death…I am trying hard to avoid it but I may not be able to do so...'

Satyagraha Continues As Congress Waits For A Gesture From Government

October, 1940, New Delhi: Under Gandhi's leadership, the chosen Congressmen have been staging Satyagraha in individual capacity and courting arrests. It seems Gandhi will continue with this form of protest. This strictly regulated movement is registering a moral protest against the British regime but falling short of causing them any significant dislocations. It seems Gandhi is following a mild policy and keeping his doors ajar to the government, hoping for a truce. But the government is taking the mildness of his policy for his weakness. It has been treating the satyagrahis harshly, putting them, one after another, in jail. It has also been, in the meantime, exploiting India to the hilt for its war efforts.

If I' m Arrested, Whole Thing' ll Be In God's Hands: Gandhi

November 17, 1940, Wardha: The arrest of Vinoba and muffling of the press in carrying news related to satyagraha had alerted Gandhi to the fact that the British government has been bent upon crushing the Congress movement. He had chosen Jawaharlal, a high-profile leader, to offer the next satyagraha. But Jawaharlal was arrested too on 31st last month. Since then, a chain of arrests of high-ranked leaders followed. On 8th of this month, Gandhi extended the scope of offering satyagraha to members of the working committee, Congress members of central and provincial legislatures and also the members of the AICC. The strategy seems to be to create public awareness through endless journeys to the prison.

As Gandhi has been sending successive satyagrahis from his panel to commit civil disobedience, the government kept herding them into jail, without showing any signs of panic. Gandhi wrote a note[98] to Vallabhbhai, almost in a mood of exasperation, saying that so long as he is not arrested he will send all the rest. In the event he too is arrested, Gandhi wrote, '...the whole thing will be in God's hands'. Today Vallabhbhai was arrested.

Political analysts see in Gandhi's strategy, action and message, visible signs of disillusionment resulting from the severity of government action. It seems, Gandhi has been temporarily taken out of depth by his wily adversaries.

Sikhs Object Strongly To Pakistan Resolution

December 1, 1940, Lahore: There is a feeling amongst the Sikhs that the Congress has not accorded the Pakistan Resolution the seriousness the matter deserved, at least so it seems, based on its reactions so far. For the Sikhs, the proposal has grave implications and they feel it imperative to deal with the matter with utmost political urgency. The Sikhs, as minority are scattered all over the proposed land of Pakistan in the north west of India with relatively larger presence in the Punjab, where they form about twenty per cent of the province's population. Their contribution to the province's economy has, however, been much larger than their proportion to the populace. Notwithstanding, the Sikhs have reportedly been the victim of discriminatory government policies and treatment under the Muslim-dominated Unionist Party led governments in Punjab. Based on such unhappy past experiences, they have strong reservations about getting transferred to a Muslim state as minority.

For past some time, the Sikhs have been letting their anxieties be known in various forums. In the All-India Akali Conference held sometime ago, Dr VS Bhatti of Ludhiana published a pamphlet demanding 'Khalistan' as a buffer state between India and Pakistan. Political observers say, such a demand was raised to oppose the idea of Pakistan. Today, the Sikhs held a general conference in the city and passed a resolution against the formation of Pakistan.

Government Succumbs To Public Pressure Subhas Released, Placed Under House Arrest

December 5, 1940, Calcutta: Subhas has been in the prison since July this year. The government considers it dangerous to set him free as the war is in full swing and the last thing it would want is to see the public erupt in a serious anti-British movement. After Subhas has been put into prison, the political protests have softened somewhat due to lack of such able and spirited leadership.

From the prison, Subhas has been creating pressure upon the government. Right from August through October, he had been writing to the home minister of Bengal requesting for his release and protesting against his unjustified imprisonment. By the end of the last month, he wrote to the governor and the prime minister of Bengal announcing his intention to go on a hunger strike from 29 November.

As he began his 'fast', there were public outcry and pressures upon the government. The coalition government, led by Fazlul Huq, has been criticised by many assembly members of the KPP, the Congress and other parties for confining him in prison. Bengal governor John Herbert, under instructions from Linlithgow, had strong reservation about releasing Subhas. However, apprehending a potentially explosive situation if anything untoward happened to Subhas while in captivity, he reluctantly consented to the Huq ministry's decision to let the dangerous foe of the Raj out of the prison. At the same time, the government has a scheme ready to re-arrest him, once he regains health. Ultimately today, his detention order was lifted and Subhas has been allowed to move to his home at Elgin Road. But he has been kept under police watch.

British Badly Entangled In North African War Theatre

December 1940, Cairo: The Italian army, under Marshal Rodolfo Graziani, had mounted a land offensive against the British army stationed in Egypt in September this year. Although the Italians had some early successes, those melted quickly against the counter-attack by General Archibald Wavell. Following the Italian discomfiture, Hitler dispatched the German Afrika Korps, commanded by General Erwin

Rommel, to help its ally. After Rommel assumed command, the British force has been having tough time. Now that the flame of war has begun to burn across vast swathes of the dark continent, the need for support from India in the form of men and material is growing by the day.

Hitler Threatens To Reduce London To Rubble

December 1940, Berlin, New Delhi: Hitler's writ runs across Europe. Britain has been hard put to offer a meaningful fight up till now. Nor does it have any strong friend in the continent to give it effective support. German aircrafts began massive bombing of London city on 7 September and thereafter, the air assault has continued at a stretch for two-and-a-half months almost without a break. The city is being bombed regularly even now and the people have almost accepted German bombings as a part of daily life.

Besides aerial attacks, the people of Britain have also been living under the fear of land invasion by the German force, whether from across the English channel or through the paratroopers. In a nutshell, Great Britain is under severe stress and clueless as to how to neutralise the Axis threat. Her dependence on India for war support is at a peak.

However, in India, the Congress, the main political party, has no desire to take advantage of the war situation. Its top leaders, including Gandhi and Jawaharlal, have been repeatedly expressing sympathy for the British and the Allies and waiting for a change of 'British heart'. The recent individual satyagraha has been specifically designed to register moral protest, but never to embarrass the British regime.

Britain on the other hand, though surrounded by hostilities all around, does not want to concede any space to the Congress. She knows pretty well that her success in the war against Hitler depends heavily on war support from Indian soil and she cannot just withstand a mass movement, if launched at this juncture. But still, she is keeping a brave face and taking a dangerous gamble. Possibly, she has understood well that the Congress would not be able to overcome its ideological compulsions and pose it a serious challenge.

Subhas, ex-president of the Congress and an ardent nationalist leader, is out of prison but continues to be under police watch. He is keen that at this critical juncture India should leverage Britain's vulnerabilities and snatch her freedom from the 'falling grasp' of the British government. He is actively mulling ways and means to use the international situation to India's advantage.

Is The Civil Disobedience Movement Showing Fatigue?

January 12, 1941, Sevagram: The individual civil disobedience by people chosen by Gandhi has been going on, though it is yet to have discernible impact on the government. Today Gandhi has issued a set of instructions[99] to the satyagrahis saying that this struggle is not likely to conclude soon. Significantly, he has asked those of the civil resisters who have been awarded with short-term imprisonment to repeat civil disobedience till the end of the struggle. And in the event the government does not arrest the civil resisters, Gandhi advised them to walk in the direction of Delhi, even if a few miles in a day thriving on such food as may be provided to them by the villagers. Significantly, Gandhi has been strict in choosing the satyagrahis and he has now made it clear that once the officer-bearers are arrested, their replacements may not be provided. Gandhi said if he himself was arrested, 'everyone will be under the discipline of his or her own conscience'. Political observers are sighting signs of fatigue and some kind of listlessness in the ongoing Satyagraha.

SUBHAS ESCAPES FROM HOME
Countrywide Commotion, Red Alert Declared

January 27, 1941, Calcutta: Today the newspapers in the country have carried the sensational story of Subhas escaping from his house at Elgin Road in the city, giving a slip to the round-the-clock surveillance. Police have launched massive search and enquires into the circumstances leading to his disappearance. There are varying accounts but no one is sure of the fact. His family sources say, Subhas may have left house unannounced in spiritual pursuit and that he had once done so in his student life.

However, according to knowledgeable sources, he had escaped from his house as early as the 16th-17th January night, purely on a political mission and at present he is in Kabul, well beyond the reach of the British Raj. He is on his way to Germany via Russia. They say, upset by the Congress' ambivalence, and the lackadaisical and even pro-British approach by other parties which were only helping the British government to retain its hold over India, Subhas has chosen this course of action—to move out of the country and join hands with the 'enemies of the enemy' to expel the British from India. He considers Germany, Italy and Japan as the likely sources of help in India's freedom struggle. His destination is Germany. He is proposing to reach there through USSR, a neutral country. He believes that, inspired by Socialist and Communist ideologies that country would extend support for India's freedom struggle.

Communal Issue Settlement More Important Than Academic Discussion Of Politics: Sapru

January 28, 1941: Concerned at the way the British regime has been using India extensively for its war activities and at the unbridgeable gap between the Congress and the League on the communal issue, TB Sapru, former president of the All-India Liberal Federation, got in touch with both Gandhi and Jinnah. He urged both of them to resolve their differences in the broader interest of the country. Today he has written[100] a long letter to Gandhi, identifying lack of settlement of the communal issue as the root cause of all the ills. He has stated that although he is a non-political person, yet he was ready to do everything possible to pave the way for the settlement of the communal issue. According high priority to this issue, he has written: '...I attach far greater importance than I do to mere academic discussions of this political theory or that'. Referring to Gandhi's reservations about Jinnah's rigidities, Sapru suggested that given Gandhi's stature, Gandhi ought to give a lead and initiate a dialogue. He said, 'You are, however, a man of infinite courage and you are big enough to rise superior to petty considerations of a conventional character'. However, it is difficult to say what impact the letter would have on the proposed 'talk', given Jinnah's stand that in any dialogue, Gandhi and Congress could represent only the Hindus and Gandhi finding such a stand as absurd.

Akali Dal Rethinks Strategy, Abandons Congress 'Line' Wants Sikhs To Join War Efforts In Large Numbers

January 1941, Lahore: In September 1939, the Congress had asked the British government to declare its war aims before it could decide on whether or not to extend war-support. At that time, the Akali Dal too had adopted a similar approach and insisted on knowing from the government its goal in pursuing the war. However, since then, there have been significant changes in the Dal's thinking. Two important reasons seem to be the confused Congress policy on 'war support' and its inadequate response to the Pakistan Resolution by the Muslim League. On a stocktaking, the Dal is realising that the numerical strength of Sikh soldiers in the British Indian army has dwindled and it feels the embittered relations between the government and the Sikh Community in recent decades, which worsened in 1939, has contributed to this trend. In the context of the changing political scenario, it realises too well the need for enhanced Sikh presence in the army.[101]

Master Tara Singh had, last year, tried to convince the Congress about its revised assessment and reach a consensus on this issue. But the Master got a strong rebuff from Gandhi. Convinced of the correctness of his view, he resigned from the Congress Working Committee and began to pursue his own line of thinking aggressively. The Dal went ahead and formed the Khalsa Defence League under the leadership of the Maharaja of Patiala, with sympathy and support from them and Giani Kartar Singh among others. To the British government, this has been a welcome development. The British Indian army has been on massive recruitment drive among the Sikhs.

The government has asked Sikander Hayat Khan, the prime minister of Punjab, to establish communication with Akali leaders to facilitate the process.

Muslim League Opposes Congress Satyagraha

February 22, 1941, Delhi: The working committee of the AIML met here today. The committee reaffirmed the Pakistan plan of the League. It has also expressed its opposition to the ongoing civil disobedience movement by the Indian National Congress.

Muslim League In The Footsteps Of Gandhi?

February 23, 1941, Delhi: The AIML Council held its meeting here and declared a slew of constructive programmes to be taken up by the League at the provincial, district, city and primary level. The activities envisaged under the ambit of the programme would include promotion of cottage industry, spread of education through night school, prohibition of interest on loans for marriage and funerals, avoidance of intoxicants and gambling, promoting brotherhood amongst Mussalmans, using Panchayat as low cost dispute settlement mechanism, emphasis on rural upliftment programme.

Political analysts see similarity of this initiative with Gandhi's constructive programmes. If implemented properly, they feel, it would help galvanise the community as a strong support base for the League.

This Gigantic Autocracy Is Greatest Blot On British Rule

February 23, 1941, Sevagram: Gandhi has written a foreword to his colleague and disciple Pyarelal's treatise, titled, 'Status of Indian Princes', compiled on the basis of authentic sources. His words show the radical way in which his views on this privileged community have altered over the last two or three decades. In the '20s and late '30s, he played a key role in restraining the Congress enthusiasm in getting involved in the States' People's Movements.

The Rajkot experience had jolted him. But the unabashed manner in which the princes are collaborating with the British in the prosecution of the war, in total disregard to the welfare of their subjects, have caused no lesser shock, dismay, grief and anxiety. He has expressed his present assessment[102] in a scathing manner by calling 'the existence of this gigantic autocracy' as the 'greatest disproof of British democracy' and also 'perhaps the greatest blot on British rule in India'. He also made a prophetic observation—that the 'system will break under its own intolerable weight'. Even though these words are by way of 'foreword' to a publication, political observers are attaching considerable importance to the utterances. They look at Gandhi's words as political statements which may influence Congress policies on States' People's Movements.

Non-party Leaders' Conference Assures War Support

March 13-14, 1941, Bombay: TB Sapru has been urging both Gandhi and Jinnah to talk and arrive at a settlement on the communal issue. He had even suggested that Gandhi convene a conference to sort this issue out. Since there was no satisfactory outcome, Sapru has held a 'Non-party Leaders' Conference' here over two days.

At the end, the conference has adopted a resolution[103] that pledges India's support for the British war efforts, but urges the British regime not to exploit India's communal discord for its own gain. It recognised the fact that there has been a deadlock in the matter of communal settlement, but suggested a way forward in the immediate future. The resolution urged that the executive council of the Governor General be reconstituted and with the exception of the Viceroy himself, and the commander-in-chief, filled exclusively with non-official Indians prominent in public life.

Further, the key portfolios including defence and finance be allotted to the Indian members and they be given opportunity to work with full responsibility and authority, and that 'the reconstructed government should be treated on the same footing as the Dominion governments'. The resolution has also placed a demand that His Majesty's Government should simultaneously issue a declaration that within a specified period after the conclusion of the war India would enjoy freedom at par with Britain and other dominions.

The Conference claims that such an arrangement would facilitate a more efficient prosecution of the war. With active involvement by the Indians and all the political parties, it would meet the constitutional aspirations of a large body of Indians. Sapru, the president of the Conference, has been authorised to convey the resolution to the Viceroy.

According to political analysts, the initiative may appeal to His Majesty's Government. However, its 'future' is suspect, given the strong objection the Congress has in giving up its civil disobedience movement and policy of non-cooperation, unless its demands for independence are met.

Japan Concludes Non-aggression Pact With Russia

April 13, 1941, Moscow: Today Japan has entered into a non-aggression pact with Soviet Russia. Political observers are attaching high degree of significance to this new development.

They suspect that Japan has been silently preparing schemes for wresting the Southeast Asian countries from the discredited European nations. While making forays in this part of Asia, it wants to keep its position in Manchukuo safe, which lies in the possible range of a Soviet attack. Great Britain has been suspicious about Japanese design on its Asian colonies. This new treaty is causing her considerable disquiet. As for Soviet Russia, the motivation about the pact seems to be able to secure its eastern border and be able to concentrate on the European war. Significantly for Russia there are confusing signals emanating from the Balkan countries. War has begun to rage in several of them, including Greece and Yugoslavia.

Subhas Is In Germany, Has To Start From Scratch

April 1941, Berlin: Subhas has reached Berlin from Moscow by the fag end of last month on an Italian passport, under the assumed name Orlando Mazzotta. Here, he has established contacts with the foreign office of the Nazi government. According to his preliminary observations, his task to advance the cause of Indian independence here may be far harder than he had anticipated.

The Nazi government, intoxicated by its series of victories, is obsessed with its own interest. It is least empathetic to others' causes, unless it finds they would be useful to its own scheme of conquest of new territories. Significantly, Germany lent helping hands to Indian revolutionaries during the first World War. At that time, a network of several Indian revolutionaries. many of them being Communists, were operating in Germany. There is practically none at present. Hitler had already persecuted Communists of all shades out of Germany, ruling out any space for the Indian left in his country. So Subhas has to start from the scratch.

Congress Aims At Consolidating Hindu Power: AIML

April 12-15, Madras: The All-India Muslim League has held its 28th session in this southern port city. Jinnah, in his presidential address, said that the League would never submit to one constitution and one central government in India. A resolution was passed, providing for amendment in the League constitution to accommodate the demand for Pakistan. In another resolution, the League has condemned the civil disobedience movement being conducted by the Congress.

AXIS FORCES STEAMROLL YUGOSLAVIA

April 17, 1941, Belgrade: After conquest of the prosperous west Europe, Hitler is concentrating on the Balkans in the east. He has been using a policy of carrot and stick to bring these countries under Axis domination. In November last year. Hungary, Slovakia and Romania joined the Axis bloc. After persuasion and threat, Bulgaria followed suit early last month. Yugoslavia resisted and it has been facing Hitler's fury. Today the Yugoslav army has capitulated while the German and Italian forces have run through the country and occupied some of its major cities.

Greek Resistance Melts Before Mighty Germans

April 23, 1941, Athens: Italy, inspired by its Balkan aspiration, launched an invasion of Greece from occupied Albania in October last year but could not make much headway as the Greeks put up determined resistance. When victory seemed far fetched for the Italians, things were made simple by the German forces which joined the war on the 6th of this month. The Greeks could not hold on any further and offered surrender. Italians are likely to take over the control of the newly-conquered country.

Civil Disobedience Has Fallen Flat In India: Amery

April 25, 1941, Sevagram: Amery, Secretary of State, while moving a resolution in the House of Commons for proclamation of extension of the governors' assumption of powers of the legislators in the provinces of British India, has made some statements that raised controversy in India and hurt the Congress badly. There are allegations that he has projected, to the British Parliament and the world at large, a false and deceptive picture of the state of affairs in India.

He has smugly attributed the lack of progress in determining the nature of constitution for India to the lack of agreement between the Indian political parties on the communal issue, being fully aware that the British regime has been actively promoting the disharmony through its policy of divide and rule. Amery has also stated that India has been voluntarily supporting the British war efforts, which is far from truth. But what has hurt the Congress and Gandhi no less is Amery's assessment of the ongoing satyagraha. Amery has paid no heed to the fact that the Congress has been studiously limiting its movement to one single objective, ie. to be able to exercise the right of 'freedom of speech'. Instead of appreciating the Congress gesture, Amery has made an observation that the civil disobedience movement has fallen flat. Today Gandhi has issued a press statement, taking exception to Amery's speech. Gandhi observed Amery had a contemptuous disregard for the actual situation in India. He also opined that Amery was devoid of the elementary grace to acknowledge the studied moderation of the Congress in its desire not to embarrass the British government.

GERMANY INVADES RUSSIA

June 22, 1941, Berlin: A great twist in the ongoing war has startled the world today. Hitler has reportedly sent over three million soldiers, 3,500 tanks and 5,000 aircrafts to unleash an unprecedented blitzkrieg upon an unsuspecting Soviet Russia, with which Germany had inked a mutual non-aggressive treaty. The non-aggression pact has now been rendered a farce. The invasion began at dawn and marked the start of a long haul operation, as is apparent from all available indications. Today alone 1,200 Russian planes were destroyed.

Some say Stafford Cripps, British envoy to Moscow, has played a key role in bringing about the rift between these two powers. Churchill had been forewarning Stalin about an impending German invasion but only unsuccessfully. In the aftermath of the attack, an agonised Britain has assured all help to Russia against Germany. US president Roosevelt has also promised to extend all support to Russia as America has been offering to Britain.

International political observers, however, feel that the Germans have begun to overstretch their resources. In India, this sudden change of equation amongst the major European nations has come as a breather for the British government. Some segments of Indian people, not insignificant in terms of percentage, are turning pro-British because of their attachment to the socialist state of Soviet Russia.

Desperate Viceroy Expands His Executive Council

July 21, 1941, New Delhi: The war situation is turning grimmer. The need to generate war support from India to Britain is increasing in commensuration. Under such circumstances, the Viceroy, who had waited unsuccessfully for long for the Indian parties to strengthen his cabinet, has today announced his decision to expand the executive council. Viceroy Linlithgow has sought to effect major changes in his executive council, through expansion, as well as separation and redistribution of existing porfolios. Significantly, the two newly created portfolios for 'information' and 'civil defence' reflect the current concerns of the government of India. The expanded executive council will have strength of twelve as against seven hitherto. The number of Indian members, chosen from outside the Congress and the League, has been raised from three to eight.

The Viceroy has also announced the setting up of a thirty-members strong National Defence Council. Created to enlist the non-official Indian opinion with the ongoing war efforts, this new body will be as representative of public opinion as possible and its members will be from native states and other elements of national life in British India. It will operate only as an advisory body, as a safety valve and aim at improving relations between the federal government on the one hand, and the Indian states and the provincial governments on the other. The government is looking at the prospect of channeling Indian ability for war purposes through this new mechanism.

Communists Sommersault, Now To Support Britain

July 1941: When Hitler and Stalin entered into a war pact in 1939, the Communists went against the Allies, on the logic that in the confrontations between the fascist and the imperialists, Germany was lesser of the two evils. Now that Germany has invaded Russia, the Comintern has instructed Communists all over the world to back the peoples' war. As a result, the Communists in India have started drumming up support for the British government. This has come as a welcome relief to the latter.

Jinnah Asks Muslims To Resign From Defence Council

August 24-26, 1941, Bombay: The constitution of the National Defence Council, which was primarily an offshoot of the emergency need of HMG, and which aimed, prima facie, at garnering support of Indians of all communities over the heads of the Indian political parties, was not well-received by the latter. Jinnah, in particular, had condemned the initiative.

Irrespective of Jinnah's stance, last month three Muslim premiers, viz. Sikandar Hayat Khan of Punjab, Fazlul Huq of Bengal and Muhammad Saadullah of Assam had joined the National Defence Council (NDC) of the Viceroy at the latter's request, without obtaining Jinnah's nod. Soon after coming to know of the fact, Jinnah had criticised the Viceroy for approaching these Muslim League premiers behind his back. These three leaders have also been the recipient of his fury. They contended having acted as premiers of provinces but that plea did not assuage Jinnah. Today, while addressing the AIML working committee meeting here, Jinnah has called upon all the three to forthwith resign from the NDC. According to reliable information, both Sikandar Hayat Khan and Saadullah might oblige soon. However, Fazlul Huq is reportedly rigid and he considers Jinnah's move as needless interference in the domain of a provincial premier. It may be difficult to bring him around. In another resolution the working committee gave ten days notice to Sultan Ahmed and Begum Shah Nawaz to resign from the expanded executive council and the National Defence Council respectively.

Subhas On His Mission In Nazi Land

August 1941, Berlin: Subhas has been trying to build an infrastructure in Germany which can be used to advance the cause of Indian independence. He had met Ribbentrop, the foreign minister of the Nazi government, by the end of April when they tried to figure out the relevance of each country to the other's cause. Following that meeting, the German government started a special bureau for India, attaching it to the Information department of the Foreign office under the charge of an undersecretary. Subhas has been able to attract some bright Indian students and competent patriotic Indians from Germany and Nazi dominated Europe to the cause of Indian independence. He is planning to start an India Centre to carry forward his planned activities. He also has plans to raise an armed force that would eventually fight the Indian war of independence against the British. One of his immediate and key objectives is to make Germany and its allies issue a declaration in favour of Indian independence to be able to place that issue at the global centre stage. But so far, he has not been able to convince the Nazi dispensation. Subhas realises the task is daunting, but he is pursuing his plans in earnest. The fact that the Nazi government is aware of Subhas's alienation with Gandhi and Gandhian Congress leaders has no doubt been weighing on its perception of Subhas's potential impact on Indian minds. However, Subhas, through his charismatic and energetic persona has been able to present himself as a credible and valuable face of the Indian nationalist leadership. Last month, he was accorded quasi-diplomatic status by the Nazi government.

Individual Satyagraha Completes A Year – A Marvellous 'Contrive' That Keeps Both Opponents Contented?

Gandhi's individual Satyagraha programme in the form of civil disobedience has run for about a year. Vinoba Bhave was the first leader to commit the symbolic civil disobedience. He was followed by Jawaharlal Nehru and Brahma Dutta, a Gandhi ashramite. Thereafter, hundreds of Congress leaders including the Congress president, Abul Kalam Azad, followed suit. Till now about 20,000 Congressmen have courted arrests. Critics say, this low-key movement, interestingly, is a panacea to many problems. Though hyped up by the nationalist press, it has not caused much problem for the government in its war efforts. The latter has continued to heavily draw Indian men in the army and also supplies for the war-efforts. The rank and file of Congress also do not seem to be unhappy because despite this symbolic protest at the national level, Congress' continued involvement in local government bodies enables them to keep sharing the fruits of power. The top leadership is satisfied that the Congress has been registering at least some kind of protest against the insults heaved upon it by the government, at the same time, without risking any serious reprisals.

Huq Resents Jinnah's Diktat, Shoots Letter To Liaquat

September 8, 1941, Calcutta: Fazlul Huq, the prime minister of Bengal, has reacted angrily to Jinnah's instruction that he resign from the Defence Council of the Viceroy, a mechanism put in place by the latter for better coordination with the provinces to ensure war preparation and supplies. Huq was resisting the move for some time, but Jinnah kept insisting. Jinnah was considering the League prime ministers' acceptance of such office, without his permission, as an affront to his authority. Peeved and frustrated at such interference, Huq now not only decided to drop out of the Defence Council but he also resigned as a member of the working committee and the council of the All-India Muslim League. Today he has written a letter[104] to Liaquat Ali Khan, secretary of the AIML, voicing concern that by imposing such measures the League leaders of Muslim minority provinces are actually harming the interests of Muslims in the Muslim majority provinces like Bengal and Punjab. Incidentally, the prime minister of Punjab, who was bullied too, had fallen in line earlier, though unwillingly. Huq said these central leaders even fail to appreciate the kind of unique responsibilities that are cast upon the premiers of the Muslim majority provinces. Huq has been deeply resenting the interference by Jinnah in Bengal's affairs and his own sphere of functioning as the prime minister. Today his anger burst forth. Huq is clearly bitter, very bitter.

Atlantic Charter Hope For Oppressed Nations, Not India

September 9, 1941: The ongoing great war has brought some momentous changes in the long-held attitude of the leading imperialist countries towards the less fortunate nations, which have been the victims of occupations and or repression by external or sometimes even internal powers aided by the former. It seems, the hard experience of losing successive battles to the Nazis and the Fascist forces have begun to make them empathise with the fears, hopes and aspirations of the oppressed countries.

On 14th of last month, US president Franklin Roosevelt and British prime minister Winston Churchill had formulated the eight-points Atlantic Charter[105] wherein they said, they respected the right of all people to choose the form of government under which they wanted to live, and they also wished to see sovereign rights and self-government restored to those people who had been forcibly deprived of them. The charter had aroused great hopes in India that she will get her long-sought-after freedom, at least at the end of the war.

Much to the dismay of the Indians, Churchill has today clarified before the House of Commons that the right of self-determination incorporated in the Atlantic Charter does not apply to India and other parts of the empire. By way of clarification, he added, 'At the Atlantic meeting we have had in mind, primarily, the restoration of the sovereignty, self-government and natural life of the States and nations of Europe now under the Nazi Yoke...'[106] The people in India are feeling cheated. Churchill's stand on India in relation to the Atlantic Charter is raising question about the sincerity of British intention.

SOUTHEAST ASIA THEATRE OF INDIAN STRUGGLE

October, 1941, Bangkok: Over two million émigré Indians have been living in Southeast Asia, especially in Burma, Malaya, Thailand, Philippines, Singapore and adjoining areas. Then there are also a scattered Indian population in Japan, French Indo-China, and certain pockets in China, including Shanghai, Hong Kong etc. The might of the Japanese army has kindled hope in them that they too can play a part in India's freedom struggle with Japanese help. They have witnessed how Japan has been helping Burmese nationalist leaders like Anug San in their fight against the British regime. The manner in which the British have been trampling non-violent movements by Indians and blatantly misusing Indian men and resources for their war purposes are causing them great ire and making their resolve stronger.

In Bangkok, there are two prominent organisations of Indians. Of the two, the Indian Independence League is dominated by the Sikhs, with linkage to the erstwhile Ghadar Party, whereas the other, viz. Thai Bharat Cultural Lodge has all major Indian communities as its members. Two leaders of the Indian Independence League, viz. the elderly Amar Singh and the young Pritam Singh, have been working together with Major Fujiwara of the Japanese Armed Forces, to raise an Indian national army by recruiting from the Indian soldiers captured by the Japanese in course of their conquest of Southeast Asia. They are visualising the scope for launching an armed freedom struggle against the British Raj through an Indian liberation army.

Japan Mulls Ultimatum To America

November 5, 1941, Tokyo: Though the presence of the US Pacific Fleet in the Hawaii has been acting as a deterrent to her territorial ambitions in Southeast Asia, Japan still ventured in Indo-China in June this year and was able to conquer it by July, causing great irritation to the US. President Roosevelt has been tightening the economic sanctions and enforcing export-ban more rigorously.

The efficacy of such trade bans has been on the rise as Britain and the Dutch government in exile have been following US footsteps. Roosevelt also ordered the freezing of all Japanese assets. In April this year, Japan had tried for a diplomatic resolution of its feud with the US by deputing her ambassador to America to initiate talks but the mission failed. Apparently placed in a stifling environment, Japan sought a solution by finding a hardliner prime minister, Hideki Tojo, to take over the reins in the middle of last month. Today, the new prime minister has decided to undertake a fresh round of trade diplomacy through the Japanese ambassador Nomura in US and in the event of its failing, deliver an ultimatum to the US, seeking removal of the economic sanction or face the consequences. This is being seen by political observers not only as a desperate but a loaded political move as well.

Subhas Has Crossed To The Enemy: Government

November 10, 1941, New Delhi: Government of India has announced today in the Central Legislature that Subhas Chandra Bose, a member of the Legislature, has gone over to the enemy.

AIML Warns Government Not To Tinker With Constitution

November 16, 1941, New Delhi: In its meeting held here, the working committee of the Muslim League has criticised the British government for enlarging the Governor General's executive council, with people who represent nobody but themselves. The committee has also demanded that the government should take no further steps or make no further adjustment in future, even within the framework of the present constitution without approval and consent of the AIML.

Subhas' Brother Sarat Bose Arrested

December 11-12, 1941, Calcutta: Fazlul Huq had been much dissatisfied with the central leaders of the AIML. This created new political possibilities. Sarat Bose, since suspended by the Congress, has the major chunk of Congress members of the assembly loyal to him. In a bid to put an end to the communal politics of the League, Sarat, the leader of the opposition, mobilised the members of the KPP, the Congress, the Hindu Mahasabha, the nationalists amongst the Indian Christians and the Anglo Indians, Labour members and the scheduled caste members under the banner of the Progressive Coalition and invited Huq to head it. Fazlul Huq has joined the new coalition along with a faction of the Muslim League members and formed a new government. It is expected that the new government would pursue secular agenda in governance. This development has caused deep disquiet to the AIML leadership. Huq has been expelled from the League. The provincial AIML members have been asked by the central leadership to hound Huq. They have begun a malicious campaign against him in earnest. Top leaders like Huseyn Shaheed Suhrawardy, Khwaja Nazimuddin and Ispahani have joined hands to attack Huq.

The British governor of the province is also unhappy at the change. The British regime has deep suspicion of Sarat Bose, a very popular leader amongst both Hindus and Muslims. With Subhas, his brother, being out of India and capable of creating problems of unknown dimension for the British, the governor felt it would be unwise to let Sarat play an important role in the government of an important province such as Bengal. He was arrested so that he would not be able to keep in touch with the new government and lend it strength. According to sources, he is likely to be sent to a prison far away from Bengal. By this, the governor hopes to weaken the new government and thus do a favour to the Muslim League.

Government Orders Release Of Congress Satyagrahis

December 3, 1941, New Delhi: Since last year, when the individual Satyagraha was launched, many Congress leaders and workers were arrested and awarded prison terms. Now, the government has ordered their release. Many political observers are attributing the softening towards the Congress to the rapidly developing Japanese military threat in Southeast Asia.

JAPANESE BOMBERS POUND PEARL HARBOUR
USA Caught Unaware

December 7, 1941: Last month Japanese prime minister Tojo had served an ultimatum on the US to lift trade sanction or face consequences. Predictably, that demand was ignored. Today, Japan has carried out the threat. A large fleet of Japanese aircrafts conducted two rounds of massive bombing over Pearl Harbour, the new base of the US Pacific Fleet.

A huge fleet of 183 fighter planes took off from an aircraft carrier floating on the ocean at about 230 kms away from Pearl harbour, and congregated on its sky at about 7:55am. Although the fleet returned after unloading huge amount of explosives and causing large scale devastation to the harbour, the ordeal was not over. A repeat attack followed an hour later when another large fleet of 167 bombers revisited the US naval base and pounded their targets ruthlessly. To add to the ferocity of the attack, a fleet of midget submarines also joined in this daring operation. According to estimates, the Japanese assault has left over 2,300 people dead and over 1,100 injured. Amongst military targets, twenty one ships were sunk and 323 aircrafts were destroyed or damaged.

The US force was not prepared for such a surprise assault and failed to retaliate in a manner they would wish to. Nevertheless, they could inflict some damage to Japanese submarines and aircrafts, especially after they recovered from the stupor of the first phase of the Japanese attack.

Fortunately for the US navy, its aircraft carriers were in the deep sea for exercise, and, escaped unhurt. It is learnt that Admiral Isoroku Yamamoto, a former student of Harvard University, played a role in planning and executing the operation against the country of his alma mater.

According to political analysts, this attack would give US an opportunity to join the war on the side of the Allies and assume a more open and effective role, now on. Japan, they contend, has multiple objectives. She was already stifled by the economic sanction and this was culmination of her series of acts of persuasion. She can utilise the temporary paralysis of the US Pacific fleet to implement her military plans in Southeast Asia. The analysts are of the view that a Japanese invasion of Southeast Asian countries including the Philippines is on the cards.

Shyamaprasad Replaces Sarat In Bengal

December 11, 1941 Calcutta: The British regime has promptly struck the fledging alternative political initiatives in Bengal. The arrest of Sarat has come just before Fazlul Huq was about to announce his new cabinet. Huq, has, however gone ahead with the task in consultation with Sarat, lodged in Presidency jail. Shyamaprasad Mukherjee of the Hindu Mahasabha has replaced Sarat as the heavyweight minister from the Hindus. Though Sarat has wider acceptability among both Hindus and Muslims, Shyamaprasad is seen as a leader of equal stature in terms of competence.

Young Officer To Raise Indian Liberation Army

December 15, 1941, Malaya: Pritam Singh of the Indian Independence League and Major Fujiwara have been scouting the Indian prisoners of war (PoW)—their aim is to raise an Indian national army in Southeast Asia. Now that the Japanese army has reached Malaya through Thailand, capturing large number of Indian soldiers, their activities have increased manifold. In course of inspection, they have come across Captain Mohan Singh, a young army officer of 1/14 Punjab regiment of the British Indian army, and found him a good prospect to lead the proposed liberation army. Mohan Singh, a patriot and person of independent spirit has agreed to shoulder this enormous responsibility. Though a lower-ranked officer, he is a confident man with potential to handle great tasks.

Students' Fury Fell Saadullah Government In Assam

December 13, 1941, Shillong: Assam has been boiling for past some time for several reasons—infiltration from eastern part of Bengal, alleged manipulation of census data by the Saadullah ministry and blatant extortion of money in the name of 'war'. On 4th of this month, a Congress legislator had brought an adjournment motion on the issue of alleged manipulation of census data by the ministry. This reflected ongoing waves of anger in the province against alleged suppression of Hindu population in the latest census data. Though the premier and some of his colleagues clarified that the ministry had no hand in the matter and the motion was got rid of, the discontent continued to simmer. Five days thereafter, RK Chaudhury, the finance minister in the cabinet tendered his resignation. Since then, the political activities began to intensify even more. Five 'no-confidence' motions were brought against the ministry. Today, the house allowed three of them. However, premier Saadullah informed the house that he had tendered his entire cabinet's resignation on the ground of joint responsibility yesterday.

Gopinath Bordoloi, the opposition leader, took up the issue of the alleged police atrocities upon the agitating students of Cotton College in Gauhati. Thereafter, a no-confidence motion was taken up and it was passed by 56-0 votes. Premier Saadullah walked out of the House on the ground that his ministry had resigned already.

The Exit Of The Saadullah Ministry

There had been simmering discontent against the Saadullah ministry in the province on account of its many unpopular policies and programmes. The natives had been suspecting the ministry of following a policy of supporting immigration of Muslims from neighbouring Bengal to alter the demographic profile in Assam.

He had launched a 'Land Development Scheme' in terms of which the government opened vast tract of agricultural lands to the people who had migrated from Bengal before a 'cut off' date. To mitigate public grievance against the scheme, the indigenous landless people of the province were also made eligible. But local people read into the true purpose of this dangerous plan, which could potentially upset the demographic profile of the province. According to one estimate, in 1939-40 alone, the Saadullah government made available one hundred thousand bighas of land to the Muslim immigrants from Bengal. This has been scaring the indigenous people. The recent census data that showed reduced figures of Hindus aggravated their concerns. The last straw on the camel's back was the ministry's blunt attempts at raising men and money to support the British war efforts. As the Japanese threat began to appear in the eastern border, Saadullah even proposed to raise an Assam Regiment and urged upon Assamese of all classes to join the armed forces. He has been in the vanguard of a campaign to raise money to help the British war efforts. He set up a provincial war aid committee, which has branch offices at various district head quarters. What is worse, the officials at various government offices have reportedly been collecting contributions from the public covertly and overtly—voluntary and also by coercion.

The extortionist measures adopted by the regime had been antagonising the people in general. The students came forward to vent popular anger. On 6 December, the students of Cotton College in Guwahati paraded the streets shouting 'not a man, not a pie to the imperial war'. The police first lathi charged and then allegedly fired at the student demonstrators, arousing deep disdain and anger against the government. In its aftermath, Gauhati had observed a day's Hartal.

His critics say, Saadullah had made full use of the Congress legislators' absence in the assembly due to their preoccupations with Satyagraha, to pursue his policies vigorously without fear of opposition. The people were enraged and the Assam stories made rounds even at other places in the country. Things came to such a pass that the Congress high command advised Assam legislators to return to the assembly and frustrate the design of the Saadullah government. After the government chose to deal brutally with the student agitation against the war extortion, a flash point was reached. The end of the Saadullah ministry has come through a democratic process in the Assembly House.

India Is A Constellation Of Nations – Hindus And Muslims Are The Two Major Ones: Jinnah

December 25, 1941: In an interview to the *News Chronicle,* Jinnah wanted the British public and the British statesmen to understand that the stand of the Muslim League was vitally different from the Congress. Referring to the statements by top Congress leaders like Gandhi, Jawaharlal and others demanding immediate independence as a pre-condition to the war cooperation, Jinnah has hinted that the one hundred million Muslims have nothing to do with the demand of independence raised by these leaders. He asserted that there was no such thing as the Indian nation. India, he contended, was a constellation of nations with Hindus and Muslims being two major constituents.

Sowing Seeds Of Indian Freedom Struggle In Europe

December 1941, Berlin: Subhas has been able to achieve two important objectives towards the cause of the Indian freedom struggle . First, he has set up the Free India Centre, which was instituted on 2nd of the last month with headquarters in Lichtensteinallee. The centre is carrying out valuable propaganda in favour of Indian independence and against the British Empire. Competent Indians like MR Vyas, NG Swami, Abid Hussain and a few more have become involved in the functioning of the centre and they are making important contributions. The centre plans to make regular radio broadcasts in various Indian languages for the cause of Indian independence through German transmitters. It also has plans to publish monthlies and books to communicate to people and governments in the continent the imperatives of the Indian freedom struggle.

Second, Subhas has been able to raise an Indian Legion in the German land. Through remarkable initiatives, he has persuaded the Nazi government to enter into an agreement with the Italian government to transfer the Indian soldiers captured by the latter in the battles against the British in North Africa to Germany. The Nazi government has also consented to impart training to those Indian prisoners of war, who would agree to join the proposed Indian Legion.

Mission: Liberation, Indian Legion Trains In Germany

December 1941, Berlin: Indian divisions of the British army have been fighting in different war theatres, including the middle east and north Africa. In the course of battle, few thousands of Indian soldiers have fallen into German and Italian hands. In May 1941, at the initiative of Subhas, selected PoW were brought from Lamsdorf and Cyrenaica camps to Berlin. Subhas and his associates in the Free India Centre have been campaigning amongst these prisoners of war to join the Indian Legion and take part in the Indian freedom struggle. Though the initial response was tepid, the strength of the legion has been growing gradually with the passage of time. Arrangements have been made for their training under the German army.

Japan Begins Southeast Asia Campaign Hong Kong Succumbs, Manila Totters

December 31, 1941, Manila: On the very next day following the Pearl Harbour blitzkrieg, both US and Britain declared war on Japan. After three days, ie. on the 11th instant, Germany and Italy came out in support of their Asian ally and declared war on the United States. All of a sudden, the war has discovered a new dimension both in terms of geographical span and intensity.

Unshackled from the diplomatic niceties, the Japanese forces proceeded to carry out their plan in Southeast Asia without losing time. Before the US fleet could regroup in Pearl Harbour, the Japanese army invaded Hong Kong on the very next day. Japan also began the invasion of the Philippines simultaneously. Japanese aircrafts began to bomb Luzon and shipping at Manila Bay. They also attacked a couple of places north of Luzon. This was followed by land invasion on 11th December at Luzon. As days passed, the Japanese army, air force and navy scaled up their aggresion. The US-Filipino forces, devoid of support from mainland America, began to wilt in that heat. While Hong Kong fell to them a couple of days ago, the Japanese forces managed to capture Sibul springs, Luzon about a week ago thereby breaching the final defensive line north of Manila. It appears the fall of Manila, the capital of the country, has now become imminent. Though complete capture of the Philippines may take more time, US forces under General MacArthur have been gradually retreating to Batan, Java and Australia.

The ease with which the Japanese have so far overcome the joint resistance by the US-Filipino forces suggest they may be able to achieve their remaining targets in Southeast Asia without much difficulty.

Japanese Advance Raises Stormy Speculations In India

In India, till now, the question facing the Congress was whether or not to launch a national struggle to force the British to concede freedom to India, or at least, give a definite time frame when they would do so. Now a different set of possibilities has arisen—the British being defeated by the Japanese in the eastern front and the prospect of the Japanese advancing into India. Obviously, such a possibility implies a war between the two powers. In such a situation, the Congress has to decide whether or not it should support the British and if so, whether actively or passively—or to remain neutral and watch. It also has to ready itself to respond to a situation of Japanese conquest and the possibility of their making attempts at replacing the British as the new colonial master. Such myriad questions are troubling Congress leaders. These are no longer academic but have already entered into the realm of distinct possibilities.

Amongst the top echelon of the party's leadership, there are significant differences of perception. Gandhi is of the opinion that the Japanese may not enter into India if the British leave the country. He also feels that in the unlikely event of their harbouring imperial ambition in India, the Congress would counter them with non-violent resistance. Jawaharlal, Azad and a few others are, however, deeply suspicious of Japanese motive. They are convinced that any Japanese attempt to advance into Indian territory must be nipped in the bud and they want that the Congress should help the British government in its fight against the Japanese.

Congress Hints At War Cooperation For 'Freedom'

December 23-30, 1941, Bombay: The Congress Working Committee met here to take stock of the current situation, Indian and global. It recognised that the world is sinking into a deeper abyss under the assault of the fascist forces, and there were now more countries and people who required help and fillip. The committee has also observed with anxiety that the war has now approached the frontier of India. However, the Committee resolved that only a free and independent India can undertake defence of the country on a national basis and play its role for the world's sake and world freedom. The hint is clear that before Britain or the Allies can expect India's support for the war, she must be made a free country.

Gandhi Disillusioned At Congress U-turn

December 30, 1941, Bardoli: Gandhi has reacted to the just-adopted resolution of the Congress Working Committee, with a mix of pain and stoicism. He saw in the resolution, the Congress's readiness to lend war support if Britain acceded to its demand for India's freedom. This was, Gandhi pointed out, a 'U-turn' from the Congress resolution adopted in Bombay in September 1940, when the party had declared its unflinching commitment to 'non-volence' and invited him to lead the Indian struggle. He felt the Congress has once again made it clear that it was ready to participate in the war if only the British government acceded to its demand of India's independence. Dismayed by the new development, Gandhi today wrote to Azad, Congress president, to relieve him of the responsibility to lead the party. He still believed that non-violence was the only way to save India and the world from self-extinction. In his letter, Gandhi declared his resolve to continue with his mission of non-violence alone. Having recognised the validity of Gandhi's contention, the Committee acceded to his request and relieved him of the responsibility. Interestingly, however, the committee, without addressing Gandhi's point of objection, sought to assure him that the Congress would continue to adhere to the policy of nonviolence.

Roosevelt Wants Britain To Reconcile With Indian Leaders

December 1941, Washington: US president Roosevelt has been impressing upon Britain to secure willing cooperation of Indians in the war efforts. It is true, even without that, Britain has been liberally drafting men and material from India. However, political analysts say, Roosevelt's main worry lies in pre-empting any internal uprising, especially in the event of a Japanese attack in the eastern front. The British government in Delhi seems to be listening to the US president's concerns. They have released Azad and Nehru from jail. More releases are likely.

FOUR
Empire Strikes Back
1942-1943

EMPIRE STRIKES BACK

GIVE INDIA 'DOMINION STATUS' AT ONCE
Moderate Leaders Cable Churchill

January 2, 1942, New Delhi: The fast-evolving war scenario across Europe, Africa and Asia has been causing grave concerns in India. To numerous Indians, British vulnerabilities against Japanese have been exposed and they realise the necessity of a national government to be able to mobilise the entire nation effectively against any foreign aggression. Today, many moderate leaders, led by TB Sapru, have sent a wire to British prime minister Churchill urging him to accord dominion status to India immediately, expand the Viceroy's executive council so as to make it assume the form of a national government, and restore the governments in provinces presently under governor rule.

Japan Runs Through British Defences In Southeast Asia

January 15, 1942: While Manila could hold the Japanese for some days essentially due to heavy presence of US forces, the other Southeast Asian countries are falling like nine pins. Four days ago, the Japanese army captured Kuala Lumpur, the capital of Malaya and despatched amphibious forces to conquer the Dutch East Indies. Today, it has begun invasion of Burma by attacking Victoria Point at the country's southern tip. The intention seems obvious—move up northwards and capture Rangoon by driving the British away.

THE MANY DIMENSIONS OF THE JAPANESE INVASION

Japan's power-packed entry into the arena on the side of the Axis Bloc has changed the complexion of the conflict substantially. If Germany has so far been running its steam-roller in Europe, Japan has launched violent assault upon both the US territory in the Pacific as well as vast swathes of the British empire in Southeast Asia in quick succession.

The raw power backing its invasion has surprised both its enemies and friends. Even its ally Germany, the much-feared European giant, has been greatly impressed. Japan had made a powerful statement of its might by its onslaught upon Pearl Harbour. She has followed up that Pacific blitzkrieg by sinking two great British battleships, viz. Repulse and the Prince of Wales in the South China Sea. The foray of its army in Southeast Asian lands has been even more spectacular. Hong Kong fell to them early and easily. In the Philippines, the Japanese army has captured Manila by forcing American general MacArthur to retreat to the Bataan peninsula. It has overrun the British forces in most parts of Malaya, commenced invasion of both Dutch East Indies and British Burma in quick succession. Adding to the Allies' worries, the Japanese army is in the course of a lightening march to the impregnable British post of Singapore.

While they are earning these swift victories, hundreds of prisoners of war, mostly Indians have been falling into their hands. Whereas the eastern aspirations of the Japanese are causing great disquiet in the British government, to Subhas, keen to wage an armed struggle against the British, the unfolding war scenario in this part of the world is opening up interesting possibilities. From Berlin, he is keeping a keen watch over the war situation in the east and the progress of the Japanese invasion.

Released Prisoners In No Mood To Revisit Prison: Viceroy

January 17, 1942: New Delhi: Though the moderates as well as the Congress leaders have been trying to mount pressure on Britain to grant India dominion status and national government, the Viceroy and his regime are in no mood to endorse these demands. Lest the British government in London turn soft fearing intensification of the Congress Satyagraha at a time when Japanese are posing a threat, the Viceroy has reassured the HMG that things are really not that bad here. Not only has the government the support from constituencies like the 'princes' but also some non-Congress political parties, the Muslim League being most prominent amongst them.

Generally, the communal parties have been in competition in extending manpower support to the government to raise the share of their community in the armed forces. As for the Congress, its individual civil disobedience movement has ceased to sting the government. Today, Viceroy Linlithgow has wired[107] to Amery, the Secretary of State, mentioning that 'the movement had gathered some strength in the opening months of 1941 chiefly in the UP' and by May some 14,000 Satyagrahis were in prison. However, now it has lost momentum. New entrants have rapidly dwindled and they stand outnumbered by the prisoners released after they served their term. The Viceroy has added that these time-expired prisoners 'showed no inclination to obey Mr Gandhi's injunctions to seek re-imprisonments'.

SINGAPORE FALLS TO THE JAPANESE

February 15, 1942: The Japanese army has dealt a devastating blow to the British Empire as it conquered the impregnable British island fortress of Singapore. The defending British army was more than the invading Japanese force in number, but they meekly capitulated to the invaders. It is reported that the British had stationed a large stock of quality artilleries but those were anchored to the ground and pointed to the sea whereas the smart Japanese launched a land attack and encircled about 90,000 strong defenders. Colonel Hunt surrendered, practically without a fight. About 60,000 Allied soldiers and officers, vast majority of them Indians, were taken by the Japanese as prisoners.

India Must Fight Like A Tiger Against This Aggression Viceroy Wants Chiang Kai-shek To Convince Indians

February 16, 1942, New Delhi: Chiang Kai-shek, along with his wife, has been in the course of a highly significant political visit to India to serve a common cause with Britain and America against their common enemy—Japan.

The Japanese army are already in Burma and threatening to cut down the route of the Allied supply to the nationalist government of China from its base in India. Both Chiang and the British Viceroy in New Delhi want that the Indian leaders, more particularly of the Congress, play a proactive role in organising Indians to extend help in the ongoing war efforts to defeat and drive away the Japanese from Burma. Chiang has something to offer to Indians in return—his open support for their cause of self-determination. He is even prepared to take up the Indian case with American president Roosevelt with whom he has considerable rapport.

Amongst Indian leaders, Chiang has a warm relationship with Jawaharlal, which grew last year when the latter paid a visit to China. The government is hopeful that the meeting of these two leaders in India would help the common objective, given Jawaharlal's professed sympathy for the cause of democracy and the Allies. But it has reservations about Chiang meeting Gandhi. Churchill, Britain's prime minister, also has been against the two meeting each other.

The Chiang couple began the tour of India following their arrival in Delhi on 9th of this month and they are likely to conclude their visit in a week's time. Today the Viceroy has written to Madame Chiang reminding her of the 'mission' and urging her to ensure that the core message is delivered to the Indians forcefully: '...I hope you will ponder this matter with due care, and that, in your own clever way - you will take steps before you depart to acclaim... as loudly as you may, your profound conviction that India must fight, like one of her own tigers, this wicked aggression.'[108]

The Viceroy has added that he attaches highest importance to the final message that the Generalissimo would deliver at the time of leaving India.

INA GROWS IN STRENGTH IN SOUTHEAST ASIA

February 17, 1942, Singapore: The fall of Singapore and the capture of tens of thousand of Indian PoW came as a windfall to Captain Mohan Singh and Major Fujiwara who have been out on a recruitment spree. They reportedly spoke to as many as 45,000 captured Indian soldiers. Although many of them suspected the Japanese intention and thought of Mohan Singh as a Japanese stooge, the visit has not gone waste. According to available reports, a good number of prisoners have joined the fledgling Indian National Army.

It's Time To Deal The Final Blow Upon The Raj Subhas Speaks To India From Berlin

February 19, 1942, Berlin: Subhas had so far concealed his identity in Germany for security reasons. In the wake of the British collapse in Singapore, he has possibly reckoned that the slide in British fortune has become irreversible and the time has arrived to deal the final blow on it, in cooperation with friendly nations. Azad Hind radio began broadcast from Germany last month. Today, through a radio broadcast,[109] Subhas has invoked Indians to rise to the occasion. He said:

'For about a year I have waited in silence and patience for the march of events and now that the hour has struck, I come forward to speak. The fall of Singapore means the collapse of the British Empire, and the end of the iniquitous regime which it has symbolised and the dawn of a new era in Indian history...'Referring to the cross-sections of people and parties who have been supporting the British war efforts he said, '...the British oppressors have endeavoured to create divisions among the Indian people... we find in India, those who openly support British imperialism. There are others who, whether intentionally or unintentionally, help the British cause...'

Thereafter, Subhas, while trying to invoke patriotism in the common people, sought to separate them from the leaders in India, supporting the British regime. He also declared that at this stage, he has decided to side with the enemies of the British to clinch freedom for the country:

'There is, however, the vast majority of the Indian people who will have no compromise with British Imperialism but will fight on till full independence is achieved... During this struggle... we shall heartily cooperate with all those who will help us in overthrowing the common enemy… The hour of India's salvation is at hand...'

Political analysts say, such direct communications to the countrymen by a top nationalist leader, criticising those supporting the British regime, is likely to create pressure on Congress leaders with regard to the formulation of the party's policies.

Muslim League Condemns Sapru Initiatives

February 21, 1942, New Delhi: The All-India Muslim League Working Committee held its meeting here. Jinnah presided over the meeting. The committee took a sceptical view of the intention of the 'non-leaders' conference' held under the presidentship of TB Sapru. The working committee described the conference's initiative as a conspiracy by the Hindu leaders to 'torpedo' the Muslim League's demand for Pakistan under the garb of interim change in the executive council. The committee warned that such a demand, if acceded to by His Majesty's Government, will constitute a breach of the government's pledges to the Muslims.

Chiang Kai-shek-Gandhi Meeting Passes As Non-event

February 22, 1942: Chiang Kai-shek and his wife concluded their India visit yesterday. Despite initial reservations on the part of the government, they were allowed to meet Gandhi in Calcutta four days ago. There was much hype about the meeting of the two tall Asian leaders but the event passed off without much consequence. At the end, Chiang felt Gandhi's strategy of non-violence may be alright in the Indian case, but it was not relevant to the dynamic world situation, including his country. He also came to the conclusion that Gandhi lacked vision of the international situation.

Political observers say, Chiang could not materially change the Congress stand on the issue of extending help to British war efforts. They also suspect the ability of the Chinese leader to help the Indian cause of self-determination.

Generalissimo Came Empty-handed, Left Empty-handed: Gandhi

February 25, 1942, Sevagram: Gandhi has summed up the experiences of his recent meeting with the Chinese leader, Chiang Kai-shek, in a letter written[110] to Vallabhbhai today. Gandhi's candid observation has been that the Generalissimo 'came empty-handed and left empty-handed. He amused himself and entertained me'. In terms of usefulness of the visit to the Congress, Gandhi's opinion was captured in this pithy sentence: "He had only one thing to say: 'Help the British anyhow. They are better than the others and will improve further hereafter.' "

American Pressure Mounts Churchill Sets Up India Committee Of War Cabinet

February 26, 1942, London: Government indifference to the January Resolution of the Congress offering cooperation was a repeat snub to the Congress leaders. Things possibly would have continued that way had the Japanese advance not become menacing.

After completing the Malaya campaign, the Japanese army dispossessed the British of Singapore and took tens of thousands of British and Indian soldiers as prisoners. Thereafter, they have been advancing towards Burma and it seems that they will be able to knock on the Indian door before long. This has infused some fear in the British Government. In these circumstances, US President Roosevelt has been repeatedly advising Churchill to conciliate the Indian leaders. Even Chiang Kai-shek of China and Lester Pearson of Canada have been trying to persuade Churchill to come to an understanding with Indian leaders without delay.

Eventually, the stream of advices has made the British prime minister establish an India Committee of the Cabinet with Clement Atlee, Leo Amery, Sir Stafford Cripps, Sir John Simon, Sir John Anderson, and Sir James Grigg as members. The committee has worked out a declaration with regard to granting dominion status to and constitutional development in India.

Prominent Muslim Leaders Cable War Support To Secretary Of State

March 5, 1942, London: For the war-ridden British Government, India continues to be the key resource base in fighting its enemies across continents. Though the Congress has been attempting to utilise this dependence for securing complete independence, several Muslim leaders, especially of the League, are working at cross purposes. Some prominent Muslim leaders have come forward with assurances of support to the government on more acceptable terms, thereby, giving it good measure of comfort. Last month, Firoz Khan Noon, a prominent Muslim leader from Punjab and a member of the Viceroy's executive council, had sent a long telegram[111] to Amery, Secretary of State for India, warning His Majesty's Government against design and arm twisting by the Congress under the threat of movements.

He had expressed his reservations about wholly 'Indianising' the executive council for the fear of Hindu majority and insisted that if this was done, the government must ensure that the Muslims have 50%

seats in the Indian cabinet. He has mentioned that the only reason the Congress could not create disturbance in India is because the Muslims have not joined them. He has repeatedly reminded Amery about the role the Muslims have been playing in the war effort and warned HMG against ignoring the pledges given to them. Today Hassan Suhrawardy, another important Muslim leader, sent Amery a wire message[112] saying, 'Muslims have contributed and are eager to contribute all material support in war effort in much greater proportion to their population strength'. He simultaneously hinted at the 'quid pro quo', ie. that the Muslims 'will resent any far-reaching decision without adequate investigation and hearing different groups'.

Japanese Forces Enter Rangoon

March 9, 1942, Rangoon: Today Rangoon, the capital of Burma, has fallen to the Japanese forces. Following the attack of the Victoria Point last month they advanced through the long narrow southern tail of the country, demolishing every resistance put up by the colonial British government of that country. While a 150 strong Japanese fleet of fighters and bombers roared in the Burmese sky vanquishing a meagre RAF fleet of 35 aircrafts, their army established unquestionable domination over the land battle. The Japanese victory here has been no less spectacular than those in Malaya, Dutch East Indies or the Philippines. On entering the capital city of Burma today, they found the British forces, together with the loyal Burma division, have escaped to the north of the country.

All Indian Forces Must Be Rallied To Repulse Japanese Churchill Announces Cripps Mission To India

March 11, 1942, London: British prime minister Churchill had reconstructed his War Cabinet last month to be able to prosecute the war more efficiently. The cabinet also formed an India Committee to deal with India-specific issues. In view of the rapidly-expanding Japanese military invasion against the USA and British interests in the Pacific, East and Southeast Asia, protecting India and her political stability have emerged as a priority for both Britain and America. Today, Churchill has announced to the House of Commons that Stafford Cripps would visit India on behalf of the war cabinet, with proposals for the settlement of the Indian question. Stafford Cripps is a prominent Labour Party leader and recently appointed as Lord Privy Seal. A member of, both, the war cabinet and its India Committee, Cripps has been known for his sympathy and favourable disposition to the Indian cause. He has been chosen by Churchill possibly because of his credibility amongst Indian leaders and his remarkable diplomatic acumen. Cripps would carry the draft declaration of the British government to be used for conducting negotiations with the Indian leaders. He is to meet various interest groups in India to achieve his mission. Churchill has justified the Cripps mission on the ground that it has become imperative to rally all the forces of Indian life to guard their land from the Japanese invaders, and to meet the crisis that has arisen in consequence thereof.

Subhas From Berlin, Rashbehari From Tokyo Question Motive Behind Cripps Mission

March 13, 1942, Berlin: In a radio broadcast from Berlin to the Indian people, Subhas has referred to the Stafford Cripps mission. He said, the mission was meaningless and that today no 'Indian is prepared to trust empty British promises of freedom after the war.' He said, Churchill and his government would soon realise they would not be able to hoodwink the Indians any longer. In a message through radio, Rashbehari Bose, another revolutionary leader from Tokyo, also opposed the Cripps mission.

How Does The 'Scorched Earth Policy' Matter To An Enslaved Nation?

March 22, 1942, Sevagram: British Indian government has begun to consider Japanese threat a real one in the eastern border. The government in close circles, has begun to hint at the 'scorched earth' policy—of destroying crops, bridges and industrial establishments in the event it has to retreat to the Indian heartland, in the face of Japanese advance through the east. Gandhi has however reacted strongly to such a strategy. Today he has written[113] in the *Harijan* expressing his strong disapproval: 'I see neither bravery nor sacrifice in destroying life or property for offence or defence...'

He has made the point amply clear that in the ongoing war, India is not fighting but her conquerors are. If in the course of a battle her present conquerors (British) are defeated by a new conqueror ie. the Japanese, it might make little differences to the vast multitude of inarticulate masses. Of the Indian soldiers, he wrote that they are not a national army but professionals who will 'as soon fight under the Japanese or any other, provided they are paid for fighting'. He has, therefore, made a powerful case against the adoption of 'scorched earth policy' by a country which is reeling under foreign rule. Political observers are sure of the ire that Gandhi's article is bound to cause to the British regime.

Cripps Arrives In Delhi, Cautious Optimism In Air

March 23, 1942, New Delhi: Stafford Cripps has arrived here today and been cordially received. Though Gandhi himself would not engage with Cripps, he has decided to remain in Delhi personally for the next few days to watch over the progress of the negotiations. He is cautious because there is much at stake and a wrong pact could make the nationalist cause suffer beyond redemption. It may be recalled that Subhas, from distant Berlin, is repeatedly cautioning the Congress leadership about the danger in the negotiation with Cripps at this juncture. The central objective of the Cripps mission, he apprehends, is to secure the support of Congress to the 'war efforts' by intriguing it.

We Wont Allow The Camp-followers To Sit On Our Chest

March 23, 1942, New Delhi: The Muslim League has been keen that its demand for Pakistan does not get diluted in these turbulent times induced by the global war. Today the League has held 'Pakistan Day' in several places. In a big meeting held at the Urdu Park in the city,

Liaquat Ali Khan presided. Jinnah too was present. Addressing a large congregation, he assured them that 'we have nothing to fear'. Saying 'our cause was just and fair', he made it clear that the League did not want to embarrass the British. At the same time he cautioned that no help would be given to the camp-followers who would like to sit on 'our chest' after the victory. He also sought to reinforce his much-repeated message that Muslims are not a minority but a nation. Probably he also wanted his message to be heard by Stafford Cripps, HMG's emissary, who has been camping in the city in search of a solution to the Indian constitutional question.

Japan Drives Out British From Andaman & Nicobar

March 23, 1942: The Japanese navy has driven out the British from the Andaman and Nicobar and taken possession of these islands. This has come as another major setback to the British.

Gandhi Wants Azad, Jawaharlal To Negotiate With Cripps

March 23, 1942, New Delhi: To Gandhi, a discerning politician, the motive of the British Government behind deputing Cripps at this juncture is clear. He does not have much hope that the cause of Indian independence would receive a fillip through this exercise. Cripps, even though a sensible and level-headed leader, will have to act within the strict boundaries set for him by the Churchill government.

According to several reports, this fresh initiative by HMG owed more to pressure from the US than to Churchill's own war strategy. Gandhi is also acutely aware that the sole motive behind the Cripps mission is to obtain willing cooperation of the Congress to the Allied war efforts, whereas he, based on his conviction in non-violence, has been against supporting any of the parties to the war. In the circumstances, Gandhi has decided to stay away from participating in the talks with Cripps while party president Azad assisted by Jawaharlal would be holding the negotiations on behalf of the Congress.

Cripps Holds Press Conference, Sends Mixed Signals

March 29, 1942, New Delhi: Since his arrival here about a week ago, Cripps at first held parley with the Viceroy, the members of Viceroy's executive council as well as the Viceroy's official advisors. Four days ago he gave copies of the proposal of the war cabinet to Indian leaders. Gandhi met him a couple of days ago, though, in a personal capacity. Cripps has been holding parleys with a wide spectrum of Indian leaders including inter alia Azad, Jawaharlal (Congress) Jinnah (League), Sikandar Hayat Khan, Fazlul Huq (both provincial premiers), Savarkar (Hindu Mahasabha), Ambedkar and MC Rajah (Depressed Classes), Sapru and Jayakar (Liberal), leaders of Sikhs, Indian Christians, Anglo Indians, Europeans and representatives of Indian states. Though the details of his discussions were not made public, these have been reportedly positive so far. According to sources close to the Congress, Cripps assured them that the executive council would be reconstituted like a 'cabinet' in the dominion states.

Today, the media had the first opportunity to get an official version of what was on offer to India from HMG. Cripps opened his press conference almost with a bang. He stated that the object of the draft declaration was to create a new Indian Union with Dominion Status for which an elected body would be set up to frame a new constitution immediately upon the cessation of the war hostilities. Meanwhile, the executive council of the Viceroy would be Indianised and it would have the status like a cabinet in the dominion states. The proposed new Indian Union would have the choice to remain within the Commonwealth or opt out of it. The constituent assembly of the new Union can, if it chooses, start with a declaration of 'independence' in the interim period. Cripps then brought the ecstatic audience down to earth when he made it clear that the proposals of the free Indian Union encompassed only British Indian provinces and not the Indian states. Worse still, the provinces would have the choice of joining the proposed Indian Union or emerging as independent entities. He further added that for the time being, the defence of India was Britain's paramount concern and its responsibility will continue to be exclusively with HMG and it could not be expected to be transferred to an Indian defence member.

Circumscribing what initially seemed to be a generous offer with regard to transferring power of governance to Indian hands, he clarified that though the reconstituted 'executive council' will have much greater freedom, it would function under the existing constitution. This was so because making the council responsible to the legislature, instead of the Viceroy, required change in the constitution, and that was out of question during the war. However, the working of the council could, Cripps clarified, certainly be improved by changing the convention or adopting a new convention. The veteran diplomat wanted Indians to understand that his proposals were a package deal. In other words, the scheme goes through as a whole or it gets rejected as a whole.

Indian Expatriates Congregate In Tokyo

March 28 to 30, 1942, Tokyo: The expatriate Indians in the vast stretches of East and Southeast Asia are meeting here to discuss ways and means to take their struggle for Indian independence to the next level. They reckon that to achieve this goal, they need to strengthen both their civilian organisation, ie. the Indian Independence League and the military wing, viz. the Indian National Army and bring in better coordination between the two. This conference is expected to give a roadmap for action.

Their present endeavour is being supported by the Japanese government. The veteran freedom fighter Rashbehari Bose is playing a lead role. He escaped from India in 1915, settled here and right since then, he has been working for the cause of Indian independence in this part of the world. He has been able to build up rapport with important people in Japan and this is proving useful. The conference is being attended by the delegates from the Indian Independence League (IIL), the Thai Bharat Lodge (TBL), the Indian National Army (INA) and other Indian organisations and persons.

The conference has decided to spread the branches of the IIL across the vast stretches of Southeast Asia, and strengthen the INA. It has also resolved to form a five-member executive body of Council of Action in the next conference at Bangkok planned to be held in near future, which is expected to be attended by a larger number of delegates.

Japan Will Destroy Anglo-Saxon Power: Japanese PM

March 28-30, 1942, Tokyo: As the Tokyo conference of the expatriate Indians get underway, the Japanese army is set to complete their conquest of Burma. This development has heartened the delegates. They feel that the scene of action has now been shifted to the eastern border of India.

The goodwill message, sent by Japanese prime minister Tojo to the conference, has also been significant in this connection. He has written that the Japanese empire is determined to fulfil their mission of destroying the Anglo-Saxon power. He added that while doing so, the Japanese government well recognises the fact that Britain plans to make India the base of its defence in the East. His statement clearly reveals Japanese intention of expelling the British from India. To the Indians, the challenge would be one of leveraging the Jap-British rivalry, and playing their own role with diplomacy and courage to secure independence for their motherland.

Let The Dead Past Bury Its Dead, Let's March Together

March 30, 1942, New Delhi: The waves of hope and optimism generated by the series of meetings that Cripps held with Indian leaders began to transform into speculation and sceptcism following his press briefing yesterday. Today, Cripps, in a radio broadcast, outlined the British offer to the Indians in greater details. He spoke about both the long-term proposal involving the constitutional issue and the short-term proposal that dealt with the 'executive council'.

After he laid the scheme before the Indians, Cripps made an emotional appeal to them to consider it seriously for the sake of India's defence, for India's freedom upon foundations wrought by Indian themselves, and for friendship between India and Britain. He exhorted Indians to forget the past and march hand-in-hand to secure a better world: 'Let the dead past bury its dead, and let us march together side by side through the night of high endeavour and courage to the already waking dawn of a new world of liberty for all the peoples...'[114]

SALIENT FEATURES OF CRIPPS' PROPOSAL

The object of the Cripps proposal is to create a new Indian union in the form of a dominion which would be at par with every other dominion in the British empire in every respect. Soon after the war ends, an elected body of representatives would frame a new constitution for India and provision will be made for participation of Indian states in the constitution-making body. The entire lower houses of the provincial legislatures shall constitute a single electoral college for sending representatives to the constituent assembly by a system of proportional representation.

While HMG would accept and implement the new constitution, any province unwilling to accept the new constitution would be allowed to retain its present constitutional position. There would, however, be provision for accession of such a province to the Indian union at a later date, if it so decides. For such provinces which do not want to join the Indian union, HMG would be agreeable to a new constitution for them, giving them status at par with the Union of India. Indian states will have the choice of joining the constituent assembly of the Indian Union. The representatives of the Indian states in the constitution-making body of the new union would be appointed by their rulers.

There would be a treaty between the constituent assembly and HMG about transfer of power which would deal with all relevant issues including, in particular, protection of racial and religious minorities. In case of Indian states, irrespective of their joining the Union of India, they would have to enter into new or revised treaties with the authorities concerned.

As regards the short-term proposal involving the executive council, Cripps has been comparatively vague. However, he made it clear that till the war ended and the new constitution was framed, the defence of India shall be with HMG. At the same time, the HMG expected much greater participation of the Indians in the executive council and their effective participation in the counsels of their country, commonwealth and the world. His Majesty's Government also relied upon them in the task of organising military, moral and material resources in cooperation with the Indian people.

JAPANESE AIRCRAFT CARRIER ENTERS BAY OF BENGAL

April 1, 1942: After helping the Japanese conquest in the Philippines, Malaya and Java, Ryujo, the light aircraft carrier of the Imperial Japanese Navy has entered into the Bay of Bengal today, raising the possibility of launching invasion on both Ceylon and India.

Japanese Planes Bombard Indian Coastal Towns

April 6, 1942, Visakhapatnam: The Japanese threat has begun to materialise. Japanese warships have become active in the sea in the Southeast of India and they have reportedly sunk fifteen enemy freighters. Bombers operating from Ryujo, which entered the Bay of Bengal five days ago, carried out raids on the eastern coastal town of Visakhapatnam and Cocanada. It may be noted that the Japanese army is already deep inside Burma. There are some rumours that the Japanese may carry out a pincer attack on India, using both sea and land routes at the Assam border. Many are seeing the attacks today as an ominous signal of a likely land invasion in the near future.

Roosevelt's Envoy Joins Talks, Light At The End Of Tunnel?

April 8, 1942, New Delhi: Cripps' radio broadcast on 30th March, more specifically his long-term proposal concerning the constitutional aspect, had so disillusioned Congress that it decided to reject the proposal. The implication of the long-term proposal, in a nutshell, was division nay, the balkanisation of India. On 2 April, Azad carried the CWC resolution rejecting Cripps's proposal in person to his meeting with Cripps. However, both the parties agreed to keep its 'publication' in abeyance and continue with the discussion on the short-term issues, more particularly the powers of members of the proposed new executive council and the distribution of responsibilities relating to defence of India, to explore if the two sides could arrive at an agreement, at least in this area.

Azad was reportedly assured by Cripps in their initial meetings that HMG will confer the executive council with wide powers and the Viceroy would, in terms of the new proposal, become a titular head and he will have the same relation vis-à-vis his council as the King has with the cabinet in Britain. While Azad has been negotiating under the impression of such a near autonomous 'executive council', Cripps made little efforts to change Azad's ideas. Later, Cripps cited constitutional difficulties to make any legal change to guarantee the new system and insisted that the Congress rely on British promises in this regard. Congress leaders were disappointed.

Even while they were trying to grapple with this disillusionment, the talks tumbled on another issue—the segregation of powers and functions between the Indian defence member in the council and the British commander-in-chief. Cripps has been firm that the C-I-C must have complete power over all such areas and functions necessary to carry out war activities. The Congress, on the other hand, felt the Indian Defence member must have a say on important policy decisions and also appropriate status since most of the government resources and activities during the war period were largely determined by the war department.

Four days ago, Cripps arranged a meeting of the Indian leaders with the C-I-C to make them understand the technical aspects of the issue, which reportedly cleared some areas of misunderstanding. The credit for this small progress can, to some extent, be attributed to Col Louis Johnson, a personal envoy of the US President, has also been taking part in the negotiations with the consent of Cripps. After several rounds of hectic negotiations with Cripps and the Viceroy on one side and the Congress and Johnson on the other, Cripps has eventually formulated a proposal that has found Congress acceptance. Today Cripps has sent the proposal with his recommendations to HMG.

Rift Between Cripps And Viceroy
HMG Supports Viceroy, Cripps Rewinds His Offer

April 10, 1942, New Delhi: Cripps mission has met with a sudden death. The proximate reason for the debacle seems to be a serious communication gap between Cripps and the Viceroy. Though the Viceroy was, by and large, involved in the negotiations, Cripps had sent his final proposal a couple of days ago to London without taking the

Viceroy in confidence. Cripps' final proposal on the Indian defence member issue had accommodated some of the Congress demands but the Viceroy felt this would hamper the war efforts. He rushed his objections to the Cripps proposal to HMG. Upon considering the contentions of both sides, HMG decided that it could not concede to the reduction of the power of the C-I-C in any material respect as long as the war continued.

Things changed completely thereafter. Yesterday Azad experienced a sense of failure due to HMG's rejection of the Congress demand on the issue of the 'Defence Member'. But he was baffled when Cripps went back on earlier assurances about the very nature of the proposed executive council. Cripps clarified that the executive council would continue to function under the present constitution and the improvement, if any, has to be effected only through suitable conventions. Further, the issues of 'convention' would arise only after a settlement was reached and it was a subject matter of discussion with the Viceroy.

The Congress, convinced that the British offer was on a hasty retreat, sought to salvage its ethical ground. Today, in a long letter to Cripps, Azad, as the Congress president, while stating why it could not accept the Cripps proposal, reiterated its demand of a 'national government' in the form of a cabinet government with full powers together with a supplementary demand that the HMG accepts the Congress position in the matter relating to 'defence' as it would be crucial for the functioning of the national government.

Cripps sent his reply immediately. He clarified that a cabinet government could not be formed without making changes of most complicated character and that on a very large scale in the constitution which was not possible during war. Under the present circumstances, the members of such a cabinet would be nominated by major political parties and it would not have any accountability. No less importantly, Cripps argued, such a mechanism would pave the way for dictatorship of the majority over the minorities. On the 'defence' issue he has made it plain that defence was the paramount duty and responsibility of the HMG while unity of command was essential in the interests of the Allied help to India. Political observers feel that there is hardly any scope for further negotiations left.

Past Distrust Has Proved Too Strong To Allow Agreement

April 11, 1942, New Delhi: Today the Congress Working Committee published its resolution of 2nd April, rejecting the Cripps' proposal. Azad also sent Cripps a reply which expressed feelings of hurt and surprise. It also made accusations. Azad sought to rebut the stand Cripps now adopted with regard to such key issues as 'formation and empowerment of national govrnment' and 'defence formula'. Based on the course of negotiations and shifting stand of Cripps over time, Azad observed that the British Government clearly seemed to be giving priority to holding on to its rule in India by promoting discord and disruption than organising an effective defence for the country against impending invasion. Though the two leaders exchanged letters, it was clear that the spirit that animated their 'dialogue' initially has died.

Tonight Cripps spoke to Indians through a radio broadcast. He lamented that the Congress has been repeatedly demanding declaration of Indian independence and a constituent assembly for framing of a new and free constitution for India and HMG, through his proposal, accommodated both of them, but to no avail. He thereafter dwelt at length as to why the demands that the Congress made could not be met. He claimed that the offer he brought, was to help India along her road to victory and to 'freedom'. 'But', Cripps regretted, 'for the moment, past distrust has proved too strong to allow of present agreement'.[115]

Roosevelt Fails To Persuade Britain, Cripps Leaves India Mission Unaccomplished

April 12, 1942, New Delhi Washington: US president Roosevelt has been keeping an anxious eye over the Cripps mission. He has been keen about securing willing cooperation of India in the Allies war efforts generally and in particular to be able to neutralise Japan. Recently he stepped up pressure on Churchill to concede India's demands for self government and in return secure her total cooperation in the Allies war efforts.

The tidings reaching him from Delhi and London were

disappointing however. On being briefed that Cripps was about to return home, Roosevelt sent a telegram[116] to Churchill through his trusted adviser Harry Hopkins, urging the British prime minister to postpone Cripps' departure and make a final attempt to strike an agreement with the Indians.

He pointed out the public perception in his country that the talks are failing due to the British Government's unwillingness to concede the right of 'self-government' to Indians, even though Indians have been willing 'to entrust to the competent British authorities technical military and naval defence control'. The US President has urged Churchill to give an opportunity to the component groups in India to form a nationalist government similar to the one in US under the Articles of Confederation now so that the Indians can, over time and through trial and error, determine upon their own form of constitution and future relationship with the British empire. He finally asserted that if, despite making such an offer, Cripps still could not evoke an agreement from the Indians, the US people would be satisfied that 'the British Government had made a fair and real offer to the Indian people'[12] and hold the Indian people clearly responsible for the breakdown.

Today Cripps left for London at the instruction of Churchill notwithstanding the last hour persuasion by the US President. His departure is being seen as an abrupt action without giving the process a fair opportunity. Obviously, Roosevelt will be disappointed. Here in India, Cripps' suddenly calling off his mission, has left several Congress leaders shocked, surprised and dismayed.

Agree To Pakistan, Take Our Cooperation: League

April 15, 1942, New Delhi: In a press statement, Jinnah has expressed willingness to political adjustments with others, if all parties agreed to Pakistan and the Muslim demand for self-determination while the details may be settled after the conclusion of the war. Coming at a turbulent time marked by the shadow of external threat and recent failure of the Cripps mission, Jinnah's statement is being viewed as politically significant.

Parched Soil Of India Needs Blood, Tears Of Her Children

April 16, 1942, New Delhi: Sir Stafford Cripps the master diplomat, has left India leaving behind debris of ill feelings. He had generated hills of false hopes and then refused to accept their ownership and returned home in a huff. Even Roosevelt found it difficult to reconcile with the fact that such an important mission could be abandoned in such irrational manner—not providing Indians with a chance of self-government when, in return, Britain could get them to willingly and extensively participate in the Allied war efforts. Amongst Indian leaders, the general reaction has been one of intense disappointment and this was reflected best in Jawaharlal's statement. [117]

> '...We want to live our lives in our own way without interference from any outsider, and to get rid of this world of non-official Excellencies and Highnesses... Our appetite for freedom is insatiable. It was not what we wanted that we told Cripps but something we considered essential and irreducible if we were to shoulder effectively today's burden and defend this dear country to the utmost... It surprises me how far we went in our desire for a settlement... The War is upon us... Our time in India itself is coming and therefore we went to uttermost limits of concession in talks with Cripps for we were anxious to face this peril with the organised power of the State and our masses functioning together. That is not to be now...Whether we remain up or down we shall do it bravely with dignity...Our blood and tears will flow; maybe the parched soil of India needs them so that the fine flower of freedom may grow again.'

Japanese Threat Looms Large In South India, Towns Emptied, Government Offices Moved Inland

April 18, 1942, Madras: The Japanese threat has been on the rise. After they established control over the Bay of Bengal, several ships have been sunk. The air raids over Visakhapatnam and Cocanada have already spread terror amongst people.

A communique[118] sent by the governor of Madras to the Viceroy today, reveals a state of sheer panic in the southern part of the country. It mentions of a report that 'a large Japanese force was on its way to south India and the spearhead could be expected to arrive any day after the 15th' April. The report caused several troops movement and the government offices have been pushed into the interiors—half to Ooty and another half to Chittoor district. It mentions that towns are being emptied and also of deep resentment in people for want of appropriate defence equipments to counter the Japanese aggression.

Resist Any Attempts To Commit Active War Support To The British: Gandhi To Vallabhbhai

April 22, 1942, Sevagram: With Japanese presence in Burma as well as in the Bay of Bengal, and their sporadic attacks on the marine vessels and bombing of a few coastal cities, tension has begun to grip both the British Government and the Indian political parties. Considering their lightening success in expelling the British from Southeast Asian countries, the threat from the Japanese war machine can be ignored at one's peril.

Obviously upset at the unfolding events, the British regime has been inviting foreign legions into India to fortify her borders. American soldiers have begun to arrive already. Talks of scorched earth policy are being heard more frequently. Not only are the British Government, many in the Congress are also exercised by the border threat. Recently Jawaharlal has issued a press statement resolving to launch guerrilla warfare against the Japanese, in the event they invaded India.

In the above backdrop, the AICC is scheduled to meet at Allahabad in less than a week's time to take a call on the emerging situation. It is expected to provide a roadmap to the party and the people. Gandhi has been seemingly upset by Jawaharlal's press statement and the emotional upsurge in many Congressmen and leaders desiring to fight against the Japanese, even if that tantamounts to fighting side by side with the British. He holds this as contravention to the principle of non-violence.

He does not want the people to get emotionally swayed and abandon this golden principle. Today he has written[120] to Vallabhbhai, who would attend the AICC meet at Allahabad, urging the necessity to stick to the core principle of non-violence. He suggested that it would be advisable for the latter to resign from the committee if 'they do not adopt an unambiguous resolution of non-violent non-cooperation'. Gandhi has also instructed him to oppose the 'scorched earth policy' and proposals to invite foreign troops into the country.

IT IS A QUESTION OF CHOOSING THE LESSER EVIL

April 23, 1942, Madras: The Japanese threat at the eastern border and the suspect British ability to defend India has been disconcerting to many Indians. A willing partnership between the Congress and the British regime, which was the aim of the Cripps mission, could have worked as a bulwark against the Japanese. But Cripps failed to invoke the necessary agreement. More than other Congress leaders, Rajagopalachari has probably been hurt by this failure. At the same time, any indigenous initiative to form a national government at the centre so that Indians could defend themselves also seems impossible because the Muslim League has been rejecting such an idea unless its demand of Pakistan is acceded to 'in principle'. To tide over the impasse, Rajagopalachari, an unconventional thinker and a pragmatic leader, has taken an unprecedented initiative. Today, the Congress members in the Madras provincial legislature have passed a resolution recommending to the AICC that the Congress should acknowledge the League's demand for separation and that negotiations should begin immediately to secure an agreement on the issue, so that a national government may be installed to meet the present emergency. The resolution has questioned the wisdom of sacrificing the chances of the formation of a national government for the doubtful advantage of maintaining a controversy over the unity of India. It is a question of choosing the lesser evil, the resolution contended.

I'll Fight Bose If He Comes To India With The Japs

April 24, 1942 Guwahati: The Japanese have driven out the British from Burma. There are reports that after a long victory run, they are regrouping in Burma and might launch an offensive upon Imphal anytime. Though Subhas is still in Berlin, there are rumours that he might move to Southeast Asia and undertake an Indian armed struggle with assistance from the Japanese to drive out the British from India.

Jawaharlal, who is in Assam, seems to be completely against any such move. Today, in a press meet here, he denounced Hitler and Japan and said he would fight them to the end. He said he would also fight Subhas Bose and his force if Bose came to India with the Japanese. He said Bose has acted very wrongly, though in good faith.

Cripps Proposal: A Post-dated Cheque On A Failing Bank

April 1942: As Gandhi had wanted, Azad and Jawaharlal negotiated with Cripps on behalf of the Indian National Congress while keeping their colleagues in the working committee regularly appraised and simultaneously availing of the benefit of their views. Cripps, on his part, explored ways and means to obtain willing support of the Congress. The draft declaration of the British Government that he brought with him had assured India dominion status at the end of the war. It obviously presupposed British victory which, however, seemed to be a matter of speculation as of now. Further, the nature and form of the future government of India and modalities of its formation as envisaged in the Cripps' proposals seemed vague. Worse, even in their obscurity, they seemed to incorporate the seeds for Balkanisation of India.

In return for these questionable offerings, Cripps wanted India to rise as one body and lend her complete might to Allied war efforts under British leadership. Ironically, Indians were expected, at the same time, not to have any effective say about defence policies and programme of actions relating to their own country during the war time. Gandhi summed up these assessments in a single sentence, saying that the proposals were in the nature of a post-dated cheque on a bank that seemed at the moment to be failing.[121]

Political India Buries Cripps Proposals

It was after a detailed appraisal that the Congress had decided to withdraw from further negotiation with Cripps. The other political parties too have chosen to reject his proposals, each for its own reasons. Significantly, Cripps mostly held negotiations with Congress leaders, Azad and Jawaharlal, which made Jinnah and the League leaders unhappy. On the flip side, it gave them the advantage to watch the course of negotiations and bargain thereafter, if such an opportunity arose. However, on the whole, the League found no attraction in the proposal and need to intervene. It rejected the offer although the proposal gave scope, even if somewhat far-fetched, to the Muslim majority provinces to come out of India and establish Pakistan. Jinnah has been critical that the proposals did not expressly recognise the entity and integrity of the Muslim nation. He has been keen that any proposal must have to unequivocally recognise the Muslim right of national self-determination. He felt that Cripps' proposal fell short of that requirement. Jinnah was also uncomfortable about the procedure for drafting the constitution, which he felt was left vague in Cripps' offer.

Sikhs have rejected the offer because under the proposal, Punjab, being a Muslim majority province, could opt out of the Indian union, thereby putting Sikhs to the permanent subjugation of the Muslims.

Ambedkar has rejected it as he thought the proposal would facilitate Caste-Hindus' domination over the depressed classes.

Gandhi's Draft Resolution Raises Doubts Over British Ability To Defend India

April 27-May 1, 1942, Allahabad: Over the last few months, the Japanese forces chased the British and British Indian troops away from Malaya and Singapore, and then entered Burma in hot pursuit. The demoralised British and British Indian troops have been evacuating Burma and taking refuge in Assam and Manipur in India.

The presence of the Japanese across the Indo-Burma border has not only been causing deep disquiet in the British rulers, Gandhi himself is a worried person. He has grown doubtful about the British ability to defend India against the Japanese in the event of the latter choosing to invade the country. In such a situation, Gandhi sees the distinct possibility of the pent-up communal passion breaking out in the form of violent communal riots across India.

The Cripps mission was a breather and aroused some expectations. However, with its failure, the flicker of hope that the British might entrust the destiny of the country to the Indians has extinguished. The threats of Japanese invasion and the questionable British ability to defend India have begun to exercise the Congress once again. The Congress Working Committee has been meeting here since 27 April to address this issue. Though Gandhi is not attending it, he had drafted a lengthy resolution and sent it to Jawaharlal to be put before the AICC. The resolution contended that the British presence in India is acting as the red herring, attracting the Japanese into the country and they would retreat if the British left India. If after the British quit India, Japan still attack her, the Congress would offer non-violent resistance, it has added.

GIST OF GANDHI'S RESOLUTION

The salient features of Gandhi's resolution[122] put before the AICC are:

a. The Congress is of the opinion that Britain is incapable of defending India and whatever she does is for her own defense. The conflicts between Indian and British interests are eternal.
b. British Government has no trust in Indian political parties… the Indian army is segregated from general people of India… the policy of mistrust continues and that is the reason the national defence is not entrusted to India's elected representatives.
c. Japan does not have any quarrel with India, she is warring against the British empire. India's participation in the war was purely a British act. If India was freed, her first step will probably be to negotiate with Japan.
d. If the British withdrew from India, India would be able to defend herself in the event of Japanese or any other external aggression.
e. The British contention that their presence in India is necessary to give protection to the princes of native states is unfounded—the princes need have no fear from an unarmed India.

f. The question of majority and minority is a British creation and would disappear upon their withdrawal.
g. The committee appeals to Britain to let go her hold on India, for her own safety, safety of India and for the sake of world peace.
h. The committee assures the Japanese government and people that India bears no enmity, either towards Japan or any other nation. But in the fight for her freedom, while India welcomes universal sympathy, she does not need foreign military aid. The committee hopes Japan will not have any designs on India. But if Japan attacks India and Britain makes no response to its appeal, the Congress will offer non-violent non-cooperation to the Japanese force.
i. When the two sides are fighting against each other, the Congress does not propose to put any obstacles before the British as these will tantamount to placing 'our country' deliberately in Japanese hands.
j. With regard to the scorched earth policy (being pursued by the British), the resolution says, despite its non-violent resistance, if any part of India falls into Japanese forces, Indians may not destroy their own crops or water supply etc. if only because it will be their endeavour to regain these later.
k. On the issue of the introduction of foreign soldiers in India during the war, the committee feels that it is harmful to India's interest and dangerous to the cause of freedom. The Congress committee appeals to the British Government to remove the foreign legions and henceforth stop their further introduction.

Crucial AICC Resolution – Jawaharlal Prevails Over Gandhi

May 1, 1942, Allahabad: The AICC session has been in progress here since April 29th. Coming together in a turbulent time and keen to chalk out the party's next course of action in the aftermath of the collapse of the Cripps mission, the members deliberated on Gandhi's resolution. Jawaharlal was upset about quite a few things in it including a somewhat friendly reference to the Japanese and objection to the presence of foreign soldiers in India.

The latter has been a crucial component of the war strategy of the Allies, whose cause he consistently sympathised with. Jawaharlal has been convinced about the need of Allied troops' presence in India for defending her against possible Japanese invasion. He put forth his views forcefully and this has led to the rejection of Gandhi's resolution—a rare occurrence in the annals of the Congress. In its place, Jawaharlal has introduced another resolution, that in several respects is akin to Gandhi's draft resolution but has some key differences.

First, the important features common to both the resolutions. These are: (a) In the event Japan invades India, the Congress will offer complete non-violent non-cooperation to the Japanese forces; (b) The Congress will continue its non-cooperation with the British. However where both the British and the Japanese are fighting, the Committee will not put any obstacles for the British.

Next, the important differences: Jawaharlal's resolution a. avoids all 'friendly references' to Japan or her people b. does not expressly state that Britain was incapable of defending India against invasion; c. says that if India were a free country and she was forced to the war, she would have undertaken her defence with a 'national army' (incidentally, it constitutes a serious violation of Gandhi's principle of 'nonviolence'); d. does not make any express appeal to Britain to leave India forthwith, but only states that under the given condition, it is impossible for the Congress to render it any cooperation e. is silent about the Committee's stand on the 'scorched earth policy'; f. does not raise any demand for sending back the foreign soldiers from Indian soil, nor does it ask to stop getting more of them in future, but merely criticises the British Government for importing them by arguing that past experiences prove these are dangerous for the cause of freedom of India. After prolonged deliberations, Jawaharlal's draft has been passed.

I Need No Credentials When I Speak To My Own People: Subhas

May 1, 1942, Berlin: The British Government, anxious about Subhas' collaboration with the Axis countries and his serial radio broadcasts addressed to the Indians, has been trying to malign his image by calling him as enemy agent and betrayer of his own country. In a speech broadcast through Berlin Radio today, Subhas sought to dispel any misgivings in the minds of his countrymen when he said:

'...I have laughed whenever I have heard Britain's paid propagandists calling me an enemy agent. I need no credentials when I speak to my own people... My allegiance and my loyalty has ever been and will ever be to India and to India alone, no matter in which part of the world I may live at any given time.'[119]

Rejection Of Cripps Is A Matter Of Joy And Pride For Indians: Subhas Speaks Over Radio From Germany

May 1, 1942, Berlin: In a broadcast from Berlin, Subhas has expressed his happiness that India has rejected the Cripps offer. He opined that the offer that promises independence in future against cooperation to be offered by the Indians immediately, as contemptible. He described the rejection as, 'a matter of joy and pride to Indians in every part of the world.'[123]

VIVISECTION OF INDIA? NO WAY, Vehement AICC Snubs Rajagopalachari By 120-15 Votes

April 29 - May 2, 1942, Allahabad: The resolution passed last month by the Madras legislature at the behest of Rajagopalachari recommending to the AICC that the Congress accedes to the League's demand for separation for the sake of forming a national government immdiately, had created extensive surprise and discontentment amongst Congressmen. In the AICC session underway here, Rajagopalachari has been vehemently opposed.

Undaunted, he resigned from the working committee and thus, freeing himself from concomitant obligations, moved a resolution stating that in the event the League agrees to support the demand for independence and join the national government, the Congress would concede the League's demand for separation from India, subject to some safeguards. The AICC has rejected the resolution by a whopping 120-15 votes, so intense has been the opposition to what most members thought of as a proposal for India's vivisection. The AICC did not rest content with the rejection but the fury spilled over and engendered a counter-resolution that sought to seal any future venture in the line of the resolution just defeated. Thus, another member, Jagat Narayan Lal moved a resolution that pointed out that any proposal to disintegrate India or give any component state or territorial unit the liberty to secede from the Indian Union being detrimental to the interests of the people, cannot be agreed to by the Congress. It was passed by 92-17 votes.

Resolution Doesn't Say What I Wanted To Tell The World

May 5, 1942, Sevagram: Gandhi has been unhappy that the draft resolution he had sent to the AICC meet was substituted by another. In a letter written today to Azad, the Congress president, he has voiced his disappointment. Noting that there was a 'vast difference' between the two resolutions, Gandhi pointed out that what he had intended to tell the world was missing in the resolution that was finally adopted.

Gandhi also referred to the major differences of opinion amongst the committee members that had surfaced in the recent AICC meet and suggested that it was better that the dissenting members left the committee. In this connection, he has opined that Azad should accept the resignation of Vallabhbhai and five or six other members and form a new committee.

Subhas Persuades Mussolini On Axis Declaration About Indian Independence

May 5, 1942, Rome: Subhas has been working hard to get a tripartite declaration by Germany, Italy and Japan in favour of the Indian independence. He has not been able to get any commitment from Nazi Germany. He recently travelled to Italy and held a meeting with Mussolini when he made a strong and convincing case for India's freedom. At the end of the meeting today, Subhas was able to persuade the Italian premier to take initiative on the matter. It is learnt that Mussolini has telegraphed the German authorities, urging them to proceed at once with the declaration.

Japanese Drive Out British, Chinese Forces From Burma

May 20, 1942, Imphal: After conceding Rangoon, the British regime had determined to confine the Japanese to the south of Burma. Not allowing them to come closer to India, emerged as a key British priority. In this, they were fully supported by America and Generalissimo Chiang Kai-shek, the head of the nationalist government of China.

America has been helping Chiang's government against the occupier Japanese regime in China. After losing Rangoon, the road from Rangoon to the Yunnan province of China which served as a supply route became unavailable to the Allies. As a result, the Ledo Road airstrip in north eastern Assam bordering north western Burma could alone be used to airlift American supplies and its protection emerged as a key concern for both America and the Generalissimo. All three parties were therefore unanimous that the Japanese had to be kept below the Prome and Toungoo line, situated at about 150 miles north of Rangoon. Chian Kai-shek grew so concerned that he sent the Chinese V, VI and LXVI armies to join the British forces and hold the Japanese. The British inducted William Slim, a veteran general leading the Allied forces in the Middle East, into the Burma war theatre. He formed the Burma Corp and tried to resist the Japanese.

But nothing worked. As the Japanese forces began to move north, the combined resistance melted rapidly. The Chinese armies were badly shattered. The VI Chinese army has virtually disintegrated. Several have retreated into China. But many have forfeited that opportunity. One full Chinese division is reportedly scouting for opportunity to escape to India.

The British forces were continuously attacked and harassed so much that Slim had to escape to Imphal, in India along with his beleaguered Burma Corp. Today he has surrendered his surviving troops to 4 Corps head quarters here. The Japanese troops have now practically no adversary in Burma and they have free run up to the east bank of the Chindwin River facing the entire Assam front. To the British regime, the Japanese presence in such close proximity is creating a scare. Imphal the eastern most Indian town, to the west of Chindwin, has become vulnerable to Japanese invasion.

Subhas Bose Meets Adolf Hitler
Much Awaited Tête-à-Tête Delivers Little

May 29, 1942, Berlin: In the wake of the Japanese conquest of British territories in Southeast Asia, Subhas has been giving serious thoughts to shift to the eastern theatre of action, for which he needs an invitation from Japan and logistical assistance from Germany. Here, he has founded the Free India Centre and raised the Indian Legion from amongst the Indian PoW. But he finds the scope rather limited due to a lukewarm German approach to the issue of Indian freedom. Today, accompanied by Ribbentrop, the Foreign Minister, Subhas has met Hitler, the head of the Nazi government for the first time since his coming to Germany.

Subhas had expected the meeting to open up several interesting possibilities in the ongoing war against the British. In comparison, it was uneventful. Hitler pointed to the enormous geographical distance between Germany and India. He also opined that any declaration in favour of Indian independence at this stage would be premature. However, he dwelt at length on the Japanese conquest over Britain in Asia and agreed to help Subhas to travel to Japan. Cautioning against air travel, Hitler has agreed to provide a submarine at his disposal. After today's meeting, Subhas is disillusioned. The silver lining is Hitler's promise of assistance to him to travel to East Asia. Subhas is keen to utilise the offer.

Sikh 'No' To Domination By One Community: Akali Dal

Although the Unionist Party in Punjab has nominally been a secular political outfit, its policies, particularly those adopted since the conclusion of the Sikandar-Jinnah pact, has been tinged with communal bias. Things obviously grew worse since the adoption of the Pakistan resolution by the Muslim League a couple of years ago. The Sikhs are particularly upset. In the event the Pakistan proposal is acceded to, they apprehend that they will be the worst-affected community. Sikhs, in general and the Akalis, in particular, have been vehemently opposing any move to partition India. Leaders like Master Tara Singh and

Kartar Singh are preparing to fight the Pakistan proposal with grit and determination. Challenging the resolution, Master Tara Singh has already announced that Pakistan can be created only over their dead bodies.It may be mentioned that the Sikhs are scattered all over Punjab and they do not have overwhelming majority in any one well-defined geographical area to be able to claim as their own to the exclusion of the others. However, confident in own abilities and strength, they do not feel the need to make such partisan demands either. They only want to live in a province where no single community has absolute domination. In other words, the Sikhs would be comfortable provided all the three communities Hindus, Muslims and Sikhs are present in normal proportion. Tara Singh had even written to the Cripps Commission suggesting that though the Sikhs do not have domination over any particular area, a province could certainly be created in which the Sikhs would not be dominated by one single community.

Good Intention And Perseverance Fall Flat Congress Finally Mulls Hard Option

June, 1942, Wardha: Congress is groping for a direction. There have been serious differences between Gandhi and many others, especially Jawaharlal, about the desirability of the Allied troops being stationed in India. To the British, the presence of the armed forces of the 'allied countries' in India is logistically important to pursue war against the Axis powers. But Gandhi has been insisting upon their removal from Indian shores. Jawaharlal has a radically different opinion. He has been insisting that the presence of these forces would be indispensable to defend India against the Japanese.

At the same time, the Congress does not also want to be seen as a British stooge. The image of a weak, compromising party would cause further damage to its already tenuous hold over its own workers and Indians in general. It not only wants to remain at the vanguard of the national struggle but also likes to be perceived by the public as playing such role.

To bring about a reconciliation between these two imperatives, he party has again approached Gandhi. He can resolve contradictory orces with consummate skill. However, Gandhi's own stand on the emoval of the Allied troops has been a bone of contention between im and the Jawaharlal camp and the party had to sort this issue out.

Now, to the relief of the Congress leaders, a compromise has been eached on this issue and it has been decided that the Allied troops vould be withdrawn after India becomes free. With this key issue esolved, the Congress has been able to persuade Gandhi to be back on he saddle and guide the party. Gandhi is now expected to formulate trategies for the next stage of the freedom struggle.

llied And Axis Forces Get Into See-saw Mode

une 1942: Hitler's decision to overstretch his resources by invading ussia appears to have been a strategic blunder. Similarly, Japan's ssault on Pearl Harbour that inducted the USA as a party to the War lso seems to be working against the Axis powers as a whole. In an ct of major retaliation, the US Navy has recently inflicted a crushing efeat on the Japanese naval power. In a sea battle off Midway Island, it as sunk four large Japanese aircraft carriers. Now, in the continent of frica, German superiority has come under stiff challenge. There are arly signals of a trend reversal in the war across the world. The Allied owers, at long last, have begun to see rays of hope. In the Axis camp owever, Japan's success in Southeast Asia is being seen as a positive evelopment. After the conquest of Philippines, Malaya, Hong Kong nd Singapore, its armed forces remain deeply entrenched in Burma. successful invasion of India can again reinforce Axis superiority y dismantling one of the main resource bases of the Allied power.

ata Steel A Casualty Of 'Scorched Earth Policy'?

une, 1942, New Delhi: Gandhi had strongly written in *Harijan* gainst the 'scorched earth policy' three months ago. By now the panese threat has increased manifold and the policy is being iscussed more vigorously in government circles.

According to sources, the government may destroy bridges, factories and industrial establishments, in the event its forces are compelled to retreat from the eastern provinces into the heartland due to Japanese advance. Boats in the coastal areas of the Bay of Bengal are already being destroyed in hundreds and thousands, at the cost of disrupting the movement of food grains especially in Bengal. Rumours are floating that should the Japanese army manage to enter into Assam and Bengal, even the Jamshedpur steel factory of the Tatas would also be destroyed to prevent its falling into the Japanese hands. There is all-round anxiety and unrest amongst people in these areas.

After Tokyo, Emigré Indians Assemble At Bangkok, Vow To Liberate Their Motherland

June 15 to 23, 1942, Bangkok: Over hundred delegates representing nearly three million Indians settled in places like Malaya, Burma, Thailand, Java, Sumatra, Borneo, the Philippines, Japan, Manchukuo, Nanking, Shanghai, Canton, Hong Kong and adjoining places assembled here to discuss plans to liberate their motherland. This conference came in the wake of the previous one held in Tokyo three months ago. Rashbherai Bose was elected as the presiding chairman. The importance of the conference can be gauged from the fact that many dignitaries and diplomats, including ambassadors of Japan, Germany and Italy participated in the proceedings. A message from Subhas was read out.

It was decided to proclaim the Indian Independence League as the apex civilian body that would work to achieve the goal of Indian independence. After the Tokyo conference, the delegates worked hard to spread the branches of the IIL throughout the region. Now it was decided that numerous other Indian organisations in the Southeast Asia would merge into the IIL. The Indian National Army was declared as the military arm of the movement with Mohan Singh as its general officer commanding (GOC). The conference specified the Council of Action as its executive body, which would be a steering committee. Rashbehari Bose has been elected as the president of the Council of Action.

There would be two members each from the civilian and military wing. N Raghavan and KPK Menon would be the civilian members, Mohan Singh and Lt Col GQ Gilani would represent the military. In the conference, Capt Mohan Singh, GOC of the INA voiced some apprehension on the status and functioning of the INA. At his insistence, the IIL has sent a bunch of queries to the Japanese government and requested for an item-wise reply. Some of these are in regard to (a) placing all Indian soldiers in territories of Japanese occupation under the control of the INA; (b) obtaining clarification on the status of the INA, insisting it should be treated at par with the Japanese army; (c) using INA only for the purpose of Indian independence; (d) securing guarantee by the Japanese government that after liberating India from the British, the Japanese will respect the territorial integrity and full sovereignty of India, etc. Many of these are clarifications cum requests.

As the conference concluded, a new tide of hope and optimism was seen in delegates and also the local Indians. The Independence League, assisted by an armed wing, viz. the INA, in combination with the formidable Japanese military power, was being perceived as a challenger to the once mighty but now tottering British empire. There was yet another golden hope. The conference invited Subhas Chandra Bose to come over to Southeast Asia and take over the leadership of the League.

Forward Bloc Declared Illegal

June 23, 1942, New Delhi: The British Government has declared the Forward Bloc an illegal organisation. It is wary of the plans and programmes of Subhas, aimed directly against Britain and does not want any political organisation within India to lend Subhas or his programmes any kind of support - overtly or covertly.

It may be mentioned that Sarat Chandra Bose, the elder brother of Subhas and known to be sympathetic to Subhas and his causes, has been languishing in a distant prison in the Madras province. The government had earlier arrested him on the charge of conspiracy with the Japanese consul in Calcutta. Fearing an invasion in the eastern border, the government is keeping keen vigil over everyone it suspects capable of creating unrest in India and helping the enemy.

Viceroy Inducts Indian Members In His Council

July 2, 1942, New Delhi: As the British Government faces an imminent Japanese threat from across Burma, the Viceroy has today expanded his executive council. He has carved out a war department from the defence department and placed it under the charge of Lord Wavell, the commander-in-chief. The other part has been entrusted to Sir Firoz Khan Noon, an Indian. The Viceroy has also inducted five additional Indian members now including inter alia BR Ambedkar, JP Srivastava, and Jogendra Singh in his cabinet. Political experts see these changes as an attempt to bestow to his executive council the cosmetic look of a 'national government'. The Congress is, however, not satisfied. It is growing increasingly tense over the Japanese presence in Burma. The party is likely to review the emerging situation in the forthcoming meeting of its working committee and take some hard decisions.

CONGRESS WANTS BRITISH RAJ TO QUIT INDIA

July 6-14, 1942, Wardha: The Congress Working Committee has just concluded a crucial meeting to formulate its policies and programmes in a politically grave situation where India's border has become exposed to potential Japanese invasion and the colonial regime does not seem competent to defend the country, but at the same time would not let India free so that Indians can rise to defend themselves. The working committee deliberated the underlying issues with Gandhi as its guide, to forge an appropriate response.

At the end, the CWC has passed a resolution that has indicated a sea change in the Congress position with regard to ongoing political negotiations with the British regime. It declared that the Congress has been compelled by circumstances created by the British regime to demand the latter's immediate withdrawal from India and unless they do so, the Congress would change gear ie. switch from individual civil disobedience to mass civil disobedience to force the issue.

The resolution does not strike assent in some of the top leaders. Azad, the Congress president, is not convinced. Rajagopalachari vehemently opposed it. However, Gandhi loyalists like Patel, Kripalani and Rajendra Prasad relied on Gandhi's judgement completely. At the end, most of the leaders realised that there is hardly any alternative to this resolution to save the Congress from enormous divisions and drifts. Both Gandhi and Jawaharlal described it as an open rebellion, even if it would be non-violent.

KEY FEATURES OF THE CWC RESOLUTION

The resolution[124] expresses Congress' conviction that the British rule in India must end immediately especially, because being in bondage, India can play 'no effective part in defending herself and in affecting the fortunes of the war that is desolating humanity'. Her freedom is necessary not only in her interest but also for world safety and ending Nazism, Fascism, militarism, and other forms of imperialism and the aggression of one nation over another.

The resolution clarifies that the Congress has been carrying out satyagraha in a manner not to embarrass the British prosecution of war and with the hope that carried to the logical extreme, the real power will be transferred to people's representatives. However, the actions of the British Government, especially revealed through the Cripps mission, confirms that they want to keep India under their subjugation. This has created much bitterness in Indian people against the British and there is growing satisfaction among Indian people at the success of the Japanese. The Congress is upset at these and it is keen to again convert such 'ill will' into 'goodwill' for the British. It also wants to build up resistance amongst people against aggression or invasion by Japan or any other foreign power.

On the vexed question of communal settlement, the resolution says the presence of foreign power has made it impossible to achieve any agreement on the issue so far. But the people will sort this issue out after the foreign power withdraws.

As regards the formation of the successor government after withdrawal by the British, the resolution proposes that responsible men and women of the country will come together to form a provisional government and evolve a scheme for convening a constituent assembly to prepare a constitution applicable to all sections of people.

On the relations with Great Britain in future and fighting against the aggressors at present, the resolution says, the representatives of the provisional government of free India and Great Britain will confer for adjustment of their future relations and for cooperation between two countries as allies in the common task of meeting the aggression presently. In this connection, the Congress is agreeable to foreign troops being stationed in India in order to ward off or resist the Japanese or other aggression and to protect and help China. The resolution has clarified that the Congress' insistence on withdrawal by the British from India does not refer to their physical withdrawal but their withdrawal as the 'ruler of the country' only. The resolution recognises that there may be a lack of stability in the country following the withdrawal by the British but adds that these were inevitable and have to be faced for the cause of freedom.

Terming all these demands as reasonable and just, the resolution has said that the Congress would be pleased if they are accepted. If not, the party apprehends that there would be progressive deterioration in the situation and also weakening of India's will and power to resist aggression. In such an eventuality, the resolution has concluded, the Congress will be reluctantly compelled to utilise all the Non-violent strength it has gathered since 1920 in launching a struggle under Gandhi for the vindication of India's political rights and liberty.

Quit India – Congress Resolves Inner Contradictions?

Right since September 1939, the Congress has been insulted and humiliated by the British regime time and again. Assured of cooperation by other sections including the native rulers and various communal political parties, the government has been ignoring the Congress and gathering manpower and other resources for war with impunity. Torn asunder by its own contradictory ideological compulsions, the Congress has literally been in self-imposed captivity. Things have come to such a pass and the party suffered such dent in its image that its tenuous hold over the people of India, including even its own members, has begun to slacken.

The working committee had to resuscitate the party's image as a fighter and the premier rival of the British Raj.

There have, however, been important differences of opinions amongst top leadership as to the course of action. Intense deliberations were held over the past two weeks. Gandhi wanted the British to leave India, leaving Indians to their fate. He felt that in such an eventuality, the Japanese would not invade the country. Still, if they did and attempted to occupy the country, the Congress would organise non-violent opposition to them. Jawaharlal, Azad and their supporters, on the other hand, were expecting the British to defend India against any Japanese invasion. They felt the British were already under pressure and any fresh movement would only embarrass them and encourage the Japanese to invade the country. The view held by a large section of the members was that the party must not appear as supplicant of the Empire, and it was time to chisel up its fighting image.

Finally, Gandhi resolved the conflicting viewpoints. It was decided to ask the British to quit India. The discord on the issue of 'foreign troops' was resolved by agreeing to allow their presence in India in terms of a treaty between the Allies and the government of free India. This gesture, the Congress hoped, would allay many misgivings about India's stand vis-à-vis the two warring blocs. The resolution expressed sympathy in favour of the Allied powers supporting their global fight in favour of democracy and freedom. The resolution blew hot and cold. It appealed to the sense of justice of the British to leave India. Simultaneously it issued grim warnings of mass struggle in the event the British chose not to heed to its request. It added the party's concerns that the continuation of the British rule was weakening India and making it progressively more incapable of defending itself. It asked the British to quit India forthwith and leave Indians to their fate.

Significantly, Gandhi, while addressing the members announced that this time the workers would not court arrests voluntarily. On the contrary they would resist arrest and submit if only physically forced to do so. Notwithstanding the aggressive tone and tenor of the resolution, Gandhi, in his characteristic style, has given indication that the Congress would still be open to negotiations with the government. Meanwhile, the resolution also needs to be ratified by the AICC scheduled to meet early next month.

AN IDEA FOR WHICH THE TIME HAS DEPARTED?

The resolution asking the British to leave India under the threat of a national movement adopted by the Congress has created a commotion and its likely impact is being intensely debated. Many political analysts feel that the Congress has already lost precious time in taking this stand. Way back in 1939, Subhas repeatedly appealed to Gandhi to serve the British the ultimatum to give India freedom, coupled with a threat of nationwide non-violent Satyagraha to force the issue. That was possibly the time to act because Britain was under tremendous pressure from Germany and the Axis camp. On the other hand, the Congress had a clear upper hand, being in charge of the governments in majority of the provinces. But Gandhi had repeatedly rejected Subhas's pleas, saying that India was not prepared to launch a nationwide movement.

The Congress not only forfeited the initiative by not acting in 1939 but worse still, allowed a communal party like the Muslim League to take a giant leap for the vivisection of India through the Pakistan Resolution in 1940, ie. within a year thereafter.

Right since September 1939, when the Congress ministries resigned in the provinces, the party had been making itself increasingly irrelevant to the government. Not only did it render

> itself bereft of administrative powers, it was so paralysed by its inner ideological contradictions that it could never effectively prevent the British government from drafting Indian men and material liberally for the purpose of the war.
>
> Now, when Congress has adopted such a bold resolution, its hold over it own members, the Indian people and other resources are considerably weaker. Both the Muslims and the depressed classes have been drifting away from it. On the other hand, Britain has come out of the eclipse and the trend of the world war has begun to show early signs of reversals. As such, the British government is expected to deal with the Congress challenge with firm hands.

Viceroy Refuses To Grant Audience To Mira Behn

July 17, 1942, New Delhi: Gandhi, in pursuing a strategy mix of confrontation and conciliation, had sent his trusted messenger Madeleine Slade (alias Mira Behn) to the Viceroy in Delhi. Even though the resolution of 'Quit India' was a clear act of sedition from the viewpoint of the government, Gandhi wanted Mira to explain to the Viceroy in person the circumstances that led the Congress to adopt such a resolution and also to explore the possibility, even at the eleventh hour, of a solution to the impasse that would be acceptable to both.

But, the Viceroy seemed to be angry. He already had reports of the working committee meeting and the resolution. He had also heard reports of Gandhi and Jawaharlal describing the proposed movement as an 'open rebellion, even if non-violent'. Exasperated by the pressure of the war, the Viceroy seemed to be in no mood to discover the subtle aspects of the oxymoron—a 'non-violent rebellion'. Obsessed with only the 'rebellion' part of the phrase, he has reportedly begun to prepare for a heavy clamp down on the Congress and its leaders. He even refused to see Mira Behn. The latter had to content herself by briefing the Viceroy's private secretary and report back to Gandhi. The message from New Delhi is loud and clear. It is ominous.

Japan Would Be The Sole Beneficiary Of This Mass Movement: Rajagopalachari Warns Gandhi

July 18, 1942, Madras: Since the Congress Working Committee passed the resolution demanding British withdrawal four days ago, India has been in the grip of palpable tension. Amidst unrelenting waves of various shades of emotions sweeping the country, Rajagopalachari has written to Gandhi, attacking the proposal with a set of compelling arguments. The letter is signed by him, together with three others.

In essence, Rajagopalachari while conceding the primacy of demand for complete independence of India from foreign domination has contended that the state is not a superstructure but one intimately interwoven with every form of activity of people. It is impractical to think that as one government withdraws, another takes its place automatically. Unless another government simultaneously replaces the incumbent in an orderly and planned manner, there exists the threat of the dissolution of the state and the society itself. Such a thing would be possible only if the Congress and the Muslim League, two major parties, evolve a joint plan with regard to the provisional government to ensure an orderly transition of power and the continuity of the state.

However, such a possibility does not exist at present. Further, the coexistence of a free Indian government and Allied troops in the country are likely to lead to the military take over of all government functions, which by implications, would tantamount to reinstallation of the British Government in worse form. The proposal, therefore, is an invitation to anarchy and the call for direct action is likely to be crushed by the authorities in power. Therefore, when responsible leaders are removed, the movement runs the risk of being converted into fifth-column activity by the enemy. The only beneficiary of the resultant chaos would indeed be Japan.

Rajagopalachari has thus registered his dissatisfaction. He ended hoping that the movement 'will operate as a protest with an international appeal and bring about a fresh approach towards a political settlement for India without actually plunging the country in direct action'.[125]

Beware Of Congress And Gandhi, Remain Vigilant: Jinnah Warns Muslims

July 23, 1942, Bhopal: Today while speaking to the press here, Jinnah has expressed concerns over the dangerous political situation that has arisen due to the Congress' intransigent political move, giving a call for direct action. He has referred to the Congress resolution and Gandhi's speeches in this connection. In view of the extraordinary situation, he has advised Muslims to remain vigilant.

Government Lifts Ban On Communist Party Of India

July 24, 1942, New Delhi: Today, the government has lifted the ban on the Communist Party of India. The party has been following a pro-British policy right since the time Germany invaded Russia, the Mecca of Communists. The government has been receiving intelligence reports about such change in approach on the part of the Communists. Now the threat emanating from the belligerent Congress seems to have acted as the trigger to lift the ban on it. The Communists would add to the stock of anti-Congress political constellation, giving the government support and moral legitimacy. Further, given the Communists' hold over the workers' union and the need to keep the factories running during the war, this gesture may prove beneficial to the government.

Congress Is Aiming To Establish Hindu Raj Under The Aegis Of British Bayonet: Jinnah

July 31, 1942, Bombay: Jinnah has been keeping a close watch over the Congress call to the British to withdraw from India. A statement[126] issued by him to a foreign press betrayed his unhappiness, irritation and suspicion. He has described the latest decision by the working committee to launch a mass movement unless the British withdrew as an attempt by Gandhi and the Congress at blackmailing the British and coercing them to 'concede a system of government and transfer power to that government which would establish a Hindu raj immediately under the aegis of the British bayonet' and, thus placing Muslims and other minorities at the mercy of the Congress raj.

Conflict With Government Escalating Fast, Gandhi Has Little Time To Work Out Plan Details

Battle lines between the government and the Congress are being rapidly drawn. As regards the government, it has decided to nip the movement in the bud. This is 'war time' and it cannot afford the luxury of allowing a mass movement to pick up momentum and act thereafter. According to reliable sources, the government wants to resort to summary action and stifle the movement 'here and now', lest it dislocates its war plans and activities across the globe. It is taking guard, expeditiously. The Congress has many problems. It has lost much of its fighting sheen due to inner-party dissensions over ideology. Right since 1939, the Congress, driven by panic and ideological confusion, has been doing a series of flip flops—pulling itself sometimes closer and sometimes away from Gandhi. Then, if the two years (1937-39) of being 'in office' corrupted many Congressmen, the next nearly three years of being 'away from it' denuded it of its political and financial muscles. No less importantly, the Congress workers and leaders have been far from any mass movement for about a decade now. On top of everything, Gandhi has very limited time to plan the details this time unlike the past two major movements of non-cooperation and civil disobedience, both of which he had planned meticulously. The net result is that he has not been able to organise his party men to his satisfaction, to wage an all out war against the powerful British regime.

Defend Your Country, Protect World Freedom: Viceroy

August 7, 1942, New Delhi: The British government has reacted to the Congress call for direct action with alacrity. Refusing to accept the Congress party as the mouthpiece of India and laying stress on the fact that great sections of India's population have already been supporting the British war efforts, the goverment in a resolution[127] condemned the Congress proposal. In essence, the government said the acceptance of the Congress proposal would be wholly incompatible with their responsibility to the people of India, to the Allies and it would cripple its efforts in the cause of human freedom in general. It has castigated the Congress for impeding the process of constitutional development time and again but for which India would have achieved self-government by now. The government promised that after the victory in the war, Indians will be given full opportunity to erect the final structure of their country's constitution. In the meantime the government stressed upon its responsibility to defend the Indian people against anarchy internally and the Japanese externally. It also mentioned about its commitment to discharge its role vis-à-vis the Allies and the humanities, especially Russia and China, both facing Axis aggression. The government has exhorted the people of India to unite with them 'in resistance to the present challenge of a party' and to lay aside all political differences for the defence of India, and to protect not only their own future but also that of the freedom-loving people of the world.

Political analysts say, through this document the government has sought to address not only the Indians, but also the rest of the world, especially the Allies, to justify a slew of tough measures that they might be contemplating against the Congress in the immediate future. Cleverly, the government in its own resolution, has skilfully used the Congress arguments like 'world freedom', 'danger to democracy' etc. against the party.

Continuation Under This Rule Is Degrading AICC Warns Of Mass Struggle At Widest Possible Scale

August 7-8, 1942, Bombay: Since the working committee meeting held last month, not only has the war situation in the world and its impact on India worsened, the British Government further hurt its relationship with the Congress by conducting a police raid on the AICC office. The police laid hands on some working notes of the proceedings of the last working committee meeting.

On that basis, the government has begun to project Congress top leaders like Gandhi and Jawaharlal as supporters of the Japanese invasion. Three days ago, Jawaharlal issued a press statement condemning the government for adopting such 'discreditable and dishonourable tactics'. Last month, the working committee had adopted a resolution asking the British to leave India. Today the AICC has put its stamp of approval to that proposal. In its resolution[128] the AICC has called for ending British rule in India immediately and observed that its continuation is 'degrading and enfeebling India' and progressively reducing her capability to defend herself and contribute to the world freedom.

By citing the worsening situation in the Russian and Chinese front, the Committee stated that the increasing perils to world freedom warrant that the Allies ought to examine their policy of domination of the subject and colonial countries. Freedom granted to India, the Committee concluded, would release the energy and enthusiasm of her vast people and enable her to fight the aggressors alongside the Allies—using arms as well as non-violent means. It went on to claim that India's freedom would change the very course of the global war in favour of the Allies.

On the modalities to bring about the above outcome, the Committee has proposed the immediate setting up of a provisional national government representing all important sections of Indian people upon the declaration of Indian independence. It assured that the government of free India will then become an ally of the UN. The provisional government, the resolution said, will evolve a scheme of representative constituent assembly, which will prepare a constitution acceptable to all sections of people. Freedom of India would be a symbol and a prelude to the freedom of the other Asiatic nations under foreign domination.

The committee has appealed to Britain and the UN on the above lines, but it has, at the same time, sanctioned a mass struggle on non-violent lines on the widest possible scale, utilising the full non-violent strength that the country has gathered since 1920. The Committee has urged Indian people to face the danger, hold together under Gandhiji's leadership and carry out his instructions as disciplined soldiers. It said, if a time comes when no Congress committee can function, every man and woman has been instructed to function within the four corners of the general instructions issued. Finally, the Committee has sought to clarify that the Congress has no intention of gaining power. When it comes, it will belong to the entire people of India.

Karenge Ya Marenge
GANDHI SPELLS OUT THE MANTRA

August 7-8, 1942, Bombay: After three long years of vacillation, the Congress has finally stuck its neck out. It has thrown the boldest challenge in its fifty-seven years of history to the British Government. Congressmen can clearly see severe reprisal measures looming large. To the historical Congress-Government equation, a third force ie. Japanese, though invisible, has now begun to exert influence. The outcome of the prospective battle with Japan in the Indo-Burma border can upset the bilateral equation significantly. By its present decision, the Congress has pushed itself to an uncharted terrain, where it will not only have to fight the British to the finish, but also tackle other imponderables, if and when these arise. Such complex situation warrants the highest quality of leadership. For obvious reasons, all the Congressmen and leaders are banking upon Gandhi to navigate[129] them to the destination. To the assembly of Congressmen and leaders listening to him with rapt attention in the AICC session, Gandhi spoke these electrifying words:

"I, therefore, want freedom immediately, this very night, before dawn, if it can be had... You may take it from me that I am not going to strike a bargain with the Viceroy for ministries and the like. I am not going to be satisfied with anything short of complete freedom… Here is a mantra, a short one, that I give you. You may imprint it on your hearts and let every breath of yours give expression to it. The mantra is: 'Do or die'. We shall either free India or die in the attempt: we shall not live to see the perpetuation of our slavery."

Though Gandhi has always stood for nonviolence and it is understood that he expects people to adhere to that golden principle under all circumstances, here in this AICC session in Bombay, he has not highlighted it in the manner that he has done in the past. At the same time, he has made it clear that even if the entire leadership are in prison, the movement must continue and every man and woman has to act within the four walls of the general instructions. 'Take a pledge', he exhorted the people, 'with God and your own conscience as witness that you will no longer rest till freedom is achieved and will be prepared to lay down your lives in the attempt to achieve it. He who loses his life, will gain it; he who will seek to save it, shall lose it. Freedom is not for the coward or the faint-hearted'. The import of such powerful words, according to the political observers, seems to be that once begun, the movement must not be stopped and people may have to make judgements for themselves sooner or later.

Wait For My Meeting With The Viceroy, Gandhi Urges Patience

August 7-8, 1942, Bombay: Though the AICC resolution and Gandhi's speech infused the audience with a spirit to plunge into action forthwith, he has advised them to have patience and wait for his final signal. He said that before launching this 'do or die' struggle, he would like to wait upon the Viceroy and plead with him to accept the Congress view points, which he said may take two or three weeks. In the meantime, he advised people to carry out his 14 point constructive programme and be in readiness. Political observers are not quite hopeful about the feasibility of such a meeting, given the refusal by the Viceroy to meet Mira Behn, Gandhi's representative last month.

GANDHI ARRESTED AT DAWN
Countrywide Crackdown On Congress Leadership

August 9, 1942, Bombay: The AICC session had concluded late last night amidst great excitement. During that time, the government was giving finishing touches to its elaborate plan to round up the top Congress leadership in one sweep by next dawn break. The commissioner of police of Bombay presented himself at the Birla House, where Gandhi was camping in the city, to take him into custody. Gandhi was about to sit for his first prayer. Another senior police officer went to arrest Abul Kalam Azad, the Congress president who was a guest at the house of Bhulabhai Desai. Included in the list of arrested persons were Jawaharlal, Vallabhbhai, Sarojini Naidu, GB Pant, Asaf Ali and several others.

By late morning, all of the top leaders were brought to the Victoria terminus railway station. The place presented an unusual spectacle.

Normally inundated by daily commuters at this hour, desolate platforms were dotted by posse of police and security forces ready to receive and escort the top Congress leaders.

A corridor train departed with almost the entire top rung leaders aboard. Besides Gandhi and Azad, the other prominent leaders included Jawaharlal, Vallabhbhai Patel, Sarojini Naidu, GB Pant, Asaf Ali, Shankarrao Deo and Pattabhi Sitaramayya. Gandhi was put in a separate compartment and only Sarojini Naidu was allowed to accompany him. Gandhi and Sarojini were taken out of the train at Poona, and placed in the Aga Khan Palace prison. The train moved on to Ahmednagar to lodge other leaders in the jail attached to the fort there. These leaders were handed over by the police to military officials.

The action of the government was lightening and decisive, aimed at nipping any potential mass movement in the bud.

Congress Socialist Party Leaders Go Underground

August 10, 1942: In a pre-dawn sweep, the Bombay police had arrested the top echelon of the Congress leadership yesterday. There has been no let up in the crackdown. It is being learnt that the police has managed to arrest all leaders who had assembled in the city to attend the AICC session.

The police have been chasing Congress leaders across the country and resorting to large-scale arrests. Even middle-level leaders are not being spared. The government is determined not to allow any leaders of consequence to remain free to be able to lead the masses. However, according to reliable sources that a number of fire-brand Congress Socialist Party leaders have managed to go underground, evading the police dragnet.

League Tells Muslims To Stay Away From 'Quit India' Stir

August 16-20, 1942, Bombay: The AIML Working Committee held a five-day long meet here. Jinnah presided. Several resolutions were adopted. One called upon the Muslims to stay aloof from the Congress. The Quit India movement launched by the Congress was described as detrimental to the Muslim interest. The League expressed willingness to negotiate with any party to set up a provisional government and mobilise resources for prosecution of war on the condition that Muslim demands were met. In another resolution, the committee invited attention to the demand for a separate homeland for Muslims, which it claimed, was in accordance with the UN charter.

Political observers say, the countrywide unrest let loose by the Quit India Movement has the League leaders worried about its eventual outcome, though the government repression has begun in earnest. In such a situation of uncertainty, the League is in a hurry to protect its turf by hyping up its demand.

Give Us A Chance, We Welcome Both Authority And Responsibility, Says Muslim League

August 21, 1942, Bombay: Although the League has neither been creating any obstacle, nor embarrassing the government in the prosecution of war, Jinnah today, in a press interview, gave an indication of the feasibility of a larger and fuller scale of Muslim help and support to that cause on the basis of a quid pro quo. Jinnah suggested that if the government gave the League real share and authority in the governance of the country, the League would welcome such responsibility and share the burden in the war effort.

British Governor Revokes Section 93 Installs Saadullah To Quell Disquiet In Assam

August 25, 1942, Shillong: The province of Assam, sharing border with Burma, has been militarily strategic to British India, more so, after the Japanese armed forces have driven its forces out of Burma. Since then the scope to send Allied help to Nationalist China using Burmese roads has ended. Instead, the Allied countries, especially America, have been using the Ledo Road airstrip in the northern part of the province to route their supplies. On its part, Britain has been preparing for a future war against the Japanese to be launched from the Assam-Burma border. These activities require peace and stability in the province. However, right since the time Gandhi was arrested following his 'Quit India' call to the British, this province has grown restive, and got engulfed in protest, chaos and disruptive activities. The local Congress Committees and 'Shanti Vahinis' have been leading the mass movements in various parts of Assam. Alarmed at the prospect of disruption in military supplies and movement of transport vehicles, Robert Reid, the provincial governor, has today revoked Section 93 and allowed Saadullah to form a new ministry. In the past, Saadullah, as the premier of the province, had adopted a high pro-British policy, enthusiastically supported British war efforts and in return obtained the tacit endorsement of the governor for large-scale immigration of Muslim people from Eastern Bengal into Assam. With his taking over the reins again, a gnawing fear has begun to envelope the province that the pro-immigration 'Land Development Scheme', which was scrapped last year, may be resuscitated.

Clampdown On Nationalist Forces
Subhas Calls Indians To Intensify Stir

August 31, 1942, Berlin: In the aftermath of Gandhi's Quit India call, Subhas is making use of two more radio stations—the Congress Radio and the Azad Muslim Radio, encouraging people to stand up against the British Raj. In a radio broadcast from Berlin today, Subhas expressed full support to the 'Quit India' call. He passionately appealed to people at home to hold fast and fight the colonial government. It may be recalled that he had repeatedly urged Gandhi to issue a similar call way back in 1939, which was ignored by the latter. However, Subhas is not complaining. To him the issue is more important and it is 'better late than never'. He wants India to get rid of the British regime anyhow.

Quit India Movement Grows Violent, Spreads Fast

August 1942: Within Congress, Rajagopalachari had raised serious opposition to the 'Quit India' resolution. Following its passage by the working committee last month he quit Congress. However, on the other extreme, Socialist leaders have been vigorously supporting the call. A number of these leaders have managed to escape arrest and go underground. While their identities are being carefully protected by the masses, these leaders are coming forward to lead the agitated workers and common people.

Soon after the arrest of Gandhi and other leaders became a public knowledge, people have been coming out on the streets in large numbers. There have been demonstrations, strikes, processions and meetings, especialy in mills and factories. The textile mills in Ahmedabad and Madras remained closed for days. Apprehensive of a possible dislocation in the war supply, the government has been tackling the situation with an iron hand. Government oppression has been facilitating emergence of a new breed of young leaders. They have begun moving to the countryside to organise the peasants in villages and people in moffussil towns.

Churchill Wants Viceroy To Crush Congress Movement

Although, the bulk of the Congress leadership have been imprisoned, mob fury has been bursting forth across the country and the shape it is likely to assume is indeterminate as of now. Gandhi's battle-cry 'do or die' has infused millions of Indians with a revolutionary zeal. In the absence of leaders who could direct their protests along non-violent lines, the masses are increasingly resorting to aggressive actions, causing damage to public properties. The British regime is a worried lot. That Britain and her allies have been able to slowly turn the tides against their enemies owes in no less measure to the resources she has so far mobilised from India. The country is being used as a base for Allied war operations including as the only route for sending US help to embattled China. Any major disruption here could prove fatal to the Allied overall war plan. What is more worrying is the prospect of a Japanese invasion of India. Churchill, the British prime minister, is vexed. So also is the Secretary of State for India, Amery. They are not prepared to take any chance and brook public agitations. It is being learnt that Churchill has given Linlithgow, the Viceroy, a free hand to crush the movement that has begun to erupt. There are also reports that Amery, with the hindsight of British success in quelling the Kurd rebels in Iraq, has suggested to Linlithgow the most cost-effective method to dismantle popular agitation—by dropping bombs or spraying machinegun bullets from aircraft. The government is also resorting to public flogging of agitators and imposing collective fines on villages, even if a single person participates in the movement. However, the wily government, to create a fissure between two communities, is exempting Muslim villages from collective fines—it is trying to project the 'Quit India' Movement as a Hindu movement.

'Quit India' Call – Differences Manifest Amongst Parties

August 1942: Though Congress decided to take the leap into the hydra-headed fire of open rebellion, some political parties, including its perennial adversaries, are standing behind the British Government, each for its own reasons. The Muslim League is seeing this Congress' move as an opportunity to come closer to British Government. Jinnah has severely castigated the Congress for its 'Quit India' call, warned the Muslims against joining the agitation and assured the British Government of the Muslim support. Hindu Mahasabha feels the Congress decision, at this juncture, is inappropriate. Even organisations of depressed classes are not supporting the Congress stand. The Communist Party of India is also opposing the Congress call. The reasons are not far to see—in the revised global scenario, there is a growing collaboration between Russia and Britain in fighting the Axis power led by Nazi Germany.

Government Uses British Troops To Tackle Protestors

September 1942, New Delhi: Since the 'Quit India' movement burst out, agitators have been attacking government properties and causing extensive damages. Post offices, railway tracks and stations, police stations, telegraph cables and government buildings have been the targets of mob violence and also sabotages. Hundreds of post offices and rail stations have suffered serious damages. Violent mobs have been attacking scores of police stations and government buildings and even putting many of them to fire. The intensity of the violence has been most pronounced in Bihar. Finding the police inadequate to tackle the rampaging mob, the government has been deploying British troops to quell them.

The Indian National Army Is Emerging As A Force

September 1, 1942, Singapore: Mohan Singh has been working hard to raise the strength of and impart training to the Indian National Army. By now, the first division of INA has acquired the strength of 16,300. He is however not satisfied. Singh is keen to raise a second division from a surplus of 24,000 volunteers and he is in need of adequate equipment and training facilities. The Japanese army, however, has not been providing the INA with sufficient arms and infrastructure. Singh has also to contend with another irritant. Quite a few opportunists have entered the INA just to avoid the rigours of Japanese prison camps. There are reasons to apprehend that these elements may switch over to the British camp at the next available opportunity. He is trying to plug these loopholes and organise the INA as a professional, battle-ready army and add to its strength.

People Are Machine-gunned From Aeroplanes

September 7, 1942, Talcher: The public protests and agitations are spreading despite severe government repression. From cities and towns, waves of discontents are travelling into villages. The intensity of public fury is more in places where there are pre-existing deep-seated grievances. The charged-up political ambience has been acting as a catalyst in bringing about hasty marriages between the local issues and the patriotic national agenda, in turn giving birth to quite a few turbulent movements. These are being fanned by an all-round expectancy that the British rule is likely to end soon. This is emboldening the aggrieved and enraged masses to strike hard at their native enemies, whom they accuse of being British protectorate.

In Talcher, a native state in the eastern India, the people have been angry with their king for his despotic rule. Imbued by the flame of the 'quit India' call, the subjects of Talcher have formed 'Praja Mandals' across the state and managed to bring the entire state except the headquarter under their control and administration. Driven by panic, the king of Talcher sought help from the 'political department' of the British Government. This set up a stage for confrontation between the opposing camps. Today, people armed with crude weapons clashed with the British army and air force. The mob was dispersed by use of machine guns from aeroplanes. After this incident, many activists of the Praja Mandals have gone underground.

Violence Engulfs India, Army Called At Several Places To Crush Angry Mob

October 3, 1942, New Delhi: Protests and agitations in response to the 'quit India' call by the Congress have spread to various parts of India, attracting sharp government reprisals. In the face of severe repression administered with alacrity, open expressions by the public of discontent and protest actions have been rendered nearly impossible. As such, the present movement against the government is turning subterranean and assuming increasingly violent form. Although Gandhi has been known for his conviction of 'non-violence', the movement is gradually acquiring a vigorously violent form in which the pent up grievances of the masses against both the British and also their native tormentors are exploding in sporadic acts of violence and sabotage.

The government has, however, different perspective on the violence. It sees intelligent planning and pattern into the acts of violence. In his report[130] to the Secretary of State for India, sent today, Viceroy Linlithgow has argued that the series of incidents, mostly sabotages, have not been 'spontaneous' but outcome of careful planning. He has contended that these began after two or three days of the arrests and occurred 'with similar objectives in widely separated areas'. These involved carefully chosen targets—being 'mainly essential communications and Government property'. Further, 'many acts, particularly sabotage of railways and roads, displayed technical knowledge...' He observed 'there was marked absence of sabotage of valuable machinery and plant in factories even where strikes occurred'. Finally, he noted a 'disciplined abstention from interferences with Muslims', ostensibly to avoid communal troubles. Viceroy identified Bihar and Eastern UP as the most affected parts of the country and assigned large parts of the responsibilities for the violence in Bihar, United Provinces and the Central Provinces to the CSP and Forward Bloc.

Muslim League Finally Gets A Grip Over Sind

October 23, 1942, Karachi: Although Allah Bux had to resign in the aftermath of Manzilgah, he managed to stage a smart comeback in March last year by manoeuvring the ouster of Bande Ali, his successor. In his second term, although he had GH Hidayatullah as a minister, Allah Bux depended on the support of Hindu members and his government had generally been following a pro-Congress line. After Congress gave the 'Quit India' call a couple of months ago, Allah Bux too responded by renouncing his colonial titles and expressing his pro-Congress views. In the process, he attracted British wrath and was dismissed by the government few days ago. Following his ouster, GH Hidayatullah formed a coalition ministry with two members of the Muslim League, one non-League Muslim and two Hindu members in his cabinet. Hidayatullah had resigned from the Muslim League last year but was expected to rejoin it and that possibility began to fetch him support of the League legislators. Today he has rejoined the Muslim League. For the first time, the provincial cabinet of Sind has a clear domination of the Muslim League. In fact, many are calling it as the first League ministry in the province. To Jinnah, even such a perception has strategic importance for the Muslim League—it enhances his negotiating power. It might act as another step towards the League's goal of Pakistan.

India Is Critical But Under Control

December 1942, New Delhi: The government has been using brute force to deal with the current agitation including liberal use of the army and even air force. More importantly, it has managed to enlist support from some sections of Indian people and establishments against the Congress movement. The Communist Party, the Muslim League, the Unionist Party, the Hindu Mahasabha, the Liberals, landlords, rich merchants and the princes of native states have been supporting the government against the movement.

On its part, the government is not letting go of any opportunity to create schism in people. On the one hand, it has imposed a system of mass punishment implying penal action on an entire village even if a single villager participates in the anti-government movement. On the other hand, it has exempted the Muslim majority villages from the purview of such penalty. It wants a political message to be engraved in the hearts of the Muslim population—that the current movement is only a Congress movement and they ought to boycott it.

With such policy mix of brute force and cunning, the government seems to have survived the initial blast of a potentially dangerous mass upheaval. Now, with the Congress leaders held in complete seclusion and incapable of posing fresh problem, the government is looking at the future with more confidence.

Its major worry now seems to be the prospect of a Japanese invasion.

Mohan Singh Arrested By Japanese Army

December 29, 1942, Singapore: In a shocking development that dealt a body blow to the morale of the INA, Mohan Singh, their GOC, has been taken into custody by the Japanese military police. Singh's growing communication gap with both the Japanese army and the Council of Action members, seem to have resulted in this unfortunate event.

In the Bangkok conference held last June, the IIL had sought several clarifications from the Japanese authorities, especially involving the status and scope of operation of the INA. The Japanese gave a blanket reply, but it was too vague and evasive, without addressing IIL's specific concerns. This made the Council of Action serve an ultimatum on the Japanese government. Meanwhile, Mohan Singh had deputed an INA team to Burma at Japanese request and one of the team members defected to the British Indian army. This created mistrust between

Mohan Singh and the Japanese army command. Recently, Mohan took a stand not to extend further cooperation with the Japanese army command, unless all the points raised by the June conference were properly clarified. This foot-down approach by the GOC of the INA led to complications in the relationship between the Council of Action and the Japanese army command. Rashbehari tried to sort out the issues but failed. The problem aggravated as complaints against Mohan Singh began to surface even within the Council of Action. Raghavan, the civilian member, felt that Mohan Singh was gathering too much power and taking important decisions such as deputing teams to Burma on his own without consulting the Council of Action.

In the aftermath of all such unsavoury developments, Rashbehari, as the president of the Council of Action dismissed Mohan Singh. Today the Japanese Military Police has arrested him.

Rashbehari Prevents Dissolution Of INA

December 1942, Singapore: Mohan Singh was preparing for the worst and had drawn up an order dissolving the INA in anticipation, which was issued on 21st of this month ie. eight days before his arrest by the Japanese. It was sought to be implemented after Singh was arrested. This created great confusion and chaos. However, Rashbehari Bose is trying to do the damage control and preserve the organisation. Many INA officers are supporting him. They feel Mohan Singh did not have the authority to dissolve the INA. This is the general feeling as well, because both IIL and INA are important organisations, reflecting aspirations of millions of Indians and they could not be sacrificed for the sake of individuals, however important they may be. Every one is hoping Subhas would take over the leadership of the IIL and INA, and put at rest the controversies.

Indian Legion – A Laboratory Of Patriotic Experiments

December 1942, Berlin: Indian Legion has grown into a fine force of four battalions comprising over 3,000 soldiers and officers, drawn mostly from the Indian PoW transferred mostly from Italy to Germany during the present year. They have been trained by German officers and are being treated as a part of the German army till the time they get to form part of the army of the independent Indian government. This status is to safeguard their interest in the event of their capture by the enemy. Subhas has been firmly emphasising that they could be used only against the British—when, where and how, would depend on the course and outcome of the ongoing war.

Subhas has been working to a scheme by making a fusion of Indian soldiers belonging to various religious, ethnic and other groups at the unit level and ensuring that everyone is inspired by an overarching spirit of nationalism and patriotism.

The Indian Legion, it seems, is creating some interesting lexicons and conventions inspired by deeply nationalistic spirit in which it is steeped. All the soldiers of the Legion have developed a practice of greeting each other with the words 'Jai Hind' (a short form of Jai Hindustan). They have also begun addressing Subhas as 'Netaji'. Though Subhas initially objected to this appellation, he had to give in to their love and abiding respect for him. The Legion has adopted the tricolour Congress flag as its own with a springing tiger in it. It has also adopted Tagore's *Jana Gana Mana* as its anthem.

AZAD PUNJAB – Tara Singh Clarifies Akali Demand

December 1942, Lahore: Dissatisfied with the Cripps proposal, Akalis have been pushing for Azad Punjab. The word 'Azad' led to widespread misunderstandings about Akali intentions, though on several occasions they sought to clarify that they did not intend to have an independent state for the Sikhs.

To set all doubts at rest, Master Tara Singh has now clarified[131] that Punjab of his vision would consist of 40% Muslim, 40% Hindus and 20% Sikhs. This is in consonance with their submission to the Cripps Mission earlier stating that in the proposed province, that the Sikhs should not be dominated by any one single community.

Gandhi And Linlithgow Trade Charges

January 13, 1943, New Delhi: On the eve of the New Year, Gandhi had written to Viceroy Linlithgow unloading the feelings of hurt from inner recesses of his heart. Five months ago, he was removed lock, stock and barrel from the centre stage of Indian politics at one jerk, into a desolate prison in Poona. No opportunity was given to meet the Viceroy to explain the Congress point of view. Such distrust, such antagonism, such bitterness for a person like him who has been professing friendship with Britain for decades! Such harshness for a leader who, right since 1939, has been steering the Congress movement with so much of discretion including in the form of low-key 'individual satyagraha' lest it dislocated the British war efforts! And all these coming from a Viceroy with whom, of all the previous Viceroys, he had the longest period of interaction and friendship! In his script, Gandhi has sounded dismayed, hurt and uncharacteristically sad.

The tone and tenor of his letter virtually reprimanded the Viceroy in the manner a friend would do another, for the latter's lack of discretion, tolerance, trust and far sight. Gandhi gave a detailed account of all of these in his letter. Gandhi also added that in such moments of trial, he would have to observe fast to crucify flesh—the option for a Satyagrahi in such circumstances. The only way he can avoid doing so is if the Viceroy can convince him of his errors in the whole episode.

Though in turn, Gandhi had hoped for a soft admission of lapses, some words of regret, an urge for reconciliation and an olive branch from his Viceroy friend, he was administered a stunning rebuff by the Lord of India. Linlithgow has sent his reply today. Holding Gandhi singularly responsible for imposing the strongest hurdle in the British war efforts, when the Allies have been fighting a life and death battle with the dreaded Axis, he has launched a severe counter-offensive against Gandhi using 'words' as weapon. Surely Gandhi could not be so naïve as not to anticipate what impact a call for mass civil disobedience, a call for an open rebellion, or a mantra of 'do or die', or a slogan of 'British, you Quit India' could have on vast millions of Indians, with Gandhi himself acting as the chief priest of the 'Yagna'?

Was that not the time to spare every single waking minute for war preparation instead of playing with words, arousing hostile emotions in people and conducting laboratory experiments with nuances of Satyagraha? Who else, if not Gandhi, was to be held responsible for the extensive damage done to the government properties, disruptions in the factory, uprooting of railways, vandalising post offices, burning policemen alive and attacking military supplies?

If You Decide To Retrace Your Steps, You Have Only To Let Me Know: Viceroy To Gandhi

January 13, 1943, New Delhi: Gandhi was not ready for the vehemence of Linlithgow. In his letter, he had attempted to convince his Viceroy friend that the blame for the chaos following the 'Quit India' call aptly laid on the government and this led to barter of accusations. Linlithgow wrote he was much disappointed because neither Gandhi nor any of the working committee members condemned the stream of violent activities that were underway in the country, even though they regularly read about them in the newspapers. However, what probably upset Gandhi even more than these open charges is the arrogance of the Ruler. Like a headmaster disciplining an errant school boy, Linlithgow wrote: 'If you wish now to retrace your steps and disassociate yourself from the policy of last summer, you have only to let me know and I will at once consider the matter further...'.[132]

I Must Resort To The Legitimate Weapon Of A Satyagrahi To Fight This Unjust Battle: Gandhi

January 29, 1943, New Delhi: Gandhi has been upset by the intransigence and bellicosity in the tone and tenor of Linlithgow's 13 January letter, which betraying his Viceregal authority, made the chances of a reconciliation look bleak. Linlithgow placed the entire blame for the August movement and its aftermath at Gandhi's doorstep. Deeply upset, Gandhi has today replied[133] to that letter at length and tried to refute the list of allegations levelled by Linlithgow against him and the Congress. He made a desperate attempt to persuade Linlithgow to see the whole matter from the Congress viewpoint too. But if still 'I cannot get soothing balm for my pain', Gandhi wrote 'I must resort to the law prescribed for Satyagrahis, namely, a fast according to capacity'. Not to leave the Viceroy in any doubt about his resolve, Gandhi also specified his programme, 'I must commence after the early morning breakfast of the 9th February, a fast for 21-days, ending on the morning of the 2nd March...'

Use Of Fast For Political Purpose Is Blackmailing Linlithgow Lashes Out At Gandhi

February 5, 1943, New Delhi: Today Linlithgow has shot off another scathing missive to Gandhi, dismissing at one stroke, the large body of arguments Gandhi had assiduously built up in his letter of 29th January trying to lay the blame at the government's door. After hearing out Gandhi, he pronounced his judgement[134]: 'But I fear that my view of the responsibility of Congress and of yourself personally for the lamentable disorders of last autumn remains unchanged...' He was critical of Gandhi's decision to fast: 'I hope and pray that wiser counsels may yet prevail with you...' Linlithgow made it clear that the responsibility and consequences of that 'action' would lie with Gandhi. Having said this, he sought to offer wise counsel mingled with a statement of strong disapproval of Gandhi's plan: 'I would welcome a decision on your part to think better of it, not only because of my own natural reluctance to see you wilfully risk your life, but because I regard the use of a fast for political purposes as a form of political blackmail (himsa) for which there can be no moral justification...' According to reliable sources, Linlithgow has discussed the issue with Churchill and the consensus between the two is that the government will make no attempt to compromise with Gandhi, nor try to dissuade him from fasting. Political observers rule out any reconciliation between the Congress and the government, at least till the conclusion of the war. With Gandhi and rest of the top leadership of the Congress inside prison, that party has been rendered politically inert, at least for the time being.

My Appeal Will Now Lie At The Highest Tribunal For Justice: Gandhi To Linlithgow

February 7, 1943, Aga Khan Palace, Poona: The letter the Viceroy wrote to him the day before, has completely disillusioned Gandhi. It has hurt him immeasurably. Linlithgow suggested that by his decision to fast, Gandhi had made an attempt 'to find a easy way out'. In his rejoinder sent today, Gandhi has reprimanded Linlithgow for imputing such a base and cowardly motive to him. Then he once again went at length to refute every allegation Linlithgow hurled at him.

However, based on the tone and tenor of Linlithgow's letters, Gandhi seemed to have given up hope that the Viceroy would at all take an impartial and fair view. He has thus decided to go ahead with his proposed 'fast'. 'You have left me no loophole for escaping the ordeal I have set before myself', Gandhi wrote to Linlithgow[135], adding that the fast would be his appeal to the Highest Tribunal for justice, which he had failed to secure from the Viceroy.

Bound For The East, Subhas Begins Hazardous Undersea Journey By German Submarine

February 9, 1943, Kiel: Since he met Hitler, Subhas has been exploring ways and means to travel to Southeast Asia. However, Japanese leaders kept changing their minds about his presence there. After they made up their mind, it took time to decide upon his mode of travel. Considering the war situation, air travel from Germany proved to be a risky proposition. Notwithstanding, he had plans to fly from Rome on last October but in view of the war-induced hazards, the flight was cancelled. At last, the Nazi dispensation has arranged a submarine for his journey. Today he has boarded a U180 German submarine in the Atlantics. Abid Hasan is accompanying him as his private secretary and assistant. The German submarine is expected to transfer the VIP passengers to a Japanese submarine on the high seas.

Gandhi Begins Long Fast In Prison Government Prepares For The Worst

February 10, 1943, Poona: Gandhi has been in the prison in the Aga Khan Palace here for the last six months. He is upset that the government has been holding the Congress and him personally responsible for the violence and chaos engulfing the country since August last year. He is convinced, if at all, it is the government which has brought things to such a pass whereas the Congress has been acting all through with considerable restraints and empathy. He also felt that the government's violence has been on a gigantic scale, compared to the protestors.

Gandhi had intimated the government of his intention to go on a twenty-one days fast with effect from the ninth of the present month, for self-purification and also to protest against the government's accusations against him. The government has been so irritated and cut up with Gandhi that it has chosen to ignore his programme and made no attempts to pacify or restrain him. Linlithgow has warned that he would consider Gandhi's fast as an act of political blackmail.

It is also being learnt that the prison authorities have arranged bundles of sandalwoods inside the palace to conduct Gandhi's funeral, should he, at his advanced age and in poor condition of health, not be able to survive the ordeal of the long fasting. Gandhi has begun the fast today as scheduled.

New-look INA Emerges: IIL-INA Relations Redefined

February 15, 1943, Bangkok: Since the dismissal and arrest of Mohan Singh, Rashbehari has been a troubled man, trying his best to salvage the IIL and resuscitate the Indian National Army by restructuring it. Upon being asked at the individual level, most of the officers and soldiers of the INA have expressed their willingness to serve and fight for the liberation of India. A news has also been doing the round that Subhas Chandra Bose is likely to take over as the president of the League. This is infusing new life in IIL and INA. INA has been reorganised and brought under the authority of the IIL. This is expected to put an end to a longstanding conflict of authority between the two organisations. Lt Col Bhonsle has been appointed as INA's director of the military bereau.

He would be assisted by Lt Col Shah Nawaz Khan as chief of general staff, Major PK Sahagal as military secretary and Major Habibur Rahman as the commandant of the officers' training school. The army has been placed under the command of Lt Col MZ Kiani.

Sind Cabinet Passes Resolution Demanding Pakistan

March 3, 1943, Karachi: In less than six months since it assumed office, the Muslim League-dominated and Hidayatullah-led Sind cabinet has taken a significant step. Today, it has passed a resolution somewhat on the lines of the 'Pakistan resolution' adopted by the League in 1940, demanding separate land for the Muslims. The resolution was moved by GM Syed, a member of the working committee of the AIML. Significantly, only 27 members were present and of them, 24 voted in its favour. Interestingly, this initiative faced opposition from two camps. Three Hindu members, two of them being ministers, voted against. What was probably more significant politically was the reservation of the Sumroo group in the legislatures who flagged opposition against initiatives to combine Sind with other provinces—whether Baluchistan, Punjab or any other. Political analysts see this as a manifestation of Sindhi sub-nationalism. Notwithstanding such opposition which could at best be considered as feeble, the adoption of the resolution has come as a boost to the Muslim League's stance and strength.

The Congress may be upset over its decision to demit office in several provinces and thus allow the League to seize initiatives. Its decision is proving particularly costly in communally-sensitive provinces like Sind, and Assam and the Muslim majority province of the NWFP.

Japan Creates Burma Command In Rangoon

March 27, 1943, Rangoon: Japan has reorganised its forces in Burma as the Burma Area Army, with headquarters in Rangoon. To be led by Lt Gen Masakazu Kawabe, this new command evidences the growing importance of this area to the Japanese government. Kawabe will report to Field Marshall Hisaichi Terauchi, the head of the Southern

Expeditionary Army, with headquarters in Saigon. Political analysts are attaching considerable significance to this new development. A section of them feels, it has been a defensive action by the Japanese to be able to meet any Allied invasion, especially from British India. Another section is noticing larger political objectives behind this move. They point out to the prospect of an Indian liberation struggle by the Indian National Army to be launched from Burma supported by the Japanese army. This is in alignment with the Japanese objective of destroying the Anglo-Saxon power. The new command would serve both these objectives, they contend

Fazlul Huq Succumbs To Political Intrigues

March 28, 1943, Calcutta: The Fazlul Huq ministry has finally succumbed to the continuing intrigues and machinations by both the Muslim League and the British governor of Bengal. Huq had formed the first coalition ministry with the League in 1937 and remained at its helm for nearly four years.

He also happened to be the president of the League in the province. Their relationship grew worse nearly sixteen months ago when Huq broke away from the League and formed an all-party ministry as the head of the Progressive Coalition. Sarat Chandra Bose had played a pivotal role in that change over, and his group of Congressmen was a key constituent of the new coalition. Right since then, the League opposed the Huq government vigorously, both within and outside the legislative assembly.

On his part, the British governor, John Arthur Herbert too had been against this multi-party coalition right from its beginning. He had played a decisive role in sending Sarat to prison even before the cabinet took oath, for the latter's alleged link with the Japanese consul. In recent times, the presence of the Japanese army in Burma and the gradual building up of the INA have been reminding the British Government of the need to take extra care of the border provinces like Assam and Bengal politically. Political observers say Herbert was looking for an opportunity to dislodge the Huq-led progressive coalition ministry.

Huq himself contributed to his downfall, when he failed to tackle a rapidly-worsening famine situation engulfing Bengal. Ironically, much of it was caused not by lack of production of rice in Bengal but due to deliberate government policies. Since the war started, the Allied military had a preferential claim over rice produced in the province resulting in the exports of sizeable quantity.

Then, as the threat of Japanese invasion loomed large on the eastern border of India, the British Government resorted to a 'denial policy' and in accordance therewith, destroyed about 30,000 country boats in August last year without informing Fazlul Huq. This produced a cascading effect on rice supply from Burma and also movement of rice across coastal areas aggravating the famine condition. On the whole, Huq could not tackle the situation properly. While the famine began stalking large areas of the province, the British Government and bureaucrats not only usurped his power to intervene in the emerging crisis but refused to keep him even in the loop. The Federal government used the instrument of ordinance to cripple Huq's efficacy in handling the food and essential commodities. It even intervened on the issue of law and order.

Huq has been a common foe of both Muslim League and the British governor. The inability of his government in tackling critical administrative issues such as famine afforded the governor the opportunity to hunt him down. Today he had sent for Huq and asked him to submit his resignation on the assurance that he would take steps for forming an all party ministry in Bengal. When Huq submitted his resignation, it was accepted with alacrity–in a matter of two hours.

Governor Installs League-led Ministry In Bengal

April 24, 1943, Calcutta: Though Fazlul Huq had resigned as the premier of Bengal on the assurance of the governor, the latter went back on his words. Instead of exploring the option of an all-party government, governor Herbert imposed Section 93 and began attempts to bring the Muslim League into power. His brash, high-handed and inequitious attitude and action drew flak from several quarters including Viceroy Linlithgow and even HMG.

Though Fazlul Huq's resignation was accepted on that very day, Herbert could not install the next ministry for almost a month due to internal feuds within the League. Nazimuddin, with his base in East Bengal and Suhrawardy, a Calcutta based politician, have both been contenders for the top job. Eventually, Nazimuddin was chosen by Jinnah as he was perceived to be more pliant to the central leadership of the League. Today Nazimuddin has taken over the reins. His cabinet includes ministers from the Muslim League, but in keeping with the past tradition, he has also inducted Hindu ministers to give due representation to the large Hindu minority in the province. Incidentally, the replacement of Huq by a Jinnah loyalist signals another achievement by the AIML, coming soon after making a debut in Sind.

Jinnah Taken Out In Colourful Procession From Daryaganj To Chaman–i-Pakistan

April 24-26, 1943, Delhi: The capital city has just witnessed a three-day long session of the AIML. There was outpouring of enthusiasm amongst members and delegates surrounded by the local Muslim population. People turned up in large numbers. President Jinnah was taken out in a colourful procession from Daryaganj to Chaman-i-Pakistan, being the venue of the session. The Muslim League National Guards and students participated. Political heavyweights like Muslim ministers from Punjab, Sind and Assam were present.

In its main resolution, the League criticised the government for not granting the Muslims self-determination. It said that the League will resist any attempts to impose any kind of federal constitution with force and exhorted Muslims to be prepared to put up efforts and sacrifice to achieve the goal of Pakistan. Amongst other resolutions adopted, one condemned the government for levying collective fines on Muslims in some villages disregarding the League's clear stand that it had nothing to do with the Congress-convened Quit India Movement.

According to some political observers, Jinnah and the League are happy at the way the Congress has been removed from sight and the way that party fell from the peak of glory during 1937-1939 to its present predicament, with all its ministries gone and its top leadership languishing in prison. They say, 'time' has presented Jinnah with a unprecedented opportunity to spread the influence of the League amongst Muslims all across British India, without fearing any effective political opposition.

British Offensive At Arakan Comes A Cropper

May 11, 1943, Maungdaw: Right since April last year, the British regime has been very uneasy with the presence of the Japanese armed forces in Burma. It poses not only military but also political risks. Anxious to protect its Indian empire and regain the lost colony of Burma, the regime has been launching scattered attacks in Burmese territories to test the Japanese might before waging a full-scale battle. Last year, post monsoon, a guerrilla regiment led by Brigadier Orde Wingate was airlifted into a number of inaccessible but strategically important places in the heart of Burma, where they destroyed several transportation and communication links. This year, the regime formed the 15 Corps under the leadership of General Slim which was to operate in the Arakan sector in the southwest of Burma. This sector borders the southeast of the eastern Bengal and the new Corps has its headquarters in Chittagong.

The Allied forces began a campaign in Akyab island, Mayu range and Kaladan valley in December last year and achieved some measure of initial success. One of its units captured the Maungdaw town at the estuary of Naf River. But the irked Japanese thereafter launched strong counter-offensive and inflicted heavy damages to their enemy, so much so that Slim has been made to rethink his strategy. Today he has decided to evacuate Maungdaw town, an important position that was gained at considerable expense. This appears to be a setback, indeed.

Allies Turn The Table On The Germans In Africa

May 12, 1943, Tunis: German General Erwin Rommel's undisputed sway over the 'dark continent' has at last begun to wane. The aura of German invincibility in the tank war across Africa under his leadership is melting under the pincer attack of the forces of British General

Bernard Montgomery from the south and the east and US General Eisenhower in the west.

Since November last year, when a contingent of fresh 140,000 US soldiers landed in Africa, the Allied power's aggression has been on the rise. As the two Allied generals are converging upon Romell's African posts, these have been falling successively to their combined might. The Allied victory is also being welcome by the natives. Only last week, the Allied army received a rousing welcome as it entered Tunis. Today the Allies have scored a decisive victory, and probably a clinching one, over the Axis by forcing about 275,000 German and Italian troops to surrender in Cape Bon peninsula, the far north-eastern part of Tunisia.The chain of victories in Africa is giving the British Government some measures of comfort, though they are still much worried about the Japanese, who are breathing over the shoulder on India's eastern border.

Aurangzeb Khan Forms Ministry In NWFP

May 25, 1943, Peshawar: Today Sardar Aurangzeb Khan has formed a new ministry in the NWFP, sending ripples in political circles across the country. The NWFP has been a source of major worry for both the Muslim League and the British Government. The domination of Congress- Khudai Khidmatgar coalition and the miserable condition of the League in this overwhelmingly Muslim majority province has been consistently challenging Jinnah's claim that the Muslim League is the sole representative of the Muslims in India. He could neither digest this condition nor deny the fact.

The performance of the League in the 1937 provincial election has been a crying shame, where the party could not even open its account. Another six years have passed since then, yet Jinnah has not been able to make any breakthrough, such has been the popularity of the Khan brothers in the province.

On its part, the British Government has also been antagonistic to Khan Abdul Ghaffar Khan, and the alliance between his Khudai Khidmatgar and the Congress. During the tenure of their government, the Khan brothers had taken several steps against the feudal and tribal lords, who have been the main patrons of the British regime in this strategic border province. When the Congress ministry here resigned in 1939, the British Government went on an overdrive to ensure the emergence of a political alternative to the Congress-KK alliance. According to some reports, the Viceroy held confabulations with Jinnah in Delhi on this matter. Feroze Khan Noon, one of the executive council members has been in touch with the governor to explore possibilities on the ground.

George Cunningham, the governor, went the whole hog to raise a political alternative to the Khan Brothers led Congress. The extant circumstances in the province were helpful. In the fifty-members strong legislature, at least twenty two belonged to the Congress-KK alliance. But with ten of them being in prison and another seven seats falling vacant, the governor could prop up a political lightweight, Sardar Aurangzeb Khan, without much difficulty. Holding the hand of the governor, Aurangzeb has cobbled up a rag-tag coalition. He secured support from twenty Muslim members, some of whom he allegedly bought. Aurangzeb managed to pull a few Sikh and Hindu members to his side as well.

A creation of the British Government, Aurangzeb is likely to advance the goal of the Muslim League. The longevity of the new ministry is certainly suspect, as neither Aurangzeb nor the League has mass support in the province. Nevertheless, Jinnah is looking at the development as another important achievement for the League. Though there is no League member in the cabinet, the premier has declared allegiance to the League. A seed has been sown. Jinnah is sure it will bear fruits. It is just a matter of time!

BENGAL FAMINE – Natural Disaster Or British Revenge?

Bengal has been in the throes of a terrible famine. The situation has turned hopeless with poor people succumbing to the scourge of starvation in hundreds and thousands. Not only in villages, hungry people arriving in towns and cities in large numbers begging for morsels of rice, have been dying in the footpaths amidst extreme indifference on the part of the rich and the government.

Intriguingly, the severe shortage of food grains and their skyrocketing prices have arisen more due to the government policies than natural conditions. Rice production in the province over the last two years has not been much different than the normal level. But the government has been diverting bulk of it to its ever-bulging armed forces, fighting global wars to defend the British Empire. Then, it has been following a 'scorched earth policy' in eastern India, in anticipation of a possible invasion and occupation of Assam and Bengal by the Japanese army. In accordance with that policy, it has already destroyed thousands of boats in the eastern coast, traditionally used to ferry food grains across places.

But what is even worse seems to be a British policy to chastise the people of Bengal for raising a flag of revolt and creating bottlenecks in extending war support, as symbolised through Subhas's actions. Churchill is displaying a visceral hatred towards Bengal. He even rejected a humanitarian offer of shipload of wheat by the Canadian prime minister Mackenzie as a gift to India, on the pretext that this would upset the careful logistical planning that is going into the war efforts. He has also vetoed a couple of fledgling initiatives by the Viceroy to ameliorate the sufferings of the starving masses of Bengal.

To the famine struck-people of Bengal, the role of the provincial government, headed by Nazimuddin, is proving to the last straw on the camel's back. Though most of the policy-making on procurement and distribution of food grains during the wartime have been taken over by the federal government, the provincial government is adding to the woes of the starving masses by its ineptitude, incompetence and corruption. As hoarders and profiteers are making the most of government policies and administrative weaknesses, there are allegations against Suhrawardy, the food and supplies minister, for making matters worse by his communal bias and attempts to harvest personal fortune from the peoples' miseries.

Subhas Reaches Japan, Invited To The Diet

June 16, 1943, Tokyo: After a long and arduous journey including a transfer by a rubber dingy from the German U Boat to a Japanese submarine in the turbulent waters of the Indian ocean, Subhas reached Sabang island naval base on 9 May, and thereafter undertook successive journeys to reach Tokyo. On the way to the Japanese capital, he tried to cultivate a network of relationship with influential civil and military leaders who are likely to be supportive of the cause of Indian independence. Here he met Tojo, the Japanese prime minister, couple of days ago and a rapport has ensued soon between the two leaders. Subhas was invited to the Japanese parliament today where Tojo has declared the Japanese government's resolve to do everything possible to help Indian independence. Such a categorical assurance on behalf of a major world power is being viewed in political circles as significant and one that may help Subhas to take the freedom struggle to its culmination.

Indian Blood Must Be Shed for India's Freedom: Subhas

June 19, 1943, Tokyo: Subhas has held a press conference here and made two radio broadcasts by announcing his presence in this part of the world. In his speech to Indians, he sought to reassure them about Japanese intention. At the same time, he stressed that while the Axis powers could only help Indians, Indian freedom could be obtained only with Indian blood. He wanted the ongoing civil disobedience programme in India to develop into an armed struggle, for, freedom, he said, could come only when people on large-scale received their baptism by fire.

Jinnah Unfurls League's Flag In Baluch Capital

July 2, 1943, Quetta: With the Congress leadership locked in prisons, the Muslim League has been on a dream run in the north western region of India. After Sind and NWFP, it was time to declare its suzerainty in British Baluchistan. In the provincial conference of the League, Jinnah, the League president, today hoisted, what the League claimed as the 'national flag' in the soil of Baluchistan. Speaking on the occasion, Jinnah said that the Muslim nation in India so far did not have a flag of its own. Now on, they have it.

Rashbehari Passes On 'Baton' To Subhas

July 4, 1943, Singapore: Today, at a conference of delegates of Indians from East Asia assembled here, Rashbehari Bose has handed over charge of the Indian Independence League to Subhas. Unprecedented enthusiasm has been in evidence in the Greater East Asia to attend the momentous event. Large numbers of émigré Indians, committed to the cause of Indian independence, have converged as delegates in this island city to witness the historic event—beginning of Indian freedom struggle in a place, so far away from their motherland!

To their delight, Subhas has also assumed command of the Indian National Army simultaneously. His very presence has kindled new hopes among the soldiers and the civilians alike. Subhas accepted the heavy responsibility with humility, praised the three million strong expatriate Indians settled in various parts of East Asia for their burning patriotism and thanked them for reposing confidence in him.

'On The Road To Freedom You Will Face Thirst, Privation, Forced Marches And Death'

July 4, 1943, Singapore: In his presidential address[136] in the conference of delegates from East Asia, Subhas has called upon the vast number of Indians to 'line up in one solid phalanx under one leadership' and prepare for the struggle to free their motherland.

There have been misgivings in several minds about Japan's intention in giving help to the IIL. Subhas addressed these concerns and tried to alleviate them based on his personal experience of international politics. He hinted at an aggressive patriotic programme, but warned that some time would be needed for the Indians to prepare for the mission ahead. Once the IIL and the INA were ready, Indian struggle would be brought in line with the struggle of the tripartite countries against the common enemy.

Subhas sought to emphasise that irrespective of support of Japan, Indians would have to fight their own battle for freedom and the road ahead indeed was hard. Reckoning that the enemy was 'at once powerful, unscrupulous and ruthless', Subhas reminded them of the sacrifice they would have to undergo: 'In this final march to freedom you will have to face hunger, thirst, privation, forced marches and death. Only when you pass this test, will freedom be yours.'

Baluchistan – Muslim League's New Bastion

July 6, 1943, Quetta: The Muslim League has begun to fortify its position in the capital of the distant province of Baluchistan in the northwest. The provincial Muslim League has held its first session here which Jinnah presided over. His lecture, trumpeting the onward march of the Muslim League, was listened to, enthusiastically, by a sizeable crowd. Jinnah explained how the League has transmuted a scattered mass of Indian Muslims, who were politically disorganised all these years, into one single nation. He declared proudly: 'Now we have one flag, one platform, and one voice.'

HOW DANGEROUS IS SUBHAS TO THE BRITISH GOVERNMENT?

July 14, 1943, New Delhi: Subhas has been in East Asia since May and visited Tokyo in the middle of last month. His activities are now being widely publicised and this, possibly in accordance with a well-deliberated strategy by him and the Axis powers. The intelligence agencies of the Allies in the East and Southeast Asia have been maintaining vigil over his activities. Military intelligence of the government of India has compiled a dossier on Subhas and his activities. Marked as a 'most secret' note,[137] it reveals a few important and interesting details:

In many interviews granted to the Axis countries' journalists, Subhas has been expressing his conviction in an Axis victory and also the liberation of India with Axis (not merely Japanese) help. He has also stressed upon the strategic need of an armed revolt in India, to occur at the time an invasion is launched in her eastern border.

Commenting on Subhas' strategy, the note says, '...that while praising and thanking Japan, Bose never forgets to refer to Germany and to Axis sympathy for India'. It records that after his taking over the Indian Independence League, the latter has assumed a new level of importance: 'Before his coming the IIL was only publicised in connection with Japan. SC Bose clearly intends to raise the movement into a national campaign for freedom, supported by all three Axis powers.'

While admitting Subhas's 'great drive and political acumen' and 'his prestige in Indian revolutionary circles, his understanding of both Indian and English character', the note apprehends that those will be of 'real value to the Japanese.' The note has referred to his wireless messages to India in English, Hindi and Bengali, and to Germany and Indians in Germany in German, exhorting all Indians outside India to join and help him to organise a 'gigantic force to sweep the British from India'.

The note assesses that Subhas can make some gain out of the 'economic distress and political deadlock' but links the chances of causing a major revolt in India to his being able to win over the Congress Party en bloc. Significantly, it concludes by observing: 'Had he arrived in East Asia last August or even during Gandhi's fast, his prospects would have been much better .'

League Wins By-elections In Afghan Province

July, 1943, Peshawar: At long last, the Muslim League has been able to savour a small measure of electoral success in the fort of Khan Abdul Ghaffar Khan. The League candidates won last four by-elections. However, the credit for this goes more to Cunningham, the governor of the province, than the League. The Khan brothers have been languishing in the prison and the government has been systematically persecuting the Khudai Khidmatgar workers. Working to a scheme, he had been distributing position and patronages to intermediaries, feudal and religious persons, so that they, with their power and influence, swing voters in favour of the League. On its part, the Muslim League has done precious little to deserve these victories. In a way Cunningham has ensured that the League scores goal in the open field. Jinnah has, however, been quick to claim that the results show that the province has begun rallying under the League.

Allied Forces Set Up Southeast Asia India Command

August 25, 1943, New Delhi: Four days ago the Allies announced setting up of the Southeast Asia Command here. This is being seen as a response to the debacle faced by the British in the East and Southeast Asia. It reflects the British resolve to retrieve their lost Asian colonies and American determination to keep channelling help to their Chinese ally by regaining the supply routes through Burma. Louis Mountbatten, chief of combined operations in the European sector, has today been named as the Supreme Commander of this new establishment. American Lt Gen Joseph Stilwell, presently the Commanding General of the China-Burma-India Theatre, would be the deputy commander. The new command is expected to coordinate the war efforts of the Allied forces in Burma, Ceylon, Malaya, Dutch East Indies, Siam and Indo-China. Clearly the Allies are expecting the new command to deliver important results.

The appointment of Mountbatten has evoked mixed responses in the Allied commanders. While some important persons including American President Roosevelt and Britain's prime minister Churchil have backed him for the post, several top commanders including US General Montgomery have reservations about his suitability for the position. Mountbatten's critics are pointing out that his track record as a naval commander was disastrous and it has been no better as the chief of combined operations, his present assignment. In fact, his unprecedented elevation as the chief of combined operations in March last year despite his poor track record as a naval captain had at that time raised several eye brows. Confirming his critics, Mountbatten, as the chief of combined operations, carried out a botched-up operations in the small French port of Dieppe across the English channel, in which the Allied forces not only suffered an ignominous defeat in German hands but also sustained loss of over a thousand precious lives of Allied soldiers. The present appointment, which constituites another level of elevation, has therefore surprised many Allied commanders. Mountbatten is, however, fortunate to have good commanders, including William Slim in this war theatre, who are both good at strategy formulation and carrying out war.

Italy Surrenders Unconditionally

September 8, 1943, Washington: In July this year, when a strong Allied force converged on Sicily, threatening the very security of Italy, Mussolini was arrested and placed under detention in an unknown destination in central Italy. Since then, Italy's surrender was almost a foregone conclusion and only a matter of time. The end came three days ago when prime minister Pietro Badoglio signed an unconditional armistice with the Allies. Today US President Eisenhower has announced the fact of Italy's surrender and signing of the armistice.

Though Italy was the weakest amongst the Axis trinity, it was a potent force ideologically. Mussolini professed the political doctrine of 'fascism' that combined radical patriotism with absolute dictatorship, and this, no doubt, appealed to a large number of people for some period of time. Militarily, though without many distinctions, Italy had fought a number of battles including in North Africa, against the Allies forces over colonial possessions in the African continent. It also played a prominent role in the war in the Balkan countries in Europe, albeit on several occasions it had to summon German help to clinch victory. Many say, Italy was often a beneficiary of the German war machine and it was usually a one-sided help.

Hitler was never respectful of the Italian military might but had a personal liking for Mussolini. He has been outraged at the act of the new Italian government and considers the armistice with the Allies as an act of sheer treason. The Allies, especially Britain, is however, relieved. They are now left with two major foes to contend with.

Incidentally, Mussolini was the first premier amongst the Axis powers who had agreed to issue a declaration in favour of India's freedom as early as 1941, when persuaded by Subhas.

Jinnah-Khizr Summit Makes No Headway

September 1943, Bombay: Soon after being ensconced as the prime minister of Punjab on 7 January this year, Khizr Hayat Tiwana has been put under relentless pressure by the Muslim League. A young premier of 41 years of age, Khizr is shrewd and level-headed but he is not experienced enough to tackle the political moves of the astute League supremo, Jinnah. His predecessor, the departed veteran Sikandar Hayat Khan, had to summon all political skill at his command to keep Jinnah and the Muslim League at bay in Punjab. Sikandar had managed to keep the Hindu leaders and workers in the Unionist Party by his side, while having simultaneously, a pact with Jinnah.

He also enjoyed the full support of the British regime—both governor and the Governor General—which made his task easier. Significantly, the British considers Punjab as a strategic province and it has traditionally regarded the Unionist Party as its best bet ahead of the Congress and the League. In turn, the Unionist Party has remained pro-British through years. Owing to the proximity between the two, following the death of Sikandar Hayat, the British governor had played an important role in choosing Khizr as his successor. Khizr continues to enjoy the British support, which is his important wherewithal in his fight against Jinnah. Jinnah resented this British-Unionist Party linkage and he had serious objection to the manner in which Khizr was chosen as the prime minister of the province, without holding due consultation with the Punjab Muslim League.

To Jinnah, Punjab has been the cornerstone of the proposed Pakistan and he has been keen to establish Muslim League hegemony over the province. As long as Sikandar was alive, he could not achieve much except passing the 'Lahore Resolution' proposing a homeland for Muslims.

There was a pact between the two leaders but Sikandar used it to his own advantage. Jinnah did not want to give the same chance to Khizr. Before the new premier got entrenched, Jinnah wanted the provincial League to foreshadow Khizr's Unionist Party. Accordingly, he wanted the Unionist Party-led government to be called as the Muslim League ministry. Khizr found that demand unacceptable. Besides, compelled by the need to safeguard own status, Khizr, being at the head of a coalition government, had to keep his non-Muslim support base intact. The British governor Bertrand Glancy has been keen that Khizr does not succumb to Jinnah's pressure.

In his ongoing cold war with Khizr, Jinnah has been effectively leveraging the 'Pakistan' issue to attract and consolidate Muslim opinion in Punjab, both within the Unionist Party and outside, to the advantage of the League. Khizr has been feeling the heat of Jinnah's strategy. He came down recently to Bombay to talk to Jinnah and sort out the irritants between the two parties. Khizr could achieve little from this meeting. It is clear, Jinnah will not allow him to retain both Muslim and non-Muslim support base simultaneously. Either he has to be a commander of the Muslim League in Punjab or face its opposition. But Khizr is a man of firm will and he is unlikely to succumb easily. He has returned to Punjab with empty hand. He is mulling his next strategy carefully.

'I Still Remain Your Friend' : Gandhi To Linlithgow

September 23, 1943, Poona: Lord Linlithgow, the present Viceroy, is about to end a long tenure in India. His rule has elicited more criticism than praise. One of the strong allegations against Linlithgow has been that he actively sought to accentuate the communal divide amongst Indians, more than all of his predecessors, to serve British interests.

He has also been accused of being unduly vindictive towards the Congress, so much so that his partisan policies and undemocratic actions threatened to tilt the scale of political power permanently in favour of the League. Gandhi, in particular, has been harbouring a deep sense of hurt not so much for being put into jail but for the Viceroy holding him responsible, unjustifiably so, for the countrywide violence that broke out since 9 August 1942.

He had exchanged several letters with Linlithgow to clear the latter's misgivings but Linlithgow, to Gandhi's mind, adamantly stuck to own views. Today Gandhi sent the outgoing Viceroy a letter[138] which could be deemed as a farewell message. But unlike a customary farewell that recollects pleasant moments and fond memories, praises the good deeds of the outgoing dignitary, Gandhi's missive has been uncharacteristically sharp and bitter.

Gandhi wrote that on the eve of Linlithgow's departure, he would like to send him 'a word'. This contrasted to the normal practice of sending one's 'best wishes' on such occasions.

Immediately thereafter, without any prelude, Gandhi gave vent to his deep hurt: 'Of all the high functionaries I have had the honour of knowing, none has been the cause of such deep sorrow to me as you have been.' Then Gandhi complained about the unfair allegations that Linlithgow had charged him with: 'It has cut me to the quick to have to think of you as having countenanced untruth, and that regarding one whom, at one time, you considered as your friend.' In the penultimate sentence before conveying his 'good wishes', Gandhi made it clear that Linlithgow's erroneous conduct was not commensurate with the dignity of a great nation: 'I hope and pray that God will some day put it into your heart to realize that you, a representative of a great nation, had been led into a grievous error.' Gandhi ended the note with five loaded words: 'I still remain your friend.' Obviously, Linlithgow may not be pleased to receive such a scathing review of his policies and actions from a top Indian leader such as Gandhi.

Top General Takes Over As The New Viceroy

October 20, 1943, New Delhi: After remaining at the helm for a long seven-and-a-half years Lord Linlithgow has demitted office and Field Marshall Viscount Wavell has, today, taken over as the new Viceroy. Wavell was the commander-in-chief and responsible in large measure for the suppression of the 'Quit India' movement. The appointment of the top soldier to the post of the Viceroy has surprised many and engendered reservations in some quarters. Linlithgow's long rein solved few problems and left India more divided than ever. People are keeping fingers crossed now that a soldier has taken over.

Slim Shifts Headquarters Of 14th Army To Coomilla

October 1943, New Delhi: General William Slim, the new commander of the 14th Army (formerly Eastern Army), has shifted his headquarters from Barrackpore at the outskirt of Calcutta to Coomilla, a district town in eastern Bengal, which is closer to both Imphal and Arakan, the two fronts where Slim expects the next round of engagements with the Japanese forces to happen. His strategic goal to get optimum air support from the RAF and American aircrafts will get a fillip as John Baldwin, leading the Third Tactical Air Force too is shifting his unit's headquarters to the same town.

The 14th Army has three corps—4 Corps under Lt Gen Geoffrey Scoones in the Assam front, 33 Corps under Lt Gen Montagu Stopford acting as the Group Reserve and 15 Corps under Lt Gen Philip Christison in the Arakan. Additionally, Slim has a brigade of guerrilla warriors led by Brig Orde Wingate under his command. Though not a main strike force, Wingate's guerrillas have been performing useful role by disrupting enemy logistics.

Mission: Liberation Of Motherland Subhas Prepares INA For Impending Struggle

October 1943, Singapore: Subhas has been preparing for an armed freedom struggle to be launched across the Indo-Burmese border. While waiting for the Japanese nod for the right time, Subhas has been working tirelessly to strengthen the Indian National Army through sustained recruitment and continuous training. By now, the second division of the INA has been commissioned and the third division is in the process of formation.

Subhas has also formed a women's brigade, a unique initiative, and named it after the Rani of Jhansi, the famed Indian queen Laxmi Bai who fought valorously against the British in 1857. Since he took over the charge, the total strength of the INA has almost doubled. The soldiers and officers are being imparted not only military training, but also political, to infuse in them a sense of pride as an Indian and a spirit of nationalism and patriotism. His experience in organising a disciplined, energetic, patriotic force in the form of the Indian Legion in Germany is helping him.

The Japanese, themselves overstretched, are not providing sufficient resources to the INA. Subhas is trying to raise resources from the local Indians. He is also taking care to ensure that the paucity of arms, ammunitions and other supplies are compensated by fierce commitment to the freedom of the motherland.

'Provisional Government Of Free India Is Entitled To And Claims The Allegiance Of Every Indian'

October 21, 1943, Singapore: The world has come to see a new face of the long colonised India, so far taking recourse only to non-violent movements for her emancipation. Today Subhas has announced the establishment of the provisional government of Free India.

Since taking over as the president of the IIL three-and-a-half months ago, Subhas has been touring East and Southeast Asia including inter alia Malaya, Thailand, Burma and Indo-China, reorganising the headquarter and branches of the IIL, and encouraging Indians to join the Indian National Army. Under his dynamic leadership, the IIL has been able to departmentalise its various activities both at the headquarter and also at the branch and even sub-branch level. Keeping in mind the future needs, Subhas has re-organised the IIL in a mould capable of rendering services like established government departments. During this period, the INA has also emerged remarkably stronger in terms of number, training and equipments. Subhas has reckoned that the freedom struggle would call for 'total mobilisation', meaning that the endeavour would be holistic, encompassing men, material and money.

Although Indians in this part of the world have been keen that the battle for freedom be launched as early as possible, Subhas has waited till now to ensure that both the IIL and the INA grow confident to handle the enormous challenges that would be concomitant to beginning India's freedom struggle from such a distant land.

Today he has announced his first major step, ie. the formation of the provisional government of Free India, alias the Azad Hind Government. Delivering a stirring speech[139] as the president of the provisional government, Subhas said that the National Army has imparted both reality and seriousness to the present Indian bid for freedom and he expressed his conviction that once this army reaches the Indian soil, it would bring about a revolution, forcing the end of the British rule. He called upon Indian people to pursue the final struggle against British and all their allies with valour and perseverance, and with full faith in final victory. As the steward of the battle for emancipation of the motherland, he said that the provisional government 'is entitled to, and hereby claims, the allegiance of every Indian.'

British Government No To IIL Help For Famine Victims

October 21, 1943, Singapore: Subhas has issued a statement saying that the British Government has rejected a humanitarian offer of the Indian Independence League to provide free rice of one hundred thousand tons as a first instalment to the famine-struck people of India, who have been dying in thousands, out of starvation. Subhas has attributed the monstrous famine to the deliberate British policy of diverting food grain to the Allied forces over the last four years on a sustained basis. He has condemned the British Government for its insensitivity and brusque refusal of the IIL's offer to help fellow Indians. It appears, the British government has kept Indians in complete darkness about the IIL offer.

FIVE

ASSAULT FROM THE EAST

1944-1945

ASSAULT FROM THE EAST

AZAD HIND GOVERNMENT DECLARES WAR ON BRITAIN AND USA

October 24, 1943, Singapore: Last night at about 12:05 am the Council of Ministers of the provisional government of Free India declared war against Britain and the United States of America. In the late afternoon today, Subhas addressed an ecstatic audience of about 50,000 Indians in Padang, opposite the city's municipality building. Even as Subhas declared that it would be a 'war', a 'bloody war' and a 'war to the finish', the air was rent with relentless patriotic slogans. Subhas reminded his followers that they should be ready to sacrifice all that they have, including their lives, to be able to translate this 'war declaration' to 'action'. Thereafter, when he asked them to raise their hands if they still approved of the 'declaration', there was thunderous applause and the sea of humanity stood as one delivering its verdict.

Japan Cedes Control Of Andaman & Nicobar To Azad Hind Government

November 5, 1943, Tokyo: The Azad Hind Government has no landed territory yet to claim its sovereignty upon. In deference to its request, the Japanese government has agreed to cede limited jurisdiction over the Andaman and Nicobar islands to it. The Azad Hind Government will also have jurisdiction over Indian territories as and when conquered from British India.

Recognition For The Government Of Free India

November 19, 1943, Singapore: The provisional government of Free India has so far been recognised by seven other countries besides Japan. The recognition has come from Burma on 24 October, Croatia on 27 October, Germany on October 29, national government of China and Manchukuo, both on 1 November, Fascist Republic of Italy on 9 November, the Philippines and the Thai government today.[140] The stream of recognitions has boosted the confidence and sanctity of the provisional government. Having secured an international standing, it is feeling emboldened to begin its armed struggle for freedom against the Anglo-American powers.

According to political analysts, the British Government is growing concerned about these unfolding events.

Subhas, Tojo Discuss INA Role In Impending Invasion

November 24, 1943, Saigon: A Japanese invasion against the British and Allied powers along the Indo-Burma border is taking shape with urgency. Early this month, Subhas visited Tokyo and conferred with Japanese prime minister Tojo on the nature and extent of the INA's participation in the proposed undertaking. On this issue, he had sharp differences with Field Marshall Terauchi, the head of the Japanese Southern army, who wanted only marginal participation by the INA for espionage and propaganda purposes. Subhas convinced the prime minister that the whole of the INA first division ought to take part in what would be the crucial war of Indian independence. Subhas also expressed urgency about rapidly building up two more divisions of the INA, keeping in view requirements that are certain to emerge in the foreseeable future. He also pressed for securing better control over the espionage mechanism, including inter alia Spy Schools. On his way back to Singapore, Subhas arrived here via Nanking, Shanghai and Manila. In each of these places he met the heads of the Independence League, top Japanese officials there and also INA officials. Here, he has met Terauchi. In the light of his talk with Tojo, Subhas reviewed INA's role again with the Japanese General. They arrived at the agreement that the INA first division would move to Burma to take part in the coming offensive.

Jinnah Calls Gandhi's Arrest Justified

December 23, 1943: In a press interview today, Jinnah has justified Gandhi's arrest and incarceration. Jinnah said Gandhi was arrested for threatening the government with a mass movement. He further said that reason demands that Gandhi withdraw that threat.

DIVIDE AND QUIT: MUSLIM LEAGUE'S NEW SLOGAN

December 24-26, 1943, Karachi: The Muslim League held its session here. Jinnah presided with GM Syed as the chairman of the reception committee. It has adopted a catchy slogan 'Divide and Quit'[141] that is ostensibly aimed at the British Government while sending a barbed message to the Congress, its political rival, that partition of India is now just a matter of time. In his speech, Jinnah said, 'We shall never rest content until we seize the territories that belong to us and rule over them.' Ironically, the whole Congress leadership is in prison.

The League has resolved to form a Committee of Action to organise Muslims across the country to resist any attempt to impose on them an unitary constitution and also to prepare for their struggle to achieve Pakistan.

Massive Offensive Planned On Imphal-Kohima
INA To Launch War Of Liberation

December, 1943, Singapore: The Japanese war plan against British India has been code named U Go. In terms of the plan, the joint forces of Japan and the INA would launch an attack on Imphal and Kohima across India's eastern border. INA at present has three divisions, adding up to strength of about 30,000. Out of these, the first and the second division, in part, comprise Indian PoWs, who are experienced soldiers whereas the third one is raised from the civilians of East Asia and they are being imparted training.

The first division of the INA would take part in the battle. It has four brigades, viz. Subhas brigade, Gandhi brigade, Azad brigade and Nehru brigade. To start with, one battalion of the Subhas brigade would fight the West African division of the Allied Forces in the Kaladan sector in Burma, whereas two others would join the invasion force in the Chin Hills. Depending on the course of the war and their performances, the soldiers of the first division of the INA would be inducted and used, including in the front line in Imphal, Kohima and beyond. The second division will be sent to action after Imphal is taken over by the joint force, while the third division will be held in reserve in Malaya. The Azad Hind Government proposes to start five new divisions from Indian prisoners who would fall into INA's hands during the course of the Imphal and Kohima offensive.

Men, Material And Money
India Has Been The Key To British War Efforts

December, 1943, New Delhi: Whether the government admits or not, the war success of Britain has relied, to a considerable extent, on the British Indian army and the war materials and equipments sourced from India. At the start of the Second World War, Indians numbered around 1,90,000 in the British Indian army. By now their number has increased to 2,000,000 - more than ten fold. What is more, the Indian soldiers have fought valiantly in several war theatres like in the Middle East Asia, Kenya, Sudan, Ethiopia and Burma. Congress' diffidence in challenging the government had allowed such indiscriminate conscription, whereas nothing was offered in return by the British regime—not even a promise of independence at the end of the war! Another malady, which is escaping immediate public scrutiny is the ballooning public debt the British Indian Government has been incurring to finance its war efforts on such a gigantic scale. At the end of the day, this would fall on the hapless Indians.

INA Fire Will Reduce British Imperialism To Ashes

January 1, 1944, Singapore: In a radio broadcast today, Subhas has responded to the expectations of vast number of Indians that the provisional government begin the armed struggle without delay. He has sounded the war bugle saying that the INA now stands ready to strike. Subhas said that three million Indians in East Asia have emerged as a compact revolutionary body, ready, to sacrifice their all for India's freedom. He said[142] that at their back was the invincible INA, which, will kindle the fire of revolution in India and that 'will reduce British Imperialism to ashes'. He has assured Indians back home that INA will soon cross the border and free India.

Subhas Shifts Headquarters To Rangoon

January 8, 1944 Rangoon: Operation U Go is waiting to be launched. The first division of the INA is poised to join Mutaguchi's three divisions in the invasion of Imphal and Kohima and thereafter advance into the Assam plains. However, their immediate programme is to join the Japanese army in an offensive in the Arakan, a ploy to divert British attention from Imphal.

Subhas has moved northwards—from Singapore to Burma, to come close to India and launch the war of independence, finally. Today he has arrived at Rangoon—the capital of Burma, situated 25 miles to the north of the Gulf of Martaban in the Andaman Sea. Along with him, the headquarters of the Azad Hind Government and also the INA have been shifted here. The present independent government of Burma, led by Ba Maw and supported by Japan, has been friendly to the provisional government of Free India.

Today, Japanese General Kawabe held a party in honour of Subhas and the staff officers of the INA. Though Subhas has a rapport and direct communication link with Tojo, the Japanese prime minister, he has to depend on Kawabe and Mutaguchi for mode of deployment of the INA units in the forthcoming invasion. As has been his consistent stand, Subhas has reiterated his keen desire that the INA soldiers be given the opportunity to pay for their country's freedom by shedding their blood ahead of others. Kawabe did not make any commitment. But he has reportedly assured Subhas that the INA units will be given the chance whenever opportunities arise.

INA To Fight As An Independent Allied Army

January, 1944, Rangoon: Subhas has been able to secure the consent of the Japanese establishment that the INA will fight as an allied, independent army, albeit within the overall command of the Japanese army. Subhas has worked out the operational details with General Kawabe. It has been decided that INA's participation would not be lesser than at the battalion level. Out of the four brigades of INA's first division, the Subhas brigade with its three battalions, would herald the Indian armed offensive against the British. However, it was decided that the troops of the Special Services Group (SSG), numbering around 250 in each group would be attached to each of the Japanese divisions. They would act as guide of the Japanese army and undertake espionage, propaganda and conversion activities amongst the enemy ranks in the proposed invasion in the Imphal sector. About 250 soldiers of the SSG have been operating already in the Arakans, helping the Japanese against the British forces.

If Two Officers Of Same Rank Meet, Each Would Salute Without Waiting For The Other

January, 1944, Rangoon: In the course of discussion between commanders of the two armies, several sensitive operational issues have come up. The Japanese are likely to deploy their three divisions numbering over 90,000 troops in the coming invasion while the INA first division with all its four regiments put together would number about 9,000. Clearly the Japanese army, enormously proud of their recent military success and their racial origin, considers itself as the dominant partner. But Subhas has not been allowing any factor to undermine the self-esteem of the troops of the Indian National Army. On all contentious issues, Subhas has been talking directly to the top generals without giving any scope to Hikari Kikan (a department of the Japanese army keeping liaison with Azad Hind Government) or the lower level Japanese army officers to complicate things. Subhas has reportedly convinced General Kawabe that the INA would abide by its own Army Act, instead of the Japanese military law. On the tricky issue of 'hierarchy', it has been decided that if officers of the two armies of equal rank meet, each would salute the other without waiting for the other to do so.

The Subhas brigade is already in Rangoon, preparing to go to the front. Majority of them are likely to fight in the Imphal border at a height of four to five thousand feet, but they do not have adequate woolens nor do they have advanced arms and adequate ammunitions. Without a shade of doubt, they are considerably ill-equipped than their Japanese counterparts. But they seem to be filled with exceptional patriotic fervour and they certainly rank high in confidence.

Kawabe Issues Invasion Order

January 19, 1944, Rangoon: Today Lt Gen Kawabe has issued a detailed order to Lt Gen Mutaguchi to, launch an invasion on Imphal before the onset of Monsoon.

Japanese Brutalities In Andaman & Nicobar Islands

January 30, 1944: Though the Imperial government of Japan had conceded the sovereignty of Andaman and Nicobar islands to the Azad Hind Government, the Japanese navy has continued to retain its near-full control over the administration. No doubt, the Azad Hind Government has appointed Lt Col AD Loganadan as the governor, but he has practically no control over the administration. The Japanese have been ruthless and completely intolerant of any opposition to the Japanese interests. Today, in a macabre action, they have shot as many as 44 Indian civilians to death on the suspicion that the latter were engaged in espionage. Ironically, many of the victims were members of the Indian Independence League, the mother body for the Azad Hind government. Over the last two years, Dr Diwan Singh, a leader of the Indian civilians had been courageously working to protect the islanders from the atrocities of the Japanese forces. He was tortured to death.

Today's incident has raised serious questions about the attitude and intentions of the Japanese. It has also betrayed the vulnerabilities of the Azad Hind government in protecting its own people.

British Forces Advance In The Arakans Once Again

January 1944, Chittagong: Even before the Japanese could launch the planned invasion, the British regime has launched an attack in the Arakan front across the Eastern Bengal-Burmese border. In a well-planned move directed by General Slim, the 15 Corps led by Lt Gen Christison in the Arakans have begun an exercise to capture some areas in the coastal belt from the Japanese. Last year the British bid to occupy territories in this sector was not only foiled, but its forces were badly mauled. The present move seems to be a renewed bid by a better-prepared force.

Kadam Kadam Badhaye Jaa

Subhas Gathers INA Force Against British

February 3, 1944, Rangoon: It has been a red letter day for the INA. Its first division is now poised to make its debut in the upcoming invasion of India in a bid to throw the British rulers out of her soil. Today three battalions of the Subhas brigade, the first of the division's four regiments, passed in review. While Subhas delivered an electrifying speech and reminded them that the unfurling of the national flag at Delhi's Red Fort was the INA's final objective, the troops of the freedom army stood at ease and listened to him as he laid down the vision of the liberation war, a 3,000 strong assembly of INA men and officials listened to him with rapt attention. The INA units appeared as pictures of India in full splendour—people of several religions, provinces and ethnicities stood shoulder to shoulder. Their spirit on display was 'a living tribute to the unity of India'. At the end, Shah Nawaz, the commander of the brigade, visibly emotional, came near and with tearful eyes promised Subhas victory or a heroic death in the battle field.

One of the three battalions is bound for the Arakans sector lying to the west of Rangoon, while the other two are to move to the Chin Hill across the Chindwin river, towards the north. The first battalion would fight along with the Japanese force and try to evict the West African division from the Kaladan valley in that sector. The troops left Rangoon by trains. At Prome junction, they would change for final destination

Allied Forces Survive A Nightmarish Attack

February 1944, Chittagong: The Japanese response to the British transgressions in the lower Burma over the last couple of months came in the form of a huge retribution. Taking the Allied army by complete surprise, the Japanese forces, accompanied by a small contingent of the INA, gave them a severe jolt in the Akyab-Mayu-Kaladan sector. Divided into three groups, they had, in the first week of this month, in a sudden and well-disguised action seized Taung Bazar, managed to cut off two Indian divisions of the Allied forces for nearly 48 hours. Sealed off from all sources of help through the land routes and forced into a hostile geographical terrain, the Allied forces for some time faced threats of large-scale annihilation.

According to reliable sources, the Japanese plan was to complete the destruction of these two divisions and then move into Chittagong, the eastern Indian port city and thereafter, begin a long march to Delhi through Bengal. Slim was very upset at this development and felt 'it was a real Japanese breakthrough and looked nasty'.[143] Panicked, he mobilised every available resource—both army and RAF—to tide over the grave crisis. The joint forces were eventually thwarted. But INA has been taking heart from its impressive debut in the liberation war.

Japanese Forces Launch Surprise Attack In Tiddim

March 8, 1944, Tiddim: The U Go offensive in the Imphal sector had begun a couple of days ago at a place far south of Imphal. The Japanese 33rd division had delivered the first attack near Tongzang about 20 miles to the south of Tiddim. One of its regiments pounced upon a detachment of the 17th Indian division and assaulted them badly. Today, another regiment of the same Japanese division crossed Manipur River several miles south of the British position at Tiddim. But intriguingly, it began to move towards the north through the hills using tracks. The sudden presence of two Japanese regiments well within the Indian border has sent alarm bells ringing in the British force.

Slim Asks For Urgent Reinforcement From Arakan

March 13, 1944, Tiddim: Coming at the back of two serious incursions over the past one week, panic gripped the British forces at Tiddim today when suddenly strong Japanese forces appeared about 60 miles north of Tiddim. It is being feared that the Japanese, adept at jungle warfare, have already heavily infiltrated the Tiddim-Imphal road. Their intention appears obvious—to isolate the 17th division at various places between Imphal and Tiddim, surround the troops and annihilate them.

To add to the British woes, today the Japanese forces were also seen assembled in strength at the south of Kabaw valley, lying to the east of Imphal. This force, being led by Major General Tsunoru Yamamoto has the backing of medium tanks, powerful artillery. It is also accompanied by troops of the Indian National Army and the Burma National Army. According to sources, Yamamoto is planning to mount attack on Imphal, using the Sittaung-Palel-Imphal Road.

Clearly disturbed by the scale and suddenness of the Japanese attack near Tiddim and the massive enemy build-up in the valley, Scoones, the commander of the 4 Corps has today ordered the 17th division to retreat to Imphal. Slim, his boss and the commander of the 14th army has, together with Baldwin, the commander of the Third Tactical Air force, met Mountbatten and made out a strong case for immediate airlifting of troops from the Arakan to Imphal. According to sources, Mountbatten has agreed to increase the allocation of aircrafts from the present eight to thirty Dakotas or their equivalent by diverting the additional aircrafts from the Ledo Road sector as a special case.

Allies Retreat To Imphal Amidst Japanese Ambush

March 14, 1944, Imphal: The troops of the 17th division began to retreat to Imphal in a long column on foot while the provisions and the wounded soldiers were carried by vehicles. As they marched north towards Imphal, the soldiers destroyed bridges behind and planted mines and booby traps on the road and camps they abandoned. Some of the Japanese began to follow the tail of the retreating column cautiously.

Imphal – A Helicopter View

Imphal, situated at a height of 2000 ft, is militarily the most strategic place for the British in India's eastern front. Spread over an area admeasuring 40 miles by 20 miles, it is a plateau surrounded in all sides by impassable mountains. To its south and west lies the Chin Hills of the Arakan range while to its east extend mountain ranges of 2000-4000 ft peaks stretching over a few hundred miles. It is the most suitable platform for the Allies to launch an attack on Burma in the central front.

Imphal depends for its supplies on Dimapur—the latter being the last railhead in the east of India. From Dimapur, the metre-gauge rail track extends northwards over a stretch of nearly 200 miles to Ledo Road from where the American supplies have been regularly sent by air to China. That air route extends over the tall mountains spanning between the two countries. America has been using this 'hump route' to send aid to the Chinese government led by Chiang Kai-shek. Dimapur has several supply depots where food, fuel and other equipments for the armed forces operating at the frontier like Imphal and beyond are stored.

The road from Dimapur to Imphal passes through Kohima which lies to its southeast at a distance of about 45 miles. As it approaches Kohima, a small sleepy garrison town situated at a height of 5,000 ft above the sea level, the road gradually slopes up and enters a dense hilly terrain. Several hills like the Naga Hills, Garrison Hill, FSD Hill, Treasury Hill surround Kohima. Beyond this town, the road slopes down and connects to Imphal about 80 miles to the south. At Imphal, the road forks out—one enters the Kabaw valley and the other proceeds towards Tiddim. Both these roads almost run parallel to the course of the Chindwin River in the east, flowing from north to south and happens to be the natural border between India and Burma.

Considering the strategic importance of Imphal, the Allied command has taken a wide range of measures to improve the place in terms of communications, roads, air strips and supply dumps. As a result of manifold initiatives, Imphal, which was at best a big village in 1942, has now emerged as an important military base. Tens of thousands of workforces have been engaged to build 'basha camps, hutted hospitals, supply dumps, ordnance depots, engineer parks, and wide tarmac roads'.[144] Air strips have been developed too and the RAF has set up a base here.

Massive Offensive Across Chindwin
Joint Forces Advance Like A Ball Of Fire

March 16, 1944, Homalin: The 15th and the 31st—two mighty divisions of the Japanese 14th army—were for past some days deployed at a wide stretch of land along the east bank of the Chindwin River, starting from Tanga in the south to Tamantha in the north. Last night, both these divisions made a swift and massive movement. They crossed that great river and began a march towards Imphal and Ukhrul.

The two divisions have been ordered to advance 'like a ball of fire', and they are adhering to the instructions by moving through roads and numerous jungle tracks with great rapidity. On the way, several advanced units of the 20th Indian division of the Allies have faced the brunt of their fury and suffered heavy casualty. The general mandate by Lt Gen Mutaguchi to his forces has been clear—to annihilate the enemy in the advanced positions, without giving them a chance to retreat to their base in Imphal.

Unionist Party? What's That?

March 21, 1944, Lahore: Today, in a meeting with the Muslim members belonging to both Treasury and Opposition benches of the Punjab assembly, Jinnah stunned everyone by claiming that there was no Unionist Party in Punjab and the present coalition ministry was one of the Muslim League. Elaborating, Jinnah described the Jinnah-Sikander Pact as a misnomer and added that neither he nor the League was a party to it. In fact, it was a document drawn up by Sikandar Hayat Khan, the former premier of Punjab, to demonstrate to the world that the province of Punjab was present in full strength behind the Muslim League.

It was an initiative by Sikander and Jinnah could not obviously object to such a gesture. Jinnah recalled that in 1937, when Sikandar, following his return to Punjab after the Lucknow session of the Muslim League, sent him 70 forms signed by members of the Punjab Assembly agreeing to become members of the League. Right from that day onwards, Jinnah contended, all of them ceased to be members of the Unionist Party. And from that very year, Jinnah added that, the Unionist Party ceased to function.

Political analysts say Jinnah's move has been a wild political gamble. He has thrown an open challenge to Khizr and this daring act could make the Unionist Party a permanent enemy of the League. But the fact that he has taken this position may be due to his conviction about the growing public support for the Muslim League in Punjab. He may also have been driven by the urgency in securing Punjab for the League, by exploring every conceivable strategy. Punjab is, after all, the pivot for the proposed state of Pakistan!

Subhas Exhorts Indians To Help Armies Of Liberation

March 21, 1944, Rangoon: Even as a full-scale war has broken out between the two sides, Subhas, in a radio broadcast today, said that the INA 'has launched its offensive and, with the cooperation of the Imperial Nippon Army, is marching shoulder-to-shoulder in the common fight against the common foe—the Anglo-Americans and their allies.' On this occasion, Subhas has exhorted Indian people,[145] 'who are the bone of our bone, the flesh of our flesh, to render all help—direct or indirect' to the armies of liberation. He also called upon the Indian soldiers and officers in Britain's armies to refuse to fight for their despotic rulers and actively join the ranks of the INA. Subhas has urged the Indians working in various departments of the British service to render all possible help in the liberation struggle. At the end, he reminded Indians that this was the golden opportunity for them to fulfil the long-cherished aspirations for freedom: 'If you rise to the occasion and do your duty, freedom will be yours before long.'

And... You Were Prepared To Take Political Advantage Of Our Military Straits!

March 28, 1944, New Delhi: War cloud continues to envelope the world. Though the Allies have been able to prevail over the Axis powers in several fronts, the Japanese threat has already manifested in the eastern border. In addition, famine has been stalking India, ravishing her vast millions. Languishing in Aga Khan Palace prison in Poona, Gandhi is unable to see any light. Today a letter[146] from Viceroy Archibald Wavell has made him more disconsolate. Wavell's letter brought to him the message of continuing mistrust of the Congress by the Raj and heaped on him some more humiliation.

Wavell, the present Viceroy, was an army general and is supposed to be a man of action rather than of diplomacy. However, the language of his letter too has been hurting. If the previous Viceroy Linlithgow's words used to be piercing in the cloak of reasoned civility, Wavell's messages are open, blunt and direct. Wavell has held the Congress and Gandhi directly responsible for India's current predicament. He quoted his own bitter experience about how he was affected as the

Commander–in-Chief when the vital supply lines to the Burma frontier was destroyed by the Congress supporters in India. This was followed by undisguised indignation conveyed through a volley of words that aimed at injuring Gandhi's pride: '...and it is clear to me that you had lost confidence in our ability to defend India, and were prepared to take advantage of our supposed military straits to gain political advantage.'

Wavell made it clear that the present Congress policy has been hindering India's progression to 'self-government and development'. To the anguish of Gandhi, he has clarified that in regard to the political settlement, the British position continues to be the same as it was two years ago when Cripps visited the country. His Majesty's Government expects Indians to frame their constitution on the basis of the agreement amongst the communities. Conscious of the fact that such an agreement is still elusive, Wavell has suggested the priority to restore the economy over the political agenda. Then came his sermon that simply dismissed the primacy of the Congress in Indian political space and the party's long-held ideological mooring: 'I believe that the greatest contribution that the Congress Party can make towards India's welfare is to abandon the policy of non-cooperation and to join wholeheartedly with the other Indian parties and with the British in helping India … in economic and political progress....'

Political observers say that such a missive from the crown representative suggests that practically nothing has changed in the British policy in regard to the Congress and there is no chance for that party to regain its former importance as a political party, notwithstanding its sustained battle for freedom and the attendant miseries, hardship and sacrifice.

Press Will Make Capital Out Of Delays Or Setbacks

March 29, 1944, New Delhi: The British regime is faced with grave peril in the eastern border of India. The Allied army in the Imphal front has been completely surprised and forced into fighting a grim, defensive war by the joint forces. Added to the military might of the formidable Japanese, the participation of the liberation army of the Azad Hind Government in the invasion has created great political risks for the British. While massive troops are being airlifted to the battle front, Wavell, the former chief commander and presently the Viceroy, continues to be a worried man.

Today in a communiqué[147] to Amery, Wavell has mentioned about an 'under-current of anxiety' and also the apprehension that 'the Congress press will not hesitate to make capital of any delays or local setbacks that may occur'. Wavell, however, has been satisfied with the Allies' preparation to thwart the threat under Mountbatten's overall leadership and he reckons that the air superiority that the Allies have 'is likely to be decisive' which can be used both for supply purposes and the movement of troops.

Notwithstanding the advantages, Wavell sounded realistically worried about the impacts of the enemy broadcasts over civilian people in the contiguous areas: '...we cannot expect people in eastern Bengal and Assam not to listen to Japanese broadcasts, and civilian morale in those parts must for some time be in a delicate state...' It looks obvious that the Allies will try to counter the last mentioned risk through massive counter propaganda.

Stopford Sets Up Headquarters In Jorhat

April 5, 1944, Jorhat To tackle the crisis arising out of the massive Japanese attack on the Assam front, Lt Gen Stopford has, in accordance with Slim's instructions, shifted the 33 Corp's headquarters here, a place about sixty-five miles to the northeast of Dimapur. He moved in here a couple of days ago. Stopford has been instructed to 'cover concentration of troops as far forward as possible' and secure Dimapur, defend Kohima and protect the railways to Ledo as the American airfields there are being used for sending supplies to China.

Joint Forces Invade Kohima

April 6, 1944, Kohima: Last night, almost one full division of the Japanese army burst upon this small strategic town. Slim's forces had till then attempted to resist this 31st Japanese division, led by Major

General Kotoku Sato, at several points like Ukhrul, Sangshak and lastly at a place about 30 miles east of Kohima. These determined defenders fought tooth and nail, were able to retard the lightning speed of the Japanese but eventually retreated—some of them to Kohima and some others to Dimapur. By the time the Japanese launched a full-scale attack on this town, there were at best a couple of thousand soldiers to defend it. Even this small body of troops was not a compact unit, but an assortment of the Assam Battalion, the Nepalese army units, some companies of the loyal Burma regiment and miscellaneous troops.

The thrust of the Japanese attack was terrible. Almost in one single sweep, they occupied several strategic positions including the main source of the town's water supply. The defenders were overwhelmed though they kept fighting to their last breath. Their slender hope to be able to resist the Japanese for some time got a fillip when part of the Royal West Kent Regiment, the leading battalion of the 161 brigade of the 5th Indian division, managed to enter the town from the northern side last night under the cover of darkness even while the Japanese attack was in full swing. This brigade was sent from Dimapur to Kohima, anticipating an imminent Japanese attack. While only one of its battalions could manage to enter the town, the rest have been left stranded on the road. By today morning the Japanese have closed round the town and cut off the Kohima-Imphal Road.

Today, the small body of defenders have been left inside the town to face a formidable force of nearly 12,000 troops, ie. almost the full strength of a division. Slim and his junior commanders never imagined that an attack of such scale and speed could take place at such a high altitude. Logistically, this town with its complicated topography, can hardly support more than a regiment of troops while the Japanese have brought almost an entire division here. Slim has become even more alarmed at the prospect of Sato's forces advancing through tracks to Dimpaur and capturing that important rail head. Sato could leave a small contingent at Kohima and direct the main body of his force to Dimpaur, which is even more poorly defended.

Subhas Sets Up Temporary Headquarters At Maymyo

April 7, 1944, Maymyo: Subhas has set up temporary headquarter in this small scenic hill town lying nearly 42 miles to the east of Mandalay. The Azad Hind Dal, tasked with setting up government apparatus in the occupied Indian territory, whenever called upon, has preceded him here. AC Chatterji would function as the Chief Commissioner of the Occupied Indian Territory.

Compared to Rangoon, Maymyo is nearer to the Manipur basin where a fierce battle is raging presently. Moreover, Mutaguchi, the commander of the 15th Army, has his headquarters here. The INA in the front has no proper signal equipments to keep in touch with the headquarters. Staying close by the Japanese General will help Subhas keep track of the war situation in general and INA troops in particular. Further, the INA troops arriving from Malaya via Rangoon are making their way to the front from here.

League Wants Assam To Be Part Of Independent Pakistan

April 8-9, 1944 Barpeta: To the relief of the Viceroy, Assam, presently under the pro-British premier Saadullah, has been extending good measure of help to the Allied forces engaged in a fierce battle with the Japanese army and the INA in Imphal and Kohima. In turn, the Muslim League has been using the British dependence on it to tighten its hold over this Hindu majority province. The Assam Provincial League held its conference here and Chaudhury Khaliq-uz-Zaman presided. In his speech, Khaliq emphasised that Pakistan is the only solution to the Muslims against the vagaries of the majorities. The conference concluded that both the provinces of Bengal and Assam, should together form an independent sovereign state to be known as Eastern Pakistan.

RAF Airdrops Water In Motor Tyres For Besieged Troops

April 15, 1944, Kohima: For the last nine days Kohima has been witnessing 'round the clock' bloody war—probably the bloodiest in the whole sector so far. Sato's forces have been launching relentless attacks over their enemies but have not still been able to inflict a conclusive defeat upon them. There have been heavy casualties in both sides. If one single factor has still kept up the morale of the British forces, it has of course been the numerous sorties by the Royal Air Force which has been dropping food, medicine, reinforcements and, of course, the much needed 'water' to the utterly thirsty soldiers in 'motor tyres'.

From the trend of the battle here, it appears Sato has no plans to proceed to Dimapur before the enemy is completely annihilated in Kohima and he gets full control of this town. Benefiting from Sato's 'Kohima first' strategy, Slim has, by this time, strengthened his forces considerably. Beginning from the 17th of the last month, thirty aircrafts have been ferrying in reinforcements from the Arakan and India's interior to both Imphal and Dimapur. By now the whole 5th Indian division has been transported to Imphal and to Kohima through Dimapur. No less importantly, the 2nd British division has arrived in Dimapur too. Now the British forces in Dimapur and Kohima are numerically as strong as the Japanese. More are on the way.

Today, one of the regiments of the 2nd British division sent to Kohima from Dimapur has joined hands with the remaining battalions of the 161 brigade of the 5th Indian division that was left stranded between Kohima and Dimapur for the last nine days. The two brigades of two different divisions have joined hands, and they have begun to march towards Kohima. The course of the battle in Kohima seems poised for a change in favour of the Allies.

Subhas Stands A Chance To Break Allied Position

April 1944: As the Indian National Army is standing at the eastern gateway of India along with the formidable Japanese army, the British Indian empire has come under grave peril. If the British resistance in Kohima crumbles, the liberation army could manage to reach the plains of Assam and thereafter attempt to descend on the Gangetic plains of Bengal and that could set the whole country aflame.

Articles published in the western press including in America, are pointing out this danger. Opinion pieces written by political experts are sharply critical of Subhas and condemn him as being a tool, puppet or agent of the Axis nations like Germany and Japan. However, the authors simultaneously pay grudging admirations to the young Indian leader's diplomatic skill, ambition, courage, patriotism and his rapid metamorphosis as a prominent leader on the world stage. Apprehensions are also being voiced that Subhas stands a realistic chance of breaking through the Allied position in Imphal and Kohima, which would be nothing short of a catastrophe for the British in particular and the Allies in general, who have otherwise managed to turn the tide against the Axis power in Europe, the Pacific and Africa.

To avert this imminent danger, the British Government has been studiously following a policy of silence about Subhas and the provisional government of Free India. Simultaneously, they are projecting the invasion as attempts by greedy Japanese to occupy India and the INA soldiers as Japanese stooges. The Indian soldiers of the British Indian army have no idea, whatsoever, about the real story of the sacrifice, patriotism and purpose of their counterparts in the INA.

Missing The Wood For The Tree? Faux Pas By Japanese?

William Slim, the commander of the 14th Army, has been both surprised and relieved at Major General Sato's strategy of not making attempts to take over Dimapur by skirting Kohima. For Sato, the commander of the Japanese 31st division that is fighting in Kohima, it would have been a rather easy task as Dimapur, poorly defended, would have quickly succumbed to Sato's tenacious and aggressive soldiers. Slim had feared that Sato would direct the major part of his forces to Dimapur, leaving a detachment at Kohima. If only Sato could take Dimapur, the entire Brahmaputra valley would have laid open to the joint forces including the rail and road to Ledo. Instead, Sato decided that the joint forces should repeatedly hammer the small town of Kohima till it is captured completely, whereupon he would advance to Dimapur. But a small body of defenders under instructions from Slim 'to fight to the last man', continued to frustrate Sato's efforts with their steely resolve and by leveraging the unique topography of the place. Now, with the progressive arrival of forces from the

Arakans and India at this battle theatre, things have begun to look somewhat better for the Allies.

Political analysts concurred with Slim's assessment. Kohima, they felt, was of little consequence compared to Dimapur. This small town with a weak defence could certainly be left to a detachment and the core of the 12,000 strong force could launch a lightning invasion of Dimapur. The occupation of that railhead and the vast supply base would have been much easier, both due to its poor defence and uncomplicated graphic position. Once Dimapur came into the possession of the joint forces, the Allied army in both Kohima and Imphal would have been permanently cut off from overland supplies. Even more important was the fact that the joint forces could then reach the Assam plains and thereafter, march to Bengal where the INA and the Japanese forces could have a role reversal in the matter of leadership. That would have led to rousing mass upheaval against the British. The decision to stick to Kohima and allowing the Allied forces to strengthen their forces in Dimapur has been a strategic blunder, they opine. According to some reports, there has been a lack of strategic thinking on this issue even in the Burma Area Army headquarters in Rangoon. Differences of opinion between Kawabe and Mutaguchi on the issue of attacking Dimapur have also been rumoured. To make matters worse, Sato was also reportedly harbouring differences with his boss Mutaguchi.

Rescue Forces Enter Kohima Under Cover Of Artillery

April 20, 1944, Kohima: The tight Japanese squeeze over Kohima has begun to slacken. The near-complete sway over the sky by the RAF has been making important differences. Though still in a bind, the Allied forces have been able to get the injured evacuated and receive reinforcement through the aerial route. They have also been receiving supplies of food, medicine, fuel and equipments in the same way. On the other hand, the Japanese have already run out of their ration. Their supply route, stretching up to the Chindwin, has been coming under frequent attacks by the guerrillas of the LRP brigade. They have practically no means to treat their injured soldiers too.

Taking advantage of their fatigue and frustration, the Allied Command has begun to send fresh troops to Kohima by repairing the road from Dimpaur. The 6th brigade of the 2nd British division from Dimapur managed to enter Kohima under cover of RAF and artillery fire. It relieved the fatigued soldiers of the garrison. Though the Japanese forces continue to hold the vantage positions in the town and the surrounding hills, they are unlikely to be able to maintain their grip over Kohima for long, unless the logistical environment is changed in their favour.

Jinnah Engineers Rebellion Against Khizr

April 30, 1944, Sialkot: Jinnah, in order to take up his fight with Khizr to the next level, came to Lahore in March this year and held series of parleys with the latter. His mission is to place the Muslim League on firm footing in Punjab, and that without delay. Jinnah wants the Unionist Party-led ministry in Punjab to be known as the League ministry. He also wants Khizr to make the Muslim League fully functional in the province. Through a series of political and public meetings, Jinnah has been trying to attract Muslim members of the Unionist Party as well Muslims of the province to the Muslim League. He has been leveraging the twin issues of 'Islam' and 'Pakistan' to achieve his goal. Khizr is feeling the heat—a slow and silent migration of Unionist Party supporters to the League has begun, thanks to Jinnah's prolonged presence in Punjab and active propaganda.

If Jinnah is squeezing him from one side, Khizr is under pressure from both Chhotu Ram, a senior leader of the Unionist Party and also the British governor, Glancy. They have been repeatedly advising him not to succumb to Jinnah's plan.

Khizr's problem compounded when his important cabinet colleague, Shaukat Hayat Khan, began to issue statements that the League's demands were not unreasonable and the Unionist ministry should accept the League discipline. Things became alarming when a group of about twenty legislators began to support the Punjab

Muslim League. Under such adverse circumstances, Khizr has now recommended to the governor for the dismissal of Shaukat. Jinnah was able to engender discontent amongst Union Party members by projecting himself as a victim of Khizr's high-handedness.

Thereafter, Jinnah furthered his political objective by holding a conference of the Punjab Muslim League party here. It was presided over by Abdur Rab Nishtar, a cabinet minister of the neighbouring NWFP. In the conference, Jinnah has issued an open call to all the Muslim members of the Punjab assembly to declare that their allegiance was to the Muslim League and to no other. He also demanded that the coalition ministry should come to be called that of the Muslim League Party. He is determined to decimate the 'Unionist Party' from Punjab.

GANDHI RELEASED FROM PRISON

May 6, 1944, Aga Khan Palace: Over the last few months, Gandhi's health has been deteriorating. His wife and worthy life partner Kasturba Gandhi died on 22 February this year in this very prison, an event that caused him deep hurt. Recently, his health condition has turned serious.

A team of doctors comprising General Candy, IMS and Dr BC Roy examined him. Three days ago they reported that Gandhi's condition was serious and he runs the risk of developing coronary or cerebral thrombosis. The government has now decided to release him[148] unconditionally, on health grounds.

Some political observers are, however, not ruling out a link between Gandhi's release and the fierce battle that has been raging in Imphal and Kohima. Subhas has been making repeated radio broadcasts addressing Indians to help the liberation army. The British propaganda machinery has been working overtime to neutralise his broadcasts through massive disinformation campaign. At the present juncture, when the top Congress leadership are in prison, small spark of rumours can make the country explode. They say Gandhi's public presence could have a reassuring effect on people and also act as a protective amulet for the government.

Gandhi Regiment Suffers Early Setback, Tries To Regroup

May 8, 1944, Khanjol The Gandhi regiment, the second major constituent of the INA's First division, overflowing with patriotic spirit, joined the battle front at the fag end of last month. Inayat Kiani, the brigade commander, was immediately asked by the Japanese commander, Yamamoto, to rush to Palel and join in an impending assault on the airport there. The Japanese were to attack that 'strategic facility' from the east and the Gandhi brigade was asked to simultaneously mount the assault from the south. Excited and eager to make a debut with such an important action, Inayat rushed a company there without wasting time and then followed up with his forces. Unfortunately, the advance unit reached the spot after the Japanese operation was carried out. To compound their miseries, it was ambushed by a well dug-in and disguised contingent of Gurkha troops on its way. Thereafter, a sustained confrontation took place between the two sides and it cost the Gandhi regiment nearly 200 lives. This was a dampener at the very 'start'. But the regiment did not lose heart. Inayat withdrew to Khanjol and set up the regiment's base.

Here too, his forces have had confrontations with the enemy following which they were pushed out of the place a couple of days ago. But today the regiment has recaptured Khanjol and it has established its firm grip over the place. The regiment has also occupied Mittongkhune, another strategic village on the next spur of mountain. Now positioned well in the strategic Tamu-Imphal sector, the regiment is preparing to protect the left flank of Yamamoto's Japanese forces. His forces have been mounting waves of attacks on Slim's army, along the Tamu-Sabong-Palel-Imphal Road. In fact, this can be seen as the most potent of all Japanese attacks in the battle for Imphal.

Joint Forces Surround Imphal, Torment Defenders

May 10, 1944, Imphal: Imphal has been encircled by the joint forces from several sides. This town, like the hub of a wheel, has been connected to its hilly circumference by six 'unevenly spaced spokes', each of the spoke representing a road or track coming from: (a) Kohima in the north; (b) Iril river valley in the north-northeast; (c) Ukhrul in the northeast; (d) Tamu-Palel in the southeast; (e) Tiddim in the south and (f) Silchar-Bishenpur in the west. The joint forces, deeply entrenched in the surrounding hills, have been launching relentless attacks on the defenders of Imphal by advancing through these spokes.

Though under severe pressure, the defenders of Imphal have been strengthened by reinforcements brought in by air. Besides the three divisions of the 4 Corps headquartered here, additional troops have been brought from the Arakans and India. Together with a tank regiment and active support of the RAF, they have been managing to prevent the joint forces from reaching the town. Most battles are taking place either along the spokes or in the circumference of the wheel. The allied defenders have been moving forward daily along the spokes to thwart the 'relentless' tides of attacks, while the joint forces have been making every effort to achieve a breakthrough.

Like Kohima, the marked difference in the air power of the two warring sides has been making an important difference in the outcome of the battle here. While the Allied transport aircrafts are evacuating the injured, bringing in fresh troops and supplying food, fuel, and equipments, the RAF fighter and bomber aircrafts are almost acting like the Allied army's extended hand. They have been bombing and strafing the joint forces ruthlessly and regularly.

With bulk of their aircrafts sent to the Pacific, the Japanese air force has generally kept a low profile in this ongoing battle. Today was an exception. A fleet of 25 Japanese aircrafts attacked Bishenpur in a bid to obtain a decisive advantage for the joint forces. However, they failed to deliver. Worse, some of the aircrafts were felled by Allied gunners. Undaunted by reverses, such as the one that happened today, the joint forces seem determined to continue with their aggression and invasion of Imphal.

Subhas Brigade Heads Towards Kohima

May 16, 1944, Chin Hills: Unable to achieve a decisive breakthrough in Kohima despite best attempts, the Japanese army commander has asked for INA's help in that sector. Having rejected INA's repeated requests earlier for a front role in the past, the Japanese request now came as a surprise to the divisional commander Zaman Kayani. Without wasting time, Shah Nawaz the commander of the Subhas brigade at Kayani's instructions, has mustered the third battalion and a part of the second battalion of the brigade presently not engaged with the enemy. He is about to start and pursue a long journey with his forces from the spine of the Chin Hills through the Kabaw valley to Kohima via Ukhrul. Though the journey would be long, arduous and the mission very challenging, they are, riding on their spirit and enthusiasm, hoping to leverage their knowledge of the local areas and their readiness to sacrifice lives to achieve a breakthrough in that key battle front. Military experts are, however, not much hopeful. They say the Japanese request has come too late and by now Slim has strengthened the British position in both Kohima and Dimapur. Unfortunately, the Subhas brigade has no transport of its own and must rely on the Japanese arrangement. Further, the monsoon has set in and the rain-lashed mountains are making movement difficult.

Mahatma Was Released Due To INA's Advance: Subhas

May 18, 1944: Today in an interview with *Yomiuri Hochi*, a Japanese newspaper, Subhas has asserted that the British attempts to check the advance of the joint force will be useless.

He mentioned that the joint forces have already pierced through the defences of a huge army put in place by the British and in a short time, this army will bring an end to British rule in India. Saying that the war of India's liberation can never be lost, Subhas has claimed[149] that 'Mahatma Gandhi's release was primarily due to the Indian National Army's advance.' He also sounded a word of caution saying that 'Britain wants to come to an agreement with the Congress, but that will be another defeat'.

Muslim League Expels Khizr From Party

May 28, 1944, Lahore Following his 'Mission Punjab' last month, Jinnah was able to drive a wedge and create inner torment in the Unionist Party. One of its important fallouts was the suspension of Shaukat Hayat by that party after he had recommended a pro-Muslim League line to Khizr. The Punjab premier was already angry about Jinnah's meddling in Punjab politics and Shaukat's growing allegiance to Jinnah. Recent developments provoked him to go further and recommend dismissal of his cabinet colleague to the British governor. The friendly governor acted with alacrity and removed Shaukat. It is now Jinnah's turn to retaliate in order to keep the fight against Khizr raging. Yesterday, the AIML Committee of Action held a meeting here and expelled Khizr from the membership of the League for his open defiance of the aims, objects and rules of the AIML. Acting in tandem with the central body, today the provincial Muslim League has declared 'all out war' against Khizr. It has not only welcomed the 'expulsion' decision by the committee of action, but also issued a clarion call to Muslims of Punjab to rally behind the Muslim League.

Sato Lifts Siege Of Kohima

May 31, 1944, Kohima: Sato's forces could not convert the advantages of the early blitzkrieg at Kohima. Though for a few days they enjoyed a huge numerical advantage over their enemy, Sato could not convert it into a conclusive victory. Over the next several weeks, large British reinforcements have arrived at Dimpaur. The RAF has been evacuating the wounded, delivering reinforcements and dropping arms, ammunitions and food. Its fighter planes are also taking part in the war covering its troops and strafing enemies.

The Japanese domination of the town had come under challenge in the middle of last month, when the 161 brigade of the 5th Indian division and 5th brigade of the British second division had forced their way into the town under RAF cover and heavy artillery fire. Since then the British have been introducing new forces in phases. As a result, by the 10th of this month, there were two brigades of the British second division, one brigade each of the 5th and 7th Indian divisions and one Indian motorised brigade inside Kohima.

The hugely improved strength of the British force, aided by the RAF, gained superiority over the Japanese division. The challenge before them, thereafter was one of dislodging the Japanese from their deeply entrenched strategic positions in the surrounding hills overlooking the town.

That gradually turned into a hand-to-hand fighting. In that stage of confrontation, the wearied Japanese forces began to wilt. Unlike their enemy, the Japanese wounded could neither be evacuated nor reinforced. Corpses piled up. Worse, their supply line stretching up to the Chindwin river came under frequent attacks by the LRP guerrillas. In the last few days, the British attacks on tired and starved Japanese forces grew intense. For all practical purposes, their continuation in the town has become untenable. Today Sato, the commander of the 31st division, has ordered the siege of Kohima to end.

Yamamoto's Force Continues To Threaten Imphal

May 31, 1944, Tamu: The Japanese army has been ordered to lift the siege of Kohima. But they are still managing to cling to high ground to prevent the British forces from moving southwards from Kohima, and attacking the Japanese besiegers of Imphal from their rear. Notwithstanding the setback at Kohima, the battle for Imphal is going on with full fury.

Their northern side still protected by the damaged Kohima-Imphal Road and the continued vigil by the Japanese army still clinging to Kohima and its outskirts, Mutaguchi's army has been delivering the major assault on Imphal from its southeast side, ie. up the Tamu Road. Here the Japanese forces, under Yamamoto, have been making relentless attempts to get a breakthrough. His forces have been protected by the Gandhi regiment on the right and the Azad regiment on the left.

I Pleaded As A Prisoner, Now I Plead As A Freeman For Permission To Meet My Colleagues: Gandhi

June 17, 1944, Poona: Gandhi has begun to explore the possibility of a negotiated settlement with the British regime. He had written to the Viceroy while he was in prison, but received no response. In another attempt to break the ice between the Viceroy and the Congress, he has written to the Viceroy stating that he would like to, as wished by the people of the country and several others out of India, take initiative for the general good. And for that he needed to know the mind of the Congress Working Committee.

He has sought permission from the Viceroy to meet his colleagues still incarcerating in prison. Reminding the Viceroy that earlier he had pleaded as a prisoner for permission to see them, Gandhi added, 'I plead now as a free man for such permission'.[150] And if the Viceroy wished to see him before that, Gandhi offered to turn up before him.

Kohima-Imphal Road Is Now Clear

June 22, 1944, Imphal: That the ongoing battle in Kohima held no hope of victory for the joint forces was clear before May came to an end. On the 31 May, Major General Sato had ordered his division fighting in Kohima to lift the siege of the town. Accordingly, the troops withdrew from the garrison town and retreated into the surrounding wild country.

That marked the end of one phase of the battle, but the Japanese army continued to pose challenge to their enemy across the entire stretch of the road between Kohima and Imphal. To re-open the road, one British division, one Indian division and the guerrillas of the LRP regiment had started from Kohima on the 6-7th of the present month towards Imphal. They cruised along with the twin mission (a) repairing the damaged roads and bridges; (b) fighting the surprise attacks by the joint forces on the way. From the opposite side, another Indian division of the 4 Corps began to march from Imphal to the north. The two forces today met at the 109 mile stone.

The union of the two forces has signalled the end of the siege of both Kohima and Imphal. However, military experts do not consider this to mean the complete rout of the joint forces as yet. Living in the hilly terrain in strength, they retain the ability to launch attacks, and they have been doing so in select areas around Imphal.

Monsoon Torments Joint Forces No End

June 1944, Imphal: Though the lack of provisions and medical facilities had been tormenting the joint forces against their well-provided enemy who have access to a steady supply of food, medicine, fuel, arms, equipments and also fresh soldiers, they were still fighting a highly unequal war with exceptional grit and determination. But, now the monsoon has broken their back. As usual, in this period of the year, the rain lashes the whole hilly terrain with all its might.

Torrents of water have obliterated the narrow roads and tracks. In several places the strong currents of streams have been washing away the supplies coming from distant Burma across Chindwin. Two more factors have added to their woes: First, the guerrillas of the LRP regiment are carrying out attacks on their supplies en route. Second, the RAF has been chasing and strafing the soldiers of the joint forces at sight.

Father Of Our Nation! Bless This Holy War For India's Liberation: Subhas To Gandhi

July 6, 1944, Rangoon: Despite the reverses suffered by the joint forces, particularly in Kohima, Subhas is convinced that the course of the war could even now be turned in favour of the joint forces if only they could dislodge the Allied forces from Imphal without delay and secure a foothold in that strategic town. Though he has been urging Indians to help the Liberation army and throw their full weights against the Anglo-American forces, nothing worthwhile has happened on ground. Gandhi was released a long two months ago, on 6 May to be precise, but he has been ill. Moreover, he also chose to remain indifferent to the happenings in the eastern front, and in fact, adopted 'Maun' for a crucial fortnight following his release.

Today, Subhas has issued a frantic appeal[151] to him. In a radio broadcast addressed to Gandhi, Subhas has gone great lengths in explaining the rationale for the present war. Subhas said that every Indian would have welcomed if India could secure her freedom through Gandhi's method of non-violence but 'things being what they are', there is no alternative left but to 'wade through blood'. He sought to reassure Gandhi that Japan bore no evil intention about India and he could, with all his experience and understanding of international politics, vouchsafe this. He emphasised that three million strong expatriate Indians have been supporting this last war of independence as one solid body. Subhas said, having experienced the might of the British forces, he was confident of a victory in the war. He also sought to assure Gandhi that as soon as victory over the British regime was accomplished the provisional government would hand over the responsibility to a government elected by 380 million Indians. At the end, he made an anxious appeal to Gandhi.[152] Addressing him as the 'Father of the Indian Nation', Subhas has urged him to help this grim war of liberation:

'India's last war of independence has begun. Troops of the Azad Hind Fauj are now fighting bravely on the soil of India and in spite of all difficulty and hardship they are pushing forward slowly but steadily… Father of our nation: In this holy war for India's liberation, we ask for your blessings and good wishes.'

The Japanese Army Decides To Retreat

July 8, 1944, Rangoon: Though the siege of Kohima and Imphal were lifted last month, the joint forces continued to operate from the surrounding hilly terrains and make the lives of the Allied forces difficult. Undaunted by bombings and air strafing, they kept coming back hard at their enemies as and when opportunities arose, often courting heavy casualties.

But with every passing day their capacity to fight has been dwindling. Acute shortage of food, provisions and armaments, growing injury and no facilities for the evacuation of the injured soldiers and absence of facilities for medical treatment locally have been severely afflicting them. Compared to their well-sheltered enemies, the joint forces have been virtually living in bivouacs—exposed to the bare 'elements'. Added to that, the rampant monsoon has been playing havoc with their lives. It has not only ended the last chance of receiving supplies from across the Chindwin in distant Burma, but also afflicted them with unspecified diseases. The emaciated soldiers are still fighting but with no prospect of victory. Under such circumstances, the Burma Army Area Command has, in consultation with Japanese prime minister Tojo, reportedly decided to abandon the invasion.

Even If The Whole Army Becomes Only Spirit, We Will Not Stop Advance: Subhas

July, 1944, Rangoon: Subhas is greatly upset at learning about the Japanese decision to retreat. Though the Japanese army has given up, he wants INA soldiers to continue and fight to the finish. Subhas has reportedly told Kawabe[153], 'Though the Japanese Army has given up the operation, we will continue it... we will not repent even if the advance of our revolutionary army to attain independence of our homeland is completely defeated… Even if the whole army becomes only spirit, we will not stop advancing toward our homeland. This is the spirit of our revolutionary army.' Kawabe, while expressing his full sympathy on this issue, has sought to impress upon Subhas the futility of continuing to fight in such hostile circumstances.

Let Us First Have Sympathy For Ourselves!: Subhas

July 12, 1944, Rangoon: In a radio broadcast today,[154] Subhas has sought to acquaint Indians about the massive disinformation campaign being carried out by the British Indian Government, using the All India Radio (AIR) and lamented that some educated Indian men and women have been carrying out these activities for paltry monetary gain. Subhas said, the AIR has been projecting him as an unpopular leader in India who was removed from the Congress presidentship, who had thereafter to leave Europe due to differences with the German government and has now developed differences with the Japanese government as well. Stories have been planted that the Japanese government has become disillusioned with Subhas because there was no uprising in the country after the joint forces had marched into India.

The AIR is also concocting stories, Subhas said, in conjunction with some disgruntled elements, about Japanese atrocities on Indian soldiers taken as prisoners and also projecting the Japanese as being anti-religious, more particularly anti-Islam. Subhas observed that initially the British propaganda machine sought to project the INA as a puppet army, which has been forced to fight 'Japan's war'. But unable to explain as to how a puppet army could fight so bravely and so stubbornly, the propagandists are now calling the INA as a rag-tag army with poor rations and poor equipment. Subhas took pride in the INA's grit and determination in fighting under conditions of extreme hardship, which is natural for a revolutionary army, anywhere in the world. To the vehement criticism that Subhas, by siding with the Japanese, is in effect acting against interest of the nationalist China, Subhas answered, 'It is alright to talk of sympathy for China, for Russia and for other countries. But let us first have sympathy for ourselves. Let us first do something to liberate ourselves.'

He said, Japan's help was needed for India's liberation, as there was no other country who could stand against a powerful empire such as the British. He said the three million Indians in East Asia standing rock solid for the cause of India's freedom have seen the Japan of today and her new policy all over East Asia and they are convinced of Japan's sincerity. Above all, the fight that is going on inside India is no longer Japan's war, it is India's own war of liberation. At the end, he has given a clarion call to Indians to come, join and make the task of liberating the country easier.

GANDHI'S NEW PROPOSAL FOR POLITICAL SETTLEMENT

July 12, 1944, London: Today Great Britain has watched with interest an interview[155] given by Gandhi to Stuart Gelder of the *News Chronicle* during 4th to 6th this month. This is the first comprehensive interview by the Indian leader since he came out of prison on 16 May followed by a 'silence for a fortnight' after his release. Significantly, with Wavell showing no inclination to hear any proposal from the emaciated Congress with its top leaders still reeling under prison, Gandhi has leveraged a powerful foreign media to send a message to the His Majesty's Government that the Congress is ready to cooperate, provided the government demonstrates its sincerity to Indian aspirations for freedom.

Gandhi, while stating that he had no authority to act in the name of the Congress, has, nevertheless, spelt out the conditions for cooperation with the British Government:

a. The Congress would be willing to participate in a national government which would be in charge of civil government, while the Viceroy and the Commander-in-Chief would remain in full control of the British and Indian armies;
b. The provisional national government, composed of members of the central legislature would be the 'responsible government' while the Viceroy would be only its constitutional head;
c. The defence portfolio would be with the national government, which will be able to render valuable help through advice and assistance on military affairs;
d. Recognising the indispensability of the Allies having to carry out war against Japan using Indian soil, the Congress will acquiesce in their continued operation in the country, subject to the condition that the financial burden will not be on India;

On the issue of the 'civil disobedience', Gandhi has made it clear that he has no intention of offering civil disobedience now as he 'cannot take the country back to 1942'.

In regard to the endemic differences between the Hindus and the Muslims on the constitutional question, Gandhi has said that he has approved the proposal of Rajagopalachari, already submitted to Jinnah, for arriving at a communal settlement.

The interview has attracted attention in Britain and aroused keen interest in India. With bulk of the Congress leadership locked up, and the communal Muslim League seeking to usurp the entire political space, the much-revered Indian leader has returned to the political arena through this fresh initiative. People do realise that even though the British sought to decimate the Congress through a strategy-mix of punishment, humiliation and neglect, Gandhi is trying to recover lost ground with diplomatic finesse. The present proposal, after long hibernation, is probably a beginning!

Gandhi Confirms His Political Proposal To Viceroy

July 15, 1944, Panchgani: With a view to begin a negotiated political settlement for India's freedom, Gandhi had last month sought permission from the Viceroy to meet members of the CWC, still in prison. But he was disappointed. In a fresh initiative, he thereafter gave an interview to the *News Chronicle* with an understanding that before being published, it would be shown to the Viceroy. But it was probably hard for the newsman to wait that long. It has already been published in both India and England. Today Gandhi wrote to Wavell, expressing regret for its premature publication but confirming its authenticity. He urged that the proposal be examined and his earlier request to meet his colleagues be considered too.

With Rajagopalachari's Formula In Hand, Gandhi Keen To Meet Jinnah

July, 1944, Panchgani: While Gandhi has written to the Viceroy trying to force open a channel of political negotiations, he has made up his mind to explore an agreement with Jinnah. He has been acutely aware how bluntly and unashamedly the British regime has been using the Congress-League differences to their own advantage. In the oppressive gloom and despair that surrounded him in the Aga Khan Palace for nearly two years, Gandhi saw a ray of hope in February 1943 when Rajagopalachari visited him with a formula that aimed at solving the endemic communal problem between Hindus and Muslims in India.

Rajagopalachari claimed that he designed it on the basis of the 1940 Lahore Resolution of the Muslim League, by agreeing to the legitimate and reasonable aspirations of the League. The formula recognised the right of the Muslims for self-determination, but provided for a common central government for two separate 'states' to look after some common strategic areas like defence, communication, commerce etc. Gandhi was a quick convert to the formula to take India out of the quagmire, given the obduracy of the League to divide India at any cost and the British nakedly leveraging the Congress-League rift to perpetuate their rule.

Rajagopalachari had sent his formula to Jinnah in April this year and followed it up with a telegram by the end of the last month. Jinnah had replied on the 2nd this month, stating that the League could consider it if such a proposal came directly from Gandhi. Gandhi is reportedly considering proposal to meet Jinnah and take the matter forward.

THE RAJAJGOPALACHARI FORMULA

Under the Rajagopalachani formula,[156] the Congress agrees to the right of self-determination by the Muslims in the Muslim majority provinces, subject to some safeguards for the non-Muslim people. Its cardinal features are: After termination of war, a commission will be appointed to demarcate contiguous districts in Muslim majority provinces in the North West and East; Plebiscite will be conducted amongst all inhabitants of these areas based on adult suffrage or any other appropriate method; If majority wants a separate sovereign state, this will be given effect to, subject, however, to the right given to the people of the border districts to join either of the two states; In the event of separation, the two states shall have, by agreement, common arrangement for defence, communication, commerce or other essential purposes; Any transfer of population will be on voluntary basis; These terms shall be binding only in case Britain transfers full power and responsibilities for governance of India to the Indians; Subject to the terms as regards the constitution for free India as mentioned above, the Muslim League should endorse the Indian demand for independence and cooperate with the Congress in forming a provisional interim government for the transitional period.

Gandhi Writes To Jinnah Seeking A Dialogue

July 17, 1944, Panchgani: Gandhi has come out of prison after nearly two years of incarceration. In the meantime, the political ambience has changed radically and a new political equation between the old actors is incipient. Over the last couple of years, while the Congress has been almost moribund, Jinnah turned out to be the major beneficiary of

British largesse as a quid pro quo for the League's benign stand on the issue of war efforts. During this period, he has been touring provinces and communalising the Muslims of the country through highly-provocative speeches, without having to face any kind of opposition or resistance either from the government or political adversaries, especially the Congress. All along, he has used the 'Pakistan Resolution' as his trump card.

Out of prison, Gandhi has resumed negotiations for India's freedom. However, he knows that in the changed conditions, the British would insist even more that the Congress first settle the communal question with the Muslim League before raising the issue of Indian independence with them. Gone are the pre-war days of 1937 to 1939 when Congress had been ruling over eight out of eleven provinces, and the League under Jinnah was tottering. The picture is very different and Gandhi now needs to win over Jinnah's confidence to be able to place a meaningful demand before the British government. Rajagopalachari has been prodding Gandhi to initiate dialogue with Jinnah to settle the communal question. Accordingly, Gandhi has made the first move. In a letter[157] written to Jinnah in Gujrati, he made an appeal: 'There was a time when I was able to persuade you to speak in our mother tongue.

Today I venture to write in the same. I had already invited you while I was in jail… Let us meet when you wish to. Please do not regard me as an enemy of Islam and the Muslims here. I have always been a friend and servant of yours and of the whole world. Do not dismiss me...' Not all agree to the efficacy of Gandhi's approach. Some political observers who know both these leaders well say that Gandhi's action has not been diplomatically mature. Gandhi ought to know that Jinnah never really considers him as the enemy of Islam or Muslims but accuses him of being so with a view to deriving political mileage. Therefore, any interactions on such basis are bound to be artificial and Jinnah alone is likely to derive its benefit. Even within the Congress, not every one agrees with Gandhi's move. Azad, the Congress president, strongly feels Gandhi's overtures towards Jinnah are wrong and it is only giving Jinnah more legitimacy and prominence, with no benefit accruing to Congress.

INA To Abandon Imphal Campaign

July 18, 1944: About a week ago, Japan had indicated to Subhas that its army in the Indian sector was left with no alternative but to retreat and that the military operation has simply become unviable and continuation would only mean loss of more precious lives. Initially Subhas was in favour of the INA continuing and fighting to the last man to set up a high glorious tradition of patriotism and valour. But later, practical considerations weighed in and he thought it better to retreat to be able to resume the struggle at a future time. Today Col MZ Kiani has ordered all regiments of the first division of the Indian National Army to withdraw and retreat to Burma.

Japan Orders Withdrawals Of Forces From India

July 18, 1944, Rangoon: The Japanese-Burma Area Army command has issued orders to its forces to withdraw from India into Burma.

Gandhi & Azad Regiments Fight Amidst Adversities

July 18, 1944: The verdict of the battle for Imphal has been delivered and the Japanese army has decided to retreat. Preparations are on for safe withdrawal to Burma and necessary rear-guard action. By now all the surviving troops of the three INA regiments including the Subhas brigade are on the Tamu-Palel Road. Their ration and supplies have been severely affected. Since the campaign began, the INA headquarters, were despatching these through trucks from Yeu railhead to Kalewa in the Chindwin, beyond which these were sent through animal transport. Once in the hills, these had to be carried only on human back.

The monsoon upset even this fragile arrangement. While the supply schedules from Burma have been disrupted of late, the movements in the rain-splashed mountains have become extremely difficult. The miseries of the INA troops aggravated as the Hikari Kikan, the intermediary, has diverted the stock meant for them to the Japanese troops, and that, on several occasions. Notwithstanding irregular ration, inadequate clothings and blankets, ineffective arms and limited ammunitions, all of which in combination have already taken toll of many of the INA men, both the Gandhi regiment and the Azad regiment were till recently still doing their jobs of protecting the Japanese flanks, in earnest. The Gandhi regiment was initiating some guerrilla actions.

On its part, the Azad regiment conducted several raids on British supplies sent from Imphal eastwards down the hill slopes. Despite their much-depleted strength, both the brigades were withstanding all odds and continuing to fight the enemy. Both the regiments have now been doing a fighting retreat in accordance with their HQ's instructions.

For The Vanquished INA Men, It Is Still A Victory

> Both, the Japanese and the INA men, are retreating, negotiating treacherous mountain slopes and tracks amidst torrential rains. With supply lines dismantled by the monsoon and the country not offering anything to fill their stomach, the weary and starving soldiers—many of them infested with dysentery, malaria and Naga sore, but having no medicine to take—are trudging along like half-dead.
>
> On both sides of the track, corpses of their colleagues lie scattered, mostly decomposed. Amidst such scary sights, some of these retreating men seriously ill and completely drained out of energy, are unwillingly abandoned by their fellow soldiers, as every man who can still walk has to preserve the last drop of his strength to somehow take the next step forward.
>
> Like the Japanese, nearly half of the INA men who had turned up for the battle have perished in the war because of hunger and disease.
>
> The survivors had offer from the enemy to desert the INA and come over to the King's side. RAF planes had distributed leaflets assuring them of sympathetic treatment. But the prospect of safety, food and even passage to home could not allure more than a tenth of the total force. The rest has opted to embrace privation, hunger and even death rather than to fail the cause

of India's freedom. The malnourished, ill, scantily-dressed INA men are returning in discipline to Burma, holding their heads high. They have, of course, been beaten militarily, but they continue to dazzle in moral halo!

SEAC Formulates Plan 'Capital' To Wrest Burma

July, 1944, New Delhi: After the siege of Imphal and Kohima was lifted, the Allied Command became confident of a decisive victory. Full Japanese retreat, it reckoned, was only a matter of time. In a high level meeting, Slim, the commander of the 14th army, Baldwin, the head of the Third Tactical Air force, and Mountbatten, the Supreme commander of SEAC, agreed upon a plan code named 'Capital' that aims at wresting Burma from the Japanese by leveraging the momentum of the recent victory.

The crux of the plan is that the 14th Army, supported by 221 Group RAF, would move into the plains between Chindwin-Irrawaddy Rivers and thereafter attempt to capture Mandalay across the Irrawaddy in the heart of Burma. Further, to accentuate the pressure on the Japanese military regime, Christison-led 15 Corps in the Arakans supported by 224 Group RAF would attempt to secure some advanced positions in that region. Finally, the plan envisages a culmination of these operations by launching an amphibious assault on Rangoon through both the sea and the air around March 1945, before the monsoon sets in. If successful, this would mean not only the driving out of Japanese but also extinction of INA's hope to liberate India.

Gandhi's Offer Of Cooperation For War Efforts Ill-conceived And Ill-timed?

July 27, 1944, Panchgani: Right since he was released from prison, Gandhi has been facing conspicuous indifference from the Viceroy despite his overtures. He had used the media to float a political proposal to the British Government early this month. Later, on 15th of this month, he had confirmed about the authenticity of the interview to Wavell. But even that has not helped to break the ice.

Today he has written[158] to the Viceroy offering that he would advise the Congress to extend full cooperation in the war effort, provided the government makes a declaration of immediate Indian independence and agrees to a national government responsible to the central assembly subject to the proviso that during the pendency of the war, the military operations should continue as at present without involving any financial burden on India.

Political observers are, however, shocked to observe that Gandhi, by offering support for war-efforts, has made a vital compromise with his life-long principle of 'non-violence'. Further, they have reservation about the impact of his appeal at this juncture, when the government has been able to overcome the Japanese-INA invasion in the eastern border. They point out that the threat in Imphal was at its peak when Gandhi was released in May, and it remained so for some weeks thereafter, when Subhas kept appealing to Indians in general and Gandhi in particular. Little doubt that at the present juncture, things have become easier for the government. The Viceroy may not be eager to respond!

Recall Governor: Jinnah Escalates Fight Against Khizr

July 30, 1944, Lahore: Jinnah sought to escalate his fight against Khizr to the next level. As part of it, the AIML Council held an important meeting in Lahore, challenging Khizr's authority over his own province. The attendance of the Muslim premiers of Bengal, Sind and NWFP in the meeting added to the clout of the proceedings. In one of the resolutions, the council condemned the Punjab governor's action in dismissing Shaukat Hayat. It went further and called upon both the Government of India and His Majesty's Government, to recall the governor.

Allied Forces Initiate Moves To Wrest Burma Back

August 6, 1944, Imphal: In accordance with the SEAC plan, the Allied forces have decided to pursue their agenda to wrest Burma back from the Japanese. The 33rd corps, led by Stopford, has taken over the charge of the central front at Imphal. The proposed invasion has been planned from here. Today Slim has issued instructions to Stopford to pursue the forces retreating towards Kalewa and Sittaung, occupy Sittaung, and if possible seize Kalewa and establish a bridgehead there. The new bridgeheads would be used as springboard for launching major offensives in the heart of Burma in the coming months.

Wavell Gives Cold Shoulder To Gandhi's Proposal

August 15, 1944, New Delhi: Wavell has responded to Gandhi's recent political proposal. Quoting Gandhi's letter of 27 July and written[159] in typical imperial bureaucratic style he has given enough hints that the British regime is determined to perpetuate its rule by exploiting the country's communal divide. Wavell has ruled out any possibility for a responsible national government at this stage. Further, he has clarified that the offer of unqualified freedom could be considered only upon cessation of the hostilities and that would be possible only on the basis of agreement between all major elements in the national life—a necessary condition to protect the interest of the minorities. In the meantime, Indian leaders could participate in an interim government, under the present constitution. Wavell ruled out dividing responsibilities for defence and military from other responsibilities of the government as long as the war did not come to an end. On Gandhi's concern about financial burden of the war, Wavell reminded Gandhi that it was an exclusive matter between HM Government and the Government of India. If at all, either of the two could alone discuss this matter.

On the whole, Gandhi is finding the response of the Viceroy dampening. Recognising that this regime has been bent upon exploiting the communal discord, Gandhi is likely to strive hard for a settlement with Jinnah.

Why Give Jinnah So Much Importance?

August 15, 1944, Sevagram: That Gandhi was contemplating to go to Jinnah for a talk was news. Gandhi has decided to walk up to Jinnah's home in quest of a solution for the communal issue by disregarding urgings and warnings from numerous leaders, persons and organisations cutting across political ideologies. Shyamaprasad, Abul Kalam Azad, Khizr Hayat, KM Munshi and several others have opposed this venture. Some of them reasoned, some attempted to persuade and some even warned him.

Savarkar has reportedly said that Indian provinces were not private properties which Gandhiji and Rajaji could make a gift of to anyone they liked! Early last month, the All-India Sikh Conference held at Amritsar had rejected he Rajagopalachari formula and voiced the apprehension that in course of the dialogue, Gandhi 'will further surrender to the Muslim League'.[160] Many have been opposing the Rajagopalachari formula for the sole reason that it envisages the vivisection of the country. Following the Sikh conference, Master Tara Singh had addressed a letter to Gandhi highlighting the Sikh concern. Today Gandhi has replied seeking to alleviate Tara Singh's anxiety: 'We shall come to no final terms. The smallest interest will have the same weight as the largest…'[161] Despite Gandhi's assurances that he was not going to finalise anything and that any agreement the two may arrive at will be subject to review and suggestions by wider public, the critics of his plan are not convinced. They contend that given Jinnah's obduracy and obsession about Pakistan, the summit is going to collapse anyway. Then why vest Jinnah with so much importance and accord legitimacy to the demand for 'Pakistan'? After all, it is nothing more than a mere 'concept' today?

As Pakistan Becomes More Probable, Sikhs Grow Keen About 'Azad Punjab'

August 20, 1944, Amritsar: The entire Congress leadership except Gandhi continues to be in prison. On the other hand, the Muslim League has been cultivating a cosy relationship with the British Government. In 1940, they passed the Pakistan Resolution and Jinnah had demanded that a new state of Pakistan be created out of Muslim majority provinces in the North West and the East. The former included Punjab. Right since then, the Sikhs have been worried. The political hibernation of the rival Congress over the last two years and the close proximity of the League to the British have been helping it carry forward its mission of Pakistan. After the Congress leadership were sent to the gaol, the League has been continuously adding to its strength. In Punjab, it has been building up base at the expense of Khizr's Unionist Party. In Bengal, the League has managed to grab the provincial government led by its member Nazimuddin. In Sind, it has propped up a League dominated ministry under Sir Hidayatullah. Even in the NWFP, it has managed to secure the allegiance of the new prime minister, Aurangzeb Khan. In Assam, another politically sensitive border state, it has the Saadullah-led ministry, which is loyal to the League. It is therefore clear that the League has been continuously adding to its political power and inching ahead towards the goal of Pakistan.

The turn of events across India has been suggesting that League's demand for Pakistan can no longer be taken lightly. Akali Dal has been very touchy on this issue for obvious reasons. During July last year, it had raised the demand for Azad Punjab though did not doggedly pursue this demand. But present circumstances are making the Dal leadership more apprehensive. In fact, many Sikhs were unhappy at the role the Congress had played earlier. The restlessness in the community created differences between the nationalist Sikhs and the more radical faction. In March this year, Tara Singh parted ways with Kharak Singh and resigned from the Dal in protest against the latters' activities. The radical group has become much more impatient by now. The prospect of Gandhi-Jinnah talks has escalated their anxieties further. They are looking at it as attempts to reach an agreement on Punjab over their heads. Today, they held an All-India Sikh Convention at Teja Singh Samundri Hall here.[162] Giani Kartar Singh, a prominent Sikh leader, has called for 'Azad Punjab' comprising Ambala, Jullundur, Lahore, Multan and Lyallpur divisions. Other top-ranked Sikh leaders like Master Tara Singh, Sadhu Singh Hamdard and Giani Sher Singh have supported him.

Wavell Calls Governors To Discuss Post-war India

August, 1944, New Delhi: The trend of the world war has been changing in favour of the Allies for past some time. Now that the Japanese-INA threat at the eastern border has also receded, the government in New Delhi has heaved a sigh of relief. Wavell, the

Viceroy, has called a conference of all provincial governors to discuss plans for post-war India. He knows that the government is now in a position to call the shots and even regulate the course of negotiations. The agenda includes:

a. consultation with principal Indian political parties
b. continued governance of India under the existing constitution
c. formation of a constituent assembly
d. negotiate a treaty for governing the transfer of power

Significantly, the conference proposed equal number of Hindus and Muslims in the Viceroy's executive council. This move is likely to influence the composition of the federal government and the process of eventual power transfer from Britain to India. According to critics, this proposal is patently unfair, considering the demographic profile of India marked by an overwhelming Hindu majority. However, the British government now seems to have decided to bluntly reward the Muslim League for its war support.

Kimura Takes Over Burma Area Army Command

September 1, 1944, Rangoon: There has been an important change in the Japanese-Burma Army area command here. Lt General Hyotaro Kimura has been appointed as the new commander of the Burma Area Army. He replaces Lt General Kawabe whose health has taken a knock recently. Kimura is reported to be one of the best Japanese generals and has now been assigned a difficult assignment.

Gandhi At Jinnah's Home, All Eyes On Malabar Hills

September 9, 1944, Bombay: Gandhi today reached Jinnah's home amidst intense media glare. He seemed hopeful that he would convert Jinnah to the Rajagopalachari Formula. He derives his confidence from the fact that this formula is based on the Lahore Resolution of the Muslim League. Gandhi has been contending that while the resolution was only an idea, Rajagopalachari has converted it into a practicable proposition by giving it a body. For Gandhi the maiden day, however, was not quite pleasant.[163] Jinnah repeated his charge that Gandhi came to the summit in his personal capacity, without representing the Congress or any other organisation. This was an injustice, Jinnah alleged, because Gandhi committed no one but himself while as League president, he was committing that organisation. Gandhi argued that he came with an open mind and he was ready to convert or get converted. He told Jinnah, 'You can change my views if you can and I will support you wholeheartedly.' At this, Jinnah was little enthused and hoped that if he could convert Gandhi, he would be able to make Gandhi his 'Ali' and that in the latter case, he could expect Gandhi to commend his scheme to the Congress and the nation. Gandhi, on his part, highlighted similarity between the Lahore Resolution and the Rajaji Formula. Jinnah was not convinced. He began to bombard Gandhi with numerous questions, almost like doing a 'cross-examination' in a law court. If Gandhi had thought the two parties could work out the finer details of the Rajagopalachari Formula in a spirit of goodwill and cooperation, Jinnah's attitude today has served him with a message that there is no hope on that count. Jinnah formulated a series of queries relating to proposals embodied in the Rajagopalachari Formula and put the onus on Gandhi to convince him. A key difference arose over Gandhi's clear stand that he could never ask the British to impose partition on India, while Jinnah insisted on 'partition and Pakistan' before independence is granted. Though upset by Jinnah's attitude, the ever-optimist Gandhi took everything in his stride. He is reportedly preparing for a better understanding and appreciation of his viewpoints by Jinnah on the next day.

Subhas Voices Reservations About Gandhi-Jinnah Talks

September 12, 1944, Rangoon: In a radio broadcast[164] today, Subhas has expressed deep apprehension about the Gandhi-Jinnah talks. He feels Gandhi has been keen to come to an agreement with the League even if it meant conceding the League's demand for Pakistan. Subhas said, 'It is clear that Gandhiji and other Congress leaders wish to compromise with Britain after settling with the League. We must act instantly, if we are to prevent this'. Saying that the Indians in East Asia are fighting for a free and united India, he expressed his firm hope that this mission would certainly be accomplished, however long and bitter the struggle may turn to be. 'Therefore', he said, 'we shall never be a party to any compromise with Britain'. Saying that he has great respect for Jinnah and that he is neither opposed to the League nor its illustrious leader, Subhas made it clear, 'But, I vehemently oppose the Pakistan scheme for the vivisection of our motherland.' He has warned the millions of Muslim young men about the British design to keep them under permanent subjugation through such a scheme: 'Therefore, my friends', Subhas cautioned them, 'you must remember that if you want freedom you must fight for it and kick the British out. There should be no compromise with Britain. Our divine motherland shall not be cut up.'

GANDHI-JINNAH PARLEY COLLAPSES

September 28, 1944, Bombay: The much-hyped talk between Gandhi and Jinnah, which had started on 9th this month, and was held almost on daily basis, met with its demise yesterday. Jinnah was the first to come with a statement[165] to the press pronouncing the 'end' on the same day. Jinnah said, Gandhi, upon his arrival, had assured him that he was really open to conviction and conversion to the Muslim League Lahore Resolution of March 1940. Jinnah lamented that though Gandhi came to the discussion only in his individual capacity and he, notwithstanding that limitation, and only in deference to Gandhi's wishes, carried on the parley and placed before Gandhi 'everything and every aspect of the Muslim point of view', he failed in his task of 'converting Mr Gandhi'.

Today Gandhi in a press interview[166] announced the failure of the dialogue with deep regret. However, he preferred to call the 'breakdown' as an 'adjournment sine die'. At the same time, he failed to conceal his bitter feelings about the malignant influence of a 'third party' on the outcome. He also seemed to have ventilated his frustration about Jinnah's rigidity, saying that, 'A mind enslaved cannot act as if it was free...' At the end, he left the judgement to the countrymen, especially the League members, to judge whether or not his approach was reasonable enough to meet the Lahore Resolution. Based on the wider public opinion, the two leaders should be willing to revise their stand, he contended.

Why Did Gandhi-Jinnah Talks Break Down?

There were several reasons that contributed to the breakdown. The fundamental of these being Jinnah's dogged insistence that Gandhi accept Muslims in India as a separate nation and Gandhi's equally strong persistence that both Hindus and Muslims together constitute a single nation. In a sense, other differences issued out of these two strong contradictory positions held by the two leaders. Jinnah wanted India to be 'divided' rather than 'partitioned' between the two major nations, viz. Hindus and Muslims. He was against a mutilated, disfigured Pakistan which would be the case if the territories for the latter were to be carved out on the basis of plebiscite carried out on contiguous districts in the Muslim majority provinces. If at all plebiscite had to be resorted to, Jinnah insisted that it ought to be done only amongst the Muslims and not all the inhabitants. Betraying his deep distrust of the Congress, Jinnah insisted that the division of the country ought to take place in the presence of the British and that both Hindustan and Pakistan must get their independence simultaneously from the British. Gandhi on the contrary, insisted that Hindus and Muslims were members of the same family. At the same time, the Muslims have right of self-determination. If they really want to live separately in certain parts of India, like in the North West and in parts of the East, they should be allowed to do so but only after ascertaining their mind. For this purpose he advocated the methodology of plebiscite as spelt out in the Rajagopalachari formula. Gandhi also insisted that the presence of the British was responsible for the perennial communal disharmony in the country and as such they must leave first, following which the Indians could settle the issue of partition amongst themselves. Though Gandhi, on principle, has been vehemently against the vivisection of India, yet he gave in to the 'partition' as envisaged in the Rajagopalachari proposal because of the stalemate created by the League, thereby blocking any chance of constitutional development. If the division had to take place, he pleaded that this ought to be as between two brothers. In this regard, he highlighted another important feature of Rajagopalachari's formula, ie. the two states should have a common central government taking care of the strategic mutual interests like defence, communication, commerce and the like. Jinnah summarily dismissed these contentions and said there was no question of two completely sovereign, independent states having a common central government. Political analysts feel in this whole exercise Jinnah shone as a brilliant lawyer ready to tear Gandhi's reasoning asunder. He was at his argumentative best and exposed several technical flaws in Rajagopalachari's Formula that Gandhi recommended. On his part, Gandhi came to the table as a leader of men with compassion in heart and appeal in mouth, in a bid to save Indians from the ruins of vivisection. He did not want to win arguments but strove for a solution and he relentlessly pursued this cause, trying to convert Jinnah till the last moment. Unfortunately, there was no meeting ground. Jinnah has been riding on the high horse backed by a series of political successes coming his way right since 1939. He saw little reason to reconcile unless his rival made an abject surrender in the negotiation table. The first clause of that surrender deed would have required Gandhi to accept Muslims as a separate nation. Despite all his modesty and humility, Gandhi could never accept this. With both Jinnah and Gandhi steadfast on their respective views on this point, the talk was doomed to fail. That's what has happened.

Subhas Visits INA Men In Their Sick Bed

September 1944, Maymyo: The INA men who eventually made it to Burma through the Chin Hills, Yeu and Chindwin rivers were brought to the mainland for rest and treatment. Subhas has been visiting various camps and hospitals in upper Burma to interact with the sick, and lift their morale. At Yeu, he met several INA men brought in by trucks. At Maymyo, the INA hospital run by the Rani of Jhansi regiment has been full to the brim. According to reports, his visit and his sympathetic yet energetic persona has had considerable impact on the ailing soldiers. Several expressed their eagerness to march to the battlefield as soon as he would give them the order.

New Battle Of Panipat Will Be Fought In The Eastern Hills, Subhas Calls For Renewed Struggle

October 21, 1944, Rangoon: Today, on the occasion of the first anniversary of the provisional government, Subhas has reviewed[167] the international and Indian situation and also the activities of the government. The failed invasion of Imphal could not cow down his spirit. Taking the ongoing adversities in his stride, Subhas has expressed hope and optimism that the provisional government and the INA would certainly be able to achieve the freedom of India, although it is bound to be a long and hard struggle.

He drew the outlines of the future battle that would be waged against the British. Calling that impending struggle as the new, battle of 'Panipat', he insisted that it would be fought on the eastern front stretching from Chittagong to Imphal and Kohima. Once this line is broken and the victorious liberation army enters the plains of Assam and Bengal, Subhas said, there would be mass uprising and the British will have to flee for their lives. Subhas highlighted the extraordinary strategic value of the Eastern Hills which had made the British fight there to the last man. In that great battle, he contended, the British were ultimately saved by the monsoon. Even if the liberation army could not take Imphal in its first strike, Subhas said that was not the end of the world, 'I shall go so far as to say that if we have to attack Imphal not once, but ten times, before that city falls, we should be fully prepared for it.' Subhas has urged everyone—Indians in East Asia, the soldiers of the INA and Indians at home to prepare for the next offensive and be ready to make supreme sacrifices. At the end, he has assured his countrymen in India that the provisional government would fight shoulder to shoulder with its allies, travel the long road to New Delhi and hoist the National Flag at Viceroy Wavell's house. He beckoned them to come and 'join us when we give the signal'.

Japanese Army Failed INA: New Japanese PM

November, 1944, Tokyo: Subhas, accompanied by a few top officials of his government, has arrived in Tokyo on first day of this month, in response to an invitation by the Japanese government. He has met General Koiso Kuniaki, the new Japanese prime minister. Subhas was received well by the new regime. Japan has presently been in the midst of its Operation 'Ichi-Go', a massive military manoeuvre in China to destroy the American air base in that country and to secure a vertical geo-corridor running from northern China to the south, touching French Indo-China. Clearly, Japan still has vested interest in Burma and she is keen to guard against an incipient Allied attack on that country. The two leaders discussed the 'defeat' in Imphal threadbare and both agreed that the causes for it could be largely attributed to the Japanese army, particularly the 'racial and military arrogance' at its lower level. The summit level-talk went well.

Subhas wanted communication between the two governments to take place in future at the highest possible levels. At the political level, he wanted Japan to appoint an ambassador to the provisional government. As regards the military affairs, he wanted direct communications between the commanders of the two armies, through translators. He wanted the role of Hikari Kikan to be confined only to issues of simple military liaison. In the Imphal campaign, there were instances of the Japanese army mistreating the INA men that caused avoidable hurt and animosity between the two armies. Subhas argued that the INA should be allowed to abide by its own army code even in relation to any offences committed by its men against the Japanese army, and there was agreement on the issue. In matters relating to ration and supplies which had played havoc in the failed expedition, Subhas wanted an overhauling in the present system and this too was agreed upon.

Will Sapru Deliver, When Gandhi and Jinnah Failed?

November 19, 1944: For decades it has been obvious that India could not expect any constitutional progress unless the major political parties were able to resolve their differences on the communal issue. The breakdown of Gandhi-Jinnah talks a couple of months ago, created new pessimism in the country on the prospect of settlement of the communal issue. Thereafter, it was out of question for lesser mortals to take up this challenge. In the circumstances, it took a veteran liberal leader like Tej Bahadur Sapru to begin a new enterprise.

Due to his initiative, the standing committee of the Non-Party Conference today appointed a Conciliation Board to 'examine the whole communal and minorities question from a constitutional and political point of view'. For the above purpose, the Board would establish contacts with leaders of different parties, including the minorities, who are interested in the issue, understand their points of views and recommend solutions to the standing committee within a period of two months. The Board will comprise non-political persons of eminence including judges and Englishmen. The participation of parties in the exercise will be voluntary and so would be their acceptance of the Board's recommendations. Sapru envisaged that the endeavour will transcend the conventional and partisan way of looking at the communal issue by politicans to a scientific and judicial level.

Subhas Sketches Vision Of 'Free India' To Students

November 22, 1944, Tokyo: In his eventful visit to Japan's capital, Subhas, besides meeting the Japanese prime minister and top officials, attended the first anniversary of the Greater East Asia Co-Prosperity Sphere, delivered a compelling speech and attracted limelight. Today he spoke to a different audience. To the students of the Tokyo University, he expounded his thoughts on the fundamental problems of India. He stressed on the need for industrialisation and highlighted its benefits, including its role in raising a modern army. As regards two key social issues of 'poverty' and 'illiteracy', he saw the need for quick and drastic reforms and clearly advocated the role of the state.

He argued that Socialism could address this issue effectively and that an authoritarian regime that was committed to serve the masses and act as their servant could handle this enormous task well. He envisioned that free India would synthesise the good points of nationalism, socialism and communism. Post-independence, the country would be founded on the pillar of national unity and planned economy. On the issue of internationalism, he argued that this ought to be a gradual extension of systems of regional cooperation in order to be meaningful and sustainable. He had words of appreciation for the Coprosperity Sphere in this connection. At the same time, he had harsh words for the British Commonwealth in its present form. He wanted it to be transformed into an association of free nations or else disintegrate.

Subhas Picks Up A Mixed Bag In Japan

November 30, 1944, Shanghai: Subhas has arrived here from Tokyo today. During his stay at the Japanese capital, he was able to persuade the Japanese government to accede to many of his demands. At the same time, he has had a few major disappointments, too. Subhas wanted the INA to play a larger role in the coming Burma war. With three of the four regiments of the first division no longer battle-worthy, he was keen that the third division of the INA be brought from Malaya to Burma to fight by the side of the second division against the Anglo-American forces. But the Japanese government did not agree.

It wanted the third division to remain in Malaya and protect it in the event of any Allied invasion. Secondly, Subhas wanted to move the existing artillery and the AFV battalion equipped with British Bren-carriers, along with the cart and animal transport companies (raised by the INA) from Malaya to Burma.

In the Imphal campaign, the INA fought with no equipment heavier than the light machine gun. They did not have adequate and effective access to the stock of 'mortars'. No less importantly, they were badly handicapped by lack of transport. Subhas sought to address these inadequacies but the Japanese did not agree, citing continuing Allied air attacks as reason.

The third issue, of course, was a political one with enormous significance. Subhas foresaw an inevitable break-up in the alliance between the Anglo-American block and Soviet Russia, and he wanted to utilise this emerging rivalry to common advantage. He even volunteered to initiate the process of a suitable diplomatic tie with that country. But the Japanese government rejected his proposal. He has left Tokyo, carrying the burden of these unfulfilled aspirations. However, not a man to be disheartened, Subhas is trying to make the best of the current situation. From Shanghai, he is likely to visit Saigon, Malaya and Singapore before returning to Burma. Raising finance, toning up the working of the League and visiting INA training camps are amongst his immediate objectives.

Third Allied Bridgehead Comes Up In Kalewa

December 4, 1944, Kalewa: Stopford's forces have, as per plan, built three bridgeheads in the east bank of the Chindwin river inside the Burmese territory. The first of the three was set up opposite Sittaung in September, the second one opposite Mawlaik in November and the third one was set up last night at Kalewa. These three bridgeheads are likely to be the launching pad for the Allied invasion of Mandalay through the Shwebo plains in central Burma. The Allied forces have not faced any significant opposition so far. According to reports, after suffering heavy losses in the recent Imphal-Kohima invasion, the Japanese forces are being re-organised in central Burma and they are planning to counter their enemy in the loop between the two great rivers, viz. Chindwin and Irrawaddy. That venue strategically suited them. The Indian National Army of the provisional government of Free India are also preparing for the impending battle. Their aspiration to reach India through Imphal has no doubt failed. But Subhas has not given up hope. If the Allied force could be delivered a crushing defeat in Burma, the prospect of a new invasion of Imphal would certainly re-open.

INA Gears Up For The Second War

December, 1944, Rangoon: With the war clouds gathering over Burma, the INA is preparing to play its role as assigned by the Japanese army. Three constituents of its first division, viz. the Subhas, Gandhi and Azad regiments are presently in Pyinmana. Though these regiments still have experienced soldiers and ammunition, their troops are not in battle worthy condition, so badly had they suffered during the Imphal campaign. But the fourth guerrilla regiment of the first division viz. the Nehru regiment is ready to take on the enemy. It was late in arriving in Burma to be able to take part in the Imphal campaign and therefore, remained unscathed. Led by Lt Col Gurbaksh Singh Dhillon, it is expected to make its debut in this war. The regiment has now been stationed in Myingyan, a place little above the confluence of Chindwin and Irrawaddy in the central west part of Burma. Dhillon is expected to protect adjoining areas of the river bank from enemy attack, if any. The fifth guerrilla regiment of the INA second division and the first infantry regiment are also in Rangoon, the latter still waiting for its heavy equipment to reach here by sea. The second INA division has shifted its headquarters to Rangoon already. The INA leadership has been taking every care to keep their morale high.

British Celebrate Victory Over Japanese And INA Wavell Confers Knighthood On Slim, Commanders

December 15, 1944, Imphal: General Slim has rendered British Raj invaluable services by thwarting the dangerous joint offensives by the Japanese and the INA at Imphal and Kohima. He led the Allied forces at the eastern border of India with exemplary courage, valour and intelligence. The joint offensive was perhaps the most dangerous challenge to the British Empire, as it was propelled by the formidable Japanese military prowess and the politico-patriotic strength of Subhas and the INA. If the top political leaders in the country could have provided a spark, India would have exploded like a huge storehouse of gunpowder, ejecting the British.

Now that the challenge has been met, the British Government is breathing normally. Slim has been gradually advancing the war front inside the Burmese territory, where his forces have been engaged in internecine warfare with the Japanese and the INA, in a bid to recapture that country for the Raj. In order to recognise the valiant war fought by Slim, his army and also the Allied forces, Mountbatten, the supreme commander of the Allied forces in Southeast Asia came to Sylhet to thank the American Combat Cargo Groups personally. Thereafter, he has arrived Imphal. Here, in front of the Scottish, Gurkha and Punjab regiments, Viceroy Wavell has knighted General Slim and three corps commanders viz. Christison, Scoones and Stopford for their contribution in the victory.

Sahgal, Dhillon Prepare Soldiers For Coming Battle

December, 1944, Rangoon & Myingyan: Lt Col Prem Sahgal, military secretary to the Supreme Commander of the INA took charge of the fifth guerrilla regiment early this month. Since then, several hundred officers of the first infantry regiment too have joined this regiment and it has been renamed as the second infantry regiment. Majority of the troops in the regiment are civilians, mostly Tamil men recruited in Malaya. Prem has been training them hard at Mingaladon camp in the northern part of the city. Gurbaksh too has large number of civilians in his fourth guerilla regiment, recruited from amongst people of south Indian origin of Malaya. Many of his troops are plantation workers, difficult to train. In Myingyan, Gurbaksh is trying hard to infuse discipline and make them a good fighting unit.

Is The War Again Changing In Favour Of The Axis?

January 10, 1945, Rangoon: Subhas has held a press conference here in which he expressed the hope that the course of the great war was entering the third phase and the Axis powers are regaining the initiative. Incidentally, last month, Germany in a major counter offensive carried out a blitzkrieg from the Ardennes to Antwerp in north-west Europe. In the process it caught two inexperienced American divisions defending that sector on the wrong foot and inflicted unprecedented damage killing thousands of the US soldiers.

The Allied force is clearly on the defensive there and it has been fighting tooth-and-nail to repulse the continuing German offensive. Japan has also been, as an outcome of its sustained Ichi-Go offensive, able to achieve its military objective in south central China, including destroying the airfields to which US supplies were meant to be sent from Ledo Road in north Assam. Both these military victories by two major Axis powers have been spectacular to say the least. Though inside Burma the British have been gaining upper hand by the day, Subhas is seemingly looking at the bigger picture. He is probably looking at these twin developments as harbinger of another decisive turn in the ongoing great battle. At this juncture, he has said that India ought to play its rightful part.

Battle Rages Across Banks Of Irrawaddy

January 17, 1945, Mandalay: The war situation in Burma has been intensifying. Since early last month two Indian and one British divisions entered into the Shwebo plain lying within the Chindwin-Irrawaddy river loop through Sittaung, Mawlaik and Kalewa bridgeheads understandably, with the aim to seize and capture Mandalay.

The original Japanese plan was to attract the bulk of the Allied forces within this loop where they would have a long and stretched supply line from their Indian bases, and to annihilate them there with a superior force. Though both rivals were enclosed by two mighty rivers the over-confident Japanese possibly saw 'Chindwin' threatening the back of the Allied, completely ignoring the Irrawaddy at their own back side.

However, things are not working out in the way the Japanese thought they would. The Allied forces have overcome their supply problems, thanks to the RAF and the United States Army Air Force (USAAF). Their aircrafts are making numerous daily sorties to bring in troops, vehicles, food and fuels into the battle areas. Still worse for the Japanese, the Allied fighters and bombers, holding complete sway over the sky due to the near absence of the Japanese aircrafts, have been strafing and bombing the ill-equipped Japanese ground troops almost at will.

Riding on the strong air support, one Indian division of the Allied forces have, by steadily pushing the Japanese forces eastward, proceeded so much as to reach the west bank of the Irrawaddy opposite to Thabeiikkyin (aerially 63 miles north of Mandalay) and they have been able to sterilise large areas of that bank of Japanese forces. Thereafter they have been able to set up a bridgehead in the east bank at Kyaukmyanung and send three battalions to strengthen it.

Today there was a severe counterattack on the bridgehead by the Japanese forces, but it was repulsed. This has stepped up the threat of invasion of Mandalay considerably. With control over west bank of the Irrawaddy getting gradually lost, the Japanese are now building up massive forces in the east bank of the river, hoping to inflict a decisive defeat on the Allied forces in that sector.

Bhulabhai Desai Submits Blue Print For Interim Government

January 20, 1945, New Delhi: Today Congress leader Bhulabhai Desai has met Viceroy Wavell and presented a scheme proposing participation of both Congress and the League in the interim government in the centre. Desai claimed that he has had informal discussions with Liaquat Ali Khan about it. Desai said that the scheme had Gandhi's endorsement and Jinnah's knowledge and tacit approval. Broadly, it envisaged parity of Congress and the League seats in the executive council, while twenty percent seats would be reserved for others. The interim government would function within the existing constitution but it would be completely Indianised, except for the Viceroy and the C-I-C. The scheme proposed that the Viceroy should invite Desai and Jinnah to take initiatives. They would consult the groups and recommend names. The selection will not be confined to members of the legislatures.

As for the provinces, coalition ministries shall be installed in Section 93 provinces. In the rest, the existing ministries would not be disturbed, though adjustments would be possible, subject to agreement between the parties. Significantly, the scheme did not envisage any constitutional initiative. Its makers felt it would be appropriate to think about the long-term issues after the interim government has worked together for a year or so. In terms of the scheme, no elections need be held in the immediate future either for the provinces or the centre. There have been rumours for past some time about the ongoing talks between Desai and Liaquat. Today's meeting of Desai with the Viceroy has strengthened them although no version was available from the League's side.

Desai-Liaquat Pact Is Utter Lie And Nonsense

January 22, 1945, Bangalore: The country has been agog with unconfirmed reports that Bhulabhai Desai and Liaquat Ali Khan have almost reached an agreement on the formation of an interim government. According to sources, Desai has already got endorsement of his initiative from Gandhi and the Viceroy has also, in his communications with HMG, reported about the relevance of the 'agreement' in the context of its suitability to the HMG's broad scheme of power transfer. However, reporters were in for a shock when Jinnah blasted away the reports appearing in a section of the press claiming that there has been an agreement between Liaquat and Desai with the consent of Gandhi and him. Jinnah said he knew nothing of it and described the report as a lie and nonsense. According to political analysts Jinnah's attitude and comment, regardless of factual accuracy of the talks, effectively buries the prospect of any negotiations between the Congress and the League through this channel.

Subhas Weighed In Gold On His Birthday

January 23, 1945, Rangoon: The tidings from the banks of the Irrawaddy in the Mandalay sector have been bad for the Japanese, the INA and also the Burmese national government led by Ba Maw. While one Indian division is entrenched at Thabeinkkyin at a short distance from Mandalay in the north, the other two divisions are gradually trying to approach the city from its west and south. Notwithstanding the inflow of discouraging reports, enthusiastic Indians in Rangoon, both the army-men and the civilians, insisted on celebrating birthday of Subhas in a befitting way. He was reportedly weighed in gold against his wishes and local people of Indian origin, cutting across economic classes, donated substantial amounts of money to enable the provisional government to pursue the battle for Indian freedom. A group of highly motivated young men and women promised in blood to form suicide squads in the battle against the invading enemy.

This Time I Do Not Want A Single Man To Go Over To The Enemy: Subhas

January 26, 1945, Rangoon: Although the war has been raging mostly in central Burma, directed at Mandalay, there are also concerns about Allied invasion of Yenangyaung oil-field area in the southwestern part of the country. That sector has been under the care of the Japanese 72 independent mobile brigade. INA forces have been assisting them. Today the second infantry regiment, led by Prem Sahgal, ready to move to the front, paraded before the Supreme Commander. Addressing them, Subhas exhorted them to fight valorously and finish the Allied forces. However he also alerted them that their enemy was numerically larger and better equipped. Subhas cautioned them, the battle won't be an easy one and might result in hunger, thirst, privations or even death. He reminded them that it was not of course, for the cowards or the unfaithful to shoulder that enormous task. Even at that penultimate hour, Subhas offered a chance to any one who was not sure of himself, to withdraw. But he cautioned that this time, he did not want that a single man should go over to the enemy.

Slim's Army Surpises Japanese At Nyaungu

February 14, 1945, Nyaungu: To the north of Yenangyaung, the areas lying from Chaulk to Pakokku on both banks of Irrawadddy, have been strategically important for the defenders as these areas are the gateways for Meiktila. Recently there were reports of movements of Allied troops in the Pakokku area followed by incidents of some serious clashes. In the opposite east bank, the Nehru regiment led by Dhillon has been entrusted with the sector between Chaulk and Nyaungu- a stretch of several miles. For about a fortnight, the regiment was put on high alert. According to reports, the Allied forces seen in or near Pakokku during last few days are no stray forces.

The fact is that one full division of Slim's 14th Army suddenly appeared at the west bank of the Irrawaddy opposite to Nyaungu, administering great shock and surprise to the Japanese army. Managing to disguise itself from the prying enemy eyes this division, by taking a long but strategic route through hilly terrain and its flanks protected by Lushai and East African soldiers, had marched southwards from Kalewa up the Myittha River valley to Gangaw and thereafter moved further south to reach Pauk at the west bank of the Irrawaddy opposite to Nyaungu. From Pauk, contingents of the Allied forces have been moving up to completely clear off the west bank of Irrawaddy of the defenders.

The invasion of Pakokku has been reportedly a part of this plan. According to confidential sources, another full division has also been rapidly arriving here and a bulk of it reached Pauk two days ago. These combined forces further aided by tank, artillery and airforce, plan to cross the river near Nyaungu and thereafter launch an assault on the highly strategic town of Meiktila. A good motorable road passing to the north of Mount Popa connects Nyaungu to Meiktila involving a distance of about 60 miles. If the report is correct, the British choice of Nyaungu to ford the great river has been strategic.

Not only is the expanse of Irrawaddy narrow here, the place is a also junction between the operational territories of Japanese 15th Army in the north and 28th Army in the south and therefore a kind of 'no man's territory'. Dhillon's regiment has been left in charge of this sensitive stretch. Last night under the cover of darkness, a company of the South Lancashire had crossed the river about a mile to the north of the Nyaungu town and set up a base at a cliff top in the east bank. Today, the rest of the South Lancashire and some other troops attempted to cross the river at the same place and also at a place opposite of Pagan. Pagan is situated about six miles south of Nyaungu in the east bank of the river.

Nehru Regiment Resists Enemy Attempts

February 14, 1945, Nyaungu: Dhillon found it difficult to cover several miles long stretch along the east bank of Irrawaddy with only three battalions consisting of about 2000 soldiers in all. His regiment had only four machine guns, three light mortars with limited ammunitions. Other arms were only rifles. Notwithstanding these handicaps, one of his battalions inflicted considerable damage to the enemy attempting to cross the river by boats at Nyaungu and Pagan and resisted the enemy's attempts at crossing for some time. But the small, ill-equipped INA troops could not stand the might of a fully equipped 'division' for long.

The enemy continued to make attempts to ford the river in motorised boats under the cover of heavy artillery and tank fire. Eventually, Hari Ram, the commander of the battalion which had earlier in the day wrecked several enemy boats with machine gun fire, lost nerve and he surrendered with 100 men to the enemy. Slim's men have taken full advantage and begun to cross the Irrawaddy in strength in both these points. According to reports, before the day light expired, they were able to set up a bridgehead in Nyaungu in the east bank. Dhillon has, with the rest of this battalion, retreated to Tithee village where his reserve battalion has been camping. An open fight against a much powerful enemy was out of question. He needed a safe area to re-organise his men.

INA Second Division Arrives At Mount Popa

February 18, 1944, Mount Popa: Prem Sahgal, leading the 2nd infantry regiment and holding the concurrent charge of the INA second division, reached Yenangyaung, 50 miles south of Nyaungu yesterday and heard about the debacle faced by the Nehru regiment there, three days ago. Now Slim's forces, securely lodged at Nyaungu, posed grave threat to Meiktila, with both places connected by a tankable road. At Yenangyaung, Sahgal met Japanese general Yamamoto Tsunoru who has been leading the 72nd independent mobile brigade and Kanjo Butai, a smaller force consisting of two infantry battalions.

Yamamoto had already rushed some of his troops northwards to drive away the enemy from the newly built bridgehead at Nyaungu or at least to confine them. He asked Sahgal to rush to Mount Popa and operate against the enemy in co-ordination with his forces, and with the Kanjo Butai. Though the road connecting Nyaungu with Meiktila was not through Mount Popa, it would be possible for Sahgal from his base at Popa not only to launch flanking attack on enemy using that road but also deny him access to Mount Popa and its adjacent areas.

Sahgal has reached Mount Popa today with a few men of his regiment and set up his base there. Some staff of the second division headquarters have also joined him. Located in between Nyaungu and Meiktila, Mount Popa with its top at about 'four thousand feet above the surrounding country' and with its high slopes and numerous streams is likely to be an ideal base for a guerrilla force. Majority of the second infantry regiment men are still on the way. They have left Prome and are heading towards Mount Popa on foot.

Subhas Dissuaded From Going To The Frontier

February 26, 1945, Meiktila: Subhas is here in course of a visit to the front, accompanied by Col Shah Nawaz, the commander designate of the INA second division and Mahboob Ahmed, his military secretary. Subhas has been eager to visit the INA troops at Mount Popa, to talk to them and lift their morale. By now Dhillon commanding the Nehru regiment has also reorganised his remaining troops and set up his headquarters at Kyaukpadaung within 10 miles of Mount Popa. Sahagal's ranks have also been swelling, with his forces arriving gradually and both his regimental and the second division's headquarters having been set up the western slope of Mount Popa. The forces of the two INA commanders aided by the Japanese Kanjo Butai, have been carrying out guerrilla attacks upon the enemy in the surrounding areas with mixed success.

Today, while Subhas was preparing for a visit to Popa, reports arrived that one Indian division and a tank brigade of the 14th Army have been inching up towards Meiktila from the Nyaungu bridgehead and that the enemy was only 20 miles away from Meiktila. Under the circumstances, Shah Nawaz and others strongly persuaded Subhas to give up his plan to visit Mount Popa and return to Rangoon.

Meiktila Falls To The Allied Forces

March 3, 1945, Meiktila: Meiktila has fallen to the Allied forces today. Supported by the RAF, the 17 Indian division and a tank brigade which had crossed Irrawaddy near Nyaungu recently launched a strong attack upon the heavily fortified town on 28th last month. These forces passed through the Nyaungu-Meiktila road. Neither could Yamamoto's forces nor the INA regiment at Mount Popa hold them down. However, once at the gate of the Meiktila, Slim's forces were fierecely opposed by the Japanese defenders of the town. A few days of grim fighting that eventually turned hand-to-hand inside the town settled the victory.

The Allied command is now expecting Kimura to divert forces from other places including the Mandalay battle theatre to retake Meiktila. This would help them to execute an 'anvil and hammer' strategy with Meiktila acting as the anvil. Once forces are diverted to this town, the hammer would fall on the weakened Japanese force in Mandalay. The only way Kimura can avoid the trap would be to recover Meiktila quickly and that, without sacrificing Mandalay. Unless he can do so, the Japanese days in Burma are likely to be numbered.

League Ministry Melts In KK-Congress Heat

March 12, 1945, Peshawar: Aurangzeb had been running a League led ministry in the NWFP, exclusively by the charity of the provincial British governor. With the improvement in the war situation, the government has been adopting a liberal view on Congress leaders. Dr Khan Sahib was one of the leaders set free. According to reports[168], Khan Sahib was in favour of removing the weak ministry of Aurangzeb and obtained Gandhi's consent to take over the reins in the NWFP once again. Back to the home province, Dr Khan Sahib moved a 'no-confidence' motion against Aurangzeb ministry and it was passed by 24-18 votes. It is learnt that the governor of the province has decided to invite Dr Khan Sahib to form the next ministry. He has asked Aurangzeb to continue as the caretaker PM. It is reported that the governor wanted a commitment to support prosecution of war against Japan from Khan Sahib and he has agreed.

Khan Sahib Recovers NWFP From League

March 16, 1945, Peshawar: Dr Khan Sahib has formed a new ministry in the NWFP. For him, the immediate priorities include release of his brother Khan Abdul Ghaffar Khan and other jailed members of the Khudai Khidmatgar.

The return of the Congress to office in the NWFP led to some speculations about the party's replicating the strategy in other provinces. This is causing disquiet among its political adversaries. However, sources close to the party's top leadership are ruling out such a possibility. It seems that the Congress does not want to pursue the 'come back' policy in respect of other provinces, not at least in the immediate future. In NWFP, the Congress was keen to rescue the province from both the 'Muslim League' and also 'communal fanaticism'.

Japanese Lay Siege Around Meiktila, INA Stands Guard At Mount Popa

March 20, 1945, Mount Popa: Kimura's forces led by General Honda have besieged Meiktila and they have been launching waves of attack on the town. Recapture of Meiktila is the last hope of the Japanese army to be able to repel the invaders and turn the tide of the war. One Indian division and a tank brigade have been defending Meiktila very stubbornly. But they have been completely cut off from the rest of the 14th army. Now supply and reinforcement could be delivered to them by either air or overland through the Nyaungu - Meiktila road.

In the circumstances, heavy responsibilities have been placed on Yamamoto's forces and also the INA regiments operating in Mount Popa and adjoining areas. They have been required to check British movement overland and if possible to destroy the bridgeheads on the banks of the Irrawaddy. Japanese forces have gained some measure of control of the west bank. In the east bank side, notwithstanding their obvious limitations in terms of number and armaments, the INA regiments led by Sahagal at Mount Popa and Dhillon at Kyaukpadaung, have also been harassing the enemy through guerialla attacks, especially during the nights. But neither the Japanese forces nor the INA regiments have been able to dislodge the British from their bridgehead. In fact they have not been able to reach within 25 miles of Nyaungu till now. Frequent clashes are happening between the two sides in this sector. The INA forces are holding their base.

New Forces Join INA At Popa

March 20, 1945, Mount Popa: Both Sahgal and Dhillon have been trying hard to restrict the enemy forces' movement between Nyaungu and Meiktila in or around Mount Popa, besides carrying out raids on them occasionally. Situation is becoming difficult, with the war gradually turning in favour of the British. Desertions have started and even instances of suborn occured this month and Dhillon court martialled four soldiers in order to maintain discipline in his regiment and awarded them death sentence. The verdict was endorsed by Sahgal, the acting divisional commander. Amidst such adversities, the two commanders and their regiments have, however, been achieving modest measure of success. With the help of Kanjo Butai, they have been dominating over 60 sq miles of country bounded by Mount Popa, Pyinbin and Welaung. Notwithstanding the fact that the British forces have decisive superiority in terms of numbers and equipments, they have been able to inflict damages upon the enemy by conducting a series of surprise raids. Today the third and the last battalion of the 2nd infantry regiment reported at Popa. This is a morale booster for the INA regiment though the overall ambience is gloomy. In Mekltila, the Allies have been able to airdrop a whole division and this has helped them to disperse the Japanese siege. The Allied forces have reportedly been able to subdue the Japanese in Mandalay city too.

Mandalay Falls: End Of Hope For Indian Armed Struggle?

March 20, 1945, Mandalay: Hopes of the Azad Hind Government to continue to wage armed struggle for India's independence from Burma is almost extinguished as the city of Mandalay has fallen to Allied powers. This city, which was the capital of ancient Burma, has a special place in the psyche of the Burmese people. The inability to protect it has considerably dented the image of the Japanese in their eyes.

Over last couple of months the Allied Command was able to induct two Indian divisions and one British division in the east bank of Irrawaddy within attacking distance of Mandalay. All the three anchored themselves in their respective bridgeheads. Japanese forces launched several serious assaults to liquidate these but failed. The need to divert forces to Meiktila also hampered their efforts. The final blow on Mandalay was delivered by Major General TW Pete Rees, the energetic commander of the 19th Indian division. His forces reached the outskirts of Mandalay twelve days ago and gradually forced their way into the city by successively demolishing a series of strong opposition. Fort Dufferin, the last bastion of the Japanese in the city, fell last night when the defenders abandoned the fort and escaped under the cover of darkness, reportedly through the drains. Political observers consider this to be an end to the Azad Hind Government's liberation struggle from Burma, for all practical purposes.

How Can A Muslim Majority Province Take Orders From Mr Gandhi? – Jinnah

March 23, 1945, Delhi: Jinnah has been much enraged by the Congress returning to office in the NWFP and this event has widened the gulf between him and the Congress. On the occasion of the 'Pakistan Day', he has issued a message in which he poured out his anger and frustration: 'It is not possible to believe that any Muslim can tolerate a ministry in a Muslim-majority Province, which takes orders from, and is subject to the control of, Mr. Gandhi at Sevagram or the Congress, who are deadly opponents of Muslim aspirations.'[169]

Saadullah Forced To Reconstitute His Cabinet

March 23, 1945, Shillong: The Saadullah ministry's cosy relationship with the British regime has been continuing at the expense of the native population of the province. The people have been reeling under oppressive measures like bans on meetings, rallies, speeches and imprisonment of the political opponents on a large scale. The opening of the land of the province to immigrants from Bengal has been another issue of anxiety. Though Bordoloi, the former premier and the provincial Congress leader was released from jail in 1942 due to health reasons, he, by and large, was rendered a passive spectator of the miseries of his people. With most of its legislators in prison, the Congress as a party was not able to confront Saadullah in the Assembly. By November last year, however, following release of some of his colleagues from prison, Bordoloi began to initiate some political action. Now the Congress strength, after the release of some more legislators have grown to 18 and this has made Saadullah's position somewhat shaky. With approval from Gandhi, Bordoloi has entered into an arrangement with Saadullah, following which he has agreed to support the Saadullah government subject to a set of conditions which include inter alia the release of political prisoners, removal of the ban on civil liberties, scrapping of the pro-immigrant land development schemes, reconstitution of Saadullah ministry on all-party basis and entrusting the revenue ministry to RK Choudhury. Today, Saadullah has resigned and then reconstituted his cabinet.

Nazimuddin-Suhrawardy Conflict Brings Down League Ministry In Bengal

March 28, 1945, Calcutta: The running feud within the Bengal Muslim League between the Dhaka axis led by prime minister Nazimuddin and the Calcutta axis led by Suhrawardy has culminated in the ouster of the Nazim-led government following the defeat of the government budget by 106-97 votes in the assembly.

A cold war of sorts had been going on right since April 1943 when Nazimuddin, prompted by governor Herbert, formed his government. Jinnah was uncomfortable at this initiative. He had suspected the change-over to be British design to expose the ineptitude of the Muslim League to govern this sensitive province in exceptionally difficult times marked by inflation, scarcity, famine and war time conditions. But the provincial League continued to trudge on its own dynamics in disregard to the views of the central leaders, including Jinnah.

Over the next two years, a piquant situation prevailed in the Muslim League organisation in Bengal. On the one hand, the Nazim led League government, hard-pressed by the conditions of scarcity and economic woes, had been suffering loss of credibility amongst the masses. The common people gradually turned against this government which was perceived to be friendly to the Muslim landed gentries and aristocrats, the traditional patrons of the provincial Muslim League. On the other hand, Abul Hashim, a leader of the Suhrawardy camp and known for his distinct Socialist leanings, had been vigorously campaigning amongst the poor peasantry across the province on issues like abolition of zamindari, permanent settlement, equality and socialism. These being the issues dear to the hearts of the rural masses, Hashim was able to take the Muslim League close to the huts, hearths and hearts of millions of peasants across the province. In districts like Barishal, Dhaka and Tippera, the membership of the League grew phenomenally in recent times.

Thus, within the League, if Nazimuddin and his government emerged as the villain to the masses, Hashim has acquired the halo of a crusader eventually benefiting the Suhrawardy camp. The changing dynamics was reflected today when as many as twenty-one members of the League crossed floors to defeat the budget of Nazimuddin government's budget leading to the fall of the government.

Political analysts are observing two significant changes occurring in the character of the Muslim League in Bengal. First, it has begun to grow as a mass-based party; second, the gradual emergence of Suhrawardy in the party hierarchy. They reckon that he may have a strong claim to the top job, in the event the League is able to form the government again.

Slim's Army Prepares For March To Rangoon

Marach 31, 1945: After the victory at Mandalay, Slim's army has now come out of the eclipse at Meiktilla. The siege by the Japanese forces has collapsed. The Allied Command has now activated the next and final part of its Burma campaign, ie. to march to Rangoon and capture the capital city before the onset of the monsoon. Rangoon still continues to be the head quarters for Japanese general Kimura and Subhas, the supreme commander of the INA. Both of them are reportedly keeping watch over the moves of the Allied forces.

Sapru & Co Cannot Torpedo Pakistan

April 2, 1945, New Delhi: Jinnah has been sharply critical of the initiatives moderate leaders like Sapru and others have been taking from time to time to facilitate the transfer of power to Indian hands. He has been suspecting them of protecting the interests of the Congress and working to the League's detriment. Referring to the report of the Conciliation Committee, appointed by the Standing Committee of the Non-party Leaders' Conference sent to HMG recommending mechanism for both formation of interim government and framing of future constitution of India, Jinnah today made some observations which betrayed both antagonism and sarcasm.

He said that Sir Sapru and his associates have been changing labels and attempting to torpedo Pakistan but that they won't succeed. In this connection he recounted that Sapru's initiatives were initially called 'all-party conference', and then changed to 'no party conference' and the latest initiative was organised under the label of a 'conciliation committee'.

RAF Bombs Legyi, INA Machine-gunners Retaliate

April 2, 1945, Legyi: Mandalay has fallen and the siege of Meiktila has collapsed. The British forces have begun to clear the areas from Nyanugu to its east and south. Though for all practical purposes the hope of a victory over the Allied forces has now extinguished, the remnants of two INA regiments in the Mount Popa area are still launching scattered assaults on enemy forces. On 30th last month Sahagal had, in course of a daring night operation targeted at Pyinbin, tumbled on an advanced guard of the heavily equipped second British division at a place situated in the middle of Setsetyo and Pyinbin.

Though he was able to somehow escape with his regiment, he had to shift his forces here. Situated at about five miles from the top of Mount Popa, Legyi 'is like a saucer with high grounds all sides' and is a good defensible position. It offered excellent opportunities to observe enemy movements and also attack by taking cover of its 'spurs and gullies'. No less importantly, the enemy has no way to assess his strength of troops and ammunition, except by way of air reconnaissance.

The British forces did just that today. The RAF bombed and machine gunned the INA base here in daylight. Sahagal's regiment drove the enemy aircrafts away by directing counter firings from machine guns. However, the machine gun operator who fought valiantly against the enemy fighter planes in the day deserted the INA regiment as the night fell. Coming after a heroic defence put up against the enemy only hours ago, this incident has come as a dampener to the rest.

Sweet Victory At Legyi Is Shattered By Desertion

April 3, 1945, Legyi: The RAF attack, yesterday, had found out the 'grid' of the INA's Legyi base. Expectedly, a full-scale overland attack by a powerful brigade of the British division unfolded on INA's position today as the daylight broke out. Aided by Japanese intelligence input about the enemy movement in advance and with the Japanese force protecting its left flank, the machine gunners of the INA regiment assaulted the enemy forces on their right from concealed and well dug positions. It was a remarkable victory by a small regiment over a much superior, fully equipped brigade, made possible by grit, determination, courage and of course good strategy. But, the joy of the triumph was shattered by the night when an entire battalion led by Khazan Shah, who had earlier proved himself a valiant commander, deserted the INA base. Worse, he was followed by three platoons and the mortar section. Under the circumstances, Sahgal has decided to abandon the position at Legyi and move back to Mount Popa where he plans to chalk out the next course of action in consultation with Shah Nawaz. Incidentally, Shah Nawaz had taken over charge as the commander of the INA second division few days ago.

INA Second Division Is Set To Retreat

April 10, 1945, Mount Popa: The position of the INA in Mount Popa and adjoining areas has become clearly impossible against the huge enemy force advancing in that sector. Today the RAF bombers raided the INA's field hospital at Kyaukpadaung, killing and wounding over a hundred people. Shah Nawaz, the commander of the second division, has issued orders for withdrawal of the INA from the sector. The left-over troops are likely to begin their retreat towards the south of the country soon.

First Infantry Regiment Lays Down Arms

April 19, 1945, Magwe: The 1st infantry regiment of the INA had delayed joining Mount Popa as they were waiting for their equipment in Rangoon. By the time they left that city, hopes were still alive and the INA was covering Mount Popa well. But things changed rapidly after the Japanese siege of Meiktila collapsed. On the way to their destination today they reached in the vicinity of Magwe and encountered a powerful contingent of the enemy tanks and Bren gun carriers. News of a conclusive Allied victory was doing the rounds putting this INA regiment into utter confusion. The headquarters of the regiment with one battalion, surrendered forthwith. Others dispersed into the country in a disorganised manner. It appears they too may not be able to avoid being captured for long.

Large Body Of INA Troops Taken As Prisoners

April 23, 1945: Pyu: Post victory at Mandalay, the Allied force, divided in two large groups and each supported by a tank brigade, have been marching southwards to Rangoon—one on the rail track and the other alongside both banks of Irrawaddy. Today the second group was passing through Pyu, a place little over 30 miles south of Toungoo and about 118 miles north of Rangoon. According to Allied sources, this group captured 150 officers and 3,000 soldiers of INA on the way. The sources claimed that the INA men surrendered. There was another report that General Kimura has just shifted his headquarters from Rangoon to Moulmein to its east. Analysts are attaching considerable significance to his action and interpreting it as the Japanese army's intention to leave Burma.

Subhas Leaves Rangoon

April 24, 1945, Rangoon: Though there are four to five thousand of INA troops present in Rangoon and adjoining areas, the question of giving a fight to the British forces was ruled out after the Japanese army left the city a day ago. Subhas has also been advised strongly to leave Burma. Today, he has left the Burmese capital, entrusting the INA forces under the care of Loganadan, with instructions to ensure their orderly surrender. Earlier, considering their contribution, the INA headquarters promoted Loganadan along with JK Bhonsle, AC Chatterji, MZ Kiani, and Shah Nawaz to the rank of Major General, while both Prem Sahagal and GS Dhillon were elevated to the rank of Colonel. A convoy consisting of Bhonsle, Chatterji, Kiani, large number of troops of Subhas brigade and members of the provisional government belonging to Malaya as well as women members of the Rani Jhansi Regiment accompanied him. From the Japanese side, Hachiya, the Japanese ambassador to the provisional government and Isoda, the chief of Hikari Kikan too travelled along with Subhas. He has decided to travel by land knowing fully well the risks of enemy attacks en route. He has declined to use aircraft and chosen to move along with his convoy. They started at dusk to avoid air attack and took the Pegu Road. Their immediate destination is reportedly Moulmein, from where they would board trains for Bangkok.

Free India Will Repay Its Debt To You With Gratitude In A Gracious Manner: Subhas Bids Adieu To Burma

April 24, 1945, Rangoon: Much against Subhas's hope and assessment, the war in Burma was won by the Allied forces. According to reports, large body of Allied troops have been marching towards Rangoon. In fact, they had already crossed the Prome-Toungoo axis and were now about 100 miles away from Rangoon. The Japanese government as well as the Council of Ministers of the provisional government of Free India strongly advised Subhas to leave Burma without delay. Subhas has started for Bangkok today.

On the eve of his departure, he has thanked the Indians in Burma for their splendid contribution to the 'total mobilisation' in respect of the war of liberation fought by the Azad Hind government. When the history of India's 'Last War of Independence comes to be written', Subhas said,[170] 'Indians in Burma will have an honoured place in that history'. He has also acknowledged with deep gratitude the debt to the people and government of Burma, hoping that 'The day will come when Free India will repay that debt of gratitude in a generous manner'.

To the INA soldiers and men left behind, he paid a wholesome compliment[171] for their bravery—whether in the plains of Imphal, hilly Kohima, jungles, oil installations or other locations in Burma. Reposing his absolute confidence in his worthy colleagues he said: 'I am leaving in your safe hands our national tri colour, our national honour and the best traditions of Indian warriors'. An incorrigible optimist, Subhas bid them adieu saying: '...the darkest hour always precedes the dawn. India shall be free and before long'.

Sahgal Surrenders, Taken To Allanmyo Enemy Army Headquarters

April 27, 1945, Allanmyo: Divided into two groups, the retreating regiments of the INA travelled southwards from Mount Popa. Shah Nawaz and Dhillon stayed at the head of one team while Sahgal led the other. They travelled in bullock carts only during nights to avoid detection and air assaults. Under continuous threats of enemy attack and plagued by lack of provision, they kept marching towards

Rangoon changing their routes occasionally to escape detection. Incidentally, Slim's forces too, moving towards Rangoon, have been combing large tracts of the country including the routes of their retreat as part of the 'Union Jack' manoeuvre. This game of hide-and-seek could not go on indefinitely as the enemy was rapidly gaining control over the whole country and also the cooperation of the natives. Four days ago, Sahagal and his men were approached by a battalion of the 20th Indian division in Magyigan village, a little above Allanmyo. To avoid a bloody but meaningless encounter, he offered to surrender with his men. Today he has been taken to the divisional headquarter of the enemy army at Allanmyo.

FINALLY GERMAN PHOBIA EXORCISED
Allied Tanks Roll On Berlin Streets

April 30, 1945, Berlin: The Allied victory has been on the cards for past some time. It has been a question of winding up the proceedings. A couple of months ago, Churchill, Roosevelt and Stalin had met to plan the final stages of the war and to decide on their post war areas of influence. The German military prowess has been soundly crushed and if at all, Germany had merely been waging a defensive war to defer her absolute surrender. Today, the last bastion has crumbled. The Soviet tanks have entered the periphery of Berlin and the Red Army has encircled the city. Berlin with an area nearly 350 square mile is now likely to surrender any time. Hitler reportedly attributed the debacle to a heinous intrigue by the Bolsheviks and the Jews. According to unconfirmed reports, the undisputed dictator has finally shot himself to death in a bunker to avert being captured by the Allies.

The curtain has nearly been drawn on the war theatre. The sole surviving worry of the Allies, is the Japanese military machine. Though Japanese forces are retreating to the home islands from various parts of the world, they have not been completely vanquished. Recounting past experiences, the Allies are not ruling out Japanese capacity to spring surprises. US and Britain want to be sure. All allies' eyes are on Japan now.

Allied Forces Enter Rangoon

May 3, 1945, Rangoon: Subhas had left Rangoon[172] under the charge of Col. Loganadan to effect an orderly transfer of the city to the advancing Allied force. Loganadan has been maintaining law and order in the city since then with the help of INA soldiers under his command. In the evening today, a brigade of the Allied forces entered the city unopposed. The surrender of the large body of the INA troops in the city has become imminent.

GERMANY SURRENDERS

May 7, 1945, Reims: Today Col Gen Alfred Gustav Jodl, the Chief of Staff German forces signed the articles of surrender in this French city at the forward head quarters of General Dwight D Eisenhower. It has marked the official surrender of Germany to the Western Allies and the Soviet Russia and also the conclusion of the Great War in Europe after 5 years 8 months and 16 days.

Subhas Reaches Bangkok With His Convoy

May 15, 1945, Bangkok: Subhas had left Rangoon on 24th last month with his convoy and reached here today. After crossing the Sittang river, the whole convoy was on foot. Subhas was offered transport but he refused to avail this personalised facility. Subhas preferred to walk with the group all the way though he was not well and his feet developed bad blisters.

They walked nearly 80 miles over six long days to reach Moulmein in the lower Burma. From there they boarded a Bangkok-bound train but that too ran only during nights to escape from air attacks. Eventually, the convoy has reached Bangkok safely. Subhas has devoted himself again to the numerous matters relating to the provisional government, League and the INA. Of course, to chalk out the next course of action has been rendered enormously complicated by the recent course of events.

Shah Nawaz And Dhillon Surrender

May 17, 1945, Pegu: Shah Nawaz and Dhillon were gradually losing members from their team as they continued with their tortuous march to the south of the country, departing from the planned route as and when possibilities of a brush with the enemy forces arose. They were heading to Rangoon to unite with the main body but on arrival at Prome they heard that all the parties were heading to Moulmein. Wearied and fatigued by the long journey, they changed mind and made one last attempt to escape to Siam in the east through Toungoo. But all through their way to the south, the enemy forces moved ahead of them and took control of the country. That made their escape to Siam difficult. Four days ago, Shah Nawaz, realising that they were in a hopeless condition, gave general permission to all those of his team to surrender if they so wished. Thereafter, yesterday, the two commanders with a heavily depleted team of less than fifty members were trapped in a forest near Pegu. Today they surrendered to a patrol from the Punjab Regiment of the 5th Indian division.

HMG's New Political Initiative
Wavell To Hold Talks With Indian Leaders

June 7, 1945, New Delhi: With the war in Europe concluded, the threat of INA liquidated and Japan being on its last leg, the British Government, much relieved, has been planning to resume the task of constitutional progress in India. It was last discussed in 1942 during Cripps' visit. Viceroy Wavell was called to London in March this year and he held long discussions with the British Government. A set of proposals aiming towards constitutional advancement was formulated. It was decided to offer these for the consideration of the Indian political leaders. The details are yet to be released. However, according to informed sources, these contain a potentially contentious issue that provides for the reconstitution of the Viceroy's executive council through a scheme of balanced representation of all communities. The authors of the scheme identified four distinct major Indian communities, viz. Caste Hindus, Muslims, Depressed Classes and the Sikhs. To satisfy the criterion of 'balanced representation', they envisaged five seats each for the Caste Hindus and the Muslims and one seat each for the Depressed Classes and the Sikhs. The scheme has not yet been tabled in the British Parliament. The Viceroy also has not so far made any formal announcement to the people in India. He plans to hold a conference of the Indian political leaders to take counsel with him, with a view to the formation of a new executive council. Meanwhile, he has begun the process with some leaders. Quite predictably, the manner in which the 'balanced representation' has been conceived by the government has stirred a hornet's nest cutting across parties.

Today BR Ambedkar, JP Srivastava and NB Khare submitted a joint note[173] stating that the proposals as regards the representations are unfair. They added that Caste Hindus should have a majority over Moslems and the Depressed Classes should have more than one member.

According to political analysts, the move of the British Government is patently iniquitous. Considering the demographic ratio of about 3:1 between the Hindus (including the depressed classes) and the Muslims, a 6 to 5 seats offer in the council smacks of palpable bias. They also contend that segregating 50 million non-caste Hindus and offering this vast population only one seat may be a strategy so as not to make the partiality glaring. But the affected leaders cutting across political parties have understood the British game plan. If the Viceroy had thought that they will accept the ignominious offer passively, he has been proved wrong.

It Is A Strange And Sinister Kind Of Political Arithmetic

June 7, 1945, Bombay: The offer of only a single seat in the proposed reconstituted executive council has angered BR Ambedkar. Apart from submitting a joint note, he has also written a letter[174] to the Viceroy today questioning the rationale behind envisaging only one member of the untouchables in the executive council when they number as many as 50 millions. He has cited statistics that the Muslims are being offered as many as five seats while they number 90 million and Sikhs with only six millions people are also offered one seat. Calling this a strange and sinister kind of political arithmetic, Ambedkar wrote such a scheme was 'revolting to' his 'ideas of justice and common sense'. He wrote he was shocked '...that His Majesty's Government with all their profession of being trustees for the Scheduled Castes... should have treated their wards in such an ill-liberal, unfair and unjust manner and far worse than enlightened Hindu opinion would have done'. Describing the proposal as a death knell to the Untouchables, he wrote that it would undo their efforts over the last fifty years for their emancipation. Before concluding the letter he has hinted that the proposal might force parting of ways between the British Indian Government and the Scheduled Castes. He has finally urged the Viceroy to communicate his proposal to His Majesty's Government. His proposal is clear - he wants that 'Untouchables' should get due representation in the executive council and he has demanded this ought to be at least three members.

Wavell Drops Shyamaprasad From Conference

June 9, 1945, New Delhi: Today Viceroy Wavell has written[175] to the Secretary of State stating that he has decided to drop Shyamaprasad Mukherjee of the Hindu Mahasabha from the proposed conference. As reasons, he mentioned series of anti-British and anti-Allies articles being published by Mukherjee's *Nationalist* paper and his apprehension that the latter would refuse to cooperate with the Viceroy and other leaders.

Wavell Calls Conference Of Leaders In Simla – A Blunt Move To Communalise Post-war Politics In India?

June 14, 1945, London: Today the details of the much-awaited British proposal[176] to improve upon the constitution of India were revealed. Secretary of State for India has placed the proposal before the British Parliament in London. The King also referred to this new proposal in his speech proroguing the Parliament today. Here in India, the Viceroy communicated it to the people of India through a broadcast.

Far from talking about 'independence', the primary focus of the proposal is on reconstituting and Indianising the executive council of the Viceroy with the exception of the C-I-C and the Viceroy himself. The new council will effectively pursue the war against Japan, and carry on with the governance till the time a permanent constitution comes into effect. The formation of the interim government will, in no way, prejudice a constitutional settlement. On the contrary, it would consider means by which an agreement could be reached on the working out of a permanent constitution. Other key features are: (i) the placing of the portfolio of external affairs in charge of an India member; (ii) the appointment of a High Commissioner by the HMG in India, as in other dominions; (iii) the assurance that the Viceroy, though he would continue to exercise his constitutional power as the head of the government, would do so only 'reasonably'. At a later stage, following the formation of the reconstituted 'executive council', the issue of restoring elected governments, advisedly coalition, in Section 93 provinces would be taken up. The decision regarding release of political prisoners would also be taken by the said council.

The proposed reconstituted executive council would have a balanced representation of main Indian communities, including equal proportion of Muslims and Caste Hindus. The Viceroy said he would call a conference of Indian leaders, both from the central and provincial politics, to take counsel with him with a view to the formation of a new executive council.

The Viceroy would invite a list of names from members of the conference from amongst which he would select future members of the council and forward these to the King Emperor for appointment.

The Viceroy has proposed to confine the prospective participants to important leaders like (i) premiers of provincial governments or those who last held the office (ii) leader of Congress Party and leader of the Muslim League in Central Assembly (iii) leaders of Congress and the Muslim League in Council of State (iv) leaders of nationalist parties and European groups in the Central Assembly; (v) N Siva Raj to represent the Depressed Classes (vi) Tara Singh to represent the Sikhs (vii) Gandhi and Jinnah as the recognised leaders of the two main parties. He is proposing to invite all these leaders to the Viceregal lodge in Simla for securing their advice.

New Constitutional Proposal A Multibagger For The British Regime?

Though the statement of policy was issued today, Viceroy Wavell had already issued invitations to some Indian leaders and the method of ensuring 'balanced representation' in the council has already begun to raise huge controversy. There is deep discontent amongst different pockets about the parity formula which has absolutely no relevance to the demographic profile of the country. Political analysts agree. Not only 'parity', the analysts also look at the proposal as deft move by the British Government to force the 'caste Hindu' tag on to the Congress. To accomplish this, it has (i) linked representations in the council to the religion and caste and not to political parties; (ii) it has divided Hindus into Caste Hindus and Depressed Classes; (iii) it has invited representatives of the Depressed Classes, the Muslims and the Sikhs, implying that the only other group of Caste Hindus is automatically linked to the Congress. This imposition is both humiliating and provocative to that party which has been the oldest political outfit with its members from all communities and which claim to represent Indians of all shades.

Analysts also opine that the British Government is trying to achieve multiple objectives through this interim arrangement: (a) chastising the Congress for withholding support to war efforts (b) denting Gandhi's image by securing promise of cooperation from the Congress for war efforts against Japan, in violation of his ideology of 'non-violence under all circumstances' (c) driving the wedge deeper between Congress and the League and also amongst communities (d) ensuring Indian help for pursuing war against Japan.

Top Congress Leaders Walk Out Of Prison

June 15, 1945, New Delhi: The conference convened by Wavell is set to open on 25th of the current month. The government had invited Gandhi but he declined, saying he represented no institution and that the function of representing Congress belonged to the

Congress president or any person nominated by him. The Viceroy has acknowledged his suggestion but insisted that Gandhi still come over to Simla. In his wire,[177] the Viceroy has stated, 'Whatever the technical position may be I shall value your help and hope you will accept invitation which was telegraphed to you last night….'

Today the government has released members of the Congress Working Committee who were still in detention, apparently with a view to facilitating the party's participation in Simla Conference. As regards other detenus connected to the 1942 movement, the onus of taking decision has been left to the new central government and the governments in the provinces.

PROFILE OF INA MEN

June 15, 1945: The Allied forces have by now successfully resisted the joint invasion by the 95,000 Japanese and 9,000 INA forces. Though the British regime was predominantly worried about resisting the invincible Japanese, it of course perceived the INA forces as a political risk, if not so much a military one, with unpredictable impact. Not unexpectedly, therefore, the British military machines have been endeavouring to acquire an understanding of the morale, motivation and strategy of these men whom they had vanquished in the war but who despite their acute paucity of arms, equipments and provisions exhibited valour, gallantry and patriotism of very high order. Recently one senior INA officer (a former Indian Army Officer) commanding a guerrilla regiment was captured and interrogated and this gives an interesting insight.[178]

If the responses and replies of the officer are relied upon, the major part of the INA consisted of willing, patriotic soldiers with commitment to the cause of Indian independence. The acid test of this was in the actions of the INA soldiers after defeat began to loom large. They discarded the easier option of offering surrender at Imphal but chose to retreat to Burma through the tortuous routes embracing starvation, disease and various other sufferings to live another day to fight for their country's freedom. Further, those who were able to return to Burma alive, had given an exemplary display of determination, courage and valour in defending Kyaukpadaung, Popa and the oilfields against the resurgent Allied attacks.

Another significant thing that came to light out of the interrogation was the general belief of the INA men that their mission failed essentially because they did not have adequate equipment. Notwithstanding their defeat, they were sure that even their failed mission would bring about a surge of nationalism in the entire Indian army. On the much discussed INA's claim that a 'rebellion in the British India Army' would be catalysed by the 'liberating army' which was poo-poohed by the British with equal disdain, the captured officer expressed his belief that this would most certainly have occurred and universally so, if only the INA were able to penetrate into the plains of Bengal and, of course, not until then.

Desai-Liaquat Pact Laid Foundation Of The Simla Talk

June 15, 1945: Even though Jinnah had given an unceremonial burial to the Desai-Liaquat pact by terming it as 'lie' and 'nonsense', Desai today derived some consolation as Gandhi publicly commended the hard labour he had put in together with his League counterpart. Today in a statement, while criticising the overtly communal approach adopted in the Simla proposal, Gandhi praised the Desai-Liaquat proposal for not adopting such colouring and for its emphasis on 'sections of Indians' with regard to representations in interim government. Gandhi stated that Desai had consulted him and had made a genuine attempt to solve the communal tangle. Gandhi, in fact, went on to say that Desai-Liaquat pact had laid the foundation for the present initiative ie. the conference at Simla.

Congress Wary Of The 'Caste Hindu' Tag

June 18, 1945, Panchgani: Gandhi was invited by Wavell to the conference to be held later this month in Simla. He had declined and suggested that the Viceroy ought to invite the Congress president or any person nominated by the president, following which the government invited MAK Azad. Today Gandhi has cabled[179] to Wavell thanking him for directly inviting Azad and observed 'Members being free at conference to accept or reject proposals clears ground for invitees to attend conference. This leaves them free to discuss the pros and cons at conference.' However, Gandhi has been steadfast in his opposition to two conditions of the proposal: (a) parity between Muslims and caste Hindus in the executive council; (b) Congress being forced to identify with Caste Hindus.

Yesterday Gandhi had sent Wavell a cable expressing his deep reservations about the 'parity formula'. Significantly, he did not question the propriety of the ratio per se, although considering the demographic profile of the country, it was abundantly clear that the ratio was highly distorted in favour of one community at the expense of the rest. He has rather opposed the rationale of the 'Fixity of Parity' saying that it would lead to 'religious division' getting officially stereotyped. If the parity between the Caste Hindus and Muslims was unalterable, Gandhi warned that the Viceroy would end up, quite unconsciously, defeating the purpose of the conference.

Observing that his concern for 'parity' has made no impact on the Viceroy, Gandhi in another cable sent today warned him yet again on its inherent danger. Going further in his protest, he said he would advice Congress not to participate in the 'executive council'. As regards the second point, he has clarified that the 'Congress has never identified itself with caste or non-caste Hindus' and can never do so, even to gain independence which will be 'one-sided, untrue and suicidal'. He has also added that the Hindu Mahasabha is the body claiming to represent solely Hindu interests. But even the Mahasabha would refuse to identify itself only with one section of the Hindus.

However, significantly, and to the relief of the Viceroy, Gandhi has not insisted upon withdrawal of these two features of the proposal as a pre-condition for the Congress to participate. At the end of the wire, he has mentioned subject to the wishes of the Congrees Working Committee he would attend the conference in spite of his strong views. Wavell seems to be comfortable with Gandhi's communiqué as the latter, by not boycotting the conference, has given him scope to introduce two new conditions which could become an integral part of any political negotiations to be carried out in India henceforth.

Subhas Cautions Gandhi Against Wavell Initiative

June 19, 1945, Singapore: Subhas is in Singapore. He is anxiously watching the political developments in India. Through radio broadcasts, he has warned Indians from Singapore about the danger of falling into the British trap laid by Wavell through a conference to be held a few days later in Simla. Subhas said the real purpose of the conference is to get, with the approval of Indian nationalists and full connivance of the Congress, half a million troops with materials to fight Britain's war in the Far East and that by being a party to it the Congress would not only distract from its long-held principles but also give up their quest for 'complete independence'. Subhas said Britain has planned to use these new Indian soldiers as fodder to fight war in Malaya, Thailand, Indo China and Japan in hard conditions. Subhas pointed out that these troops will have to confront the INA forces in East Asia who would fight to the last man. Besides, Subhas reminded the Congress leaders that the Congress by coming to an agreement with Wavell, would be tricked into agreeing to vivisection of India and reduce itself as one of the several political parties in the country.

Gandhi Warns Azad Of Possible Pitfalls

June, 1945: Simla: Congress president MAK Azad is here with his party colleagues to attend the conference called by the Viceroy. Gandhi too has come here in his individual capacity on special invitation by Wavell. Though he is not a participant, Gandhi is monitoring and advising the Congress team.

The summer capital is in political ferment and it is difficult to rule out secret agreements and understandings worked out by the leaders of political parties inter se or with the government. Today Gandhi has written to Azad,[180] cautioning him against probable pitfalls. He has expressed his anxiety on the basis of a report about Azad agreeing to form a cabinet. Gandhi has made it clear that the CWC has not given Azad the right or permission to form a cabinet and emphasised the primacy of the CWC in such a matter. Gandhi has also advised Azad that he must take the Congressmen who are present into confidence in anything he does and also he 'should put everything in writing'.

Gandhi has particularly warned Azad about his standing objection to the 'parity' formula. He wrote that he has been shouting against it and would continue to do so, even if he was alone. 'I shall refuse to be a party to it...' Gandhi continued, 'I do not care if the negotiations breakdown on this....' Gandhi warned a national government at the centre, formed on this basis, would be laid on a wrong foundation. Expressing his strong view, Gandhi clarified that 'In this respect I am neither a Hindu, nor belong to any other religion. I belong to all faiths or to none....' Clearly he wants Azad to take due care about this point in the deliberations in the conference.

Khizr Seeks Protection Against Muslim League

June 23, 1945, Lahore: Since his dismissal from the Khizr cabinet about a year ago, Shaukat Hayat Khan has acquired the halo of a political martyr. He has been addressing numerous public meetings of the Punjab Muslim League. On the other hand, Jinnah has been making a villain of Khizr by calling him a traitor to the Muslim cause. The League has been able to attract Muslim masses on the issue of Pakistan. Even religious divines like the Sajjada Nashin and Pirs have been joining the League in droves. An ominous trend of communal polarisation has already set in the province. The League leaders from other provinces have also been adding fuel to the fire—some of them even visited Punjab and criticised Khizr's dismissal of Shaukat. Khizr has been realising that the ground beneath the Unionist feet is slipping and its prospect in the forthcoming election is getting increasingly bleak.

Khizr's worries have multiplied on getting hints that Wavell, the Viceroy, is likely to hold a conference to install a popular interim government in the centre which, by dint of the proposed mechanism of its formation, will essentially be a coalition government of the Congress and the League. In such an eventuality the League, on the strength of the new found lever of power at the federal level, would raise the risk of intervention in Punjab to an unacceptable level. It could even lead to the demise of the Unionist Party. Therefore, Khizr has requested[181] the Viceroy, in the event a popular government is installed at the centre, there must be a representative of the Unionist Party in it.

Congress Shy And Jinnah Riding High
A New Trend In Political Negotiations

June 24, 1945, Simla: The conference of prominent Indian leaders is set to begin tomorrow. On the eve of that august event, Viceroy Wavell has today met few top political leaders including MAK Azad, Gandhi and Jinnah. Tonight he has sent a cable to Amery,[182] summing up his perception of the 'positions' of key Indian leaders on the issues proposed to be taken up in the conference.

Congress president Azad did not raise objection to the 'parity' formula between Muslims and the caste Hindus. Though Azad bitterly criticised the tag of the 'caste Hindu' being attached to the Congress, he did not want to push this issue beyond a point. Azad however remained firm as regards the 'method of selection' of the members and wanted the Congress to have a voice in the selection of non-Hindus as members of the executive council. He made it clear that 'Muslims in particular must not be selected by an exclusively communal body'.

Based on his interaction with Gandhi, Wavell felt that the present government initiative was on the whole acceptable to him. On the issues of parity and method of selection, his views were similar to that of Azad. 'In spite of severe pressure to the contrary', Gandhi was prepared 'to accept parity between caste Hindus and Muslims' but he was firm that 'it must be open to the Congress to put forward the names of Muslims or Scheduled Castes' as members of the council. Both the leaders also agreed to help the British in pursuing war against Japan, one of the core conditions of the conference.

Wavell met Jinnah too. The British regime has already favoured him by imposing the dual conditions of 'parity' and 'caste Hindu' tag to the Congress. But Jinnah demanded more. In course of informal talks with Wavell, he proposed two more conditions: first, in regard to the mode of handling matters in the interim government, by insisting that 'if majority of Muslims were opposed to any decision, it should not go by vote'; second, Muslim League alone must be given the right to nominate all Muslim members to the new council.

Political analysts feel even before the Conference has taken off, a new trend seems to have set in with regard to the bargaining powers of the Congress and the League as well as the role of the government as a mediator. The British regime, London and New Delhi acting in concert, have given a political 'master stroke', outwitting the Congress. By bringing its leaders out of the long and gruelling prison stay after three long years and offering them spoils of power in a jiffy, the government has been able to make it compromise with its long-held ideology and convictions. Its leaders appeared to be in haste to compromise with whatever terms the British offered. Jinnah leading the League, on the other hand, has been able to humble and insult Congress - his main political rival. He was now keen to extract more pound of flesh for having helped the British with their war efforts at the critical period.

Viceroy Orders Temporary Break, Seeks Nominations

June 29, 1945, Simla: At the end of hard work of last few days, the Viceroy gave the participants here a break, but with an important homework. The Congress, the League and the representatives of various interest groups have been asked to discuss and send him a list of their nominees to be considered for appointment as members of the new executive council. Each could send more names than their quota, including names of worthy outsiders. The Viceroy, however, would have the final say—to choose from these lists and recommend those he finds most suitable. Though he has not announced any specific date for reconvening the conference, it is expected to resume once the list of names reach him.

Jinnah Puts Up Road Block At Simla

July 9, 1945, Simla: Right since the time the Viceroy adjourned the conference, the hill city has been amidst intense political activities. The decision-making bodies of the parties, including interalia the working committees of both the Congress and the League, have been deliberating on relevant issues, with 'quota' and the 'right to nominate' occupying centre stage. Sivaraj, the leader of the Depressed Classes, has reiterated the latter's demand that their 'quota' in the executive council be calculated using the same ratio as for the Muslims. He has also questioned the right of the Congress to nominate members of the Deperessed Classes.

The working committee of the Muslim League in its meeting, held on the 6th July, officially endorsed two demands which Jinnah had informally discussed with Wavell on the eve of the conference. First of its demand is to have some kind of an additional safeguard, besides the Governor General's veto, to protect Muslim interests from any majority driven decision taken in the new executive council. Its second demand is to have the exclusive right to nominate all Muslim members to the council.

The Congress also held its working committee meeting on 3rd July, but the party did not intend to put up any road block to the proceedings of the conference. It only made clear that the party would, under no circumstances, give up its right to nominate persons of any religion and or community. Today Wavell has written to Jinnah, expressing his inability to concede to the two fresh demands of the League. Jinnah has acted with remarkable alacrity. In a matter of hours he has shot back his reply, saying that the League would not be able to send the list of names under such circumstances. The latest position taken by the League has driven the conference to a quagmire.

Jinnah Adamant, Wavell Refuses To Budge

July 11, 1945, Simla: The entire political arithmetic so carefully worked out by the British regime, is likely to go haywire because of the two additional demands put forth by Jinnah.

Though Wavell has so far been accommodating Jinnah and the League in more than one way, he is no longer able to help the latter.[183] Out of the five prospective Muslim members for the executive council, Wavell has been determined to take one from the Unionist Party, a long trusted ally of the British, while agreeing to take four from the Muslim League. Today in a meeting with Jinnah, he has made his intentions clear. Jinnah was incensed.

Wavell tried to persuade him but without success. Jinnah has been angry with Khizr and the Unionist Party and now he has vowed zero tolerance for it. Jinnah also made it clear that he was rigid about incorporating an additional safeguard to protect Muslim interests in respect of decisions taken in the executive council. Wavell did not agree to these demands as well. Things have become difficult after Jinnah refused to submit the League's list of names for the executive council. Political observers say the conference has begun to totter.

Simla Conference Collapses

July 14, 1945, Simla: The much-hyped conference has ended here without an agreement. Neither non-League parties nor the Viceroy could convince Jinnah to withdraw his two additional demands, which appeared lopsided, and unjust. However, the Viceroy can still smile for more than one reason: first, he has been able to establish a new set of power equation in the matter of political negotiations in India by pushing the Congress to the backseat; second, he could expose the bitter acrimony amongst Indian political parties to the world; third, he has secured the commitment of all these parties to cooperate with the government for pursuing war against Japan. On top of all these, Wavell has also managed to earn sympathy from all for having tried genuinely to bring about an agreement among the Indian political parties on the constitutional settlement.

League's The Culprit: Azad To Wavell
Congress Trying To Strangle League & Pakistan: Jinnah

July 14, 1945, Simla: Wavell's conference has ended today amidst confusion and mutual distrust,[184] Wavell had offered to own up responsibilities for the failure but Congress president Azad pointed out that it was indeed the Muslim League who, by refusing to give up its claim to nominate all Muslim members, brought about the collapse. Rajagoplachari also held the League responsible. But Jinnah sought to disassociate himself or the League from any contribution to the failure by insisting that the two core conditions, viz. the right to nominate all Muslim members and the provision for Muslim 'veto', were perfectly legitimate concerns of the League and that the Congress and the League were looking at the issues from completely different angles. Jinnah has been against conceding any ground to the opponents even as an interim arrangement expressing the fear of the League '...that Congress would make use of interim arrangement to consolidate their position and gradually strangle League and Pakistan'. Master Tara Singh, the Sikh leader, had obviously another set of concerns. He sought to let out the Sikh voice in his concluding speech, saying that 'Sikhs could accept Pakistan only if Muslims agreed to separate Sikh State'.

Hindu Mahasabha Not Invited – Impact On Outcome

Although Wavell had invited political parties and representatives of various hues including Muslim, Sikhs, Scheduled Castes, Europeans etc, he did not send an invite to the Hindu Mahasabha. There are reports that this was a planned move by Viceroy Wavell. Significantly, in September last year, Jinnah, at the outset of his parley with Gandhi, had made it a precondition that the latter must admit the Congress as representing Hindus while he, on behalf of the League, would represent the Muslims. In the circumstances, Gandhi had found the 'omission' of Mahasabha as deliberate and exceptionable. At one point of time, he said that if the omission of Hindu Mahasabha was a method of putting the Congress in its place and treating it as a sectional or Hindu body, the Congress would avoid the whole affair. However, he did not pursue the matter further treating the government's stand as arising out of 'ignorance'. The Hindu Mahasabha, on its part, could not advocate its own case for inclusion beyond a point. It sharply criticised the 'parity formula' and had called for a 'Hartal' on 8 July. But there was no strong pressure brought on Wavell to review the arrangement.

Critics say that in the absence of Hindu Mahasabha as a participant, it became convenient for both the government and the League to brand Congress as the representatives of the Hindus. They contend, if the Muslim League represented the essentially communal viewpoints of the Muslims, Hindu Mahasabha did so for the Hindus, whereas the Congress claimed to represent the secular viewpoints of both the communities.

Had Mahasabha also been present in the conference against the League, the status and importance of the Congress as a representative body of both the communities would have gone up—it could have had more decisive say in the proceedings and its final outcome.

Failure Of Wavell Meet – A Ringside View

The conference held here from 25 June has ended yesterday without a result. Political observers are not surprised. They say that right from the beginning there were multiple and contradictory claims by the participants on some core issues, which remained irreconcilable till the end. They have made some interesting observations on individual groups:
The Congress came here as 'underdog'. Its top leaders were released on 15 June. They were almost herded into the conference after three long years of incarceration in the 'prison'. The government insulted the Congress by labelling it as a representative of the 'Caste Hindus' and treating it almost at par with the Muslim League while determining the ratio of the members in the new executive council. While in the existing central legislature the numbers of the Congress and the League happen to be 57 and 30 respectively, the revised ratio in the form of a parity between caste Hindus and Muslims gave the League an unfair advantage. Even if the 'parity' factor was somehow shoved down its throat, Congress found it even more painful to accept the exclusive tag of representing the 'Caste Hindus only'. In course of the conference, the emaciated Congress tried meekly to display its representative character by nominating two Hindus and three non-Hindus including one Christian, one Parsee and one Muslim being its president MAK Azad. Jawaharlal and Vallabhbhai Patel were the Hindus. When its right of choosing a Muslim member was also questioned by Jinnah, it thought it could bear the burden no more and decided to disengage. As regards the Depressed Classes, in early June, Ambedkar had strongly demanded that they ought to have at

least three members in the council. This, of course, made the other groups wary fearing this could come at their expense. Sivaraj, the representative of the Depressed Classes, echoed the demand here.

Khizr Hayat Tiwana, the premier of Punjab, attended the conference with other provincial premiers—present and past. A political rival of Jinnah, Khizr pressed for the nomination of one representative of his Unionist Party to the Viceroy's executive council. He has been nervous of AIML's nagging interference in Punjab, the chance of which would increase in the event of the Muslim League monopolising the entire quota of Muslim ministers in the federal government. Khizr felt his own party's presence, however small, in the executive council would act as a check upon the AIML. The fact that Khizr has been in the good books of the British Government, both in Delhi and London, raised a strong possibility that his request would be examined favourably. He was successful in his mission and he made Wavell choose one from his party to be one of the five Muslim members in the council. Not only that, Wavell stuck to this in the face of a belligerent Jinnah till the end and this proved to be one of the important reasons for the breakdown of the conference.

On its part, the AIML persisted in its claim that it was the sole representative of the Muslims in the country and it alone had the right to choose the Muslim members of the executive council. Sticking to this stand was essential for the League not only to pin down Congress to an artificially contrived non-Muslim silhouette but also to keep other ambitious Muslim leaders like Khizr Hayat Tiwana in check.

All in all, there were too many claims and counter-claims. Wavell apparently wanted to take the process of transfer of power forward through this conference. However, every party wanted to register its claim 'here and now'. Sorting these out proved to be impracticable. No surprise that the conference failed to reach any degree of consensus despite deliberations for nearly three weeks.

Why League Behaved The Way It Did In Simla?

Out of the many interesting facets of the recent Simla Conference, the strategy of the Muslim League stood out ahead of others. On the eve of the conference, the political clout of the League, after witnessing explosive growth since August 1942, had begun to attract some amount of doubt and cynicism. Khizr in Punjab has for long been antagonistic to Jinnah and the League and their enemity has been growing bitter by the day. In Sind, there has been an unmistakable emergence of Sindhi sub-nationalism which did not sync with the League's priority for a single state of Pakistan.

The League-led government in Bengal gave way to the governor's rule in March. With the gradual re-emergence of the Congress, the NWFP ministry, earlier led by Aurgangzeb Khan, was reclaimed by Dr. Khan Sahib. Due to the same reason, the Saadullah ministry in Assam came to depend on the Bordoloi-led Congress Party for its survival.

Under such circumstances, the League had to, in order to achieve its long-term political goals including Pakistan, revamp the perception of the government, political rivals and most importantly the Muslim masses about its strength. According to several political analysts, the League, through its aggressive and seemingly unreasonable posturing in the Simla Conference, has attempted to achieve that very goal. No doubt, Jinnah-led League, has assumed high degree of risks in the process. The efficacy of its strategy will be tested in the general elections, when held.

Muslim League Demands Immediate Elections

July 15, 1945, Simla: The uncompromising stand of the League, that it alone should be given the right to nominate all Muslim candidates for the executive council, was a key reason for the Simla conference to collapse. While most of the other participants felt that the League's stand was unjustified, the League was of the opinion that its support amongst the Muslims of the country has been underestimated by its adversaries. The issue in question was whether or not the League could be considered as the sole authoritative representatives of the Indian Muslims. The working committee of the AIML met today to discuss the subject. The committee has reasoned that the strength of the League in terms of support from the Muslims must not be judged on the basis of its electoral performance in 1937.

Things have changed vastly over last few years and there are groundswells of support for the party from the Muslims all across the country. The committee contended that these changes, over past few years, reflected in several byelection results and numerous floor crossings from rival parties to the League in various provinces. Therefore, the working committee has contended that another election held now would settle the representative strength of the League beyond dispute. Accordingly, it has adopted a resolution demanding immediate elections to both central and the provincial legislatures.

INA Prisoners Herded In Ships, Despatched To India

July 1945, Rangoon: Due to the very manner of their deployment in the just-concluded Burma war, there were concentrations of INA troops at certain places making it easy for the advancing British forces to capture them. Such was the case with the remnants of the second infantry regiment accompanying Sahagal, the first infantry regiment at Magwe, men marching with Shah Nawaz and Dhillon near Pegu, the residues of first three regiments of the first division at Pyinbin and of course, a few thousand troops in or around Rangoon.

After regaining its lost colony of Burma, the victorious British regime had sent nearly 750 INA prisoners from Rangoon to India by ship in May. Again this month, a large number of INA men taken captives have been sent by a number of ships to Chittagong and Calcutta from Rangoon. According to reports, these prisoners are being treated unfairly and denied the minimum facilities that ought to be extended to prisoners of war as per international convention. Evidently, the British regime is treating them as 'traitors' and a mix of vengefulness and contempt is influencing its policies vis-a-vis these INA men.

Allies Meet To Weed Out The Last Enemy

August 2, 1945, Potsdam: A key conference held here in Germany, right since 17 July, has concluded. Three premiers, viz. Truman from USA, Joseph Stalin from Soviet Russia and Winston Churchill met to deliberate on post-war world order, areas of influence of the major Allied powers, peace treaties concluding the rest of the war and related critical issues. During the course of the conference, Clement Attlee, who, upon the victory of the Labour Party in the general election held last month replaced Churchill as the prime minister of Great Britain, joined the deliberation.

The Allies, in particular the USA, have been upset that the war in the Pacific was still raging and the Japanese suicide bombers were launching regular attacks on the Allies' ships, causing significant losses in terms of lives and properties. While the leaders discussed various issues as per agenda, they seriously examined the strategies that would force Japan to surrender. During the conference, Truman had reportedly informed Stalin about his country's making of a new weapon capable of unprecedented mass destruction. In the middle of the proceedings, ie on 26th last month, the Allied powers issued an ultimatum to Japan to surrender or face prompt and utter destruction.

Gandhi Played A Wire-puller in Simla: Jinnah

August 6, 1945, Bombay: Following the abortive conference in Simla, Jinnah is back here. He looks to be bitter with the proceedings in Simla. He has opined that with the war nearly concluding in Europe, it is now time to work for the final constitutional settlement in India rather than to grope for erecting an interim arrangement for governance. Jinnah has been upset that his demands were not accepted in 'toto' by Wavell. He has also expressed his unhappiness about Gandhi's presence in Simla without any representative capacity, only at the behest of the British. He has accused Gandhi of playing the role of a wire-puller in Simla.

Political observers say Jinnah's accusations are unfounded. Gandhi, in fact, played rather a benign role throughout the conference even to the detriment of Congress interest by allowing the party to overlook the 'Caste Hindu' tag and to make it agree to the 'parity formula'. Jinnah, they say, has developed an oversized political ambition and is now taking advantage of the growing British dependence on him in recent years. He is finding any opposition to his request irksome.

AMERICA DROPS ATOM BOMB ON HIROSHIMA
World Stunned, Japanese War Machinery Jolted

August 6, 1945, Tokyo: In a matter of about ten days since the Allied powers issued the ultimatum from Potsdam, USA has benumbed Japan, nay, the world by shock and awe. It attacked Japan with the atom bomb, apparently to bring her into expeditious submission. Today, an American aircraft 'Enola Gay' dropped uranium bomb, nicknamed 'Little Boy', on the thriving Japanese city of Hiroshima.

This is the first 'war application' of the monstrous weapon of mass destruction in the planet and has wrought unprecedented havoc. It has exterminated about one-third of the city's three hundred fifty thousand people and swept several large buildings out of the earth. According to eyewitnesses who have survived the macabre attack, they saw a noiseless flash followed by light brighter than a thousand suns, immediately before the calamity struck. Most of the victims succumbed quickly but worse is the fate of the survivors—all disabled to various degrees by the radiation. Whereas blood and tears have swept the earth, the skies of this city are rented by panic cries and heart wrenching wailings.

REPEAT ATOM BOMB ATTACK ON NAGASAKI
Truman Threatens More Attacks

August 9, 1945, Tokyo: US bombers came back to haunt Japan again. Within three days of pulverising Hiroshima, in a gruesome repeat attack, an US aircraft has today dropped a plutonium bomb, nick named 'fat man', upon Nagasaki, another thriving Japanese city, killing about seventy thousand people.

The world is stunned by this repeated brutal attack. There are widespread condemnations describing the US bombings as disproportionate acts of revenge. Even some of her allies are finding these unwarranted. However, US president Truman is unfazed, unrepentant. In a chilling warning, he has demanded immediate surrender by Japan, failing which he has held out the threat of more such attacks. The British Government in India is now able to shed its Japan phobia completely. In the current scenario, Japan's surrender seems to be a matter of days. Its policy on the issue of Indian independence and negotiation with Indian political forces are likely to be influenced by the event.

Japan's Backbone Is Broken

August 9, 1945, Manchuria: Japan has been reeling under the impact of two successive atom bomb attacks by America. Her miseries have been compounded further as a vast Soviet army has invaded Manchuria in northern China, which has been under Japanese control. Russia declared war against Japan yesterday. Experts say that this is the last nail on the coffin of the Japanese military might. Japan may have to surrender any time now.

Subhas Orders War Memorial On Island City

August 16, 1945, Singapore: In the aftermath of attacks on Hiroshima and Nagasaki, followed by the Soviet invasion of Manchuria, Japan's surrender is being seen as a foregone conclusion. The Allied forces have been on hot chase to reclaim the lost colonies of the Western countries in Southeast and East Asia. They could reach Singapore in a few days' time. Japan formally surrendered yesterday and Subhas has decided to leave Singapore soon. But his final destination has not been announced. According to some sources, Subhas was considering opening up channels of communications with Soviet Russia and wanted to reach the Manchurian front with Japanese help.

For the past few months he has been, through radio broadcasts and meetings, prophesying an impending rivalry between the Anglo-American powers and Soviet Russia, now that the war has come to a close. After Japan's surrender, Russia would probably remain one rare, though remote, option for him to carry forward his unfinished struggle for India's liberation.

Meanwhile, Subhas wanted a war memorial to be constructed in this beautiful city as a mark of respect to the warriors of the INA who laid down their lives to liberate their motherland. Yesterday, he assigned this challenging task to Cyril John Stracey, an Anglo Indian Officer of the INA—to ensure that an appropriate 'war memorial' comes up on the sea face of the city, before the Allied forces land up there.

Before leaving for Bangkok, his immediate destination, Subhas instructed Major General MZ Kiani to represent the Azad Hind Government and to protect the interests of the Indian community in Malaya and maintain order in Singapore. It is evident that the Allied powers will march into Singapore before long.

No Politician Has Such Hold Over Men Of Indian Army

August 20, 1945, Delhi: The battle of Burma has been conclusively won by the British Raj and the defeated troops of the Indian National Army are being herded into prisons in India and Malaya. But the Raj is upset that the bulk of the INA force, both rank and officers, continue to remain committed to their ideology, viz. expulsion of the British and freedom of India. Worse, Subhas and the INA have begun to transform into a legend and influence sizeable sections of the Indian army personnel.

This is unprecedented as the Indian army has, barring the only time of the Sepoy Mutiny, remained steadfast in its loyalty to their British masters through centuries. The British Indian army has served British interests at various war theatres across the world with remarkable devotion, often without recognition.

Today, Viceroy Wavell has expressed[185] his anxiety about Subhas to Frederick Pethick-Lawrence, Secretary of State for India: 'This is the first occasion on which an anti-British politician has acquired a hold over a substantial number of men in the Indian Army and the consequences are quite incalculable.' In his letter, Wavell has also alerted him about the danger that would be posed to the Raj, in case Subhas was brought to India as prisoner and desired that such a possibility be scrupulously avoided.

Victory On Hand, Government Announces Elections

August 21, 1945, New Delhi: The plan of Indianisation of the executive council and constitutional intiatives had stumbled at Simla. In its aftermath, communal temperature began to soar and within a month following the 'death of dialogues' in the hill capital, disturbing jargons like 'civil war' have begun to do the rounds. In such ominous, gloomy ambience, the sudden, swift victory over Japan has brought the British regime its smile back. With external threats vanished, now HMG has begun to address the Indian problems afresh. Viceroy Wavell has been in close touch with HMG on these issues.

Today, he has announced that the elections to both centre and provincial assemblies will be held in the forthcoming winter. He is slated to visit England in the next few days to hold detailed discussions with HMG on election, reorganisation of the Viceroy's executive council and the next round of constitutional initiatives.

SUBHAS CHANDRA BOSE DIES IN AIR CRASH?

August 23, 1945, Taipei: Today, the Domei Agency of Japan has revealed to the world the news of the death of Subhas Chandra Bose, the head of the Azad Hind Government, in an air crash on 18th of this month.

Subhas had reportedly left Singapore for Bangkok on 16 August. He was accompanied by SA Ayer, Abid Hassan, Habib-ur-Rahman and two other senior officials of the provisional government. According to sources close to the Azad Hind Government, Subhas planned to reach Tokyo to finalise the modalities of surrender. In the Singapore meeting, it was earlier decided that the Azad Hind Government should surrender independently and Subhas wanted an agreement on that count with the Tokyo regime. However, another version said his final destination was Manchuria. On the 17th, he, alongwith the senior officials, reached Saigon. There, he was offered a seat in a bomber plane that was bound for Dairen, a Manchurian port city. Shidei, a Japanese army officer, travelling in the same aircraft was to negotiate the surrender of the Japanese Kwantung army with the senior Soviet army officials in Manchuria occupied by Soviet forces.

The source giving this news claimed that Shidei was to introduce Subhas to top Soviet army officials. At Subhas's insistence, the authorities allowed one more seat in the bomber plane. Subhas asked Habibur-Rahman to accompany him while the remaining officials were supposed to follow later by available flights.

By the evening of 17th, they reached Tourane. The next day morning they resumed their journey by the same plane and landed at Taihoku in Formosa. At about 2:30 pm, the plane again flew from Taihoku for the next destination. However, the aircraft is reported to have crashed soon after the take-off in the outskirts of the Taihoku airport itself. Many people, including political observers, are unwilling to believe the above reports and especially the death of Subhas. The news of death of the Head of a government coming so late after the event, has been raising several doubts as regards its authenticity. Even Mountbatten, the supreme commander of the Allied force in Southeast Asia, seems to be suspecting the authenticity of the story. From his present headquarters in Kandy in Ceylon, he has ordered an enquiry into Subhas's alleged death.

A Flaming Sword Forever Unsheathed In Defence Of India: Sarojini

August 1945: As the news of his death reached India, Sarojini Naidu said that myriads of men and women felt a deep personal bereavement. Continuing, she paid her tribute, 'His proud, importunate and violent spirit was a flaming sword forever unsheathed in defence of the land he worshipped with such surpassing devotion. A greater love hath not man than this, that he lay down his life for his country and his people.'[186]

Subhas Undoubtedly A Patriot, Though Misguided: Gandhi

August 24, 1945: Subhas has got rather a brief, critical obituary from a man whom he reverentially addressed as the 'father of the nation'. Today Gandhi has expressed his feelings about Subhas's death in the air crash in a letter to Rajkumari Amrit Kaur. He has written: 'Subhas Bose has died well. He was undoubtedly a patriot, though misguided.'[187]

The remaining part of his short letter refers to the trivia. Critics say that Gandhi's ideology of non-violence has fashioned this short and seemingly unkind comment.

Britain Threatens Harsh Punishment To INA Prisoners

August 27, 1945, Delhi: A couple of days ago MZ Kiani, the commander of INA, surrendered to the British 5th division in Singapore with rest of the INA troops. This marked the end of its independent existence. Meanwhile several thousand INA men, officers and soldiers, have been brought into India through the ports of Chittagong and Calcutta. While some have been lodged in prison-camps in Bengal, most have been sent to north, west and north-western parts of India. Apart from Jhingergacha and Nilganj (near Calcutta), the INA men have been kept in camps at Kirkee (near Poona), Bahadurgarh (adjacent to Delhi), Red Fort in Delhi, Attock, Multan and other undisclosed locations. The government has been tight-lipped about the actual number of the prisoners and the places of their detention. At the same time, Auchinleck, the Commander-in-Chief, has been categorical about the need to administer harsh punishments to these 'traitors' who had sworn loyalty to the King Emperor but later held weapons against Him. On more than one occasion, he has made it clear that several hundred of these prisoners were not only guilty of 'treason' but they also inflicted brutalities upon their Indian colleagues and British troops, and therefore deserved either death sentence or transportation for life.

Today the government has issued a press communication stating its decision to hold trials for the INA prisoners.

Polls Will Show Muslims Solidly Behind Pakistan: Jinnah

September 5, 1945, Karachi: After whatever all he did or omitted to do to help the British war efforts, Jinnah has been of the opinion that the British should be beholden to him. Therefore, the Viceroy's siding with Khizr during the Simla Conference on the issue of nominating Muslim members irritated him. He feels the League now commands the support of the largest number of Muslims across the country,

Punjab included. He reckons that these facts shall be proved beyond doubt through elections which the League may fight with its agenda of 'Pakistan'. In a press conference today, he has advocated early general election and asserted that Muslim India solidly stands for Pakistan.

Mountbatten's Soldiers Blow Away INA 'War Memorial'

September 8, 1945, Singapore: In deference to the last wish of his leader, John Stracey had ensured that a war memorial came up in Singapore in a record time. Facing the sea, stood the gallant memorial inscribed with the words 'Unity, Faith, Sacrifice'. These three words symbolised the spirit of the INA. When the British forces landed here, the proud INA war memorial greeted them. Today, in an act of meanly revenge and against military ethics, the soldiers of Mountbatten blew up the sacred memorial with dynamite. As the British carried out this dastardly act of vandalism against the war dead, the local Indians and the imprisoned INA soldiers watched with helpless rage.

Clement Attlee's Barbed Offer To Indian Politicians

September 19, 1945, London: Today in a broadcast to India, Clement Attlee, the British PM assured that India will have independence at the earliest possible date. However, in the same breath he also appealed to Indians to settle their differences and decide their own destiny. Attlee is very much aware about the irreconcilable differences between the Congress and Muslim League on some critical issues and more importantly, the provocation provided by the Wavell government that are making it even more difficult for these two warring parties to come to an agreement.

Elections To Central, Provincial Legislatures In Winter

September 19, 1945, London, New Delhi: Both Attlee, the British prime minister in London and Wavell, the Viceroy, in New Delhi have announced today that the Labour government seeks an early realisation of self-government in India and for this purpose intends to hold elections to central and provincial legislatures in the coming winter. Wavell said the results of the polls would determine the composition of an assembly to draft a constitution for a united India and also the executive council of the Viceroy. To determine the constitution-making body, which has so far proved to be a complex task, it is necessary to know the mind of the electorates of British India and the representatives of the Indian states. Prime minister Attlee appealed to Indians to work unitedly to frame a constitution that will be deemed fair and equitable by all parties and interests in the country. In fact, following the collapse of the Simla round table conference, the elections now hold the key to a political solution in the country.

Not A Hair On The Head Of INA Men Must Be Touched

September 21, 1945, Bombay: After long incarceration, Sarat Bose was released from prison a week back. He was held in detention right since December 1941, without justifiable reasons. The news of his release was widely cheered by people in Bengal and the rest of India including Bombay. He has arrived here in connection with the AICC session. Today he has lashed out at the government for its ill treatment of the INA prisoners. His statement has been hard-hitting and it is clearly aimed at pressurising the government to reconsider the scheme of 'trial' of these men.

Blasting away at one stroke the cobwebs of accusations the British regime has been weaving around the INA men by calling them misdirected men, stooges of Japanese, traitors, cowards, anti-national and various other bad names, Sarat said,[188] 'it was shameful to say INA men toadied to the Japanese'. As a matter of fact, he affirmed that these men had resisted the Japanese, and that stubbornly, when necessary. Sarat lamented that while the country owed gratitude to these valiant soldiers, they were being held prisoners. Then he dared the government that 'not a hair on the heads of the brave soldiers of Indian freedom must be touched.'

This is being seen by political observers as the first powerful statement coming from a leading Indian politician that could, besides challenging the government, also influence the Indian thinking and feeling about the proposed trial of the INA men in coming days.

Congress Signals Its Support To INA Men

September 23, 1945, Bombay: The three-day session of the AICC that began on 21st has concluded today. Significantly, it was held at Gowalia Tank Maidan from where nearly three years ago, the party had issued the 'Quit India' call to the British Raj. After spending nearly three long years in prison, the top echelon of the party leadership, visibly in an act of symbolism, picked up the thread where it was left and renewed its demand for India's 'independence'. At this juncture, the issue of the proposed trial of the INA men held as prisoners came to the party as God sent. Sarat Bose, who had recently made out a strong case in favour of the INA men through the press, was heartily cheered by a 30,000 strong crowd in the Congress pandal. Jawaharlal advanced the case further. In the session, he moved a resolution saying that 'it would be tragic if these men were to be punished for having laboured, however mistakenly, for the freedom of India.' An amendment was proposed to delete the words 'however mistakenly' but Jawaharlal reportedly did not agree to the deletion.

According to political analysts, Jawaharlal, by moving a resolution on the INA men and at the same time suggesting that 'these men had laboured mistakenly', has given a clear signal that the Congress Party has decided to take the issue forward, perhaps aggressively, but on its own terms and to its own advantage. They feel that these words were incorporated discreetly to fit in the 'INA' issue to the Congress's professed ideology of 'non-violence'.

League Conquers Fresh Ground In The North West

October 3, 1945, Peshawar: Two more major political successes have come to Muslim League. Nawab Mohammad Mumtaz, a highly influential and big Tiwana landlord, has joined the League in Punjab. This is being seen as a setback for Punjab premier Khizr. In the NWFP, where the League, in the face of fierce opposition from the Khan Brothers, has so far laboured hard without success, got a boost as the Afghan Jirga, an organisation of consequence amongst the Afghan people, decided to swell its rank. Earlier Abdul Qayum Khan, a heavyweight Congress leader, had joined the League within a month of the collapse of the Simla conference. On the 20th of last month, Mian Iftikharuddin, President of the Punjab Provincial Congress, switched his allegiance to Jinnah and the League. The influx of three heavyweight Muslim leaders over the past three months from the rival parties are, of course, good tidings for the League.

No Less Than Fifty 'Black' Prisoners Would Be Hanged

October 20, 1945, New Delhi: The central cabinet has taken a stock of the INA men. According to sources close to the government, about 43,000 people had enrolled as members of the Indian National Army in Southeast Asia. Contemptously called as JIFFs, or Japanese Indian Fifth Column by the British dispensation, this army had 20,000 men from Indian army and another 23,000 civilians recruited from the expatriate Indians, mostly from Malaya. The members of the Germany based Indian Legion, again contemptuously called Hiffs, who are in Europe or have been captured number 950. The government has categorised them under three heads, viz. white, grey and black. The men about whose loyalty the government has no doubt have been classified as 'white'. They are being treated as 'recovered prisoners of war' and they would continue to serve the Indian army. The 'grey' category included those men whose loyalty was weak and breached under propaganda but they were not fundamentally disloyal. The government intends to discharge them from services. The government said the 'black' prisoners were those whose conduct merited trial for a criminal offence or whose release will be dangerous. According to sources, the men categorised as 'black' are the hard core members who deeply believed in the ideology of the INA and whose loyalty to the British has been irrevocably broken.

According to the Cabinet note[189] issued today, so far the government has been able to recover 16,000 INA men and interrogated 11,300 of them. Based on the interrogation, the prisoners have been categorized as follows: Black 2565; Grey 5091 and White 3,644. The authorities have come to the conclusion that the offences committed by the 'black' category of prisoners are serious enough to warrant 'death' or 'transportation for life'. They are also sure that the punishment of 'death' is certain to be imposed, confirmed and executed in at least 50 cases.

Irrespective of the gradation, there are visible signs of contempt, malice, and derision in the British regime's approach to the INA men in general. And flowing through all these, there is an undercurrent of silent, determined rage, and a deep vindictiveness to teach these 'traitors' a lesson.

Congress May Even Suborn The Indian Army, Panicky Wavell Writes To Pethick-Lawrence

October 22, 1945, New Delhi: Even two months ago, basking under the glory of a conclusive victory in the great war, the British regime was sure it would get the Indian people to share its anger and indignation against the 'so called' Azad Hind Government, the Indian National Army and the INA prisoners. But shockingly, unintended developments have begun to occur. Although the Congress has, by and large, been economical about Subhas, it has cherry-picked the issues of the provisional government of Free India and the 'INA trial' and the party has been pursuing them, in particular the latter issue, aggressively.

It has formed the INA Defence Committee, with several legal luminaries to defend the accused INA men. The party has been glorifying the valour and patriotism of the INA men. The local Congress committees have been according public receptions to the released INA men. In most political meetings, the INA has become the 'must discuss' topic. According to press reports, Jawaharlal, the premier Congress leader, has been raising the favourite INA slogans such as 'Jai Hind' and 'Chalo Delhi' in his meetings, and the people have been responding with wild enthusiasm.

Political analysts say that the Congress has been able to blend the revival of the 'Quit India' call of 1942 with the highly emotive issue of the 'INA trial' to deeply embarrass the British regime. Viceroy Wavell has been writing to the Secretary of State for India, explaining how the top Congress leaders were delivering violent, anti-British speeches by leveraging the mass sympathy for the INA. On 9th of this month, he wrote there were talks of Nehru's plan was to make use of the INA and large quantities of arms smuggled into India from Burma - both to train Congress volunteers and use as a Congress striking force against the government. He seems to have developed a phobia on this count. Today Wavell has again written[190] to Pethick Lawrence about his apprehension that the Congress may suborn the army which would be the most dangerous development in the near future.

Jinnah Warns Syed Not To Meddle With Candidates

October 26, 1945: The Muslim League party in Sind has been through internal turmoil for past sometime. There has been a tussle between two factions led by premier Hidayatullah and provincial League president GM Syed. The bickering between the two groups came to full public view when the Syed-led group abstained from the meetings of the central and the provincial parliamentary boards of the League held yesterday, where the names of the candidates for the provincial and central legislatures for the forthcoming elections were announced. It is not difficult to guess that a rebellion is on the ferment. In anticipation, Jinnah has today cautioned Syed not to defy the decision of the central Parliamentary Board about the candidates whose names have been cleared.

Remember! India Adores The Men On Trial: Gandhi

October 29, 1945, Poona: Even though several Congress leaders have been striking hard postures against the government on the issue of the INA trial, the British regime had hoped that Gandhi, being the most ardent advocate of non-violence, would not endorse the populist stand of other Congress leaders. But even that hope was dashed today.

As Gandhi opened his mind on the issue today in a letter,[191] the government, already upset at the trend of things, grew anxious. In his letter written from the 'Nature Cure Clinic' here, addressed to Sir Evan Jenkins, Gandhi began in an apologetic tone 'This I write in fear and trembling, lest I may be overstepping my limit'. Then he introduced a subtle logic as to why he is taking up the issue of the INA even though they had waged a violent war. 'Though I can have nothing in common with any defence by force of arms', Gandhi added, 'I am never blind to the valour and patriotism often displayed by persons in arms, as seems to be the case here'. Thereafter, he rendered a piece of advice which could as well be treated as a veiled threat: 'And can the government afford to ignore, the almost, if not the wholly, unanimous opinion of Indians of all shades of opinion?' Pointing out that 'India adores these men who are on their trial', Gandhi has left the decision to His Excellency. But the government has been left in no doubt as to what does the tallest mass leader of the subcontinent want it to do.

Why Not Make INA Nucleus Of Indian Army? – Vallabhbhai

November 1, 1945: The trial of the INA men was to begin on the 8th of the last month, but it has been rescheduled to be held on the fifth day of the current month. Meanwhile, the issue has been picking up momentum with every passing day. Today Vallabhbhai's riposte[192] to Auchinleck's statement on the issue of 'complete Indianisation' of the Indian army has exploded on the British regime like a bomb shell. Auchinleck had earlier expressed inability to lay down any time limit for 'Indianisation' as the matter depended, he claimed, on the interest evinced by young Indians to enrol as army officers. Taking a dig at the British Commander-in-Chief's statement, Vallabhbhai pointed out: 'Does he not know that Mr Subhas Chandra Bose organised an army of 60,000 and a women's brigade in under a year?' And, he added, 'It is this very army the British Government is trying to disband now'. Then came another broadside that caused the government deeper anxiety. Vallabhbhai asked if the British were serious about giving India independence, why did they not make the INA, the nucleus of the army to be? According to sources, his statement has been causing considerable disquiet in the government.

INA Trial Opens In Red Fort, India Is In Flames

November 6, 1945, Delhi: Yesterday, the INA trial opened up at the Red Fort here. It began with three top INA commanders —Major General Shah Nawaz, Col Prem Sahgal and Col Gurbaksh Singh Dhillon. The first of these three was a divisional commander while the other two commanded a regiment each. Notably, all of them gave a reasonably good account of their leadership against the British forces. They were accused of treason and for committing brutalities by putting their subordinate soldiers in the INA to death. The Congress' INA defence committee turned up in the court room in strength. As many as thirteen legal luminaries, including Sir TB Sapru, KN Katju, Bhulabhai Desai, Sir Dalip Singh, Asaf Ali and Jawaharlal attended the opening of the trial. Today, major newspapers across the country flashed the news of the event under big headlines. Some of them devoted several pages to the trial and carried many engrossing stories about the Azad Hiind Government and the Indian National Army, hitherto kept hidden by the British Government. The *Hindustan Times* carried the photos of the three accused, who by now have turned into national heroes. In addition, the newspaper also managed to publish a file photo of the women of the Rani of Jhansi regiment marching with rifles on their shoulders. The detailed newspaper coverage and bits and pieces of the facts of the provisional government and the stories of valour and sufferings by the Indian National Army seem to have set the whole country aflame. Today Madurai, in the southern part of the country, exploded with anti-British rage. The police had hard time in tackling the protesters and eventually opened fire. Two persons fell to police bullets and several were wounded.

Congress May Use The INA To Spearhead Revolt

November 6, 1945, Delhi: The surging public interest and support to the INA men cutting across caste and community, and the rising tides of anti-British sentiment for having put these national heroes to trial and humiliation have been upsetting the Viceroy no end. Today he has written[193] to Pethick-Lawrence, the Secretary of State for India, confessing that the government in India is facing great difficulty, in fact, so great that he feels the need for support and guidance from HMG. Wavell has complained that top Congress leaders like Vallabhbhai, Jawaharlal and Pant are making statements to provoke mass disorder. Wavell has added that these leaders are taking the credit for the 1942 disturbances, glorifying the INA and asserting that the British could be turned out of India in a short time. They have warned that the officials who were responsible for suppressing the 1942 movement would be tried as war criminals and punished.

Wavell has alleged that they are contemplating to contest elections, and thereafter, serve an ultimatum to the British and organise a mass movement like in 1942 on a much larger scale if their demand is not heeded. Wavell has raised doubts about the genuineness of the Congress policy of non-violence. He has also lamented about Gandhi not doing enough to control things: 'Gandhi's influence is believed to be on the side of moderation but he has said and done practically nothing for weeks….' Wavell expressed his worst fear that the Congress is counting on the INA, as the spearhead of their revolt and it would suborn the Indian army if it can and the party even hopes to impair the loyalty and efficiency of the police.

INA TRIAL BRIDGES COMMUNAL DIVIDE

From mid 1943 to mid 1945, the British Indian government either shielded Indians from the news of the Azad Hind Government, INA and Subhas Chandra Bose or presented them with purposeful distortion. During the battle of Imphal and Kohima, they managed the information flow with consummate skill. As a result, the Indian soldiers fighting on the Allied side had no proper idea about the INA and the Azad Hind Government. The INA, on the other hand, survived on minimum ration and fought with antiquated and inadequate arms, but they brimmed with patriotism and established a new watermark of excellence in terms of commitment, valour and gallantry.

After they were brought back to India as prisoners, these facts were gradually known. The long-suppressed nation, including its men serving the armed forces, discovered in the INA men, virtues that the people of a self-respecting nation ought to possess. The whole country came to admire their spirit, patriotism and heroics. Indians demonstrated waves of anger and disdain against the British regime, which was attempting to demonise these national heroes. The British Indian Government had called

> their patriotism 'treachery' and wanted to impose exemplary punishments. The INA men, in the process, acquired larger than life images. Their sacrifice became proverbial, their heroics legendary, and their patriotism the saga of national pride. The people of the country have begun to think that the INA men can do no wrong and that the government has been out to wrong them. Gauging the public mood, it is clear that any attempt to discredit and punish these heroes will meet with violent popular disapproval.
>
> The British Government is clearly feeling uncomfortable at the gradually consolidating public opinion in favour of a pan-India nationalism that is growing, cutting across religious divide, to challenge the moral right of the British to rule India. The fact that the government unwittingly put a Hindu, a Muslim and a Sikh officer on trial is bringing all three major communities together against it. The government is upset—it can ill afford to allow, for whatever reason, the religious divides to be bridged which it has so assiduously cultivated over long decades in order to be able to rule the Indians.

Subhas Usurping Gandhi's Place In Popular Esteem

November 10, 1945: Henry Twynam, the governor of the Central Provinces and Berar, has been repeatedly reminding the Viceroy about the explosive condition of the country in the wake of the trial of the INA men. A fortnight ago, he had written[194] that he was not able to recollect any period in which there have been such venom and such unbridled attacks on the government and its officers.

He compared these with the Irish revolution that never allowed any 'let up' in the campaign against British rule and never to 'let the flame of animosity die down until independence is achieved'. He has been particularly upset by Gandhi's lack of intervention to reinstall the supremacy of the creed of 'non-violence' amongst the Indians and the Congressmen in these violent, emotive times. He feels Gandhi was gradually fading into the background and revolutionary leaders like Nehru and Patel are coming to the forefront. Today he has sent another missive[195] to the Viceroy wherein he has complained about the Congress leaders making every effort to 'prepare a mass mentality in support of another violent struggle'. Once again he has complained about Gandhi's continued 'silence' that 'furnished no encouragement to moderate Congressmen and this', the governor wrote, 'takes him away from the masses'. Twynam has referred to his sources suggesting that 'Subhas Chandra Bose is rapidly usurping the place held by Gandhi in popular esteem....'

Calcutta Erupts In Unprecedented Fury

November 22, 1945, Calcutta: The city witnessed unprecedented public fury over the issue of the INA trial. Yesterday, the university students had taken out a big protest procession from Wellingdon Square in central Calcutta, aiming to reach Dalhousie Square, the city's prime district housing both government and corporate headquarters. When they were prevented by the police, a large number of onlookers joined their ranks. The massive body of protesters then picked up confrontation with the police, following which lathis and brickbats were exchanged liberally. The situation grew so bad that the police opened fire. But even that did not deter the demonstrators. They dug in and continued to fight. An extremely uneasy situation ensued and that continued through last night. In the morning today, the demonstrators moved in two columns—one from Bowbazar and another from Dharmatala—the destination being common, ie. Dalhousie square.

As they attempted to surge ahead, tens of thousands of people joined the march and then the sea of people broke through the police cordon. Upon reaching their destination, the demonstrators turned riotous and burnt several British and American army vehicles. The police fired several rounds and great chaos followed. Mob violence continued. Eventually, the army was called in to tackle the mob violence.

The ferocity of the protest has surprised and shocked the government. They are surprised that they could not so far gauge the extent of popular sentiment in favour of the INA. The incident has been practically an eye opener.

Normalcy Returns To Calcutta

November 24, 1945, Calcutta: Pro-INA violence had gripped the city on November 21 and 22. Though the army was called in on the second day, the impact of the event could be felt till yesterday, as large number of municipal workers and water workers too joined in the agitation. This resulted in throwing large part of civic life out of gear. Today normalcy has returned to the city. According to preliminary reports, several scores of people were killed while hundreds of people sustained injuries. Over 150 vehicles, including many army vehicles, were burnt.

India As Turbulent As During Sepoy Mutiny: Twynam Best Thing To Do Is To Cut Our Losses: Cunningham

November 27, 1945, New Delhi: The tide of pro-INA sentiment cutting across communities and the country-wide protests, some of these violent, have been causing the government deep disquiet. Wavell's anxieties have increased manifold as one after another, the governors of the provinces are advising him to urgently review the government policy on the INA trial. Glancy, the governor of Punjab, had ten days ago, mentioned to him about the rising sympathy of Indians in his province in favour of the INA men. He then suggested that the number of trials in future should be reduced only to a few.

He also noted that the people of Punjab have been very angry over 'treason' charges against the INA men. Yesterday, Sir Henry Joseph Twynam, governor of the Central Provinces & Berar, wrote[196] that he was sceptical of the Indian army's reaction if they were ordered by the government to fire upon the mobs. He went to the extent of comparing the present situation to the one prevailing at the time of the Sepoy Mutiny. Today, George Cunningham, the governor of the NWFP, categorically advised[197] the government not to initiate any further proceedings against any one as he felt Indian opinion has clearly been against the INA trial. He has expressed his anxiety that the issue is daily becoming an Indian versus British one, and irrespective of the final outcome of the trial, 'This anti-British bias will persist in each man's mind'. Describing the trial as the 'most difficult problem' he has faced in India, Cunningham today advised the Governor General, 'the best thing to do is to cut our losses'. With several of the governors expressing their deep-seated reservations, the government is expected to scale down its target and mode of future trials. Auchinleck has already taken the cue. He has recently proposed not to press 'treason' charges against the accused in future.

Congress For 'United India', League Wants 'Pakistan' Election Results Show Extreme Polarisation

December 1945: In terms of the announcements made in September by the British prime minister and the Viceroy, elections to the central legislatures were held and the results are now out.

The Congress Party has registered impressive wins in the general constituencies. On the whole, out of a total 102 seats, it won 57 (as against 36 in 1934), followed by Muslim League (30), Europeans (8), Independents (5) and Akalis (2). Significantly, the Muslim League has won all the 30 seats reserved for Muslims. It fought this election—on one plank— 'If you want Pakistan, vote for Muslim League'. In a way, the League made it a referendum for the Muslims of the country. The Congress stood for united India and against the vivisection of the country. It tried to mobilise all Muslim parties, which had differences with the Muslim League. However, the results show that the Muslim voters have stood solidly behind the Muslim League. The results are a clear indicator that the hard work done by Jinnah in communalising the Muslims since 1937, and his single-minded perusal of the demand for Pakistan has paid rich dividends. Jinnah can now claim with greater confidence that the Muslim League is the most qualified if not the 'sole' representative of Indian Muslims.

Beware Of Congress' INA Propaganda: Auchinleck

December 22, 1945, New Delhi: The ability of the Congress in leveraging the INA issue and the depth and intensity of Indian emotions in this regard has taken Auchinleck, the Commander-In-Chief, by surprise. In the light of the experience since 5 November, when the trial began, he is not in a position to discard the possibility of a mutiny in the armed forces. Today he has sent a communiqué[198] to his chiefs of staff, warning them that the nationalist Indian members of the armed forces could fall prey to the vigorous Congress propaganda that has been extolling the Indian National Army as true patriots and condemning the government. In the event, their morale were to deteriorate 'gravely owing to continued propaganda and some units mutinied', Auchinleck apprehended that the mutiny 'might become general, even if in some cases half-hearted'.

Syed Raises Flag Of Rebellion Against League In Sind

December 26, 1945, Karachi: GM Syed, the president of the Sind Muslim League, was one of the prime propagators of the idea of Sind's secession from the province of Bombay. He had also played an important role in crafting the Pakistan Resolution in 1940. Syed has been visualising Pakistan as a federation of independent Muslim states, with Sind being one of them.

Now that the probabilities of Pakistan has increased somewhat, realities are confronting thinking politicians like Syed. He is able to foresee huge influx of Muslims from India's heartland into the north-western states like Sind and others that would federate into Pakistan and the burden that would be placed on the latter's resources as a result. He wants to be sure that Sind would have the autonomy to deal with such issues. Reportedly, he has differences of opinion on the connected issues with both central and some of the provincial leaders.

In recent months, Syed has experienced conflicts and confrontations on a number of issues with Sir Hidayatullah, the premier. He also fell out with the central leadership of the League, especially on the tendency of the central leaders to interefere excessively in the matters of the province. In October, the central parliamentary board of the party had ignored him in selecting candidates for the provincial and central legislatures in the forthcoming elections. He was further warned by Jinnah not to affect any changes in the CPB's list. Things have only worsened since then. Today he has resigned from his membership of the working committee of the AIML, protesting the manner in which the central leadership has been handling Sind matters. He has gone to the extent of putting up candidates to contest in the Sind Assembly election against those nominated by the CPB. Political observers are not hopeful about Syed's prospects, given the rising tide of sentiments in favour of Jinnah and Pakistan in Sind.

Conciliation Board Publishes Its Report

December 27, 1945, Bombay: Even as the Congress and the League show no sign of coming together on any proposal for a negotiated transfer of power from the British to the Indians, liberal leaders like TB Sapru, MR Jayakar, NG Iyenger and Jagdish Prasad endeavoured hard to frame a comprehensive proposal providing for a constitutional plan. The Conciliation Board appointed by the Standing Committee of the Non-Party Conference in November last year has published its report today. It made comprehensive recommendations covering short-term and long-term issues. Briefly, it provides for a. a single state in the nature of federation of British Indian provinces and Indian states; b. the accession of the states to the federation from time to time on terms agreed; c. no right of secession of the provinces; d. joint general electorate with reservations for minorities; e. parity of Hindus (excluding Scheduled Castes) and Muslims in union legislature (lower house) and union executive; f. protection of minority rights through appropriate provisions. The proposal has found the idea of Pakistan impractical.

Native States: Jawaharlal Paints Realistic Picture

December 31, 1945 to January 4, 1946, Udaipur: AISPC is holding its general meeting in this lake city after a gap of nearly six years. Since it held its last meeting in Ludhiana way back in 1939, there have been drastic changes in the political ambience in the country. At that time, the Congress was fighting for freedom and creating pressure on the British Government in various manners. The government is now ready to concede to reasonable aspirations of the political parties of British India and it is for these parties to come to an agreement and put up their demands. In the changed condescending environment, Indian political parties have begun to harbour the ambition of absorbing a sizeable part of the Indian India into the proposed Indian state. They are, therefore, of the opinion that in the present juncture, the future of few hundred native states requires to be assessed more realistically.

Jawaharlal, as the president of the AISPC, has laid down a vision for these states. His prognosis is that most of these would be absorbed in the British Indian provinces and that hardly fifteen to twenty large states might enter into the federation as autonomous units, with their rulers as constitutional heads. However, Jawaharlal is for democratic representation even with respect to the princely states and is contending that the representatives of these states in the constituent assembly should be democratically elected. Further, there should be full responsible governments in the federating states.

AIML Comes Down Hard On Sind Rebels

January 2, 1946, Meerut: The AIML Action Committee has decided to chastise GM Syed and quell the rebellion before it can spread. The committee has decided to impose capital punishment upon the rebel leader. It has expelled Syed, together with ten others, for opposing the official candidates in the elections.

Verdict From Red Fort, Top INA Commanders Set Free

January 3, 1946, Delhi: The verdicts on the trial of the first three accused, viz. Shah Nawaz, Prem Sahgal and GS Dhillon were delivered today at the Red Fort. The authorities had rejected the sanctity of the INA and its Army Act under which these three officers had imposed death sentences to their subordinate soldiers. Considering the government's obstinate, unreasoned stand, the accused officers were advised by their counsels to deny actually putting any of the court-martialled soldiers to death. The legal luminaries, spearheaded by Bhulabhai Desai, put up a spirited defence of the three INA officers. At the end, the three were held guilty of waging war against the King Emperor but spared the charge of murder. Shah Nawaz was found guilty of abetment of murder. The court pronounced sentences of cashiering (or, dismissal from service), forfeiture of pays and allowances and transportation for life. However, the three were told that the last and the harshest of the three sentences, ie. transportation for life, has been remitted by the Commander-in-Chief. This implied that the three officers would be free to step out. The news spread fast and there were celebrations across India. Political analysts see the verdict as a definite signal of weakening government resolve to proceed further with the trial. The intense public opinion in favour of the INA men has, they feel, certainly influenced the outcome. They also feel, the government will be cautious in holding further trials.

Another INA Trial Opens At Delhi Cantonment

January 9, 1946, New Delhi: Even as the trial of three top INA commanders ended last week, a new one has begun in Delhi Cantonment today against Captain Abdul Rashid. He was charged with waging war against the King Emperor and for the brutal treatment of Indian army men held as Japanese prisoners of war in the Bidadari camp in 1942. Rashid had defected from the British Indian army to join the INA and was placed in charge of that camp. He was charged along with two others, viz. Singhara Singh and Fateh Khan. Rashid refused the Congress offer for legal defence and wanted to be defended by the defence committee set up by the Muslim League. He also wanted to be tried separately, claiming that a different set of circumstances applied to his case.

Shed Blood When Called Upon, Now Cast Vote: Jinnah

January 11, 1946, Delhi: Both the Congress and the Muslim League are satisfied with their electoral performances. Following the notifications of the results of the elections to the central legislature, the Congress has been claiming it is the biggest, strongest and most representative political organisation in the country. The Muslim League is equally upbeat, having secured every Muslim seat which for the first time has given some measure of legitimacy to their claim of being the sole representative of country's Muslims. The League is celebrating its remarkable victory today. Here Jinnah addressed an enthusiastic gathering and said Muslims were powerful, well organised and prepared to shed blood for Pakistan. However, the time for that has not come. The elections are shortly due in several provincial assemblies. For the present they should cast their votes in support of Pakistan and Muslim League.

Wavell Addresses Indian Princes

January 17, 1946, New Delhi: Early this month Jawaharlal's speech in the AISPC Conference in Ludhiana, laying down a vision of the Indian native states, had exercised their rulers for understandable reasons. However, their anxieties were considerably alleviated after hearing the Viceroy. In the twentieth annual session of the Chamber of Princes, Wavell at first acknowledged their significant contribution to the recent Allied war victory. Then he impressed upon them the need for a satisfactory solution to the framing of a constitution upon which depended the happiness and prosperity of Indian people. Thereafter he came to that vital issue. Referring to the fact that the native rulers' relationships with the crown were guaranteed by their treaties and engagements, he sought to comfort them: 'I can assure you that there is no intention on our part to initiate any change in this relationship or these rights without your consent.'[199] The nervous rulers, in return, spelt out their noble intention of reforms, presumably as an amulet against future democratic threat either from their own people and or the political parties from British India, the Congress in particular. The Princes promised substantial reforms in the interest of their states and people. Political analysts are sighting potential tension between these political parties and the native Princes, given their conflicting aspirations.

Assam Gives A Clear Mandate To Congress

January, 1946, Shillong: The results of the provincial assembly election are out. A key issue for the electors in the province was its natives' concern to preserve its demographic integrity. On this issue, the Congress shared common concerns with the Tribal League and their alliance has paid handsome dividends. Congress has secured absolute majority, pre-empting any scope for the governor to manipulate, as he had done in the past. The party has won 58 out of a total 108 seats in the provincial legislature as against 33 in 1937.

Saadullah, it may be recalled, was ousted in 1941 in the wake of a student movement. However, he was later brought back by the British governor to the chagrin of the native population. Thereafter, exploiting the political void in the province due to the absence of the Congress Party in the assembly, he managed to stick to power till 1945. During this period, taking advantage of the war conditions and the virtual absence of any opposition, his ministry pursued immigrant-friendly policies more aggressively. Apparently to support the British war efforts, his government had raised a slogan 'grow more food' but under this guise, it opened three districts of the province for settlement to immigrant cultivators from Bengal. Some critics say that even the Viceroy did not believe in the genuineness of the slogan and saw it as a planned effort to 'grow more immigrants' in the province.

A common scare about an impending revolution in the demographic profile in both the plains and hills of the province had brought the Congress and the Tribal League together in the recent election and it was widely believed that the coalition, more particularly the Congress, would do well.

Sind Electorate Polarised, Verdict Not Clear Enough

January, 1946, Karachi: The electorate of Sind has delivered its verdict and it has some interesting facets. There were three key planks in the election campaigning by the parties. The Congress propagated the theme of 'undivided independent India', the Muslim League demonstrated its unflinching commitment to 'Pakistan' while the rebel group, led by GM Syed, advocated the cause of Sindhi sub-nationalism. Syed did not oppose Pakistan but nor did he want the interests of Sind to be subjugated to any other entity—whether Punjab, or any other province or a monolithic Pakistan. The verdict showed that unlike the previous election in 1937, the Hindus have solidly stood behind the Congress. The party secured 18 seats now as against only 7 then.

Together with the four successful nationalist Muslims members, the party has a bloc of 22. But the performance of the Muslim League has been stellar. From a 'blank' in 1937, the party has been, riding on a strong 'Pakistan' wave, able to secure as many as 27 seats reserved for the Muslims. The rebel League candidates led by GM Syed ended up with only 4 seats, while 4 other independent Muslim candidates have also made the cut. Though badly mauled, Syed can, if he wants to form the government, hope to secure support from the Congress bloc of 22 and the 4 independent Muslim candidates. In such a scenario, 3 European members elected to the assembly would hold the key to ministry formation. It would be interesting to see if Jinnah would reconcile with Syed and form a League ministry or prefer a path of confrontation.

Abdul Rashid Awarded Seven Years' Imprisonment

February 6, 1946, New Delhi: The verdict in the Abdul Rashid case is out today. Rashid had denied that he had joined the INA to fight the British. He insisted that he was intrigued by the Hindu-Sikh conspiracy to take INA into India piggybacking on the Japanese, expel the British and make India a place where no self-respecting Muslim could live. Like other Muslim men who joined the INA, Rashid claimed, he too joined to safeguard Muslims against such a conspiracy. However, his defence did not work and he was awarded seven years of rigorous imprisonment for brutal treatment of Indian army men held as prisoners.

INA Trial Brings Congress, Muslim League Closer

February 12, 1946, Calcutta: The verdict in the Abdul Rashid case has stirred hornet's nest. While the Muslim League, frustrated that its defence committee, unlike the Congress's, failed to acquit the accused officer, cried hoarse alleging discrimination. Jawaharlal from the Congress Party too called the judgment 'unfair'. Though many in the INA fraternity felt disgusted about the stand Rashid took, the pervasive pro-INA climate has sparked off anti-British protests in several pockets. The most intense demonstration has erupted in Calcutta.

In a re-enactment of the November 1945 scene, students once again assembled yesterday at Wellingdon Square and attempted to march to Dalhousie Square. Significantly, Muslim students turned up in numbers in yesterday's demonstration. Like on the last occasion, the police barricaded their way. Unbridled exchanges between lathi and brickbat followed. The violence quickly grew intense and the police fired bullets. Several vehicles and roadside shops turned victim of the confrontation. However, with the hindsight of past experience, the government called in the army to tackle the situation without much delay.

Today, the authorities allowed the demonstrators to march to Dalhousie. According to reports, over a lakh of people including Hindu and Muslim students, Congress and League cadres, Communists, and women joined the procession. The crowd demanded not only fair treatment to Rashid but also shouted slogans in favour of Hindu-Muslim unity. According to reports, the Government has been disturbed at the signs of an emerging unity between the two communities. According to unconfirmed reports, more than a dozen people have lost their lives and a few hundred suffered injuries, some of them serious, during these two days, such has been the intensity of the agitation.

'Netaji's Lessons are Sacrifice, Unity and Discipline'

February 12, 1946, Poona: In a letter written to Rajkumari Amrit Kaur a couple of days after Subhas's death was announced in the newspapers, Gandhi had done a curt and somewhat unkind appraisal of Subhas, describing him as a patriot, but misguided. However, since then he seems to have changed his assessment[200] somewhat. Now, in a detailed article in the *Harijan*, while differing with Subhas's method of freedom struggle, he has admitted that the 'hypnotism of the Indian National Army has cast its spell upon us'. Talking of what Subhas offered to the nation, he said, 'The lesson that Netaji and his army bring to us is one of self-sacrifice, unity irrespective of class and community, and discipline.'

Gandhi has acknowledged Subhas's signal contribution to forging communal unity and spirit of nationalism across all communities. Incidentally, the Congress is in dire need of such a spirit in the countrymen in the present difficult times when the rising secessionist demand of the League is about to tear the nation apart. The government is exploiting the communal card so blatantly that the Congress simply seems out of depth to tackle the issue. On the other hand, the League is trying to bully it under the indulgent eyes of the British Government. No doubt, the INA had proved itself as the epitome of communal harmony. Such spirit alone can save India from being divided. Gandhi seems to have recognised this fact in his article.

Unless Their Sentences Were Remitted, Indian Army Would Have Dissolved

February 13, 1946, New Delhi: The fact that the three INA officers were set free at the end of a month long trial, after calling over a hundred witnesses from India and outside including Malaya, Singapore, and Japan has created deep disquiet amongst some sections of the British bureaucracy, army establishment and pro-British media. *The Statesman,* which followed the trial closely, expressed its disgust at the final outcome. Yesterday, Auchinleck attempted to explain[201] his decision to remit the sentences of the accused INA officers to one of the powerful pillars of the British Raj, ie. the top echelon of the British commanders, who have been supposedly unhappy on this issue. Auchinleck wrote that by allowing commutation of sentences of the three accused persons of the INA, the government has been able to avert a violent internal conflict.

This was so, Auchinleck reasoned, as 'a generally genuine feeling' prevailed amongst Indian officers in the Indian Army that the accused were 'patriots and nationalists' and 'even if they were misled, they should be treated with clemency as true sons of India'. Auchinleck has added that the great majority of the Indian army officers, while admitting the gravity of the offense committed by the accused, were practically sure 'that any attempt to enforce the sentence would have led to chaos in the country at large and probably to dissensions and mutiny in the Army culminating in its dissolution, probably on communal lines.'

Today Auchinleck has forwarded the copy of his above communiqué to Viceroy Wavell.

Khan Charisma Still Works – NWFP Snubs Jinnah

February 18, 1946, Peshawar: Notwithstanding a League-led ministry's rule from May 1943 to mid March 1945 and all kinds of manipulations by Cunningham,[202] the governor, including favours and patronages to vested interests, the Congress, led by the Khan Brothers, has emerged winner in the elections, winning 30 out of a total of 50 seats. In this election, the League stressed the themes of 'Islam in danger' and 'Pakistan'. In spite of such blunt attempts to communalise the voters, the League has achieved limited success by winning 17 seats reserved for Muslims. In this hugely Muslim majority province, the cry 'Islam in danger' sounded ridiculous. The majority Pasthun Muslims preferred their province to be part of undivided India (for which the Congress stood) instead of being part of Pakistan, where they were likely to be dominated by the Punjabis. The Congress has been able to project Muslim League as the 'cat's paw' of the British and this worked amongst the 'independence-spirited' Pasthuns. The Congress also tried to win over large number of tenant farmers by promising them land to be taken away from the big Khans. On the whole, the election result of this Muslim majority border province has come as a huge morale booster for the Congress. It is hoping that it would be able to use the poll verdict to its advantage while conducting the final negotiation with the British Government to decide upon terms and conditions of India's independence.

Muslim Bastion That Still Remains Elusive

The seed of Muslim League was laid in the Aligarh movement in UP and its presence and activities were, for long, more pronounced in provinces where Muslims lived as minority community. It appears the feeling of insecurity due to Hindu domination had concerned the Muslims in those provinces more than in the hugely Muslim majority provinces like Sind and NWFP or even provinces like Punjab and Bengal which had considerable Muslim population. In fact, to the people of the provinces with clear Muslim majority, issues like 'Islam in danger' had lesser appeal—the people of NWFP, for example, found such election slogans absurd. Therefore, fashioning the spread of the League to these provinces, which are supposed to be the parts of the proposed Pakistan, has been a demanding task. Jinnah has so far done it in a masterly fashion. His performance has been all the more spectacular, as he has also simultaneously made the League's appeal grow at a frantic pace in Muslim minority provinces and also provinces like Punjab and Bengal, by surcharging the people with vigorous communal campaign. In the 1937 provincial elections, the Muslim League had failed to win any seat in Sind and managed to secure only two seats in Punjab. In the recent elections, it has emerged as the single largest party in both these provinces—stellar electoral achievements! Besides it has also vastly improved its performance in Bengal and several Muslim minority provinces. The League's only failing so far has been its inability to make a dent in the NWFP. In that border province, with an overwhelming percentage of people being Muslims, Khan Abdul Ghaffar Khan-led Congress has yet again humbled Jinnah and the League in the recent election. The tall Pathan stalwart is, through his victory, still protecting the Congress image as a repository of Muslim confidence. To Jinnah, on the other hand, the NWFP lingers as a major and bitter challenge.

MUTINY BREAKS OUT IN ROYAL INDIAN NAVY

February 18, 1946, Bombay: The Indian marines in the Royal Indian Navy have been aggrieved by the policies of racial discriminations by the authorities for long. Their discontents are bursting out now. One of the fallouts of the recent World War was the global exposure of the Indian soldiers to the working conditions of defense personnel in countries across the world which only made them feel bitter about the discriminations practised on them by the British. Over last few months, the legend of the INA and the nationwide outcry against the public trial of the INA soldiers, have kindled in them a new sense of self respect and dignity. They submitted a memorandum to the authorities pointing out grievances and seeking redressal of discriminatory practices within a specified time, failing which they threatened to resign in a body. But the British Government, seemingly intoxicated by their recent war successes, chose to ignore.

Today the ratings at the HMIS Talwar, a shore establishment in the city for signals training, began a hunger strike protesting against hardships on pay and food, and outrageous racial discrimination and in particular the derogatory references by their commander to their national character. The ratings thereafter held a mass meeting in Bombay in pursuance of their earlier decision. The authorities have called out British troops and placed all ships of the Royal Indian Navy in charge of British officers and men. There are reports that the government has been trying to suppress the movement with iron hands. But it is worried because the disaffection in civilians has begun to spread amongst the armed forces. Coming on the eve of fresh attempts at transferring power to Indian political parties, these unfolding events are causing great disquiet in both the government and the Congress leaders.

Britain's Cabinet Ministers To Visit India

February 19, 1946, London: Today, Pethick-Lawrence, Secretary of State for India, has announced in the parliament that the HMG would depute a team of three cabinet ministers to India who would, in association with the Viceroy, discuss with Indian political leaders and seek agreement on constitutional issues and interim government aimed at early realisation of self-government in India.

Jinnah Insists On Two Constituent Assemblies

February 19, 1946, New Delhi: Two important objectives of the present elections were to: (a) elect people's representatives who can form the constituent assembly and frame a constitution for India and, (b) form an interim government in the centre. But buoyed by the striking success of the Muslim League in the elections, Jinnah has decided to accentuate the demand for 'Pakistan' right away. He has strongly insisted that there should be 'two' constitution-making bodies, not one. On the issue of 'interim government', Jinnah has demanded that before the League decides to participate in the 'interim government', other parties must accept the principle of 'Pakistan' and declare so.

CSP, Communists Support Marines' Protest

February 21, 1946, Bombay: A protest strike by the Indian marines against racial discrimination and unjustified treatment by authorities that began three days ago in the naval barracks here have snowballed into a major crisis. The government, instead of assuring to look into their grievances, adopted a tough posture and countered the ratings with force. It confined the strikers to their barracks, using Maratha battalions and armed police.

The issue had been boiling over for last three days and has assumed a dangerous form today. In the morning, the two sides exchanged fires. The striking marines thereafter managed to gain access to several ships anchored at the port and took control of the sophisticated guns installed therein. They have demanded withdrawal of the government forces guarding the barracks but the government, in turn, has hardened its stand. In the meanwhile, the complexion of the crisis changed radically after the Congress Socialist Party (CSP) and the Communists pledged their sympathy in favour of the striking marines. The government apprehends that the impact might now percolate to Bombay city. [203]

Mutineers Show White Flag, But Government Worried

February 23, 1946, Bombay: Since yesterday, the city has witnessed unprecedented violence. Bombay observed a general '*Hartal*' yesterday in sympathy with the striking marines in which the Communists and the students played key roles. There were widespread confrontations with the government forces. The mob offered determined resistance and fought pitched battles with the army and the police, who opened fire to tackle the situation. Scores of people were killed and many more injured but the mob refused to give in. In the evening, Jawaharlal and Vallabhbhai held meeting in Chowpatty in the city, and condemned the violence. The tension was carried over to today as well. There were chaos and violence in the city for major part of the day. The government in Delhi was upset as the unrest amongst the Indian marines, which had earlier spread to Calcutta, intensified there during the course of the day.

The situation in Bombay improved in the late hours today. There are reports that both Patel and Jinnah have persuaded the striking marines to surrender. In the evening, the marines offered to lay down arms.

Though the mutiny has seemingly ended, its intensity and social as well as political connectivity, are causing the government much disquiet. According to official sources,[204] the week-long incident in Bombay has left 228 civilians dead and 1,048 of them injured while 34 police officials were injured and three constables killed. Besides, there were extensive damages to government properties.

Punjab Polls Show Division Among Three Communities

February 24, 1946: The results of the elections to the Punjab Legislative Assembly were declared today. For the first time over two decades, the Unionist Party has suffered serious electoral reverses managing to win only 20 seats, whereas, the Muslim League and the Congress have emerged as two potent forces, quite opposite to what happened in 1937. This province too reflects deep polarisation of votes on the basis of religious affiliation. Though not able to achieve the majority, the Muslim League has emerged as the single largest party, winning as many as 73 seats (out of a total 86 reserved seats) followed by the Congress with 51 seats. For the seats reserved for the Sikhs, the Akali Dal sought to assert its monopoly and as a result it had confrontations with the Congress in several seats. However, benefitting from the trust reposed by the Sikhs, the Akalis secured the bulk of the reserved seats. They finished with a tally of 22 seats.

There is a clear disenchantment with the Unionist Party as the voters possibly viewed it as ineffective against the rising tide of the League. Thus, its Hindu supporters seemed to have shifted their patronage to the Congress and the Muslim supporters voted the League.

Like elsewhere, the League had made 'Pakistan' the major election issue in Punjab as well, which encouraged Muslim voters to support its candidates. On the contrary, Congress contested on the plank of unified India and against partition, thus pulling most Hindu votes. Akalis raised the issue of protecting Sikh interests in the context of the League's demand for Pakistan and the Congress' apparent indifference to their concerns. Sikh voters trusted the Akalis. Muslim League is euphoric with its massive victory in Punjab. Jinnah is happy that the Muslim League can now pursue its demand of Pakistan with greater legitimacy.

The Message Of The Naval Mutiny

The mutiny in the Royal Indian Navy that had erupted in Bombay, spread like wild fire in various ports of the country and involved ten naval establishments including in Karachi, Madras, Calcutta, Cochin, Lonavla, Jamnagar, Visakhapatnam, Mandapam, Andaman & Nicobar, and, 45 ships besides miscellaneous ships and four flotillas. The political consciousness of the rebellion was manifest as the ratings had taken out processions and not only burnt the American flag in the US Information Office but also hoisted the Congress, Muslim League and the INA flags. The rebellion was severe in Karachi and Calcutta. The latter was badly affected by the agitation on 21 and 23 February.

To the relief of the government, the rebellion finally came to an end on the 23rd. The government, scared by the rebellion in the armed forces, which happens to be its mainstay in the country, has been comforted by Vallabhbhai's opinion that indiscipline in the services should not be encouraged and that the government may tackle the issue including using 'immediate discharge' as the main form of punishment. Gandhi has also criticised the strikers for mutinying without the call of a prepared revolutionary party and without the guidance and intervention of political leaders of their choice.

Notwithstanding the ethical and strategic implication of the mutiny, it seems that the government is feeling uncomfortable at the possible INA effect on the strikers.

As for the outcome, many demands of the strikers regarding welfare measures are likely to be accepted. Simultaneously, the authorities are resorting to large number of court martials and dismissals from the services.

Notwithstanding the gesture and support of some eminent Indian leaders to the government of India in tackling it, the rebellion has served the British government with a clear warning that Indian defence personnel have become impatient, they no longer want to serve their colonial masters.

Battle Won, Yes, But Is The War Lost?

Subhas had made a determined bid to expel the British from India by a joint invasion with the Japanese, launched at the eastern border. But the British won that battle. They inflicted decisive defeats on the Japanese and the INA, first in India and then Burma. Many would argue that the responsibility for the 'failure' attached essentially to the Japanese army—their faulty strategy, overconfidence, arrogance, and inability to make proper use of the INA—at the right time and place.

It was well known that the INA, on its own strength, came nowhere near the British forces, whether in terms of number of troops, equipments, arms, ammunitions et al. The two had pre-decided that the Japanese would break the outer shell of British defence of India and once they entered the plains of Assam, the INA would take over. The liberation army expected to receive overwhelming mass support from then on. The Japanese failed to do their bit and the INA had little chance to carry out their assigned role. Notwithstanding the above, barring some weaklings, the men of the INA displayed courage, valour and patriotic spirit befitting a liberation army. Many died, many succumbed to hunger and disease, many were captured, but not many deserted even under extremely adverse conditions.

The impact of the Indian National Army, however, travelled

far beyond the battle field. It was able to kindle spirit and self-respect in the Indian armed forces and masses, once facts about their sufferings and sacrifices were made public. The mutiny in the Royal Indian Navy could be seen as the latest evidence of the INA's impact on Indians in general and the Indian armed forces in particular.

The manner in which India reacted to the issue of the INA prisoners and their trial has been deeply distressing for the British. Though they were looking to Indians to be beholden to them for having driven out the Japanese and brought in these 'Japanese stooges' back to India for due punishment, the whole country rose up against them! Even the Congress Party, which once wanted the British to defend India against the Japanese attack, was now singing praises of the provisional government of Free India and comparing it to the French government in exile of Charles De Gaulle!

The British found such reactions extraordinary, bewildering, and smacking of ingratitude. As days passed, public resentment against the INA trial soared. Its own governors from the provinces kept sending alarming reports. The situation was compared to that of the Sepoy Mutiny period and the attack on the government and its officers were found to be similar to the relentless assaults by the Irish revolutionaries on the British. Some British officials began to doubt the loyalty of the Indian army. More than one provincial governor brought pressure on the Viceroy to drop the treason charges, mitigate sentences, reduce number of trials, or even stop these altogether.

The government also sensed veiled Indian political opposition to the continued use of the Indian army in the Dutch East Indies and French Indo-China, where Britain was using the Indian army to help other European countries recover their lost Asian colonies. Steeped in such adversities, what added to the government's anxiety was the fact that it could not hope to get sufficient number of British troops in India to suppress any violent movement, should that actually occur. The people of war-weary Britain are clamouring for the return of their boys to the home country. All these, in combination, are signalling that continued British rule in India and for that matter in the East and Southeast Asian colonies have come under serious threat.

In a nutshell, it seems that the British, by defeating Subhas and his INA, had won a battle, but it is poised to lose the 'war', which would be the case if they are to give up their colonies in India and the rest of Asia. This may be the 'end outcome' of the assault that Subhas had launched from the East!

SIX

Last Chance Of Unity Lost In Squabbles?

1946

LAST CHANCE OF UNITY LOST IN SQUABBLES?

NEHRU'S IDEA IS TO BUILD LARGEST BONFIRE AND THROW LIGHTED TORCH: VICEROY

March 5, 1946, New Delhi: Viceroy Wavell has been upset with the role played by the Congress and Jawaharlal in regard to the INA issue. Today he has written[205] to Pethick-Lawrence referring to the 'sporadic cases of indiscipline in the forces reported by the War Department'. He is especially upset about Jawaharlal's activities and apprehends that the latter might exploit the issue in negotiations with the Cabinet Delegation. While appreciating MAK Azad, the Congress president, for the responsible line taken on the INA matter, Wavell has accused Jawaharlal for 'practically inciting the services to mutiny'. Then he sought to explore Jawaharlal's motive in his communiqué. He said, 'Nehru's idea seems to be to build the largest possible bonfire into which he can throw a lighted torch if negotiations with the Cabinet Delegation do not go well.'

INA Legacy Conquers British, But Stumbles At The Communal Politics Of India

Before the issue of INA trial hit India, the Congress party, forced to wear the 'Caste Hindu' tag and reconcile to the 'parity' formula in the Simla conference, was seething in impotent anger. The government, through these twin impositions, implicitly conveyed that the treatment was a punishment for the party's role in 1942. As such, when the INA issue unfolded, the party acted with remarkable alacrity as summed up in Jawaharlal's cryptic words, 'The veil has at last been lifted.' Significantly, all these days, the government did everything possible to hide news relating to Subhas, the Azad Hind Government and the Indian National Army from Indians.

Little did it realise that if trials of INA men were to be conducted as the government announced they would, a floodgate of information was bound to open up.

The Congress had several scores to settle with both the British regime and the Muslim League – that of giving up power in eight provinces in 1939 without any reward, of being repeatedly asked by the British regime to secure prior agreement with the Muslim League as a pre-condition for any important political negotiation, of being thrust into the gaol for three long years, of losing Muslims voter to the League, and the last being forced to wear the 'Caste Hindu' tag and agree to the 'parity' formula. With the 'INA' issue on hand, the party probably senses that the hour of retribution is on hand. It cultivated the intense pro-INA and anti-British passion of the Indians of all communities. Riding on the peak of the surging emotion of the countrymen, the party leaders began to batter the regime so hard that the entire government grew nervous.

The leaders of the Congress were quick to identify an important legacy that the party could appropriate and flaunt to both the government and political rivals with telling effect—the high watermark of communal harmony in the INA, the like of which India had not witnessed probably ever in her entire British rule. Congress began to do this exercise with consummate skill and reap political benefits. In a matter of a few months since the

Simla Conference, the party could regain its past importance or probably more than that. But the League led by Jinnah, refused to allow the Congress to sway the Muslims of the country with the INA card. Acting against the very philosophy of the INA about communal harmony, the League went ahead to divide the very INA men on communal lines. It floated its own Defence Committee and offered to render legal support to the Muslim men and officers.

Such has been the force of the communal politics, that the League's strategy was successful in attracting some INA men, Abdul Rashid being one of the early beneficiaries. And when such haloed INA men began to succumb, the strategy began to work its magic upon the Muslim masses.

That the League will not give up an inch to the Congress was evident when it threatened to oppose INA's Shah Nawaz's candidature for a reserved seat in Punjab legislative assembly from Rawalpindi in December last year, because he was proposed by the provincial Congress. His INA background was of no consequence. The League thus practically forced Shah Nawaz to retract.

The League's attempts at communalising the INA legacy found an extreme expression in course of a joint Hindu-Muslim students' protest programme against the verdict in the Abdul Rashid's case in Madras. In February this year, the students of both the communities had met to chalk out a common protest programme when the Muslim students objected to the shouting of 'Jai Hind' on communal consideration.

A unity between these two communities of students that was just fledgling could be saved by acceding to their demand on the counter-condition that the Muslim students would not shout 'Pakistan Zindabad'.

The Madras incident showed that the INA spirit in the matter of communal harmony is fast going into a coma in India. Finally, Jinnah has come forward to perform its last rituals. His latest demand for two separate constituent assemblies have put paid to the dream of an united independent India. Clearly, the INA spirit could overpower the British Raj but it is not proving strong enough to fight the domestic communal politics. When such high ideals could be slaughtered at the altar of 'debased' communal politics, and that with such impunity, the present developments could be seen as bad omens pointing to a fratricidal future for the country!

League's Bid Foiled, Unionist-Congress-Akali Coalition Ministry In Punjab

March 7, 1946, Lahore: There have been intense political negotiations and manoeuvrings in Punjab since the poll verdicts were announced. Although the Muslim League emerged as the single largest party in the recent election, it did not have the half-way majority to form the government. The League had attempted unsuccessful negotiation with Congress. It had also opened talks with the Akalis but these fell through on the issue of 'Pakistan', which the Akalis vehemently opposed and the League declared as 'non-negotiable'.

The Unionist Party, till recently the premier political player ruling Punjab, had some understandings with the Muslim League for some years. But its relations with the League were going downhill as the rift between Khizr and Jinnah kept worsening. After being badly thrashed in the recent election, it has joined hands with the Congress and the Akali Dal. Together, they command majority in the legislature. Unionist Party's leader Khizr Hayat Tiwana has, today, been invited by the governor to form ministry and he has proceeded to constitute a coalition ministry with the Congress and the Akali Dal as the principal partners. Top Congress leaders Vallabhbhai and Congress president Azad have reportedly worked hard with both Akali leaders and Khizr to bring about the coalition.

Having emerged as the single largest party, the Muslim League had been pinning its hope to form the ministry but it failed to find the required coalition partners. It is furious to see the opportunity slip away. The League has been looking at Punjab as the fulcrum of the proposed Pakistan and it was literally pining for securing the lever of power here. There are early indications that the League leaders would not brook the others ganging up against them. They are bitter with the Unionist Party and viewing Khizr Hayat Tiwana's action as a kind of betrayal. Political observers say the League may whip up communal politics and generate political disturbances in the province.

SGPC Endorses Demand For Sikh State

March 9, 1946, Amritsar: The Sikhs have been disquiet over what they perceive as the neglect of their interest in the ongoing political negotiations. In the Simla conference, there was distinct proposal to safeguard the interest of both Hindu and the Muslims but neither the British regime included the Sikh, the third largest religious community, in it nor the Congress made a pitch for a similar protection for them. Meanwhile, the proposal of Pakistan has been adding to their discomfort and anxiety. As a result, a large section of the Sikhs deemed it appropriate to take up the cudgel and fight for their own interests. Before the recent elections got under way, they, led by Sardars Baldev Singh, Joginder Singh and Bahadur Ujjal Singh, formed the Panthic Pratinidhi Board (PPB) to act as an organised political body that would also fight the elections against opponents including the Congress. The PPB has been demanding separate homeland for the Sikhs and also adequate safeguards for their person and property in the event of division of India. Today, the PPB got an important endorsement to their demand for an independent homeland for the Sikhs from the SGPC, the highest religious body of the Sikh community.

Committed To Protect Minority Rights, But Cannot Allow Unjustified Veto

March 15, 1946, London: Even as the Cabinet Mission Team prepares for visit to India Clement Attlee, the British prime minister has issued a statement[206] saying that the team members are going to India with 'the intention of using their utmost endeavours to help her to attain her freedom as speedily and fully as possible'. It was for India to decide about the form of the government, he said, adding that 'our desire is to help her to set up forthwith the machinery for making that decision'.

He also made an observation that could potentially agitate Jinnah and the League. Probably frustrated by the repeated scuttling by the League of past initiatives for framing a constitution, Attlee observed that the HMG has been mindful of the right of the minorities and wanted that they lived without fear. At the same time it could not allow a minority to place their veto on the advance of the majority.

Attlee touched upon another subject that has been of much sensitivity to Britain, ie. whether or not India would remain within the British Commonwealth. Commonwealth is a free association of free peoples, he emphasised. However, it was purely India's right to decide. In the event, she elects for independence, Attlee said, 'It will be for us to help to make the transition as smooth and easy as possible'.

Jawaharlal Falls To Mountbatten's Charm?

March 19, 1946, Singapore: The issue of INA trial had hit India like tidal waves. Faraway from India, in Malaya too, the local Indians have been agitating against the maltreatment of the local INA prisoners by the British Military Administration (BMA) through strikes and protests. Thousands of them, mostly local recruits in the INA's third division were made prisoners by the British when they recaptured Malaya after Japan had surrendered. Jawaharlal, on a visit to Malaya to examine their treatment and condition, arrived here yesterday. He was probably surprised by being the beneficiary of a lavish reception hosted by Mountbatten, the supreme commander of the SEAC in this island city.

Mountbatten nearly extended state honours to Jawaharlal, ostensibly as the representative of the All-India Congress. Both rode in open car on the city street while people gathered in large numbers to greet him. Mountbatten hosted a dinner in the Government House in Jawaharlal's honour. According to reports a kind of rapport has ensued between the two in a brief period.

Today, Jawaharlal was to lay a wreath at the INA war memorial in a public function but he reportedly agreed at Mountbatten's request to keep it simple. Though the beautiful memorial was demolished earlier at Mountbatten's order, a simple wooden replica was erected hurriedly for today's purpose. Later in the day, Jawaharlal addressed a mammoth gathering in the Jalan Besar stadium in the city. Nearly one lakh people gathered to hear him. When the enthusiastic crowd raised the usual slogans of the INA that were anti-Imperialism and emphasised the need to be ready to shed blood for freedom of India, he sternly reminded them that the time for violence and armed struggle was passé and also that now, constructive action and the constitutional path constituted the only road to reach that goal. Nehru's speech came as a big disappointment to the audience and soon the slogans died and the crowd drifted away.

According to political analysts, the local Indians were much disillusioned today. They had earlier seen in Subhas a highly charismatic leader imbued with fierce patriotism and a firm believer in expelling British from India by force. The unfinished mission of liberating the motherland, for which they made enormous sacrifice and the premature death of Subhas had caused them enormous grief. They probably wanted to see similar uncompromising spirit in Jawaharlal. Jawaharlal has been a leader of great stature.

The news of his visit aroused unprecedented enthusiasm in numbers of expatriates Indians here, but his actions and utterances came as huge disappointment to them. The analysts point out that, Mountbatten, the military general, has earned a major diplomatic victory from the visit of the famed Indian leader. He can hope that the resentment of the local Indians against the BMA, over the issue of treatment of INA prisoners may pose him lesser problems, now on.

Akali Dal Restive, Demands Separate State For Sikhs

March 22, 1946, Amritsar: Sikhs are disquiet over the prospect of Pakistan. The growing might of the Muslim League in the province and its increasing belligerence are aggravating their apprehension. Although the Akali Dal is a coalition partner in the Khizr ministry, it feels, the threat of Pakistan is looming large over Punjab's head. In a bid to protect the interests of the Sikhs, the Dal has today passed a resolution[207] demanding a separate state for the Sikhs.

Cabinet Mission To Explore Process Of 'Power Transfer'

March 24, 1946, New Delhi: The Cabinet Mission, comprising Lord Pethick-Lawrence, Secretary of State for India, Sir Stafford Cripps, President of the Board of Trade and AV Alexander, the First Lord of Admirality arrived here today. The team will hold extensive discussions with Viceroy and members of his council, provincial governors, various political parties, interest groups and individuals to arrive at agreements on the modalities of transfer of power to the Indian hands, culminating in the independence of the country. Its frame of references are said to involve only the British Indian provinces and not the princely states. It also envisages the transfer of power to united India in the form of a confederation of states or provinces. Lord Wavell, the Viceroy, is also expected to involve himself with the Cabinet Delegation to help the team in carrying out its assignment.

We Come With No Plan In Our Head

March 24, 1946, New Delhi: Today the members of the Cabinet Delegation interacted with the press. They seemed to be keen to remove misgivings in any quarter and create a perception that they have come with an open mind and that they were committed to develop a mechanism on the basis of discussion with various interest groups and agreement, at least between the major political parties. Stafford Cripps made it clear that they had no predetermined scheme either on paper or in their head but they would try to develop a plan in coordination with the Indian parties, which would pave the way for setting up an interim government and help India realise her goal of independence.

Pakistan Without Calcutta Would Be Asking A Man To Live Without Heart: Jinnah

April 4, 1946: The Cabinet Mission team has set about its task in earnest. Its two primary goals are securing agreement between major parties on framing of constitution for the country and forming a new 'interim government' at the centre. The team has been holding parleys with the Viceroy, the members of his executive council and the provincial governors. Talks with major Indian parties including the Congress and League have just begun. Congress Working Committee has authorised Azad to negotiate with the Cabinet Team on behalf of the party. Accordingly, Azad is likely to meet the Cabinet Mission team in a couple of days. The core concern of Congress is clearly to avoid the vivisection of the country. However, keeping in view the League's adamant stand on a separate Muslim homeland, the partition can be avoided probably by agreeing to near-full autonomy to the federating provinces. Much deliberation is going on within the party simultaneously. On its part, the Muslim League is projecting its demand of 'Pakistan' as non-negotiable and insisting that only its finer details need be chalked out. Earlier, Rajagopalachari had, advanced a formula agreeing to Pakistan provided the population in the non-Muslim majority contiguous districts of Bengal and Punjab were given a choice to join India. But Jinnah has been strongly opposing any proposal to divide Bengal and Punjab. He is not prepared to accept a truncated or smaller Pakistan. He wants five provinces in their entirety. Understandably, to create pressure on the Cabinet Team and political rivals, Jinnah reportedly said Pakistan without Calcutta would be like asking a man to live without his 'heart'.[208] Such strong views on the part of the top leaders of the two major parties are certain to make the task difficult for the Cabinet Mission team.

Chorus Of 'Pakistan' Rents Delhi Is Cabinet Delegation Listening?

April 7-9, 1946, New Delhi: While the team of the Cabinet Mission has been camping here and interviewing various cross sections of leading Indians, the Muslim League has held a politically significant event to celebrate its unprecedented electoral success. More than 800 League members newly elected to both, the central and provincial, legislatures attended. The League used the occasion to bring back the demand for Pakistan at the centre stage with an important modification[209] in the scheme. The Lahore resolution had demanded an independent State in which the constituent units will be autonomous and sovereign. In a lengthy resolution passed here, the AIML has demanded 'a sovereign independent state comprising of Bengal and Assam in the North East and the Punjab, North West Frontier Province, Sind and Baluchistan in the North West zone'. It also demanded two separate constitution-making bodies for Pakistan and Hindustan and provision to safeguard interests of the minorities.

Another important resolution has authorised the League to participate in the 'interim government' in the centre. At the same time it warned that any attempt to impose a constitution or interim government contrary to their demand will be resisted by all means. According to political observers, Jinnah, by a clever choice of venue sought to deliver a political message to the Cabinet Delegation – that the Muslims of India stood rock behind their demand of Pakistan.

Verdict Of The Provincial Elections 1946

In the general election for provinces held during January to April, Congress has achieved majority in all provinces except Bengal, Punjab and Sind. On the other hand, the Muslim League has reaped rich benefits of communal politics, in which it assiduously engaged itself since 1937. Jinnah consistently kept 'Islam' under spotlight to evoke the feelings of a separate nationhood in the Muslims. As corollary to this, the League made this election as a kind of referendum on the issue of Pakistan.

The fact that these strategies have paid handsome dividends shows that the League has been able to communalise the vast majority of the Muslims.

Its performance has been particularly impressive in Bengal, Sind and Punjab. In each of these three provinces, the League carried out extensive propaganda to arouse religious fanaticism and communal passion. It has emerged as the single largest party in Bengal, capturing most of the reserved seats which amounted to about half of the total seats. Its splendid success came essentially at the expense of the Krishak Praja Party, another Muslim dominated party with largely secular outlook and agenda. The Congress party election plank was 'undivided India' and it reaped massive votes from Hindus and non-Muslim communities.

It has increased its tally in almost every province over its 1937 results—Assam 58 now over 33 in 1937, Bihar 98 (98), Bombay 125 (86), Central Provinces & Berar 92 (70), Madras 165 (159), Orissa 47 (36) & United Provinces 153 (134). In the Muslim majority provinces the party's performance was more spectacular. It has been able to consolidate the non-Muslim, especially the Hindu votes who have been most apprehensive about the prospect of 'partition' and 'Pakistan'. It secured 51 in Punjab over 18 in 1937, Sind 18 (7) & Bengal 86 (54). In another Muslim majority province, NWFP, the party had achieved a stellar victory by securing 30 seats as against 19 in 1937.

Hindu-Muslim Parity Thrown To The Wind
Suhrawardy's Cabinet Emits Communal Bias

April 23, 1946, Calcutta: Results of the provincial elections in Bengal held last month reflected deep polarisation. The Muslim League has received unprecedented endorsement by the Muslim electorates giving it a single party majority in the Legislature. It almost trebled its seats from 40 in 1937 to 113 this time. It, thus, not only monopolised the reserved seats for the Muslims but in the process, squeezed the space of Krishak Praja Party, a relatively secular Muslim dominated party which happened to be a key player in the previous election and regime.

Congress bagged ninety percent of the Hindu votes, thus winning 86 seats compared to only 54 in 1937 election. For some time talks of a coalition ministry between the League and the Congress went on but failed. Now Muslim League leader Huseyn Shaheed Suhrawardy has formed the League led ministry with the help of European and Independent members. However denying the long-established convention of keeping a 'near parity' between Muslim and Hindu ministers, he has offered Hindus only 3 berths out of a total of 11. As if to tease the 'caste Hindu' dominated provincial Congress, he has included two scheduled caste representatives in these three cabinet berths. Hindus in general are suspecting his fairness. They already have accumulated grievances against him as the culprit for not only mishandling the Bengal famine but adopting communal bias in administering relief. Many of them feel his ineptitude, corrupt practices and communal bias had caused tens of thousands of deaths in the province as he happened to be the food and civil supplies minister during that period.

Choose Between Sovereignty And Size

> The Cabinet Delegation has so far met numerous Indian leaders of political parties and interest groups as well as eminent persons. It has held several rounds of meetings with the leaders of the Congress and the League, they being two major political parties. Unfortunately the Delegation could not elicit an agreement between these two on the future constitution of British India. Jinnah remained fixated to his demand for Pakistan. Under the circumstances some progress, if it can be called so, was achieved when the delegation made it clear that Jinnah has to make a choice between sovereignty and size. In other words, if he remained adamant about an independent and sovereign Pakistan, the League would have to reconcile with truncated or moth-eaten Pakistan as the non-Muslim majority areas of Punjab and Bengal will secede from it and join India. On the other hand, if the two states agreed to form part of a union, he could have all the Muslim majority provinces without truncation. Jinnah has been unhappy at both of these mutually exclusive proposals but he realises he will have to choose one.

Cabinet Team Moots Undivided India Invites Party Leaders To Simla

April 27, 1946, New Delhi: The Cabinet Mission Team have, by now, held extensive discussions with major leaders of Congress, Muslim League, Sikhs, Scheduled Castes, Depressed Classes, Hindu Mahasabha, and Indian States besides liberal leaders like Sapru, Jayakar and others. The team is finding it difficult to reconcile a wide spectrum of views elicited in the process. What has been troubling it the most is the radically different positions taken by the Congress and the League, two major parties, on the issue of 'partition'. The delegation has held a series of parleys, a few of them back-to-back, with Jinnah and Azad in the last few days in search of an agreement. On that basis, today the delegation has sounded these two parties as to if they could jointly strive to work on a scheme based on the following fundamental principles about the future constitution: a. one Union government dealing with three key subjects, viz. external affairs, defence and communications; b. two groups of provinces—one Hindu and another Muslim majority, dealing with subjects which the provinces in the respective groups want to be dealt with in common at the group level; c. the provinces will deal with all other subjects and they will be vested with residuary sovereign rights; d. the issue of Indian states joining the Union government will be subject matter of separate negotiation. While both the Congress and the League wanted to have further clarifications about the proposal, the Cabinet Delegation, hopeful of eking out an agreement at last, has requested the presidents of the Congress and the League to send four members each from their parties to Simla for further deliberation.

Discussions Over, Consensus Out Of Reach

May 12, 1946, Simla: After extensive deliberations for nearly two months, the Cabinet Mission had mooted a concrete proposal for constitutional development and convened a conference in Simla on fifth of the present month, inviting both Congress and the Muslim League with a view to reach a consensus on some key issues such as 'nature of the union', 'modalities of drawing of constitution', etc. On behalf of the Congress, top leaders like Azad, Jawaharlal, Vallabhbhai and Abdul Ghaffar Khan attended whereas Jinnah, Liaquat Ali, Ismail Khan and Abdur Rab Nishtar represented the League. Even Gandhi stayed in the summer capital to tender advice, if needed. They discussed the scheme of an undivided India with two clearly divided groups of provinces based on the two major religions. But there were disagreements on several issues including a. the sequential order in which constitutions were to be framed for the union, groups of provinces and individual provinces, b. scope and extent of authority of the union government, c.compulsory grouping of provinces, d. manner of seceding by a province from the

Union after 10 years, e. manner of safeguarding minority interests, f. parity of representation as between groups of provinces in the union legislature and executive, etc. The differences were too wide to be reconciled. Today the delegation has admitted that the conference has failed to evolve an agreed plan. It has also announced that in view of the continuing disagreements it intends to issue, in course of next few days, a statement of their views as to the next steps to be taken.

Cabinet Mission Publishes Its Plan

May 16, 1946, New Delhi: The Mission Team said it had made exhaustive attempts to bring together the Congress and the League to an agreement but failed. It had considered the partition of India but found weighty reasons—administrative, economic, military and above all unwillingness in large segments of populations against it. At the same time, the Mission recognised the fears and concerns of the Muslims in regard to the protection of their religion, culture, economic and other interests in an undivided India. In comparison, the Indian states, the Commission observed, were cooperative and they agreed to cooperate in the new development of India and they could be made to join the Federation before the paramountcy lapsed on the basis of negotiations. Having regard to these diverse but important considerations, the Mission has rejected the plea for partition but at the same time favoured full autonomy for the provinces subject to a minimum of Central subjects. In accordance therewith, it has put forward a set of proposals[210] and it recommended that these ought to be the basic form of and the foundation upon which Indians can frame the Constitution of India. The Mission suggested that in the meanwhile an interim government may be set up to carry on with the governance.

KEY FEATURES OF 16 MAY STATEMENT

As per the Cabinet Mission Plan, the Union should have both executive and legislature comprising of representatives of both, British Indian provinces and Indian states. It should deal with three subjects, viz. foreign affairs, defence and communications and have power to raise necessary finance for the above purposes. Any major communal issue in the legislature should require decision by majority of each of the two major communities present and voting as well as majority of all members present and voting.

The Indian states shall have all subjects and powers other than those ceded to the Union and also all residuary powers.

The provinces should have all subjects other than the three envisaged for the Centre and have all residuary powers. The plan has divided British India into three 'sections' – A, B & C. The Hindu majority provinces of UP, Bihar, CP, Orissa, Madras, and Bombay are placed under section A. The Muslim majority provinces in the north-west, viz. Punjab, Sind and NWFP together with British Baluchistan are listed under section B. Bengal, another Muslim majority province, together with Assam, a Hindu majority province are placed in Scetion 'C'.

The number of members in the constituent assembly would be comprising 292 from the provinces, 4 from Chief Commissioners' Provinces and not more than 93 from the Indian states. While the provincial legislative assemblies will elect their representatives to the constituent assembly by single transferable vote, the method of selection of the states' representatives would be decided in consultation. Each province will have a quota on the basis of its population, roughly in the ratio of one for every million. This quota will be further divided amongst the three major communities, viz. General, Muslim and Sikh in the ratio of their population within the province. The representative of each community will be elected by members of that community in the respective provincial legislature. The interests of other communities who could not expect to send their representatives on account of their numerical inadequacy have been protected by an Advisory Committee - a special mechanism. The elected representatives from all provinces will meet together as one body in Delhi, decide upon the general order of business, elect a Chairman, set up the Advisory Committee and thereafter divide themselves up into three 'sections'.

For writing the constitution, the provinces will require to sit in their respective 'sections'. The section would draft constitution for the provinces constituting it. It was also open to the section to draft a constitution for the 'group'. The constitution for the union of India will thereafter be drafted by the members of the provincial assemblies designated for this purpose together with the representatives of the Indian states.

It has been left open to a province to elect to come out of the 'section' to which it was assigned, but only after the new constitutional arrangements have come into operation and this could be done through a decision in the legislature formed following the first general election held under the new constitution.

Yet another provision of far-reaching consequences requires the constitution of the Union and the groups to incorporate a clause that allows any province, by a majority vote in its legislature, to call for a reconsideration of the terms of its constitution after an initial period of ten years and at ten-yearly intervals thereafter. The Cabinet Mission plan has coupled this proposal with formation of an interim government in the centre by the elected representatives of political parties. This interim government, having the support of the major political parties, shall be completely Indianised. However it is yet to announce the details of the government, more particularly its composition. The choice of joining the British Commonwealth has been left to independent India.

There Are Only Two Forces That Bind This Document, Honour And Necessity

May 20, 1946: The exact implications of the Statement of 16 May are not quite easy to comprehend. Gandhi, the astute politican and one with extensive legal training, has now presented his views[211] on the document before the country. Before doing so he had to study the 'state papers' issued by the Cabinet Mission and the Viceroy for last few days. He did 'clause by clause' investigation to be able to understand its spirit, technicalities and also some inherent contradictions of grave nature. Today he has expressed his opinion in the *Harijan*. On the whole, Gandhi has found it to be 'the best document the British Government could have produced in the circumstances'. However, he made a significant observation that the Statement has no compulsion in it. It is rather an appeal and advice. The true import of the Statement, Gandhi assessed, lay in its 'voluntary' nature. There is nothing in it binding in law. Its two binding forces according to him, are 'honour' and 'necessity'. Gandhi felt the voluntary character of the Statement demanded that the liberty of the individual provinces should be unimpaired. It should be left to a province to join or leave a 'section'. In this connection, a grave technical error inherent in the simultaneous presence of two contradictory clauses, viz. Para 15 and Para 19 in the Statement, did not escape his attention with regard to their potential to create bitter disputes between the major parties. While the basic emphasis of the proposal has been 'provincial autonomy' which was buttressed by Para 15 (5) providing that the provinces have the right to form group, para 19 sought to take away that very right by 'compulsory grouping' of provinces into certain predefined 'sections' and laying down a set of procedures for framing of constitutions—provincial, group and the union. Gandhi suggested that such contradictions could be resolved by highlighting the basic 'voluntary' nature of the proposal and the stress upon the key theme of 'provincial autonomy'. In this connection, he dwelt upon the peculiar situation applicable to the Sikhs and the provinces of NWFP and Assam who would be potential sufferers of the provision of 'compulsory grouping' and contended that the voluntary character of the Statement demanded that the liberty of individual provinces as regard to the 'section' should be unimpaired. Para 19, Gandhi has contended, only 'proposes' but does not 'order'.

Congress Senses Mischief In 16 May Statement

May 24, 1946, New Delhi: The Congress Working Committee has responded to the Cabinet Mission proposals with scepticism. The Committee has noted that the plan did not offer any worthwhile improvement over the present position in the matter of 'interim government' which would continue to function as the 'executive council' of the Viceroy. The desirable thing would have been to make the cabinet responsible to the central legislature, the committee observed.

The committee expressed its reservations about the proposed manner of securing representation in the constituent assembly from Baluchistan, Coorg, Indian states and the European community. More importantly, it voiced its difference of opinion on the provisions spelt out for building up the constituent assembly. In particular, it noted a serious discrepancy in the Cabinet Team's fundamental assumption about the 'autonomy' to the provinces and provisions relating to the mode of their participation in constitution making. It observed that on one hand, the Statement provided that provinces should be free to form 'groups'. On the other hand, it has pushed them into predefined 'sections' which would settle 'provincial constitutions' and further decide if any 'group constitution' shall be set up.

The Committee saw that the reconciliation of such inconsistencies would be in allowing the respective provinces to make their choices as to whether or not they would like to belong to the 'section' to which they were allotted. The Committee was of the opinion that the constituent assembly is sovereign as far as framing of constitution is concerned and it will be open to it at any stage to make changes and variations. At the end, the Committee observed that it was not able to give a final opinion on the proposal as the Statement did not provide a full picture.

Is Statement Of 16 May A 'Gateway' To Pakistan?

June 5-6, 1946, Delhi: The AIML Council held its meeting here and discussed the Cabinet Mission Plan. The council criticised the Cabinet Mission for discarding the League's demand for Pakistan and for using harsh words while setting it aside. However, it also noted that the Cabinet Mission had simultaneously recognized the Muslim fears, reservations and anxieties of being subjugated to the Hindu rule perpetually.

'...notwithstanding the affront offered to Muslim...' by the Cabinet Mission, the council, having regard to gravity of the situation and actuated by a desire for a peaceful settlement of issue of Indian constitution, agreed to the proposal for the overwhelming reason that the prospect of Pakistan was inherent in this plan by 'virtue of the compulsory grouping of the six Muslim provinces, in sections B and C...'[212] Significantly, besides the stipulation of compulsory grouping of the provinces the Cabinet Mission Plan also provides an exit route to the Provinces after ten years.

The reactions of two major political parties viz., the Congress and the Muslim League to the Cabinet Mission Plan are public by now. It has become clear that the two have radically different views on 'grouping of provinces' and 'sections'. The AIML resolution has warned that the ultimate attitude of the League will 'depend on the final outcome of the labour of the constitution-making body and on the final shape of the constitutions' emerging 'from the deliberations of that body jointly, and separately, in its three sections'. Political analysts are reading into these 'differences' the seedlings of a major political storm.

Would Assam Be The Flash Point Of A Bitter War Between Congress And League?

The Cabinet Mission proposals have been engaging the attention of the Indians – political parties and politically aware people alike. Though drafted carefully by a team of four eminent persons, a critical evaluation exposes its inconsistencies which could generate severe conflict between two major parties in days ahead. The authors of the plan have, at the beginning, acknowledged that it was their 'recommendation' and that they intended it to be only the 'broad basis of the future constitution'. They expected it would get the 'two major communities to join' to set up the constitution-making machinery. In other words, they gave an impression that the plan would bring the feuding parties together and start the process of setting up the constituent assembly. They acknowledged that it was not their object to lay out the details of a constitution on some given lines 'but to set in motion the machinery whereby a constitution can be settled by Indians for Indians'. It seemed that they intended to bring together the major and rival political parties together so that they cooperate, strive and frame a constitution that is good for all Indians. It would be a process calling for interaction, dialogue and agreement.

Seen against the above backdrop, the compulsory grouping of the provinces into pre-determined 'sections' vide Para 19 seemed contradictory. It was all the more glaring because in paragraph 15, the plan simultaneously provided that 'Provinces should be free to form Groups with executives and legislatures... and each Group could determine the Provincial subjects to be taken in common'.

Probably, such contradictions as stated above would have been ignored but for forcing Assam into section C together with Bengal. It is true that the compulsion of grouping created dissatisfaction in Sikhs in Punjab and also the people of Congress-led NWFP for fear of being pressurised by the Muslim majority of Punjab, but generally speaking the categorisation of the rest ten provinces into sections A & B corresponded to their demographic profile. However, squeezing Assam, a clearly Hindu majority province into section C together with Bengal, a Muslim majority province and with population six times as large as hers, not only seemed unjust but also raised the prospect of its getting bullied while framing its own provincial constitution. It has been difficult to find any rationale for this except that the province was for some years ruled by pro-Muslim League regime due to Congress policy of abdication and the largesse shown by the British governor.

It is therefore probable that Assam would resist this grouping. On its part the Congress is likely to plead that Assam should be given a choice as to the 'section' it would want to be a part of. If that freedom is denied to the province, the Congress may take up the cudgel. Considering the fact that the League has a deep-seated ambition about Assam, a full scale war is likely to break out sooner rather than later.

Government Shelves Wavell's 'Breakdown Plan'

June 6, 1946, London: The dim prospect of securing Congress-League agreement on transfer of power in India that became manifest since the Simla Conference last year had prompted Viceroy Wavell to chalk out an alternative plan for a time-bound 'transfer of power'. Now, as the labour of the Cabinet Mission Team over two months seems to be facing a 'dead end', the Labour government in Britain, led by Attlee, discussed Wavell's breakdown plan that envisages gradual withdrawal of British from India. In course of deliberations in a cabinet meeting the government decided against withdrawal from India by a specific date, which happens to be a core feature of the plan. While noting that the lack of agreement amongst Indian leaders on a plan of independence has been a roadblock in India being conferred freedom, the British cabinet simultaneously felt it could not allow chaos to take over the country by any of its plans or actions. The cabinet has been of the view that it has to observe its responsibilities until Indian leaders are able to agree on a basis for accepting the British offer of 'independence'. Though the government driven by these reasonings has serious reservations about the Wavell plan, the prospect of an agreement between the Congress and the League on a common plan of independence continues to be very bleak.

INNER VIEW OF THE BREAKDOWN PLAN

Right since mid 1945 when the Simla Conference was abandoned, Viceroy Wavell has been convinced of one thing – the near impossibility of bringing about an agreement between Congress and League leaders. Then onwards, Wavell has been labouring hard on an alternative plan that could be used to transfer power to Indian hands while protecting British interests – politically and commercially. He christened it as 'breakdown' plan—the name actually meaning one that could be invoked if the negotiations between the Indian parties break down and their leaders fail to arrive at an agreement. Because of its contingent nature, it has also been referred to as 'reserve plan' or a 'backup plan' by some.

Wavell's plan has evolved over time. His advisers Evan Jenkins (now Punjab governor), BV Rau and VP Menon provided important inputs in devising it. Wavell is reportedly keen about preserving the unity of India, post independence. But having realised the uncompromising attitude of Indian parties, particularly, the League's obsession with Pakistan.

Wavell, through this plan, has attempted to dissuade its leaders by establishing that the Pakistan they have been asking would be an unattractive one. He devised it in a manner to make the country's vivisection appear repulsive by both the Congress and the League, such that it was likely to bring them together and make them agree to the plan of united India.

Breakdown Plan envisages withdrawal of the British from India in more than one phase. In the first phase, the Raj proposes to transfer the power in the Hindu majority provinces of Bombay, Madras, Central Provinces, Orissa, Bihar and United Provinces to Congress whereupon the British Indian government would withdraw its officials and army to the remaining areas of British India, likely to be the parts of Pakistan. These latter provinces could continue to be governed by the present constitution. They will have the benefit of observing the Federation of provinces being run by the Congress and then decide whether to join it or remain independent or form another Union. However, in Bengal, Punjab and Assam if the Muslim majority areas opt to form a separate union, the 48 million strong non-Muslim minorities of these three provinces would have the option of joining the Federation run by the Congress. This would, by enforcing partition of these provinces, create a small, weak and unattractive Pakistan. Wavell reckoned that the very prospect of partition of these three provinces would discourage Muslim League from claiming Pakistan and make them settle for unified India with a suitable constitution.

Another core feature of the plan is that it specified a date by which the Raj would transfer the power to India— undivided or divided. In the event the rest of India did not opt to join the Federation, the British in the subsequent phase, would hand over power to one or more provinces individually or to another Federation. In any case, as per the plan the British would withdraw from the country by March 31, 1948.

Between Devil And Deep Sea, We Want Neither, Say Sikh Conference

June 9-10, 1946, Amritsar: Sikhs have been upset by the terms of the Cabinet Mission proposal. An All Parties Conference of the Sikhs was held here to discuss the proposals mooted in the May 16 Statement. Over 800 representatives of the community from NWFP, Delhi and United Provinces have thronged here besides those from various parts of Punjab. It was felt that the Cabinet Mission Plan met some demands of the Congress, and some of the Muslim League. But for the Sikhs, the plan would be an unmitigated disaster. Thus the Congress can find in it the provision for a virtual federation of states in the united India, whereas Muslim League has begun to see in it a virtual Pakistan. But in either case, Sikhs would be under perpetual domination by the Muslims in their own province. It may be recalled that Akali leaders have been asking for a province where no single community should dominate the Sikhs. Such a possibility is clearly absent in the Cabinet Mission Plan. Today, the Conference has let known the Sikh dissatisfaction by formally rejecting the proposal[213]. It has also been reported that several leaders held the British regime, more than even Jinnah and the League, primarily responsible for ignoring the Sikh interests and advocated a policy of violence against them to correct the injustice.

Sikhs Have A Special Place In Punjab : Secretary Of State These Are Empty Rhetorics: Master Tara Singh

June 11, 1946, Amritsar: Master Tara Singh, is deeply upset, at the Cabinet Mission statement of 16th May. The fact that the Muslim League has conveyed its acceptance of the plan is causing him greater disquiet. As per the Cabinet Mission Plan, Punjab is placed under section B along with Sind & NWFP, all the three being Muslim majority provinces. Again, within Punjab the Sikhs form hardly twenty per cent of the total population. If the constitution for Punjab is drawn up at the 'section' level, the Sikh interest is certain to be ignored and there is every likelihood of placing them under permanent subjugation of the Muslim majority.

Master Tara Singh had written on 25th last month to Secretary of State voicing his concerns. He had queried what was the use of the government saying that it considers Sikhs as one of the main communities, when the Cabinet Mission Plan treated them with utter neglect? He wondered if there was any hope for the Sikhs getting rights at par with the Hindus and the Muslims. He also posed a question that if majority of section B frame a 'constitution' but the Sikh community does not agree, would it ensure a deadlock?

Today the Secretary of State has sent him a riposte[214] advocating that the Cabinet Mission Plan was best for the Sikhs and it is a better option than either the creation of Pakistan or partition of Punjab. He attempted to assuage Tara Singh saying that Sikhs have always a special place in Punjab and that their importance would not depend on mere numbers. The constituent assembly as well as any future government will give them due importance, he concluded. These assurances sounded empty rhetoric to Master Tara Singh. Yesterday the Sikhs in a representative conference held at Amritsar rejected the Cabinet Mission Plan. Now the Secretary of State's letter has hardened their resolve to protect their interests. The Sikhs as a community are likely to escalate their protests.

Congress-Muslim League Spar, Wavell To Go Ahead With Interim Government

June 16, 1946, New Delhi: Even as the Congress - League differences on the 'constitution making process' remain a potentially explosive issue, Viceroy Wavell has been finding road blocks in the matter of forming the interim government as well. There have been simmering dissensions between the two parties about its composition and over the right of nominating Muslim members to the executive council but the Congress insists that such a claim is patently unfair.

In view of the above discord between the two parties which seems to be irreconcilable and considering the challenges of governance that lay ahead of the post-war reconstruction-needy India, the Cabinet Delegation and the Viceroy have decided to put forth their own proposal for the interim government. Wavell has, in a statement issued today, invited fourteen prominent Indian leaders to join his executive council. He has made it clear that simultaneously, the constitution-making will proceed on the basis of the Statement of 16 May. The list of fourteen includes six belonging to the Congress including a representative of the Scheduled Castes, five from the League and one each from the Sikh, Indian Christian and Parsee communities.

A government communiqué said [215] 'In the event of the two major parties or either of them proving unwilling to join in the setting up of a coalition government on the above lines, it is the intention of the Viceroy to proceed with the formation of an interim government which will be as representative as possible of those willing to accept the Statement of May 16'. The Viceroy has clarified that the composition of the interim government proposed by him was only an expedient to solve the present difficulty and to obtain the best available coalition government. He also directed the provincial governors to immediately summon the respective legislative assemblies and proceed with the elections necessary to set up the constituent-making machinery.

Jawaharlal On A Rescue Mission In Kashmir, Has To Be Rescued Himself

June 20, 1946, Domel: In Kashmir, there has been simmering popular discontent against the Maharaja's rule. Sheikh Abdullah, the leader of the National Conference, has been spearheading a popular movement against the autocratic regime. Sheikh had even presented the case of the people to the Cabinet Mission team and urged for self-government for the Kashmiri people by bringing Maharaja Hari Singh's oppressive regime to an end. The infuriated Maharaja got Sheikh and his colleagues arrested. They have been languishing in jail.

At this, Jawaharlal, with ancestral linkage to Kashmir and also being an avid follower of local politics had rushed to this princely state with Asaf Ali and Dewan Chaman Lal to arrange for legal aid to the Sheikh and his colleagues. They entered Kashmir's territory by crossing the Kohala Bridge yesterday and were arrested at nearby Domel. At Congress office in Delhi, the worried Congress leaders got in touch with the Viceroy who then talked to the supposedly eccentric Maharaja, convinced him and then arranged to send a special aircraft from Delhi to bring the arrested leaders back. This episode indicates that any political negotiations with this ruler will be a difficult task.

Congress Backs Out, League Jumps In

June 25, 1946, New Delhi: While the dominant view of the Congress Working Committee (presently holding a meeting here on the Cabinet Mission proposals) has been against joining the interim government, Jinnah has sensed an opportunity in the Congress stance, and held a meeting of the working committee of the League immediately. The committee has adopted a resolution accepting the scheme of 16th June. Today Jinnah also met the Cabinet Delegation and the Viceroy. He has sought to impress upon them, albeit unsuccessfully, that the League ought to be given chance to form the interim government , should the Congress refuse to take part in it.

Constituent Assembly? Yes. Interim Government? No. Congress To Adopt Dual Policy On These

June 26, 1946, New Delhi: The proposal for forming the interim government in terms of the Statement of 16th June has been engaging the political parties in the country. The Sikhs, who had earlier rejected the 16th May proposal, rejected this proposal as well, while both the League and the Congress were engaged in evaluating its pros and cons. Meanwhile Jinnah has stoutly objected to the nomination of any non-League Muslim as member of the interim government.

On 22nd this month, Wavell, in a letter to Azad, has expressed his inability to consider any Muslim nomination from Congress and requested him to bear with it. The composition of the interim government was only an expedient to solve present difficulty and would not be a precedent, the Viceroy assured Azad. Congress has been incensed. Being the representative of Indians of all castes and creed, and the largest and the oldest political formation in the country, it found such back room political maneouvering patently unjust. It vehemently objected to the League's stand that it could not nominate a Muslim member in the interim government. The Congress Working Committee has today adopted a comprehensive resolution wherein it has stated that it can never give up its national character and accept an artificial and unjust parity or agree to the veto of a communal group. Congress president Azad has conveyed the decisions of the working committee to the Viceroy rejecting the proposal of interim government[216].

As regards the 16th May Statement, the committee expressed several reservations including inter alia the provision on grouping of provinces which, it felt, has treated provinces like NWFP and Assam as well as some minorities, especially the Sikhs, unfairly. Notwithstanding, the committee decided that the Congress would join the proposed constituent assembly in terms of Cabinet Mission's Statement of 16th May with a view to drafting the constitution of a free, united and democratic India. At the same time the party president has made it clear to the Viceroy that on some of the provisions of the 16th May Statement, including on the issue of 'grouping of provinces', the Congress has its own interpretation.

Acceptance Of Cabinet Mission Plan Mixed Feelings In Congress

June 26, 1946: The Congress continues to have several objections to the proposals of May 16 and June 16 as suggested by the Cabinet Committee. However, considering the proposal in its entirety, the feelings within the party are seemingly mixed. One section including the party president Azad is happy essentially because it saves the country from being partitioned. Gandhi too has reportedly found the proposal a good and an honest effort by the British government. But not all agree. Even several orthodox leaders are not enthusiastic. Then there is strong unhappiness in the left wing. Congress Socialist leaders, in particular, are vociferously opposing the scheme.[217] Prominent CSP leader Jayaprakash

Narayan also opposed the working committee resolution accepting Statement of 16th May and said it would be dangerous for the Congress to participate in the proposed constituent assembly.

Interim Government: Congress Refuses League Is Refused, Jinnah Is Angry

June 27, 1946: In a meeting with Jinnah, a couple of days ago, the Cabinet Delegation and the Viceroy had informed him that the scheme of 16 June for formation of interim government has fallen flat following the Congress rejection. But as both the Congress and the League accepted the 16 May proposals, the Viceroy decided to wait for some time to give a chance to a coalition government and therefore he intended to defer the issue of interim government to a later date. In the meantime he wanted to carry on with a caretaker government. Jinnah had been hoping that in view of the Congress' refusal to join, the League will be called in to form the interim government. Jinnah has reacted strongly to the Viceroy's action. He has cautioned the Viceroy against any attempt to whittle down in any way assurances given to the Muslim League or to change or modify the basis of 16 June Statement. In such an eventuality, Jinnah warned, the British government will forfeit the confidence of Muslim India. He has disapproved any attempt to postpone the formation of the interim government. Incidentally, in his statement of 16 June, the Viceroy had announced that he would aim at inaugurating the new government on 26 June thereabout.

Cabinet Mission Team Returns

June 29, 1946: The Cabinet Mission team has left India for London.

Provinces Elect Their Representatives To The Constituent Assembly, Sikhs Boycott

July 1946, New Delhi: The elections to the provincial assemblies held during January to April this year have, on the whole, catapulted the Congress and the League to the centre stage. Out of the total of

1,585 seats in eleven provinces, these two parties together won as many as 1,348. While the League with a tally of 425 claimed more than 90 per cent of seats reserved for the Muslims, the Congress, barring the Sikhs, dominated all the non-Muslim constituencies and bagged as many as 923 seats. The Akalis in Punjab claimed the lion share of the seats reserved for the Sikhs. With such compositions the provincial assemblies recently elected their representatives to the 'constituent assembly'. In terms of the Statement of 16 May, the provincial assemblies were to elect their representatives to the constituent assembly.

The number of representatives that a provincial assembly could send to the constituent assembly was determined roughly in the ratio of one for every million people in that province. To ensure a fair representation across major religious communities, this allocation was further divided amongst Hindus, Muslims and Sikhs in ratio of their population to the respective province. It was further provided that the representative of each community in a province shall be elected by members of that community in its legislative assembly.

The proposed constituent assembly would consist of an aggregate of 389 members comprising of 292 to be elected from the provinces, 93 representing the Indian States and 4 to represent the Chief Commissioners' provinces. The elections to the constituent assembly have been concluded during this month but the Sikhs, unhappy and upset with the Cabinet Mission proposals, boycotted it. The Congress has monopolised the 'general' seats claiming as many as 203 out of a total of 212. Besides it has won 5 reserved seats that included 4 Muslim and 1 Sikh. The Muslim League has also registered an impressive victory, having won all but 7 seats reserved for the Muslim community. Barring 4 to Congress, it had to concede 3 reserved seats to the Unionist Party.

Keeping in view Jinnah's intermittent demand for Pakistan and 'two separate constituent assemblies' there were certain measures of apprehension as to the peaceful conclusion of the election to a single 'assembly' for the proposed Union of India. All eyes would henceforth be upon the assembly to begin its work though Sikh boycott is causing some measure of consternation.

New President's Statement On Plan Stirs AICC

July 6-7, 1946, Bombay: The AICC has met here to consider the working committee's acceptance of the Cabinet Mission proposal of May 16th. Jawaharlal, who was earlier elected as the president of the party, formally assumed the 'responsibility' in this session. This is his fourth term as the Congress presdent.

Though there were other weighty contenders for the post of the president including especially Vallabhbhai who enjoyed the confidence of overwhelming numbers of Provincial Congress Committees, Azad, the outgoing president had proposed Jawaharlal's name and urged for unanimous election.[218] Gandhi himself wanted Jawaharlal to be the next president and he had earlier made known his mind to Azad.

As the president at this crucial juncture his views on the recent Cabinet Mission Plan were eagerly solicited by both the media and Congressmen. Jawaharlal indeed touched the subject in his winding up speech in a way that took most by surprise and left some, including a few top leaders shocked. For past nearly two months, some measures of expectations were growing about the Congress and the League coming together, to write the future constitution of the undivided India. At the same time, however, the relationship between the two parties continued to be fragile and sensitive and warranted delicate handling.

Against this background, Jawaharlal, as the president of the Congress made an explosive statement. Stating his views on the two plans—long-term (16th May Statement) and short-term (16th June Statement)—he made it clear that it was not the question of the Congress accepting either of the two plans.

It was, he emphasised, a question of their entering into the constituent assembly, and nothing more. They would remain in the assembly as long as they felt that would serve India's interest. To clarify his ideas further, Jawaharlal said that 'We are not bound by a single thing except that we have decided for the moment to go to the Constituent Assembly'.

'Constituent Assembly Can Change Or Modify' Jawaharlal's Comment Explodes Like A Bomb

July 10, 1946, Bombay: After the Congress Working Committee had accepted the long term part of the Cabinet Mission Plan last month, the AICC ratified it three days ago. However, in his winding up speech in that session, Jawaharlal had delivered a strong message that the Congress would refuse to get tied down by the 'letters' (meaning the procedures) of the 16 May scheme. Jawaharlal said that the Congress party would be animated and guided by its 'spirit' in working out the future constitution of the Union of India and the provinces.

He had, by his speech, upset several top leaders including former president Azad who apprehended that such an uncompromising attitude on the part of the Congress could throw the entire plan for an undivided India into jeopardy. Today, Jawaharlal has moved another step ahead. If he had earlier spoken to the inner audience of Congressmen, today he declared the Congress attitude to the Cabinet Mission Plan to the global audience.

In a press conference Jawaharlal, in reply to a question, clarified that Congress would enter the constituent assembly 'completely unfettered by agreements and free to meet all situations as they arise.' He rejected the modality proposed in the Statment.

He sought to explain that the 'mechanism' of 'grouping' envisaged by the Statement was just not workable or practical and it was bound to collapse because of the opposition of one or the other constituent provinces of the 'sections'. In reply to a specific query by a reporter, whether the AICC ratification meant that the Congress has accepted the Cabinet Mission Plan in its entirety, the president, gave further clue to the probable Congress strategy. He said that that the Congress has agreed to participate in the 'constituent assembly'. However, the constituent assembly would be free to change or modify the proposals the way it deems fit. This has exploded like a bomb on political India.

Jinnah Condemns Jawaharlal's Interpretation

July 13, 1946, Hyderabad: Jinnah gave a loaded political reaction to Jawaharlal's views and interpretations of the Cabinet Mission Plan expressed in the recent Congress session and also to the press. Jinnah has issued a statement today saying that 'Pandit Nehru's interpretation of the Congress acceptance of the Cabinet Mission's proposals of 16 May is a complete repudiation of the basic form upon which the long-term scheme rests and all its fundamentals and terms and obligations and rights of parties accepting the scheme.' According to political analysts, Jawaharlal's action has re-opened the issue and Jinnah, in the new situation, is mulling over the options available to League.

Is A Genuine Opportunity Lost?

> CMP has been the latest development in the course of a negotiated political settlement between Britain and India. It raised a faint prospect of avoiding partition and Pakistan. On the flip side, as some political analysts see, the offer of 'independent united India' has been a bait in lieu of which the Congress has been called upon to accept the onerous provision of 'compulsory grouping' and specific procedures for framing of constitutions for the provinces and the groups. The pre-defined classification of the provinces into specified 'sections' and the onerous procedures with regard to framing of constitutions, made even more prickly by subsequent enunciation of the 'rule of simple majority' to settle differences at the 'section' level, allowed opportunity to the League to subdue the free will of large populations in four provinces, viz. Assam, Punjab, Bengal and NWFP. As a result the scope of a healthy political discourse between the major political parties to undertake the constitution framing activities based on the free opinions of the widest numbers of people has been stymied, nay, throttled. To be able to come out of this captivity and fashion the emergence of a sovereign, independent, undivided India based on the cooperation of the major communities poses a complex

challenge calling for great tact, determination and courage. It calls for great statesmanship and tact on the part of the Congress, the largest party to respond to the challenge. Jawaharlal's recent statements, seen in many quarters as nothing less than 'explosive', have polarised people. Those who endorse his speech and press interview say a wild, boisterous energy could alone blast away that carefully fabricated contraption by the British. Jawaharlal through his bold statement, they say, has purveyed that force and sought to dismantle any League-British conspiracy with regard to suppressing the will of a large number of people in framing their own constitutions. But according to his critics Jawaharlal ought to have remembered that the Congress has as its rival Jinnah, the wily politician who was obsessed with the idea of Pakistan and he needed little pretext to abandon his commitment to CMP and revert back to the claim for Pakistan. The case of undivided India, they point out, could be advanced by one of the two ways – (a) the Congress with its appeal to the largest segments of people could stand resolutely against the British in a political trial of strength; (b) the Congress could convince the people of all communities, especially the two major communities, about the benefits of undivided India and outclass Jinnah and the League in terms of statesmanship and vision. They say unless Jawaharlal can culminate this action piece into either of the above two strategies, his utterances may lapse into intemperate outburst throwing the Cabinet Mission Plan to disarray without being able to open a new vista to the goal of independent undivided India.

Viceroy Invites Congress And League To Form Interim Government

July 22, 1946, New Delhi: The attempt made by the Viceroy last month to install an interim government of 14 members had fizzled out after the Congress refused to be a part of it. What hurt the Congress badly was the Viceroy's assurance to Jinnah that he would not accept the Congress nomination of a Muslim as a member of the interim government. The recent deterioration in communal relations in the country has prompted both HMG and the Viceroy to begin a fresh round of initiative in this matter without delay. Considering the fact that earlier two attempts at formation of interim government were hampered by media publicity, the Viceroy has now desired that at least the preliminary stages of negotiations in this fresh round of initiative be conducted on a strictly personal and secret basis.

Today, the Viceroy has sent a confidential communication to the presidents of both the Congress and the League which incorporated the proposal for the formation of the interim government and solicited their participation. It envisaged a 14 member executive council consisting of 6 members (including one scheduled caste representative) to be nominated by the Congress, 5 members by the League and 3 members of minorities (including 1 Sikh) to be nominated by the Viceroy. Learning from the past, the Viceroy proposed that neither the Congress nor the League would be entitled to object to the names submitted to him by the other party. The major portfolios would be distributed equitably between the two major parties. As regards the sensitive subject of 'major communal issue', the Viceroy would welcome a convention to be set up for its settlement with the assent of both the major parties. As regards the status of the interim government, the Viceroy has made it clear that though constitutionally it cannot have the same status as a 'dominion cabinet', HMG will bestow upon it the greatest freedom in carrying out the day-to-day administration of the country.

Congress Questions Viceroy On Issue Of Political Independence

July 23, 1946, New Delhi: Jawaharlal, the Congress president, has promptly responded to the Viceroy's proposal for the interim government. He has raised two important objections: (a) the interim government was not being offered full political independence; (b) the Viceroy is retaining the right to nominate the representatives of the minorities. Jawaharlal has made it clear that the Congress may not be inclined to take up this offer unless the issue of political independence of the interim government is settled. According to sources, the Congress response has upset the Viceroy. At the same time, the turbulent communal situation may not allow him to cease trying for an interim government with participation of the major political parties.

League To Go For 'Direct Action' To Wrest Pakistan

July 27-29, 1946, Bombay: Jawaharlal's comments on the Cabinet Mission Plan generated a gnawing suspicion in the League that the Congress intends, by using its majority, to not only dishonour the provisions relating to 'grouping of provinces' but make the 'constituent assembly' function as a sovereign body, unfettered by limitations of functions or procedure envisaged by the Statement of 16th May scheme. The postponement of the formation of the interim government by the Viceroy in an allegedly dishonest manner has added to the League's anger. In a meeting of its council, the AIML has adopted a resolution that has accused the British government of appeasing the Congress even though that party gave a wrong interpretation to the statement of 16 May and extended only conditional acceptance of the Plan. Alleging that the British government was sacrificing interests of the Muslim nation and weaker sections of people to placate the Congress, the council has resolved to withdraw its acceptance of the Cabinet Mission's Proposals conveyed to the government last month.

Critics say, Jinnah had agreed to the Cabinet Mission Plan proposal on the calculation that it would help the Muslim League to eventually reap bigger rewards than by enforcing Pakistan at the present juncture. But the Congress intention as reflected in its president's statement has made Jinnah's calculations go haywire and the contours of the future negotiations on transfer of power has become fuzzy.

Muslim India Won't Rest Content Without Pakistan

July 29, 1946, Bombay: The AIML Council met here to take stock of recent political developments in the country. In another resolution the League has alleged that the Congress is bent upon setting up 'Caste Hindu' Raj in India in connivance with the British government. Mentioning that

Muslim India has exhausted all peaceful solutions of the Indian problem by compromise and constitutional means, the resolution made it clear that the Muslims would not rest content without achieving Pakistan and they would resist any attempt to impose constitution-making machinery or setting up of any interim government without the consent of the League. The council exhorted that the Muslim nation 'stand to a man' behind the League and begin preparing for 'direct action' to wrest a separate homeland for a Muslim nation.

League Declares 16 August As 'Direct Action Day'

July 30, 1946, Bombay Today, the working committee of the Muslim League met at Jinnah's residence and fixed 16 August as the Direct Action Day for Pakistan to be observed throughout India.

WE WANT PAKISTAN – JINNAH'S WAR CRY

As a matter of fact, the Muslim League had accepted the Cabinet Mission Plan ahead of the Congress. Though the Plan rejected the separate state of 'Pakistan', its provisions allowed for large measure of provincial autonomy and even the scope for seceding from the Union at a later date. In other words, it could be used to create a strong Muslim state In the future. The League accepted it on 6 June and right from 8 June onwards, Jinnah has been in correspondence with the Viceroy about formation of the interim government. This betrayed his eagerness to wield the lever of power at the federal level. On 25 June, he appraised the Viceroy of the League's decision to join the interim government subject to some conditions.

In the meanwhile, the Viceroy kept waiting for the Congress' acceptance of the plan before taking the next step. Jinnah felt this as unfair and an appeasement of the Congress.

On 26 June, after about twenty days from the date of the League's acceptance, the Congress finalised its response to the Cabinet Mission proposals. It accepted only the Statement of the 16th May of the Cabinet Mission, which dealt with the framing of the constitutions. But, exhibiting its clear disapproval of the principle of 'parity' between the Congress and League and also on the issue of the right of nomination of members by parties to the interim government, the Congress refused to join it. Jinnah expected that the League would be given the chance to form the government when the Congress refused. But the Viceroy, thought it unwise to form his executive council without the Congress representatives. Under the evolving circumstances he proposed to set up a temporary caretaker government pending an agreement between the major parties for which, he felt, the negotiations could resume. Jinnah was upset and he demanded that the election to the constituent assembly be postponed as both the matters were interlinked.

Jinnah, however, kept the League in a state of readiness to join the interim government, whenever the occasion arose. On 1st July, the 'central parliamentary board' of the League had nominated eight leaders as candidates for the executive council, which included Jinnah, Liaquat Ali Khan, Abdur Rab Nishtar, Sir Feroze Khan Noon, and four others. But, with no invite coming to the League thereafter, an impatient Jinnah wrote to Attlee and Churchill in London on 6 July expressing dissatisfaction about the manner of handling of negotiation by the Viceroy and the Cabinet Delegation.

In the midst of such uncertainties, Jawaharlal's press interview on 10 July caused a commotion. Jinnah read into his utterances the Congress' insincerity and intention to bend the plan according to its convenience by leveraging its majority in the constituent assembly. Much exercised by the turn of events, the council of the League held a meeting during 27 to 29 July in Bombay and revoked its acceptance of the Cabinet Mission Plan. The League held both the Congress and the Viceroy responsible for its revocation decision. It contended that Muslim India has exhausted without success all efforts to find a solution of the Indian problem through peaceful and constitutional means. Pronouncing its verdict that the scheme of 'unified India' was now buried, the League has reverted

> back to its demand for Pakistan and it has proposed 'direct action' to achieve this goal. It seems the Cabinet Mission Plan has come under grave peril and the clamour for Pakistan has acquired a new life-force.

Jinnah Alleges Bias Against League In Government

July 31, 1946, New Delhi: Jinnah reacted to the invitation of the Viceroy for the formation of the interim government, expressing his deep displeasure. In his communiqué, he recounted item by item, how the Viceroy's proposal has deprecated the League's demands: (a) violation of parity, which was equal in the earlier offer being 5:5, now became favourable to Congress as 6:5; (b) the Congress being given the right to nominate one Scheduled Caste representative; (c) the Congress being allowed to nominate a Muslim representative though the League had so long fought tooth and nail on the issue and it was one of the prime reasons for the collapse of the Simla conference last year. Jinnah also expressed unhappiness about the manner in which the 'minority safeguard' was provided for in the proposal. In view of the above, Jinnah contended that there was no chance of the working committee of the League accepting the offer to join the interim government.

Wavell Asks Congress To Form Interim Government

August 6, 1946, New Delhi: Viceroy Wavell has been in an unenviable situation. His government has been facing the prospect of countrywide violence and chaos in the wake of the League's call for 'direct action'. The new interim government remains to be formed as yet while the League has in the meanwhile, revoked its acceptance of the Cabinet Plan. The League has accordingly expressed its unwillingness to join the interim government and has preferred to go for 'direct action' to realise its goal of Pakistan. According to sources, the Viceroy was instructed by the HMG to ignore Jinnah and invite the Congress to form the interim government. He was also advised to summon the constituent assembly by the first week of the next month.

Today he has invited Jawaharlal, the Congress president, to make proposals for the formation of the interim government. The Viceroy wrote that Jawaharlal could discuss with Jinnah about the matter if he wished and that a coalition government would certainly be welcome. As regards the issue of political independence of the interim government, the Viceroy sought to address the Congress concern saying that though constitutionally it would not be a dominion cabinet yet HMG will grant it full freedom for carrying out the day-to-day business of governance.

Viceroy Attempts To Bring The League Around

August 8, 1946, New Delhi: It was a tough decision for HMG and the Viceroy to invite the Congress to the exclusion of the League. The Viceroy today wrote to Jinnah in which he referred to the League's recent resolutions rejecting Cabinet Mission Plan and adopting the course of direct action. Informing Jinnah that he has invited the Congress to form the interim government, the Viceroy hoped that the League would respond positively to the invitation for a coalition government, if made by the Congress. Clearly, he has sent a signal that he is prepared to ignore the League's acts of omission and commission if it agrees to join in forming the government. Probably, he is attempting to persuade Jinnah to give up the line of 'direct action' and not leave the seat of power to the Congress alone.

Congress Comes Closer To Sikhs

August 9, 1946: In the steadily rising political temperature arising out of the Congress-League confrontation, the Sikhs have been finding themselves in a corner, with HMG and the Viceroy showing little sensitivity to their concerns. They had earlier rejected the Cabinet Mission Plan. They also decided to boycott the elections to the constituent assembly. In a politically significant development, the Congress has now decided to extend its helping hands to the Sikhs. In a resolution adopted today, the Congress Working Committee admitted the injustice that has been meted out to the community by the Cabinet Mission Plan in its proposal. Assuring Sikhs of all possible support to remove their legitimate grievances and secure adequate safeguards for protecting their just interest, the resolution urged them to reconsider their decision to 'boycott' the constituent assembly.

Congress Accepts Cabinet Scheme 'In Its Entirety' CWC Makes A Tactical Move

August 8-12, 1946, Wardha: As the political temperature keeps soaring in the aftermath of the Muslim League's call for 'direct action' and in the midst of the continuing stalemate in the matter of both the interim government and the constituent assembly, the invite of the Viceroy for government formation has reached Congress. To the League and other critics, the offer prima facie looked 'biased' in favour of the Congress as the latter's acceptance of Statement of 16 May was qualified and it sought to interpret several of its clauses in its own way. Under the circumstances, the Congress Working Committee has met here and passed a resolution[219] that seeks to address these issues. A part of the resolution says: 'The Committee wish to make it clear that while they did not approve of all the proposals contained in this statement, they accepted the scheme in its entirety'. Having expressed this general commitment, the resolution reiterated that the scheme had inconsistencies and added that the Congress interpreted it 'to resolve the inconsistencies contained in it and fill the omissions in accordance with the principles laid down in that Statement'. It left the questions of interpretation to be 'decided by the procedure laid down in the Statement itself'. The resolution also elaborated on the sovereign character of the constituent assembly.

Congress Accepts Viceroy's Invitation Jawaharlal To Negotiate Details

August 8-12, 1946, Wardha: The Congress Working Committee considered the Viceroy's offer to the Congress president to make proposals for formation of the interim government. Though the Viceroy said he would be happy to see a coalition in the interim government, the matter was left to the Congress president. The prospect of the League joining the coalition in the extant circumstances appeared unlikely. Though the Viceroy's offer clearly fell short of granting complete political independence to the interim government that rendered the post of the Viceroy as merely the constitutional head, the working committee accepted the offer. It has authorised Jawaharlal to negotiate with the Viceroy on the issue.

Jinnah Challenges Competence Of Assam Assembly

August 12, 1946, Bombay: Post Cabinet Mission Plan, politics in the country has been moving along two different strands—one with regard to the drafting of the 'constitutions' and the other involving formation of an interim government.

In regard to the former, the efforts are at best moving with interruptions. A serious difference has arisen with regard to the interpretation of 'grouping of the provinces' and the issue has become knotty with respect to the province of Assam.

This province in the north east of British India had, under the Saadullah government, been the victim of planned demographic invasion from neighbouring Bengal. The new Congress ministry and also the Congress Party have been uncomfortable with the province being grouped along with Bengal, a Muslim majority province in section 'C'. Not only that, due to large size of Bengal's population (about six times that of Assam), section 'C', inclusive of both the provinces, also has Muslim majority amounting to about 51.6%. The placement in such a 'section' and the apprehension that the 'constitutions' of the 'province' and the 'group' may be drafted by rule of majority have been causing grave concerns to the provincial Congress. The Assam Assembly while electing its representatives to the constituent assembly also passed a resolution giving a mandate to all the members of the Constituent Assembly elected from Assam to resist all or any attempt to set up a 'group constitution' for the settlement of questions relating to any subject in which the province of Assam is interested or concerned or for any such question being dealt with by any such group of provinces on the basis of majority votes.

Jinnah has been eyeing Assam as a potential component of the proposed Pakistan and he has been heavily relying on the provision in the Statement of May 16 on 'grouping of provinces' and 'section' to subdue that province. He has begun to sense potentials for greater trouble for the League in these directives. In a statement issued today he has questioned the competence of the Assam Assembly to give such directions to the representatives of the constituent assembly.

It appears a major dispute on the compulsory grouping of provinces for writing the constitution is on the cards.

'Direct Action Day' Declared As Public Holiday Congress Walks Out Of Provincial Assembly In Protest

August 12, 1946, Calcutta: The Suhrawardy-led Muslim League government of Bengal has declared 16th August—the date for Direct Action—a public holiday. The Congress, the opposition party in the provincial legislature, is finding this extraordinary, communally motivated and highly objectionable. To lodge its protest against the government's policy in giving effect to a party decision in such blatant manner, the Congress, led by Sarat Chandra Bose, has today staged a walkout in the Bengal Legislative Assembly. They are suspecting obvious foul play by the Muslim League and the Bengal government on the day of the 'direct action'.

Sikhs Withdraw Policy Of Boycott Decide To Join Mainstream

August 14, 1946: In the first week of July, Sardar Baldev Singh, the leader of the Panthic Pratinidhi Board (PPB) had written to British PM Clement Attlee, complaining about the injustice done by the Cabinet Mission by placing Punjab in section 'B' and demanding an appropriate safeguard for the Sikhs in the context of such an unfair placement. But Attlee in his reply blamed the PPB for boycotting the constituent assembly without giving it any assurances. Deeply aggrieved, the PPB met on 10 July and reiterated its resolve to boycott the constituent assembly. However, in these days of rapid political development, the PPB's resolve has today undergone a radical change. The Board met here to consider the emerging situation and the recent Congress invitation to join the process of constitution making. The Board has agreed to respond to the Congress invitation and accepted the Statement of 16 May. The PPB adopted a resolution lifting the embargo on the 'constituent assembly' to give it a fair trial and advised the Sikhs to return their representatives to the constituent assembly to safeguard their interests. Political analysts are looking at today's decision of the Sikhs as a significant development, especially with regard to the province of Punjab. The induction of the Sikhs is also expected to strengthen the Congress voice in matters of political negotiations with the League and HMG.

Punjab Tense On Eve Of Direct Action Day

August 14, 1946, Lahore: As the day of Direct Action draws nearer, the tension is brewing across the country, more so in Punjab and Bengal. In Punjab, the Muslim National Guards, an armed private army of the League has been secretly storing arms and ammunitions. The League is also spreading communal hatred through pulpiteers and newspapers. On the other hand, the Akalis are organising the Sikhs to counter any attacks by the Muslim National Guards. The tension is in palpable.

Muslims Are No Believers In Ahimsa: Abdur Rab Nishtar

August 1946, New Delhi: Following the call of 'direct action' given by the League, there are widespread feelings that the League is up to some mischief and that especially in Bengal, it is likely to misuse its ministry and the state power to achieve its political goal using questionable means. Muslim League leaders are breathing fire and brimstone. To a question on the issue, Jinnah warned, 'I am not going to discuss ethics...' Taking an oblique dig at the Congress and Gandhi, Liaquat Ali said: 'We cannot eliminate any method.' If Liaquat's utterance was suggestive, Abdur Rab Nishtar, League leader from the NWFP, sounded candidly violent.

Noting that Pakistan now could be achieved only through shedding of blood, he said that if opportunities arose, the blood of non-Muslims must be shed for 'Muslims are no believers in ahimsa'. In Bengal, Nazimuddin, one of the top League leaders corroborated as well as elaborated on Liaquat: "There are a hundred and one ways in which we can create difficulties, especially when we are not restricted to non-violence. The Muslim population of Bengal know very well what 'Direct Action' mean...we do not need to bother to give them any lead." These utterances[220] ought to put Viceroy Wavell on guard. The Congress is hoping that Wavell will take due precautions to avert violence. But according to some political analysts, though Wavell has given a chance to the Congress to form the interim ministry, reportedly under pressure from the HMG, his sympathy actually lies with the Muslim League. If true, this has dangerous implications.

Interim Government: Jinnah No To Jawaharlal Invite

August 15, 1946, Bombay: Events are happening fast. Only three days ago, Viceroy Wavell had invited Jawaharlal, the Congress president, to form an interim government at the centre. Though Jinnah had already rejected the Cabinet Mission Plan, Jawaharlal, in a seemingly calculated political strategy, wrote on the very next day to Jinnah requesting for the League's cooperation in the formation of the interim government. He followed up the written initiative by paying a personal visit to Jinnah's residence in Bombay today. According to available reports, Jinnah made clear his dissatisfaction about the Viceroy's offer to the Congress. He also enquired in details about Jawaharlal's plan and especially if the Congress would nominate any Muslim member to the cabinet, an issue about which the League has zero tolerance. There was no favourable outcome at the end.

Political analysts say the meeting was held in an atmosphere of mutual distrust and under the shadow of the ominous call of 'direct action' by the League. They say, the Congress was not hopeful of any result and that Jawaharlal's action was a political strategy, Jinnah's reaction was also on the expected line. Jawaharlal has exited from Jinnah's house empty-handed. The paths of the two are clearly divergent. Thus, as Jawaharlal is mulling the modalities to form the interim government without the League, Jinnah seems to be preparing to deal a body blow to the Congress aspiration for a united India through its programmes of 'direct action' to be observed vigorously throughout the country tomorrow.

League's Direct Action Day – Ominous Signals All Around

August 15, 1946, Calcutta: Normally 'direct action' days are observed through strike, protest meetings and processions. However, if sources are believed, this Direct Action Day may be very different. The Muslim League, angry with the imminent formation of the central government under Jawaharlal, wants to prove that it is not prepared to accept the Congress hegemony but bent upon achieving its goal of Pakistan. In Sind and Bengal, the two provinces where the League is at the seat of power, it has officially declared the Direct Action day as public holiday. It seems, the League has singled out Bengal, to register its protest through a highly communal agenda. It is being heard that the League leaders with active connivance of the pliant bureaucracy in the province, has a planned carnage in the city of Calcutta. The city is in the grip of unprecedented tension.

DIRECT ACTION DAY BECOMES THE DARKEST DAY
Brings Unprecedented Shame, Violence To Glorious City

August 16, 1946 (Friday), Calcutta: The glamorous, beautiful city of Calcutta, known to be the pride of the British Empire in the Orient, has been suddenly gripped by an inferno of communal frenzy in the wake of the Direct Action Day call by the Muslim League. Like a bolt from the blue, a catastrophe has suddenly descended on it. Planned and initiated by the Muslim League, a ghastly riot, fuelled by base human instincts, has meandered through the streets and alleys, lanes and by lanes of the city taking toll of countless human lives. By dusk, hundreds of corpses, many of these brutally mutilated lay scattered in homes, lanes and streets and dogs were seen sniffing at the dead. Women, molested and raped with impunity, were left to mourn for the dead. Properties worth crores of rupees have been reduced to ashes. Panic and fear have gripped the city.

All these gory events seem to be part of a well-planned strategy of the Muslim League. The League has decided to go the extra mile to deliver a strong message to the Congress top leaders and the British regime, that it would not now settle for anything less than Pakistan. Having decided to direct the full blast of the programme of communal carnage to Bengal, the Suhrawardy-led League government hatched the plot carefully with eye on details. Though the call was to be observed across the country, Bengal was chosen for maximum impact. Bengal happens to be the province that has the maximum Muslim population and under Jinnah's scheme, an undivided Bengal including Calcutta, would be invaluable to the proposed Pakistan. If this important port city, with over seventy per cent people being Hindus, can be cowered to submission, annexing the whole of Bengal would be a cake walk. Suhrawardy, the main architect of the massacre has been putting the jigsaws in place for past some time. As the prime minister, he has been inducting Muslim policemen from the northern and north western parts of the country, who were expected to play a partisan role in cases of communal riots. He has also connived with the British bureaucracy to render them ineffective once communal riots unfolded.

This Black Friday began with numerous processions of communally surcharged people in the city streets. They converged into a huge meeting in the vast Maidan in the heart of the city convened to sensitise people about the demand for Pakistan. Many of them, hired goons of the League, were armed with lethal weapons fit enough to conduct mass murders. After series of violent and provocative speeches, the mob looted a reputed arms shop on the Chowringhee Road, adjoining the Maidan and then started to spread out to central and northern parts of the city. Thereafter began the killing by communal targeting of the Hindus, at first in ones and twos, then in tens and by the late noon in hundreds. Males were murdered upon sight, women molested, raped and their shops and houses consigned to leaping flames. Murderous mobs trotted the streets, brandishing dangerous weapons and shouting slogans demanding creation of Pakistan.

By late night, at the time of going to the press, the city was completely under curfew. Around midnight, a terrible thunderstorm hit the city that kept the hooligans at bay temporarily. But before long the communal gangs again fanned out spreading terror in householders across the city. Heartrending wailing and mourning were pierced by intermittent communal slogans. The city sky at several areas was red with the flames of the fires devouring houses and shops.

Is Calcutta Riot A Handiwork Of Suhrawardy?

August 16, 1946, Calcutta: According to some reports, Suhrawardy, the prime minister, spent the day at the police headquarters at Lal Bazar, not to prevent the genocide but rejoicing the success of the Direct Action Day and possibly dreaming the annexation of the whole of Bengal to the proposed Pakistan. These reports allege he stayed put there for long hours to ensure that the police remained aloof and the mayhem by the armed goons continue unabated.

The manner in which the ghastly massacre was carried out by preempting the intervention of the law enforcing agencies clearly suggested that Suhrawardy compromised almost the entire British bureaucracy with consummate ease. It was easy for him to befool governor Frederick Burrows, a Labourite and an ex-leader of Railwaymen's Union in England, who has little experience as an administrator. As the city reeled under extreme violence and cried in desperation, Suhrawardy sent him on a guided tour of the neutral areas where Burrows's amateurish eyes and ears could not find actionable abnormalities. The army was available in large numbers in The Fort Williams within the city, ready to step in. However, they were not called in until 2 am and that too in limited number in a few areas as desired by the Suhrawardy government.

Fierce Retaliation Shocks Suhrawardy

August 18, 1946, Calcutta: After the Muslim League sponsored goons ran amok in Calcutta for almost a-day-and-a-half under the lenient bureaucracy, indulging in murders, rape, loot and arson with gay abandon, the majority Hindu community began to come out of the shock and stupor and by later half of yesterday they organised themselves for self-defence and counter attacks, wherever possible. The local youths collected arms of all descriptions and began to gather together. The city branches of the Hindu Mahasabha had reportedly stored arms in anticipation of a riot in the aftermath of the Direct Action Day. Their members came forward to lead in the counter-attack on the Muslim minority in the city. The strength of the forces of retribution went up significantly as the minority Sikh community, traditionally aggressive, and also the Hindi-speaking people of the majority community from the north and west of Bengal joined hands. Their counterattack has snowballed into strong retaliation against the Muslim dwellers of the city. In the initial phase of this payback, the police continued to remain indifferent which, in a demographic profile of 70:30, worked to the advantage of the majority community avengers. Today, Hindus were seen retaliating fiercely in the south and southeast areas of the city including Ballygunge, Bhawanipore, Kalighat, Tollygunge, Alipore,

Kareya, Jadavpur and Garia. They also gained the upper hand in central Calcutta. Areas between Bowbazar and Manicktala were the worst affected.

By today evening, the counter reprisals have become severe, no less savage than the original riots, making the minority community lose all hopes of life and property. Although the government, surprised by the severity of the revenge attacks are using both police and the army, they have not been able to stem the murderous members of the majority community who are in no mood to relent without settling the score. In the chain of events over the last three days, the city streets have bathed in human blood but the thirst for it does not seem have been quenched.

It is being learnt from some sources that today Suhrawardy was seen crestfallen, repenting his inability to protect the Muslims in the city in spite of heading the provincial government. Political observers say his sense of guilt should be overwhelming, having subjected innocent, hapless people of both communities to vicious communal orgies by misusing the state machineries to achieve ulterior goals.

Tales Of Horrors – The Fallouts Of The Direct Action

August 20, 1946, Calcutta: According to a government source, the direct action violence in Calcutta has left nearly 4,400 people dead, over 16,000 injured and about a lakh of people homeless. In Punjab, the outbreak of violence was reportedly, much lesser. However, under apparent tranquility various communities have reportedly been accumulating weapons and getting ready for open war any time.

Savagery, Enthusiasm For Murder Were Terrible: Wavell

August 21, 1946, Delhi: The riots in Calcutta first broke out on 16 August, led by the hired goons of the League and this continued for almost two days. The Hindu retaliation began on 18 August and continued through 19 August. Today Viceroy Wavell has appraised Pethick-Lawrence, Secretary of State for India, on the issue. Wavell has written[221] that according to information available to him, the 'savagery and enthusiasm for murder was terrible', that the parties of one community would lie in wait for one of the other community and once grabbed would 'cut him to pieces with shouts of joy'. Wavell has wondered at how 'All ordinary human feelings seem to have completely deserted a considerable proportion of the population of the city'.

Even the army had difficulties in containing the bloody confrontation between the two communities. Eventually, five battalions of British and four battalions of Indian and Gurkha troops had to be deployed to regain control over the city. According to Wavell's report to Pethick-Lawrence, the riot-affected citizens have been asking for more British battalions to be deployed as they have seemingly lost faith in the impartiality of the indigenous forces.

According to political observers, it is surprising to see how the communal amity that was on splendid display only in January this year on the issue of the trial of INA's Abdul Rashid, vanished in thin air. This ghastly riot, they feel, has exposed the 'achilles' heel' of the Indian freedom struggle—how the demon of communal politics can in one sweep devour the good senses and wisdom of the people in general! They also feel there is an undercurrent of glee in Wavell's note because this unprecedented fratricide would strengthen his stand that the Congress must come to an agreement with the League on the issue of formation of the interim government.

POLITICAL RAMIFICATIONS OF THE CALCUTTA RIOT

It is becoming clear that the Muslim League had planned the communal violence in great detail, in order to create a countrywide commotion and thereby reinforce its demand for Pakistan. It also wanted to strengthen the claim of the proposed Pakistan over the whole of Bengal, including the city of Calcutta. Its calculation seems to have been that if it gets away with brutal massacre of Hindus in this Hindu majority city, people will be too terrorised to oppose the inclusion of the entire province in Pakistan. The League government benumbed the administration in order to carry out its diabolical plan and towards this goal it was able to secure the tacit support of British officials.

Critics hold Viceroy Wavell and governor Burrows responsible for abetment in this sordid event, as they had enough advance intelligence but did precious little to prevent its occurrence.

Insiders say, despite meticulous planning, Suhrawardy failed to achieve his goal in full measure. It is true that the series of events proved the inevitability of Pakistan to an extent, given the kind of bad blood created amongst the communities. However, the strong Hindu backlash suggested the impracticability of ceding of whole of Bengal to Pakistan in the event a separate land for Muslims was indeed carved out of India. What has been most lamentable is that the age-old amity between the two communities has become a casualty of political machinations and politicians' avarice.

Rise Of Suhrawardy, Architect Of Pogrom?

Huseyn Suhrawardy has been known as an adroit politician but his integrity remains suspect. His critics say that he has been keeping his personal interests above the country. They accuse him for his lack of scruple and practising politics not out of any public spirit but as a tool to wield power and amass wealth. Some of them even charge him with moral depravities.

Highly educated and intelligent, he quickly made his way up through the ladder as a career politician. Born in Midnapore in West Bengal, and having studied in St Xavier's College in Calcutta, he qualified as a barrister in England. He started his political career with the Swarajya Party, became deputy mayor of Calcutta Corporation in 1924, at the age of 31 and deputy leader of the Swarajya Party in the Bengal provincial party. Later on he switched over to the Muslim League for the long political haul.

Within the League, he has been indulging in bitter intra-party politics. In the provincial League, he has been leading the Calcutta axis and engaged in a perpetual battle with the Dhaka axis led by Nazimuddin. Suhrawardy was a minister in the cabinets of Fazlul Huq and Nazimuddin. As the food and supplies minister in the Nazimuddin government during the famine between 1941-1944, he acquired infamy for administrative ineptitude, seeking personal goals through people's miseries and communal bias in administering relief. He came to occupy the centre stage of the provincial Muslim League, exploiting his association with Abul Hashim, a League leader with Socialistic leanings who fought hard battles against the establishment on issues that affected the poor peasantry like abolition of Zaminadari and such others. While Hashim, seen as a pillar of the Calcutta axis, by his untiring work brought the League close to hundreds and thousands of peasant households in many districts of East Bengal and Tippera and helped in the transition of the League into a mass based party in Bengal, Suhrawardy emerged as a major beneficiary.

He leveraged the growing popularity of his group in composing webs of intrigues, engineering defections in Nazimuddin camp and finally ousting Nazim's government in a voting on the budget last year. In the election that followed during the winter, Suhrawardy emerged as the leader of the victorious Muslim League which managed to secure a single-party majority.

While forming his cabinet this year, Suhrawardy had sent an unmistakable signal of his intention of playing communal politics. Whereas right since 1937, prime ministers like Fazlul Huq and Nazimuddin always maintained a near parity between their Muslim and Hindu cabinet colleagues, Suhrawardy sent that tradition packing. In his cabinet of eleven members, he included only three Hindu ministers.

His relations with Jinnah have been based on convenience rather than trust. Though Suhrawardy resents the overlordship of the central leaders, he has been comfortable in cooperating with Jinnah in playing communal politics. On the issue of Jinnah's call of the 'direct action day', Suhrawardy went overboard to make a success of it, and surely he has expectations of rewards. According to political analysts, he may claim his pound of flesh at a later date.

Interim Government To Take Over On 2 Sept Viceroy Announces Team

August 24, 1946, New Delhi: Today the Viceroy has announced a new interim government at the centre. He has named twelve members and left two places vacant in a 14-member body. There have been rounds of consultations in the preceeding fortnight between Jawaharlal and Wavell about the composition of the interim government. Jawaharlal has been keen that the cabinet should be representative of the main elements in the country and also that all seats must be filled up to lend the government strength and create public perception about its solidity. However, the Viceroy has chosen to leave two seats vacant. The members named are Jawaharlal, Vallabhbhai, Rajendra Prasad, Asaf Ali, Rajagopalachari, Sarat Bose, John Mathai, Baldev Singh, Shafat Ahmed, Jagjivan Ram, Syed Ali Zaheer and CH Bhaba. The Viceroy described his latest initiative as a momentous step towards freedom of India.

New Government Not To Trespass On The Field Of Provincial Administration

August 24, 1946, New Delhi: Though the Viceroy has sent enough feelers to Jinnah that he was open for the League to join the interim government upon which the cabinet will be reconstituted, there has been simmering tension in the capital about the self-imposed exile of the League. The Sikh move of reconsidering their policy of withdrawal and sending Baldev Singh into the cabinet, was a welcome relief and contributed to the representative character of the interim government. The Viceroy welcomed the members of his new executive council whom he described as representatives of a very large body of political opinion in India. At the same time he also delivered a politically significant guideline to the new government to the effect that 'the new government had neither the power nor any desire to trespass on the field of provincial administration'. Political analysts see this as an attempt to appease the Muslim League governments in the provinces. The blanket nature of the directive or guideline gives a license to the indiscreet provincial governments to misuse state machineries for narrow political ends, they argue. Moreover, the Congress has always advocated the case for a strong centre. Giving in meekly to such dictum of the Viceroy, especially with the hindsight of the political machination by the Bengal government, is rasing questions about the sagacity of the Congress leaders.

If A Blood Bath Was Necessary, It Would Come About In Spite Of Nonviolence

August 27, 1946, New Delhi: Viceroy Wavell developed almost a serious disconnect with the Congress during the course of a meeting with Gandhi and Jawaharlal this evening. Just back to Delhi after a visit to riot-torn Calcutta he had called the two top Congress leaders for a discussion to end the political log jam. Incidentally, earlier this month he had invited the Congress to form the interim government, but that offer not yet given effect to. In the meantime, the League flexed muscle through its call of 'direct action'. Surely, it is out to convince Wavell of the dangers of civil war that lies ahead should he proceed to allow Congress alone to take over the reins of power at the centre.

During their parley, Wavell had faithfully retransmitted the 'danger' he perceived through the Calcutta episode and sought to impress upon the two Congress leaders the necessity of coalition government at both, the centre and Bengal to avert a civil war. There was only one impediment to that goal, Wavell argued. It was that the Congress ought to accept the 16 May Statement's provision about 'groupings of provinces' and 'sections'. While accepting that it would be difficult for the Congress to reopen negotiations with the Muslim League, Wavell still wanted them to do so as the 'country expected it as a result of what had happened in Calcutta'. But Gandhi did not agree. He put up a defence of the Congress interpretation, legally and logically. Unable to meet the force of Gandhi's logic, Wavell burst forth saying that he was a solider, a plain man and not a lawyer.[222] Nevertheless, he knew perfectly well 'what the Mission meant' and that the 'compulsory grouping' was the crux of the plan. That made no impact on his guests. So also was his veiled threat that unless the Congress fell in line, he 'could not undertake the responsibility of calling together the constituent assembly'.[223]

Congress has been, for many years, relying upon the mechanism of the constituent assembly to create an undivided independent India which would take over the country from the British. Congress has also been keen that the opinions of the Indians, cutting across creed and caste, at the widest possible scale, are freely expressed and considered in the making of the country's constitution. The import of the Viceroy's threat, as perceived by the Congress, was that it ought to compromise these sacred principles in the face of exhibition of brute force such as what happened in Bengal recently, resulting in unprecedented bloodshed.

Wavell—having delivered the ultimate threat about non-summoning of the constituent assembly, began to think that he would, thereby, succeed in making the Congress accept the provisions of 'grouping' and 'sections'. But, he was nonplussed by a statement from Gandhi towards the end of the meeting, saying: 'If a blood bath was necessary, it would come about in spite of non-violence'.[224] Coming from the great pacifist, these words sounded ominous to the Viceroy. Still, before the meeting ended, Wavell, almost hoping against hope, handed over to Jawaharlal the draft of a Statement he expected from the Congress accepting the above two provisions to end the logjam.

Don't Expect Congress To Bend Before Brutal Exhibition Of Power

August 28, 1946, Valmiki Mandir, New Delhi: In the meeting with the Viceroy that concluded hours ago, Gandhi had expressed the Congress dissatisfaction about the latter's way of handling of the matters of interim government and constituent assembly. Gandhi was offended at Wavell's dictatorial approach. Based on the proceedings of the meeting, Gandhi has now pieced together a letter[225] expressing his feelings while simultaneously delivering a strong political message to the Viceroy. Referring to the repeated assertion by Wavell that he was a plain man, a solider and not a lawyer, Gandhi hinted that being a solider was not good enough to act as the 'crown representative' and that some measure of legal knowledge was essential too. Wavell could not ignore law, Gandhi wrote, not at least those, of which he happened to be the co-author. If need arose, Wavell could indeed secure able legal help. Gandhi wrote: 'You should be assisted, if necessary, by a legal mind enjoying your full confidence'. Gandhi then referred to Wavell's 12th August public announcement inviting the Congress to form the government from which he was now trying to back out. He dared the Viceroy to recall that action, form another ministry, and possibly use arms for maintaining peace and order. On the contrary, Gandhi wrote, the Congress does not hope to govern the country with the help of the British arms. In a pithy reference to the Calcutta riots, for which both the British and the League government of Bengal could be held responsible and which were presently being used to bully the Congress. Gandhi wrote, 'Nor can the Congress be expected to bend itself and adopt what it considers a wrong course because of the brutal exhibition recently witnessed in Bengal. Such submission would itself lead to an encouragement and repetition of such tragedies.' Then he proceeded to pin the Viceroy down for these unfortunate events, attributing these 'to the continued presence in India of a foreign power strong in and proud of its arm'.

Gandhi assured that the Congress knew the minds of both the Hindus and the Muslims, more than Wavell or any Britisher. Still, if Wavell could not trust the Congress wholly, he should reconsider his decision of having already invited the Congress to form the interim government, Gandhi contended. At the end, Gandhi asked Wavell to convey the whole of his letter to the British Cabinet in London. It is being reliably learnt that Gandhi is likely to take up the issue with Attlee and other members of the British cabinet, either directly or through other channels to force Wavell to form the interim ministry with the Congress, as already announced.

Viceroy Plans To Go Ahead With Interim Government
Jinnah Calls Viceroy's Declaration Double Betrayal

August 28, 1946, Bombay: Yesterday, the Viceroy had called both Gandhi and Jawaharlal and demanded that the Congress give an undertaking that it would comply with the government's interpretation of the Statement of May 16. Wavell reckoned that this would not only remove the road block to the convening of the constituent assembly but also bring the Muslim League back to the interim government. He asked Jawaharlal to put the issue before the CWC to know its opinion.

Both Gandhi and Jawaharlal took serious objection to Wavell's approach. The Congress, thereafter adopted, a two-pronged strategy to counter the Viceroy's sudden change of position on such a critically-important political issue. It shot two sets of communications one to London and another to the Viceroy—the first to bring in pressure from HMG and the second to confront the Viceroy with facts and reasoning.

Late last night, Gandhi wrote a letter addressed to Wavell and he also sent a cable to his trusted aide Sudhir Ghosh[226] in London to take up the matter with prime minister Attlee. Gandhi had suggested that Ghosh must impress upon HMG about the inept handling of sensitive political issue by the Viceroy of India and that he was indeed in need of assistance from an abler and legal mind.

Jawaharlal sent Wavell a sharp rejoinder stating that the working committee has rejected the proposition and made it clear that the Congress has been all through consistent in its interpretation of the provision relating to 'sections' and 'grouping of provinces', and this has been known to both the Viceroy and HMG. It has also been willing to refer any disputes in this regard to the Federal Court. In such circumstances, it criticised the Viceroy's recent attempts to impose interpretation of the Cabinet Mission upon it. The CWC also sharply crticised the Viceroy's stand on deferring the summoning of the constituent assembly, as undue delay could potentially undo the entire structure built up over the past few months.

The Viceroy has seemingly capitulated to the two-pronged attacks from Gandhi and the HMG — more due to pressure from London, that he must not dither any longer, at least not in respect of allowing the interim government to take office. The HMG additionally instructed the Viceroy to try to convince the Congress to defer the summoning of the constituent assembly till October. Wavell has announced that the interim government will take office on 2 September. Today, Jinnah while addressing a reception in Bombay has reacted angrily to these developments and called the Viceroy's action amounting to 'double betrayal'.

Observe It As A 'Day Of Mourning' Across India: League

September 1, 1946: Congress is poised to take over the reins of the interim government at the centre tomorrow. Wavell had tried to summon his powers to obstruct the Congress for some days. But his resistance wilted after Clement Attlee intervened. Infuriated at the prospect of the Congress taking up the reins of the federal government the Muslim League has decided to observe tomorrow as a 'day of mourning' countrywide and display black flags. There are reports that on the eve of installation of the interim government communal tensions are brewing in several parts of the country, especially Bombay, Punjab, Bengal and Bihar.

Jawaharlal Forms Government, Says Door Open For ML

September 2, 1946, New Delhi: Today Jawaharlal has taken over as the vice-president of the council of ministers. His cabinet which has fourteen berths includes Vallabhbhai Patel, Rajendra Prasad, Sarat Chandra Bose, Jagjivan Ram and C Rajagopalachari (all Hindu members); Aruna Asaf Ali, Shafaat Ahmed Khan and Syed A Zaheer (all Muslim members); Baldev Singh (Sikh member); CH Bhabha (Parsee member) and John Mathai (Indian Christian member). Two cabinet berths have reportedly been left vacant for Muslim League at the insistence by the Viceroy. Nehru has said his doors are open for the Muslim League and has assured he would restructure his cabinet, once the League decides to join the government.

Communal Hatred Grips Bombay, Claims Over 200 Lives

September 5, 1946, Bombay: Jinnah's call to observe September 2 as a 'black day' and as 'the day of mourning' had given rise to communal tension in different parts of India. In Bombay, a riot broke out a day before the designated 'black day' when the Muslim League supporters went on a rampage. The administration came down promptly and heavily on the rioters and deployed both police and the army to control the situation. Notwithstanding, communal hatred continued to retain its vicious grip over large sections of Hindus and Muslims. Swift and clandestine attacks on the innocent people of the opposite communities, mostly by stabbing, have been going on. Northern parts of the city have been the worst affected. Today a heavy monsoon downpour in the city had for some time dampened the malicious enthusiasm of the goons, but before long they returned to resume the carnage. According to reports, over 200 people have so far been killed and more than 600 injured. The victims belong to both the communities. So far, around 2,000 people have been taken into custody.

Jinnah Says 'Probably Yes' To Interim Government

September 25, 1946, New Delhi: Today Jinnah met the Viceroy and the two have reportedly conducted important political negotiations. Clearly uncomfortable at leaving the interim government and the constitution-making initiatives at the hands of the Congress alone, the Viceroy has been trying to persuade Jinnah to bring the League into the government and also into the constituent-making process. In course of the their meeting, Jinnah sounded somewhat positive about joining the cabinet but remained evasive about the latter. In regard to the former, he has been trying to bargain. In fact, in his last meeting with the Viceroy on 16th of this month, he wanted to secure some exclusive rights for the League to the detriment of the Congress but failed to get any assurance. Today he tried again.

He wanted that the vice-presidentship of the interim government should be rotated between the Congress and the League. The Viceroy, instead, offered the League the vice-chairmanship of the coordination committee of the cabinet. Jinnah has now agreed to refer the issue of joining the interim government to the working committee of the League. Considering his hold over the League, this gesture was considered to be good enough.

However, on the issue of joining the 'constitution-making' process, Jinnah said the matter has to be referred to the council of the AIML. Before that, it was necessary to obtain clarifications on several essential matters, including especially the procedures to be followed in regard to making provincial and group constitutions and their inter-relationship with the Union constitution. Jinnah said he could not be rushed in this matter. Political analysts are reading into today's meetings Jinnah's strategy—to enter into the interim government without committing to enter the proposed constituent assembly.

Nominating A Muslim
It Is Not A Question Of Right But Duty: Gandhi

September 26, 1946, New Delhi: In continuation to his meeting with Jinnah, the Viceroy held meetings with both Jawaharlal and Gandhi to know their views about the League joining the interim government. Both of them welcomed the decision but they refused to give up the right of the Congress to nominate nationalist Muslims as member of the executive council. Gandhi put his views succinctly. If it was a question of a 'right' for the Congress, it could be foregone. But it was a matter of 'duty' and could not be compromised. Much to his relief the Congress leaders did not impose any hard condition for taking the League members on board, eg. extracting a simultaneous commitment from the League to join the proposed constituent assembly.

'Muslims Tired, Probably Sorry That They Started It'

October 3, 1946, Bombay: The vicious communal riot that gripped the city from the beginning of this month seems to be finally coming to an end. There were a few distinct phases[227] of the carnage. On the first three days, ie. 1 to 3 September, Muslim communal elements went on the rampage, apparently to do justice to the call for the 'black day'. During this period, 65 Hindus were killed while 22 Muslims died at the hands of rioters of the other community. Over the next two days, the trend was reversed with 67 Muslims and 41 Hindus dying. Thereafter, till the 14th of the month, the administration secured better control and the death count declined for both the communities. However, catching the administration off-guard, the riot again raised its ugly head in the second fortnight and continued till the end of last month. In this second spell, 67 persons were killed of which 41 were Muslims.

Today Andrew Clow, the governor of Bombay, has written[228] a letter to Wavell, sharing his perception on this month-long riot and its impact. Clow, while observing that the riot having been initiated by the Muslims has claimed over 390 lives of people of both communities. He has added that it has, worryingly, also transformed now into an economic attack on the Muslims. Hindu milkmen are now deserting their Muslims masters while Hindu mill-owners are not employing Muslim workers. Clow has noted that such Social and economic apartheid are hurting the Muslims more and felt that: 'Now Muslims are tired and probably sorry that they had started it.'

Ghastly Riot Breaks Out In Noakhali

October 10, 1946, Calcutta: The fire of communal riot has again reared its ugly head in Bengal. For the past few days, Dacca was gripped by communal riots. There were several incidents of stabbing, murder and looting in that city. Now the communal frenzy has spread to Noakhali in Bengal's distant eastern part. According to early reports, the hooligans encouraged by the Muslim League have hatched a massive conspiracy in those faraway 'difficult-to-reach' rural areas to massacre the helpless Hindu minorities. Today trouble brewed in Ramganj Police Station area in the north-west corner of Noakhali, and soon vicious attacks on minority Hindus spread across wide stretches of the district, forming part of a carefully planned out programme of carnage. There are reports of murder, rape, arson and other atrocities having broken out in a number of villages. People in utter distress called for police help but none came.

League Wants To Nominate A Scheduled Caste Member

October 13, 1946, New Delhi: The Viceroy's attempts at getting the Muslim League on board has been proving to be a tortuous process involving Jinnah, Jawaharlal, and Gandhi with the Viceroy being in the centre. Jinnah has been going in circles on issues like reserving the right to nominate Muslim members by the League alone, the acceptance of the League as the sole authoritative representative body of the Muslim, rotation of vice-presidentship, mode of settling major communal issues in the council, allowing the League say over future appointments of representatives of the minorities and so on. Most of these demands were not acceded to. The Viceroy, however, agreed to cede to the League the vice-chairmanship of the coordination committee of the cabinet. Today, Jinnah has surprised the Viceroy by asking whether the League can nominate a representative of the scheduled castes or other minorities as the Congress has been allowed the liberty to nominate Muslim members. The Viceroy said the League could do so but wondered if this would not harm the cause of a smooth, harmonious relationship between the two parties in the matter of carrying out the governance of the country!

We're Sending Men To The Council To Protect Muslims, Minorities From The Congress Raj: League

October 14, 1946, New Delhi: Right since 2nd September, when the Congress formed ministry at the centre, both Wavell and Jinnah have been disquiet. Wavell has been attempting to convince Jinnah to change his mind and join the government. With efflux of time, Jinnah too has been alarmed at the prospect of the Congress consolidating its hold over the lever of power. Against this background, the working committee of the AIML met here and held lengthy deliberations during 7-14 October.

The committee disapproved the basis and the scheme of setting up the interim government. But with regard to the danger which the committee thought was posed to Muslims and other minorities by the Congress government, and for other 'weighty and obvious reasons' it decided to send five League members to join the executive council. In a letter written yesterday, Jinnah had informed the Viceroy that in the interest of Muslims and other minorities it would be fatal to leave the entire administration of the central government to the Congress. Today the League has nominated its five members—Liaquat Ali Khan, II Chundrigar, Abdur Rab Nishtar, Ghazanfar Ali Khan and Jogendra Nath Mandal. In the evolving political situation, Wavell has reportedly insisted on a fair distribution of the cabinet responsibilities, with at least one of the key portfolios being given to the League team. Accordingly, negotiations have begun between the Congress and the League. Gandhi has been in the capital as the tortuous political negotiations keep going.

The Congress leaders have been peeved at the nomination of JN Mandal, who happened to belong to the scheduled caste and was a member in the League ministry in Bengal. Gandhi saw no generosity in this nomination, keeping in view the League's questionable communal track record in that province. He felt that it was not a good augury for a harmonious relationship.

Muslim League To Join Interim Government

October 15, 1946, New Delhi: The government has issued a communiqué today stating that the Muslim league has decided to join the interim government and the King Emperor has appointed five of its nominees as members of the Viceroy's executive council. Before giving his final nod, the Viceroy had made an attempt to make the 'right to join the government' conditional on the League giving a firm commitment that it would revoke its Bombay resolution of July 1946 on 'direct action' and also accept the 16 May Statement. But Jinnah managed to evade both the issues for the time being by insisting upon certain guarantees from the Congress. He also added that it would require a council meeting to be called to revoke the Bombay resolution, which of course, would take time. The Viceroy left the matter there by advising Jinnah that the needful should be done at the earliest, and gave the green signal to the League to enter the council, much to the chagrin of the Congress.

We Must Face Issue Or Retire From Public Scene Jawaharlal To Wavell On Noakhali

October 15, 1946, New Delhi: As the hard political negotiations for portfolio distribution involving the Congress and the League are in full swing in the capital, endless tidings of the distress and miseries of the helpless minorities of Noakhali and Tippera are hitting the Congress politicians already in power. Today Jawaharlal, the vice-president of the interim government, has, in a letter[229] complained to Governor General Wavell that 'A vast area of Bengal has ceased to have any Government functioning, any security, and has just become the happy hunting ground of the worst elements in the community' and that 'Mass slaughter, arson, burning of human beings, rape, abduction on a large scale, forcible conversions and all manner of other horrible things are happening'. Jawaharlal pointed out all these were going on in the name of provincial autonomy and though the governor of the province and the Governor General himself could intervene to stop these infernal proceedings, they were allowing the same to continue indefinitely. Jawaharlal hinted that it is a terrible responsibility for 'all those in charge' to rise to the occasion and posed the question to Wavell: 'What is the good of our forming the Interim Government of India if all that we can do is to watch helplessly and do nothing else when thousands of people are being butchered and subjected to infinitely worse treatment?' At last he sought to drive home the urgency of the matter. 'I feel that we must face this issue somehow or else retire from the public scene', he wrote.

Taking into consideration the continuing, studied apathy of the governor of Bengal and the Governor General about the happenings in Noakhali, political analysts are doubtful if such mild urgings by Jawaharlal would hurry Wavell into action against the Suhrawardy government. Incidentally, Jawaharlal, after holding out the threat of 'quitting public office' in this letter, has written another latter on the same day to Wavell on the modalities of reconstituting the interim government, now that the League was poised to join in. This too, the analysts feel, may encourage Wavell not to take Jawaharlal's threat of 'quitting public office' seriously.

No Law-giver Can Give Interpretation Of His Own Law

October 21, 1946: The provincial assemblies had elected their representatives to the constituent assembly almost three months ago but the latter has made no headway till now. In the face of sustained and determined opposition by the League, the inauguration of the Assembly has been deferred more than once. The bone of contention has been the 'sections' and 'compulsory grouping of provinces', which have been central to the League to realise its ambition of gaining control over the NWFP, Assam, whole of Punjab and Bengal. Congress on the other hand has been claiming that the inherent contradictions in the Statement of 16 May could be resolved only on the basis of the premise that the provinces have freedom of choice in this regard, which also happened to constitute the essential spirit of the whole scheme. The situation grew complicated since the Viceroy and the Cabinet Delegation have, instead of confronting the Congress argument logically or acceding to the party's request to refer it to the Federal Court, been broadly supporting the interpretation of the League. Today Gandhi sent a strong message to both the Viceroy and the Cabinet delegation, saying that it was improper for them to do what they have been doing. In an interview to Preston Grover of the Associated Press of America, Gandhi said that the State Paper recommended the device of 'grouping', which the Congress interpreted in one way, the League in another and the Cabinet Mission in a third way. He contended that 'No law-giver can give an authoritative interpretation of his own law. If then there is a dispute as to its interpretation, a duly constituted court of law must decide it.'[230]

Muslim League Members Take Oath
Cabinet Reshuffled, Liaquat New Finance Minister

October 25, 1946, New Delhi: Today, five members of the Muslim League have taken oath. To accommodate them, the Congress has undertaken a restructuring exercise. Two berths were left open already. Now, three members of the cabinet, viz. Sarat Chandra Bose, Shafaat Ahmed Khan and Syed A Zaheer tendered their resignations to accommodate the League members. If this was a relatively straightforward exercise, a major problem did arise in regard to the portfolio that was to be offered to Liaquat Ali Khan, the senior-most member of the League. The Viceroy wanted that a key portfolio be allocated to him. But the Congress was not prepared to give up any one of the home, defence or foreign affairs. After much churning of ideas, the Congress decided to act upon its senior leader Rafi Ahmed Kidwai's suggestion to offer the 'finance' portfolio to him. According to sources close to Congress, the presumption is that the League leader, owing to inexperience, would embarrass himself in handling this highly technical responsibility. The other portfolios allotted to the League members were commerce, communications - post and air, health and law.

There Will Be A Congress Bloc And A League Bloc

October 1946, New Delhi: The League leaders had been upset that the Congress formed the government without adhering to the terms of the Statement of 16 May and by interpreting these according to its own convenience. After entering into the cabinet, they are acutely aware that they need to oppose Congress and simultaneously create conditions for achieving the goal of Pakistan. They seem to be looking at their roles in the executive council in strategic terms to neutralise Congress power, rather than aiming at good governance for India.

Liaquat Ali has made the League's goal clear without wasting time. He said, the League is in the government to support the Pakistan issue and that he would not accept Nehru's leadership. He has also given enough hint that the interim government will consist of a Congress bloc and a Muslim League bloc and each will work under separate leadership.

The indications are loud and clear that the cabinet will struggle to survive, let alone do something positive for the country.

Minority Hindus Are Decimated In Noakhali

October 1946, Feni: The ghastly communal riots engulfed the Muslim majority districts of Noakhali and Tippera where carnage has been carried out by the goons with allegiance to the Muslim League over the helpless Hindu minorities at a stretch from 10 October to 21 October. The riots began in Ramganj police station area and the carnage soon spread to other areas including Begumganj, Lakshmipur, Sonaimuri, Sandip and Raipur. Gradually, the infernal fire began to devour the southern part of Tippera as well. Hajiganj, Chandpur and Faridganj have been amongst places badly hit.

The rioters operated with impunity, breaking bridges and putting up roadblocks, making it difficult for the army to operate. According to several sources these occurred at the directions of the Suhrawardy led government, which all through, stood as onlookers. The attacks were cruelly planned and thorough in details: slaughter of male, rape and forcible remarriage of Hindu women, destruction of property and cattle.

Critics say, it is yet another desperate move by the League government to strengthen the claim of Pakistan over the whole of

Bengal. Unlike Calcutta, this time the carnage was carried out in an area that was hugely Muslim-dominated and as such, there was no fear of retribution. The slayings were one-sided and comprehensive. Such dastardly acts have aroused countrywide condemnation.

After Calcutta, Noakhali
The Communal Inferno Rages On

> Chilling accounts of gruesome massacre of the minority Hindu community across numerous villages in the Sadar and Feni subdivisions of Noakhali district and parts of Tippera are slowly reaching the rest of the province. For about ten days, starting from 10th of the present month, the goons of the ruling Muslim League carried out a well planned pogrom across villages spread over an area of nearly 250 square miles slaying men, raping and kidnapping women and forcing them to remarry their tormentors and destroying their homes and livestock. To muzzle the flow of news, prevent any armed forces from reaching the sites and to be able to carry out the heinous agenda of barbaric persecution of hapless Hindu families in chilling isolation, the League-sponsored gangs of assassins put up numerous road blocs and destroyed bridges, de-linking the earmarked territory from all potential sources of help. The indulgent Suhrawardy government, perceived by many to have been acting as an accomplice also ensured transfer of all those bureaucrats who could impede or prevent the chains of the ghastly events.
>
> It is becoming clear that the massacre at Noakhali is the second planned attempt by the League to press home the demand for Pakistan and scare the Hindu minorities in the province in Bengal. The Calcutta riot patronised by Suhrawardy had boomeranged on the League which possibly encouraged it to select the countryside where small Hindu communities would have no chance to retaliate and could be butchered at will. The pogrom was planned in detail and implemented with exactitude such that the infernal massacre continued uninterrupted for more than ten days.

As the news began to reach other parts of the province and the country, stunned disbeliefs are turning into revulsion and anger. In Bihar, violent responses have begun to occur. According to political analysts, Suhrawardy and the Muslim League have committed an act of huge political immaturity at first by engineering riots in Calcutta and now carrying out the pogrom at Noakhali. For centuries, Hindus and Muslims have been living amicably in the province, sharing common language and culture. These twin acts may put a decisive end to that amity. If the League is keen on claiming the entire Bengal for Pakistan, it will find that task almost impossible now. Suhrawardy may have, by planned massacres in Calcutta and Noakhali, made a forceful case for Pakistan, but he has certainly lost the case for a united Bengal.

Noakhali Can Wait, Calcutta Needs Gandhi's Presence

November 3, 1946, Sodepur: The communal violence in Noakhali had broken out on 10 October and thereafter raged viciously for several days. During this period New Delhi, the capital of the country, was witnessing hectic political negotiations between the Congress and the League, with the Viceroy as the arbiter. This resulted in the League deciding on 15 October to join the interim government. This was followed by a course of hectic negotiations over distribution of portfolios and that continued till 25 October. During all those days the tidings of the communal pogrom were reaching Delhi but failing to evoke any substantial action. After the power equations between the Congress and the League were settled in Delhi, Gandhi reached Calcutta on 29 October. By that time, the wailing of the distressed Hindus of Noakhali and Tippera were renting the air of that city causing shock, frustration and anger. In Calcutta, Gandhi held discussion with prime minister Suhrawardy and governor Burrows about his decision to visit Noakhali.

Today, however, Gandhi has announced delay in departure for Noakhali as Suhrawardy requested him to postpone his journey till after the Bakri Id. Referring to the riot that has erupted in Bihar, Suhrawardy has suggested that Gandhi's presence in Calcutta may be helpful for peace. Gandhi has agreed to delay his Noakhali visit by a few days.

Bihar In The Grip Of Communal Frenzy, Gandhi Upset, Jawaharlal Acts With Alacrity

November 6, 1946, Sodepur: Even before Gandhi landed in Sodepur, a fierce riot had broken out in Bihar. It started off following a hartal observed on 28 October. According to reports, the majority Hindu community of the province reacted angrily to the disturbing reports reaching them from neighbouring Bengal. Unfortunately, their wrath fell on the hapless and innocent Muslims in the province. Hooligans and communal elements promptly began to exploit the situation. As a result the riots have turned vicious taking a heavy toll of the minority Muslims.

Gandhi, from his Sodepur Ashram, has been regularly appealing to the Hindus of Bihar to stop the atrocities forthwith. Today he has written a letter to the people of that province asking them 'Is it nationalism to seek barbarously to crush the fourteen per cent of the Muslims in Bihar?' He has also observed that Bihari Hindus are honour bound to regard the minority Muslims as their 'brethren'. He has been keeping in regular touch with Jawaharlal, the prime minister, to ensure the safety of Muslims in Bihar. To his relief, Jawaharlal has acted with alacrity to combat riots against the minorities in Bihar. He has come down to Patna with some of his cabinet colleagues to tackle the situation urgently. Despite a communally surcharged environment in parts of Bengal and Bihar, the Bakri Id celebration passed peacefully in Calcutta. Today, Gandhi has left the city with a team of 25 people for Noakhali by a special train.

Bihar Rioters Will Be Fired Upon, Says Jawaharlal Had Govt Shown Same Zeal In Bengal: Shyamaprasad

November 6, 1946, Patna & Calcutta: Today Jawaharlal has issued a stern warning[231] to the rioters in Bihar that if they did not behave, the government would fire upon and bomb them from air, if necessary. Shyamapraad Mukherjee, president of the Hindu Mahasabha, who has been extremely upset at the plight of the minorities in Noakhali and more so, by the inaction of the interim government in Delhi about the ongoing communal riot there, has today, reacted strongly[232] at Jawaharlal's apparently discriminatory attitude. In a statement,

Shyamaparasad said: 'One of the greatest surprises has been the inactivity of the "Interim" government.' He added that 'Indeed, if the members of the Interim government, some of whom now openly threaten bombing from air in Bihar, had exercised similar zeal and activity in Bengal in August last or even in October... much of India's tragedy today might have been averted.'

Bihar Swept By Unprecedented Communal Carnage

November 1946, Patna: The inferno of communal hatred has now begun to burn maliciously in the land where once Lord Buddha had attained nirvana and Buddhism flourished, singing the glory of non-violence. Such is the power of lower reaches of human emotion and instinct! The stories of the massacre of innocent, helpless Hindu males and the ravage of their women in Noakhali had spread like wild fire not only in the rest of Bengal but also to neighbouring Bihar. The majority Hindu community of this province has burst out in anger and that was directed to the local minority Muslims, who unfortunately had no role in the massacre in Noakhali. The opportunist elements, as always in such cases, have escalated the stray acts of riots into a massive atrocity against the Muslims spanning over wide areas in the province, especially its central and eastern parts. So savage and brutal has been the violence that the interim government in Delhi has been shaken to its core!

Gandhi presently in Noakhali applying balms to the victims has become deeply upset at this development, which has emerged as a new link to the grisly chain of communal hatred and violence in the country. He wants to visit Bihar. However, Jawaharlal, the prime minister and Vallabhbhai, the Home Minister, have dissuaded him as both are tackling the situation on war footing.

Devote Every Ounce Of Energy For Bihar Riot Victims

November 17, 1946, New Delhi: Right since the day the League members took charge of their portfolios, the coalition ministry has been riding rough weather. They have been working as a separate bloc under the leadership of Liaqaut in utter disregard of Jawaharlal. So far the League has neither accepted the 16 May scheme nor withdrawn its Bombay resolution proposing direct action. One of the League members has even gone to the extent of saying that the events in Bengal are part of its all-India battle for Pakistan. Vexed and irritated beyond measure, Jawaharlal has been, for past some time, impressing upon the Viceroy to instruct the League leaders to cooperate both in the work of governance and making of constitution which has only been getting deferred.

Jinnah today sought to return the pressure. In reply to a missive from the Viceroy asking him to call the council meeting of the League, Jinnah has, by giving references of correspondences of Jawaharlal and Gandhi, accused the Congress of openly violating the provisions of the 16 May Statement in regard to 'grouping' in the name of provincial autonomy. In such circumstances, Jinnah has written, it would not serve any purpose to call the meeting of the council.

Thereafter, he drew the attention of the Viceroy to the communal riots in Bihar. In view of the massacre of the Muslims in that province, Jinnah urged the Viceroy to postpone the summoning of the constituent assembly and devote every 'ounce of energy' for the restoration of peace and order. According to political analysts, both the Bihar and the Union governments have been acting with remarkable alacrity in Bihar to douse the communal fire. Notwithstanding, Jinnah has got an excuse to avoid the constituent assembly and may continue to frustrate the pleas of both the Congress and the Viceroy.

Muslim League Members Will Not Attend Constituent Assembly: Jinnah

November 21, 1946, New Delhi: Three days ago, Jinnah had written to the Viceroy urging him to postpone the inaugural meeting of the constituent assembly sine die by quoting Congress' lack of sincerity in adhering to the terms of the Cabinet Mission Plan and the 'ruthless massacre of Muslims' in Bihar.

But the Viceroy was not convinced about the League's stand. Today he requested the League to attend the proposed meet and work together with the Congress in sorting out controversial issues. The Viceroy has assured that in the constitutent assembly neither the Congress nor the League will be allowed to impose things on each other so that they can resolve the areas of disagreement in a cooperative framework. At the same time, unable to wait indefinitely, the Viceroy has today issued invitation letters for the inaugural ceremony of the constituent assembly, to be held on 9 December.

Jinnah has taken serious exception to the action of the Viceroy. In a statement issued today, he administered strong rebuff to the Viceroy and accused him of commiting 'one more blunder of a very grave and serious character'. He has alleged that the Viceroy is playing into the hands of the Congress. Jinnah has made it clear that he is determined not to allow the constitution-making activities to proceed. Jinnah has made another important statement to the effect that no early session of the AIML Council may be held to rescind or reconsider the July resolution of the League, adopted in Bombay rejecting the Cabinet Plan. In the light of the statement, it is only ethical that the League relinquishes the ministries but it seems to be in no mood to do that. To expel them would be a major challenge for both Wavell and the Congress.

League Cannot Have It's Cake And Eat It Too

November 23-24, 1946, Meerut: Congress has elected JB Kripalani as its new president since Jawaharlal took over as the vice president of the interim government. In the annual session being held here, the party has reacted angrily to the League's decision to abstain from the constituent assembly. While addressing the Subjects Committee, Jawaharlal observed that the League, with encouragement from the British government, is acting like the 'King's Party', managing thereby to hinder the process of power transfer.

There is also a growing pressure within the party that unless the Viceroy ensured that the League members resign, the Congress members of the cabinet ought to quit it. The prevailing mood in the session was that the League cannot have the cake and eat it too.

Messages Of Peace And Communal Harmony On Lips, Gandhi Criss-crosses Riot-ravaged Land

November 1946, Noakhali: Gandhi arrived here on 7th of this month and since then he has been moving across the riot-ravaged villages listening to stories of numerous incidents of unprecedented brutalities and atrocities on helpless Hindu minorities. In quite a few villages, after large-scale murders and exodus, only one or two Hindu families have been left spending days amidst extreme fear. Gandhi has been camping in the affected villages. He has been campaigning for communal amity, appealing to the Muslims, and reassuring the few surviving Hindu families. He has few chosen followers accompanying him. Communal miscreants are finding Gandhi's presence and activities obnoxious and impediments to their mission. They want him to leave Noakhali and have been trying to discourage him in various manner by displaying posters demanding Pakistan and also holding out threats to his life. There have also been instances where they have sabotaged the bamboo bridges across canals that he was likely to pass through, and spread pieces of broken glass on his pathways. Every time Gandhi has been saved by providence. Unmindful of his personal safety, Gandhi has been moving on, spreading the messages of peace and goodwill and appealing to the conscience of the tormentors.

Gandhi's presence in Noakhali has exposed the governmental ineptitude and worse, its complicity to the genocide. His continued presence here is bringing Bengal and the League government under limelight nationally and internationally. A deeply embarrassed Suhrawardy is insisting that Gandhi leave Noakhali.

Assam Roadblock In The Constituent Assembly Grouping Of Provinces Is A Settled Fact: Jinnah

November 26, 1946, Karachi: A fundamental difference exists between the Congress and the Muslim League on the interpretation of the provision relating to the right of a province to go out of a 'section'. It has blown into a major controversy in the context of the province of Assam, which has been grouped with Bengal in section 'C'. Based on its bitter experience of the past of mass scale immigration from Bengal, the Congress party in Assam apprehends that the Muslim majority in Bengal would reflect on the section as a whole and act to the detriment of Assamese people. This has prompted its Congress leaders to try to come out of the given section before the drafting of the respective constitutions gets under way.

Bordoloi, the prime minister of Assam, came to Gandhi to seek his support and could convince him of the justness of the cause. Congress is supporting Assam's right to come out of section C even before the drafting of constitutions has begun. Jinnah was addressing the press here today. Taking strong exception to the Congress stand on the issue, he said that the 'grouping of provinces' is a settled fact and it forms an unalterable element of the Cabinet Mission Plan. He added that, Assam could exercise its right to come out of the grouping only after the constitution is worked out.

Assam is clearly a Hindu majority province and therefore common people are not able to make out Jinnah's dogged insistence on her confinement to section C with Bengal, a Muslim majority province. However, to the political analysts, the reasons are clear and simple. The League has long-term interest in the province and it is therefore not ready to budge. On this issue, the British government is supporting Jinnah but Congress will not listen. As such a roadblock has arisen with regard to the proceedings of the constituent assembly.

Last-ditch Attempt To Bring Congress, League Together

The date for the first session of the constituent assembly is fast approaching and the Viceroy has already issued invitations. But the rivalry between Congress and the League on the issue of the Assembly has reached a peak and HMG has been refusing to intervene decisively. As the situation stands today, the Congress has demanded that the Viceroy expel the League members unless the League accepts the 16 May Statement while the League has dared him to do so and face the consequence. In hindsight, the blame for the present state of affairs lies at the doors of the Cabinet Delegation and the Viceroy.

First, the Statement of May 16 was so drafted and so featured that it lent itself to varying interpretations and it was but natural that political parties would compete to establish their own versions.

Second, the Congress had, right from the beginning, consistently interpreted that the provinces had freedom to choose their 'sections' and they could not be forced into any pre-specified 'section' against their will. Though the Cabinet mission and the Viceroy clarified that the Congress version was not correct and the right interpretation was that the grouping, as given in the Statement was compulsory, it did not confront the Congress with required force. More importantly, the Viceroy allowed the Congress to form the interim government without obtaining an assurance that it would adhere to the delegation's and the Viceroy's point of view in the above matter. In effect, it left the Congress free to cultivate its own interpretation.

Third, the Viceroy not only kept supporting the League's interpretation on sections and groupings (which incidentally was in consonance with the official interpretations) but he went a step further. In the month of May he, with a view to securing the League's cooperation, assured Jinnah that in the event of differences arising between the Congress and the League within a 'section', contentious issues will be decided by 'majority votes'. Statement of 16 May had no such provision and it was clearly an afterthought. Such a provision had immense political significance and hurt the Congress interests badly. The Congress was certain to contest such manipulation tooth and nail. Not only had the Viceroy thus misled the League with such dangerous assurance, but, he, at a later date, also allowed the League to join the interim government even though the League had not reversed its Bombay resolution of July, rejecting the Cabinet Mission proposal and deciding on 'direct action' to realise its goal of Pakistan.

In a nutshell the Viceroy, guided by HMG, chose not to act firm against the Congress and on the other hand kept appeasing the League with the hope that things will be sorted out in course of time. Now the inevitable has happened. It appears that the Cabinet Mission Plan is on its last leg. But its demise will of

> course be a matter of infamy for HMG. At this juncture, the HMG has reportedly decided to summon the top leaders of the rival communities to London and make a last-ditch attempt to sort out their differences. It may not be wrong to assume that HMG knows the futility of this enterprise, but it still wants the exercise to go though to save its own face and lay the blame squarely on Indians.

London Invites – Liaqaut Accepts, Jawaharlal Declines

November 26, 1946, New Delhi: India is passing through difficult times. The process of power transfer has stumbled over the disagreements between the Congress and the League over the interpretation of some key features of the Cabinet Mission Plan. The interim federal government, though it has members from both these parties, is practically in a limbo due to consistent road blocks put forth by the League members. In these tense times, the Congress is keen to carry forward the tasks of the constituent assembly which is essential to facilitate the transfer of power to Indian hands, whereas the League has serious doubts about the Congress intentions. After Jinnah declined to take part in the inaugural meeting of the constituent assembly scheduled to be held on 9 December, the Viceroy tried afresh to bring the two parties together. Congress has agreed to sit into the 'sections' but wants that the progress thereafter will hinge on the deliberations that would take place. The League on the other hand wants a guarantee in advance from the HMG that the provision of the CMP would be scrupulously adhered to. In the extant circumstances, the prospect of an agreement between the Congress and the League look almost nonexistent.

Today Clement Attlee, the British prime minister, invited Viceroy Wavell and representatives of the Congress, the Muslim League and the Sikhs to visit London to sort out their differences. The presence of the Viceroy, who was involved in the formulation of the CMP proposals, would hopefully facilitate an agreement. This invitation has come as a welcome relief to the Muslim League and Liaqaut has responded positively. However, Jawaharlal has expressed his unwillingness to avail the offer. He has argued with the Viceroy that this new initiative would undo whatever progress has so far been achieved in terms of the Cabinet Mission Plan including the formation of interim government, election to the constituent assembly and the impending inauguration of that Assembly. It would, he contended, reopen the whole process in public perception.

According to sources, the Viceroy is making all-out efforts to secure participation of the Congress leaders in London without which the exercise would be infructuous. His line of persuasion is that the conference in London may lead to the League's joining the Assembly meeting on 9 December.

Liaquat Makes Life Unbearable For Congress

December, 1946, New Delhi: When the Congress offered the finance portfolio to the League, it expected the League minister to make a mess of a highly technical job and abdicate voluntarily. Reportedly, even Jinnah had reservations about a League member accepting it. However, some of the veteran Muslim bureaucrats saw unique advantages attached to the ministry and at their advice, Liaquat took over the portfolio. It is hardly two months but Liaquat has been using his power to vet important proposals of the other ministries to the hilt to hinder their functioning.[233] By using strategies like delaying allocation or pruning of amounts etc, he is making the Congress-run ministries gasp. He has also ensured that there are clear cut divisions between the Congress and the League members and they do not see eye to eye. The agenda of the League is to paralyse the interim government from within and to render the dream of an 'united independent India' impossible.

Serious Differences In Interpretation Of Cabinet Plan Congress-League-Sikh Leaders Fail To Reach Agreement

December 6, 1946, London: The Congress position on 'sections' and 'grouping of provinces' having been radically different from both the League and HMG, the party saw little reason to visit London to reach at an agreement on the issue under the auspices of the British government. However, due to strong persuasion by Clement Attlee, the British prime minister, the party deputed Jawaharlal to London. Vallabhbhai stayed put, devoting the short time on hand to prepare for the inaugural meeting of the Constituent Assembly in India. Four Indian leaders Jawaharlal (Congress), Baldev Singh (representing the Sikh view), Jinnah and Liaqaut (Muslim League) arrived here on the 2nd of this month along with the Viceroy. Wavell's presence was considered valuable not only as the Viceroy of India but also his being the co-author of the Cabinet Mission Plan. The leaders deliberated the issue but they were not able to reach at any consensus on the matter.

During the course of the discussion, serious differences of opinion arose in regard to the role of 'section' and 'grouping' vis-à-vis the autonomy and freedom of a province. Jawaharlal, putting up the Congress view, contended that the provisions relating to 'section' and grouping of provinces are mere procedural matters. What is of crucial importance, he contended, was the 'spirit of the plan', which emphasised the 'provincial autonomy'. If provincial autonomy is of paramount importance, the provinces ought to have the right to opt out of the Section or Group, whether 'before' or 'after' the task of constitution-making is undertaken. On this point, he was opposed by both the League and the HMG who had a common view that the provisions as regards sections and groupings as stated in the Statement of May 16 were compulsory. The disagreements also extended to the mode of settling of differences within a section. The views of the two sides were fundamentally so different that, they were concluded as irreconcilable.

Statement Of 16 May Is What The Cabinet Mission Has Always Stated Was Their Intention

December 6, 1946, London: Today the British Cabinet has issued a statement announcing that the talks of the last few days involving the Indian leaders and HMG have ended without any agreement and that major problems arose in the interpretation of Paras 19(v) and 19 (viii) of the Statement of 16 May. Dwelling further on these clauses, the statement aggravated the ongoing controversy. Though the Statement of 16 May had only required the provinces to meet in 'sections' but provided no mechanism as to how differences amongst parties, if any, were to be resolved within a 'section', now HMG has, through this new statement, added that the Cabinet Mission throughout maintained the view that such differences should be settled by rule of simple majority—"the decisions of the Sections should, in the absence of agreement to the contrary, be taken by simple majority vote of the representatives in the Sections.'" This new clarification seems to be an attempt to regularise the assurance that the Viceroy had once given to Jinnah privately.

The Cabinet's statement then proceeded to establish that not only the 'written words' but the 'intention' of the Cabinet Mission must be taken into account to understand the meaning of the Plan. The Statement said that the HMG 'have had legal advice which confirms that the Statement of May 16 means what the Cabinet Mission have always stated was their intention. This part of the Statement as so interpreted, must, therefore, be considered an essential part of the Scheme of May 16, for enabling the Indian people to formulate a constitution which His Majesty's Government would be prepared to submit to Parliament.'[234]

According to political analysts these interpretations, interpolations and ruling by HMG seem like after-thoughts and attempts to cure the defects that were inherent in the original Plan. Introducing new elements of such fundamental importance in matters of political negotiations between two parties engaged in bitter rivalry could certainly be deemed as partisan and biased. These are likely to cause great affront to the Congress and harden its position.

Drafting The Provincial And Section Constitution Paras That Are Bones Of Contention

The Cabinet Mission Plan has categorised the provinces of British India under sections A, B and C. It has also outlined the procedures for drafting of constitutions at three levels. Two relevant paras, viz. 19 (v) and 19 (viii), are reproduced below: Para 19 (v) says, 'These sections shall proceed to settle provincial constitutions for the provinces included in each section and shall also decide whether any group constitution shall be set up for those provinces and if so, with what provincial subjects the group should deal. Provinces shall have power to opt out of groups in accordance with provisions of sub clause (viii) below.'

Para 19 (viii) provides, 'As soon as new constitutional arrangements have come into operation, it shall be open to any province to elect to come out of any group in which it has been placed. Such a decision shall be taken by the new Legislature of the province after first general election under new constitution'.

The Cabinet Mission has provided that the decisions at the sections, in the absence of agreement to the contrary, should be taken by simple majority vote of representatives in the sections.

HMG Snubs Congress – Wont Force Constitution On Any Unwilling Party

December 6, 1946, London: In the long statement issued today HMG gave an elaborate exposition of what have been the interpretation, intention and view of the Cabinet Mission on 'sections', 'grouping' as well as 'mode of handling differences in sections'. Conscious that these would be contested and rejected by the Congress, the statement of HMG has recommended appropriate dispute resolution mechanism. In regard to 'grouping of provinces' and 'sections', HMG urged the Congress to accept the views of the Cabinet Mission to pave way for the League to reconsider their attitude. Should differences arise in the interpretation on other questions, the same may be referred by either party to the Federal Court. Then it reverted to the matter immediately in dispute, ie. 'grouping of provinces' and 'sections'. The statement added that if in spite of this reaffirmation of the intention of the Cabinet Mission, the 'constituent assembly' is still not satisfied and wants to refer this fundamental point to the Federal Court, such reference should be made at the earliest. In such eventuality, it would be reasonable to postpone the meetings of the 'sections' until the decision of the Federal Court is known.

Thereafter, the final blow to the dream of an independent undivided India was delivered. The statement said that should a constitution be framed for India by a constituent assembly devoid of representation of a large section of her people, His Majesty's Government could not force 'such a constitution upon any unwilling parts of the country'.[235] The implications are clear - that HMG will not allow the Congress to impose a constitution on the League, if it is prepared without the latter's participation. Political analysts are viewing the British government's statement as an end to the Cabinet Mission Plan for all practical purposes. If at all, an official declaration of its demise remains to be made.

Two Board Flight To Frame Indian Constitution, Two Stay Back To Promote Pakistan

December 7, 1946, London: Jawaharlal and Baldev Singh have flown for India. They are in a hurry to be in India for the inaugural meet of the constituent assembly. However, Jinnah and Liaquat have decided to stay on. The League leaders have several sympathisers amongst the British politicians, especially belonging to the Conservatives. Jinnah and Liaqaut may probably use their extended stay to generate sympathy for the League and convince the British opinion makers about the justification for its demand for Pakistan. In the present circumstances the prospect of the League's participation in the 9 December inaugural meeting has completely disappeared.

SEVEN

Blood, Partition & Independence

1946-1947

Blood, Partition and Freedom

CABINET PLAN IN COMA, WAVELL SUGGESTS RESCUE

December 11, 1946, London: Wavell came to London to facilitate a consensus amongst Indian leaders on the interpretation of the Cabinet Mission Plan. Personally he has not been hopeful of a positive outcome and the proceedings have vindicated his opinion. With Jawaharlal, the Congress president, taking a rigid position on a couple of key provisions, the viability of the entire Cabinet Mission Plan has become suspect. Though upon referral by HMG, the authors of the 'proposals' have come forward with the clarification on the disputed clauses, the government is not at all hopeful that the Congress will agree to abide by their clarifications. Under such circumstances, Wavell has been trying to persuade the Attlee cabinet to revert to his 'breakdown plan' to accomplish the task of power transfer. On the 5th of this month he had made a plea to the British government about his plan. After the reconciliation proceedings were wound up, Wavell began to intensify his efforts. Today the plan was again discussed at the British prime minister's residence.

Constituent Assembly Holds First Meeting

December 13, 1946, New Delhi: As scheduled, the constituent assembly commenced its inaugural session here four days ago with Sachchidananda Sinha, the eldest member in chair. Held under the cloud of the boycott call by the Muslim League, 207 members attended as against 296 who were entitled to participate. As apprehended, the League resorted to complete boycott of the Assembly.

Jinnah has been sceptical about Congress intention to adhere to the clauses of the 16 May Statement and he has repeatedly made it clear that the League would avoid the constituent assembly unless the Congress comes clear and commits itself to the Statement, letter and spirit. But to his angst, the Congress, in the recent meet in London held in the presence of His Majesty's Government, made it clear that it would not budge from its proclaimed position of freedom to choose which group it wants to belong to.

However Jinnah received a boost when HMG held out a blanket assurance that it would not impose a constitution prepared in the absence of the League representing the Muslims of the country. Considering these facts and factors, Jinnah has seemingly been determined not to have anything to do with the Assembly. Incidentally, he along with Liaquat Ali Khan, have chosen to stay back for some time in England. They have been mobilising political support for the League's position there. It was thus a foregone conclusion that the League would boycott the Assembly and its decisions.

Two days ago, Rajendra Prasad was elected as the president of the Assembly. Today Jawaharlal has introduced the 'objective resolution'. It has been decided to hold the next meeting on 20 January 1947. The members are hoping against hope that the Muslim League will attend it. Princes of native states are also expected to attend the next meeting in strength. Political analysts look at what they call as the 'authorised absence' of the League at this meeting as a precursor to the birth of the second constituent assembly, and probably the birth of a separate state for the Muslim.

Neither Congress, Nor League Comply With Norms, But Both Stay On

The clarification on 'grouping' and 'sections' by HMG (that clearly goes against the Congress interpretation), followed by its advice that the constituent assembly, if it is not still satisfied, can refer the issue to the Federal Court, had challenged the legitimacy of the Congress in continuing in the interim government unless its stand on the issue was endorsed by the Apex Court.

On the other hand, the League had, by its July resolution adopted in Bombay, abandoned the constitutional method and resolved in favour of direct action. Notwithstanding, they were allowed to join the interim government due to Wavell's initiative. The League has not yet rescinded that resolution, but still continues to be in the executive council.

Interestingly notwithstanding such anomaly, neither the Congress nor the League seems inclined to leave the government. It is clear that both these parties have got entangled in intractable conflicts and the British government is not helping matters. There are likely to be twin casualties to this imbroglio – first, the capacity of the interim government to govern; second, the prospect of a united independent India

Britain Wants Time-bound Transfer Of Power

December, 1946, London: HMG is realising that the Cabinet Mission Plan has become unworkable. At the same time, it realises the impracticability of continuing the British rule over India, administratively and militarily, beyond a year or two. The appointment of British officers in the ICS stopped sometime ago. In the armed forces, a newfound self-respect amongst Indians and their declining loyalty to the Raj—both derived from the INA episode—are visible. The immediate trigger is however the steadily rising communal violence which is threatening to engulf the country and the British regime and along with it while its capacity to tackle such situation stands increasingly diminished due to gradual withdrawal of the British force from the sub-continent. Prime minister Attlee is growing impatient to transfer power to Indians and exit. However, considering the irreconcilability between the two major political parties of India on the key issues, Attlee feels that it would be sensible to fix a 'D' day for transfer of power and then go all out to achieve that target. But Wavell, the Viceroy, holds a contrary view. He feels pre-fixing a date without finding responsible Indian hands to take over the reins would push the country to the throes of unprecedented communal riots. Having ruled India for nearly two centuries, such a measure, he felt, would constitute acts of colossal irresponsibility and would tarnish the British image across the world.

Clement Attlee is not buying Wavell's theory. On the contrary, he has become suspect of Wavell's capacity to deliver. It is learnt that the HMG has already begun the process to find out a competent successor of Wavell who can deliver and not stonewall his government's initiatives.

Congress Working To A Plan For Speedy Integration Of Princely States

December, 1946, New Delhi: The news that HMG is growing impatient to exit India is having impact upon large numbers of princely states. Even a year ago, most of them were dreaming of becoming independent after the lapse of the paramountcy following the British exit. But the scenario has been changing fast and the new realities are sinking. The political ambition of the Congress has been widening with time and today it extends far beyond the British Indian provinces.

This is finding synergy with the popular aspirations in the native states to be part of the independent India. Jawaharlal, as the president of the AISPC, has been well aware of the popular desire as well as the lack of viability of most of these states—economically, militarily and politically—to stand on their own legs. It appears both he and Vallabhbhai have been working on a plan to assimilate most of these states into independent India once the paramountcy lapses.

If India Were To Be Partitioned On Communal Basis, So Also Must Be Bengal, Punjab

December, 1946, Calcutta: Shyamaprasad, a top ranked leader of Hindu Mahasabha, is pitching for partition of Bengal and annexation of the Hindu majority area of Bengal to India. All through, he was against partition of the country and worked for a united independent India. However, the recent experience of mindless rioting following the 'direct action day' call by the Muslim League government has made a deep impact on him. The planned manner in which thousands of Hindus were killed in Calcutta and thereafter severe atrocities were committed on them in Noakhali under the encouragement of the Muslim League government has convinced him about the demerit of Hindus continuing to live in a Muslim dominated state and under a government controlled by the Muslim League.

In view of such experience, Shyamaprasad has put forth the argument that if at all India as a country has to be partitioned on the communal basis, Bengal and Punjab also must be partitioned on the same ground. He is making a strong case in these lines and canvassing his view points amongst the legislators of various parties and also representing these to the government.

British Cabinet Rejects Breakdown Plan

January 3, 1947, London: Wavell's 'breakdown plan' was once discussed and rejected by the British cabinet in June last year. However, in the light of the irreconcilable differences continuing between the Congress and the League on the interpretation of the Cabinet Mission Plan, Wavell again insisted that his own plan deserved a re-visit. It was taken up for discussion several times by the India and Burma Committee during last month. In order to enhance its acceptability to the Congress, Wavell recently, had made a key change in the plan ie. the first phase of British withdrawal would be limited to four Hindu majority provinces of Bombay, Madras, Central Provinces and Orissa leaving out Bihar and United Provinces. This would not make the 'prospect of Pakistan' obvious and give the whole Plan a secular, objective look as if on the issue of joining the federation, the rest of the country would take a decision based on the experience of power transfer occurring in these four provinces.

However after few rounds of detailed appraisals, the India and Burma Committee rejected the plan for more than one reason. According to its final observations, the plan was more of a military kind and hence unsuitable for a delicate political operation. It was also criticised for betraying a defeatist attitude—as if British would be retreating under pressure from Indian political parties. Then there were legal complications. Phased power transfer would necessitate new sets of equations of the Congress-led provinces with the central government. This in turn would require changes in the GOI Act of 1935 for the interim period. Those were perceived to be vexatious, cumbersome and avoidable. Last but not the least, under the plan, protecting the interests of the religious minorities and the control of Indian army were expected to pose complex problems. Overall, the weight of demerits was considered to be heavier than advantages accruing to the HMG. The Committee took note of the objective of the British government in favour of a graceful, orderly, smooth transfer of power to democratic successor in accordance with its laid down policy.

Considering all these factors, the 'breakdown plan' was rejected today, although Wavell has not been formally communicated about it yet. This rejection also sends a message that the days of Wavell as the Viceroy may be numbered. He does not seem to possess the requisite profile that Labour government has in mind to effect the power transfer in the manner it wants.

Muslim League Ministry Takes Charge Of Sind

January 3, 1947, Karachi: The unclear verdict of the Sind electorates in January 1946 had created a piquant situation. The Hidayatullah-led rag-tag government had faced no-confidence motion from a strong body of opposition, comprising of Congress and Syed Group, both of them put together were numerically as large as the treasury bench, on more than one occasion and had to be rescued by the 3 members European group. Keeping in view its unstable nature, governor Mudie had ordered re-elections which were held last month. The League had leveraged its demand of Pakistan and the communal card, including the Bihar riot. It was able to mobilise the support of Sajjada Nashins and the Peers to corner GM Syed, who happened to be its principal target. Its strategy met with success and the League was able to secure as many as 35 seats reserved for the Muslims. As expected, the Congress further consolidated the Hindu votes and raised its tally from 18 last year to 20 this year. The remaining 5 seats went to Europeans (3) and Jamiat (2). Syed himself has been defeated though there are allegation of electoral malpractices against the League. For the time being, however, Jinnah has achieved his target. He has pre-empted any potential trouble from Sind to the demand for a single sovereign independent state of Pakistan. Today Hidayatullah has formed a League ministry. Unlike last year, he has no fears on account of 'numbers'.

Constitution Of Free India Must Be Made Without Any Compulsion On Her People

January 5, 1947, New Delhi: Considering the clarification on the interpretation of 'grouping' and 'sections' biased and against the fundamental principle of provincial autonomy, the Congress Working Committee had issued a comprehensive statement on 22nd of this month. Now AICC has met and endorsed that statement.[236]

AICC has made it clear that the Congress has always been in favour of referring disputes relating to interpretation to the Federal Court. But recent announcements by the British government have rendered such a course purposeless. Such a reference could be made by parties on an agreed basis, with both agreeing to abide by the decision given but that prospect seemed to be non-existent in the aftermath of the British government's latest statement.

The AICC has opined that the constitution of the free and independent India must be framed by her people on the basis of as wide an agreement as possible and that, without any interference by any external authority and compulsion on a province or any part of it by another province. It pointed out that the scope for such compulsion indeed existed in respect to people of Assam, NWFP, Baluchistan and the Sikhs in the Punjab.

However, in order to ensure that the constituent assembly can proceed with its task without being afflicted by the problems arising out of varying interpretations, the AICC has agreed "to advise action in accordance with the interpretation of the British Government in regard to the procedures to be followed in the 'sections'."[237] But it simultaneously made clear that this must not involve of any compulsion on a province or part of a province. And in the event any such attempts being made, the province or the part of the province would have 'the right to take such actions as may be deemed necessary in order to give effect to the wishes of the people concerned'.[238]

Political analysts feel that the AICC has gone for a collision course, with both His Majesty's Government and the League on this issue. This virtually rules out the League's participation in the constituent assembly's proceedings.

Wavell's Days Are Numbered As Viceroy?

January 8, 1947, London, Delhi: India and Burma Committee had rejected the 'breakdown plan' already. It was felt the plan would lead to an inexorable division of India in two or more parts, which was not desirable. However, thereafter the committee met a couple of days ago and decided to keep the 'breakdown plan' in reserve to be used only in case of emergency.

In that context, the League's continuing rigid stand about boycotting the constituent assembly threatened the schedule of power transfer and compelled HMG to have a second thinking on Wavell's plan. Today, Attlee has conveyed his government's decision to Wavell and requested the latter's presence in London to review the situation. However, Wavell is already back in India. He is unlikely to accept Attlee's invite knowing that his plan has been given a nice burial for all practical purposes. Worse, he realises he has forfeited the trust of the British government. He knows that his days as Viceroy in India are numbered and he will have to go back to Britain as a failure.

Constituent Assembly Resolves To Proclaim India An Independent Sovereign Republic

January 22, 1947, New Delhi: The constituent assembly held its second meeting here. As anticipated, the Muslim League boycotted the proceedings. The objective resolution was introduced by Jawaharlal on 13th last month. It was passed today.[239] It said that the constituent assembly solemnly resolves to proclaim India as an independent sovereign republic and draw up a constitution for future governance. It also pronounced the assembly's intention to bring into the independent sovereign India, entire British India, Indian states and other parts of India which are outside British India and other states and territories willing to be constituted into India.

Punjab Boils, Muslim League Cadres Fight Pitched Battle With Government Forces

January 24, 1947, Lahore: Right since the time Khizr Hayat Tiwana formed the coalition government partnering with the Congress and the Akali Dal, his relationship with the Muslim League has been reaching a new low. Failure to form the government despite being the single largest party in the legislature and also losing the Unionist party, its erstwhile ally, to rivals Congress and Akali Dal, have been stinging the League leadership. Throughout last one year, the League has been organising protests and processions against the coalition government on various pretexts, particularly on communally sensitive issues. It has also been actively promoting the Muslim League National Guard (MLNG), an armed band of volunteers who could be used effectively in the events of communal conflagrations. On its part, the Khizr government, because of its dependence on the Congress and the Akalis, has been compelled to take tough actions against protests and agitations, especially those based on communal programmes undertaken by the League and the MLNG.

On the 7th of this month the feud between the two parties became grave over a by-election to the assembly in Dera Ghazi Khan, where the League candidate had a fair chance of winning. On the election day the government clamped Section 144 reportedly for administrative reasons. But the League construed it was a deliberate act to influence the voters against the League.

Since then, series of confrontations have been going on between the League activists and the police. To prevent communal tension from rising further, the Khizr government yesterday banned both the Muslim League National Guard and Rashtriya Swayam Sevak Sangh. Things came to a head today when the police, acting on a tip off, went to search the headquarters of Muslim League National Guards in the city. In course of the search operations, seven top leaders of the League tried to obstruct the police and they were rounded up. As the news spread in the city, the students of local Islamia College turned up on the streets and staged wild agitation against the government.

Khizr Government Striking At The Root Of Civil Liberties: Jinnah

January 26, 1946, Karachi: Today Khizr government has released the arrested senior leaders of the Muslim league. They included, amongst others, eminent leaders like Khan of Mamdot, Feroz Khan Noon, Shaukat Hayat Khan and Begum Shah Nawaz. The government's action against these popular leaders has been creating Muslim sympathy wave in favour of the League in Punjab. In a statement issued from here, Jinnah has sharply criticised the Khizr government for declaring the MLNG an unlawful organisation and indulging in steps that he alleged, struck at the root of the civil liberties.

Congress Serves Ultimatum: Expel League Or We Quit

February 12, 1947, New Delhi: Led by Liaquat Khan, the Muslim League members have been pursuing a deliberate policy of obstructionism while being a part of the interim government. The Congress is finding the pinpricks too much to bear. It feels that governance itself is becoming a casualty. For own reasons, the League has not been participating in the constituent assembly. This has been adding to the tension between the two parties.

The Congress has a grudge that the League, after having rejected the Cabinet Mission proposal in July last year, was allowed to join the government without formally accepting the Plan again. Nor did it give an undertaking to take part in the constituent assembly. A week back, nine non-League members of the interim government had jointly written to the Viceroy that the League, which had not accepted the Cabinet Mission Plan, could not continue in the government. Today, Jawaharlal has stepped up the pressure. He has threatened that unless a decision is taken on this issue, Congress would leave the government.

British Rule To Come To An End By June 1948

February 20, 1947, London: Jawaharlal's threat seems to have created pressure upon the HMG. However, it has no clear cut solution to offer. It does not want nor can it afford to remove the League ministers as this would have huge political ramifications in an already communally surcharged country. At the same time, it also cannot let the Congress walk out.

The consequences of that could be simply catastrophic. In these circumstances, prime minister Clement Attlee has been able to deflect the issue somewhat by an announcement[240] in which he has stated about HMG's intention to transfer power to the responsible Indian hands not later than June 1948. He added that if by then, a fully representative constituent assembly fails to draw up a constitution in accordance with the proposals of Cabinet Mission, His Majesty's Government would consider to whom the powers should be handed over—central or provincial governments—one or more sovereign governments.

The Viceroy would carry out this exercise in consultations with Indian political parties and by discovering the Indian public opinion expressed through possible ways like plebiscite or vote of legislative assemblies.

Clearly, by this statement the HMG has re-transferred the pressure upon Indian political parties, especially the Congress, which has been keen on a strong centre and united India.

Mountbatten To Be New Viceroy Of India

February 20, 1947, London: Today, British prime minister Clement Attlee has announced the appointment of Lord Mountbatten as the new Viceroy of India. He would shortly replace Lord Wavell. HMG expects the moribund political processes in India to get a new lease of life with this strategic change.

CAN THE NEW VICEROY DELIVER?

The appointment of Lord Mountbatten, as the new Viceroy of India has surprised many, but has raised lesser controversy and criticism than when he was elevated from a naval captain to the chief of combined operations in 1942. Criticism against him around that time got iouder, when he was, in the very next year, elevated as the supreme commander of the SEAC because as the chief of combined operations, he had indulged into a highly questionable campaign in Dieppe, courting unprecedented disaster for the Allied forces at enemy's hands. However fortune at last smiled on him after he took over as the supreme commander of the SEAC. Thanks to few brilliant generals, especially William Slim, Mountbatten managed to secure for the British series of decisive victories over the Japanese in Southeast and East Asia. Post the victories in 1944 & 1945, Mountbatten reached pinnacle of popularity in Britain.

Many political analysts tracking Mountbatten's career over last two decades, are however, not quite sure about his suitability for the present assignment. They see him as a person who is charming and courageous but overconfident, dangerously ambitious, 'publicity mad' and ever-engaged in quest of personal glory. Mountbatten has blood connection to several royal families of Europe including, of course, England and has remarkable rapport with King George VI, who happens to be his cousin. His royal pedigree has given him several advantages, but unfortunately, it probably has made him less sensitive about the value of lives of ordinary humans. Such insensitivity was repeatedly displayed by him during the war campaigns he had carried out as the commander. Those no doubt signified raw courage, and passion for victory, but also poor strategy and of course scant concern for human lives including those of his own marines and soldiers. There is little reason to think that such basic personal traits in him have changed since then.

These analysts point out that Mountbatten, by virtue of enjoying the confidence of the British King George VI, prime minister Attlee and opposition leader Churchill, would carry a blank cheque from Britain's political establishment. This is a huge advantage to begin with. However, it remains to be seen as to how he would use these in the matter of political negotiations. They apprehend that driven by his innate traits and military background, he may strive to hammer out a political solution in India rather expeditiously at the cost of long-term interests of the Indians. Not only does he have personal limitations, he would also be under pressure from the British government to hasten. Significantly, the British government is almost exasperating under pressure of rising communal violence, intense rivalry between Congress and the League, the gradual withdrawl of British forces from India and the rising alienation of the Indian armed forces. The British are in a hurry to get out of this country, keeping its image and long term interests as intact as possible and it therefore wants a Viceroy who can deliver this objective—the end is important and not the means. It is hoping Mountbatten will help achieve this precious goal, better than any other.

Shyamaprasad Intensifies Call For Hindu Bengal

February 1947, Calcutta: The announcement of the British cabinet that the Viceroy would, in the matter of transfer of power, consider public opinion, has encouraged Shyamaprasad, the leader of Hindu Mahasabha, to launch a strong campaign for division of Bengal into Hindu majority west and Muslim majority east so that Bengali Hindus have at least a part of the province. He has been much upset by the ongoing efforts by some leaders at carving out an independent united Bengal. In a statement issued recently, he insisted that the British must transfer power to a strong central government in respect of the whole of British India. He has vehemently opposed cutting of Bengal from the rest of India, which, he said would perpetually enslave thirty five million Hindus to an artificial majority. He asserted that Hindus will resist any such attempts with their blood. Understandably, Shyamaprasad's extra-ordinary determination has arisen in the aftermath of the Calcutta riots and Noakhali massacre under the active encouragement of the Muslim League government. He feels the League has permanently forfeited the trust of the Hindus.

In view of the ongoing developments, the Hindu Mahasabha, although against the vivisection of India on principle, is insisting that Bengal must be divided between Hindu majority west and Muslim majority east so that Hindus have at least one part of Bengal to control, whether in a federated undivided India or as a part of the partitioned India.

League's Civil Disobedience Turns Violent In NWFP

February 21, 1947, Peshawar: With the prospect of the British exiting the country in a year or so, the Muslim League has become desperate to win the NWFP, the last bastion that it must have in order to wrest Pakistan. The provincial Muslim League has been stepping up its ante against the Khan Sahib-led Congress government. It has been running a civil disobedience campaign in Peshawar and Mardan. In a violent turn of events, today a 5000-strong mob, reportedly supporters of Muslim League, forcibly entered the garden house of Dr Khan Sahib and vandalised it while the police refused to fire at the miscreants. The situation in the province is getting increasingly tense by the day.

Liaquat Twists Capitalists' Ears, Congress Moans

February 1947, New Delhi: Liaquat Ali Khan has been improvising means to make life difficult for the Congress. As the finance minister, he has proposed hefty rise in taxes for the large businesses and capitalists, knowing fully well that the latter are the support base of the Congress. It is heard that Liaqaut is proposing to levy 25% taxes on all business profits in excess of one hundred thousand rupees. Apparently a Socialistic measure aimed at doing good to common people by taxing the rich, it disguises his agenda to torment the rival political party[241]. Liaqaut is also hoping to bring about a discord between the Socialist and the right wing groups in the Congress party through this measure.

Squeezed Between League And Coalition, Khizr Quits

March 2, 1947, Lahore: Since the police raided the headquarters of the Muslim League National Guards (MLNG) in Lahore a couple of months ago, the League has been adopting increasingly hostile posture against Khizr Hayat's coalition government. The Provincial League leadership has been emboldened by the support coming from League leaders of other provinces like Sind and Bombay. Abdullah Haroon, a prominent leader from the neighbouring Sind exhorted Muslims in his province to join MLNG and proceed to Punjab to secure civil liberties for the Muslims there. Strong boost came from the central leadership. Jinnah criticised the banning of MLNG terming the action as most high handed and unwarranted striking at the root of civil liberties. He also vehemently attacked the Punjab police's search operations in the MLNG office and arrest of some of the top League leaders.

In a bid to convert the attacks on the MLNG into national issue, the working committee of the AIML had met on 29 January, 31 January and 2 February and demanded that the constituent assembly be dissolved forthwith and also the Congress ministries in various provinces be dissolved too as they have failed to protect the Muslim population.

Buoyed by support from the central leaders, the Provincial League leaders here grew so emboldened that they began to challenge the might of the Khizr Hayat Tiwana government through series of violent agitations. Things came to such a pass that on the 7th day of last month, the police had to arrest 74 Muslim League members of the Assembly. Since then, hell has broken loose. About a fortnight later on the 24th, large number of League members and supporters came out on the streets of Amritsar to stage violent demonstrations. On Cooper street, the unruly mob fought pitched battles with the police. They returned lathis and tear gas of the police with stones and brickbats. Such was the ferocity of the confrontation that more than hundred people were injured and had to be hospitalised. The government was almost taken out of its depth by the viciousness of the incident and had to call in British troops to restore order. Since then, the province has been in the grip of tension.

It was becoming clear that Khizr Hayat Tiwana, squeezed between the coalition partners and the Muslim League, would not be able to bear the pressure for long. Today, he has tendered resignation to the governor.

Native States Represented In Constituent Assembly, Jayprakash Opposes Any Space To Princes

March 2, 1947: There has been a long debate over the mode of representation of the native states in the constituent assembly. While the British government has generally been sympathetic to the princes and agreeable to allow them a significant role in the matter of nomination, both the AISPC and the Congress Socialists have been against giving them space in this regard. Jawaharlal, personally, was for these representatives to be elected by the states' people. However, finally a compromise has been worked out. Jawaharlal as the chairman of the negotiating committee of the constituent assembly agreed to half of the states' representatives to be elected by people, provided that it was left to the states concerned to increase the number of such elected representatives—beyond the fifty per cent, presently agreed. This meant that the princes would still have significant say in the matter of nomination unless they voluntarily agree to a cut in their rights in favour of their subjects. Jayprakash Narayan has severely criticised this arrangement but Jawaharlal highlighted the expedience factor and the AISPC has endorsed his stand.

League Celebrates Khizr's Resignation

March 3, 1947, Lahore: The Muslim League is celebrating the ouster of the Khizr Hayat coalition government as a victory day in various places across Punjab including Rohtak, Ambala, Ferozepur, Gurdaspur, Gujranwala, Attock, Lyallpur, Muzaffargarh, Dera Ghazi Khan, Mianwali, besides Lahore. Today nearly two-hundred thousand workers and supporters of the League including about 500 MLNGs assembled in front of the Mochi gate in the city. In the meeting presided over by the president of the Punjab Muslim League, speaker after speaker called upon the Muslims to join the MLNG and hailed it as the disciplined army of the prospective Pakistan.

It may be recalled that soon after Khizr resigned, Evan Jenkins, the governor of Punjab, made an attempt to install a minority government of the Muslim League but he had to give up in the face of vehement opposition by the Akalis and the Congress. In its aftermath, the disillusioned League has become even more hardened and vocal on the demand for Pakistan. Jinnah has welcomed Khizr's resignation and exhorted the Muslims in Punjab to take the next step—to settle the matter with others including Hindus, Sikhs and the British government[242].

Sikhs Against Hoisting Of ML Ministry, Demand Partition Of Punjab

March 1947, Lahore: Kartar Singh, a prominent leader of the Sikh community has raised the demand for partitioning the province of Punjab. He has made it clear that Sikhs would not tolerate any attempt to hoist a League ministry on Punjab and resist it with all their might. In the meantime, the Sikhs have also been able to convince the Congress to put up the resolution for partitioning Punjab.

Communal Riots Spread Across Punjab, Situation Grim

March 5, 1947, Lahore: Communal ambience in Punjab has begun to deteriorate in the aftermath of the victory day celebration by the League. Master Tara Singh has warned the Sikhs about the sinister designs of the Muslim League and asked them to be prepared to face imminent dangers of communal violence.

The political temperature soared, when as a counter to the League's communal programme, their rivals organised anti-Pakistan demonstration. This led to fierce communal clashes resulting in the death of thirteen persons and injuries to several others. In the communally sensitive areas of Lahore, clashes had begun to erupt soon after the victory day celebration. Now, reports of communal riots are reaching the capital from several other parts of the province like Amritsar, Multan, and Rawalpindi including even the adjoining rural belts. In Amritsar, a mob tried to attack the Golden Temple that provoked the Sikhs no end. The situation is reportedly critical there.

The overall situation in Punjab has turned grave. To make matters worse, the British officials who know their days are numbered have chosen to become 'time servers'. Notwithstanding, the urgency of the situation has compelled the Raj to impose governor's rule in the province under Section 93 with effect from today.

Any Province Or Part Of A Province Willing To Join The Union Cannot Be Prevented: Congress

March 6-8, 1947, New Delhi: Congress Working Committee has met here and considered the rapidly evolving political situation. The committee has adopted few resolutions[243]. In one, it has welcomed Attlee's declaration fixing June 1948 as the time limit for transfer of power. In another, it has (in view of the facts that the ministry in Punjab was coerced to resign by resorting to unconstitutional means and that the province has since been engulfed in fire of communal violence), commended the partition of Punjab in predominantly Muslim and predominantly non-Muslim parts. In a press interview the Congress president hinted that the principle may as well be applied to Bengal. In a third resolution, the committee has invited the AIML for a meeting of representatives of both parties to consider the situation that has arisen and devise means to meet it.

In this connection, the committee sought to address the additional issues that would arise with regard to the applicability of the constitution (in the making at present) to Punjab and Bengal, two Muslim majority provinces both of which seemed to be heading towards partition. It has thus stated in its resolution that the constitution framed by the constituent assembly will apply only to those areas which accept it. The resolution provides that any province or part of a province, which accepts the constitution and desires to join the Union cannot be prevented from doing so. Thus there must be no compulsion either way, and the people will themselves decide their future. This peaceful and cooperative method, the resolution asserted, would be the only way to make democratic decisions with the maximum consent.

Shyamaprasad's Lesson On 'Two Nations' Theory

March 19, 1947, Calcutta: Shyamaprasad, Hindu Mahasabha leader, has issued a statement today saying that the division of Bengal would give two major communities in the province full freedom to develop their own culture and tradition in their respective parts. Both the communities will also surely recognise that it will be in their mutual interest to guarantee full protection to the minorities.

Political analysts say, Shyamaprasad has made Jinnah a victim of his own theory of 'two separate nations'. If Hindus and Muslims are so different that they can not live together in India, the same situation obtains in Bengal and Punjab, both of which have nearly equal numbers of people of the two communities. In fact, Shyamaprasad has gone a step further. In view of the bitter experience of the past, he wants Bengal and Punjab be divided, whether or not, India is partitioned.

Shyamaprasad has been carrying on strong campaign amongst Hindu members of provincial and central legislature in favour of partition. Barring a few like Sarat Chandra Bose and KS Ray most other Hindu leaders, including from the Congress, have been supporting him. Congress Working Committee has already passed resolutions in favour of division of Bengal and Punjab.

Mountbatten Heads For India With Blueprint Of Action

March 20, 1947, London: Mountbatten has started for New Delhi to take over as the new and hopefully the last Viceroy of India. Based on his interactions with and expectations of the British cabinet, he has a blueprint of action in mind. He would give a serious try to resuscitate the Cabinet Mission Plan and transfer power to a unitary government of British Indian provinces and the native states through the medium of the constituent assembly. But he would not force the major parties to fall in line. If this goal cannot be achieved by October, he would suggest alternative measures to transfer power by the due date ie. June 1948. He has special thoughts for the native states. He would urge and hasten them to introduce some form of democratic governance and try for a fair and just agreement with the British India with respect to their future relationship.

Viceroy's Swearing-in Over In Fifteen Minutes

March 24, 1947, New Delhi: British government's eagerness to transfer power to India is public knowledge here. In that context, the appointment and now the arrival of Mountbatten, the new Viceroy, has made the Indian political parties both expectant and simultaneously apprehensive of any bias in favour of the rival or rivals.

His remarkable background, especially his reputation as a man of decision and action is making the native political leaders watch his every move. Mountbatten, on his part, has announced his style of functioning at the swearing in ceremony itself, which was attended by Jawaharlal, Liaquat Ali Khan and other members of the Viceroy's executive council. He took only four minutes to complete his crisp, no-nonsense address and the whole ceremony lasted for a meagre fifteen minutes. It has not been the practice for the Viceroys to deliver speech on such an occasion. His speech, short and loaded, constituted a departure. Two key features were: (a) HMG's determination to transfer power within June 1948; (b) exhortation to all political leaders not to say or do things that might aggravate communal disharmony.

Thereafter, he held two separate meetings with Jawaharlal and Liaquat for long hours to get a first hand feel of the ground realities. Jawaharlal is an acquaintance who visited him at his headquarters at Singapore a year ago while he was the supreme commander of the SEAC and the two had struck some rapport then.

Neither Gandhi nor Jinnah was present in the swearing ceremony. They are however, keeping keen watch over the new Viceroy's agenda, inclination and style, which they may have to encounter soon.

Mountbatten Sets Up Team For His Indian Mission

March 25, 1947, New Delhi: Mountbatten has held his first staff meeting. In attendance were Abell George, private secretary, Captain Brockman, personal secretary, Lord Ismay, chief of the Viceroy's staff, Sir Eric Mieville, principal secretary, Lt Col Erskine Crum, conference secretary and Alan Campbell-Johnson press attaché. He proposes to hold regular round table with these members to get their inputs so that he can think on critical issues without mental reservation. This would be a daily exercise and Mountbatten proposes to process the details of his meetings with Indian leaders through this novel mechanism. Mountbatten had used similar technique during his tenure as the supreme commander of SEAC. In fact, the present mechanism would be a customised and more improved form.

Gandhi Says Partition Will Be Over His Dead Body, But Azad Not Sure

March 31, 1947, New Delhi: Gandhi was camping in the capital of the riot-torn province of Bihar engaged in dousing the communal fire and bringing back amity between two communities. Mountbatten was keen to meet him at the earliest and proposed to bring him to Delhi by his personal aircraft. However, Gandhi, in his characteristic style, refused the offer politely and travelled by railways in the third-class compartment to reach here.

Upon arrival here, he was dismayed to know Patel and Jawaharlal were veering round to Mountbatten's view on the need of partition to facilitate transfer of power. Before Gandhi started for the Viceroy's House, Congress leader MAK Azad had chance to have close interaction with him. Azad, a strong protagonist for 'United India' has been worried these days at the growing clamour for partition and several top Congress leaders' growing tendency to give in to such divisive idea.

In reply to a specific question by an anxious Azad, Gandhi asserted that so long as he was alive he would never agree to the partition of India and if the Congress wished to accept partition, it would be over his dead body. Soon after his return to the residence from the Viceroy's House, he was closeted with Vallabhbhai for over two hours. Azad saw Gandhi after that meeting and noticed perceptible change in him. Gandhi still did not favour partition but 'no longer spoke so vehemently against it'. To his further discomfort, Azad felt Gandhi 'began to repeat the arguments which Sardar Patel had already used'.[244] He has reportedly become nervous because he knows if Gandhi relents, none else can save India from being divided.

'Prevent Partition, Let Jinnah Take Over Government'

April 1, 1947, New Delhi: Soon after landing in Delhi, one of the things Mountbatten wished to do on priority, was to meet Gandhi. He knows that Gandhi has to be convinced about any solution that he may architect for transferring the power.

The first meeting between the two stalwarts was held yesterday. Today they met for the second time. If the first was a courtesy call aimed at knowing each other better, today's tete-a-tete had political contents. Gandhi, while appreciating the sincerity of Mountbatten, felt he would have to face the consequences of the sins of his predecessors. Gandhi emphasised that the British policy of divide and rule has created a situation in which the alternatives were either continuation of the British rule to keep law and order, or an Indian bloodbath. The bloodbath must be faced and accepted, he observed.

Gandhi beseeched Mountbatten not to divide India as the British planned to withdraw. Mountbatten, while sharing his personal assessment of the extant political ambience, asked if Gandhi could suggest any viable alternative to partition. Gandhi then came with an unexpected and seemingly 'out of box' suggestion that the Viceroy may dismiss the present cabinet and call on Jinnah 'to appoint an all-Moslem administration'[245] Mountbatten was amazed at this radical idea and reckoned it impracticable on the face. However, he agreed to give the idea a fair chance provided Gandhi could assure him that the Congress as an organisation would back it up. Today, reporters met Gandhi while he was on his way to his evening prayer. He looked optimistic and lively after many days. He was hoping he would be able to convince his long-time Congress lieutenants on this issue so that the partition of the country can be avoided.

However, reporters who have met some topmost Congress leaders for their reactions, have gathered contrary impression. Most of them seemed to be firmly opposed to Gandhi's idea on this issue.

Hindu Mahasabha Resolution For Bengal Partition

April 4 to 6, 1947, Tarakeswar: In the wake of the rapidly rising communal violence in the country, particularly in Punjab and Bengal, demands for partitioning these provinces have been growing louder. Following the recent massacre of Hindus and Sikhs in Punjab, the Congress had last month adopted a resolution for partition of Punjab into two parts viz. predominantly Muslim and non-Muslim majority areas.

Bengal has been a victim of repeated bouts of communal violence too. Here Hindu Mahasabha has taken similar initiative. It has held its provincial conference here and adopted a resolution[246] for the partition of Bengal. Presiding over the conference, leader NC Chatterjee said it was not a question of partition, but a 'life and death' issue for the Bengali Hindus. Shyamaprasad declared there was no other solution to the communal problem in Bengal than to partition it. The conference adopted a resolution urging His Majesty's Government to allow such portion of Bengal as are desirous of remaining within India to form a separate province within the Union of India.

Jinnah Stays Rigid On Partition

April 5, 1947, New Delhi: Since taking over as the Viceroy, Mountbatten has held the first meeting with Jinnah today. Jinnah, a man of high intellect, a barrister from the Inns Court England, the supreme leader of the Muslim League and one of the key leaders across the entire political spectrum of India, appeared to Mountbatten as formal, cold, reserved and it took considerable time for Mountbatten to unfreeze him. But the first meeting has been enough for him to understand that Jinnah was determined on the issue of partition.

Gandhi Concedes Defeat, Urges Mountbatten To Persuade Congress Leaders

April 11, 1947, New Delhi: Following his second meeting with the Viceroy held on 1 April, Gandhi held discussions with top Congress leaders like Jawaharlal, Vallabhbhai, Kripalani, Rajagopalachari, Rajendra Prasad, Ghaffar Khan and others to bring them around his view to secure the independence for united India.

But he failed to convince them on the issue of making Jinnah the prime minister to prevent the vivisection of India. He had practically no supporters[247]. Today he has written[248] to Mountbatten informing that none except Badshah (Ghaffar) Khan agreed to the proposition. Neither he could convince them nor could they dislodge him from his 'position'.

Sounding resigned, he wrote that he would, henceforth, like to represent only himself, like his friend late Andrews used to do. Gandhi requested: 'Thus I have to ask you to omit me from your consideration' and stated his intention to proceed to Patna.

It is understood from close quarters that to most of Gandhi's colleagues, the proposal seemed to one of unbridled excesses, one that could not be acceded to, even if that meant preserving the hope of independence for a united India.

Today Gandhi also met Mountbatten personally. In a two-hour long meeting between the two, Gandhi urged Mountbatten to go ahead with his plan if he had belief in it. But being the shrewd tactician he is, Mountbatten politely declined, saying he possibly could not expect success with the Congress when Gandhi himself had failed. The Viceroy has reportedly heaved a sigh of relief at Gandhi's retreat. He has excellent rapport with Jawaharlal and he reckons working with the latter would be a much easier task. With Gandhi's withdrawal from the field of negotiation, the prospect of the partition is indeed looming large!

Critics find it strange that Gandhi should abdicate negotiation at the conclusive stage of India's long decades of freedom struggle, undoing all his life's work. He is well aware of the consequences of his resignation.

Governors Brief Governor General, Bad Tidings From Punjab, NWFP

April 15-16, 1947, New Delhi: Mountbatten has been negotiating with the political leaders. Simultaneously, he has called a conference of the governors of eleven British Indian provinces to get an idea of the ground realities and also get a clearer vision into the methods and processes that would be involved for the transfer of power. All incumbent governors except Frederick Burrows from the communally sensitive province of Bengal turned up. Burrows, being ill, sent his representative to advise the new Viceroy.

NWFP, a traditional forte of Congress and Khan Abdul Ghaffar Khan, has undergone a radical change in terms of political ambience since the talk of formation of Pakistan has begun to loom large. The Muslim League in the recent months has been able to communalise the province and it expects to dislodge the Congress in the event a fresh election is held there. In Punjab, another Muslim majority province, the League, frustrated at not getting an opportunity to form the government, has been bent upon engendering communal tension. In both the provinces, the League has been adopting similar strategy. Officially it has been staging civil disobedience movements against the government. However, covertly it has been fuelling communal tension and promoting riots against the minority Hindus and Sikhs. While the governor of the NWFP favoured holding of fresh elections to take cognizance of the new realities, the governors of both Punjab and Bengal advised the Viceroy against the partition of the provinces. Mountbatten has been chalking out a plan for the transfer of power to Indian hands. He has reportedly used this conference to do a reality check on his assumptions.

League Determined To Eject Congress Ministry

April 22, 1947, Peshawar, Muslim League has been keen to deliver a strong message to the new Viceroy that the British have no option but to agree to Pakistan. In a well-planned strategy, it has been hitting the Congress ministry here relentlessly so as to remove the last vestige of the Congress from the Muslim constituency. It has been fomenting trouble across the province at such scale that Khan Sahib led government has been hard put to counter them. The growing belligerence of the League in the form of protests and processions has eventually entrapped the government by making it lose patience. After the administration has put several pro-Muslem League members in prison, the League has begun to garner public sympathy in the province. Today, League supporters resorted to violence in the capital. They cut telephone wires. Women demonstrators barged into the radio station and hoisted the League flag in the All India Radio building. Agitation has also been sweeping large areas of the province including Abbottabad, Bannu, Kohat, Nowshera, Swabi and several other places.

The dominant issue is the demand for fresh election. The League reckons that a landslide victory, which it considers a certainty in the altered political scenario now, will conclusively establish that the Muslims of the NWFP, unlike their leaders viz the Khan Brothers, solidly stand behind the demand for Pakistan.

Forces Are Gravitating Towards Partition?

April 1947, New Delhi: Mountbatten has held several meetings with top political leaders across the spectrum. He has been finding some measures of consensus among the Muslim League and the Congress on the issue of partition. The Muslim League has made it clear to him that they would insist on partition at all costs and fight a civil war if needed than agree to the 'transfer of power' to a Hindu majority Union. In Congress, there is a division on the issue. Though the party has been traditionally against vivisection of the country, its leaders like Jawaharlal, Vallabhbhai and many others have become so frustrated by the obstructionist policies of the League in the interim government and the blatantly communal policies of the League in general, that they have almost become reconciled to partition provided no coercion was brought upon people and no non-Muslim community was made to go to Pakistan against its own will.

Mountbatten is therefore finding partition to be the easiest solution for transfer of power within the given time limit. It looks he may go ahead with this option because the alternative of building a consensus for a united India would be a Herculean task, even if this might be beneficial for all communities.

The new Viceroy however has to cross a big hurdle—he has to convince Gandhi or at least neutralise him. He knows Gandhi has been firm against division of the country. He also knows that Gandhi, the tallest leader in India still has immense mass appeal.

Rajendra Prasad Turns Partition Of Punjab And Bengal Into An Open Question

April 28, 1947, New Delhi: The constituent assembly has begun its third session in the Constitution Hall here. Although the League continued to boycott the proceedings, the presence of the delegates of important native states including inter alia Baroda, Bikaner, Jaipur, Jodhpur, Udaipur, Cochin, Patiala and Rewa added to the fervour and enthusiasm. The delegates from the states promised to work hard together to frame a worthy constitution. Sir Vijayaraghavachariar, representing Udaipur, expressed the mood saying that all members would put their heads together and do a work that will be acknowledged by the posterity and the history would say: 'Blessed are these men; they did their work and they laid the foundations rightly, and on these foundations will the future history of India evolve.'

At the same time the intransigence of the League and Jinnah's dogged pursuit of the goal of Pakistan with the new Viceroy cast large measure of uncertainty over the proceedings of the assembly. HMG's punchline that it would not impose a constitution that is made without participation by a large section of the Indian population upon any unwilling parts of the country, has raised several questions. There are reports that the League, emboldened by HMG's stand, has been hoping to be able to extract its cherished land of Pakistan including the whole provinces of Punjab and Bengal. Rajendra Prasad, president of the assembly, while addressing the delegates sought to deliver the message that such a goal was completely unattainable.

He acknowledged that even though Congress had accepted the Statement of May 16, 1946, '…it may be that the union may not comprise of all the Provinces' …'If that unfortunately comes to pass,' Prasad continued, 'we shall have to be content with a constitution for a part of it'. But in such an eventuality, Prasad hinted that the same golden principle of not imposing a constitution on any unwilling part of the country must apply to parts of Punjab and Bengal as well. He put it succinctly: 'In that case we can and should insist that one principle will apply to all parts of the country and no constitution will be forced upon any unwilling part of it. This may mean not only a division of India, but a division of some Provinces.'

With Prasad's politically loaded statement, the Congress has made it clear that the question of partition of two Muslim majority provinces of Punjab and Bengal is wide open now.

Suhrawardy Plan For United, Independent Bengal

April 26, 1947, New Delhi: Suhrawardy has met Mountbatten here and contended that the Bengalis want to remain united in an independent state. He has presented to the Viceroy a scheme[249] for united, independent Bengal, to be a third state in addition to India and Pakistan. He has conceived the scheme along with other Bengali leaders like Kiran Shankar Ray, Abul Hashim, SR Bakshi and Mohammad Ali Chaudhury. He has claimed that the plan has been endorsed by Jinnah. Territorially ambitious, his plan proposes to include some parts of Assam and Bihar in the proposed state of United Independent Bengal.

It is reported that Burrows, the British governor of Bengal, is also backing the plan. The governor thinks this would be his parting gift to the people of the province. Burrows, is keen, that Calcutta remains a prime port and he has suggested some kind of international arrangement to maintain its importance.

It is being learnt that Mountbatten has responded to the plan cautiously. He has asked Suhrawardy to prove that it has wide support. To the overenthusiastic governor, the Viceroy is reported to have advised to adopt all India view and not be swayed by province-centric considerations.

Suhrawardy's Plan Gets Jinnah's Endorsement

April 26, 1947, New Delhi: Suhrawardy's 'United Independent Bengal' proposal initially navigated through rough seas, attracting criticism even within the provincial Muslim League. Besides Nazimuddin, his arch rival, Maulana Akram, another top League leader too viewed the plan with consternation. They perceived it as antagonistic to the Lahore resolution, giving call for creating Pakistan comprising Muslim majority provinces. However, such reservations were effectively tackled by Abul Hashim, an ideologue of the League who too strongly advocated for an united Bengal, though his views differed from Suhrawardy in some respects and he saw Bengal as a Bengali Muslim state, comprising both Muslims and Hindus, though uniting with Indian confederacy. He contended that the Lahore resolution did not, at the first place, envisage creating an 'Akhand' Pakistan. On the contrary, it provided for Muslim majority areas in the northwest and the east of the country to be grouped while they would constitute autonomous sovereign states. The united independent Bengal would much fulfil that condition.

However, since 'Pakistan' per se is still an emotive issue with the Muslims in general, Hashim sought to neutralise its impact upon Bengali Muslims by playing upon their fear of domination by their co-religionists from the western parts and also suppression of Bengali by the Urdu language in the event the partitioned Bengal with Muslim majority joined Pakistan as its part.

At the all-India level, Suhrawardy's Bengal plan has picked up momentum after Jinnah gave his nod. Today, in his meeting with the Viceroy, Jinnah said he would have no objection even if the united Bengal remained outside Pakistan and hoped it will be in friendly terms with Pakistan. Jinnah has reportedly urged the Viceroy not to destroy the unity of people of Bengal and Punjab which have common national characteristics such as language and culture cutting across religion. With Jinnah taking active interest in the plan, Suhrawardy's adversaries in the League are falling in line too. An added advantage has been the support line extended by Ispahani and other Muslim industrialists and businessmen with business interests in Calcutta and western parts of Bengal. They are lending strong, firm support for a united, independent and sovereign Bengal for their own reasons.

If Hindus And Muslims Can Live Peacefully In Bengal, Why Not In India – Suhrawardy Fumbles For Answer

April 27, 1947, Delhi: Suhrawardy has held a press conference here today. He issued an emotional appeal to the people of Bengal holding out the vision of a golden future for the United Independent Bengal—of being more prosperous than the rest of the sub-continent. He also promised that the government of the proposed state will cater to the aspirations of all sections of people. He declared his willingness to go 'very very' far to meet the wishes of the Hindus in Bengal if they accepted the principle of a sovereign independent Bengal. However, he failed to give satisfactory reply to a journalist who questioned him if Hindus and Muslims can live peacefully in Bengal, then why cannot they do so in India.

It is being heard that Suhrawardy has been trying to secure the support of top leaders of Congress and the League for his plan. Whereas Jinnah is reported to have blessed it, Gandhi has not. He has doubts about Suhrawardy. Planned carnage in Calcutta and Noakhali cast serious doubts about Suhrawardy's intentions and credibility. The Congress has already passed resolution for division of Bengal. Shyamaprasad has attacked this plan saying that Suhrawardy is using it as a strategy to eventually bring the greater Bengal into the fold of Pakistan.

Bengali Hindus Stage Unprecedented Protest Against 'United Bengal' Plan

April, 1947, Calcutta: Rumours of a 'United Independent Bengal' are floating thick and fast. Majority of Hindus in the province are getting increasingly restive. Reports are trickling where even Jinnah is backing Suhrawardy on the plan and he has held parley with the Viceroy. These are adding to their panic. To most of the Hindus in the province, the Muslim League has lost its credibility, thanks to the monumental contribution by Suhrawardy towards that end in more than one way. He started the process as the supplies minister in the League ministry in the early 1940s when he displayed blatant communal bias in providing relief to the famine victims. He escalated the communal politics further while forming his cabinet last year when he broke the long tradition of 'parity' in the cabinet by drastically reducing the number of Hindu ministers. The flash point was reached when Suhrawardy planned the ghastly communal riots in Calcutta in the wake of the Direct Action Day and thereafter encouraged the brutal massacre of innocent, hapless Hindu peasantries in Noakhali. In the aftermath of such communally surcharged politics practised by the League, the majority of the Hindus are looking at the plan of United Bengal as one of eternal rule by the Muslim League and successive decimation of Hindu lives, property and honour. Large numbers of Hindus in the province are therefore organising themselves and protesting. They realise they must stall the plan 'here and now'. They want Bengal to be partitioned and the Hindu majority part to join India, which alone, they believe, would be able to provide security and safety to them.

Shyamaprasad, heading the Hindu Mahasabha, has emerged as the undisputed leader of this movement. He has been able to mobilise most of the Hindu legislators—central and provincial—cutting across political spectrum in support of the movement for partition of Bengal. Significantly, a few days after the Hindu Mahasabha adopted a resolution in favour of partition early this month, the Bengal Provincial Congress Committee has announced the general principle of partition. Under Shyamaprasad's dynamic and energetic leadership, demand for the partition are being raised by various sections of Bengali Hindus—students, professionals, businessmen, shopkeepers, municipal bodies, union boards, trade associations, zamindars' association, bar association, rate payers' association, and even local clubs etc. People in tens of thousands are signing and sending petitions to the Viceroy. Even illiterates are not lagging behind. They are affixing thumb impressions. On the whole, the response is pervasive and unprecedented.

Pakistan Wave Sweeps NWFP, Congress Government In Tight Spot

April 28-29, 1947, Peshawar: The situation in the NWFP is becoming worse by the day. Muslim League's demand for fresh elections is growing strident. Under the indulgent eyes of the local

British officials, the League has been conducting civil disobedience movement in the province building up unrest and chaos. Although the Congress is presently holding power, the Muslim Leaguers are certain to reap large dividend from the 'Pakistan' wave, if a fresh election is held. The League is effectively playing upon the fear in the people of a Hindu majority centre in the event of a Congress win and the province tagging with India. New Viceroy Mountbatten just concluded a two day-visit here and he could sense popular support surging in favour of the League. Strong pro-Pakistan demonstration was organised by the League during his visit, reportedly to impress upon him the need for holding fresh elections without delay.

Riot-ravaged Kahuta – A Standing Testimony Of Bestial Communal Massacre

April 29, 1947 Kahuta: Right since last month, Punjab has been witnessing wide scale communal riots. The Muslim League, angered for not being able to form the ministry in the province has been organising communal massacres at several places in the province, particularly in western Punjab. Rawalpindi has been the worst affected where killings of Hindus and Sikhs have been most rampant and all forms of atrocities have been also been committed on these two communities for weeks together.

Last month, Kahuta, a small, quiet hamlet, hardly 25 miles away from Rawalpindi witnessed unprecedented communal violence. Inhabited by two thousand Sikhs and Hindus and about one and a half thousand Muslims, living peacefully for ages and sustaining the village economy by working together and through mutual co-operation, Kahuta witnessed its entire human habitation wiped out in one deadly night. A horde of armed Muslim fanatics swooped on the village like bolt from the blue, and put fire to all the Sikh and Hindu homes. They also stood guard, caught hold of all those who made a bid to escape, tied and burnt them. The fire eventually reached the Muslim houses as well. By morning, the entire village was reduced to heaves of debris.

Today, on his way back from Peshawar, in the NWFP to Delhi via Rawalpindi, Mountbatten was brought to the site by Evan Jenkins, the Punjab governor. The razed down town declared loudly the extent to which communal hatred has possessed the people, like evil spirit.

PUNJAB IS BURNING

Right since the resignation by the Khizr government, Punjab has been under the rule of the governor and in the throes of intense communal violence. The League had been very keen to form the next government so that it could hasten the birth of Pakistan, but its opponents, all of whom put together happened to be numerically superior in the legislative assembly, were equally determined not allow this to happen. The frustration and anger of the League have been manifesting in the form of relentless acts of communal violence. In the western and central parts of Punjab where the Muslims are in large majority, the Hindus and the Sikhs have been facing unprecedented communal atrocities. Their miseries are indeed grave because indifferent British officials, under a partisan governor, have been insensitive to the ongoing persecution. The wave of violence against the religious minorities is travelling to the neighbouring province of the NWFP as well.

Jinnah Resents 'Moth Eaten' Pakistan, Demands Whole Group B And C Provinces

April 30, 1947, New Delhi: Congress Working Committee has earlier passed resolutions calling for partition of Bengal and Punjab segregating their non-Muslim majority areas, the intent being delimiting and restricting the areas that are likely to join Pakistan. This upset Jinnah's calculations. He is very unhappy at the prospect of getting what he calls as 'moth eaten' country for the Muslim. He has now launched a campaign against the truncated Pakistan. Jinnah is demanding that

Pakistan should comprise of all provinces included in groups B and C of the Cabinet Mission Plan, which would mean Sind, Punjab, NWFP, Bengal and Assam besides the native state of Baluchistan.

But Rajendra Prasad has objected to Jinnah's new aspirations. While presiding over the third session of the constituent assembly, he clarified in a press conference that the Lahore resolution of 1940 spoke of Pakistan as comprising of areas where Muslims were numerically in the majority. The hint is that the resolution did not conceive of 'province as a whole'. Rajendra Prasad, in this connection, has also emphasised the division of the provinces, a well-known Congress stand, on which it had already adopted resolutions.

TWISTS AND TURNS: TALE OF FOUR INDIAN LEADERS

In 1944 and 1945, the Muslim League seemed to have been riding on the crest of a wave of political success. Its bonhomie with the British regime to the exclusion of the Congress had emboldened its ambition of claiming all five Muslim majority provinces including of course Bengal and Punjab in their entirety as part of the proposed Pakistan. On the other hand, the Hindu Mahasabha had been opposing the demand for Pakistan vehemently as it implied the division of the country. As to the Congress, Gandhi was somewhat accommodative. He was willing to concede Pakistan but in a truncated form on the basis of Rajagopalachari's formula. Political analysts point out in more details the interesting shift of positions by leaders and parties over the period 1944-1947

In 1944 Rajagopalachari, a pragmatic Congress leader of keen intellect was in favour of acceding to the demand for Pakistan but his formula provided for cutting away from two of its constituent provinces viz., Bengal and Punjab, those areas having non-Muslim majority population. At that time this proposition was vehemently opposed by Shyamaprasad, leader of Hindu Mahasabha, who was strictly against the vivisection of India. Gandhi, however, was convinced of its merit and he travelled to Jinnah's home urging him to accept it. Jinnah, sitting at the centre stage of Indian politics chose to turn down Gandhi's offer, hoping that he would be able to wrest all the five Muslim majority provinces in their entirety as components of Pakistan. Now in 1947, Shyamaprasad has reconciled with the inevitability of 'partition' and he has been fighting for wresting the non-Muslim majority areas from Bengal and Punjab almost on the same basis as what was proposed by Rajagopalachari. On his part, Jinnah has to climb down from his high horses and accept the truncated and mutilated Pakistan which he had refused with impunity in 1944 at the face of imploring Gandhi. No less interestingly, Gandhi himself, who had then gone to Jinnah agreeing to Pakistan proposal, is now keen to avoid the vivisection of India, by any means.

Ismay, Abell To London With 'Plan Balkanisation'

May 2, 1947, New Delhi: Today, Hastings Ismay and George Abell have left for London under instructions of Mountbatten. Ismay would present the 'Plan Balkan' to the British government for its approval. According to sources, the cardinal feature of this plan is the 'freedom of choice' allowed to the provinces of the British India as well as over five hundred princely states. While these provinces could join either India or Pakistan, Bengal and Punjab would have the freedom to split if they were divided in their choice. The chief attraction for the Indians would be extensive freedom of choice and rapid transfer of power.

Dream Of United India Almost Buried, Gandhi And Jinnah Appeal For Communal Peace

May 6, 1947, New Delhi: Gandhi has been a worried person. His dream of united, independent India is almost buried. His own lieutenants have refused to toe his line—to allow Jinnah take over the government to avoid vivisection of India. Now the only person who can ensure united India is Jinnah himself, by withdrawing the League's demand for Pakistan. The rising incidents of communal disturbances, mostly a result of political machinations, are another cause of great concern. Gandhi came down to Jinnah's residence at Aurangzeb Road to find out the last ray of hope. On the main issue, ie. preventing partition, he was thoroughly dismayed. After three hours long meeting, Jinnah released a press statement which said it all:

'We discussed two matters. One was the question of division of India into Pakistan and Hindustan, and Mr Gandhi does not accept the principle of division. He thinks that division is not inevitable, whereas, in my opinion, not only is Pakistan inevitable but this is the only practical solution of India's political problem.

'The second matter which we discussed was a letter which we both have signed jointly appealing to the people to maintain peace...'[250] Political analysts say with this meeting and the joint statement, probably the last nail has been driven into the coffin of the Cabinet Mission Plan.

'Plan Balkanisation' Devastates Jawaharlal, Mountbatten Does Damage Control

May 11, 1947, Simla: After sending his emissaries to London with the 'Plan Balkan', Mountbatten arrived here with his family five days ago. Eric Meville and VP Menon also accompanied, giving him the opportunity to hold informal talks in the cool comfort of a hill station while a scorching summer was sweeping the northern Indian plains. His most important guest of course, has been Jawaharlal who arrived here on the 8th, together with Krishna Menon. Last night post dinner, the Viceroy, acting on hunch had shown him the copy of the 'Plan Balkan' as revised and approved by London, probably to get a feel of the likely Congress response.

According to sources, this made things topsy turvy. Jawaharlal was extremely upset, going through it. He felt the revised draft constituted a major departure from the one that was earlier drafted and taken by Ismay and Abell to London. He had a chance to see that. It envisaged India as successor to British India and others as seceders. The revised one clearly held out the prospect of India getting fragmented into pieces. Jawaharlal made no efforts to disguise his strong disapproval and resentment. Realising that the Congress non-acceptance of this plan would send the process of transfer of power back to square one, Mountbatten reportedly agreed to revise it.[251] Sources claim that the new plan provides for only two successor dominion states of India and Pakistan to be carved out of the British India after partitioning Punjab and Bengal while the princely states are required to join either of these two dominions. The sources inform that Mountbatten has kept the 'new plan' confidential. The Muslim League or Jinnah have no clue to this momentous development. However, Mountbatten expects the new plan to be acceptable to them for it provides for Pakistan, even if truncated.

The chief demerit of the plan, from the Congress point of view, lay in the fact that it envisaged transfer of power to two 'dominion' states, while the party has been, right since Karachi session, demanding 'complete independence'. But the issue was explained to Jawaharlal as rather technical. He has been persuaded that the dominion state was as good as fully independent and it was entitled to frame its future constitution in the manner it liked. While the demerits were technical, the chief merit of the new plan was 'rapid transfer of power'. Jawaharlal has been convinced, so also Vallabhbhai. Though the latter is not now in Simla, VP Menon has been in close touch with him all the while and the changed scheme reportedly has his nod.

I Will Use Tank And Aeroplanes To Crush Communal Clashes: Mountbatten

May 14, 1947, Simla: Jawaharlal and Vallabhbhai Patel have already made their opinions known in favour of the partition. The ongoing interactions between Mountbatten and Jawaharlal here also confirm that negotiations are heading towards that end. Gandhi does not want the partition, but he has practically no listeners. Maulana Azad, ex-president of Congress shares many concerns of Gandhi including especially the prospects of widespread communal violence following the partition. Azad visited Mountbatten at the latter's viceregal lodge in Simla to express his fears of bloodbath that would entail the partition. However, in his characteristic no-nonsense style Mountbatten has assured Azad that he would resist any such attempts with iron hand and in fact, nip them in the bud. He said, 'At least on this one question I shall give you complete assurance. I shall see to it that there is no bloodshed and riot ... I shall not use even the armed police. I shall order the Army and the Air Force to act and use tanks and aeroplanes to suppress anybody who wants to create trouble.'[252]

Mountbatten Rushes To London With 'Revised Plan'

May 18, 1947: By the time Mountbatten chalked out the alternate plan that fetched endorsement of Jawaharlal, his earlier 'Plan Balkan' was approved by the British cabinet. The Viceroy's sudden overhauling of the earlier plan antagnoised them. Eventually, Mountbatten has managed to incorporate in it a trump card to impress upon both the British cabinet as well as the opposition leaders. He would project that he has been able to secure the consent of Jawaharlal and the Congress to accept dominion status for India even if for a limited period. From the British point of view, this would be of considerable importance. The Congress acceptance of the 'dominion state' offer, even after several decades of bitter struggle, lent the Empire with exceptional glory. According to some sources, Edwina Mountbatten, the wife of the Viceroy, endeavoured to make Jawaharlal to agree to this concessional gesture. Mountbatten has today flown to London with the 'Revised Plan'. VP Menon, the Reforms Commissioner is accompanying him.

Sarat Bose Presents Plan For Free Sovereign Socialist Republic Of Bengal

May 20, 1947, Calcutta: Sarat Chandra Bose is firmly against partition of India and Bengal, both. He has been of the conviction that the partition is no solution to the ongoing communal problem in India and it would rather add to the distress of both communities. However, now that India's partition has turned into near a certainty, he has been attempting to preserve the unity of Bengal. Today he has unveiled before the Press, his plan for a free, sovereign, Socialist republic of Bengal. Its key features are: (a) adult franchise and joint electorate;

(b) composition of the constituent assembly with thirty members of which sixteen would be from the Muslims and fourteen from the Hindus, (c) legislature to be elected after the constitution is framed; (d) elected legislature to decide Bengal's relations with rest of India, (e) coalition ministry with equal number of ministers from Hindus and Muslims, (f) equality in the services between Hindus and Muslims for the time being; etc. Sarat Bose feels socialism will be the effective shield against communalism. He is trying to secure the support of Gandhi, Jinnah and other top leaders for this plan. Though Sarat's plan like Suhrawardy's, aims at preventing the division of Bengal, there are differences as well. Notwithstanding, some distinguished leaders like Abul Hashim, Kiran Shankar Ray, and Mohammad Ali Chaudhary have pledged their support for both the plans.

Jawaharlal Blasts Jinnah's Demand For A Corridor

May 24, 1947: While Viceroy Mountbatten is in England, busy discussing with the British cabinet and opposition leaders the revised plan for transfer of power, Jinnah literally exploded a bombshell in India three days ago by demanding a long corridor of 800 miles that would connect the West and the East Pakistan. Jinnah gave expression to his new demand in the form of an answer he gave to a question put up by Doon Campbell of the international news agency, Reuters.[253] Thanks to the extensive network of this globally reputed agency, his demand is being widely circulated.

Jinnah's statement has attracted a strong reaction from Jawaharlal. In an interview given today to the United Press of America, he vented his irritation: 'Mr Jinnah's recent statement is completely unrealistic and indicates that he desires no settlement of any kind. The demand for a corridor is fantastic and absurd...'.[254] He also gave a summary appraisal of his political adversary's strategy saying that Jinnah accepts what he gets and goes on asking for more.

Political analysts feel that the new demand is a tactical move by Jinnah to test water. The strong reaction it has evoked in the Congress, however, indicates an early demise of the proposal.

Plan 'Partition' Approved By British Government, Mountbatten Arrives In Delhi

May 31, 1947, New Delhi: Mountbatten got the assent of the British cabinet to the 'plan partition'. He has arrived in Delhi from London with the crucial 'go ahead' signal. In Britain, he was able to convince not only the Labour leaders but even Churchill, the Conservative Party leader. Mountbatten has been able to do this almost impossible task of bringing the ruling and opposition leaders in the same platform by highlighting the benefits that would accrue to Britain out of the plan. First, it achieves the purpose of transfer of power in agreement with Indian political parties, and that, well within the time deadline.

Second, the power would be transferred to two dominion states, which is a dilution to Congress' repeated demand for outright independence. Third, the two dominion states would join the Commonwealth, a matter of prestige to Britain. Overall, this arrangement not only ensures an orderly transfer of power but also preserves the future political and commercial interests of Britain.

The Plan Is For Full Freedom HMG Seeks To Reassure Indians

May 31, 1947, London: HMG has approved the 'revised plan' that Mountbatten carried here which envisaged transfer of power to two 'dominion states', India and Pakistan. To convince the Indians that this was for all practical purposes 'complete independence', HMG has issued a statement to reassure them that the plan indeed granted them full freedom.

It added that it has no intention whatsoever, to frame any ultimate constitution for India and it was for the Indians to exercise that right without any fetter. Clearly there would be two constituent assemblies, of India and of Pakistan, who would constitute the legislatures of the two dominion states and to whom HMG would transfer the power.

Sarat Bose's Plan For United Bengal Hits Roadblock

June 1, 1947, New Delhi: Suhrawardy's plan of a united Bengal had floundered at the face of fierce opposition by both Hindu Mahasabha and the Congress. Shyamaprasad had transmuted the pervasive sentiment of the Hindus into determined political opposition. Notwithstanding, the burial of Suhrawardy's scheme, Sarat Bose was hitherto persisting with the plan of an Independent Socialist Republic of Bengal, with active involvement of Abul Hashim, KS Ray and few others. Gandhi had okayed the plan subject to certain safeguards and also assured Sarat that he would discuss the draft with the Congress Working Committee. Gandhi's benevolent approach to the plan was giving Sarat hope.

However, the situation has changed drastically in last few days. Congress has reconciled to the idea of partition between India and Pakistan but it wants no further dilution or division. Its idea is to give Jinnah what is 'must' but at the same time architect a strong, closely knit country from the rest of the territory. Vallabhbhai does not want to give even one inch extra land to Jinnah and Pakistan than what is absolutely necessary. Lending his solid support for the movement by the Hindus in Bengal for partition, he has warned Sarat against falling into the League's trap to convert Bengal as part of a greater Pakistan in course of time. He wanted both Sarat and KS Ray, to stand united on the official policy of the Congress. Vallabhbhai's position has been echoed in the words of Congress president Kripalani: 'All that the Congress seeks to do today is to rescue as many areas as possible from the threatened domination of the League and Pakistan. It wants to save as much territory for a Free Indian Union as is possible under the circumstances….'[255] Political experts feel that with Mountbatten having decided in favour of partition and given the hardened stance of the Congress and particularly Vallabhbhai, Sarat's plan for the Sovereign Socialist Republic of Bengal has practically little chance, if any, to succeed. But Sarat, deeply convinced that the partition would only deepen the miseries of people of both communities, is refusing to give up. He is hoping against hope.

Mountbatten Unveils 'Partition Plan' To Indian Leaders

June 2, 1947, New Delhi: Mountbatten had received the assent of British cabinet for his revised plan ie., 'plan partition' and returned to New Delhi on 31 May. Today he has convened a meeting of Jawaharlal, Vallabhbhai, Kripalani, Jinnah, Liaquat, Abdur Rab Nishtar and Baldev Singh. Before unveiling his partition plan, Mountbatten gave one last chance to these leaders of the Congress, the Muslim League and the Sikhs to resuscitate the Cabinet Mission Plan if they wished. However, each of the Indian leaders stuck to their known positions, leaving 'partition' of the country as the only alternative.

Thereafter, the Viceroy rolled out the details of the plan. Its key features are:

(a) The Congress would have to give up its demand for making a constitution before partition;

(b) Pakistan would get a truncated geographical territory (with Bengal and Punjab divided) as a final and immediate deal;

(c) Both India and Pakistan would get dominion status;

(d) British Indian provinces and the native states are to accede to either India or Pakistan as they choose;

The Viceroy has also made it clear that he expects the leaders of all the three groups to convey their acceptance before the midnight today.

LAST HOPE EXTINGUISHED, GANDHI FAILS MOTHER INDIA

June 2, 1947, New Delhi: Mountbatten, after giving the deadline to the top Indian political leaders to convey their acceptance of the 'Plan Patition' by midnight, was scheduled to meet Gandhi. For the Viceroy Gandhi would be the last but the most difficult hurdle to overcome if his 'Plan Partition' was to go through. The much acclaimed victor of many battles for the Allies in the Southeast Asia in the recently concluded World War was clearly diffident in encountering the proverbial warrior of peace and non-violence, who still held undisputed sway over tens of millions of Indians. It is true that Mountbatten already succeeded in weaning away the Jawaharlal and Vallabhbhai led Congress from Gandhi. It is also true that he had given Gandhi a chance to offer a practical alternative solution and the latter admitted his failure. Yet he knew, Gandhi could never reconcile to the vivisection of India, and that was precisely the cause for his apprehension. Mountbatten was particularly uneasy about Gandhi's 'inner voice' syndrome, which could wake up unpredictably and oppose partition. On the basis of his personal knowledge and understanding of India, Indians and Indian politics, Mountbatten was keenly aware that in the event Gandhi, even if alone, stoutly opposed his scheme of partition, the vast majority of Indians would rally behind. This could, undo all his hard work.

Also waiting for this momentous meeting with trepidation was the vast humanity in the sub-continent. To them, Gandhi was the last glimmer of hope, one who could salvage 'mother India', about to be cut into two pieces by a heartless colonial ruler with the passive co-operation of short-sighted native politicians obsessed with immediacy of power.

Unfortunately for the vast millions of Indians, that last flicker of hope extinguished without even the proverbial 'last minute flare-up'. In the meeting[256] that was conducted in the silence of a graveyard, Gandhi rather than being angry with the Viceroy, seemed to be lamenting for the limitations of his own followers who, without understanding the long term implications of this horrendous decision of partition to both the communities, gave in to the British scheme of expeditious transfer of power. The day being Monday, Gandhi had his traditional vow of silence or 'Maun'. But that did not deter Gandhi from expressing his deep frustration. Scribbling on the back of many used envelopes, Gandhi made it clear that his vow of silence of course allowed him to break it if he were in the company of high officials and had important, urgent matters at hand that warranted deliberations.

There was therefore, full justification for him to break his 'silence' and speak using all his experience, reasoning and skill of persuasion. Notwithstanding, he did not speak a word on such a momentous occasion to the top most government official. Explaining his reticence, Gandhi wrote on one another envelope, 'But I know you don't want me to break my silence.' Gandhi was dismayed, disillusioned by Mountbatten's action in dividing India. But he was heartbroken by the complicity of his own disciples in this act. Before taking leave of the Viceroy, he made a vague but apparently innocuous observation,

'There are one or two things I must talk about, but not today. But if we meet each other again, I shall speak.' These soft, gentle expressions gave out a clear indication of Gandhi's pessimism and his resigned mindset. Whatever these 'one or two things' may be, it was clear, those, in no case, would be a new crusade against partition. As Gandhi's meeting with the Viceroy ended, the last hope of the free undivided India vanished for ever. On his part, Mountbatten heaved a long sigh of relief because the final and the mightiest obstacle to his plan was overcome. After Gandhi was gone, Mountbatten was reportedly waiting for the acceptance letters from the Congress, Muslim League and the Sikhs to the plan of partition, which now appeared to be nothing more than formality.

HMG PROPOSES TO PARTITION INDIA AND QUIT

June 3, 1947, London: HMG has today issued a statement giving the contents of the 'Plan Partition' to which it has already accorded its approval and for which Mountbatten has been able to secure the consent of major Indian political leaders yesterday. HMG has reiterated its intention to transfer power to Indian hands by June 1948 or even earlier on a Dominion status basis. It clarified that it does not intend to frame any ultimate constitution for India, nor does it want to interrupt the working of the existing constituent assembly.

At the same time, the HMG added that it does not want to impose a constitution being prepared on parts of the country unwilling to accept it. In this connection the HMG has referred to the majority population in Bengal, Punjab, Sind and British Baluchistan who have been boycotting the existing Assembly. As a solution, HMG has proposed that a choice must be given to the unwilling population to have a new constituent assembly. Towards that end, the new plan provides for the provincial legislatures of Punjab and Bengal to decide as to if they would wish to have partition of their respective provinces. For this purpose, the respective assembly would meet in two parts—Muslim majority and non-Muslim majority districts. If either of these two segments decides by a simple majority in favour of partition, the province will be divided. However, if any member so demanded, the provincial legislature as a whole could meet before hand and decide which of the constituent assemblies –existing and the proposed—it would like to join in the event the ultimate decision went in favour of remaining united. However, European members would not take part in this process. In terms of the 'partition plan', the Sind Assembly will make its choice which of the two assemblies it would like to join. As regards NWFP though two of its three representatives have been participating in the existing constituent assembly, the province, in view of its special circumstances, will be given an opportunity through a referendum to choose between the two constituent assemblies. It has been left to the Governor General to find out the wishes of British Baluchistan.

The plan also requires the Governor General, in case Punjab and Bengal opt for partition of their provinces, to immediately set up boundary commissions to demarcate their boundaries for the purpose of ceding to India and Pakistan. In the event, the province of Bengal opts for partition, the plan provides for a referendum in the district of Sylhet in Assam as to whether it would like to join East Bengal or remain a part of Assam. In the event it decides to become part of East Bengal and thus Pakistan, a boundary commission shall demarcate the Muslim majority areas in the district and also the Muslim majority areas of the adjoining districts which will then be transferred to East Bengal.

Realities Of Partition Begin To Sink In

June 3, 1947, New Delhi: By last night, the Viceroy has received the formal acceptance of his plan of partition of India from the Congress, Muslim League and the Sikhs. Today, he has held a press conference where he announced the fact of acceptance of the plan in the presence of Jawaharlal, Vallabhbhai, JB Kripalani, Jinnah, Liaquat and Baldev Singh. After the announcement, Mountbatten circulated a thirty four pages closely spaced document on the 'administrative consequences of partition' amongst the leaders. The paper gave an overall view of the enormous administrative challenges that the process of power transfer would place on the two dominion states. According to reports from the Viceroy's officials, the leaders were shocked to realise that they have, now, to come to terms with the stupendous tasks that lay ahead.

Congress Throwing Us To Wolves: Abdul Ghaffar Khan

June 3, 1947, New Delhi: Things are changing very fast. Under a political climate of 'speed' introduced by Mountbatten, the Indian political parties have been required to hasten their decisions. He is in a tearing hurry to complete the power-transfer and has infused his urgency into the top political leaders of the country. Like the proverbial piper of Hamlin, he has been making them follow him. Such has been the hurry that on a number of occasions, the process of decision making in political parties has been turned upside down. Top leaders are first committing themselves and then getting endorsement by the party organisation, sometimes without due deliberations. This new trend at times is creating fissures amongst members and groups.

Today, Khan Abdul Ghaffar Khan, the Congress stalwart of the NWFP got a shock of his life when in a meeting of the Congress Working Committee convened to discuss the issues relating to his province, Gandhi spoke in support of partition. Ghaffar Khan till then had no clue that the Congress had finally consented to the plan of partition. Along with his brother Dr Khan Sahib, he has been keeping the Congress flag aloft in the northwestern border province despite ceaseless acts of hooliganism and communal disturbances engineered by the Muslim League. In fact by continuing to hold the reins of that overwhelmingly Muslim majority province on behalf of the Congress party despite all onslaughts the Khan brothers have been making a strong statement in favour of independence for the unified India. Of course they were vaguely aware of the dilemma on the part of some Congress leaders on the issue of partition. But not even in their dreams could they imagine Gandhi himself would endorse the partition of the country. After shock and surprise came sadness and anger. They felt cheated that they were not even consulted before taking a decision of such monumental importance!

The implication is obvious. The two gallant brothers have so far held out the province against the prowling League, but the Congress has, by agreeing to the partition, pushed them as meat to the League whose leaders had visceral hatred for them. NWFP has been an essential part of Jinnah's scheme of Pakistan. Now that the Congress has literally abandoned the province, the League would attempt to simply devour it. Ghaffar Khan expressed the feeling of having been betrayed by laying bare his heart: 'We Pasthuns stood by you and undergone great sacrifices for attaining freedom but you have now deserted us and thrown us to the wolves...'[257]

To the Khan Brothers, Gandhi was the last hope against partition and now it was gone. In the extant circumstances, the brothers reckon that raising the demand for an independent Pakhtoonistan, even if it is a desperate bid, may give them and the Pasthuns an amulet against Jinnah, Muslim League and Pakistan.

Mountbatten Prepares Indian Princes For 'Inevitable'

June 3, 1947, New Delhi: There had been speculations about the future constitutional position of the native states for long years. More recently many princes had dreamt of independence after the British left India as reward for their age-old loyalty and unstinted support to the Raj in the recently concluded War. Though, the partition plan literally sealed their future as independent sovereign political entities, many of them did not understand its significance. Mountbatten, the man in a tearing hurry, did not waste time to send the message across their community. Today he has conducted a meeting with the State Negotiating Committee in his chamber. Many princes including those of Bhopal, Patiala, Dungarpur, Bilaspur and representatives of Hyderabad, Baroda, Mysore, Kashmir, Gwalior, Travancore, Jaipur, Bikaner etc were present. The Viceroy made efforts to let the reality sink in them.

The audience understood from what the Viceroy said that they had no chance to save their kingdoms. Their only choice was between India and Pakistan. In the circumstances, these distressed royalties were anxious to know if it would be possible to arrange for the paramountcy to lapse before His Majesty's Government transferred the power to the British India. It looked obvious in such an eventuality that they would be able to ensure better terms in exchange of their signing instrument of accession.

PLAN PARTITION ENDS DREAMS OF NATIVE PRINCES

The approach of the British government towards the native states stands to change drastically in the wake of the adoption of the partition plan. For long, the princes have been ardent supporters of and blindly loyal to the HMG and rallied behind it whenever called upon—from World War I to World War II. In return they have been enjoying an unfettered right to rule their subjects as they liked.

The British government exercised some broad control through its 'residents'. In the initial three decades of the present century, even the Indian political parties adopted a soft policy characterised by non-intervention in their internal affairs. However, the experiences of running provincial governments (and later interim government at the centre) have broadened their ambition in terms of annexing these states to the mainland. In the late 1930s, the discomfiture of Gandhi at the hands of the rulers of Rajkot hardened the attitude of the Congress vis-à-vis the rulers of the native states. Another significant development has been the growing aspirations of the subjects of these states for representative and responsible governments.

The States Peoples' Organisations have also been longing for merger of their states with the mainland. Now the Plan Partition by compelling the native states to join either India or Pakistan has completely sealed the fate of their rulers as independent political entities. Even a year ago, the Cabinet Mission Plan held some hope for their independence once the British exited India. The situation is radically different now.

Mountbatten Announces 15 August 1947 For Transfer Of Power; Stuns Everyone

June 4, 1947, New Delhi: In a crowded press conference here on the issue of transfer of power Mountbatten was interacting with journalists from across the world. At the fag end, an Indian journalist asked the Viceroy if he had a definite date in mind for granting of independence to the two dominion states. Though the question, to many, seemed to be premature, Mountbatten in an impromptu reply said he indeed had a date in mind and it would be 15 August this year.[258]

This caused a flutter for no one really expected the Viceroy to even quote a precise date for such momentous event which involved tackling of numerous delicate issues, including holding of referendums, demarcation of boundaries, partition of provinces, splitting of armed forces, allocation of government resources, officials and many others. It was also clear that quite a few of the above were likely to be contested bitterly by the Congress and the League.

According to officials close to the Viceroy, such a spur-of-the-moment reply was not the offshoot of any careful consideration, but the typical mindset of an army General known to take spot decisions. This could, to an extent, have been influenced, according to some sources, by Mountbatten's sentimental attachment to that date which happened to be the date of Japan's surrender to the Allies, exactly two years ago.

This Hurry Could Be Ruinous!

Fixing of the D day for transfer of power as 15 August has been evoking mixed reactions of surprise and anxiety. Significantly, the mandate Mountbatten had from the British government permitted him time upto the end of June 1948.Political analysts say, a meagre period of three months is clearly inadequate to sort out multitude of complicated issues especially when the two major contending parties have deep distrust for each other. Mountbatten would have to literally run through these three months leaving many gaping holes.

They contend that the cost of the needless haste may have to be borne by the vast millions of people of the two dominion states. Unfortunately, the Indian political parties are failing to recognise the implications of this dangerously short time frame. They seem to be obsessed with power that is beckoning them—the sooner the better!

Gandhi Acquits Viceroy, Holds Indians Responsible For Partition

The partition has become a certainty. Gandhi is in gloom and despair. But Mountbatten has sought to convince him that the decision of partition has been made by the Indian politicians, not the Empire. The plan for transfer of power, he tried to persuade Gandhi, conformed to what all Gandhi himself insisted upon viz. non-coercion, self-determination, earliest possible British departure and also Gandhi's sympathetic views on dominion status.

Gandhi seemed to have concurred with the logic. He has attributed the vivisection of the country to the myopic vision and failure of political India including his own disciples rather than the Viceroy or the British government in London. Today, while addressing his prayer meeting here, Gandhi said:'The British Government is not responsible for Partition. The Viceroy has no hand in it. In fact he is as opposed to division as Congress itself, but if both of us - Hindus and Moslems - cannot agree on anything else, then the Viceroy is left with no choice.' [259] Mountbatten is breathing easy at the unconditional acquittal of the British and the Viceroy of the charges of 'partitioning India' by Gandhi, the topmost leader in the subcontinent Continent.

Mountbatten Sets Up Partition Committee

June 7, 1947, New Delhi: Mountbatten had tried to sensitise the Indian leaders about the enormous administrative challenges associated with the partition like allocation of staff, resources, institutions, records and many more between the two dominions. To facilitate the enormous task, he has set up a Partition Committee to be chaired by him with two members each from the Congress and the League while he would act as the chairman.

Congress has nominated Vallabhbhai and Rajendra Prasad to the Committee. Liaquat Ali Khan and Abdul Rab Nishtar will represent the League. Jinnah had initially expressed his reservations for such a body to be set up by the government of India. The task of partitioning the country and her resources between the two successor states constituted the responsibility of HMG, he contended. Mountbatten had difficulty in persuading Jinnah, but he has eventually succeeded.

Better Not Disrupt The Atmosphere Already Created For Partition Of Bengal

June 8, 1947, New Delhi: Sarat Bose's last hope for a united Bengal was buried today. So far Gandhi had promised a sympathetic consideration for it. According to political observers, his soft corner for it stemmed from the fact that he had seen in the plan an inherent logic against the 'partition' of the whole country. But amidst fast paced events, he has changed his mind.

Gandhi today has written to Sarat mentioning that both Jawaharlal and Vallabhbhai are dead against the proposal and that they are convinced it is 'merely a trick for dividing Hindus and the Scheduled Caste leaders' and '...corrupt practices are being resorted to, to get support for the proposal.' Therefore Gandhi has warned Sarat that unless the latter was sure about the bonafide of the scheme and has the assurance of the local Muslim League supported by the Centre, he should 'give up the struggle for unity of Bengal and cease to disturb the atmosphere that has been created for the partition of Bengal'.[260]

Cogress Eager To Accept Mountbatten As Joint Governor General

June 9, 1947, New Delhi: Keeping in view the mammoth administrative challenges that the two dominion states would confront due to and following the partition, the Viceroy's office had mooted out a proposal that Mountbatten should act as the Joint Governor General of both the states for a limited term. With the command over armed forces, administrative and financial resources a Joint Governor General would be able to ensure a peaceful transition, the proposal contended.

The Congress has been agreeable to the proposal, or even to have

Mountbatten as the first Governor General of India alone. Jinnah's position is however not clear as yet. He has been known to be in favour of three Governor Generals - one each for Pakistan and India and the third to be Mountbatten - to act as a supreme arbitrator. But Mountbatten himself has not been ready to assume such a supra-national role.

This issue can be finally resolved after Jinnah says the final word. Political analysts however, consider Jinnah's position on the issue as myopic. They feel, a common Governor General can ensure a peaceful transition. This includes not only managing a large scale cross-border human migration but also other complex issues like division of assets, etc.

No Consensus Despite Gandhi's Appeal AICC Endorses Partition By 29-15 Votes

June 14, 1947, New Delhi: Partition plan has already become irreversible - top Congress leaders have accepted, and the working committee has cleared it. The AICC nod was therefore being seen as formality. However when the AICC met to consider an official resolution moved by GB Pant to divide India, there were criticism, anger and fireworks. Sacred principles in favour of a united India were at the altar of political expediency. It became obvious that on this issue, many in the AICC did not share the thoughts of Jawaharlal, Vallabhbhai and other key decision makers.

They launched bitter attacks even though they knew the partition has become fait accompli. The members from Sind, where a sizeable Hindu population faced the prospect of eternal domination by communal Muslim League, were particularly disconsolate and vocal. Tempers ran high even though Gandhi was present and he urged the members to accept partition. Saying that he himself was against the partition all his life, he felt now a new situation had been created when there was no alternative. He said political realism demanded the acceptance of the Mountbatten plan. Emotions surged and despite Gandhi's appeal there was no unanimity[261]. The resolution was put to vote and passed with 29 voting for and 15 against.

League Rushes Leaders To NWFP Ahead Of Referendum

June 17, 1947, New Delhi: Though a referendum at this time in the NWFP is likely to give a decisive victory in favour of Pakistan constituent assembly due to the hard labour put up by the League to communalise the people, Jinnah is not taking any chance. A committee comprising of Chundrigar, Ghazanfar Ali and two others is being sent to strengthen the League organisation there and ensure a resounding success in the upcoming referendum. On the other hand, the Congress seems to have already conceded defeat.

Bengal Assembly Gives Verdict In Favour Of 'Partition'

June 20, 1947 Calcutta: Today, the Bengal assembly has voted on the issue of the partition. As per procedure, following a joint session, the legislative assembly was to meet in two parts viz. Muslim majority areas and rest of the province, each of them voting on 'partition' separately. The rule of simple majority was to be applied and if, either of the two parts, voted in favour of the partition, the partition of the province would take place.

In the joint session, 126 votes were in favour of joining the new constituent assembly of Pakistan, whereas 90 votes were cast in favour of the extant constituent assembly of India. In groups, the members from the Muslim majority areas in the east have opposed partition by 106-35 votes, whereas those from the non-Muslim areas voted in favour of the partition and the new constituent assembly by 58-21. The import of today's proceedings is clear—Bengal is to be partitioned.[262]

Maharaja Down With Colic Pain!
Viceroy Returns Empty-handed

June 23, 1947, Srinagar: Whereas most of the native states are yielding to the Viceroy's advice and persuasions by the Congress and the League, a few rulers have been vascillating or refusing to join one of the two dominions. These include Kashmir, Bikaner, Hyderabad and Junagadh. Two very large states viz. Kashmir and Hyderabad have almost put their foot down. Though unable to publicly disobey the Viceroy, the rulers of these two states are using various ruses to avoid the issue. According to some unconfirmed reports, the Maharaja of Kashmir has been planning to declare independence for his state. Like Hyderabad, Kashmir is also a huge state albeit with a contrasting demographic profile. Its people are mostly Muslim but a Hindu Maharaja is ruling over the state. Its unique location bordering both India and Pakistan vests it with enormous geo-strategic importance. Mountbatten is convinced that Kashmir will turn to be a source of unending conflict unless it decides to join either of the two dominions by the date of the power transfer. However, the Maharaja is reportedly convinced of his strength to run Kashmir as an independent state. He has also been ruthless in suppressing internal protests and dissensions and placed behind bars many protesters against his rule including Sheikh Abdullah, a popular mass leader.

Considering its strategic importance, Mountbatten himself came down to Kashmir five days ago to convince and persuade the Maharaja to decide on the accession, make an announcement on the issue by 14 August and send representative to the constituent assembly of the relevant country. The Viceroy planned to confer with the Maharaja in private, tender him advice and secure his commitment. The Maharaja, while hosting the Viceroy lavishly, had planned the all-important personal meeting with him today, being the last day of his visit. However, at the scheduled hour, the Maharaja sent a message that he was down with colic pain and that he has been advised by his physician not to exert. Mountbatten has got the hidden message and set out for Delhi. His worries have aggravated about not only the future of the state but the kind of conflict Kashmir could generate between the two dominions, unless the recalcitrant Maharaja saw reason and that, in time.

Nizam Wants Hyderabad To Be The Third Independent State In The Subcontinent

June, 1947, Hyderabad: Nizam's kingdom is spread over a huge 82,000 square miles in the heart of India. Hindus constitute eighty seven per cent of the population of this vast swathe of land and they along with other subjects are ruled by a coterie of Muslim aristocracy headed by the Nizam. He has his own army to protect the state. However, Razakars, a religious and fundamentalist militia, have a vice-like grip over Nizam and exercise undue influence over his state policies.

Nizam is too proud of his ancestry, vast kingdom and abundant resources to take the 'partition plan' of Mountbatten seriously. He has not been paying heed to repeated advice of the Viceroy to be practical and sign the instrument of accession in favour of one of the dominion states. Not only has he not attended any of the meetings convened by the Viceroy on this matter, the deputies he sent have also not been given power to commit anything concrete on his behalf to the Viceroy. Further, the messengers the Viceroy sent to Hyderabad have not been able to secure any commitment from him.

Guided by the coterie of Muslim nobility and Ittehadul-Muslimeen, a powerful pro-Nizam Muslim party, Nizam has been insisting that Hyderabad should remain an independent state and stand on an equal footing with India and Pakistan. He has also issued a 'firman' wherein he has announced that upon the transfer of power, Hyderabad would assume independence.

For obvious reasons, Nizam has been causing lots of anxieties to both the Viceroy and the Congress party. There are also unconfirmed rumours that Nizam has been negotiating with Jinnah and may join Pakistan. This is adding to the Congress' disquiet.

Punjab Echoes Bengal Verdict, Chooses 'Partition'

June 23, 1947, Lahore: Today the Punjab Assembly met to decide on the issue of partition. The rules were similar as Bengal and so also was the verdict. In the joint session held here, ninety one voted in favour of the new constituent assembly (Pakistan) as against seventy seven voting in favour of the existing constituent assembly. In the group voting, the western Punjab containing the Muslim majority areas voted against partition by 69-27 whereas eastern Punjab with non-Muslim majority population favoured partition by 50-22 votes.

Political analysts say, the outcome of the voting in both Bengal and Punjab only reflect the deep communal polarisation and near-complete break-down of mutual trust between the two religious communities.

Sind Assembly Decides To Join Pakistan

June 26, 1947 Karachi: As per the 'plan partition', it has been left to the province to decide joining either of the two dominion states. Today, the proposed state of Pakistan has got its first constituent. Sind has become the first province to decide to join it.

Today, the Sind legislative assembly in a special sitting decided that Sind should join Pakistan constituent assembly under the scheme of 3 June 1947.[263] The decision was however not unanimous and carried out by 33-20 votes.

Vallabhbhai, Rab Nishtar To Head Two States Departments

June 27, 1947, New Delhi: Mountbatten has set up two States Departments to address the issues of Indian states for the two Dominions - one headed by Vallabhbhai of Congress and the other under Abdur Rab Nishtar of the Muslim League. The department is expected to take over most of the functions hitherto being discharged by the Political Department of the Crown Representative, excepting Paramountcy, and facilitate the process of accessions of the states to either of the two proposed dominions by addressing their common concerns and formulating the contour of the final relationship.

According to political analysts, Vallabhbhai has been involved with the State Peoples' Movements for decades in several native states. He is not only well aware of the mind of the people but also well experienced in the art of political negotiation with the rulers.

He is expected to make full use of his knowledge and skill. In comparison, Abdur Rab Nishtar is not so experienced and his field of activities has also been limited. The bottom line is that the Congress is expected to be the gainer as a result. It must also be recognised that in terms of geographical area, the native states put together account for more than one-third of the sub-continent. Therefore the efficient handling of the department can indeed make difference to the final sizes of the two prospective dominion states.

Partition Committee Becomes Partition Council

June 27, 1947, New Delhi: As the date for transfer of power is nearing, the pressure has been mounting on the Partition Committee to carry out multifarious kinds of administrative functions and solve several complex problems - administrative, financial, defence related and others. To tackle the challenge, the Partition Committee has now been reorganised as Partition Council. It would be chaired by the Viceroy and will have two members each from the Congress and the League. Vallabhbhai and Rajendra Prasad will represent the Congress while Rajagopalachari will be the alternate member. The League will be represented by Jinnah and Laiqaut Ali with Rab Nishtar acting as the alternate member. The council will operate through a steering committee consisting of two senior officials—HM Patel and Mohammad Ali representing India and Pakistan respectively. The steering committee, in turn, will be assisted by ten expert committees consisting of representatives of the two countries. The expert committees shall handle and tackle all conceivable areas impinging on partition including organisation, records and personnel, assets and liabilities, central revenues, contracts, currencies and coinage, economic relations, domicile, foreign relations and the armed forces. The council held its first meeting today with Mountbatten in the chair.

Partition Of Provinces Fait Accompli, Focus Is On Demarcation Of Borders

June 27, 1947, New Delhi: Both Punjab and Bengal legislative assemblies, with their members casting votes in two stages in accordance with the formula prescribed by the HMG, already decided in favour of partition of their provinces. It is high time some measures of clarity are introduced on the territorial jurisdiction. The Partition Council met today with Mountbatten in chair. It accepted with 'surprising speed and unanimity Jinnah's proposal that Sir Cyril Radcliffe should be invited to serve as the chairman of the Punjab and Bengal Boundary Commission with the casting vote on both'.[264]

Radcliffe To Draw Boundaries Of Punjab, Bengal And Assam

June 30, 1947, New Delhi: In accordance with the decision of the Partition Council, Mountbatten has initiated one of the most contentious and communally explosive tasks—to determine the boundaries of Punjab and Bengal in order to divide these two provinces between India and Pakistan. Both these provinces have Muslim majority but marginally, and that adds to the complexity of the task. Though there are marked community-specific concentrations in the western and eastern parts, the population is almost inextricably mixed in quite a few areas of both Punjab and Bengal. Punjab presents a special difficulty where Sikhs, an economically prosperous and politically assertive community, though forming only twenty percent of the population, is widely scattered throughout the province.

In Bengal, an additional issue is in regard to Sylhet a district of Assam, over which the eastern part of Pakistan is laying its claim in view of its being a Muslim majority area. The district, would decide through a referendum, whether to remain a part of Assam or join East Bengal and thus, become a part of Pakistan. In the latter event, the boundary commission will demarcate the Muslim majority areas of Sylhet and also the contiguous Muslim majority areas of the adjoining districts of Assam. The political ambience in Bengal and Punjab are communally surcharged. It is apprehended that once the boundaries are decided upon, the minorities may resort to mass emigration to the country where they are in religious majority. The experience of 'direct action day' and series of communal riots are festering like open wounds in their psyche.

Since the demarcations of boundaries would impinge upon the lives of millions of people of the three communities, the agency entrusted with the work must not only be fair and impartial but seem to be so. Keeping this in view, Mountbatten has constituted two boundary commissions for Punjab and Bengal. The latter commission would additionally deal with the Sylhet district of Assam. The Congress and the Muslim League have named two sets of High Court Judges each to serve as members of each commission and Sir Cyril Radcliffe would serve as the chairman.

While deciding upon boundaries, the commissions are expected to take into account:

a. communal majority of contiguous area;
b. administrative viability;
c. natural boundaries;
d. communication and water or irrigation system

Critics say that the deliberations in the commission might proceed strictly on communal lines and the members of the Commission representing the Muslim and non-Muslim communities being in equal proportion, Radcliffe's role may become all the more important.

Background Of Cyril Radcliffe

It was not easy to find out a person competent to undertake such a challenging task as to demarcate the boundaries of two most communally sensitive, densely populated provinces with almost equally distributed people of rival communities. The Congress and the Muslim League, not seeing 'eye to eye' on most issues, were also unlikely to agree upon a common person. In this context, Sir Cyril Radcliffe has been a befitting choice. A barrister of eminence, a person with sharp mind and intelligence, one who has multi-disciplinary knowledge and above all a person of integrity and imbued by a deep sense of duty, he has been called upon by the British government to carry-out this professionally demanding but thankless job. His nomination has met with the approval of both Jawaharlal and Jinnah. Such a rare occurrence was possible because of Radcliffe's formidable reputation. However, squeezed between two 'to be born' hostile countries with strong claims and counter-claims over territories, he is likely to antagonise both the communities at the end. The enormity of Radcliffe's task could be gauged by the facts that the two provinces involved eighty eight million people and 175,000 square miles of geographical territories and he has to complete the task within one and a half month. Besides the usual difficulties, in Punjab, he has to contend with the vast network of irrigation channels criss-crossing the province. He also has to contend with the special issue of Sikhs, who by their sheer enterprise have reclaimed huge tracts of land from desert and converted miles and miles of arid lands into high-produce, prosperous farmland, but stand disadvantaged politically for being scattered all throughout the province. Then, important places like Lahore and Amritsar, with their unique demographic profiles comprising people of all three communities presented special difficulties. In Bengal, though the task appears relatively simpler due to the skewed distribution of the two communities in the east and the west, yet he has to contend with the extensive river networks, and abundant jute and paddy fields.

'Boundary Awards' On 16 August, A Cruel Joke On Hapless Millions?

Mountbatten has instructed Radcliffe to submit his awards on the boundaries of Bengal and Punjab by 13 August. However, he would announce these awards on 16 August. He has justified the '3 day gap' saying that the disclosure of the awards before the day of independence would mar the spirit of celebration. However, critics say that Mountbatten is being not only childish but cruel too. Firstly, he had needlessly hurried the whole process after making an arbitrary declaration of the date for transfer of power. Now on such a vital issue like boundaries, he is refusing millions of vulnerable people of both communities a chance to migrate in time under the auspices of the British Indian government, which has a command over the entire country. His plan to announce the boundary awards after the independence implies that millions of people would suddenly discover themselves being in a hosile country and having become easy prey to the hooligans of the other community. They doubt the administrative capacity and also the intention of the successor governments to handle communal disturbances that are bound to follow once the 'awards' are announced. Things are likely to be particularly bad for the minorities in Pakistan. Even Mountbatten himself would have no say as regards handling of the situation in that dominion after 14 August, they point out.

Division Of Indian Armed Forces In 1:4 Ratio Between Pakistan And India

June 30, 1947, New Delhi: If one single issue has received extraordinary attention of both the Congress and the League on the eve of the power transfer, it involved division of the Indian armed forces. It is expected to be a complicated exercise where the 'break up' would encompass battalions, regiments, installations, training institutions, equipments and ammunitions. The Partition Council has agreed without delay or dispute, to the method for division of this large force. Basic principle adopted is that India and Pakistan shall each have in their own territory Armed Forces, predominantly non-Muslim and Muslim, respectively. This would roughly work out to a ratio of 1:4 between Pakistan and India.

Congress, League Strongly Oppose Unified Command Of The Armed Forces

June 30, 1947, New Delhi: Serious disagreements have arisen between the present British commander-in-chief Auchinleck and the Indian political leaders as regards keeping the Indian armed forces under a unified command for some time after the two dominions become independent. Auchinleck is convinced that the Indian armed forces has been one of the finest secular institutions and by keeping them under unified command for two or three years, both the dominions can ensure that they have the most potent amulet against communal violence. Even Mountbatten supports Auchinleck's views. However, both the League and the Congress are opposing the idea of the unified command. They are impatient to have complete control over their respective armies no later than the date of power transfer. Jinnah and Liaquat have openly asserted that they are not prepared to take over the reins of government without their own armed forces in being. Rajendra Prasad feels if India was divided into two states, a unified army should not and could not continue for a day.

Mountbatten has intervened and insisted that General Auchinleck would remain vested with the administration of the armed forces until the partition of personal and physical assets between the two dominions are complete. As per Mountbatten's scheme, Auchinleck would be designated as the supreme commander from 15 August as distinguished from the commander-in-chief of the two dominions. Briefly he would remain in India in the administrative control of Indian armed forces. For the time he would function under the Joint Defence Council to consist of the Joint Governor General or two separate Governors-General (as the case may be) and the two defence ministers of the two countries besides himself. He will, however, not have any operational control over any unit except those in transit from one dominion to another. Therefore, he will not have any responsibility for law and order.

UNSEEMLY HASTE – IS IT GREED FOR POWER?

Political analysts are seeing ominous signs in the strong reluctance of both, Congress and the League in letting the Indian army remain unified under the British commander-in-Chief for a small window of time following the independence. To them, such attitude meant that the political leaders of both parties have not been able to appreciate how grave the communal situation could become from 14 August. It may be mentioned that the mutual distrust between the two communities was never worse than it is now. Right since July last year, successive communal riots have been occurring—in Ahmedabad (July), Calcutta (August), Bombay (September), Noakhali (October), Bihar (October) and in Punjab over last few months almost without a break. As if those in Calcutta, Noakhali and Bihar were not vicious enough, reports say the tragedies in Punjab this year have been even more. Generally speaking, in several places across the sub-continent both communities are baying for the blood of each other. These evils are only expected to aggravate manifold after the partition. Unfortunately neither the Congress nor the League has adequate experience of governance including using of military to contain serious civil disturbances. Therefore, it would have been only in the fitness of things to make use of the experience and service of the British regime for a few extra months following the partition so that the minorities in both sides could take an informed decision in an environment of safety as to whether they ought to continue in the country of their present residence or cross the border. In normal course, as per the British announcement, the time for power transfer was fixed as June 1948. Both the Congress and the League could avail the services of a common Governor General and thereby ensure the British protection for respective minorities till that time. Mountbatten, on his own, had made a reasonable and responsible proposal to remain as the Joint Governor General. But Jinnah squandered the chance. Now the second opportunity for protection of the minorities is going to be lost by the leaders' decision to partition the army. The analysts say, having remained under the British rule for about 200 years, the unwillingness to tolerate them for some more months is intriguing. They are of the opinion that such hurry and impatience could be interpreted as sheer childishness and immaturity or extraordinary greed for power. Political analysts have serious doubts about the ability of the partitioned armed forces to check communal riots. Such has been the spread of the communal venom that there is every likelihood of its creeping into and corrupting the armed forces of the two dominion states as they move towards independence. And in the event this happens, Auchinleck will practically have no scope to intervene.

Jinnah Self-selects Himself Governor General Of Pakistan

July 2, 1947, Karachi: Jinnah has selected himself to be the first Governor General of Pakistan, a constitutional position. Today, he has intimated Mountbatten about his decision. He has reportedly consulted some of his close friends on this issue before deciding. At the same time, Jinnah has hoped that Mountbatten would stay as the Governor General of India. Probably Jinnah is thinking Mountbatten's presence as the head of the government of India would be helpful not only to safeguard the interest of Pakistan especially in terms of allocation of common resources, but also to protect the religious minorities therein.

Let Us Make Laws Sitting Together Than Make Treaties As Aliens

July 5, 1947, New Delhi: Now the policies of the States Department led by Vallabhbhai have been showing results. Several important princely states had taken their seats in the third meeting of the constituent assembly in April and agreed to work hand in hand with the elected representatives of British India to frame the new constitution. Keen to convert trickles into a flood, Vallabhbhai, known as a hard political bargainer, extended to the princes, a warm hand inviting them to join the independent India. In a statement issued today he urged them to make laws sitting together as friends than to make treaties as aliens. He assured them that the business between the states and India will be as equals.

Native States Are Joining India In Droves

Vallabhbhai as the political head and VP Menon as the administrative head of the States Depratment have been putting up hard work to persuade the rulers of princely states to join the proposed dominion state of India. They have been putting two instruments viz. 'standstill agreement' and 'instrument of accession' to optimum use to gain the trust of the princes and simulatenously to create pressure on them. Recognising the fact that the core concern of these princes related to the continuation of the agreements and treatises they have had with the British Crown, the standstill agreement provided for their continuation. As regards the instrument of accession, a prince by signing it, agreed to accede his state to India and granted the latter control over specified subjects. The scope of such subjects differed widely depending on the status of the native state. Those states which have been enjoying internal autonomy under the British Crown were allowed to surrender control in respect of only three areas viz. defence, external affairs and communications. As a matter of strategy, those rulers who signed the instrument of accession have been allowed the benefit of the 'standstill agreement'. Considerable progress has been achieved in bringing around a large portion of the 565 states so far. The princes are practically under pincer attack. On one hand, the new Viceroy has made it clear that the Crown's support will not be available to them after 15 August and therefore, it would be sensible for them to negotiate the accession on favourable terms in good time. On the other hand, there has been surging pressure from the rulers' own subjects who are yearning to join India. There is a third factor too, but no less important. It is the leadership of Vallabhbhai. No Indian leader, probably, has the feel of and insight into the mood of the states' people more than him. Vallabhbhai has also been adept at real politik. He was, in a sense the pivot of the Congress high command when the party had governments in majority of the provinces. If he is somewhat awed by the rulers of the native states, he is equally trusted and adored by their masses. No wonder that under his leadership, the States Department has been scoring success and the princely states are joining India in droves.

Assam Keen To Hand Over A Resourceful District To Pakistan On A Platter?

July 6-7, 1947, Sylhet: Besides the two provinces of Punjab and Bengal, the third contentious issue between the two proposed dominion states has been a district in the east of India. After Bengal decided in favour of partition, a referendum became necessary in Sylhet. This highly resourceful district of Assam replete with its vast paddy fields, tea estates, lime and cement industries, has been in the eye of a storm for past some time. Being part of Assam, it was supposed to be a part of India. However, Pakistan has been claiming it on the ground that the Muslims constituted the majority of its population. The fate of the province has been left to the outcome of a referendum.

Sylhet is an interesting case. Economically and educationally, it has been a leading district in Assam. However most of its people are Bengali speaking, unlike other districts of the province who speak Assamese or other tribal languages. The League has been laying their claim on this district on the ground of its being a Muslim majority district, though it transpires that such a majority could only be marginal. According to electoral roll, Muslims constituted about 54.3% of the electorate, though Liaqaut Ali Khan has been claiming that the actual Muslim population is about 60.7% and therefore the value of Muslim votes need to be enhanced proportionately. His claim is being contested by the Hindu population of the district. They have raised the question of enfranchising large number of Hindu plantation workers living in Sylhet for generations. They have also been asking for bringing trade and business segments within the scope of the referendum.

At the same time, the Hindu inhabitants of the district have another kind of grievance. They have been complaining that the rest of the province, as well as the provincial Congress leadership, have literally forsaken them while the League has been leaving no stone unturned to win the referendum. Jinnah has been taking personal initiative in the issue. The two days long referendum has concluded today. The eligibility to participate was ultimately restricted to General, Muslim and the Indian Christian constituencies. There were several complaints of irregularities in preparation of electoral roll and putting up road blocks to dissuade Hindu voters from exercising their franchise. Stitching together all of these, political observers see Sylhet seceding to Pakistan a certainty.

Referendum Delivers Sylhet To Pakistan

July 12-13, 1947, Sylhet: The result of the referendum has been out and it has been on expected lines. The votes cast in favour of joining Pakistan were 239,619 while those who wished to remain part of Assam and India numbered 184,041. Though the deck has been cleared for the district to join East Bengal, some ambiguities still hang over its inhabitants. In terms of the plan of partition, the boundary commission on Bengal is also working to identify the Muslim majority areas in the district and the contiguous Muslim majority areas in its adjoining districts in Assam. Its final shape as a part of Pakistan may be known after the boundary commission delivers its report.

Congress Uses Stick And Carrot To Secure Accession

July, 1947, New Delhi: It is becoming clearer that all the princely states have to join with either of the two dominion states who would be successors to the British Empire. As days pass the rulers of these states are realising their vulnerabilities and most of them have begun making up their minds. Congress is far ahead of the Muslim League in the race to goad them to their stable. Leaders like Jawaharlal and Vallabhbhai have been particularly active. Vallabhbhai, a master in realpolitik, is using both carrot and stick to make these native rulers to fall in line. There are reports that depending on their status and inclination the princes amenable to joining India are being offered bouquet of privileges including inter alia exemption from customs duty, titular constitutional offices, ambassadorial posts, chances to enter electoral politics etc. The recalcitrant princes are being issued threats of investigations, depositions and even police actions.

Radcliffe To Draw Boundaries Of Punjab, Bengal From His Delhi Office

July 10, 1947, New Delhi: Mountbatten has asked Radcliffe to begin his work forthwith and submit his reports by 13 August, 1947 which is hardly one and a half months away. In view of the exceptionally small window of time, proper physical inspection of relevant areas of two large provinces are almost out of question. It is being learnt that Radcliffe would carry out essentially an indoor exercise in Delhi on the basis of the available maps and documents. He is keenly aware that such a methodology has several limitations and may at times, produce bizarre outcome like cutting a man's home from his tilling land or even bifurcating his residential home. Before beginning his work, Radchiffe voiced his apprehensions to Indian political leaders including Jawaharlal and Jinnah, but on their insistance he has agreed to go ahead. Critics say, the leaders are betraying their colossal insensitivity to the likely impact of such a crucial task undertaken as a drawing room exercise and carried out under such a ridiculously short time limit on the lives of tens of million people of both communities.

Radcliffe's work has been rendered more complicated as the Indian members in both his teams also seem to have serious differences amongst themselves. Each of the Boundary Commission has two members each from the Congress and the Muslim League. The Bengal Commission has Justices CC Biswas, BK Mukherjea, Abu Saleh M Akram and SA Rahman while the Punjab Commission is being served by Justices Mehar Chand Mahajan, Teja Singh, Din Mohammad and Muhammad Munir.

Despite all of them being High Court judges these members seem to be clearly divided on partisan lines and it is getting clear that Radchiffe's casting vote may be necessary to arrive at the final decision frequently.

It's Final – Jinnah The First Governor General Of Pakistan

July 10, 1997: London: On the second day of the present month, Jinnah had informed the Viceroy of his decision to become the Governor General of Pakistan due to some compelling reasons. Jinnah's decision caused upset to many including in his own party. But still, the League fell in line. On 5th of this month, Liaqaut had written to the Viceroy urging the latter to recommend Jinnah's name as the Governor General of the new dominion state to HMG.

It was clear right since then that by not agreeing to a common Governor General for both the dominion states, which Mountbatten had proposed, Pakistan would suffer more. This is simply because post-partition the majority of the common assets would be in the physical possession of India and a common Governor General would have been the best protective amulet to ensure their fair distribution. Next, and more importantly, there are issues of safety of the minorities in both the dominion states and their inter-country movement, which appear to be a certainty. Notwithstanding, Jinnah did not relent. Probably he expected that Mountbatten as the Governor General of India would in any case, take care of these concerns.

Today, Clement Attlee has declared acceptance of Jinnah as the first Governor General of proposed Pakistan.

Jinnah's Statement on Kashmir Worries Congress

July 11, 1947 New Delhi: Maharaja of Kashmir has kept everyone guessing – the Congress, the League and of course the Viceroy who looks at the indecisive Kashmir as a potential danger to the sub continent. The Congress has been trying to convince the Maharaja to sign the instrument of accession but without success. On 17th last month, Jinnah appeared in the scene with a mild, liberal stance to attract the Maharaja. In a statement he had said that it has been the policy of the League not to interfere with the internal affairs of any state. But even that had no impact. In the meantime, the Congress began to take keener interest. Both Gandhi and Jawaharlal were planning visits to Srinagar. Taking note of the Congress initiatives, Jinnah has offered the Maharaja a bait[265] now. He has mentioned that Kashmir could join either of the two dominion states or choose to remain independent. Pakistan would welcome it and sign friendly agreements with her for commonwealth of both the peoples. Clearly, Jinnah's statement has added to the uncertainty and aggravated Congress' concern.

Can One Subscribe To 'Two Nation' Theory, And Still Attend Constituent Assembly?

July 14, 1947, New Delhi: The League leadership had consistently set aside requests from both the Congress and the Viceroy to attend the first three meetings of the constituent assembly. Jinnah had made it clear that the Muslims of the country would have nothing to do with the assembly. Responding to his call, large number of Muslim representatives, barring few from the NWFP and some Nationalist Muslims, stayed away from the assembly so far. Now that the League's demand for Pakistan has been acceded and a new constituent assembly is poised to open shortly, the leadership of the League, relieved and relaxed, issued a call to the Muslims residing in areas expected to be parts of the dominion of India, to come forward and participate in the proceedings of the Indian Constituent Assembly. They have stressed this was necessary with a view to securing the rights of the Muslims in the post-partition India by incorporating adequate and effective safeguards for minorities in the constitution. In the meeting of the assembly that has begun in the Constitution Hall here, several Muslim members turned up and took their seats for the first time.

When the Secretary called out the name of Haji Abdul Sathar Ham Ishaq Sait - one of the newly arrived Muslim members, Deshbandhu Gupta, an existing member, raised a point of order demanding that it was necessary to know if the new member still subscribed to the 'two nation theory'. He also suggested, now that the partition has been decided upon, it was necessary to review the whole question and lay down that a member who did not subscribe to the 'objective resolution' of the assembly could not sign the register. However, the president disallowed Gupta's contention saying that he saw no 'point of order' issue in it and that as long as an elected member did not resign, he had the right to sit in the House.

Independence Act To Give Birth To Two Dominions

July 18, 1947, London: Indian Independence Bill consisting of 20 clauses and 3 schedules was introduced in the House of Commons on 4th of the present month. The bill has provided for two sovereign dominion states viz. India and Pakistan in the sub-continent to emerge on 15 August 1947. The territories of India would constitute all that of British India except territories of Pakistan.

The territories of Pakistan would comprise of West Punjab, East Bengal, Sind, and British Baluchistan. The NWFP and the Sylhet district of Assam would also join it subject to the results of the referendums going in its favour. The vast number of native states would have to join either of these two dominion states. The constituent assemblies of two dominion states would constitute the legislatures of their respective dominions to whom the power would be transferred. Consequently, the central legislative assembly and the council of states would get dissolved.

The Act provides for a common Governor General for the two dominions unless the legislature of either of them passes a law to the contrary. The Governor General shall be appointed by His Majesty and shall represent His Majesty for the purposes of the government of in each dominion. Till the time the constituent assemblies of the two dominions frame and pass their respective constitutions, they will be subject to the extant Government of India Act 1935 as modified by the provisions of the Indian Independence Act.

A Treaty Of Peace Without A War
Glowing Tribute To The Indian Independence Bill

July 18, 1947, London: The proposal that seeks to transfer power to two dominion states and strategically titled as the 'Indian Independence Bill' was greeted with laudatory comments by the members for being unique and noble. Lord Listowel, Secretary of State for India, while introducing the bill, described it as unique in the history of legislation in the country. Lauding HMG's initiative, he had observed: 'Never before has such a large portion of the world population achieved complete independence through legislation alone'. Listowel also had words of appreciation for the Congress choice of retaining the name 'India' for the new dominion state. The mood of the British parliament was best described by the statement of Lord Samuel in the House of Lords who described the bill as 'a moral to all future generations; it is a Treaty of Peace without a War'.[266]

Following the adoption of the bill in the House of Commons on 15 July and in the House of Lords the next day ie. on 16 July, it has received the royal assent today. By virtue of this Act, the British Raj would end on 15 August. It has also stipulated partition of India into two sovereign dominions—India and Pakistan.

PLEBISCITE IN NWFP
Pakistan Wave Sweeps The Province

July 6 to 17, 1947, Peshawar: After the Congress endorsed the 'partition plan', Ghaffar Khan and his brother Dr Khan Sahib have been desperate to find out the ways and means to slip out of the clutches of Pakistan and the League. Ghaffar Khan had conferred with Gandhi and he wanted the people of his province to be given a choice to decide upon their own future instead of summarily pushing them to Pakistan. Plebiscite was considered an option. Gandhi had taken up the matter with Mountbatten and the latter agreed to hold a referendum in the NWFP where people could choose between India and Pakistan. However, Khan Brothers, realising that the League, by its sustained propaganda and actions, has already communalised the people, insisted on incorporating a third option of Pakhtoonistan, which they said would be a separate land for the Pathans. But Jinnah vehemently opposed it for understandable reason.

Mountbatten did not want to complicate the process of transfer of power and even the Congress, which had earlier opposed balkanisation and the scheme of independent Bengal, did not evince due interest in the proposal. Khan brothers realised too well what would be the outcome of the referendum in the event of a direct contest between India and Pakistan in a communally surcharged province. They, as a protest for non-incorporation of Pakhtoonistan as one of the choices, gave call for boycott of the plebiscite. The situation grew more complicated after the Afghanistan government claimed that the territory lying to the west of Indus river was predominantly inhabited by the Afghans and they should have the right to decide about their future.

The interest of the neighbouring country had created great unease not only in the NWFP and Delhi but its ripple travelled across Thames in London. Interestingly, this development brought the British regime and the League closer in NWFP. The HMG sharply criticised the attempt of the Afghanistan government to meddle with the politics of NWFP, part of British India. Considering the tense situation in the province, the referendum was placed under the care of Brigadier JB Booth, designated as the Referendum Commissioner who conducted it, utilising the services of British officers of Indian army.

The referendum conducted over last several days has concluded today. According to political analysts, the verdict is almost foretold - in favour of Pakistan. The League is already celebrating. For the Khan Brothers, the future looks ominous. When it comes to revenge, the League may cause them such harm, which even the British did not. Dismayed, disillusioned they are preparing for the worst.

Mountbatten Reconstitutes Interim Government, Creates Two Different Administrations

July 19, 1947, New Delhi: To facilitate smooth transition of power to the two prospective dominion states, the Viceroy of the undivided India, has reconstituted[267] the interim federal government. The reconstituted executive council has two provincial administrations, one each for India and Pakistan. Each administration will deal with its own business and consult the other in areas of common interest. Under the revised arrangement, these administrations have been suitably placed under the charges of the Congress and the League ministers. As regards matters of common concern, those would be dealt with jointly by both the wings under the chairmanship of the Governor General.

Jinnah Conquers Last Muslim Bastion NWFP Decides To Join Pakistan Constituent Assembly

July 20, 1947 Peshawar: As anticipated, the people of the NWFP have given their verdict in favour of joining the Pakistan constituent assembly. While the total electorate consisted of 572,798 persons, little over half of them only cast their votes. The verdict in favour of the Pakistan constituent assembly was 289,244 to 2874. Significantly, large number of voters numbering around 49%, dissatisfied with the limited choice they had, abstained from voting. Notwithstanding the poor turnout, the result of the referendum has finally endowed Jinnah with his most sought after victory.

Fears Stalk Punjab, 50,000-strong Boundary Force To Protect People, Property

July 24, 1947, New Delhi: The 'plan partition' was recommended by Mountbatten to the HMG as a panacea for communal conflicts and the leaders of both the Congress and the League embraced it, some political analysts say, with unseemly haste.

Significantly, the communal fire that flared up following the formation of the interim government by the Congress, was kept burning by the League even after it joined the cabinet. It was only after HMG accepted the demand for Pakistan that the communal hatred had showed signs of ebbing. But the euphoria of the 'separate homeland' began to disappear again, after the issue of demarcation of boundaries of Punjab and Bengal cropped up. There are several areas in Punjab in Jullundur and Ambala divisions and also Lahore, Multan, Gurdaspur districts over which the rival communities have lodged their claims. In Bengal, with the exception of some districts in its eastern and the western parts where either of the two communities have clear majority, several districts lying in both parts of the province have intensely mixed population. For example, if Hindus are expecting districts like Khulna to be part of India, the Muslims are hoping that districts like Nadia and Murshidabad would be awarded to Pakistan. Claims and counter claims have been raised about the city of Calcutta itself. Rumours are running thick and fast due to lack of transparency in the working of the Boundary Commissions. According to some reports the Indian members of both the commissions have begun to adopt clearly partisan stands and the fate of several millions now lies at the hands of one man-Sir Cyril Radchiffe. Emotions of insecurity and fear have begun to engulf people in these two provinces. As a result the communal fire has been lit once again and it is gaining in strength quickly, especially in Punjab.

Against this backdrop, Mountbatten summoned here a meeting of the Partition Council to mull measures to douse the fire and establish peaceful conditions so as to facilitate the process of partition. Not resting with mere appeals to the parties and the citizens, the council under Mountbatten has decided to set up a 50,000 strong military force to ensure peace in sensitive places across Punjab. To be commanded by the famed Major General Pete Rees (who had played a daring role in defeating the Japanese forces in the battle of Mandalaya in 1945), this force with a high proportion of British officers would, effective from August 1, cover districts like Sialkot, Gujranwala, Sheikhpura, Lyallpur, Montgomery, Lahore, Amritsar, Gurdaspur, Hoshiarpur, Jullundur, Ferozepur and Ludhiana. Rees will be advised and assisted by Brigadier Digambar Singh and Col Ayub Khan from the Indian and the Pakistan army respectively. Post 15 August, Rees would have operational control of the forces of both the countries in the sensitive territories in Punjab and he would remain responsible to the governments of the two dominion states through Auchinleck, the supreme commander and the Joint Defence Council.

Gandhi To Be One-man Boundary Force In Bengal

July 24, 1947, New Delhi: If Punjab is sitting on a volcano, the danger in Bengal is no less. The ghastly riots following the Direct Action Day suggest that a major holocaust can befall on its people in the wake of partition, if things are allowed to get out of hand. It is being heard that Gandhi has a plan to be in Bengal before or around 15 August. In letters written today to Vallabhbhai and others he mentioned that he proposes to visit Noakhali again and may reach there after touching Srinagar, Lahore and Patna. Mountbatten is aware of Gandhi's earlier visit to riot-torn Calcutta and Noakhali last year and the kind of influence he exercised over the masses. He would be only too glad if Gandhi is in Bengal around that time. According to some reports, Mountbatten sees Gandhi as 'one man boundary force' in Bengal, another communally sensitive province.

'Be Practical' – Mountbatten's Last Hour Advice To Princes

July 25, 1947, New Delhi: The Viceroy has convened a meeting of the princes in which he made it clear once again that becoming independent on the lapse of paramountcy was not an option available to them—they have to join either India or Pakistan. A set of guidelines has been made available to help them make their choice. These are: (a) the geographical contiguity of the 'state' to a dominion; (b) demographic composition of the population of the 'state' in terms of religious faith; and (c) the choice of the ruler.

Mountbatten addressed the princes in full session here and encouraged them to sign the instrument of accession expeditiously. The Congress had already given the rulers a political offer—it would not interfere with their receiving honours and titles from the King Emperor. The Viceroy exhorted the princes to be serious and act with promptitude, reminding them that after 15 August he would not be able to act as the Crown Representative and mediate with the dominions on their behalf. The Viceroy also warned them that neither they can run away from the dominion governments nor can they hope to fight wars with the latter with their obsolete store of arms. Mountbatten offered them to protect their personal prerogatives and succession rights should they sign the instrument of accession in time.

PAKISTAN CONSTITUENT ASSEMBLY IS SET UP TODAY

August 11, 1947, Karachi: The Pakistan constituent assembly began its proceedings yesterday in the old Sind Assembly building. Jogendra Mandal was elected as the chairman for the day. The assembly later elected Jinnah as its president. It formally conferred the honorific title of Qaid-e-Azam on him. The assembly also adopted the flag of Muslim League as the flag of the proposed state of Pakistan by adding a white strip near the mast. Speaking to the assembly, Jinnah laid down his vision of Pakistan. He sought to assure citizens of all religions that they would have equal rights as citizens irrespective of their faith: 'You may belong to any religion or caste or creed - that has nothing to do with the business of the State...We are starting with this fundamental principle that we are all citizens, and equal citizens, of one State.' He also envisioned a complete fusion of citizens of all faiths in Pakistan: '... you will find that in course of time Hindus would cease to be Hindus, and Muslims would cease to be Muslims, not in the religious sense, because that is the personal faith of each individual, but in the political sense as citizens of the State.' According to reports, though Jinnah spoke like a secular visionary, the minorities remain sceptical about their future, given the communally surcharged ambience in the proposed new state.

Menon Has A Narrow Escape, Jodhpur Maharaja's Theatrics Handled Deftly

August, 1947, New Delhi: Vallabhbhai as the political head of the States Department, assisted by the astute bureaucrat VP Menon as its administrative head, has achieved unprecedented success in persuading over five hundred native states of varying sizes to join India. On 7th of this month, the ruler of Bikaner signed the instrument of accession. Today, the Maharaja of Jodhpur, another key, large state bordering both the proposed dominion states of India and Pakistan followed suit. Sources said the Maharja was undecided about his choice between the two states and he was given a blank form by Jinnah to write his wish list and assured the same would be acceded to without a question. But eventually, he was convinced and he chose India. Not only Vallabhbhai and Menon, Mountbatten also reportedly played a role in making the Maharaja take this decision. But the final part of the negotiation turned theatrical when the Maharaja, probably exasperated by the stream of coercion and persuasion for signing the instrument of accession, had in a one to one meeting with VP Menon, suddenly brandished his small revolver and threatened to shoot the latter. But Menon tackled him with tact and the Maharaja eventually reconciled. Now only three important native states have been left to take their decisions. They are Kashmir, Hyderabad and Junagadh.

Boundary Awards To Be Available Only On 16 August – Tension Grips Bengal And Punjab

August 12, 1947, New Delhi: Radcliffe is camping in the Comptroller's House in the viceregal estate. Today Mountbatten's representative went there to meet him. According to him, though both Punjab and Bengal Awards are ready, Radcliffe has not been able to complete the Sylhet award till now and it was likely to be ready only by 14 August. According to another source, all three reports would be ready by tomorrow but the Viceroy is not inclined to publish them before 16 August ostensibly for the reason that this would mar the spirit of celebration of independence. Meanwhile his programme to leave for Karachi tomorrow evening to attend Pakistan's independence has come handy as he won't be able to return before 14th evening and the following day would be a holiday in India. As such the day of announcement of the award has been pushed to 16 August.

On the eve of Pakistan's independence which comes a day before India, there are palpable tensions about boundary awards in Bengal and Punjab.

Gandhi Is In Bengal To Preserve Communal Peace

August 13, 1947, Calcutta: Gandhi has come to Bengal to prevent communal flare-up in the wake of partition of both the Country and the province. He had brought back peace in the city last year by spreading message of communal harmony. Mountbatten has been relying much on his repeating the magic. Since it is now more or less clear that Calcutta would be a part of India, Suhrawardy, the prime minister, is much apprehensive about a vigorous reprisal and has urged Gandhi to protect the Muslims in the city. Gandhi had reached Sodepur Ashram in the outskirt of Calcutta on 9th this month. Today, he has moved with his team to Hyderi House in the east Calcutta. Initially he faced angry protestors, who felt he was protecting Muslims but not doing enough to save the Hindus from Muslim atrocities in the eastern part of Bengal. However, Gandhi has pacified them. He is trying to convince them on the need to maintain peace and communal harmony. It seems he has been able to make the initial break through.

Pakistan Celebrates Independence

August 14, 1947, Karachi: Pakistan has celebrated its independence today. Mountbatten was invited for this momentous occasion. However, when he arrived at Karachi yesterday his reception was lukewarm. Jinnah had deputed Hidayatullah, the Governor-elect of Sind to receive Mountbatten, till then the Viceroy of the entire country, at the airport.

Today ceremonies were held at the Legislative Assembly and a capacity crowd filled the ground facing the Assembly House. Leaders looked enthusiastic but their overwhelming reverence to Jinnah almost enforced upon the latter a kind of summit-isolation. In his solitary space Jinnah seemed to sparkle with his towering presence. The ceremonies and celebrations were over within an hour following which Jinnah and Mountbatten rode an open car on the way to the Government House. By midday, Mountbatten bid adieu and boarded flight for New Delhi. Jinnah, in his characteristic cold and courteous manner expressed his eternal gratitude and friendship to Mountbatten.

Bloody Celebration Of Independence Minorities Massacred, Violence Grips Lahore

August 14, 1947, Lahore: Pakistan has become an independent dominion today. In Karachi, Jinnah and Mountbatten had an open car ride acknowledging the greetings of the people. The dream of a homeland for the Muslims of India has come true. However, the communal hatred has reared its ugly head on this very day, portending an ominous future for minorities in the country. According to reports reaching New Delhi, massacre of Hindus and Sikhs have already begun in the old city in Lahore - men, women and children alike. The Muslim hooligans are roaming the city perpetrating the carnage. Fire has been raging in several parts of the city. Helpless families are begging for shelter with the 'boundary forces' to save their lives. Such news reaching Delhi and the Indian leaders on the eve of the Indian independence is causing much consternation. India is scheduled to observe her independence midnight today.

Is The Worst Tragedy In Human History Set To Unfold?

August 14, 1947 New Delhi: As Mountbatten was flying back from Karachi to Delhi over the territories of Punjab, he saw several large fires dotting the landscape, their flames widely spread and fumes billowing up in the sky. Mountbatten could figure out that communal riots have begun to take their toll. Having occurred on the very day of the Pakistan's independence is indeed an ominous sign of things to come.

Gandhi's Presence Is Making A Difference

August 14, 1947, Calcutta: Calcutta was generally hostile to Gandhi till yesterday. However, the city has begun to respond to his call for peace and communal harmony. Nearly ten thousand people attended Gandhi's evening prayer meeting today. Gandhi decided to postpone his Noakhali visit and instead stay put in Calcutta at the request of Suhrawardy. He has recognised the crucial role Calcutta can play in preserving communal amity. He is reported to have said that if Calcutta returned to sanity and real friendship, then Noakhali and the rest of

India would be safe. Finding little reason to celebrate independence in the aftermath of the 'partition', he exhorted the people to observe the occasion by fasting and praying for the well-being of India.

Envelope Is Empty

August 14-15, 1947, New Delhi: After the constituent assembly passed the resolution inviting Mountbatten to be the first Governor General, Rajendra Prasad and Jawaharlal went to Mountbatten's residence to personally deliver the invitation. The road from the assembly house to the Government House was so crowded that it took considerable time for the two leaders to reach their destination. Even the Government House was full of pressmen, keen to capture this historic moment. After exchange of pleasantries, as Jawaharlal handed over to the Governor General-elect the portfolios of the new cabinet in an envelope, press photographers' cameras kept flashing. According to sources close to Mountbatten, after the Indian leaders took leave, driven by curiosity to see the content and familiarise himself with the names of the cabinet members to whom he would administer oath of office in a few hours time, Mountbatten opened up the envelope. The next experience was extra-ordinary. The envelope was empty—it had no list inside. The 'amazing guffaw' seemed to have occurred out of hectic work schedule or excess enthusiasm or it could be due to a 'sublime oversight' on the part of Jawaharlal.

'Long Years Ago We Made A Tryst With Destiny' Jawaharlal's Midnight Broadcast To Indian Nation

August 14-15, 1947, New Delhi: On the eve of the independence Delhi is wearing a festive look. The people are clearly in a mood to celebrate. Though the exodus has already started from the West Pakistan, particularly West Punjab, and the miles long caravans of the frightened, riot affected, hapless Hindu and Sikh refugees are desperately heading for India, they are as yet far away from Delhi to be able to mar the spirit of celebration.

On 14 August midnight, the constituent assembly was convened. A resolution was passed proclaiming independence and formally inviting Mountbatten to be the first constitutional Governor General of free India. In the Assembly Jawaharlal delivered an emotional speech:

'Long years ago we made a tryst with destiny and now the time comes when we shall redeem our pledge, not wholly or in full measure, but substantially. At the stroke of the midnight hour when the world sleeps, India will awake to life and freedom….'[268]

Junagadh Nawab's Emissary In Karachi, Vallabhbhai Patel Furious

August 15, 1947, New Delhi On the day of the Indian independence, a piece of news is causing disquiet in Congress. Mahabat Khanji III, the Nawab of Junagadh has reportedly sent his emissary Ismail Abrahani to Karachi three days ago with signed instrument of accession in favour of Pakistan. Junagadh has been vacillating in the matter of exercising choice of accession and it is reported to have secretly opened communication with Jinnah. The latter assured moral and military support to the Nawab in the event that he opted to join Pakistan.

Junagadh in Saurashtra region is surrounded by India in three sides whereas its fourth side opens to Arabian sea. Though ruled by a Muslim Nawab, its people are predominantly Hindus. As such, the Nawab's decision has caused much anger and disquiet in Congress. Vallabhbhai Patel, who hails from the neighbouring area, is particularly furious. Congress is mulling appropriate steps against the Nawab to secure Junagadh's accession to India.

Communal Holocaust In The Holy City

August 15, 1947 Amritsar: As if to prove that Jinnah's lofty secular address to the Pakistan's constituent assembly only a day ago was a piece of cruel satire, intense communal violence against the minorities has engulfed Lahore. It began yesterday and was manifest in a blind fury today. It seemed as though it was aimed at teaching a lesson to the Hindus and the Sikhs for daring to stake a claim on the city. The Muslim fanatics have begun a terrible massacre. It is heard that people are being beheaded and mutilated at will, with police remaining spectators, and the gutters of the city have turned red with blood. Hindu and Sikh refugees, in thousands, are bursting forth upon Amritsar, barely 35 miles away from Lahore. Last midnight India celebrated her independence. Delhi, the country's capital in particular, was ecstatic. Here in the holy city of Amritsar, ironically a ghastly celebration of Indian independence has begun today by wreaking revenge and spilling blood of Muslim men, women and children.

Over last few days, thousands of refugees have been arriving at Amritsar railway station from across the border. Today, a train arriving from Pakistan reportedly carried in all its compartments corpses of Hindus and Sikhs. This has acted as a trigger for unprecedented massacre of Muslims, including those who were fleeing to Pakistan through this holy city

Thus Punjab, east and west, has been gripped by terrible communal violence. Such is its fury that it seems to be heading for a total communal cleansing in both sides of the province. The consequences of the partition of India have begun to show up in Punjab in all its evil forms!

Last Viceroy Is The First Governor General Of Indian Dominion, Chief Justice Kania Administers Oath

August 15, 1947, New Delhi: Sir Harilal Kania, the Chief Justice of India administered oath to Mountbatten as the first Governor General of India in the Durbar Hall here. This august ceremony of transfer of power was poignantly captured by playing 'God save the King' followed by 'Jana Gana Mana'.

The next destination was Council House, where Indian national flag was to be hoisted amidst gun salute. By the time Mountbatten and other dignitaries reached, the house was packed much beyond capacity. Exuberant citizens had made their way in and they were mixed up with official guests, eager to be eyewitnesses to the momentous proceedings. Jostling for space inside the House literally forced those in the fringes pushed out of the hall into the open area. Outside the Council House a sea of humanity gathered. They besieged the round shaped architecture from all sides. Rajendra Prasad initiated the proceedings by reading out good will messages from the heads of nations across the world. In the process, he was about to commit a faux pas by leaving out the message of Truman, the US president. The embarrassment was averted after the US ambassador 'protested the omission through a loud whisper'.

Mountbatten read out the message from the King who lauded the peaceful transition. He then addressed the assembly. He 'drew maximum applause' when he referred 'his solicitude for Gandhi', the supreme commander of Indian freedom struggle. Ironically, on this august occasion, Gandhi was conspicuous by his absence. After the speeches were delivered, the tri-colour national flag of India was hoisted and a salvo of thirty-one guns was fired.

Tri-colour Flies Full Mast Over The War Memorial

August 15, 1947, New Delhi: The independence celebration concluded by hoisting the Indian national flag in the War Memorial. About a quarter million people thronged the Memorial in the Princess Park. The size of the gathering was nearly ten times more than the venue's capacity. Nearly six people claimed a chair and every inch of the land space was occupied. The immense crowd tried repeatedly to reach the dais at the centre in which stood the flagstaff. Every time they made such efforts, they had to be neutralised by the available security personnel with great difficulty. The cycle of these movements resembled unrelenting waves of a turbulent sea determined to devour a tiny island in their centre.

Mountbatten and his carriage found it excruciatingly difficult to navigate through the dense human mass and eventually had to resign when Mountbatten was still at least 25 yards away from the flagstaff. He could move no further, and had to stay in his carriage. While the flag was being hoisted he took the salute from there.

MOUNTBATTEN FACES THE INA SPIRIT, ACKNOWLEDGES

Mountbatten, who was the supreme commander of the Allied forces in the Southeast Asia, has been known for his extreme dislike for the INA and Subhas, bordering on hatred. He had described Indian National Army as dregs of Indian Armed Forces collected and mobilised by Subhas. According to many, he may have had a second thought on his assessment of Subhas and the INA today or the destiny possibly wanted him to do so.

As he entered the Council House today to take oath as the Governor General of the free India, the huge patriotic gatherings inside the hall rhythmically chanted 'Jai Hind', the words of greetings first introduced in the Indian Legion which was started by Subhas in Germany.

These two words were later transformed into a 'mantra' of patriotism by the Indian National Army. His experience in the War Memorial was no less significant. Nearly two years ago, in the month of August, his victorious army, supposedly under his instructions, had blown away the newly built INA War Memorial in Singapore by dynamite. That action was in complete disregard to War ethics and aimed at humiliating not only the INA but all patriotic Indians. Today, he came to the War Memorial constructed by the British to take salute as Indian Governor General. But he could not reach the central dais when the flag of Independent India was hoisted. Was it a stroke of destiny?

What Went Wrong? Chief Architect Of Indian Freedom Ponders

August 15, 1947, Calcutta: Delhi has been celebrating Indian emancipation from British rule of nearly two centuries with excitement. Calcutta is much subdued in comparison. The verdicts of Boundary Commissions are not yet out. Tens of thousands of people, particularly in the border areas in both the east and west sides of Bengal are spending hours in morbid fears of the communal elements. Violence is expected to breakout the moment the 'boundary awards' are announced. Blood has already begun to spill profusely in the West Punjab. Refugees, forming miles long caravan, have set out in search of safe destinations in both sides of the border. Butchering of the Hindus and the Sikhs began in the old walled city of Lahore yesterday itself. Retaliation against Muslim minorities has begun in Amritsar in earnest. The government anticipates a fierce retaliation in East Punjab and Delhi and it is trying to take precautions.

Here in Beliaghata, in the eastern part of the metropolis, Gandhi has been camping in order to spread messages of peace and communal harmony. He had come to Calcutta a year ago to apply balm to the riot victims of 1946. and here he is again. The situation in Bengal is extremely sensitive. Even a small event can trigger huge communal conflagrations on both sides of Bengal. Gandhi is acting almost like a one-man army carrying the grave responsibility to prevent any such occurrence.

He is acutely aware that the division of the country has been a blunder. He knows it would offer no solution to the communal disharmony, conflict and violence, and can rather increase it manifold. But he could not convince others, even his long trusted followers and fellow travellers, who have parted ways with him before reaching the last milepost.

With the vivisection of India his life's work has been undone. The values for which he stood and wanted the Congress to stand have been cast wayside. He preached non-violence, communal harmony and an undivided India. The country has been hacked into two, there are bloodbaths and the communities are at each other's throats. Yes, the political power has changed hands from the British to the native leaders but the soul of India has been strangulated.

Last night, when Delhi was bathing in glittering lights and Jawaharlal was delivering his 'India's tryst with destiny' speech, Gandhi, to the vast millions of Indians the prime architect of the freedom struggle, was away in Calcutta. The lamps in his Beliaghata house were put off by 10 p.m. as usual. He had little reason to cheer. Probably he was searching for what went wrong

Today Indian has woken up to freedom. The youngest nation in the world however seemed to be in no mood to introspect. Unlike Gandhi, their political Guru, 350 millions of Indians wanted to rejoice. Putting the history of acrimony and partition behind them, they seemed impatient to find their place in the comity of nations and play a decisive role in shaping the new world order.

EPILOGUE

After the bloody struggle of 1857, the way to Indian independence was finally paved by another passionately patriotic, self-effacing bloodshed on the eastern frontiers of the country. Unfortunately, the Indian political class leading the struggle from within the country failed to counter the sustained British diplomatic machinations that eventually resulted in the tragic fratricidal partition of India. While the Hindus and Muslims massacred each other, the native politicians busied themselves in laying utopian foundations for the two countries.

On eve of independence, Jinnah, in his speech in the Pakistan Constituent Assembly, drew the sketch of his dream country as one to be founded on a secular fabric, where the State would have no business with religion, where people could freely pursue their faiths, where the angularities of majority and minority would vanish, where the State would be impartial and dispense even-handed justice, and where, in course of time, politically Hindus would cease to be Hindus and Muslims would cease to be Muslims and turn to be one citizen of that great country. Facts prove that his dreams stand thoroughly shattered. Successive governments of that country have decimated the religious minorities to near oblivion, making overt and covert use of State power. Having destroyed thus the plurality of the nation, their wraths have begun to take toll of intra-religious minorities as well.

As for India, her ancient culture and heritage have been her life force for ages. Post-independence, this force has gradually but certainly succumbed to society's insatiable thirst for money and power. Corruption has been pervasive. Today, obscene opulence co-exists with abject poverty. Talents of vast numbers of young Indians remain to be harnessed. Vast masses are unemployed, and they have practically no access to quality housing, education, health care and judicial systems. Frustrations of people are manifest through proliferation of political parties. New outfits emerge every day and sell more dreams. But they quickly end up aggravating the discontent of the people.

Freedom fighters who gave away their lives for the country's independence, wanted India to show to the world an alternate, better and more humane way of living. Today's India is very far from that. Successive generations have failed to leverage the 'political freedom' to make the needed social and economic transitions. In fact, today Indian dreams are measured primarily in terms of GDP percentages! That too, with a shamefully skewed distribution.

Reaching the benefits of freedom to people at large remains a complex challenge. Its magnitude is no less daunting than the struggle to wrest freedom from the colonial rulers. And, this lies completely in the hands of young India. Vivekananda had given the clarion call of 'arise, awake, and stop not till the goal is reached'! That had inspired millions then. But this call has been lost in the sea of greed and corruption. Today India has to resurrect that spirit. She has to march ahead and finish the unfinished task of attaining all-round freedom for all Indians.

Reference

1. http://www.humsafar.info/1937.php <6.1.13>
2. *Collected Works of Mahatma Gandhi* [hereafter CWMG, Volume LXV, July 1976, p3-4
3. *His Majesty's Opponent: Subhas Chandra Bose and Indian Struggle Against Empire,* Sugata Bose [e-book]
4. *A nation within a nation: Pathway to India's partition,* Bimal Prasad, Manohar, 2000, p407
5. Towards Freedom, 1937-47: Chief Editor: P N Chopra [hereafter 'Towards Freedom'], Volume 1, p 301-2 reproducing AICC File No P-1/ 1937-38 dated 31 March 1937, ICHR, Delhi, 1985
6. *Raj, Secrets, Revolution: A Life of Subhas Chandra Bose,* Mihir Bose [hereafter Mihir RSR], p 136
7. https://sites.google.com/site/cabinetmissionplan/ss4-m-j-akbar <7.1.13>
8. CWMG: Volume 72 (e-version), p 3
9. Ibid, pp 35-38
10. http://archives.dawn.com/archives/13241 <7.1.13> & https://sites.google.com/site/cabinetmissionplan/durga-das-3 <7.1.13>

11. http://www.oocities.org/sadna_gupta/SS7_BimalPrasad.html <10.1.13>
12. https://sites.google.com/site/cabinetmissionplan/ss4-m-j-akbar <10.1.13>
13. Ibid <10.1.13>
14. *Nehru Selected Works,* General Editor: S Gopal, Volume 8 [hereafter NSW], p 151
15. http://www.humsafar.info/1937.php <8.1.13>
16. CWMG: Volume 72 (e-version), pp 370-1
17. Ibid: p387
18. Ibid: pp 380-1
19. NSW: p 565
20. *Towards Freedom,* Volume 1: p 1159
21. *Dr Ambedkar Life & Mission,* Keer, Dhananjay (hereafter Keer DALM), p302
22. CWMG: Volume 72 (e-version), p 442
23. CWMG: Volume 73 (e-version), p 5
24. http://www.humsafar.info/1938.php <10.1.13>
25. *The Collected Work of Sardar Vallabhbhai Patel,* Volume 7, Ed. Pran Chopra, page 105 – reproducing Bombay Chronicle dated 9 April 1938
26. Mahatma Gandhi, Sankar Ghose, p 268
27. CWMG: Volume 73 (e-version), pp 348-9
28. http://www.telegraphindia.com/1040123/asp/northeast/story_2815051.asp <12.1.13>
29. NSW: p388 reproducing Jawaharlal's letter dated 28 April 1938
30. CWMG Volume 74 (e-version,): pp 57-58
31. Ibid: p 54
32. Ibid: pp 86-7
33. http://www.mkgandhi.org/ebks/journalist_gandhi.pdf <12.1.13> AND, CWMG Volume 74, pp 35-37
34. https://sites.google.com/site/wwwsrisubhashcom/subhash-chandra-bose-and-assam <12.1.13>
35. CWMG: Volume 74 (e-version): pp 325-6
36. Congress President: Speeches, Articles and Letters January 1938 – May 1939, Ed. Sisir K Bose, Sugata Bose, [hereafter Bose CPSAL], p 122-126

37. CWMG: Volume 74 (e-version): p 335
38. CWMG Volume 75 (e-version): pp 13-15
39. *A Comprehensive history of Modern India,* Ed. Chopra, P N, Puri B N, Das M N & Pradhan A C, p265
40. CWMG: Volume: LXVIII, Jan 1977, pp 486-487
41. CWMG: Volume 75 (e-version), p 208
42. *A Frank Friendship: Gandhi and Bengal,* Gopal Gandhi, p283
43. CWMG: Volume 75 (e-version), pp 207-8
44. Bose CPSAL: p 199
45. CWMG- Volume 75 (e-version): pp 217-218
46. Bose CPSAL: p 137-143
47. CWMG: Volume 75 (e-version): p 226
48. Bose CPSAL: pp 149-155
49. CWMG: Volume 75 (e-version): p469-474
50. Ibid: p 252
51. Ibid: pp 295-8
52. Ibid
53. Ibid: pp 306-307
54. Ibid: p 337
55. CWMG Volume 76 (e-version): pp 55-8
56. http://www.mkgandhi.org/ebks/Mahatma_Vol5.pdf
57. CWMG: Volume 76 (e-version): p 273
58. Ibid: pp 311-2
59. *Important Speeches of Jawaharlal:* Bright J S, p162
60. CWMG: Volume 76 (e-version), pp 326-8
61. Ibid: pp 433-437
62. Ibid: pp 326-328
63. CWMG: Volume 77 (e-version), p 408-13
64. Ibid: p12
65. Ibid: p 423-4
66. Ibid: pp 425-427
67. Ibid: pp112-115
68. Keer DALM: p 330
69. CWMG: Volume 77 (e-version), p431-3
70. Ibid: p 208
71. CWMG Volume 77(e-version), p226

72. CWMG: Volume 78 (e-version), p 43-4
73. Towards Freedom: Documents on the Movement for Independence in India, Part 1: Edited by K N Panikkar, pp 38-9
74. http://www.columbia.edu/itc/mealac/pritchett/00litlinks/txt_azad_congress_1940.html <26.9.14>
75. CWMG: Volume 78 (e-version), pp69-76
76. Ibid: pp438-439
77. Ibid: pp 442-443
78. http://www.internationalpeaceandconflict.org/profiles/blogs/jayaprakash-narayan-s-statement-1#.U5tV0igVet4 <14.6.14> Also, CWMG, Volume 78: p 441
79. CWMG: Volume 78 (e-version), p 109-110
80. *The Cripps Mission: An Appraisal*, B K Mishra, p 16
81. CWMG: Volume 78 (e-version), pp 256-258
82. Ibid: p350
83. Ibid: pp386-388
84. *India Wins Freedom:* M A K Azad[hereafter Azad IWF], p 32
85. *Soul Force: Gandhi's writings on Peace,* Edited by V Geetha, p 312-verified
86. & 87.http://www.mkgandhi.org/ebks/Mahatma_Vol5.pdf pp 420-1 <27.9.14>
88. CWMG: Volume 79 (e-version), pp 466-468
89. Ibid: pp129-130
90,91. Ibid: pp139-141
92. Ibid: pp139-14
93. Ibid: pp 165-166
94. Ibid: pp 206-208
95. Ibid: pp 210-227
96. Ibid::pp 275-277
97. Ibid: pp 339-341
98. Ibid: p 385
99. CWMG: Volume 80 (e-version), pp20-22
100. Ibid: pp472-475
101. *The Sikhs of the Punjab*, Grewal J S, p 172
102. CWMG: Volume 80 (e-version), p 83
103 Ibid: pp 479-480

104. *Bangladesh: Past and Present,* Ahmed S, p 95
105. http://www.atlanticcharter.ca/backgroundinfo.php <27.1.13>
106. http://www.ihr.org/jhr/v05/v05p203_Lutton.html<27.1.13>
107. War cabinet paper W.P. (42) R2 India Office 28 January 1942: Transfer of Power [hereafter TP], Volume I, Page 83
108. MSS.EUR.F.125/124 16 February 1942, Linlithgow to Madame Chiang Kai-Shek, TP, Volume I, pp 182-183
109. Azad Hind, Writings and Speeches (1941-1943) Subhas Chandra Bose, Edited by Sisir K Bose and Sugata Bose, *Netaji Collected Works,* Volume 11 [hereafter, Azad Hind, Writings and Speeches], p 67-68
110. CWMG: Volume 82 (e-version), p 65
111. L/PO/6/106b:f 291 28 February 1942, Firoz Khan Noon wire dated Feb 28, 1942 to Amery, TP, Volume I, pp 270-271
112. MSS. EUR. F. 125/22 dated 5 March 1942, TP, Volume I, p 325
113. CWMG: Volume 82 (e-version), p121-122
114. The Transfer of Power in India, V.P. Menon: Orient Longman Ltd; Hyderbad, etc 1997 (hereafter TPI: Menon), p 125
115. TPI, Menon, p 135
116. Telegram R/30/1/t:ff 5-8 12 April 1942, TP, Volume I, p 759-760
117. Telegram, L/P&J/8/510:f 566 16 April 1942 from Linlithgow to Amery reproducing Jawaharlal's press statement, TP, Volume I, pp 789-790
118. MSS EUR F 125/70 DATED 18 APRIL 42- REPORT NO 3 OF 1942: TP, Volume I
119. Azad Hind Writing and Speeches 1941-1943, p 96
120. CWMG Volume 82 (e-version), p229
121. Mahatma Gandhi, Ghose, Sankar, p286
122. CWMG: Volume 82 (e-version), pp 231-233
123. Azad Hind: Writings and Speeches, p 94
124. CWMG: Volume 83 (e-version), pp 445-447
125. Ibid: pp 447-449
126. Ibid: p 172
127. Ibid: pp 456-458 quoting Transfer of Power Volume II pp 600-3
128. Ibid: pp 451-454
129. Ibid: p189-200

130. Telegram,MSS.EUR.F.125/23 dated October 3, 1942 from Linlithgow to Amery, TP, Volume III, pp 75-78
131. *The Sikhs of the Punjab*, Grewal J S, p 173
132. CWMG: Volume 83 (e-version),pp461-462
133. Ibid: pp279-281
134. Ibid: pp 462-465
135. Ibid: pp 282-5
136. Chalo Delhi: Writings and Speeches 1943-1945, *Netaji Collected Works*, Volume 12: Edited by Sisir K Bose and Sugata Bose [hereafter Chalo Delhi] pp 39-44
137. Note by Military Intelligence L/WS/t/1576:ff 79-80 dated 14 July 1943, TP, Volume IV, pp 74-75
138. CWMG, Volume 83 (e-version), p 425
139. Chalo Delhi, p 120
140. *The Men From Imphal -The struggle in east asia,* Abid Hassan Safrani & John A Thivy p57-58
141. http://www.nihcr.edu.pk/Downloads/Chronology.pdf <04.11.14>
142. Chalo Delhi, p 172
143. *Defeat into Victory*, Viscount Slim [hereafter, Slim] p 270
144. Slim, p 331
145. Chalo Delhi, pp 194-95
146. CWMG, Volume 84 (e-version), pp 433-435
147. L/PO/10/21 29 March 1944 Wavell to Amery, TP, Volume IV, p 544
148. Amery to Churchill, L/P&J/8/623, f 104 dated 4 May 1944, TP, Volume IV, p 950
149. Chalo Delhi, p 200
150. CWMG, Volume 84 (e-version), p 112

151&152. Chalo Delhi, pp 212-222

153. Indian National Army and Japan, Lebra, p 190
154. Chalo Delhi, pp 254-63
155. CWMG: Volume 84 (e-version), pp 148-151, 170-172
156. CWMG: Volume 83 (e-version), pp 449-50
157. CWMG: Volume 84 (e-version), p 199
158. Ibid: pp239-240
159. Ibid: pp454-456

160. Ibid: p 277
161. Ibid: p296
162. *They too fought for India's Freedom,* Ashgar Ali Engineer, p 181
163. CWMG: Volume 84 (e-version), p 369-371
164. Chalo Delhi, p 266-268
165. CWMG: Volume 84 (e-version), p 478
166. Ibid: pp 419-423
167. Chalo Delhi, pp276-284
168. Wavell to Amery, Telegram, L/P&J/8/659, f 43 dated 19 March 1945, TP, Volume V, p 712-
169. J Colville to Amery, L/PO/10/22 dated 27 March 1945, TP, Volume V, p 754
170. & 171. Chalo Delhi, pp 317-318, 319-320
172. Mihir RSR, p 274
173. Telegram, L/P&J/8/522, f 198 dated 7 June 1945, Wavell to Amery, TP, Volume V, p1094
174. Ambedkar to Wavell, Wavell Papers, Political Series, April 1944-July 1945, Pt 1, pp 207-9, TP, Volume V, pp 1094-1097
175. L/P&J/8/522 f 174 dated 9 June 1945, TP, Volume V
176. Statement of the policy of HMG made by the Secretary of State for India Cmd.6652 dated 14 June 1945: TP, Volume V, pp 1118-1120
177. Wavell to Amery, Telegram, L/P&J/8/522, f115 dated16 June 1945, TP, Volume V- p1129
178. Note by Military Intelligence (Extract) L/WS/1/1506, f126 dated 15 June 1945, Volume V, pp 1127-1128
179. Telegram, L/P&J/8/522, f108 dated 19 June 1945, TP, Volume V, p1143
180. CWMG Volume 87 (e-version), pp170-71
181. Wavell to Amery Telegram, L/P&J/8/522, f 79 dated 24 June 1945, TP, Volume V, p1151
182. Wavell to Amery, Telegram, L/P&J/8/524, ff 25-6 dated 25 June 1945, TP, Volume V, pp 1151-1154
183. Wavell to Amery: Telegram, L/P&J/8/524, ff 34-5 dated 11 July 1945, TP, Volume V, pp 1224-1225
184. Telegram, L/P&J/8/524, ff 64-5 dated 14 July 1945, Wavell to

Amery, Volume V, pp 1247-1248
185. L/PO/10/22 dated 20 August 1945, TP, Volume VI, p 107
186. *The Forgotten Army*, Peter Ward Fay [hereafter Fay] p434 quoting Hindu 26 & 29 August 1945
187. CWMG: Volume 87 (e-version), pp 398-99
188. Fay p 446 quoting Hindu dated 22 Sep 1945
189. L/WS/1/1577, ff 142-7 20 Oct 1945 TP, Volume VI, Doc 154, Cabinet India and Burma Committee Paper IB (45) 16
190. L/PO/10/22 dated 22 Oct 1945 TP Volume VI, p 375 doc 157
191. CWMG: Volume 88 (e-version), p 233
192. Fay p 450 quoting Hindu dated 2 November 1945
193. L/P&J/8/525, ff 404-7 dated November 6, 1945, TP Volume VI, p 450-54
194. L/P&J/5/194, ff 46-8 dated 25 Oct 1945, TP, Volume VI, pp 393-5
195. L/P&J/5/194, ff 35-6 dated 10 November 1945, TP, Volume VI, pp 468-9
196. L/P&J/5/194, ff 28-9 dated 26 Nov 1945, TP, Volume VI, pp 542-3
197. TP, Volume VI, p546-47, doc 243 quoting Wavell Papers
198. L/WS/1/1008, ff 166-8 dated 22 December 1945, TP, Volume VI, p 673 –675
199. The Indian Annual Register 1946 Volume 1 page 27
200. CWMG: Volume 89 (e-version), pp 402-4
201. DO No 80/V-I/46/13 dated 13 February 1946, TP, Volume VI, p 936-46
202. http, //prr.hec.gov.pk/Chapters/1159S-3.pdf <10.6.14>
203. L/P&J/5/167,ff 158-62, dated 24 February 1946 TP, Volume, VI, p1079-1084
204. L/P&J/167,ff 158-62, dated 24 February 1946 TP, Volume VI, p1079-1084
205. L/PO/10/23 dated 5 March 1946, TP, Volume VI, p 1110
206. http://www.bl.uk/reshelp/findhelpregion/asia/india/indianindependence/transfer/transfer2/index.html 3.2.13>
207. *The Punjab Crisis – an analytical study*, Anup Chand Kapur, S Chand, 1985, p 92

208. *The Sole Spokesman- Jinnah*, Ayesha Jalal, p 179, quoting notes of meeting between the Cabinet Delegation and Viceroy's Executive Council
209. http://www.humsafar.info/1946.php <3.2.13>
210. http://www.bl.uk/reshelp/findhelpregion/asia/india/indianindependence/transfer/transfer2/index.html 3.2.13>
211. CWMG: Volume 91 (e-version), pp 1-3
212. Ibid: pp 437-9
213. *The Sikhs of the Punjab* Volume, J S Grewal, p 176
214. *Modern History of Punjab*, J C Aggarwal S P Agrawal, p 56
215. CWMG: Volume 91 (e-version), pp 441-2
216. http://www.gandhiserve.org/information/chronology_1946/chronology_1946.html <3.2.13>
217. Poverty of Gandhian Philosophy, Himansu Roy, p 122-123
218. Azad IWF, p161-162
219. Ibid: 167
220. *Restoration of Split Milk*, S N Roy Chaudhury, Gyan Publishing House, New Delhi, 2011, p 185, Also IAR: 1946 Volume 2, NN Mitra, p 69
221. L/PO/10/ 23 dated 21 August 1946 : TP Volume 7, p 274
222. CWMG: Volume 92 (e-version), p460-1
223 & 224.Ibid, p460-1
225. Ibid: p 73-4
226. Ibid:pp 73-4, also pp 462-4
227. L/P&J/5/167, ff, 41-3 dated 17 Sep 1946, TP Volume VIII, pp 531-3
228. L/P&J/5/167,ff, 37-8 dated 3 Oct 1946,TP Volume VIII, pp 648-50
229. TP Volume 7 pp 175-6 quoting Wavel Papers, Official Correspondence, India, January 1946- March 1947
230. CWMG, Volume 92 (e-version), pp 382-384
231 & 232. Hindustan Standard- 6 Nov 1946, Allahabad
233. *India Since Independence Making Sense of Indian Politics,* V K Ananth, Dorling Kindersley (India) Pvt Ltd, p 32. Also, Azad IWF, 179
234, 235.CWMG: Volume 93 (e-version), pp412-4

236. 237. 238. Ibid: p 421-422
239. http://parliamentofindia.nic.in/ls/debates/facts.htm <4.2.13>
240. http://www.hindu.com/thehindu/thscrip/print.pl?file=20120615291108700.htm&date=fl2911/&prd=fline& <4.2.13>
241. Azad IWF, p 189-190
242. http://www.humsafar.info/1947.php <4.2.13>
243. http://www.cambridgeindia.org/9780521060547.asp [review of A G Noorani's book] <19.6.14>
244. Azad IWF, p 203
245. *Mission with Mountbatten*, Alan Campbell-Johnson Campbell [hereafter Mission with Mountbatten], p 42
246. *Land of Two Rivers*, Nitish Sengupta, p 478-479
247. Azad IWF, p 204
248. CWMG: Volume 94 (e-version), pp 283-284
249. The Partition in Retrospect- Ed Amrik Singh p 249 (United Bengal Plan, A G Noorani)
250. CWMG: Volume 95 (e-version), p411
251. *Mission with Mountbatten*, pp 76-80
252. Azad IWF, p 207
253. http://www.humsafar.info/1947.php <4.2.13>
254. *Mission with Mountbatten*, p 81-82
255. *Bengal Divided: Hindu Communalism and Partition 1932- 1947* Joya Chatterji, p 261
256. *Mission with Mountbatten*, p 85-86
257. http://pu.edu.pk/images/journal/studies/PDF-FILES/Shah-4%20new.pdf <7.2.15>: Abdul Ghaffar Khan, the Khudai Khidmatgar, Congress and the Partition of Inda, Sayed Wiqar Ali Shah quoting Thrown to the Wolves, Pyarelal, Calcutta, 1996, p 96-97
258. *Gandhi:Naked Ambition*, Jad Adams, p262
259. *Mission with Mountbatten*, p 93
260. CWMG: Volume 95 (e-version), p 232
261. Azad IWF, p-214-216
262. *Transfer of Power in India*, V P Menon, p 387
263. http://prr.hec.gov.pk/Chapters/308S-2.pdf <5.2.13>
264. *Mission with Mountbatten*, p 104

265. *Across the Line of Control: Inside Pakistan Administered Kashmir*, Luv Puri, Columbia University Press, © 2012, p 20

266. *History of Freedom Movement in India 1857-1947*, S N Sen, p339. Also, http://hansard.millbanksystems.com/lords/1947/jul/16/indian-independence-bill , <10.6.14>, Also, V P Menon, p 391

267. http://www.bl.uk/reshelp/findhelpregion/asia/india/indianindependence/chronology/index.html <5.2.13>, Also, V P Menon, p 392

268. *Selected Works of Jawaharlal Nehru* (SWJN) Second Series, General Editor S Gopal, Volume 3, p 135

Bibliography

Across the Line of Control: Inside Pakistan Administered Kashmir, Luv Puri, Columbia University Press, 2013

Pathway to India's Partition, Volume II- A nation within a nation, Bimal Prasad, Manohar Publishers and Distributors, 2000

A centenary History of the Indian National Congress, Volume III, 1935-1947: General Editor, B N Pande, All India Congress Committee (I) and Vikas Publishing House Pvt Ltd, New Delhi, 1985

A Comprehensive history of Modern India, Ed Chopra P N, Puri B N, Das M N & Pradhan A C, Sterling Publishers Pvt Ltd, 2003

A Frank Friendship: Gandhi and Bengal - A Descriptive Chronology, Gopal Gandhi, Seagull Books, 2008

A Gentleman's Word: The Legacy of Subhas Chandra Bose in Southeast Asia, Nilanjana Sengupta, ISEAS Publishing, 2012

A History of Pakistan and its Origins, Edited by Christophe Jaffrelot, Anthem Press, 2004

A short history of All India Forward Bloc, Rathin Chakraborty, 15th Party Congress of All India Forward Bloc 2005

Agrarian Movement in India: Studies on 20th Century Bihar, Ed Arvind N Das, Frank Cass and Company Ltd, 1982

Agrarian Movements aand Congress Politics in Bihar 1927-47, K K Sharma: Anamika Prakashan, 1989

All India Kisan Sabha: Volume 1 & 2, O P Ralhan, Anmol Publications Pvt Ltd, 1998

Ambedkar and Social Justice, Volume I & II, Publication Division, Ministry of Information and Broadcasting, Govt of India, 1990

Ambedkar Refuted, Chakravarty Rajagopalachari, Hind Kitabs, 1946

An Advanced History of Modern India, Sailendra Nath Sen, Macmillan Publishers India Ltd, 2010

An Autobiography: Jawaharlal Nehru, Penguin Books, 2004

Assam Muslims: politics and cohesion, B J Dev, D K Lahiri, Mittal Publications, 1985

Azad Hind: Writings and Speeches (1941-1943) Subhas Chandra Bose: Edited by Sisir K Bose and Sugata Bose, *Netaji Collected Works: Volume 11*, Netaji Research Bureau Kolkata and Permanent Black , 2007

Bangladesh: Past and Present, Salahuddin Ahmed, APH Publishing Corporation, 2004

Bengal Divided, Hindu Communalism and Partition 1932- 1947, Joya Chatterji, Cambridge University Press, 1994

Bengal Politics, 1937-1947, Kamala Sarkar, A Mukherjee & Co 1990

Brothers against Raj: A Biography of Indian Nationalists Sarat and Subhas Chandra Bose , Leonard A Gordon, Rupa & Co, 2000

Caste, Culture and Hegemony: Social Dominance in Colonial Bengal, Sekhar Bandyopadhyay, Sage Publication (India) Pvt Ltd, 2004

Chalo Delhi: Writings and Speeches 1943-1945, *Netaji Collected Works: Volume 12*, Edited by Sisir K, Bose and Sugata Bose, Netaji Research Bureau Calcutta & Permanent Black, 2008

Collected Works of Mahatma Gandhi: Volume LXIX, Publications Division, Government of India, July 1977

Collected Works of Mahatma Gandhi, Volume LXV, Publications Division, Government of India, July 1976

Collected Works of Mahatma Gandhi: Volume LXVI, Publications Division, Government of India, Oct 1976

Collected Works of Mahatma Gandhi: Volume LXVII, Publications Division, Government of India, Dec 1976

Collected Works of Mahatma Gandhi: Volume LXVIII, Publications

Division, Government of India, January 1977

Collected Works of Mahatma Gandhi: Volume LXX, Publications Division, Government of India, Sep 1977

Collected Works of Mahatma Gandhi: Volume LXXI, Publications Division, Government of India, Jan 1978

Collected Works of Mahatma Gandhi: Volume LXXII, Publications Division, Government of India, Mar 1978

Collected Works of Mahatma Gandhi: Volume LXXIII, Publications Division, Government of India, Apr 1978

Collected Works of Mahatma Gandhi: Volume LXXIV, Publications Division, Government of India, June 1978

Collected Works of Mahatma Gandhi: Volume LXXVII, Publications Division, Government of India, Oct 1979

Collected Works of Mahatma Gandhi: Volume LXXVIII, Publications Division, Government of India: Dec 1979

Collected Works of Mahatma Gandhi: Volume LXXXIII, Publications Division, Government of India, Sep 1981

Collected Works of Mahatma Gandhi: Volume LXXXIV, Publications Division, Government of India, Nov 1981

Collected Works of Mahatma Gandhi: Volume LXXXV, Publications Division, Government of India, Feb 1982

Collected Works of Mahatma Gandhi: Volume LXXXVI, Publications Division, Government of India, Aug 1982

Collected Works of Mahatma Gandhi: Volume LXXXVII, Publications Division, Government of India, Feb 1983

Collected Works of Mahatma Gandhi: Volume LXXXVIII, Publications Division, Government of India, May 1983

Communalism in Bengal: From Famine to Noakhali 1943-47, Rakesh Batabyal, Sage Publications India Pvt Ltd, 2005

Communism and Nationalism in Colonial India 1939-45, D N Gupta, Sage Publications India Pvt Ltd, New Delhi, 2008

Communism in India, Gene D Overstreet and Marshall Windmiller, University of California Press, 1959

Conflict between India and Pakistan, An Encyclopaedia, Peter Lyon,ABC-CLIO Inc 2008

Congress and Indian Nationalism: The Pre-Independence Phase, Ed

Richard Sisson & Stanley Wolpert, University of California Press, 1988
Congress-Muslim League Tussle 1937-40: A critical analysis, Abida Shakoor, Aakar Books, 2003
Congress President: Speeches, Articles and Letters January 1938 – May 1939, *Netaji Collected Works Volume 9*, Ed Sisir K Bose, Sugata Bose, Netaji Research Bureau Calcutta & Permanent Black, 1995
Congress Presidential speeches-a selection, Sankar Ghose, All India Congress Committee, 1975
Constitutional Development of India, Manik Lal Gupta, Atlantic Publishers & Distributors (P) Ltd, 1989
Constitutional Schemes and Political Development in India: Toward Transfer of Power, Ed Verinder Grover, Ranjana Arora, Deep & Deep Publications
Crisis in the Indian Subcontinent :Partition-Can it be Undone? Lal Khan, Aakar Books, 2007
Defeat Into Victory, Field Marshall Viscount Slim, Pan Books, 2009
Documents on North East India: Volume 4 Assam (1936-1957), Edited by Suresh K Sharma, Usha Sharma, Mittal Publication, 2006
Dr Ambedkar-Life and Mission, Dhananjay Keer, Popular Prakashan Pvt Ltd, 2005
Dr Rajendra Prasad: Correspondence and Select Documents, Volume 6: Edited by Valmiki Choudhary, Allied Publishers Pvt Ltd, 1986
Dynamics of Punjabi Suba Movement, Krishan Gopal Lamba, Deep & Deep Publication Pvt Ltd, 1999
Evolution of Constitutional History of India (With Special Reference to the Role of the Indian National Congress and the Minorities) 1773-1947, V B Mishra: Mittal Publications, 1987
Explaining Pakistan's Foreign Policy: Escaping India, Aparna Pande, Routledge, 2011
Factional Politics in an Indian State: The Congress Party in Uttar Pradesh, Paul R Brass, University of California Press, Cambridge University Press, 1965
Freedom at Midnight, Dominique Lapierre, Larry Collins, Vikas Publishing House Pvt Ltd, 2011
From Movement to Government: the Congress in the United Provinces 1937-42, Visalakshi Menon, Sage Publications India Pvt Ltd, 2003

From My Bones, Memoirs of Col Gurbaksh Singh Dhillon of the Indian National Army, Aryan Books International, 1998

Fundamentalisms and the State: Remaking Polities, Economies, and Militance, Edited by Martin E Marty, R Scott Appleby, University of Chicago Press, 1993

Gandhi and Ambedkar: Saviours of Untouchables, Sheshrao Chavan, APH Publishing.Corp, 2001

Gandhi Jinnah Correspondence and Communal Question, edited by Amalendu De, Ratna Prakashan, 1999

Gandhi The Man, His People, and the Empire, Rajmohan Gandhi,University of California Press, 2008

Gandhi vs Jinnah: The Debate Over the Partition of India, Allen Hayes Merriam, Minerva Associates, 1980

Gandhi: A Political And Spiritual Life, Kathryn Tidrick, I B Tauris & Co Ltd, 2006

Gandhi: Naked Ambition, Jad Adams, Quercus, 2011

Gandhi's Passion: The Life And Legacy of Mahatma Gandhi, Stanley Wolpert, Oxford University Press, 2002

Geographical Thought of Dr B R Ambedkar, D M Wankhede, Gautam Book Centre, 2009

Glimpses of Indian National Congress From Inception to attainment of freedom (1885-1947), T N Kundra, Regency Publications, 1996

Glimpses of Indian National Movement, M Abel, ICFAI University Press, 2005

His Majesty's Opponent: Subhas Chandra Bose and Indian Struggle Against Empire, Sugata Bose,Penguin Books, E Book

History Modern India, S N Sen, New Age International Publishers, 2006

History of the Freedom Movement in India 1857-1947, S N Sen,New Age International Pvt Ltd, 2009

History of India: From National Movement to Present Day (Vol.4), N Jayapalan, Atlantic Publishers and Distributors, 2001

History of Indian National Congress 1885-2002, compiled and edited by Deep Chand Bandhu, Kalpaz Publications, 2003

History of the United Panjab, Volume III, Dr. Bakhshsish Singh Nijjar, Atlantic Publishers and Distributors,1996

Hitler and the Nazi State, Martin Collier, Philip Pedley, Heinemann Educational Publishers, 2005

Important Speeches of Jawaharlal Nehru: A collection of most significant speeches delivered by Jawaharlal Nehru from 1922 to1946, m Editor, J S Bright, India Print Works

India and Pakistan: Crisis of Relationship, Edited by Air Commodore Jasjit Singh, Lancer Publishers Pvt Ltd, 1990

India since Independence: Making Sense of Indian Politics, V Krishna Ananth, Dorling Kindersley (India) Pvt Ltd, 2011

India Wins Freedom (The Complete Version), M A K Azad, Orient Longman Ltd, 1988

India: Struggle for Freedom: Political Social and Economic, Jayprakash Narayan, Edited by Yusuf Meherally, Hope India Publications,2006

India's biggest Cover-up, Anuj Dhar, Vitasta Publishing Pvt Ltd, 2012

India's Bismarck: Sardar Vallabhbhai Patel, Balraj Krishna, Indus Source Books, 2007

India's Partition: The Story of Imperialism in Retreat, D N Panigrahi, Routledge, 2004

Indian Muslims and Partition, Dr S M Ikram, Atlantic Publishers & Distributor, 1992

Indian Political Thought, K S Padhy, PHI Learning Pvt Ltd, 2011

Indian Summer: The Secret History of the End of an Empire, Alex Von Tunzelmann, Pocket Books, 2008

Introduction to the Constitution of India, B K Sharma, PHI Learning, 2011

Islam and the Secular State: Negotiating the Future of Shari'a, Abdullahi Ahmed An-Na'im, Harvard University Press, 2009

Islam in the Subcontinent Muslims in a Plural Society, Mushirul Hasan, Manohar Publishers and Distributors, 2002

Islam in the subcontinent, Annemarie Schimmel, E J Brill,1980

"Islam" Means Peace: Understanding the Muslim Principle of Nonviolence Today, Amitabh Pal, Preager, 2011

Islamic Jihad: A Legacy of Forced Conversion, Imperialism and Slavery, M A Khan, iUniverse, 2009

Japan and the Indian National Army, Tilak Raj Sareen, Mounto Publishing House, 1996

Jawaharlal Nehru- A Biography, Sankar Ghose, Allied Publishers, 2003

Jawaharlal Nehru: A Biography, Abridged Edition, Sarvepalli Gopal, Oxford University Press,2003

Jawaharlal Nehru: A Biography, Frank Moraes, Jaico Publishing House, 2007

Jayaprakash Narayan Selected Works, Vol 3 (1939-1946), Editor Bimal Prasad, Manohar Publishers and Distributors, 2003

Jayaprakash Narayan, A Centenary Volume, Sandip Das, Mittal Publications, 2005

Jayaprakash Narayan: Struggle With Values, Madhu Dadavate, Allied Publishers, 2002

Jinnah: Man of Destiny, Prakash Almeida, Kalpaz Publications, 2001

Jinnah's Early Politics Ambassador of Hindu-Muslim Unity, Ian Bryant Wells, Permanent Black, 2005

Jungle Alliance - Japan and the Indian National Army, Joyce C Lebra, Asia Pacific Press, 1971

Kohima 1944: The Battle That Saved India, Robert Lyman, Osprey Publishing, 2010

Land of Two Rivers: A History of Bengal from the Mahabharata to Mujib, Nitish K Sengupta, Penguin Books, 2011

Language, Religion and Politics in North India, Paul R Brass, iUniverse Inc, 2005

Lokopriya Gopinath Bordoloi: An Architect of Modern India, Lily M Baruah, Gyan Publishing House, 1993

Mahatma Gandhi, Sankar Ghose, Allied Publishers Ltd, 1991

Mission with Mountbatten, Alan Campbell-Johnson, Jaico Publishing House, 1951

Modern History of Punjab, A lookback into ancient peaceful Panjab focussing confrontation and failures leading to present Punjab problem and a peep ahead Relevant Select Documents, J C Aggarwal, S P Agrawal, Concept Publishing Company, 1992

A Comprehensive history of India: Modern India, P N Chopra, B N Puri M N Das, A C Pradhan, Sterling Publishers Pvt Ltd , 2005

Mohandas: A True Story of a Man, his People and an Empire, Rajmohan Gandhi, Penguin Books, 2007

Muslim Identity, Print Culture and the Dravidian Factor in Tamilnadu, J B P More, Orient Longman Pvt Ltd, 2004

Muslim Separatism and the Partition of India, Debadutta Chakravarty, Atlantic Publishers and Distributors, 2003

Muslims in India: Recent Contributions to Literature on Religion, Philosophy, History, & Social Aspects, Mohammed Taher, South Asia Books, 1993
My Life and Times, Sayyid Mir Qasim, Allied Publishers Ltd,1992
National Liberation , Nigel Harris, I B Tauris & Co Ltd, 1990
Nehru Jinnah Correspondence including Gandhi-Jinnah and Nehru-Nawab Ismail Correspondence, Published by J B Kripalani, General Secretary, AICC
Nehru Selected Works Vol 8, General Editor- S Gopal, Orient Longman Ltd, 1985
Nehru, Benjamin Zachariah: Routledge: London, 2004
Netaji in Germany: An Eye-Witness Account of Indian Freedom Struggle in Europe during World War II, Alexander Werth, Walter Harbich, edited by Sisir Kumar Bose, Netaji Research Bureau, 1970
Netaji Rediscovered, Kanailal Bose, AuthorHouse, 2010
Netaji Subhas Bose, Bengal Revolution and Independence, Reva Chatterjee, Ocean Books Pvt Ltd, 2000
Pakistan: A Modern History, Ian Talbot, Palgrave Macmillan, 2010
Patel, A Life, Rajmohan Gandhi, Navajivan Publishing House, 1990
Patriots and Tyrants: Ten Asian Leaders, Ross Marlay, Clark Neher, Rowman and Littlefield Publishers, 1999
Peasant Struggles in India, Edited by A R Desai, Oxford University Press 1979
People's Revolt in Orissa: A Study of Talcher, D P Mishra, Atlantic Publishers and Distributors, 1998
Phoenix from the Ashes, The Indian Army in Burma Campaign, Daniel P Marston, Preager, Westport, 2003
Political Philosophy of Rammanohar Lohia, Alternative Development Perceptions, K Gopinath Pillai, Deep & Deep Publications,1994
Politics of Identity: Ethnic Nationalism and the State in Pakistan, Adeel Khan, Sage Publications India Pvt Ltd, 2005
Politics of regionalism in India: with special reference to Punjab, Madhu Sudan Misra, Deep & Deep Publications, 1988
Poverty of Gandhian Philosophy, Himansu Roy, Concept Publishing Company, 2001

Quit India Movement in Assam, Anil Kumar Sharma, Mittal Publications, 2007

Quit India Movement: Role of Big Business, British Secret Documents, 002, edited by P N Chopra, South Asia Books, 1992

Raj, Secrets: Revolution, A Life of Subhas Chandra Bose, Mihir Bose, Grice Chapman Publishing, 2004

Rashtriya Swayam Sevak Sangh, National Upsurge, M G Chitkara, APH Publishing Corporation 2004

Rediscovering Gandhi: Hind Swaraj: Volume 1, R P Misra (series editor) In collaboration with Gandhi Smriti and Darshan Samity, Concept Publishing Company, 2007

Religion, Caste and Politics in India, Christophe Jaffrelot, Primus Books, 2010

Restoration of Split Milk, S N Roy Chaudhury, Gyan Publishing House, 2011

Roots of Communal politics: Indian National Congress Cawnpore Riots Enquiry Committee, Indian National Congress Kanpur Riots Enquiry Committee, Edited by Norman Gerald Barrier, Arnold-Heinemann Publishers (India), 1976

Saga of Satyagraha, R R Diwakar, Bharatiya Vidya Bhavan, 1969

Selected Works of Jawaharlal Nehru, Second Series, Volume 1, General Editor S Gopal, Jawaharlal Nehru Memorial Fund

Selected Works of Jawaharlal Nehru, Second Series, Volume 2, General Editor S Gopal, Jawaharlal Nehru Memorial Fund

Selected Works of Jawaharlal Nehru, Second Series: Volume 3, General Editor S Gopal, Jawaharlal Nehru Memorial Fund,

Sir Chhotu Ram: A Saga of Inspirational Leadership, Balbir Singh, Publications Division, Ministry of Information and Broadcasting, Govt of India, 2009

Social Thought of Rabindranath Tagore: A Historical Analysis, Tapati Dasgupta, Abhinav Publications, 1993

Soul Force: Gandhi's Writings on Peace, Edited by V Geetha, Tara Publishing, 2004

South Asia: From Freedom to Terrorism, Shashi B Sahai, Gyan Publishing House, 1998

State, Nation and Ethnicity in Contemporary South Asia, Ishtiaq Ahmed, Pinter,1998

Subhas Chandra Bose and Indian Communist Movement, a study of cooperation and conflict, Gautam Chattopadhyaya, People's Publishing House, 1973

Subhas Chandra Bose and Middle Class Radicalism: A Study in Indian Nationalism 1928-1940 , Bidyut Chakrabarty, I B Tauris & Co Ltd, 1990

Subhas Chandra Bose, the Indian leftists and communists, Gautam Chattapadhyaya, People's Publication House, 1997

Subhas Chandra Bose: A Biography, Marshall J Getz, McFarland & Company Inc, 2002

Subhas Chandra Bose: The Springing Tiger, Hugh Toye, Jaico Publishing House, 2011

Subhas: A Political Biography, Sitanshu Das, Rupa & Co, 2006

Terror and The Postcolonial, Edited by. Eelleke Boehmer and Stephen Morton, Wiley-Blackwell, 2010

The British Left and India: Metropolitan Anti-Imperialism 1885-1947, Nichols Owen, Oxford University Press, 2007

The Collected Works of Mahatma Gandhi Volume 72, (Electronic Book),Publications Division, Government of India, 1999, 98 Volumes

The Collected Works of Mahatma Gandhi Volume 75, (Electronic Book), Publications Division, Government of India, 1999, 98 Volumes

The Collected Works of Mahatma Gandhi Volume 76, (Electronic Book), Publications Division, Government of India, 1999, 98 Volumes

The Collected Works of Mahatma Gandhi Volume 77, (Electronic Book), Publications Division, Government of India, 1999, 98 Volumes

The Collected Works of Mahatma Gandhi Volume 78, (Electronic Book), Publications Division, Government of India, 1999, 98 Volumes

The Collected Works of Mahatma Gandhi Volume 79, (Electronic Book), Publications Division, Government of India, 1999, 98 Volumes

The Collected Works of Mahatma Gandhi Volume 81, (Electronic Book), Publications Division, Government of India, 1999, 98 Volumes

The Collected Works of Mahatma Gandhi Volume 82, (Electronic Book), Publications Division, Government of India, 1999, 98 Volumes

The Collected Works of Mahatma Gandhi Volume 83, (Electronic Book), Publications Division, Government of India, 1999, 98 Volumes

The Collected Works of Mahatma Gandhi Volume 84, (Electronic Book), Publications Division, Government of India, 1999, 98 Volumes

The Collected Works of Mahatma Gandhi Volume 87, (Electronic Book), Publications Division, Government of India, 1999, 98 Volumes

The Collected Works of Mahatma Gandhi Volume 89, (Electronic Book), Publications Division, Government of India, 1999, 98 Volumes

The Collected Works of Mahatma Gandhi Volume 91, (Electronic Book), Publications Division, Government of India, 1999, 98 Volumes

The Collected Works of Mahatma Gandhi Volume 92, (Electronic Book), Publications Division, Government of India, 1999, 98 Volumes

The Collected Works of Mahatma Gandhi Volume 93, (Electronic Book), Publications Division, Government of India, 1999, 98 Volumes

The Collected Works of Mahatma Gandhi Volume 94, (Electronic Book), Publications Division, Government of India, 1999, 98 Volumes

The Collected Works of Mahatma Gandhi Volume 95, (Electronic Book), Publications Division, Government of India, 1999, 98 Volumes

The Collected Works of Sardar Vallabhbhai Patel: 1937-1938, Volume 7, Ed Pran Nath Chopra, Konark Publishers, 1996

The Communal triangle in India, Asoka Mehta and Achyut Patwardhan, Kitabistan, 1942

The Congress ideology and programme, 1920-85: The Ideological Foundations of Indian National Congress under Gandhian Leadership and after, P D Kaushik, Gitanjali Publishing House, 1986

The Cripps Mission: An Appraisal, B K Mishra, Concept Publishing Company, 1982

The Forgotten Army: India's Armed Struggle for Independence 1942-1945, Peter Ward Fay, Rupa & Co, 1994

The History and Culture of the Indian People Struggle for Freedom, Volume 11, General Editor R C Majumdar, Bharatiya Vidya Bhavan, 1969

The History of British India: A Chronology, John F Riddick, Preage Publishers, 2006

The History of Indian National Congress (1885-1935) Volume 1, B Pattabhi Sitaramayya, Padma Publications, 1946

The INA Speaks: Being the statements of Major General Shah Nawaz Khan [and others], All India INA Enquiry and Relief Committee(India), Raj Kamal Publications, 1946

The INA Trial and the Raj, Harkirat Singh, Atlantic Publishers and Distributors, 2003

The Indian Annual Register 1937-1942, 10 volumes, Mitra, H N and Mitra N N, Gyan Publishing House, 1998

The Indian Annual Register 1946, N N Mitra, Annual Register Office

The Indian National Army and Japan, Joyce Chapman Lebra, Asia Pacific Press Pte Ltd, 1971

The Indian National Army: Second Front of the Indian independence movement, Kalyan Kumar Ghosh, Meenakshi Prakashan, 1969

The Indian National Congress: centenary hindsights, selection of papers from a seminar organised by University of Oxford, edited by D Anthony Low, OUP 1988

The Indian Political Parties: A Historical Analysis of Political Behaviour up to 1947, B B Misra, Oxford University Press,1978

The Indian Struggle 1920-1942 by Subhas Chandra Bose, Ed Sisir Kumar Bose Sugata Bose, Netaji Collected Works Volume 2, Oxford University Press, 2011

The Making of India- A Political History, Ranbir Vohra, M E Sharpe Inc, 2012

The Man Who Divided India, Rafiq Zakaria, Popular Prakashan Pvt Ltd, 2009

The Men From Imphal, Abid Hasan Safrani & The Struggle in East Asia John A Thivy, Netaji Research Bureau,1995

The Muslims of British India, P Hardy, Cambridge University Press, 1972

The Partition in Retrospect, Editor Amrik Singh, Anamika Publishers & Distributors (P) Ltd, 2000

The Penguin Gandhi Reader, Rudrangshu Mukherjee, Penguin Books India (P) Ltd, 1993

The Punjab Crisis: An Analytical Study, Anup Chand Kapur, S Chand, 1985

The Rajaji Story, 1937-1972, Rajmohan Gandhi, Bharatiya Vidya Bhavan, 1984

The Rediscovery of India, Meghnad Desai, Penguin Books, 2011

The Sikhs of the Punjab, J S Grewal, Vol 2-3, Revised edition, Cambridge University Press, 1998

The Sole Spokesman: Jinnah, The Muslim League and the Demand for Pakistan, Ayesha Jalal, Cambridge University Press, 1994

The Springing Tiger: The Indian National Army and Netaji Subhas Chandra Bose, Hugh Toye, Allied Publishers Pvt Ltd, 2009

The Transfer of Power 1942-47, Editor in Chief: Nicholas Mansergh, Assistant Editor E W R Lumby, HMSO, 1970,Volume I

The Transfer of Power 1942-47, Editor in Chief: Nicholas Mansergh, Assistant Editor E W R Lumby, HMSO, 1971, Volume II

The Transfer of Power 1942-47, Editor in Chief: Nicholas Mansergh, Assistant Editor E W R Lumby, HMSO, 1971, Volume III

The Transfer of Power 1942-47, Editor in Chief: Nicholas Mansergh, Assistant Editor E W R Lumby, HMSO, 1973, Volume IV

The Transfer of Power 1942-47, Editor in Chief: Nicholas Mansergh, Assistant Editor E W R Lumby, HMSO, 1974 Volume V

The Transfer of Power 1942-47, Editor in Chief: Nicholas Mansergh, Assistant Editor Penderel Moon, UBS Publishers Ltd,1976 Volume VI

The Transfer of Power 1942-47, Editor in Chief: Nicholas Mansergh, Assistant Editor Penderel Moon, UBS Publishers Ltd, 1978 Volume VIII

The Transfer of Power In India, 1945-47, E W R Lumby, George Allen & Unwin, 1954

The Transfer of Power in India, VP Menon, Orient Longman Ltd, 1997

They too fought for India's freedom: The Role of Minority, Edited by Asghar Ali Engineer, Hope India Publications, 2005

Towards Freedom 1937-47, Chief Editor: P N Chopra, Volume 1,Indian Council of Historical Research, 1985

Towards Freedom: Documents on the Movement for Independence in India, Part 1, Edited by K N Panikkar, ICHR,OUP, 2009

Towards Independence 1940-47: Memoirs of an Indian Civil Servant , Asok Mitra, Popular Prakashan Private Limited, 1991

Transformation in Indian History, Edited by Pratima Asthana, S Z H Jafri, Anamika Publishers & Distributors (P) Ltd, 2009

Turmoil in Punjab Politics, S C Arora, Mittal Publications, 1990

Vinayak Damodar Savarkar, Y G Bhave, Northern Book Centre, 2009

Violence Denied: Violence, Non-Violence and the Rationalization of Violence In South Asian Cultural History, Edited by Jan E M Houben, Karel R Van Kooij, Brill 1999

What Congress and Gandhi have done to the Untouchables, B R Ambedkar, Gautam Book Centre,1945

Various issues of The Pioneer, The Statesman, The Hindu, Amritabazar Patrika and Hindustan Times related to the years from 1937-47

INTERNET REFERENCES

http://ahoy.tk-jk.net/macslog/BenitoMussoliniCapturedan.html <1.2.13>

http://archive.org/stream/nationbuildingin021687 mbp/nationbuildingin021687mbp_djvu.txt <24.7.13>

http://archive.org/stream/studyofeconomicp031271 mbp/studyofeconomicp031271mbp_djvu.txt<12.1.13>

http://archives.dawn.com/2002/12/25/op.htm <24.7.13>

http://archives.dawn.com/archives/13241 <7.1.13>

http://filestore.nationalarchives.gov.uk/pdfs/large/ cab-65-53.pdf <24 .7.13>

http://hansard.millbanksystems.com/lords/1947/jul/16/indian-independence-bill , <10.6.14>

http://indiannavy.nic.in/sites/default/files/under2ensigns.pdf <24.7.13>

http://japanfocus.org/-Janis-Mimura/3657 <27.1.13>

http://militaryhistory.about.com/od/worldwarii/p/dunkirk.htm <26.1.13>

http://militaryhistory.about.com/od/worldwarii/p/World-War-Ii-Munich-Agreement.htm <13.1.13>

http://news.bbc.co.uk/2/hi/3684288.stm <27.1.13>

http://parliamentofindia.nic.in/ls/debates/facts.htm <4.2.13>

http://prr.hec.gov.pk/Chapters/1159S-3.pdf <10.6.14>

http://prr.hec.gov.pk/Chapters/308S-2.pdf <24.7.13>

http://pu.edu.pk/images/journal/csas/Currentissue/Final%20 Paper%205.pdf <24.7.13>

http://pu.edu.pk/images/journal/history/PDF-FILES/chawala.pdf <5.2.13>

http://pu.edu.pk/images/journal/studies/PDF-FILES/Shah-4%20new.pdf <24.7.13>

http://punjabiworld.com/Punjabi-Culture/Punjabi-History/1773.html < 4.2.13>

http://subhaschandrabose.org/ina_chronologicallist.php <24.7.13>

http://trove.nla.gov.au/ndp/del/article/17988662 <3.2.13>

http://ww2db.com/event/today/04/06/1942 <7.8.13>

http://www.ambedkar.org/ambcd/44C.%20Important%20

Correspondence%20Relating%20To%20Transfer.htm <24.7.13>
http://www.asiantribune.com/?q=node/9266 <7.1.13>
http://www.atlanticcharter.ca/backgroundinfo.php <24.7.13>
http://www.bbc.co.uk/history/ww2peopleswar/timeline/factfiles/nonflash/a1152299.shtml <15.07.2013>
http://www.bl.uk/reshelp/findhelpregion/asia/india/indianindependence/indiapakistan/partition1/index.html <23.11.2012>
http://www.bl.uk/reshelp/findhelpregion/asia/india/indianindependence/transfer/transfer2/index.html <24.7.13>
http://www.bl.uk/reshelp/findhelpregion/asia/india/indianindependence/chronology/index.html <5.2.13>
http://www.britishempire.co.uk/maproom/india/vpmenon.htm <24.7.13>
http://www.burmastar.org.uk/The%20Battle%20of%20Kohima.htm <24.7.13>
http://www.cambridgeindia.org/9780521060547.asp [review of A G Noorani's book] <19.6.14>
http://www.columbia.edu/itc/mealac/pritchett/00islamlinks/txt_iqbal_tojinnah_1937.html <7.1.13>
http://www.columbia.edu/itc/mealac/pritchett/00litlinks/txt_azad_congress_1940.html <26.9.14>
http://www.csss-isla.com/arch%2057.htm <7.1.13>
http://www.frontline.in/navigation/?type=static&page=flonnet&rdurl=fl2912/stories/20120629291208100.htm <24.7.13>
http://www.gandhiserve.org/cwmg/VOL072.PDF <21.1.13>
http://www.gandhiserve.org/information/chronology_1937/chronology_1937.html, 7.1.13>
http://www.gandhiserve.org/information/chronology_1946/chronology_1946.html <3.2.13>
http://www.globalsecurity.org/military/library/report/1986/RMF.htm <1.2.13>
http://www.hindu.com/thehindu/thscrip/print.pl?file=20120615291108700.htm&date=fl2911/&prd=fline& <4.2.13>
http://www.hindustantimes.com/news/specials/netaji/enlisting5.htm <4.2.13>
http://www.history.co.uk/explore-history/ww2/north-africa.html

<22.2.13>
http://www.historyonthenet.com/Chronology/timelinewwii.htm <24.7.13>
http://www.humsafar.info/1938.php <10.1.13>
http://www.humsafar.info/1941.php <27.1.13.>
http://www.humsafar.info/1946.php <3.2.13>
http://www.humsafar.info/1947.php <4.2.13>
http://www.ibiblio.org/hyperwar/ETO/East/Balkans/AG-Balkans.html <27.1.13>
http://www.ibiblio.org/hyperwar/USA/USA-WD-Ops/USA-WD-Ops-B.html <24.7.13>
http://www.ihr.org/jhr/v03/v03p407_Borra.html <24.7.13>
http://www.ihr.org/jhr/v05/v05p203_Lutton.html<27.1.13>
http://www.independent.org/newsroom/article.asp?id=1930 <27.1.13>
http://www.internationalpeaceandconflict.org/profiles/blogs/jayaprakash-narayan-s-statement-1#.U5tV0igVet4 <14.6.14>
http://www.kashmir-information.com/Miscellaneous/Bhatt1.html <5.2.13>
http://www.mkgandhi.org/ebks/Mahatma_Vol5.pdf <14.6.14>
http://www.nihcr.edu.pk/Downloads/Chronology.pdf <4.11.14>
http://www.nihcr.edu.pk/Downloads/Punjab_Muslim.pdf <24.7.13>
http://www.nps.edu/Academics/Centers/CCC/research/StudentTheses/Mahmood05.pdf <4.2.13>
http://www.oocities.org/sadna_gupta/SS7_BimalPrasad.html <10.1.13>
http://www.open.ac.uk/researchprojects/makingbritain/content/spanish-civil-war <12.1.13>
http://www.pacificwar.org.au/battaust/Britain_betrays_Australia.html <27.1.13>
http://www.pacificwar.org.au/pearlharbor/pearloverview4.html <24.7.13>
http://www.secondworldwarhistory.com/japan-ww2-events-timeline.asp <8.3.13>
http://www.telegraphindia.com/1040123/asp/northeast/story_2815051.asp <12.1.13>
http://www.telegraphindia.com/1121124/jsp/opinion/story_16231515.jsp <24.7.13>

http://www.worldwar2history.info/North-Africa/ <1.2.13>

https://sites.google.com/site/cabinetmissionplan/directactionjinnahwavellnehrujuly <3.2.13>

https://sites.google.com/site/cabinetmissionplan/durga-das-3 <7.1.13>

https://sites.google.com/site/cabinetmissionplan/ss4-m-j-akbar <7.1.13>

https://sites.google.com/site/wwwsrisubhashcom/subhash-chandra-bose-and-assam <12.1.13>

Wavell's Breakdown Plan, 1945-47: an Appraisal: Iqbal Chawla Universdity of the Punjab, Lahore: http://www.global.ucsb.edu/punjab/journal/v16_2/articles/4-Iqbal%20Chawla%20Final%2016.2.pdf <4.2.13>

INDEX

M

Q

R